CONTENTS

Lake Matheson reflections Photo: Tourism West Coast

TRIP PLANNING

NATIONAL PARKS MAPS

NORTH ISLAND REGIONAL MAPS

SOUTH ISLAND REGIONAL MAPS

NORTH ISLAND CITY & SUBURBS MAPS

SOUTH ISLAND CITY & SUBURBS MAPS

MOTORHOME DUMP STATIONS

north island travel time and distances

Distances are shown in kilometres and assume the most direct route on sealed roads where possible.
Travelling times are shown in hours & minutes and are calculated for a driver travelling at 80-100 km/hr on open stretches, with an allowance for rest stops.

Auckland •	444 8:15	342 5:35	182 3:05	496 8:20	124 1:55	500 9:05	321 6:00	626 9:20	424 6:35	365 6:20	237 4:15	521 7:40	235 3:50	282 4:05	284 4:45	201 3:20	115 1:50	390 7:50	198 3:10	457 8:00	652 9:15	295 4:55	166 3:00
Cape Reinga •		786 13:50	290 5:25	940 16:35	568 10:10	944 17:20	112 2:15	1070 17:35	868 14:50	809 14:35	216 4:30	967 15:55	679 11:50	726 12:20	728 13:00	645 11:35	559 10:05	834 16:05	642 11:25	901 16:15	1096 17:30	739 13:10	267 5:15
Chateau Tongariro •			524 8:40	431 6:55	218 3:40	468 8:25	663 11:35	314 4:50	234 4:00	251 4:20	579 9:50	207 3:10	178 2:50	94 1:30	58 0:50	250 3:45	311 4:40	283 6:05	158 2:45	138 2:45	338 4:45	263 4:15	508 8:35
Dargaville •				678 11:25	306 5:00	682 12:10	178 3:10	808 12:25	606 9:40	547 9:25	126 2:20	705 10:45	417 6:40	464 7:10	466 7:50	383 6:25	297 4:55	572 10:55	380 6:15	639 11:05	834 12:20	477 8:00	55 1:05
Gisborne •					385 6:30	176 3:40	817 14:20	452 6:45	221 3:25	582 10:25	733 12:35	397 6:05	274 4:50	337 5:25	446 7:20	291 5:00	402 7:05	167 2:55	435 7:30	469 7:15	534 8:15	201 3:25	662 11:20
Hamilton •						389 7:15	445 7:55	504 7:25	298 4:40	241 4:25	361 6:10	397 5:45	111 1:40	158 2:10	160 2:50	109 1:55	110 1:50	266 5:55	74 1:15	326 6:05	528 7:30	196 3:05	290 4:55
Hicks Bay •							821 15:05	628 10:25	397 7:05	586 11:10	737 13:20	573 9:45	278 5:35	362 6:55	450 8:50	295 5:45	406 7:50	343 6:35	439 8:15	582 10:40	710 11:55	205 4:10	666 12:05
Kaitaia •								947 15:20	745 12:35	686 12:20	109 2:15	844 13:40	556 9:35	603 10:05	605 10:45	522 9:20	436 7:50	711 13:50	519 9:10	778 14:00	973 15:15	616 10:55	155 3:00
Masterton •									231 3:20	341 5:15	863 13:35	107 1:40	430 6:35	346 5:15	342 6:05	502 7:40	563 8:25	413 6:30	442 8:00	179 2:50	100 1:50	515 8:00	792 12:20
Napier •										410 6:15	661 10:50	176 2:40	224 3:50	140 2:30	252 4:25	296 4:55	357 5:40	182 3:10	309 5:05	248 3:50	313 4:50	309 5:15	590 9:35
New Plymouth •											602 10:35	234 3:35	308 5:35	305 5:25	193 3:30	309 5:40	343 6:15	463 10:00	181 3:30	162 2:25	352 5:10	393 7:00	531 9:20
Paihia •												760 11:55	472 7:50	519 8:20	521 9:00	438 7:35	352 6:05	627 12:05	435 7:25	694 12:15	889 13:30	532 9:10	71 1:15
Palmerston North •													323 4:55	239 3:35	235 4:25	395 6:00	456 6:45	358 5:50	335 6:20	72 1:10	142 2:10	408 6:20	689 10:40
Rotorua •														84 1:20	172 2:50	83 1:30	168 2:40	155 4:15	161 2:45	304 4:25	454 6:30	85 1:25	401 6:35
Taupo •															112 1:55	156 2:25	217 3:10	189 4:35	169 2:35	220 3:05	370 5:10	169 2:45	448 7:05
Taumarunui •																227 4:05	288 4:40	301 6:30	100 1:55	166 3:15	356 5:15	257 4:15	450 7:45
Tauranga •																	111 2:05	238 5:45	149 2:30	376 6:35	526 8:00	94 1:35	367 6:20
Thames •																		323 6:55	173 3:05	425 6:55	587 8:20	205 3:40	281 4:50
Waikaremoana •																			316 7:00	430 7:00	495 8:00	240 5:40	556 10:50
Waitomo Caves •																				266 5:10	456 7:10	243 4:05	364 6:10
Wanganui •																					190 2:45	389 5:10	623 10:00
Wellington •																						539 7:55	818 12:15
Whakatane •																							461 7:55
Whangarei •																							

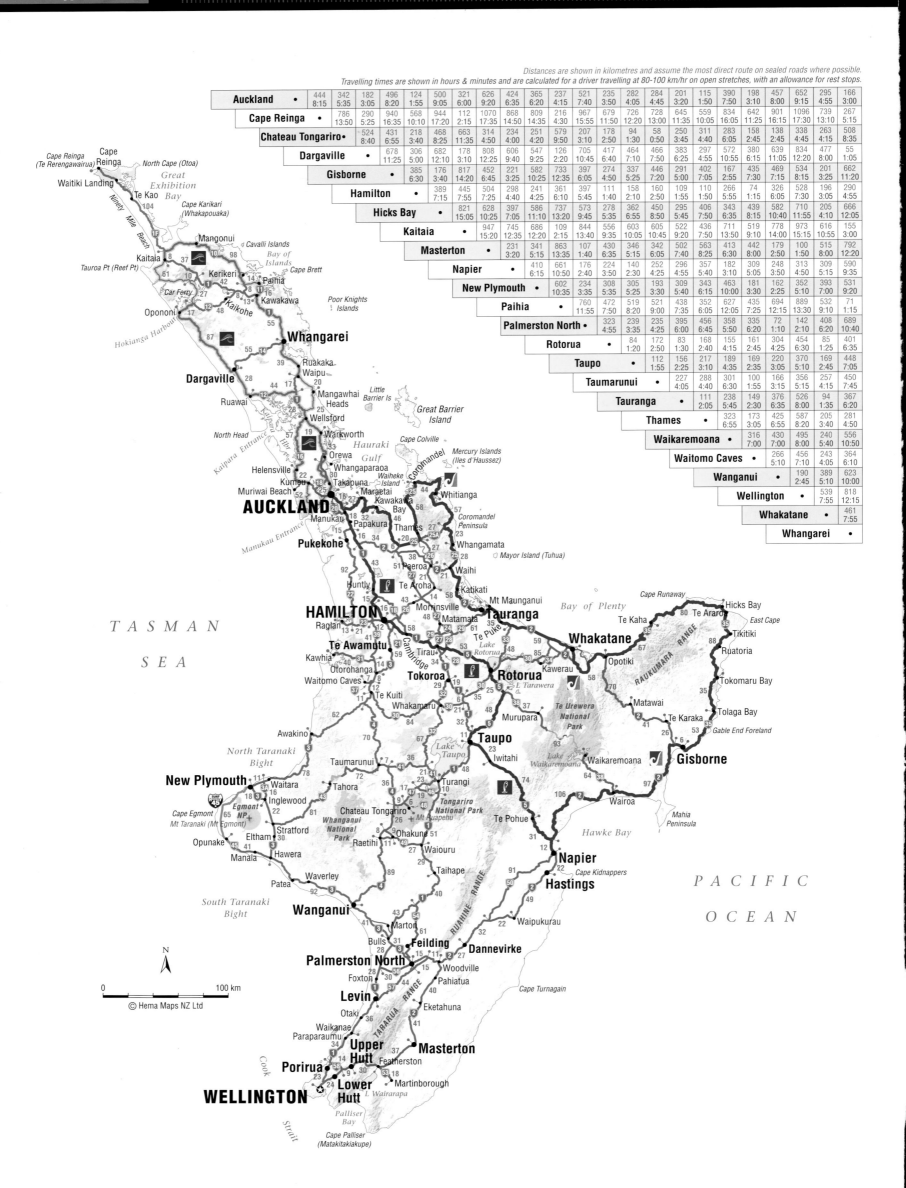

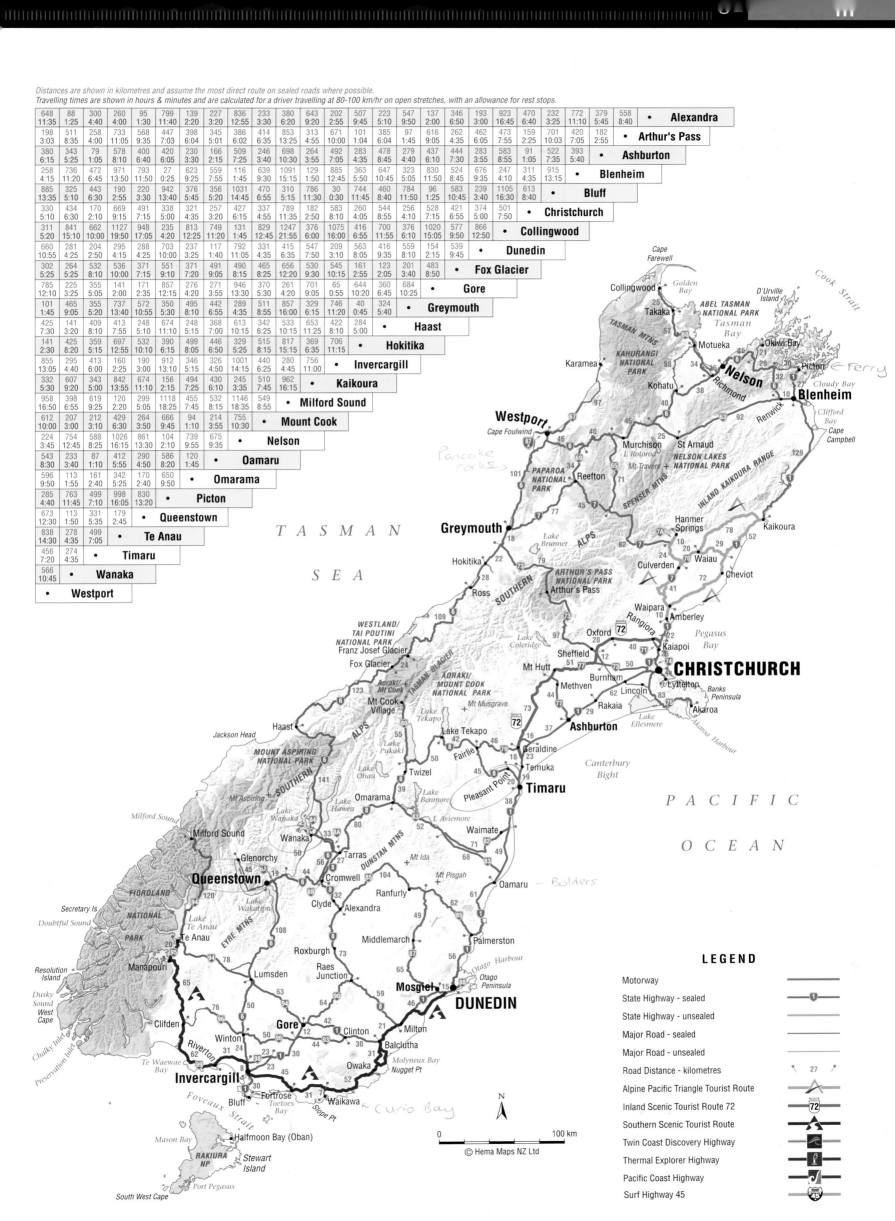

Distances are shown in kilometres and assume the most direct route on sealed roads where possible.
Travelling times are shown in hours & minutes and are calculated for a driver travelling at 80-100 km/hr on open stretches, with an allowance for rest stops.

648 11:35	88 1:25	300 4:40	260 4:00	95 1:30	799 11:40	139 2:20	227 3:20	836 12:55	233 3:30	380 6:20	643 9:20	202 2:55	507 9:45	223 5:10	547 9:50	137 2:00	346 6:50	193 3:00	923 16:45	470 6:40	232 3:25	772 11:10	379 5:45	558 8:40	• **Alexandra**
198 3:03	511 8:35	258 4:00	733 11:05	568 9:35	447 7:03	398 6:04	345 5:01	386 6:02	414 6:35	853 13:25	313 4:55	671 10:00	101 1:04	385 6:04	97 1:45	616 9:05	262 4:35	462 6:05	473 7:55	159 2:25	701 10:03	420 7:05	182 2:55	• **Arthur's Pass**	
380 6:15	343 5:25	79 1:05	578 8:10	400 6:40	420 6:05	230 3:30	166 2:15	509 7:25	246 3:40	698 10:30	264 3:55	492 7:05	283 4:35	478 8:45	279 4:40	437 6:10	444 7:30	283 3:55	583 8:55	91 1:05	522 7:35	393 5:40	• **Ashburton**		
258 4:15	736 11:20	472 6:45	971 13:50	793 11:50	27 0:25	623 9:25	559 7:55	116 1:45	639 9:30	1091 15:15	129 1:50	885 12:45	363 5:50	647 10:45	323 5:05	830 11:50	524 8:45	676 9:35	247 4:10	311 4:35	915 13:15	• **Blenheim**			
885 13:35	325 5:10	443 6:30	190 2:55	220 3:30	942 13:40	376 5:45	356 5:20	1031 14:45	470 6:55	310 5:15	786 11:30	30 0:30	744 11:45	460 8:40	784 11:50	96 1:25	583 10:45	239 3:40	1105 16:30	613 8:40	• **Bluff**				
330 5:10	434 6:30	170 2:10	669 9:15	491 7:15	338 5:00	321 4:35	257 3:20	427 6:15	337 4:55	789 11:35	182 2:50	583 8:10	260 4:05	544 8:55	256 4:10	528 7:15	421 6:55	374 5:00	501 7:50	• **Christchurch**					
311 5:20	841 15:10	662 10:00	1127 19:50	948 17:05	235 4:20	813 12:25	749 11:20	131 1:45	829 12:45	1247 21:55	376 6:00	1075 16:00	416 6:55	700 11:55	376 6:10	1020 15:05	577 9:50	866 12:50	• **Collingwood**						
660 10:55	281 4:25	204 2:50	295 4:15	288 4:25	703 10:00	237 3:25	117 1:40	792 11:05	331 4:35	415 6:35	547 7:50	209 3:10	563 8:05	416 9:35	559 8:10	154 2:15	539 9:45	• **Dunedin**							
302 5:25	264 5:25	532 8:10	536 10:00	371 7:15	551 9:10	371 7:20	491 9:05	490 8:15	465 8:25	656 12:20	530 9:30	545 10:15	161 2:55	123 2:05	201 3:40	483 8:50	• **Fox Glacier**								
785 12:10	225 3:25	355 5:05	141 2:00	171 2:35	857 12:15	276 4:20	271 3:55	946 13:30	370 5:30	261 4:20	701 9:05	65 0:55	644 10:20	360 6:45	684 10:25	• **Gore**									
101 1:45	465 9:05	355 5:20	737 13:40	572 10:55	350 5:30	495 8:10	442 6:55	289 4:35	511 8:55	857 16:00	329 6:15	746 11:20	40 0:45	324 5:40	• **Greymouth**										
425 7:30	141 3:20	409 8:10	413 7:55	248 5:10	674 11:10	248 5:15	368 7:00	613 10:15	342 6:25	533 10:15	653 11:25	422 8:10	284 5:00	• **Haast**											
141 2:30	425 8:20	359 5:15	697 12:55	532 10:10	390 6:15	499 8:05	446 6:50	329 5:25	515 8:15	817 15:15	369 6:35	706 11:15	• **Hokitika**												
855 13:05	295 4:40	413 6:00	160 2:25	190 3:00	912 13:10	346 5:15	326 4:50	1001 14:15	440 6:25	280 4:45	756 11:00	• **Invercargill**													
332 5:30	607 9:20	343 5:00	842 13:55	674 11:10	156 2:15	494 7:25	430 6:10	245 3:35	510 7:45	962 16:15	• **Kaikoura**														
958 16:50	398 6:55	619 9:25	120 2:20	299 5:05	1118 18:25	455 7:45	532 8:15	1146 18:35	549 8:55	• **Milford Sound**															
612 10:00	207 3:00	212 3:10	429 6:30	264 3:50	666 9:45	94 1:10	214 3:55	755 10:30	• **Mount Cook**																
224 3:45	754 12:45	588 8:25	1026 16:15	861 13:30	104 2:10	739 9:55	675 9:35	• **Nelson**																	
543 8:30	233 3:40	87 1:10	412 5:55	290 4:50	586 8:20	120 1:45	• **Oamaru**																		
596 9:50	113 1:55	161 2:40	342 5:25	170 2:40	650 9:50	• **Omarama**																			
285 4:40	763 11:45	499 7:10	998 16:05	830 13:20	• **Picton**																				
673 12:30	113 1:50	331 5:35	179 2:45	• **Queenstown**																					
838 14:30	278 4:35	499 7:05	• **Te Anau**																						
456 7:20	274 4:35	• **Timaru**																							
566 10:45	• **Wanaka**																								
• **Westport**																									

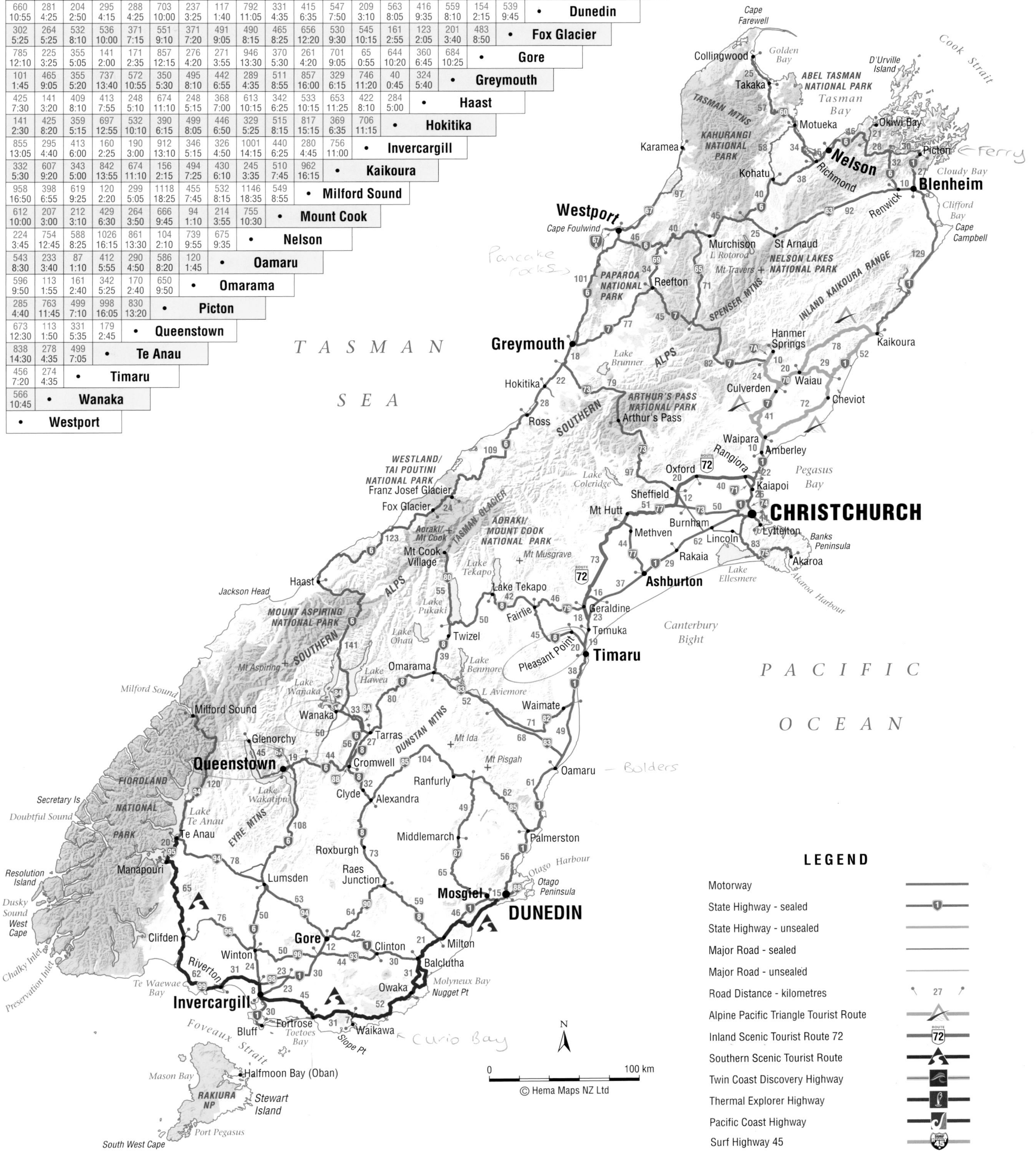

20 top things to do

1 Great Walks

There are six DOC Great Walks in the South Island: Abel Tasman Coastal Track, Heaphy Track, Kepler Track, Milford Track, Rakiura Track and Routeburn Track. Every year about 14,000 people complete the Milford Track. The North Island has three DOC Great Walks: Waikaremoana, Tongariro Northern Circuit and Whanganui Journey (a canoe trip).

2 Ski

The South Island has numerous skiing areas, including Queenstown and Lake Wanaka, as well as many areas around the Southern Alps. The North Island has three skifields: Whakapapa, Turoa and Maunganui. Whakapapa is New Zealand's largest ski field. The season in New Zealand generally runs between July and September.

3 Follow wine trails

The Hawke's Bay region is the North Island's largest wine producing area, with other major areas including Waiheke Island, Kumeu, Warkworth/ Matakana, Gisborne and Martinborough. The South Island's largest wine producing region is Marlborough, and Central Otago and the Waipara Valley are other booming areas.

4 Cruise

Around the Bay of Islands and Auckland you can charter a yacht or join a boat cruise. Another popular tour is from Russell or Paihia out to the Hole in the Rock. On the South Island, cruising is a good way to experience the numerous sounds in both the Fiordland and Marlborough regions.

5 See wildlife

Throughout New Zealand kiwis are on display at various locations, including the Kiwi House, Rainbow Springs, Mt Bruce National Wildlife Centre, the Kiwi and Birdlife Park, the National Kiwi Centre, the Orana Wildlife Park and Willowbank Reserve. The South Island's West Coast has New Zealand's only white heron nesting site, and colonies of both blue and yellow-eyed penguins. See fur seals at Cape Foulwind, the Southern Encounter Aquarium in Christchurch and the world's only mainland colony of royal albatross on the Otago Peninsula.

6 Sample local produce

Te Puke is the 'capital' for kiwifruit. Try mussels and oysters at the Coromandel, shellfish at the Pouto Lighthouse, kumara at Dargaville, honey in Warkworth, bacon and ham in Pokeno and cheese in Eltham. Visit orchards and olive groves in the Hawke's Bay region. Around the South Island sample rock lobster at Kaikoura, Havelock's greenshell mussels, the internationally-famous Bluff oysters, Mapua's smoked fish and Stirling's cheese. Buy seafood in Nelson, stone fruit in Central Otago and cheese, chocolate and Barker's fruit products in Geraldine.

7 Scenic flights

A scenic flight is the perfect way to see the South Island's more remote scenery, like the Fiordland region's sounds, the glaciers of the southern West Coast and the Southern Alps. It's also a good way to see Australasia's highest mountain and the southern hemisphere's longest glacier in Mt Cook National Park.

8 Participate in adventure activities

New Zealand is a wonderful country to experience adventure activities, like sky diving, bungy jumping, jet boating, mountain biking, bridge climbing, sky jumping, kayaking, parapenting, skiing, white-water rafting, four-wheel driving, diving, gliding and hot-air ballooning.

9 Bushwalk and tramp

Tramp in the Waipoua and Waitangi forests, Waitakere and Hunua ranges, Whakarewarewa Forest, Egmont and Whanganui national parks, and the Tararua Ranges on the North Island. Tongariro Crossing is one of the best day-walks. Around the South Island, tramp in the Abel Tasman, Kahurangi, Rakiura and Fiordland national parks. The Otago Central Rail Trail and Tuatapere Hump Ridge Track are other highlights.

10 The TranzAlpine train journey

Although it's a spectacular journey, winding through amazing scenery, the TranzAlpine train journey takes just four hours. It is a great way to travel between Greymouth on the west coast and Christchurch on the east.

11 See geothermal phenomenon and hot pools

Around Rotorua and Taupo there are numerous geothermal parks, and the world-famous Pohutu Geyser. Hot pool complexes are near Gisborne, the Bay of Plenty, Tongariro National Park, Waiwera Hot Springs, Morere Hot Springs, Tokaanu, Lake Taupo and Te Aroha. The South Island has Hanmer Springs and Maruia Springs Thermal Resort.

12 Shop

Auckland has good designer shopping, Wellington offers excellent urban shopping, and smaller cities have artworks, gourmet food products and quality knitwear. Both Christchurch and Dunedin have excellent urban shopping while other South Island towns and cities have artworks and gourmet food products. On the West Coast, pick up some jade (greenstone) jewellery.

13 Fish

Try catching trout at Turangi – the trout town of New Zealand – as well as at Lake Waikaremoana, Lake Maraetai, Whirinaki Forest Park, Kaweka Forest Park, Lake Taupo, Tongariro River, Waitahanui River and Tauranga Taupo River. Head to Whangaroa Harbour or Tutukaka for game-fishing. To catch brown trout and salmon on the South Island head to: rivers like the Buller, Karamea, Waitaki, Taieri, Clutha and Pomehaka and lakes including Rotoiti, Rotoroa, Roxburgh, Wanaka, Hawea, Te Anau, Manapouri and Brunner. The Matuara River, near Gore, is known as 'the brown trout fishing centre of Southland'. Rakaia is world renowned as a salmon fishing area.

14 Experience Maori culture

Cultural experiences can be found in Waitangi, Auckland and Rotorua. There are numerous historic pa sites and marae around the East Coast and Maori craft at Tokomaru Bay. Rewa's Village, Tamaki Maori Village and Howick Historical Village also provide interesting insights. On the South Island, see a Maori pa site at Matangi Awhea, Whakatu Marae, Te Waikoropupu Springs (a Maori sacred place) and Te Awhina Marae.

15 Bungy jump

On the North Island, bungy jump off the Auckland Harbour Bridge or leap from New Zealand's first purpose-built platform bungy jump at Taupo. At Mount Hutt, on the South Island, try a ski or snowboard bungy. At 134m, the Nevis Highwire bungy jump, near Queenstown, is the highest in Australasia.

16 Surf

On the rough west coast, board surfers enjoy the breaks of Opunake, Raglan, Piha, Muriwai and Ahipara. Highly recommended surfing venues on the east coast include: Castle Point, Gisborne, Mt Maunganui, Whangamata, Hot Water Beach, Mangawhai Heads, Waipu Cove and Sandy Bay.

17 Cave

The Waitomo region has extensive cave systems and caves can also be found at Waipu, Waiomio, Nikau Caves and Kawiti Caves. New Zealand's deepest cave, Nettlebed, is located in the South Island's Kahurangi National Park. Mt Owen Bulmer Caves, Ngarua Caves, Oparara Basin, Honeycomb Hill Cave and Te Ana-au Caves are also popular.

18 Golf

Premium golf experiences are offered at Kauri Cliffs in Northland, Gulf Harbour north of Auckland and Wairakei near Taupo. Paraparaumu Beach Golf Links is New Zealand's number one ranked course. There's a great golf course in Amberley on the South Island, and some of New Zealand's toughest holes at the Clearwater Resort's golf course in Christchurch.

19 Scenic drives

The North Island has three scenic tourist routes: Twin Coast Discovery Highway, Thermal Explorer Highway and Pacific Coast Highway. Mauao and Mount Maunganui Beach has the best beach and coastline of the Bay of Plenty. Travel through the South Island on the Alpine Pacific Triangle touring route, Inland Scenic Route 72 and Southern Scenic Highway. The Milford Road is known as one of the world's best alpine roads.

20 Mountain bike rides

Popular spots on the North Island are Woodhill, Waiheke Island, Rotorua's Whakarewarewa Forest, and the Hunua Ranges and Tapapakanga regional parks. One of the best routes is the 42nd Traverse. On the South Island, around Nelson, Reefton, Queenstown, Alexandra, Christchurch and Naseby there are numerous tracks. Good routes include the Queen Charlotte Walkway and the Otago Central Rail Trail.

25 must-see attractions

Lord of the Rings movie-set locations
See where Middle Earth was filmed. Throughout this atlas major filming locations are shown with a 🎥 symbol.

Cape Reinga lighthouse (1 A1)
The meeting point of the Tasman Sea and the Pacific Ocean

Kerikeri's old buildings (4 A8)
New Zealand's oldest stone building (1833) and New Zealand's oldest house (1822)

Poor Knights Islands Marine Reserve (4 E13)
One of the world's finest dive locations – off the coast from Tutukaka.

Auckland (7 D4)
Sky Tower, MOTAT, Kelly Tarlton's Antarctic Encounter and Underwater World, Auckland Zoo, Rainbow's End Adventure Park, Waiheke and Rangitoto Island, Bungy off the Harbour Bridge, museums, galleries

Cathedral Cove and the Coromandel Peninsula (8 D13)
Beautiful beaches for swimming, fishing and boating

Waitomo Caves (11 H5)
Glow-worms, caving, black-water rafting

Mount Tarawera (13 H6)
See the Buried Village, visit the museum and walk between the excavated dwellings

Rotorua (13 G4)
Geothermal attractions, including hot springs, mud pools and geysers

Cruise to White Island (14 E11)
Take a cruise from Whakatane to New Zealand's most active volcano

Lake Taupo area (19 E4)
Wild trout fishery, geothermal and volcanic areas to explore, bungy jump, waterfalls

Mount Taranaki (23 D5)
New Zealand's 'most climbed mountain' at 2517m.

Tongariro National Park (26 A12)
Whakapapa skifield, active and extinct volcanoes, tramping

Wellington (33 F1)
New Zealand's capital: Te Papa Museum, Wellington Zoo, seal colony, Embassy Theatre, Wellington Cable Car, Carter Observatory, Wellington Botanical Gardens, Capital E

Marlborough region (40)
Wineries, kayaking and cruising on the Sounds

Pancake Rocks blowholes (45 B5)
Limestone rocks and blowholes that make a spectacular spouting display

Franz Josef (49 G6) and Fox (49 H4) glaciers
Experience massive rivers of ice on foot or by helicopter

Mt Cook National Park (59 A7)
Tasman Glacier, the southern hemisphere's longest glacier, and Aoraki (Mt Cook), Australasia's highest mountain at 3754m

Lake Tekapo (60 D10)
Turquoise glacial lake best seen from the historic Church of the Good Shepherd

Christchurch (56 D10)
Hagley Park, tram rides, Avon River, garden tours, Southern Encounter Aquarium, Antarctic Centre, Gondola, Art Gallery

Dunedin (74 H11)
Larnach Castle, Victorian and Edwardian architecture, Royal Albatross Centre, Penguin Place, Taieri Gorge Railway, garden tours, Otago Museum, Otago Peninsula

Curio Bay (78 H11)
Fossilised forest which is believed to date from the Jurassic age; in the Catlins

Invercargill's Queens Park (127 A3)
80ha park in the CBD, with a golf course, Southland Museum and Art Gallery, aviary, Japanese garden and rose garden

Queenstown (65 H4) and Wanaka (66 D8)
Ski fields, adventure activities, Skyline gondola complex, TSS Earnslaw cruise on Lake Wakatipu, wine trails, Skippers Canyon, scenic flights, Mount Aspiring National Park, lakes Wanaka and Hawea, Rob Roy Glacier, Puzzling World, Wanaka Beerworks, Rippon Vineyard

Milford Sound (63 C7)
Bowen Falls, Stirling Falls, Mitre Peak, bottlenose dolphins, fur seals, Fiordland crested penguins, cruises, kayaking, diving, Milford Deep underwater observatory.

- Drinking Water
- Toilets
- Fireplace/BBQ
- Picnic Area
- Rubbish Disposal
- Shower
- Stream Water
- Walking Track

- Fully serviced Campgrounds have flush toilets, tap water, showers, rubbish collection, picnic tables and usually some powered sites. Many have barbecues or fireplaces, a kitchen, laundry and shop.
- A fee is charged at most DOC campsites.

Northland

Campsite	Map	Drinking Water	Toilets	Fireplace/BBQ	Picnic Area	Rubbish Disposal	Shower	Stream Water	Walking Track
Cable Bay	4 A11	✓	✓				✓		
Forest Pools	3 B6		✓		✓			✓	
Kapowairua (Spirits Bay)	1 A2	✓	✓			✓	✓		✓
Maitai Bay	2 F7	✓	✓				✓		✓
Otamure Bay	4 D13	✓	✓			✓	✓		✓
Puketi	2 K11	✓	✓	✓	✓		✓		✓
Puriri Bay	4 C12	✓	✓			✓	✓		✓
Raetea North Side	3 A4		✓					✓	
Rarawa	1 E4	✓	✓				✓		✓
Sunset Bay	4 A11	✓	✓				✓		
Taputaputa	1 A1	✓	✓			✓	✓		✓
Trounson Kauri Park	3 G5	✓	✓	✓	✓	✓	✓		✓
Uretiti	4 J13	✓	✓		✓	✓	✓		✓
Urupukapuka Bay	4 A11	✓	✓				✓		
Waikahoa Bay, Mimiwhangata	4 D12	✓	✓				✓		

Auckland

Campsite	Map	Drinking Water	Toilets	Fireplace/BBQ	Picnic Area	Rubbish Disposal	Shower	Stream Water	Walking Track
Akapoua Bay	36 D4	✓	✓		✓	✓	✓		✓
Awana Beach	36 D5	✓	✓			✓	✓		
Harataonga	36 D5	✓	✓			✓	✓		
Home Bay	6 J12	✓	✓			✓			
Medlands Beach	36 E5	✓	✓			✓	✓		
Motuihe	7 D6	✓	✓						
Motuora	6 F11	✓	✓				✓		
Whangapoua	36 C4	✓	✓			✓	✓		

Waikato

Campsite	Map	Drinking Water	Toilets	Fireplace/BBQ	Picnic Area	Rubbish Disposal	Shower	Stream Water	Walking Track
Booms Flat	8 G12		✓	✓					✓
Broken Hills	8 G13		✓	✓		✓		✓	✓
Catleys	8 G12		✓	✓	✓	✓		✓	✓
Fantail Bay	8 A9	✓	✓			✓	✓		✓
Fletcher Bay	8 A10	✓	✓	✓		✓	✓		✓
Hotoritori	8 G12		✓	✓		✓		✓	✓
Kakaho	19 C2		✓	✓	✓	✓		✓	✓
Ngaherenga	18 B13		✓	✓	✓	✓		✓	✓
Piropiro	18 C12		✓	✓	✓	✓		✓	✓
Port Jackson	8 A10	✓	✓	✓		✓	✓		✓
Shag Stream	8 H12		✓	✓	✓	✓		✓	✓
Stony Bay	8 A10	✓	✓	✓	✓	✓	✓		✓
Totara Flat	8 G12		✓	✓		✓		✓	✓
Trestle View	8 G12		✓	✓		✓		✓	✓
Waikawau Bay	8 B11	✓	✓			✓	✓		
Wainora	8 G12		✓	✓		✓		✓	✓
Wentworth	8 J14	✓	✓	✓	✓	✓	✓		✓
Whangaiterenga	8 G12		✓	✓	✓	✓		✓	✓

Bay of Plenty

Campsite	Map	Drinking Water	Toilets	Fireplace/BBQ	Picnic Area	Rubbish Disposal	Shower	Stream Water	Walking Track
Dickey Flat	10 F10		✓					✓	✓
Hot Water Beach	13 H6	✓	✓		✓				
Lake Tarawera Outlet	13 H6	✓	✓		✓	✓			
Mangamate	20 D11		✓	✓	✓			✓	
Okahu Roadend	20 D12		✓	✓	✓			✓	
Rerewhakaaitu-Ash Pit Road	13 J6	✓	✓						
Rerewhakaaitu-Brett Road	13 J6	✓	✓						
Sanctuary	20 D11		✓		✓			✓	✓

East Coast

Campsite	Map	Drinking Water	Toilets	Fireplace/BBQ	Picnic Area	Rubbish Disposal	Shower	Stream Water	Walking Track
Anaura Bay	16 J11	✓				✓			✓
Boulders	15 G3		✓	✓	✓			✓	✓
Manganuku	14 J14		✓		✓			✓	✓
Mokau Landing	21 E2	✓	✓	✓	✓	✓			✓
Omahuru (Ogilvies)	14 J12		✓	✓	✓			✓	
Orangihikoia	20 D14		✓	✓	✓			✓	
Rosie's Bay	21 E2		✓					✓	✓
Te Pakau (8 Acre)	14 H12		✓					✓	✓
Te Taita O Makoro	21 D2		✓	✓				✓	
Waikaremoana Motor Camp	21 E3	Fully serviced							✓
Whitikau	15 G5		✓	✓	✓			✓	

Tongariro/Taupo

Campsite	Map	Drinking Water	Toilets	Fireplace/BBQ	Picnic Area	Rubbish Disposal	Shower	Stream Water	Walking Track
Army Road	19 G6		✓						✓
Clements Clearing	19 G6		✓					✓	✓
Clements Roadend	19 G6		✓						✓
Kaimanawa Road	19 J3		✓					✓	✓
Kakapo	19 G6		✓					✓	✓
Mangahuia	18 J12	✓	✓		✓	✓			✓
Mangawhero	26 C11	✓	✓		✓	✓			✓
Pokaka Mill	18 H12		✓						
Te Iringa	19 G6		✓						✓
Urchin	19 J3		✓						
Whakapapa Motor Camp	26 A12	Fully Serviced							✓

Whanganui

Campsite	Map	Drinking Water	Toilets	Fireplace/BBQ	Picnic Area	Rubbish Disposal	Shower	Stream Water	Walking Track
Kawhatau	27 G5	✓	✓						✓
Ohinepane	18 G9	✓	✓	✓	✓				✓
Whakahoro	18 H9	✓	✓		✓				

Wellington

Campsite	Map	Drinking Water	Toilets	Fireplace/BBQ	Picnic Area	Rubbish Disposal	Shower	Stream Water	Walking Track
Bucks Road	33 C6		✓					✓	✓
Catchpool Valley	33 F3	✓	✓	✓	✓	✓		✓	✓
Holdsworth	34 B7	✓	✓	✓	✓	✓		✓	✓
Kiriwhakapapa	34 A8		✓		✓			✓	✓
Otaki Forks	33 A5	✓	✓			✓		✓	✓
Putangirua Pinnacles	33 G5		✓		✓			✓	✓
Waikawa	29 H5		✓					✓	✓
Waiohine Gorge	33 B7		✓		✓			✓	✓

Hawkes Bay

Campsite	Map	Drinking Water	Toilets	Fireplace/BBQ	Picnic Area	Rubbish Disposal	Shower	Stream Water	Walking Track
Everetts	20 J11		✓		✓			✓	
Glenfalls	20 J10		✓					✓	
Kumeti	30 B11		✓	✓				✓	
Lake Tutira	28 A12	✓	✓		✓				
Lawrence	28 C8		✓	✓	✓			✓	✓
Kuripapango	27 C7		✓					✓	✓
Mangatutu Hot Springs	28 A8		✓	✓	✓			✓	✓
Waikare River Mouth	28 A13	✓	✓		✓				✓

There are many more places to stay in the great outdoors managed by Department of Conservation. For details of Great Walks, walk in campsites near huts, information about huts or any other conservation information contact your nearest visitor centre or visit the DOC website: www.doc.govt.nz

DOC Hotline 0800 362 468 For fire, search and rescue call 111

Nelson/Marlborough

Acheron Accommodation House	47 E6	Toilets, Stream water
Aussie Bay	40 G9	Tap, Toilets, Picnic tables
Butchers Flat	39 H6	Toilets, Picnic tables, Stream water
Camp Bay	40 F11	Tap, Toilets
Canaan Downs	38 F9	Tap, Toilets, Picnic tables, Walks
Cobb Cottage	43 J5	Toilets, Stream water
Cobb River	37 H6	Toilets, Stream water
Coldwater Stream	43 J2	Toilets, Stream water
Courthouse Flat	42 B8	Toilets, Picnic tables, Stream water
Cowshed Bay	40 G10	Tap, Toilets, Picnic tables, Walks
D'Urville Island	40 B9	Toilets, Stream water, Walks
Elaine Bay	40 E8	Tap, Toilets, Picnic tables
Ferndale	40 F10	Tap, Toilets, Picnic tables
French Pass	40 C9	Tap, Toilets, Picnic tables, Hot showers
Harvey Bay	40 E8	Tap, Toilets, Walks
Kauauroa Bay	40 E10	Toilets, Stream water
Kawatiri	42 F11	Toilets, Picnic tables, Stream water, Walks
Kenepuru Head	40 F11	Tap, Toilets, Picnic tables, Walks
Kerr Bay	42 G13	Fully serviced
Kowhai Point	43 E3	Toilets, Picnic tables, Stream water
Lake Rotoroa	42 G11	Tap, Toilets, Picnic tables, Walks
Lake Tennyson	47 C4	Toilets, Stream water
Marfells Beach	44 E12	Tap, Toilets, Picnic tables, Walks
Mill Flat	43 C7	Toilets, Picnic tables, Stream water
Moetapu Bay	40 G9	Tap, Toilets, Picnic tables
Momorangi Bay	40 G9	Fully serviced
Nikau Cove	40 F10	Tap, Toilets, Picnic tables
Onamalut	40 J8	Tap, Toilets, Picnic tables
Pelorus Bridge	39 H6	Fully serviced
Picnic Bay	40 F10	Tap, Toilets, Picnic tables
Rarangi	40 J10	Tap, Toilets, Picnic tables
Ratimera Bay	40 G11	Tap, Toilets, Picnic tables
Robin Hood Bay	40 H11	Toilets, Stream water
Siberia	42 C11	Toilets, Stream water
Totaranui	38 D9	Tap, Toilets, Picnic tables, Hot showers, Walks
Waimaru	40 E10	Tap, Toilets, Walks
Waiona Bay	40 D9	Toilets, Stream water
West Bay	43 F1	Tap, Toilets, Picnic tables, Hot showers, Walks
Whatamango Bay	40 G11	Tap, Toilets, Picnic tables
Whites Bay	40 J10	Tap, Toilets, Picnic tables, Hot showers, Walks

*Except for kitchen and hot showers

Canterbury

Ahuriri Bridge	67 A4	Picnic tables, Stream water
Andrews Shelter	52 B10	Toilets, Picnic tables, Stream water
Avalanche Creek Shelter	52 B8	Tap, Toilets, Picnic tables, Rubbish bins, Walks
Craigieburn Shelter	52 D9	Toilets, Picnic tables, Stream water, Walks
Deer Valley	46 E13	Toilets, Stream water, Walks
Grey River	53 D7	Toilets, Stream water, Walks
Greyneys	52 B8	Toilets, Picnic tables, Stream water, Walks
Hawdon Valley	52 B9	Toilets, Stream water, Walks
Klondyke Corner	52 C8	Toilets, Picnic tables, Stream water, Walks
Lake Taylor Camping Area	46 J12	Toilets, Picnic tables, Stream water
Loch Katrine Camping Area	46 H12	Tap, Toilets, Picnic tables
Mt Nimrod	60 J13	Tap, Toilets, Kitchen, Picnic tables, Rubbish bins, Walks
Orari	61 E4	Tap, Toilets, Kitchen, Picnic tables, Rubbish bins
Otaio Gorge	68 B11	Tap, Toilets, Kitchen, Picnic tables, Rubbish bins
Peel Forest	61 C5	Fully serviced
Pioneer Park	61 F2	Tap, Toilets, Kitchen, Picnic tables, Rubbish bins, Walks
Temple	59 F4	Toilets, Picnic tables, Stream water
Waihi Gorge	61 E4	Tap, Toilets, Kitchen, Picnic tables, Rubbish bins
White Horse Hill	59 B6	Tap, Toilets, Picnic tables, Rubbish bins, Walks
Wooded Gully	52 E14	Tap, Toilets, Picnic tables, Walks

West Coast

Gillespies Beach	49 G3	Tap, Toilets, Walks
Goldsborough	45 H3	Tap, Toilets, Kitchen, Rubbish bins
Hans Bay	45 J3	Tap, Toilets, Rubbish bins
Kohaihai	37 H2	Tap, Toilets, Kitchen, Picnic tables, Walks
Lake Ianthe	50 C9	Tap, Toilets, Kitchen, Picnic tables
Lake Mahinapua	45 J1	Tap, Toilets, Picnic tables, Rubbish bins, Walks
Lake Paringa	58 B12	Toilets, Picnic tables, Stream water, Walks
Lyell	41 G6	Tap, Toilets, Kitchen, Picnic tables, Rubbish bins, Walks
Marble Hill	46 D12	Tap, Toilets, Kitchen, Picnic tables, Rubbish bins, Walks
Ottos/MacDonalds	49 F6	Tap, Toilets, Picnic tables, Rubbish bins, Walks
Slab Hut Creek	46 B9	Tap, Toilets, Picnic tables, Rubbish bins, Walks

Otago

Boundary Creek	58 J10	Tap, Toilets, Picnic tables, Walks
Cameron Flat	58 G11	Tap, Toilets, Picnic tables, Walks
Glencoe	68 J10	Tap, Toilets, Kitchen, Picnic tables, Walks
Homestead	66 E14	Tap, Toilets
Kidds Bush	66 A9	Tap, Toilets, Picnic tables, Walks
Kinloch	64 F12	Toilets, Kitchen, Picnic tables, Stream water, Walks
Lake Sylvan	64 E11	Toilets, Picnic tables, Stream water, Walks
Macetown	65 F6	Toilets, Stream water, Walks
Moke Lake	64 H14	Toilets, Stream water, Walks
Pleasant Flat	58 E12	Tap, Toilets, Picnic tables, Walks
Purakaunui Bay	79 H2	Tap, Toilets, Rubbish bins
Skippers Township	65 F4	Tap, Toilets, Picnic tables, Walks
St Bathans Domain	67 F2	Tap, Toilets
Tawanui	78 E13	Tap, Toilets, Picnic tables, Rubbish bins, Walks
Trotters Gorge	74 B13	Toilets, Picnic tables, Stream water, Walks
Twelve Mile Delta	64 H13	Toilets, Stream water

Southland

Cascade Creek	64 G10	Toilets, Picnic tables, Stream water
Deer Flat	64 H9	Toilets, Picnic tables, Stream water
Henry Creek	70 B12	Toilets, Picnic tables, Stream water
Kiosk Creek	64 H9	Toilets, Picnic tables, Stream water
Lake Gunn	64 F10	Toilets, Kitchen, Picnic tables, Stream water, Walks
Mackay Creek	64 J9	Toilets, Picnic tables, Stream water, Walks
Mavora Lakes	71 B4	Tap, Toilets, Kitchen, Picnic tables, Stream water, Walks
Monowai	70 H10	Tap, Toilets, Walks
Piano Flat	72 E11	Toilets, Kitchen, Picnic tables, Stream water, Walks
Smithy Creek	64 G9	Toilets, Picnic tables, Stream water, Walks
Thicket Burn	76 D10	Tap, Toilets, Picnic tables, Walks
Totara	64 J9	Toilets, Kitchen, Picnic tables, Stream water
Upper Eglinton	64 G9	Toilets, Kitchen, Picnic tables, Stream water, Walks
Walker Creek	64 J9	Toilets, Picnic tables, Stream water

Cape Reinga Lighthouse

Land's End, Bluff

Te ARAROA
THE LONG PATHWAY

Base image © Geographx 2006

Te Araroa – The Long Pathway

A New Zealand-long walking track – Te Araroa, meaning the Long Pathway – is taking shape from Cape Reinga to Bluff. This edition of Hema's New Zealand Road Atlas shows sections of it.

The track will be 3,000 kms long – a project headed by the private Te Araroa Trust and its eight regional trusts. Seventy percent of the distance is open for walking on existing north-south tracks though some are not yet signed with Te Araroa logos, and most are not yet linked. A further 13 percent of the trail is walkable on back-roads which connect trailheads. In consultation with local authorities and Department of Conservation (DOC) conservancies, Te Araroa Trust designed the North Island route in 1997, using many existing tracks and mapping possible linking routes.

In 2000 the Trust financed and constructed its first link track, 18km up the Waikato River. Since then, Te Araroa Trust and Te Araroa regional trusts, usually in cooperation with local authorities, have opened over 400km of new linking track, some 13% of the total distance. The DOC tracks en route are now mostly marked up with Te Araroa logos. Many of them are in the South Island, where Te Araroa Trust completed a route design in 2002. The latest track developments and trail maps for many of the walkable sections are available on Te Araroa's website www.teararoa.org.nz.

History

Much of Te Araroa's route crosses countryside and coast that is legally walkable, for example on road reserve that has been surveyed off but not built, or coastline, or down rivers where canoes are recommended, or across DOC land that is not tracked. If these 'paper' roads, beaches, forests and water sections such as the Whanganui River are included, the trail route can be described as 93% legally negotiable. For reasons of safety though, these additional routes are not shown, for they do not yet have proper definition.

Also, some of the tracks that are shown, for example the routes through the Tararua or Richmond Ranges, should be attempted by experienced trampers only.

River crossings are another hazard. At major rivers, Te Araroa Trust simply declares a 'safety zone' and it's up to individual trampers whether they cross and how. For at least two South Island rivers, the crossing is best done by 4WD vehicle or jet boat. Te Araroa Trust recommends that any trampers who attempt remote tracks or significant river crossings should first consult with the local area office of DOC. It advises that trampers must always fill in intentions forms in every hut and shelter they pass, even if they don't intend staying there. The Trust also recommends that trampers should take advantage of mountain safety and river crossing courses, available through www.mountainsafety.org.nz.

Safety

The New Zealand-long tramping route was once an aim of the New Zealand Walkways Commission set up in 1975 to encourage walkway development. The Commission put in place 130 new short tracks, but did not progress a New Zealand-long trail. NZWC was formally abolished in 1990, when control of walkways was handed over to DOC, but the Department did not pursue the long trail idea.

In the mid 1990s the long trail project was revived by a newspaper campaign headed by journalist and tramper Geoff Chapple. Te Araroa Trust was formed as keeper of the vision. At first the Trust saw its role only as encouraging those with the necessary resources to undertake construction of their sections – mainly district, city and regional councils – but in 2000 the trust became a track builder.

In 2002 the Mayors Taskforce for Jobs – an organisation which aims to stimulate employment, and includes most New Zealand district and city councils – made Te Araroa a priority project. That same year DOC signed a Memorandum of Understanding with Te Araroa Trust by which the Department agreed to support the goal, and in 2007 the Government voted DOC $3.8 million to finance construction of Te Araroa on DOC estate.

Te Araroa Trust acts now as an advisor for participating councils and DOC, as well as continuing its own track scoping, financing, and building using a construction manager and many volunteers.

Te Araroa Trust intends to open the track in December 2010.

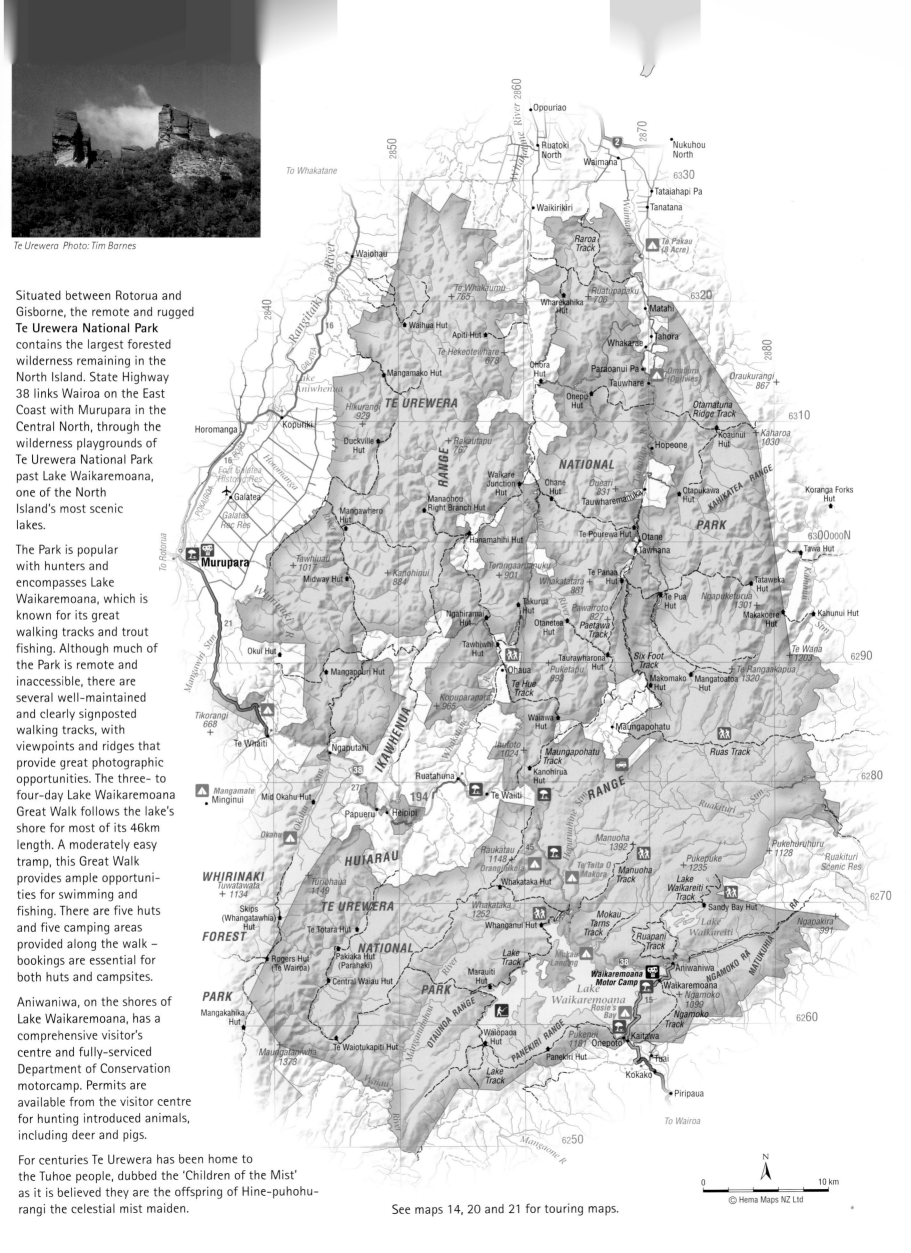

Te Urewera Photo: Tim Barnes

Situated between Rotorua and Gisborne, the remote and rugged **Te Urewera National Park** contains the largest forested wilderness remaining in the North Island. State Highway 38 links Wairoa on the East Coast with Murupara in the Central North, through the wilderness playgrounds of Te Urewera National Park past Lake Waikaremoana, one of the North Island's most scenic lakes.

The Park is popular with hunters and encompasses Lake Waikaremoana, which is known for its great walking tracks and trout fishing. Although much of the Park is remote and inaccessible, there are several well-maintained and clearly signposted walking tracks, with viewpoints and ridges that provide great photographic opportunities. The three- to four-day Lake Waikaremoana Great Walk follows the lake's shore for most of its 46km length. A moderately easy tramp, this Great Walk provides ample opportunities for swimming and fishing. There are five huts and five camping areas provided along the walk – bookings are essential for both huts and campsites.

Aniwaniwa, on the shores of Lake Waikaremoana, has a comprehensive visitor's centre and fully-serviced Department of Conservation motorcamp. Permits are available from the visitor centre for hunting introduced animals, including deer and pigs.

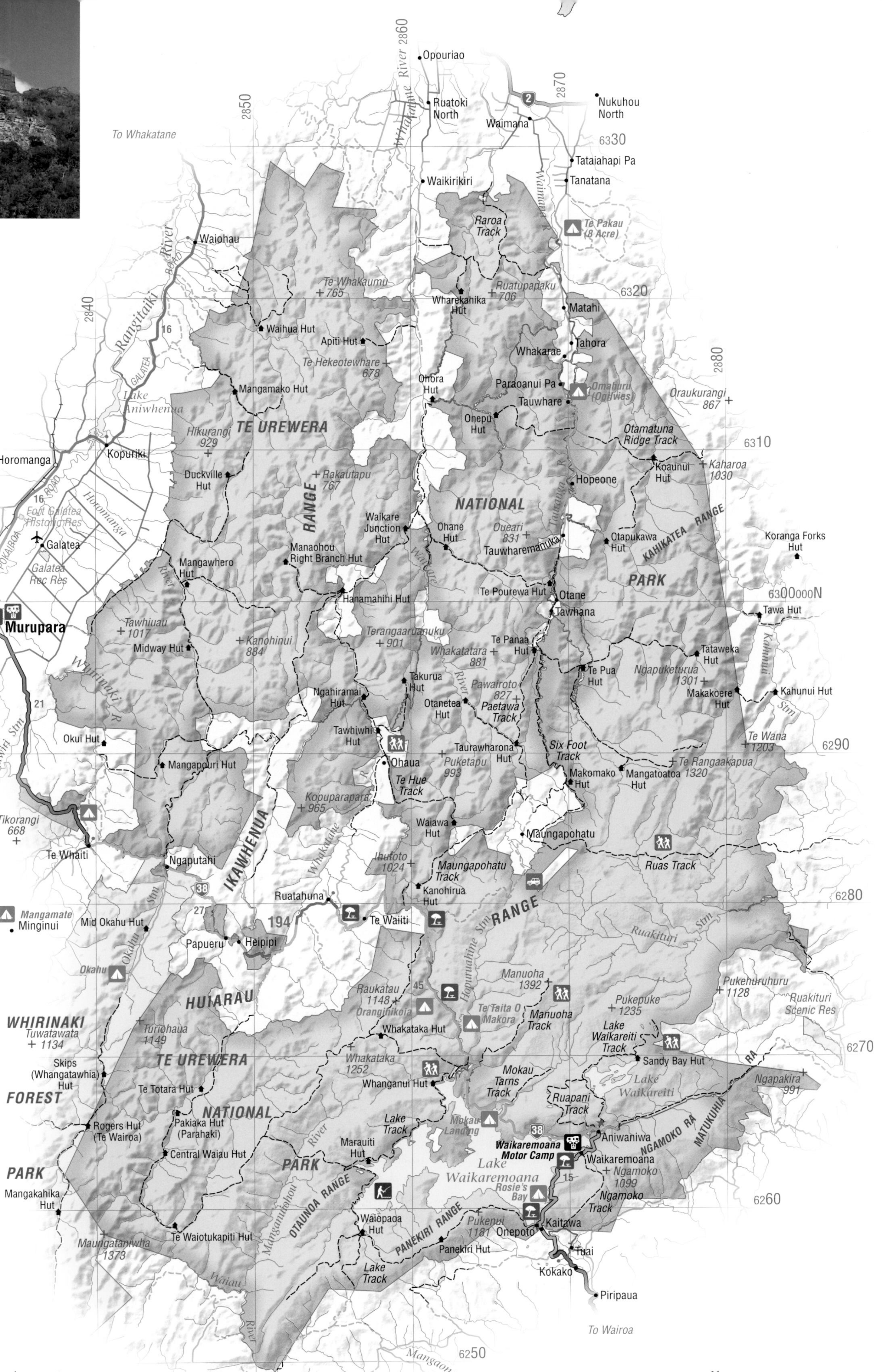

For centuries Te Urewera has been home to the Tuhoe people, dubbed the 'Children of the Mist' as it is believed they are the offspring of Hine-puhohu-rangi the celestial mist maiden.

See maps 14, 20 and 21 for touring maps.

Tongariro National Park

Lake Lahar, Mt Ruapehu Photo: Donna Blaber

Containing both active and extinct volcanoes, **Tongariro National Park** is New Zealand's oldest national park and a World Heritage area. In Peter Jackson's Lord of the Rings films, the Park's dramatic landscape was the setting for Mordor and Mount Ngauruhoe made an appearance as Mount Doom.

Forming the Park's heart are the active volcanoes: Mt Tongariro with its red, raw craters; the charred cinder cone of Mt Ngaruahoe; and majestic Mt Ruapehu's snowy crown and sinister crater lake. Scenic flights provide excellent views of the mountains' diverse peaks.

The cream of the Park's hikes is the 17km Tongariro Crossing, which provides an opportunity to experience some of the most scenic volcanically active areas. There is the option to climb to the summit of Mt Ngauruhoe or Mt Tongariro en route. It is not a round trip so transport must be arranged at one end, or you can catch a shuttle bus from Turangi, Whakapapa Village or National Park Village.

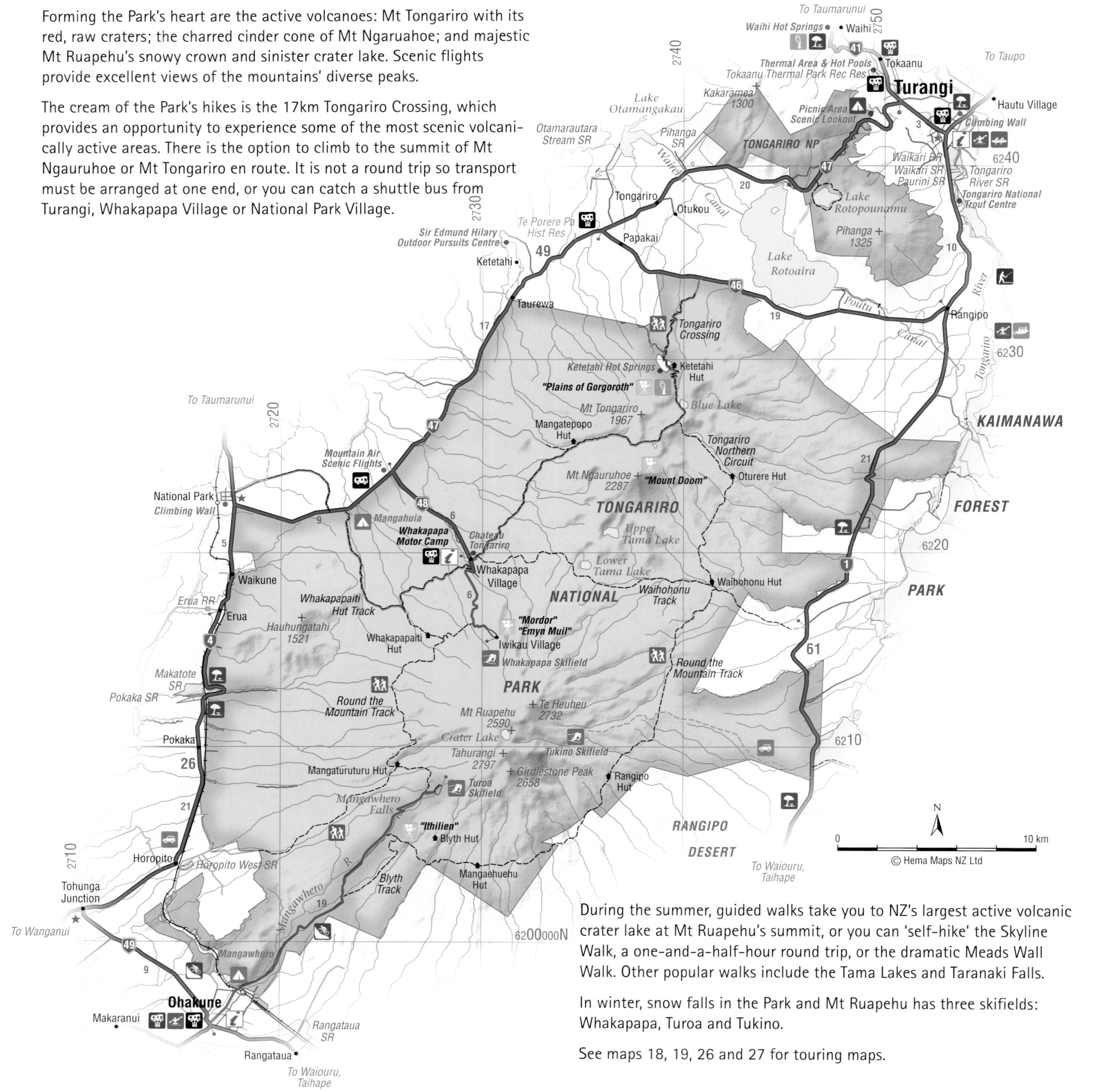

During the summer, guided walks take you to NZ's largest active volcanic crater lake at Mt Ruapehu's summit, or you can 'self-hike' the Skyline Walk, a one-and-a-half-hour round trip, or the dramatic Meads Wall Walk. Other popular walks include the Tama Lakes and Taranaki Falls.

In winter, snow falls in the Park and Mt Ruapehu has three skifields: Whakapapa, Turoa and Tukino.

See maps 18, 19, 26 and 27 for touring maps.

Arthur's Pass National Park

Trampers and climbers flock to **Arthur's Pass National Park** for its amazing ridges, screes, deep valleys, waterfalls, glaciers and gorges. Sitting right in the heart of the national park, Arthur's Pass village has basic facilities and several accommodation options. The excellent DOC headquarters has detailed maps of all the tracks in the area and enthusiastic trampers can enquire here about overnight trips. There's also a small museum, which gives some historical background, and an old Cobb and Co coach on display. Nearby, at the Alpine Chapel, you can gain great views of the Avalanche Creek Waterfall.

Since Arthur Dobson surveyed the pass in 1864, it has been a popular route linking Westland and Christchurch. Skiers, trampers and climbers have been frequenting the region since the railway was completed in the early 1920s. During the summer experienced climbers flock to Arthur's Pass to climb nearby mountains including Mt Rolleston, Mt Murchison and Mt Franklin. In winter the park is transformed by snow, making it popular with skiers and climbers.

Make sure you stop at the lookout point above the pass to see the native mountain parrots called keas and gain excellent views before heading downhill to Otira where the Caley Art Gallery has a good collection of oil paintings, hand blown glass, greenstone (jade) and Maori carvings.

See maps 45, 46, 51 and 52 for touring maps.

Arthur's Pass Photo: Donna Blaber

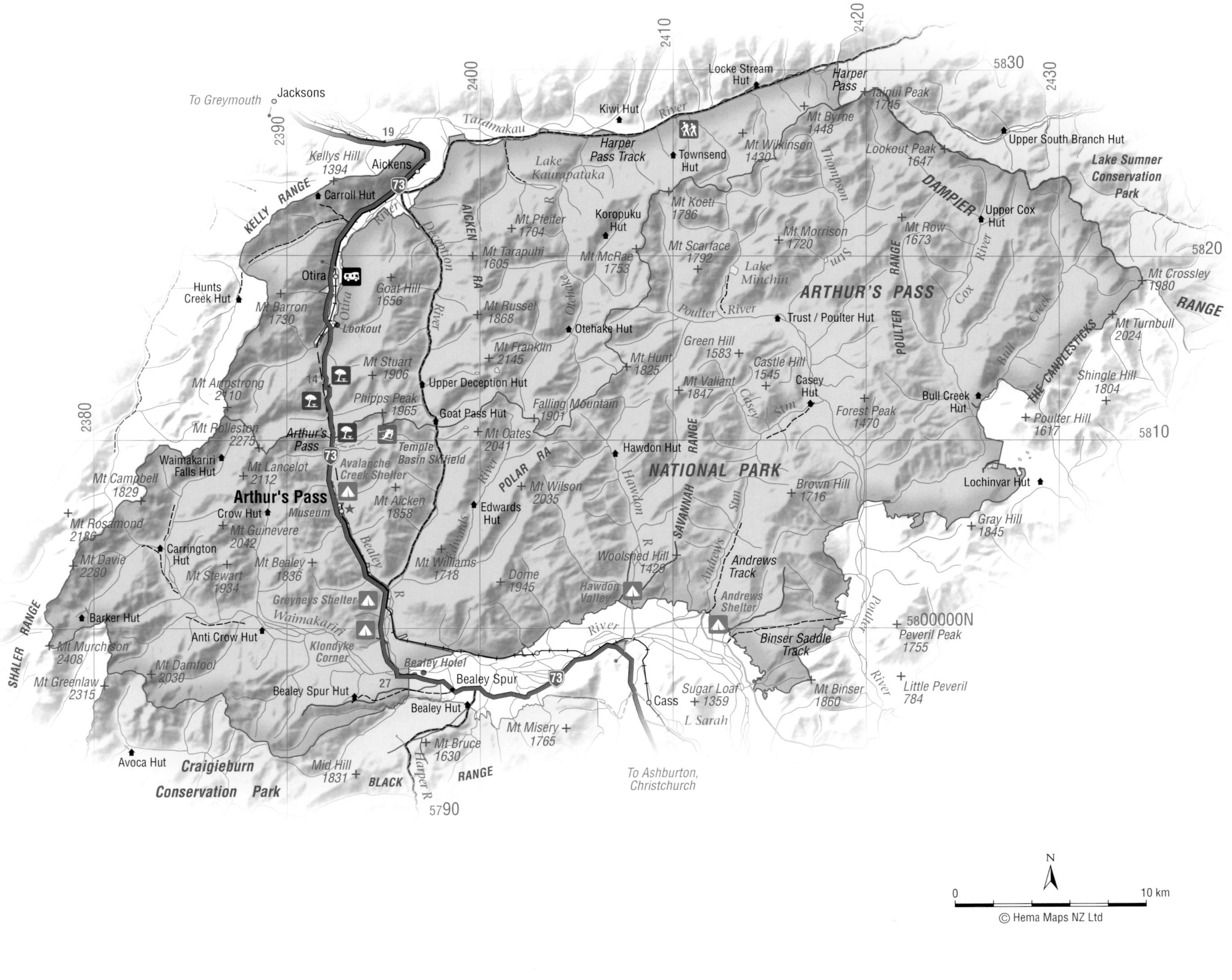

Karamea Waterfall

The vast **Kahurangi National Park** is a 400,000 hectare wilderness of native forest and nikau palms that is a haven for adventure activities. The park contains New Zealand's deepest cave: Nettlebed.

Many tracks cross this isolated park, including the Heaphy Great Walk and the Wangapeka Track. It takes four to six days to complete this Great Walk, and DOC provides seven huts and six campsites. Many a hiker emerges from the national park reporting sightings of great spotted kiwi, short and long tailed bats, and giant land snails. The quiet township of Karamea is both the beginning and the end point of the Heaphy Track.

The beginning of the Heaphy Track provides one of the region's nicest short walks. A suspension bridge crosses the Kohaihai River accessing a 40-minute side-loop that winds through an amazing nikau palm grove where these beautiful palms thrust their smooth, ringed trunks from the pure white sands of a lagoon.

See maps 37, 38 and 42 for touring maps.

Key Summit along the Routeburn Track. This magnificent view is also easily accessible from the Milford Road.

Gates of Haast Photo: Peter Mitchell

See maps 57, 58, 64 and 65 for touring maps.

Part of Te Wahipounamu, the Southwest New Zealand World Heritage Area, **Mount Aspiring National Park** has many scenic walks including the Cascade Saddle Route and Rees-Dart Track, a moderately difficult four to five day tramp along the Rees and Dart rivers. Stunning mountain scenery, alpine landscapes and the Dart Glacier are all seen en route. It is also possible to climb Mount Aspiring (Tititea), but peaks such as these and the glaciers are best explored with experienced guides from a reputable trekking and climbing company.

The Routeburn Great Walk journeys through Mount Aspiring National Park and down over Harris Saddle into the Fiordland National Park. The 32km track takes two to three days to complete, and four huts and two campsites are provided along the way.

From Wanaka, SH6 follows the northern shores of Lake Wanaka towards Makarora before the incredibly scenic drive heads through Mount Aspiring National Park then hugs the Haast River into the small settlement of Haast, on the west coast. Be sure to stop at the Gates of Haast to see the river tumbling down over massive boulders.

Aoraki/Mt Cook & Westland Tai Poutini National Parks

Fox Glacier walk Photo: Tourism West Coast

Aoraki/Mt Cook.

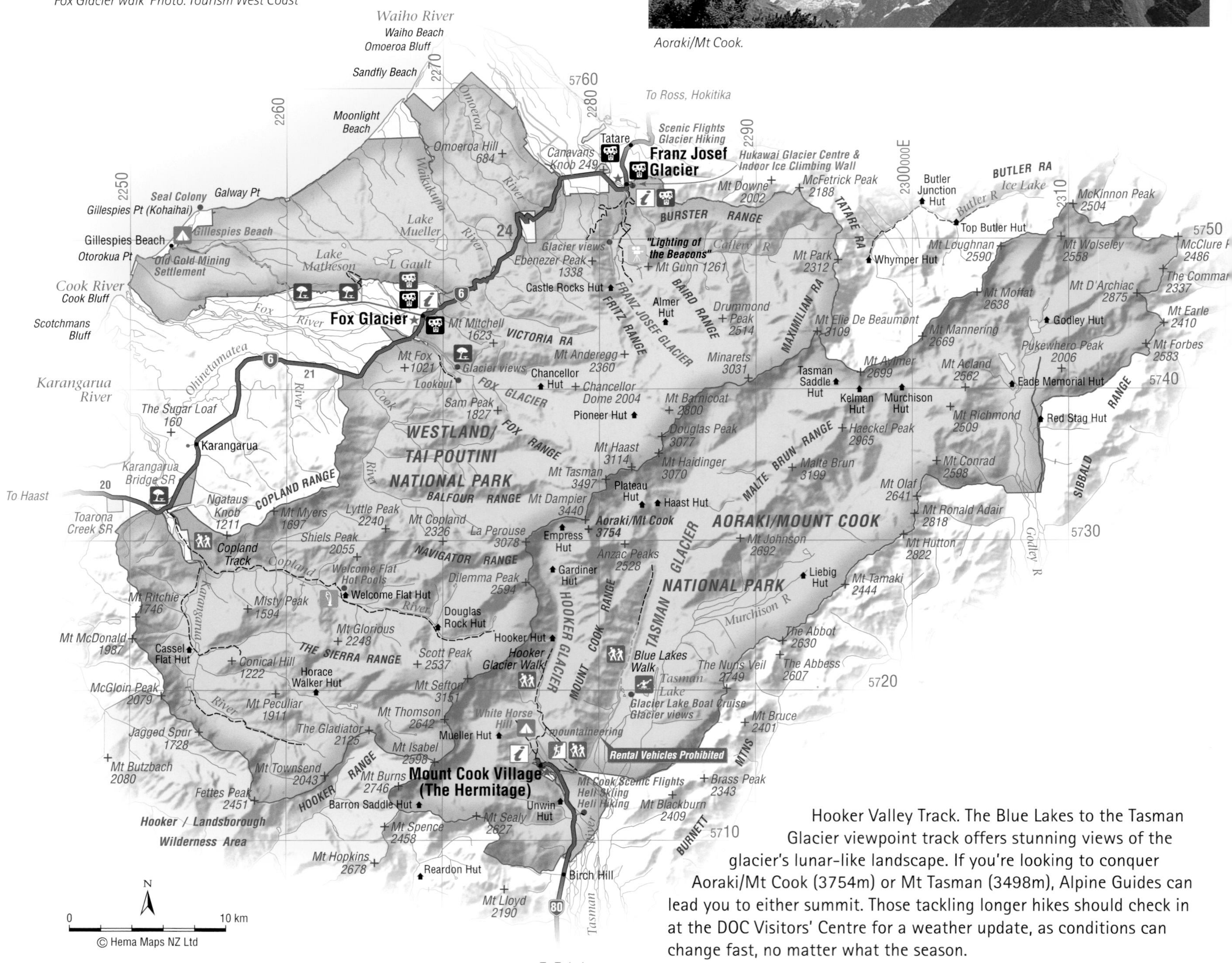

The incredibly scenic drive to Mt Cook via SH80 skirts the shores of Lake Pukaki beneath the textured slopes of the Ben Ohau Range. The tiny alpine village of Mount Cook is an ideal base from which to explore the **Aoraki/Mt Cook National Park**, which boasts Australasia's highest mountain (Mt Cook) and the rumbling Tasman Glacier, the Southern Hemisphere's longest frozen river of ice.

During the winter heli-skiing is a popular pastime and various companies provide options for guided tours. Skiers can also land on the 27km-long Tasman Glacier in a ski plane. Heli-hiking on Mt Dark's rugged ridges and wide open basins is available year round.

In the summer visitors can enjoy 4WD journeys, rock climbing and hiking or an informative cruise on Tasman Glacier Lake, beneath the terminus of the glacier. There are a number of good family walks that leave from the village, including the Bowen Bush Walk, Glencoe Walk, Kea Point and Hooker Valley Track. The Blue Lakes to the Tasman Glacier viewpoint track offers stunning views of the glacier's lunar-like landscape. If you're looking to conquer Aoraki/Mt Cook (3754m) or Mt Tasman (3498m), Alpine Guides can lead you to either summit. Those tackling longer hikes should check in at the DOC Visitors' Centre for a weather update, as conditions can change fast, no matter what the season.

The **Westland Tai Poutini National Park** encompasses the Fox and Franz Josef glaciers, whose icy tongues are surrounded by rainforest. To really experience these massive rivers of ice, take a guided tour or take a helicopter ride for a bird's-eye view.

From Franz Josef it's a short drive to the glacier's car park. To gain a good view of the Franz Josef Glacier hike to Sentinel Rock (around 10 minutes) or hike the 3km Glacier Valley Walk to the terminal face (around an hour and a half return). You can join a guided tour and hike up the face of the glacier to explore stunning ice-blue tunnels on the world's steepest and fastest-flowing commercially guided glacier.

Helicopter flights and guided walks of the Fox Glacier are also on offer and it takes around five minutes' hiking from the car park to gain a view of the glacier or 30 minutes to get close to the terminal face.

See maps 49, 50, 59 and 60 for touring maps.

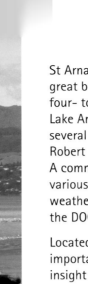

Nelson *Photo: Donna Blaber*

St Arnaud, right at the doorstep of **Nelson Lakes National Park**, provides a great base for trampers exploring the park's various tracks including the four- to seven-day Travers-Sabine Circuit. The two- to three-day hike to Lake Angelus, a stunning alpine pond, is also popular. There are also several excellent day hikes, including the Lake Rotoiti Circuit, Mount Robert loop track, St Arnaud Range track, and Whisky Falls track. A commercial water-taxi service on the lake whisks hikers to and from various points or provides cruises of the lake on demand. The latest weather report, maps, hut tickets and hunting permits are available from the DOC visitor centre in St Arnaud.

Located on the lake edge, the Rotoiti Nature Recovery Project is an important conservation site. The Bellbird and Honeydew tracks provide an insight into this work and honey-dew nectar can be seen literally dripping from the beech trees.

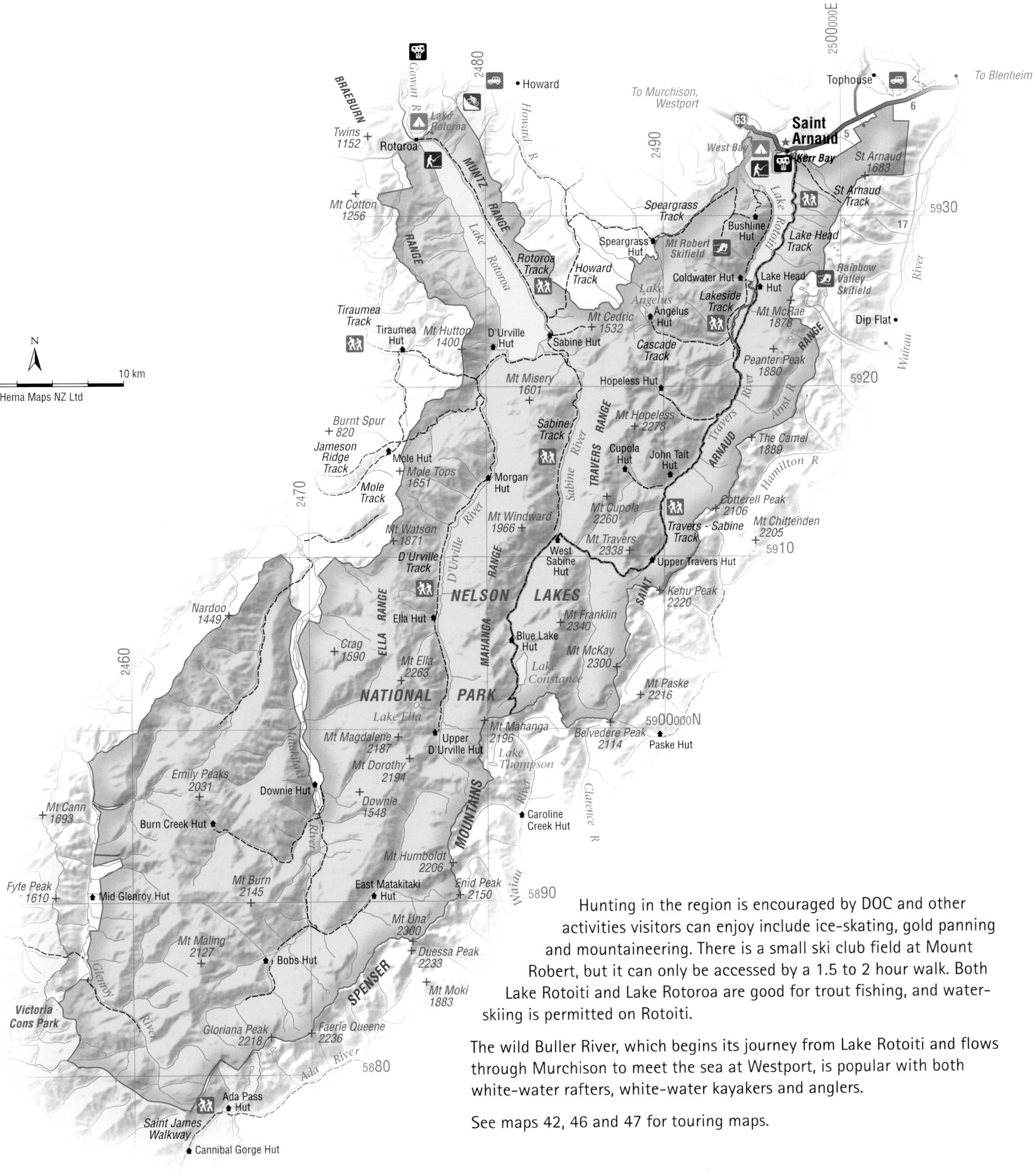

Hunting in the region is encouraged by DOC and other activities visitors can enjoy include ice-skating, gold panning and mountaineering. There is a small ski club field at Mount Robert, but it can only be accessed by a 1.5 to 2 hour walk. Both Lake Rotoiti and Lake Rotoroa are good for trout fishing, and water-skiing is permitted on Rotoiti.

The wild Buller River, which begins its journey from Lake Rotoiti and flows through Murchison to meet the sea at Westport, is popular with both white-water rafters, white-water kayakers and anglers.

See maps 42, 46 and 47 for touring maps.

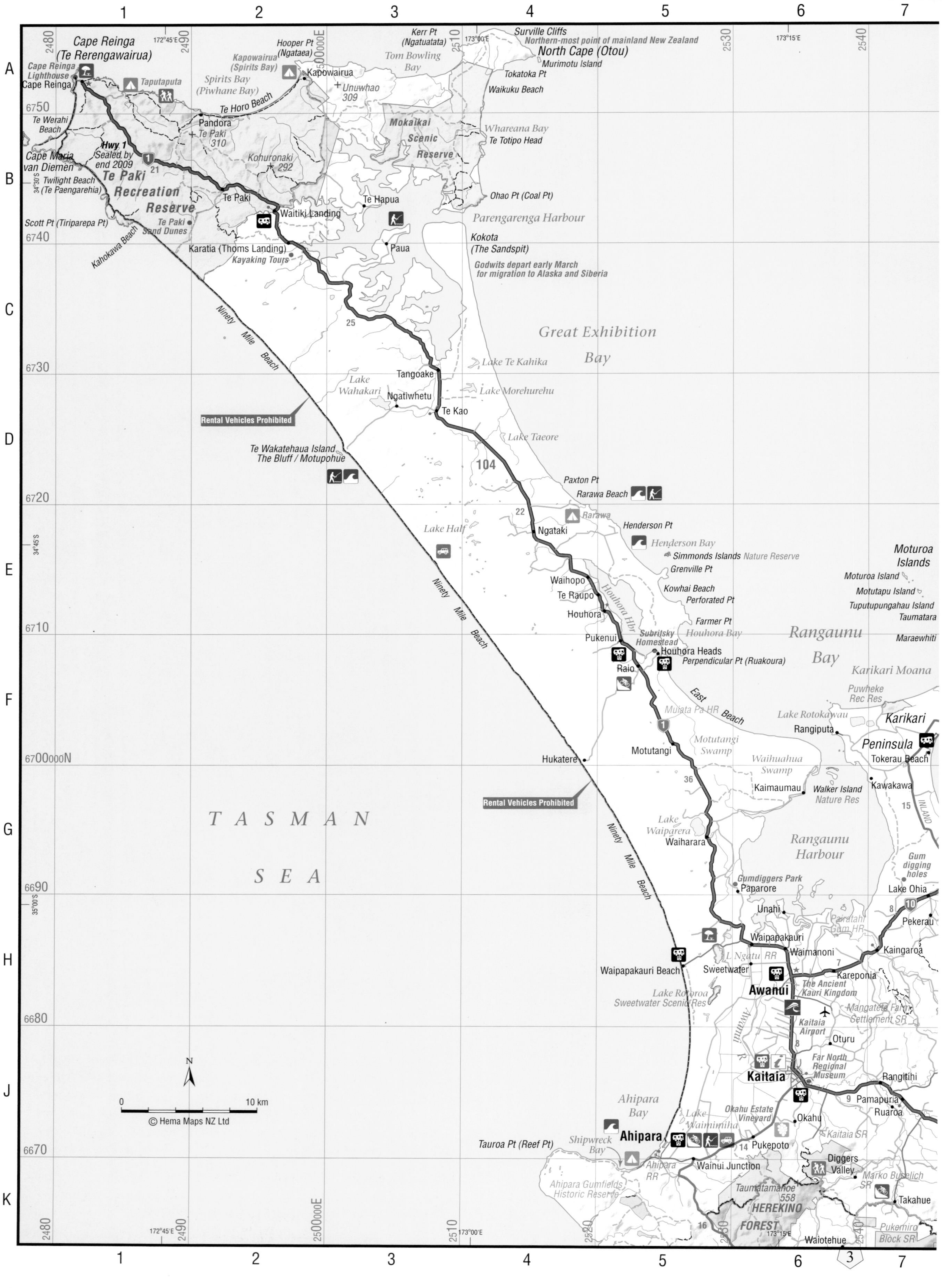

Cape Reinga (Te Rerengawairua)
Cape Reinga Lighthouse
Cape Reinga
Taputaputa
Te Werahi Beach
Cape Maria van Diemen
Twilight Beach (Te Paengarehia)
Scott Pt (Tiriparepa Pt)
Hwy 1 Sealed by end 2009
Te Paki Recreation Reserve
Te Paki Sand Dunes
Kahokawa Beach
Pandora
Te Paki 310
Kohuronaki 292
Te Paki
Waitiki Landing
Karatia (Thoms Landing)
Kayaking Tours
Kapowairua (Spirits Bay)
Kapowairua
Spirits Bay (Piwhane Bay)
Te Horo Beach
Hooper Pt (Ngataea)
Kerr Pt (Ngatuatata)
Tom Bowling Bay
Unuwhao 309
Mokaikai Scenic Reserve
Surville Cliffs
Northern-most point of mainland New Zealand
North Cape (Otou)
Murimotu Island
Tokatoka Pt
Waikuku Beach
Whareana Bay
Te Totipo Head
Ohao Pt (Coal Pt)
Te Hapua
Paua
Parengarenga Harbour
Kokota (The Sandspit)
Godwits depart early March for migration to Alaska and Siberia
Great Exhibition Bay
Ninety Mile Beach
Lake Te Kahika
Tangoake
Lake Wahakari
Ngatiwhetu
Te Kao
Lake Morehurehu
Lake Taeore
Rental Vehicles Prohibited
Te Wakatehaua Island The Bluff / Motupohue
104
Paxton Pt
Rarawa Beach
Rarawa
Ngataki
Henderson Pt
Henderson Bay
Lake Half
Simmonds Islands Nature Reserve
Grenville Pt
Kowhai Beach
Perforated Pt
Waihopo
Te Raupo
Houhora
Houhora Hbr
Farmer Pt
Houhora Bay
Pukenui
Subritsky Homestead
Houhora Heads
Perpendicular Pt (Ruakoura)
Raio
East Beach
Muriata Pa HR
Motutangi
Motutangi Swamp
Waihuahua Swamp
Hukatere
Rental Vehicles Prohibited
Kaimaumau
Walker Island Nature Res
Lake Waiparera
Waiharara
Rangaunu Bay
Rangaunu Harbour
Karikari Moana
Puwheke Rec Res
Lake Rotokawau
Karikari Peninsula
Rangiputa
Tokerau Beach
Kawakawa
Moturoa Islands
Moturoa Island
Motutapu Island
Tuputupungahau Island
Taumatara
Maraewhiti
Gum digging holes
Lake Ohia
Pekerau
Gumdiggers Park
Paparore
Unahi
Pairatahi Gum HR
Waipapakauri
Waimanoni
Kaingaroa
L. Ngatu RR
Sweetwater
Kareponia
Waipapakauri Beach
Lake Rotoroa Sweetwater Scenic Res
Awanui
The Ancient Kauri Kingdom
Mangatete Farm Settlement SR
Kaitaia Airport
Oturu
Far North Regional Museum
Kaitaia
Rangitihi
Pamapuria
Ruaroa
TASMAN SEA
Ahipara Bay
Lake Waimimiha
Okahu Estate Vineyard
Okahu
Ahipara
Tauroa Pt (Reef Pt)
Shipwreck Bay
Pukepoto
Kaitaia SR
Ahipara RR
Wainui Junction
Diggers Valley
Ahipara Gumfields Historic Reserve
Taumatamahoe 558
Herekino Forest
Marko Buselich SR
Takahue
Pukemiro Block SR
Waiotehue
0 10 km
© Hema Maps NZ Ltd

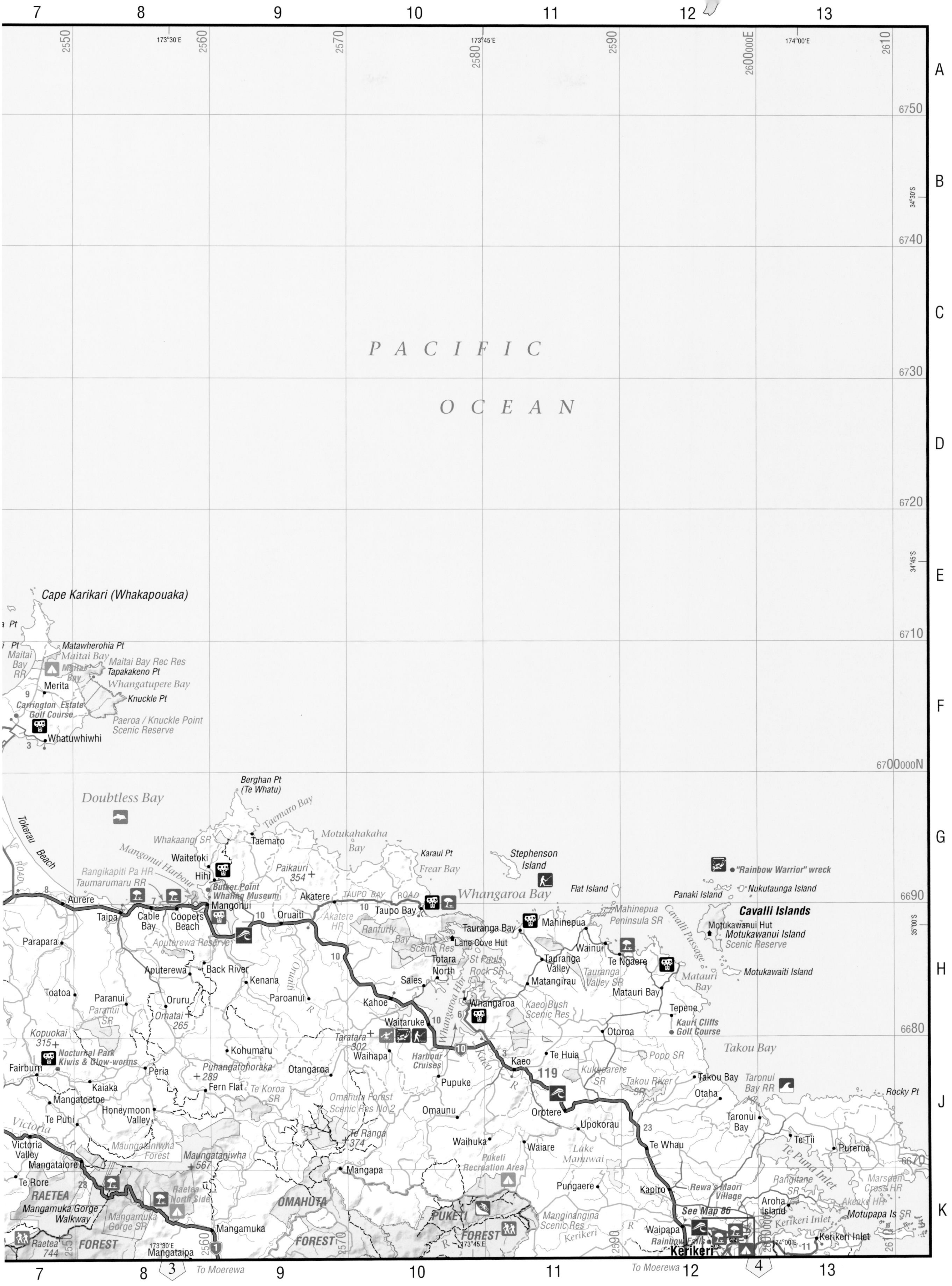

PACIFIC
OCEAN
Cape Karikari (Whakapouaka)
Matawherohia Pt
Maitai Bay
Maitai Bay Rec Res
Tapakakeno Pt
Whangatupere Bay
Knuckle Pt
Merita
Carrington Estate Golf Course
Paeroa / Knuckle Point Scenic Reserve
Whatuwhiwhi
Doubtless Bay
Berghan Pt (Te Whatu)
Taemaro Bay
Whakaangi SR
Taemaro
Motukahakaha Bay
Tokerau Beach
Mangonui Harbour
Rangikapiti Pa HR
Taumarumaru RR
Waitetoki
Hihi
Butler Point Whaling Museum
Paikauri 354
Karaui Pt
Frear Bay
Stephenson Island
Whangaroa Bay
Flat Island
"Rainbow Warrior" wreck
Nukutaunga Island
Panaki Island
Cavalli Islands
Aurere
Taipa
Cable Bay
Coopers Beach
Mangonui
Oruaiti
Akatere
Taupo Bay Road
Taupo Bay
Akatere HR
Ranfurly Bay Scenic Res
Tauranga Bay
Lane Cove Hut
Mahinepua
Mahinepua Peninsula SR
Cavalli Passage
Motukawanui Hut
Motukawanui Island Scenic Reserve
Motukawaiti Island
Parapara
Aputerewa Reserve
Aputerewa
Back River
Kenana
Oruaiti R
Totara North
St Pauls Rock SR
Wainui
Te Ngaere
Tauranga Valley
Tauranga Valley SR
Matauri Bay
Matangirau
Saies
Toatoa
Paranui
Paranui SR
Oruru
Omatai 265
Paroanui
Kahoe
Whangaroa
Whangaroa Hbr
Kaeo Bush Scenic Res
Tepene
Kauri Cliffs Golf Course
Kopuokai 315
Nocturnal Park Kiwis & Glow-worms
Kohumaru
Taratara 302
Waitaruke
Waihapa
Harbour Cruises
Kaeo R
Otoroa
Takou Bay
Te Huia
Popo SR
Fairburn
Kaiaka
Peria
Puhangatohoraka 289
Otangaroa
Kaeo
Kukuparere SR
Takou River SR
Takou Bay
Taronui Bay RR
Rocky Pt
Mangatoetoe
Fern Flat
Te Koroa SR
Pupuke
Otaha
Te Puhi
Honeymoon Valley
Omahuta Forest Scenic Res No 2
Omaunu
Orotere
Upokorau
Taronui Bay
Victoria
Victoria Valley
Te Ranga 374
Waihuka
Waiare
Te Whau
Te Tii
Te Puna Inlet
Purerua
Maungataniwha Forest
Maungataniwha 567
Lake Manuwai
Mangataiore
Mangapa
Puketi Recreation Area
Rangitane SR
Marsden Cross HR
Te Rore
Raetea North Side
Pungaere
Kapiro
Rewa's Maori Village
Aroha Island
Akeake HR
RAETEA
Mangamuka Gorge Walkway
Mangamuka Gorge SR
OMAHUTA
PUKETI
Manginangina Scenic Res
Kerikeri
See Map 86
Kerikeri Inlet
Motupapa Is SR
Kerikeri Inlet
Raetea 744
FOREST
Mangamuka
Mangataipa
FOREST
FOREST
Waipapa
Rainbow Falls
Kerikeri
To Moerewa
To Moerewa
119
173°30'E
173°45'E
174°00'E
34°30'S
34°45'S
35°00'S
2550
2560
2570
2580
2590
2600000E
2610
6750
6740
6730
6720
6710
6700000N
6690
6680
6670
7
8
9
10
11
12
13
A
B
C
D
E
F
G
H
J
K

1
2
3
4
5
6
7
To Kaitaia
Ahipara
Ahipara RR
Wainui Junction
Diggers Valley
Marko Buselich SR
Te Rore
Takahue
RAETEA
Mangamuka Gorge Walkway
Mangataiore
Maungataniwha 567
Raetea North Side
Mangamuka Gorge SR
Mangamuka
Mangapa
Puketi Recreation Area
Lake Manuwai
Pungaere
Manginangina Scenic Res
Kerikeri
PUKETI FOREST
OMAHUTA FOREST
Taumatamahoe 558
HEREKINO FOREST
Orowhano 507
Orowhana SR
Manukau
Waiotehue
Raetea 744
Waitawa SR
FOREST
MAUNGATANIWHA RANGE
Pukemiro Block SR
Mangataipa
Mangataipa Scenic Res
Mangamuka Bridge
108
Naumapa
Forest Pools
Puketi Scenic Res
Puketi
Herekino
Awaroa
Broadwood
Orawau
Pukemiro
Mohuiti
Tutekehua
Kahikatoa
Umawera
Rahiri
Waihou Valley
Herekino Hbr
Puhata
Pareokawa Water Cons SR
Papong a
Te Karae
Urungaio
Owhata
Rotokakahi River SR
Runaruna
Kohe
NORTHLAND FOREST PARK
Mata
Orira
Rangiahua
Rawhia
Okaihau
Lake Omapere
Okuratope Pa Hist Res
Te Ahuahu
Whangape
Rotokakahi
Motukaraka SR
Te Huahua
Okaka
Te Umakuri Pt
Pawarenga
Tapuwae
Mangungu
Horeke
Maraeroa
Utakura
Mangungu Mission House
Mataki 328
Mangataraire
Utakura SR
Golden Stairs Walkway
WARAWARA FOREST
Panguru
Tapuwae SR
Motukaraka
Kohukohu
Ivydale
Wairere
Wairere Boulders Nature Park
Ngawha
Kaikohe SR
Whangape Harbour
Motuti
Matawhera
Ferry
Clendon House
Rangiora
Pukewhariki 359
Motukauri
Lower Waihou
Rawene
Motukiore
Kaikohe
Ngawha Springs
Tauwhare 600
Waireia
Papua
Waima
Hone Heke Monument
Horse riding Cultural experiences
Mitimiti
Te Karaka
Onoke
Opata
Parahirahi 324
Matihetihe
Punehu
Ohuri
Reena
Hokianga Harbour
Waiparera
Rangi Point
Waitapu
Karuhiruhi
Omanaia
Moehau
Karakamatamata Scenic Res
Te Iringa
Rakautao
Oue
Taheke
Ngapuhi
Waima Valley
Punakitere Valley
Tautoro
Koutu
Whirinaki
Mangawhero
56
Punakitere
Kirioke
Lake Tauanui
Motutoa
Pakanae
Framptons Hut
Framptons SR
WAIMA FOREST
Wahaotetupua Scenic Reserve
Otaua
Opononi
Sand tobogganing
Pakanae SR
Te Raupua 781
Waima Main Range Track
Mataraua
Arai-Te-Uru RR
Omapere
Oraora
Te Wai-O-Te Marama SR
Oraora SR
Waoku Coach Road Track
Waimamaku
Waiotemarama
Labyrinth Woodworks
Wekaweka
Three Bridges
Hokianga - Kai Iwi Coastal Tramping Track
Kohekohe 464
MATARAUA FOREST
Mataraua Forest
Mataraua Valley SR
Awarua
Wekaweka SR
Kaikai Beach
PARATAIKO RANGE
Mangakahia River
Giant Kauri Trees Tane Mahuta
Waimatenui
Mangakahia River SR
Twin Bridges
WAIPOUA FOREST
Kawerua
Waipoua River
Toetoehatiko 510
NORTHLAND FOREST PARK
Waipoua Settlement
Waipoua Forest
Tutamoe
Nukutawhiti
Tapuketaru 604
Hokianga - Kai Iwi Coastal Tramping Track
Gorrie SR
MARLBOROUGH FOREST
TUTAMOE
Kaimaro SR
Opouteke SR
Opouteke
Kaitui
Mangatu
Kaitui SR
Oranoa
Donnellys Crossing
Trounson Kauri Park SR
Okaharau Road SR
Pakotai SR
Taha Moana Scenic Reserve
"Four Sisters" Kauris Guided night walks
Trounson Kauri Park
RANGE
Maunganui Bluff Scenic Reserve
Aranga
Whatoro
KAIHU FOREST
Tutamoe 770
Maunganui Bluff
82
Aranga Beach
Kaihu
Shag Lake
Lake Waikere
Kairara
TASMAN SEA
Lake Taharoa
Kaiiwi Lakes
Lake Kaiiwi
Ahikiwi
Maropiu
Kaihu SR
Waimata Settlement SR
Ripiro Beach
Mamaranui
Waihue
Maitahi
Mamaranui Farm Settlement Scenic Reserve
Awakino River
Omamari
Kaihu R
Moremonui Gully
Parore
0
10 km
© Hema Maps NZ Ltd
Baylys Beach
BAYLYS COAST ROAD
Mangatara
Mangawhare
Mount Wesley
Rehutai
173°15'E
173°30'E
173°45'E
35°15'S
35°30'S
35°45'S
6670
6660
6650
6640
6630
6620
6610
6600000N
6590
6580
2530
2540
2550
2560
2570
2580
2590
A
B
C
D
E
F
G
H
J

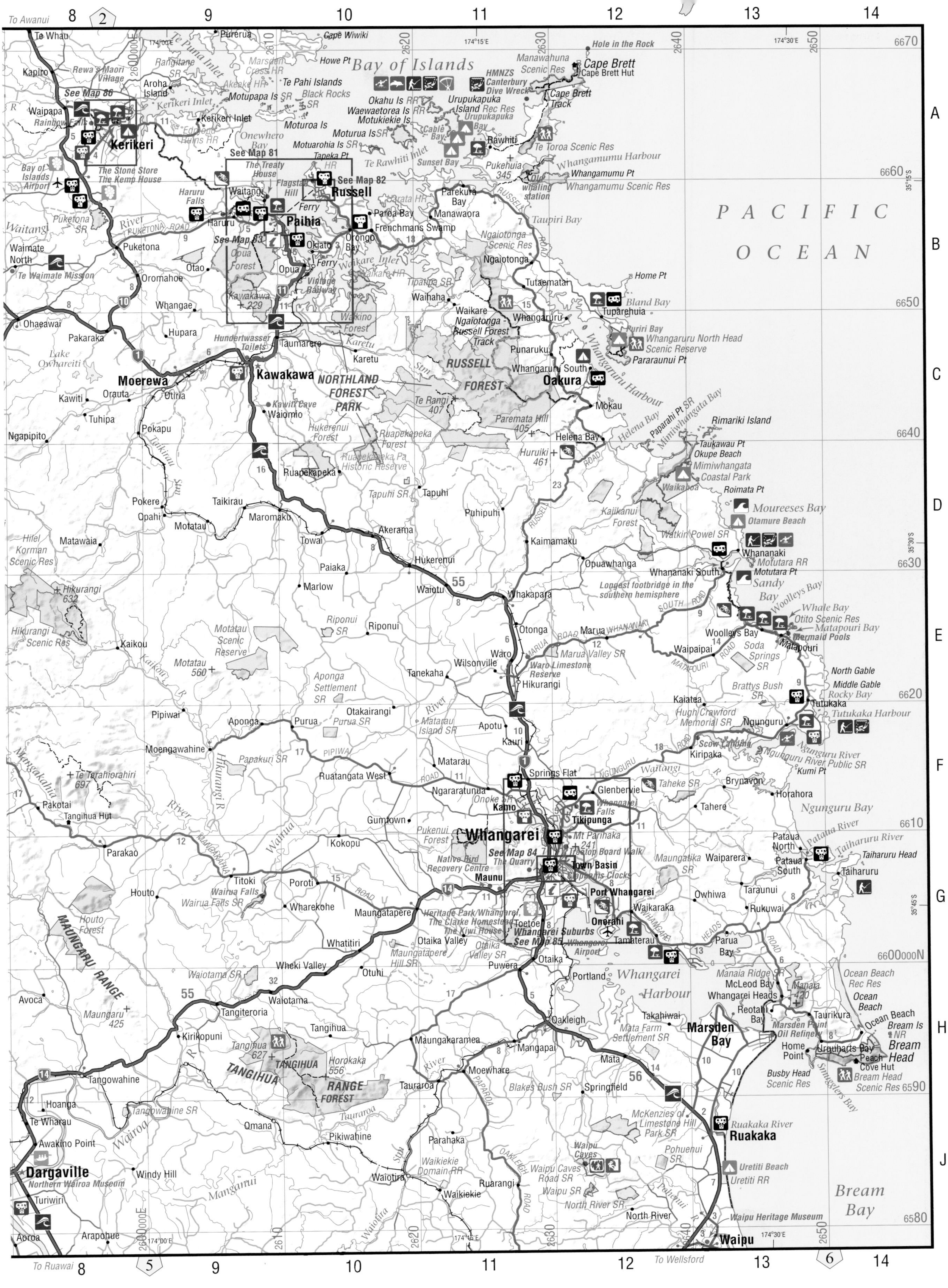

To Awanui
To Ruawai
To Wellsford
Bay of Islands
PACIFIC OCEAN
Cape Brett
Cape Brett Hut
Hole in the Rock
Cape Brett Track
Manawahuna Scenic Res
HMNZS Canterbury Dive Wreck
Urupukapuka Island Rec Res
Urupukapuka Bay
Rawhiti
Te Toroa Scenic Res
Whangamumu Harbour
Whangamumu Pt
Whangamumu Scenic Res
Old whaling station
Pukehuia 345
Te Rawhiti Inlet
Sunset Bay
Cable Bay
Okahu Is RR
Waewaetorea Is RR
Motukiekie Is
Moturua Is SR
Motuarohia Is SR
Moturoa Is
Black Rocks SR
Te Pahi Islands
Motupapa Is SR
Howe Pt
Cape Wiwiki
Purerua
Marsden Cross HR
Te Puna Inlet
Rangitane SR
Aroha Island
Kerikeri Inlet
Kerikeri
See Map 86
Rewa's Maori Village
Kapiro
Te Whau
Waipapa
Rainbow Falls
The Stone Store
The Kemp House
Bay of Islands Airport
Onewhero Bay
See Map 81
The Treaty House
Flagstaff Hill
Tapeka Pt
See Map 82
Russell
Waitangi
Haruru Falls
Haruru
Paihia
See Map 83
Opua Forest
Okiato
Ferry
Opua
Vintage Railway
Kawakawa 229
Waikare Inlet
Orongo Bay
Parekura Bay
Manawaora
Paroa Bay
Frenchmans Swamp
Taupiri Bay
Ngaiotonga Scenic Res
Ngaiotonga
Tutaematai
Home Pt
Bland Bay
Tuparehuia
Puriri Bay
Whangaruru North Head Scenic Reserve
Pararaunui Pt
Whangaruru Harbour
Whangaruru
Whangaruru South
Punaruku
Oakura
Mokau
Waikare
Ngaiotonga-Russell Forest Track
RUSSELL FOREST
Tipatipa SR
Waihaha
Waitangi River
Puketona
Puketona SR
Waimate North
Te Waimate Mission
Oromahoe
Otao
Whangae
Ohaeawai
Pakaraka
Lake Owhareiti
Hupara
Hundertwasser Toilets
Taumarere
Karetu
Kawakawa
Moerewa
Otiria
Orauta
Kawiti
Tuhipa
Ngapipito
Pokapu
Kawiti Cave
Waiomio
NORTHLAND FOREST PARK
Te Rangi 407
Paremata Hill 405
Helena Bay
Paparahi Pt SR
Mimiwhangata Bay
Rimariki Island
Taukawau Pt
Okupe Beach
Mimiwhangata Coastal Park
Waikahoa
Roimata Pt
Huruiki 461
Hukerenui Forest
Ruapekapeka Forest
Ruapekapeka Pa Historic Reserve
Ruapekapeka
Tapuhi SR
Tapuhi
Pokere
Opahi
Taikirau
Motatau
Maromaku
Towai
Akerama
Pupuhi
Kaikanui Forest
Kaimamaku
Moureeses Bay
Otamure Beach
Watkin Powel SR
Whananaki
Motutara RR
Motutara Pt
Whananaki South
Opuawhanga
Longest footbridge in the southern hemisphere
Sandy Bay
Woolleys Bay
Whale Bay
Otito Scenic Res
Matapouri Bay
Mermaid Pools
Woolleys Bay
Matapouri
Matawaia
Hiell Korman Scenic Res
Hikurangi 632
Hikurangi Scenic Res
Paiaka
Hukerenui
Marlow
Waiotu
Whakapara
Riponui SR
Riponui
Otonga
Marua
Waipaipai
Soda Springs SR
Marua Valley SR
Waro Limestone Reserve
Waro
Wilsonville
Hikurangi
Tanekaha
Kaikou
Motatau Scenic Reserve
Motatau 560
Aponga Settlement SR
Brattys Bush SR
North Gable
Middle Gable
Rocky Bay
Tutukaka
Tutukaka Harbour
Kaiatea
Hugh Crawford Memorial SR
Ngunguru
Pipiwai
Aponga
Purua
Otakairangi
Purua SR
Matarau Island SR
Apotu
Kauri
Moengawahine
Papakuri SR
Kiripaka
Scow Landing
Ngunguru River Public SR
Kumi Pt
Matarau
Springs Flat
Te Tarahiorahiri 697
Ruatangata West
Ngararatunua
Glenbervie
Taheke SR
Brynavon
Horahora
Ngunguru Bay
Pakotai
Tangihua Hut
Kamo
Whangarei Falls
Tikipunga
Tahere
Gumtown
Pukenui Forest
Whangarei
Mt Parihaka 241
Treetop Board Walk
Native Bird Recovery Centre
See Map 84
The Quarry
Town Basin
Claphams Clocks
Maungatika SR
Waiparera
Pataua North
Pataua South
Taiharuru River
Taiharuru Head
Taiharuru
Parakao
Titoki
Kokopu
Wairua Falls
Wairua Falls SR
Poroti
Maunu
Port Whangarei
Owhiwa
Taraunui
Rukuwai
Houto
Wharekohe
Maungatapere
Heritage Park/Whangarei
The Clarke Homestead
The Kiwi House
Toetoe
Onerahi
Waikaraka
Whangarei Suburbs
See Map 85
Whangarei Airport
Tamaterau
Parua Bay
Houto Forest
MAUNGARU RANGE
Whatitiri
Otaika Valley
Maungatapere Hill SR
Otaika Valley SR
Otaika
Waiotama SR
Wheki Valley
Otuhi
Puwera
Portland
Whangarei Harbour
Manaia Ridge SR
McLeod Bay
Whangarei Heads
Manaia 420
Ocean Beach Rec Res
Ocean Beach
Avoca
Maungaru 425
Waiotama
Tangiteroria
Tangihua
Oakleigh
Takahiwai
Mata Farm Settlement SR
Reotahi Bay
Taurikura
Marsden Bay
Marsden Point Oil Refinery
Home Point
Urquharts Bay
Peach Cove Hut
Bream Is NR
Bream Head
Bream Head Scenic Res
Busby Head Scenic Res
Smugglers Bay
Kirikopuni
Tangihua 627
TANGIHUA RANGE FOREST
Horokaka 556
Maungakaramea
Mangapai
Mata
Tangowahine
Moewhare
Tauraroa
Blakes Bush SR
Springfield
Hoanga
Te Wharau
Tangowahine SR
Omana
Awakino Point
Pikiwahine
Parahaka
McKenzies of Limestone Hill Park SR
Ruakaka River
Ruakaka
Pohuenui SR
Dargaville
Northern Wairoa Museum
Windy Hill
Waikiekie Domain RR
Waipu Caves
Waipu Caves Road SR
Waipu SR
Uretiti Beach
Uretiti RR
Turiwiri
Waiotira
Ruarangi
Waikiekie
North River SR
North River
Bream Bay
Waipu Heritage Museum
Aoroa
Arapohue
Waipu

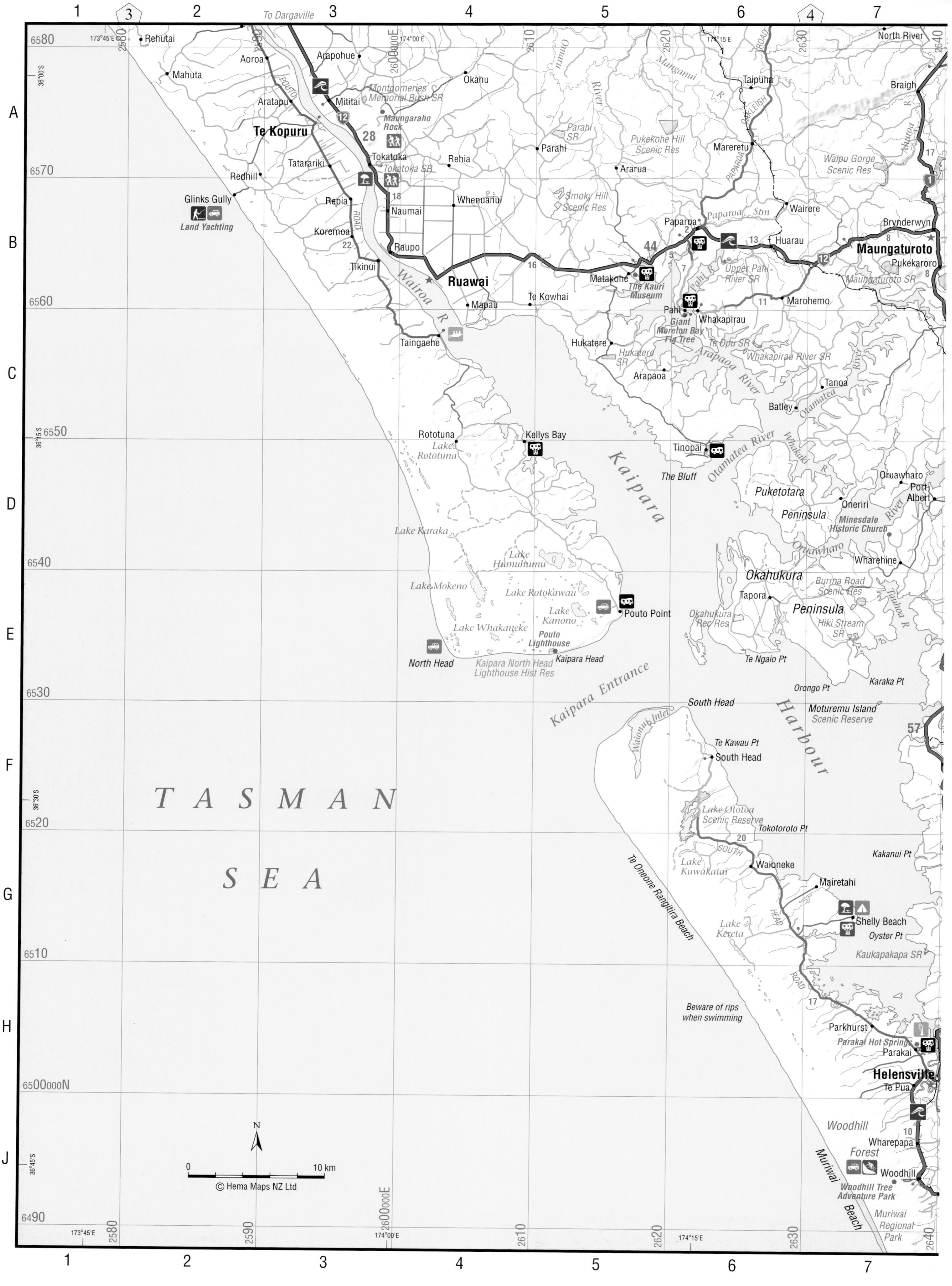
To Dargaville
Rehutai
Mahuta
Aoroa
Arapohue
Mititai
Aratapu
Te Kopuru
Okahu
Montgomeries Memorial Bush SR
Maungaraho Rock
Tokatoka
Tokatoka SR
Tatarariki
Redhill
Rehia
Parahi
Parahi SR
Glinks Gully
Land Yachting
Repia
Naumai
Whenuanui
Koremoa
Raupo
Tikinui
Ruawai
Wairoa R
Mapau
Te Kowhai
Taingaehe
Pukekohe Hill Scenic Res
Ararua
Smoky Hill Scenic Res
Taipuha
Mareretu
Paparoa
Paparoa Stm
Wairere
Huarau
Matakohe
The Kauri Museum
Pahi
Giant Moreton Bay Fig Tree
Whakapirau
Upper Pahi River SR
Marohemo
Te Opu SR
Whakapirau River SR
Hukatere
Hukatere SR
Arapaoa
Arapaoa River
Tanoa
Batley
Otamatea River
Waipu Gorge Scenic Res
Brynderwyn
Maungaturoto
Pukekaroro
Maungaturoto SR
North River
Braigh
Rototuna
Lake Rototuna
Kellys Bay
Kaipara
Tinopai
The Bluff
Puketotara Peninsula
Oruawharo
Port Albert
Oneriri
Minesdale Historic Church
Lake Karaka
Lake Humuhumu
Lake Mokeno
Lake Rotokawau
Lake Kanono
Lake Whakaneke
Pouto Point
Pouto Lighthouse
Kaipara Head
North Head
Kaipara North Head Lighthouse Hist Res
Wharehine
Okahukura Peninsula
Tapora
Okahukura Rec Res
Burma Road Scenic Res
Hiki Stream SR
Te Ngaio Pt
Karaka Pt
Orongo Pt
Kaipara Entrance
South Head
Moturemu Island Scenic Reserve
Harbour
Waionui Inlet
Te Kawau Pt
Lake Ototoa Scenic Reserve
Tokotoroto Pt
TASMAN
SEA
Te Oneone Rangitira Beach
Lake Kuwakatai
Waioneke
Kakanui Pt
Mairetahi
Shelly Beach
Oyster Pt
Lake Kereta
Kaukapakapa SR
Beware of rips when swimming
Parkhurst
Parakai Hot Springs
Parakai
Helensville
Te Pua
Woodhill Forest
Wharepapa
Woodhill
Woodhill Tree Adventure Park
Muriwai Regional Park
Muriwai Beach
© Hema Maps NZ Ltd
0
10 km
N

To Whangarei
8
9
10
11
12
13
14
A
B
C
D
E
F
G
H
J
PACIFIC OCEAN
Bream Bay
Taranga Island
Hen and Chicken Islands Nature Reserve
Sail Rock
Navire Rock
Simpson Rock
Waipu
Waipu Heritage Museum
Waipu River
Waipu Cove Wildlife Refuge
Waipu Cove
McKenzie Cove
Andersons Cove
Langs Beach
Langs Beach SR
Bream Tail
McGregor Rock
Bream Tail SR
Robert Hastie Memorial SR
Mangawhai Cliffs Walkway
Brynderwyn SR
Brynderwyn Hills Walkway
Brynderwyn Hills SR
Mangawhai Harbour Wildlife Refuge
Cattlemount 430
Te-Uri-O-Hau SR
Mangawhai Golf Course
Mangawhai Heads
Tara
Cooks Stream SR
Mangawhai Point
Pukekaroro SR
Hakaru
Kaiwaka
Te Arai Pt
Te Arai Point
Spectacle Lake
Spectacle Lake RR
Te Arai SR
Tomarata Lake
Te Arai
Topuni SR
Topuni
Pakiri SR
Tomarata
Te Hana
Logues Bush SR
Pakiri
Cape Rodney – Okakari Point Marine Res
Goat Island
Cape Rodney
Glass bottom boat rides
Snorkelling
Leigh
Jellicoe Channel
Te Ananuiarau Bay
Ngatamahine Pt
Waimaomao Bay
Te Hue Pt
Hingaia Pt
Mt Hauturu 722
Te Titoki Pt
East Cape
Little Barrier Island Nature Reserve
Waiteitei
Wellsford
Whangaripo
Omaha Eco Area
horse riding
Wayby Valley
Hoteo North
Conical Peak 385
Big Omaha
Whangateau
Reptile Park
Ti Point SR
Ti Point
Wayby
Sunnybrook Scenic Res
Point Wells
Whangateau Hbr
Omaha
Omaha Bay
Omaha Flats
Totara Peak SR
Dome Valley Forest Track
Matakana
Wilsons SR
Anchor Bay
Takatu Pt
Tauhoa
Waiwhiu
Sheepworld
Takatu
Tawharanui
Tawharanui Regional Park
Mt Harriet 229
Hoteo
Dome Valley
Warkworth District Museum
Old cement works
Buckleton Beach
Streamlands
Warkworth
Sandspit
Kawau Bay
Kawati Pt
Sharp Point SR
Mt Taylor 164
Kawau Island
Kawau Is SR
Lawries SR
Kaipara Flats
Kaipara Flats Airfield
Kourawhero
Honey Centre
Duck Creek SR
Snells Beach
Ferry
Algies Bay
Smeltinghouse Bay SR
Mansion House
Stony Hill RR
Kawau Island HR
Grey Heights 182
Kawau Pt
Mangakura
Atuanui Scenic Res
Andrews Kauri SR
Mt Auckland 305
Mt Auckland Walkway
Woodcocks
Parry Kauri Park
Hepburn Creek
Mahurangi Hbr
Scandrett RP
Martins Bay
Glorit
Pohuehue SR
Moirs Hill Walkway
Pohuehue
Kaipara Hills RR
Onehunga Stream SR
Moir Hill 358
Ahuroa
Komokoriki
Pukapuka
Burton Wells SR
Mahurangi SR
Motuketekete Island
Motuorekareka Island SR
Mahurangi
Casnell Island SR
Araparera
Armstrong Kauri SR
Puhoi SR
Mahurangi West
Mahurangi RP
Motuora
Motuora Island RR
Tuhirangi 214
Puhoi
Puhoi Cheese Factory
Saddle Island SR
Sealink ferry to Great Barrier Island
Ph (09) 300 5900 / 0800 732 546
www.sealink.co.nz
To Port Fitzroy Great Barrier Island
To Tryphena Great Barrier Island
Kakanui
Tahekeroa
Couldrey House & Museum
Wenderholm RP
Hauraki Gulf
Makarau
Waiwera
Waiwera Hot Springs
North Shore Suburbs See Map 88
Hatfields Beach
Toll Road
Orewa
Whangaparaoa Bay
Whangaparaoa Peninsula
Bird Sanctuary (Open)
Tiritiri Matangi Island
Whangaparaoa Passage
Riteakawarau 252
Kanohi
Wainui
Red Beach
Army Bay
Gulf Harbour
Kaukapakapa
Silverdale SR
Snow Planet
Silverdale
Waiau Bay
Shakespear Regional Park
Te Haruhi Bay
Okoromai Bay
Waitoki
Loch Norrie
Stillwater
Whangaparaoa
Okura Estuary SR
Piripiri Pt
Long Bay – Okura Marine Reserve
Dairy Flat
Dairy Flat Airport
Okura
Redvale
Long Bay
Long Bay RP
The Noises
Ahaaha Rocks
David Rocks
Glenvar
Toroa Pt (Gull Pt)
Albany SR
Torbay
Coatesville SR
Coatesville
Albany Heights
Browns Bay
Rakino Island
Rakino Is RR
D'Urville Rocks
Horuhoru Rock
North Harbour Stadium
Billy Goat Pt
Rakino Channel
Thumb Pt (Te Patu Pt)
Waikoukou Valley
Massey University Campus
Mairangi Bay
Rewiti
Paremoremo
Castor Bay
Rangitoto Island Scenic Reserve
Home Bay
Motutapu Island Recreation Reserve
Thompsons Pt
Waiheke Island
Owhiti Bay
Hooks Bay
Stony Batter HR
Waimauku
Riverhead
Lucas Creek
Cuthill
Milford
Beesonline Honey Centre
Huapai
Kumeu
Whenuapai
Whenuapai Airforce Base
Glenfield
L Pupuke
Matietie Hist Res
Oneroa
Palm Beach
Onetangi Bay
Gun Emplacements
Birkenhead
Kaipara R
To Auckland
7
36
6580
6570
6560
6550
6540
6530
6520
6510
6500000N
6490
2650
2660
2670
2680
2690
2700000E
174°30'E
174°45'E
175°00'E
36°00'S
36°15'S
36°30'S
36°45'S

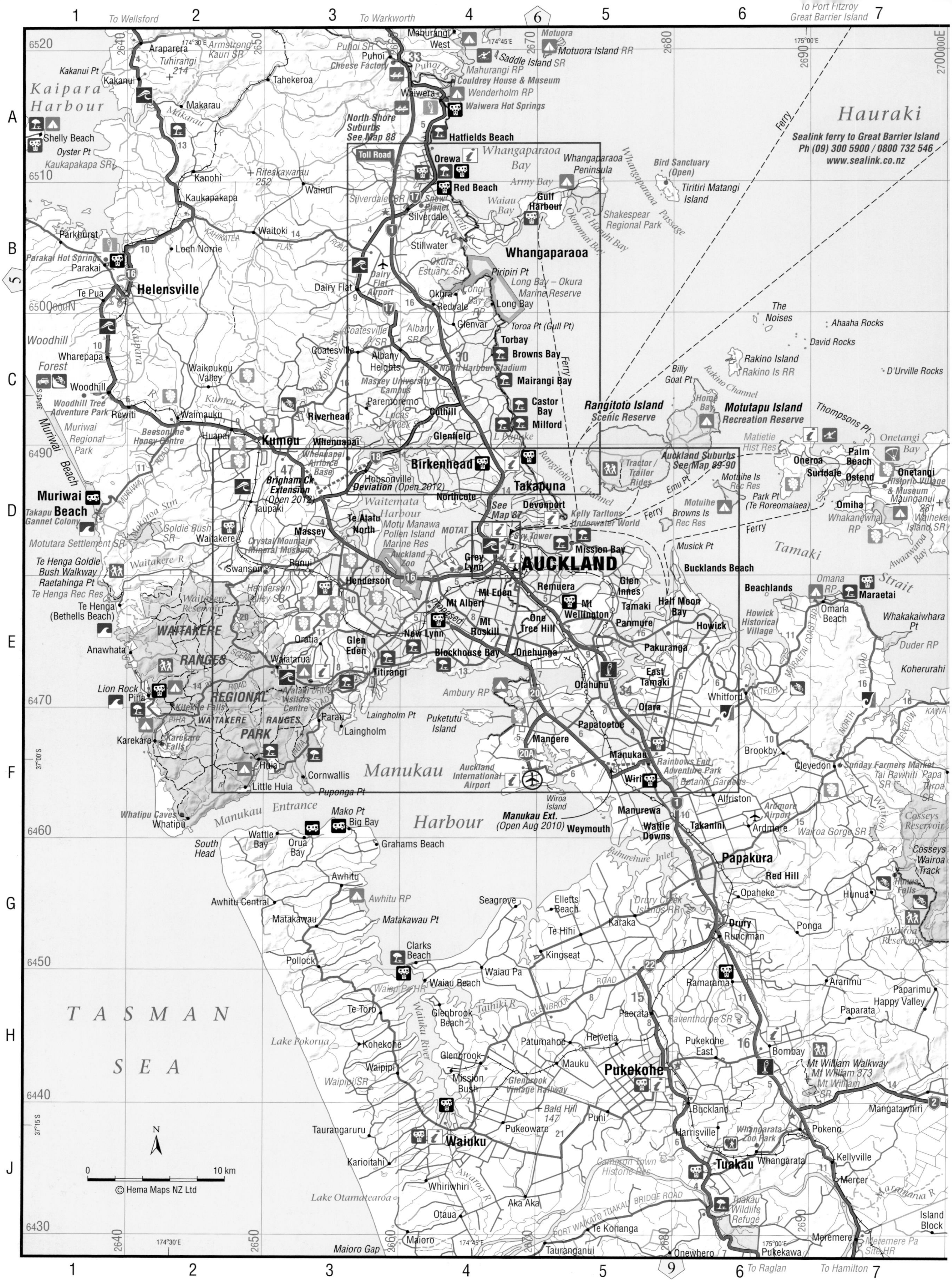
To Wellsford
To Warkworth
To Port Fitzroy Great Barrier Island
Kaipara Harbour
Hauraki
Sealink ferry to Great Barrier Island
Ph (09) 300 5900 / 0800 732 546
www.sealink.co.nz
Ferry
Araparera
Armstrong Kauri SR
Tuhirangi 214
Kakanui Pt
Kakanui
Tahekeroa
Puhoi SR
Puhoi
Cheese Factory
Mahurangi West
Motuora
Motuora Island RR
Saddle Island SR
Mahurangi RP
Couldrey House & Museum
Waiwera
Wenderholm RP
Waiwera Hot Springs
Makarau
Shelly Beach
Oyster Pt
Kaukapakapa SR
North Shore Suburbs See Map 88
Hatfields Beach
Toll Road
Orewa
Whangaparaoa Bay
Whangaparaoa Peninsula
Army Bay
Red Beach
Bird Sanctuary (Open)
Tiritiri Matangi Island
Whangaparaoa Passage
Kanohi
Riteakawarau 252
Kaukapakapa
Wainui
Silverdale SR
Snow Planet
Silverdale
Waiau Bay
Gulf Harbour
Shakespear Regional Park
Te Haruhi Bay
Okoromai Bay
Parkhurst
Waitoki
Loch Norrie
Kahikatea Flat Road
Stillwater
Whangaparaoa
Parakai Hot Springs
Parakai
Helensville
Te Pua
Dairy Flat
Dairy Flat Airport
Okura Estuary SR
Piripiri Pt
Long Bay – Okura Marine Reserve
Okura
Redvale
Long Bay RP
Long Bay
Glenvar
Woodhill
Kaipara R
Coatesville SR
Albany SR
Toroa Pt (Gull Pt)
Torbay
The Noises
Ahaaha Rocks
David Rocks
Wharepapa
Forest
Coatesville
Albany Heights
Browns Bay
North Harbour Stadium
Rakino Island
Rakino Is RR
D'Urville Rocks
Waikoukou Valley
Massey University Campus
Mairangi Bay
Billy Goat Pt
Rakino Channel
Woodhill
Woodhill Tree Adventure Park
Rewiti
Kumeu R
Paremoremo
Castor Bay
Rangitoto Island Scenic Reserve
Home Bay
Motutapu Island Recreation Reserve
Thompsons Pt
Muriwai Regional Park
Waimauku
Riverhead
Lucas Creek SR
Cuthill
Milford
L Pupuke
Beesonline Honey Centre
Huapai
Kumeu
Whenuapai
Glenfield
Matietie Hist Res
Onetangi Bay
Muriwai Beach
Whenuapai Airforce Base
Hobsonville
Birkenhead
Rangitoto Channel
Tractor / Trailer Rides
Auckland Suburbs See Map 89-90
Oneroa
Palm Beach
Surfdale
Ostend
Onetangi
Historic Village & Museum
Brigham Ck Extension (Open 2012)
Deviation (Open 2012)
Takapuna
Muriwai Beach
Taupaki
Northcote
Devonport
Emu Pt
Motuihe Is Rec Res
Park Pt (Te Roreomaiaea)
Takapu Gannet Colony
Goldie Bush SR
Waitakere
Waitemata Harbour
Motu Manawa Pollen Island Marine Res
See Map 87
Kelly Tarltons Underwater World
Motuihe
Browns Is Rec Res
Omiha
Whakanewha RP
Mauganui 231
Waiheke Island SR
Motutara Settlement SR
Te Atatu North
MOTAT
Sky Tower
Mission Bay
Ferry
Te Henga Goldie Bush Walkway
Raetahinga Pt
Te Henga Rec Res
Crystal Mountain Mineral Museum
Massey
Auckland Zoo
Grey Lynn
AUCKLAND
Musick Pt
Tamaki
Swanson
Ranui
Bucklands Beach
Beachlands
Omana RP
Maraetai
Strait
Te Henga (Bethells Beach)
Waitakere Reservoir
Henderson Valley SR
Henderson
Mt Eden
Remuera
Glen Innes
Tamaki
Half Moon Bay
Omana Beach
Whakakaiwhara Pt
WAITAKERE
Mt Albert
Mt Wellington
Panmure
Howick
Howick Historical Village
Mt Roskill
One Tree Hill
Duder RP
Oratia
Glen Eden
New Lynn
Pakuranga
Anawhata
RANGES
Scenic
Waiatarua
Blockhouse Bay
Onehunga
East Tamaki
Koherurahi
Titirangi
Ambury RP
Otahuhu
Whitford
Lion Rock
Piha
REGIONAL
Arataki Visitors Centre
Otara
Kitekite Falls
Parau
Laingholm Pt
Puketutu Island
Laingholm
WAITAKERE RANGES PARK
Papatoetoe
Mangere
Karekare
Karekare Falls
Manukau
Rainbows End Adventure Park
Brookby
Clevedon
Sunday Farmers Market
Tai Rawhiti SR
Papa Turoa SR
Huia
Cornwallis
Manukau
Auckland International Airport
Wiri
Botanic Gardens
Little Huia
Puponga Pt
Wiroa Island
Alfriston
Whatipu Caves
Manukau Entrance
Mako Pt
Manurewa
Ardmore Airport
Whatipu
Big Bay
Harbour
Manukau Ext. (Open Aug 2010)
Weymouth
Wattle Downs
Takanini
Ardmore
Cosseys Reservoir
Wairoa Gorge SR
Wattle Bay
Orua Bay
Grahams Beach
South Head
Pahurehure Inlet
Papakura
Cosseys Wairoa Track
Red Hill
Awhitu
Opaheke
Hunua
Hunua Falls
Awhitu RP
Awhitu Central
Seagrove
Elletts Beach
Drury Creek Islands RR
Matakawau
Matakawau Pt
Te Hihi
Karaka
Drury
Runciman
Ponga
Wairoa Reservoir
Clarks Beach
Kingseat
Pollock
Waiau Beach
Waiau Pa
Ramarama
Ararimu
Waiau Pa SR
Glenbrook Road
Paparimu
Happy Valley
TASMAN
SEA
Te Toro
Taihiki R
Glenbrook Beach
Paerata
Raventhorpe SR
Paparata
Waiuku River
Lake Pokorua
Kohekohe
Patumahoe
Helvetia
Pukekohe East
Bombay
Mt William Walkway
Mt William 373
Mt William SR
Glenbrook
Waipipi
Mauku
Pukekohe
Waipipi SR
Mission Bush
Glenbrook Vintage Railway
Bald Hill 147
Puni
Buckland
Mangatawhiri
Taurangaruru
Pukeoware
Harrisville
Whangarata Zoo Park
Pokeno
Waiuku
Tuakau
Whangarata
Kellyville
Karioitahi
Camerontown Historic Res
Awaroa R
Whiriwhiri
Mercer
Lake Otamatearoa
Aka Aka
Tuakau Wildlife Refuge
Port Waikato Tuakau Bridge Road
Otaua
Te Kohanga
Island Block
Maioro Gap
Maioro
Tauranganui
Onewhero
Pukekawa
Meremere
Meremere Pa Site HR
To Raglan
To Hamilton
0
10 km
© Hema Maps NZ Ltd
N

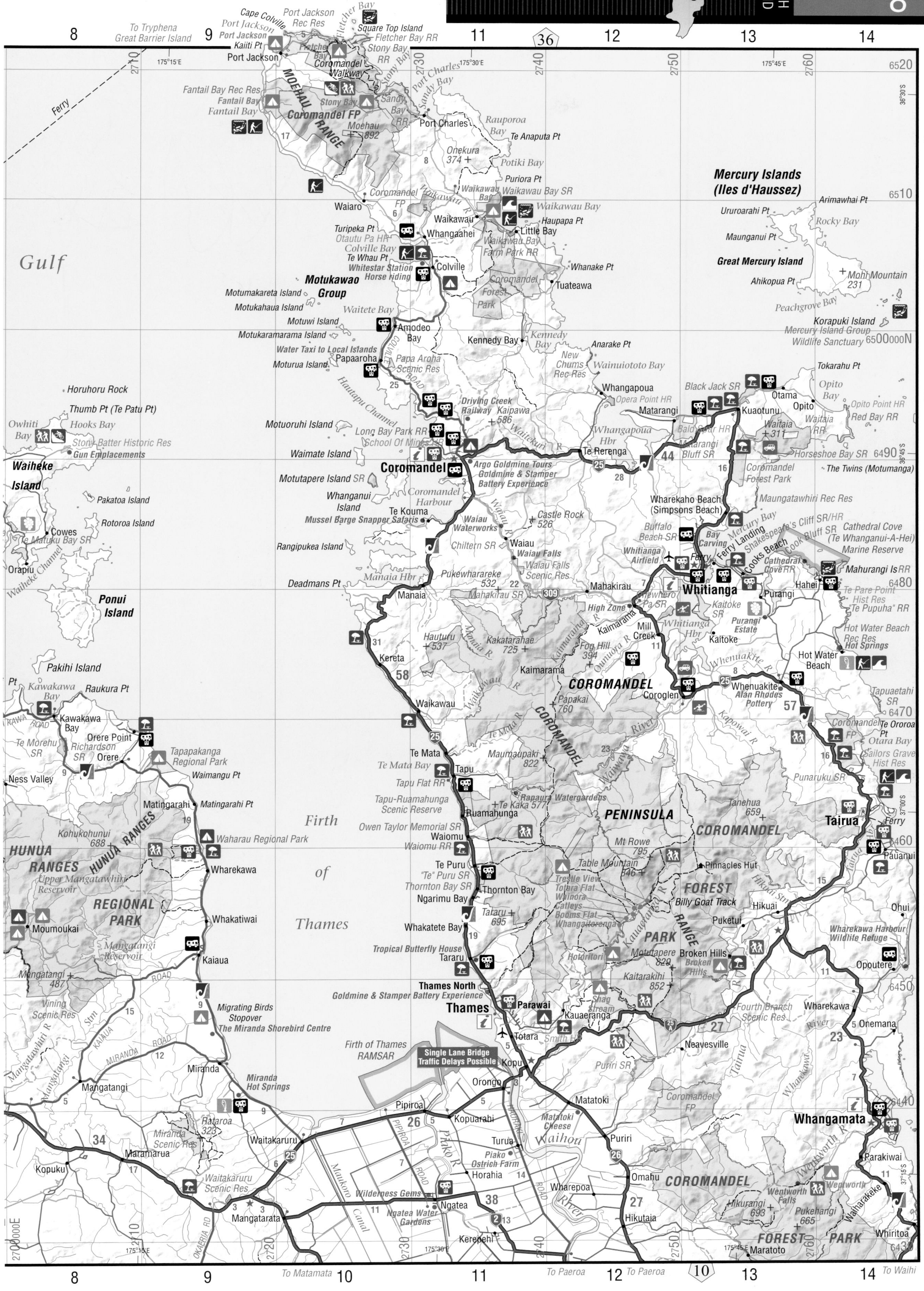

To Tryphena
Great Barrier Island
Cape Colville
Port Jackson
Port Jackson Rec Res
Fletcher Bay
Square Top Island
Fletcher Bay RR
Stony Bay
Kaiiti Pt
Port Jackson
Coromandel Walkway
Port Charles
Sandy Bay
Fantail Bay Rec Res
Fantail Bay
Stony Bay
Coromandel FP
MOEHAU RANGE
Moehau
892
Rauporoa Bay
Te Anaputa Pt
Onekura
374
Potiki Bay
Puriora Pt
Waikawau Bay SR
Waikawau Bay
Haupapa Pt
Little Bay
Waikawau Bay Farm Park RR
Whanake Pt
Tuateawa
Coromandel Forest Park
Waiaro
Coromandel FP
Waikawau
Whangaahei
Turipeka Pt
Otautu Pa HR
Colville Bay
Te Whau Pt
Whitestar Station Horse riding
Colville
Gulf
Motukawao Group
Motumakareta Island
Motukahaua Island
Waitete Bay
Motuwi Island
Motukaramarama Island
Water Taxi to Local Islands
Moturua Island
Amodeo Bay
Papaaroha
Papa Aroha Scenic Res
Kennedy Bay
Kennedy Bay
Anarake Pt
New Chums Rec Res
Wainuiototo Bay
Whangapoua
Opera Point HR
Hautapu Channel
Driving Creek Railway
Kaipawa
586
Horuhoru Rock
Thumb Pt (Te Patu Pt)
Owhiti Bay
Hooks Bay
Stony Batter Historic Res
Gun Emplacements
Motuoruhi Island
Long Bay Park RR
School Of Mines
Waimate Island
Coromandel
Argo Goldmine Tours
Goldmine & Stamper Battery Experience
Waiheke Island
Motutapere Island SR
Pakatoa Island
Rotoroa Island
Whanganui Island
Coromandel Harbour
Te Kouma
Mussel Barge Snapper Safaris
Cowes
Te Matuku Bay SR
Waiheke Channel
Oraipu
Rangipukea Island
Deadmans Pt
Ponui Island
Waiau Waterworks
Castle Rock
526
Chiltern SR
Waiau
Waiau Falls
Waiau Falls Scenic Res
Pukewharareke
532
Manaia Hbr
Manaia
Mahakirau SR
Mahakirau
Whangapoua Hbr
Te Rerenga
Waitekuri R
Mercury Islands (Iles d'Haussez)
Arimawhai Pt
Ururoarahi Pt
Rocky Bay
Maunganui Pt
Great Mercury Island
Mohi Mountain
231
Ahikopua Pt
Peachgrove Bay
Korapuki Island
Mercury Island Group Wildlife Sanctuary
Tokarahu Pt
Black Jack SR
Otama
Opito
Opito Bay
Opito Point HR
Red Bay RR
Matarangi
Kuaotunu
Waitaia
Bald Spur HR
Matarangi Bluff SR
Horseshoe Bay SR
The Twins (Motumanga)
Coromandel Forest Park
Maungatawhiri Rec Res
Wharekaho Beach (Simpsons Beach)
Mercury Bay
Buffalo Beach SR
Bay Carving
Ferry Landing
Shakespeare's Cliff SR/HR
Cathedral Cove (Te Whanganui-A-Hei) Marine Reserve
Cooks Beach
Cook Bluff SR
Cathedral Cove RR
Mahurangi Is RR
Hahei
Whitianga Airfield
Ferry
Whitianga
Purangi
Te Pare Point Hist Res
"Te Pupuha" RR
Hot Water Beach Rec Res
Hot Springs
Hot Water Beach
High Zone
Kaitoke SR
Purangi Estate
Kaitoke
Whitianga Hbr
Mill Creek
Kaimarama
Fog Hill
394
Hauturu
537
Kakatarahae
725
Kereta
Kaimarama
Whenuakite R
Whenuakite
Alan Rhodes Pottery
Tapuaetahi SR
COROMANDEL
Coroglen
Papakai
760
Pakihi Island
Kawakawa Bay
Raukura Pt
Kawakawa Bay
Orere Point
Te Morehu SR
Richardson SR
Orere
Tapapakanga Regional Park
Waimangu Pt
Ness Valley
Waikawau
Te Mata
Te Mata Bay
Tapu
Tapu Flat RR
Maumaupaki
822
Coromandel FP
Te Ororoa Pt
Otara Bay
Sailors Grave Hist Res
Punaruku SR
Matingarahi
Matingarahi Pt
Tapu-Ruamahunga Scenic Reserve
Rapaura Watergardens
Te Kaka 577
Ruamahunga
PENINSULA
Tanehua
659
Tairua
Ferry
Firth of Thames
Owen Taylor Memorial SR
Waiomu
Waiomu RR
Waharau Regional Park
Kohukohunui
688
HUNUA RANGES
HUNUA RANGES
Upper Mangatawhiri Reservoir
Wharekawa
REGIONAL PARK
Te Puru
"Te" Puru SR
Thornton Bay SR
Thornton Bay
Ngarimu Bay
Mt Rowe
795
Table Mountain
846
Trestle View
Totara Flat
Wainora
Catleys
Booms Flat
Whangaiterenga
COROMANDEL FOREST PARK
Pinnacles Hut
Billy Goat Track
Pauanui
Moumoukai
Whakatiwai
Tararu
695
Whakatete Bay
Hikuai
Puketui
Ohui
Wharekawa Harbour Wildlife Refuge
Mangatangi Reservoir
Kaiaua
Tropical Butterfly House
Tararu
Motutapere
829
Broken Hills
Broken Hills
Opoutere
Mangatangi
487
Kaitarakihi
852
Hotoritori
RANGE
Thames North
Goldmine & Stamper Battery Experience
Thames
Parawai
Kauaeranga
Shag Stream
Fourth Branch Scenic Res
Wharekawa
Onemana
Vining Scenic Res
Migrating Birds Stopover
The Miranda Shorebird Centre
Totara
Neavesville
Firth of Thames RAMSAR
Single Lane Bridge Traffic Delays Possible
Kopu
Puriri SR
Miranda
Miranda Hot Springs
Mangatangi
Orongo
Matatoki
Coromandel FP
Whangamata
Pipiroa
Kopuarahi
Matatoki Cheese
Rataroa
323
Miranda Scenic Res
Waitakaruru
Maramarua
Turua
Waihou
Puriri
Piako Ostrich Farm
Horahia
Piako R
Parakiwai
Kopuku
Waitakaruru Scenic Res
Mangatarata
Wilderness Gems
Ngatea
Ngatea Water Gardens
Omahu
Wharepoa
COROMANDEL
Wentworth Falls
Wentworth
Hikutaia
Hikurangi
693
Pukehangi
665
FOREST PARK
Waiharakeke
Whiritoa
Kerepehi
Maratoto
Matakoro Canal
To Matamata
To Paeroa
To Paeroa
To Waihi

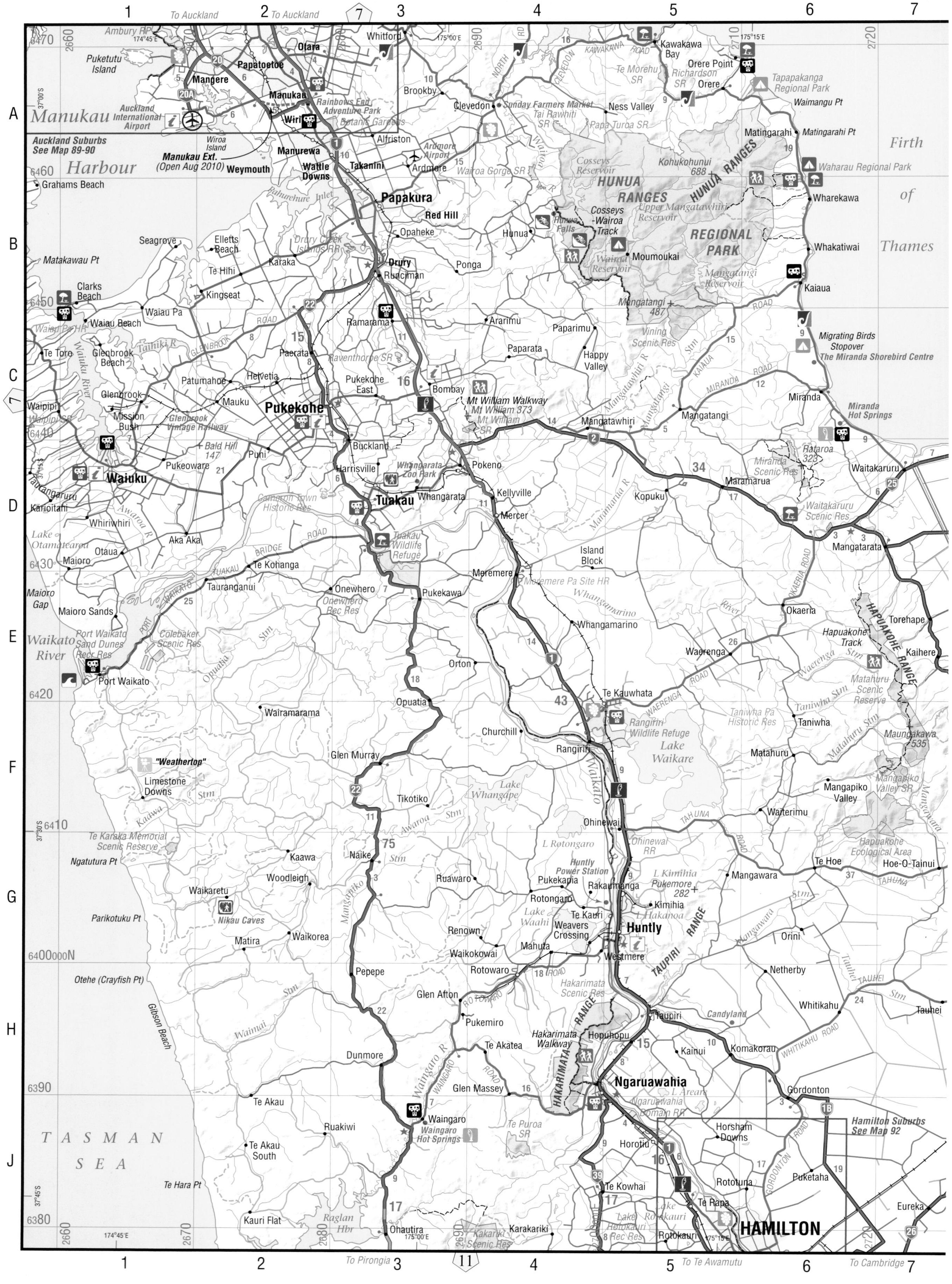

To Auckland
To Auckland
7
Ambury RP
Puketutu Island
Mangere
Papatoetoe
Otara
Whitford
Manukau Harbour
Auckland International Airport
Manukau
Wiri
Rainbows End Adventure Park
Botanic Gardens
Auckland Suburbs See Map 89-90
Wiroa Island
Manukau Ext. (Open Aug 2010)
Weymouth
Manurewa
Wattle Downs
Takanini
Alfriston
Ardmore Airport
Ardmore
Brookby
Clevedon
Sunday Farmers Market
Tai Rawhiti SR
Papa Turoa SR
Kawakawa Bay
Te Morehu SR
Richardson SR
Orere Point
Orere
Tapapakanga Regional Park
Waimangu Pt
Ness Valley
Wairoa Gorge SR
Cosseys Reservoir
HUNUA RANGES
HUNUA RANGES REGIONAL PARK
Kohukohunui 688
Upper Mangatawhiri Reservoir
Matingarahi
Matingarahi Pt
Firth of Thames
Waharau Regional Park
Wharekawa
Grahams Beach
Papakura
Pahurehure Inlet
Red Hill
Opaheke
Hunua
Hunua Falls
Cosseys-Wairoa Track
Wairoa Reservoir
Moumoukai
Mangatangi Reservoir
Whakatiwai
Seagrove
Elletts Beach
Drury Creek Islands RR
Karaka
Drury
Runciman
Ponga
Matakawau Pt
Te Hihi
Kingseat
Clarks Beach
Waiau Pa
Waiau Beach
Waiau Pa HR
Kaiaua
Mangatangi 487
Ramarama
Ararimu
Paparimu
Migrating Birds Stopover
The Miranda Shorebird Centre
Te Toro
Glenbrook Beach
Taihiki R
Paerata
Raventhorpe SR
Paparata
Happy Valley
Vining Scenic Res
Patumahoe
Helvetia
Pukekohe East
Bombay
Mt William Walkway
Mt William 373
Mt William SR
Mangatawhiri
Mangatangi
Miranda
Miranda Hot Springs
Waipipi
Glenbrook
Mauku
Pukekohe
Mission Bush
Glenbrook Vintage Railway
Bald Hill 147
Buckland
Pokeno
Puni
Pukeoware
Waiuku
Harrisville
Whangarata Zoo Park
Tuakau
Whangarata
Kellyville
Mercer
Rataroa 323
Miranda Scenic Res
Maramarua
Kopuku
Waitakaruru
Waitakaruru Scenic Res
Karioitahi
Whiriwhiri
Cameron Town Historic Res
Lake Otamatearoa
Otaua
Aka Aka
Tuakau Wildlife Refuge
Island Block
Mangatarata
Maioro
Te Kohanga
Tuakau Bridge Road
Maioro Gap
Tauranganui
Onewhero
Onewhero Rec Res
Meremere
Meremere Pa Site HR
Pukekawa
Whangamarino
Okaeria
Okaeria Road
Torehape
Maioro Sands
Waikato River
Port Waikato Sand Dunes Recr Res
Colebaker Scenic Res
Hapuakohe Track
Hapuakohe Range
Waerenga
Kaihere
Port Waikato
Orton
Matahuru Scenic Reserve
Wairamarama
Opuatia
Te Kauwhata
Rangiriri Wildlife Refuge
Taniwha Pa Historic Res
Taniwha
Churchill
Maungakawa 535
Lake Waikare
Rangiriri
Matahuru
Glen Murray
"Weathertop"
Limestone Downs
Lake Whangape
Tikotiko
Mangapiko Valley
Mangapiko Valley SR
Waiterimu
Ohinewai
Ohinewai RR
Te Karaka Memorial Scenic Reserve
Kaawa
Naike
L Rotongaro
Hapuakohe Ecological Area
Ngatutura Pt
Huntly Power Station
L Kimihia
Te Hoe
Hoe-O-Tainui
Woodleigh
Ruawaro
Pukekapia
Rakaumanga
Pukemore 282
Mangawara
Waikaretu
Rotongaro
Kimihia
L Hakanoa
Nikau Caves
Te Kauri
Lake Waahi
Weavers Crossing
Huntly
Taupiri Range
Parikotuku Pt
Renown
Orini
Matira
Waikorea
Mahuta
Waikokowai
Westmere
Otehe (Crayfish Pt)
Pepepe
Rotowaro
Hakarimata Scenic Res
Netherby
Gibson Beach
Glen Afton
Whitikahu
Tauhei
Pukemiro
Taupiri
Candyland
Hakarimata Walkway
Hopuhopu
Hakarimata Range
Te Akatea
Kainui
Komakorau
Dunmore
Waingaro R
Ngaruawahia
L Areare
Glen Massey
Gordonton
Te Akau
Ngaruawahia Domain RR
Waingaro
Waingaro Hot Springs
Te Puroa SR
Horsham Downs
Hamilton Suburbs See Map 92
Ruakiwi
TASMAN SEA
Te Akau South
Horotiu
Rototuna
Puketaha
Te Hara Pt
Te Kowhai
Te Rapa
Eureka
Kauri Flat
Raglan Hbr
Lake Rotokauri
Lake Rotokauri Rec Res
Ohautira
Karakariki
Kakariki Scenic Res
Rotokauri
HAMILTON
To Pirongia
11
To Te Awamutu
To Cambridge

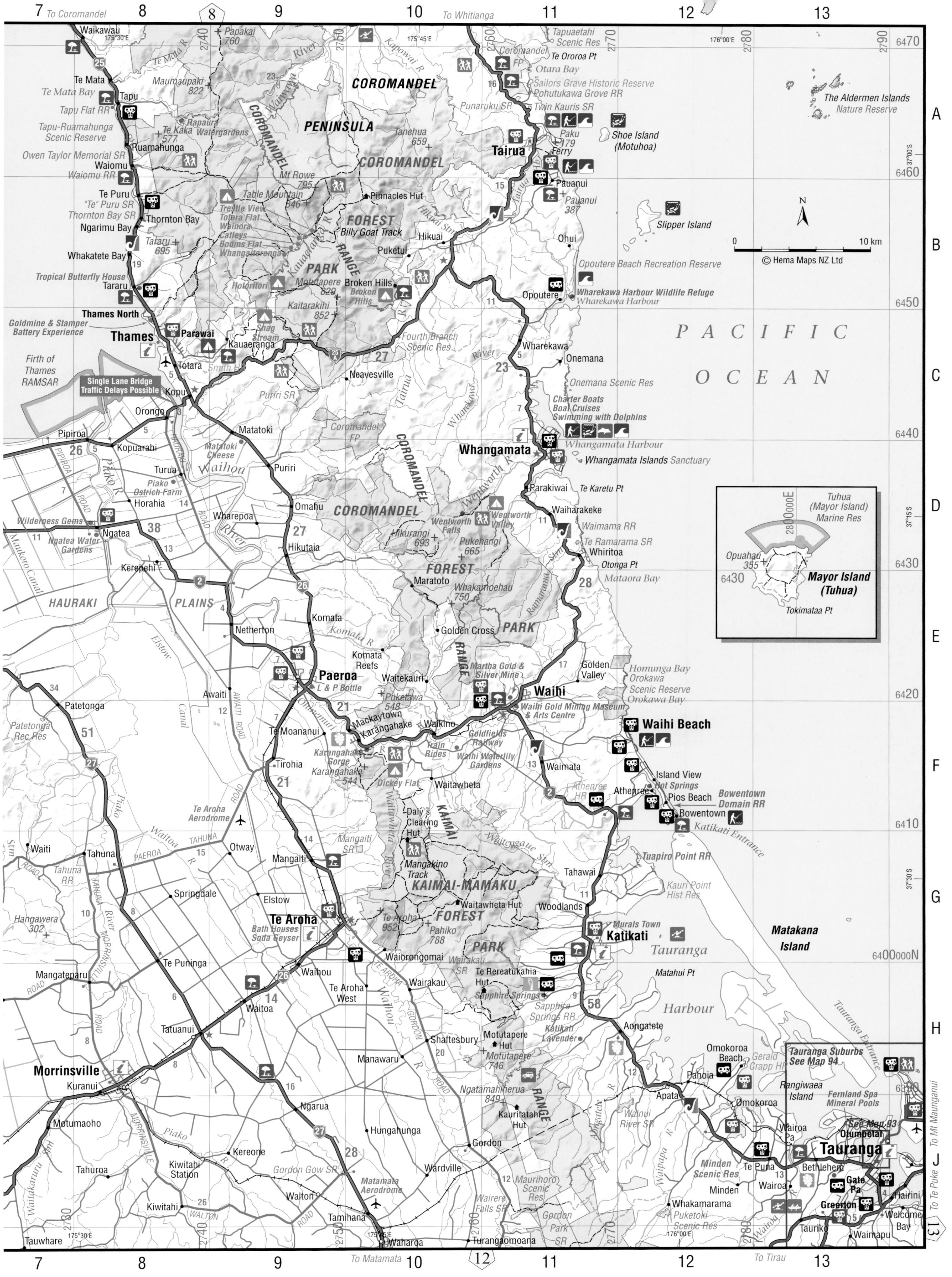

To Coromandel
To Whitianga
To Matamata
To Tirau
To Te Puke
To Mt Maunganui
COROMANDEL
PENINSULA
COROMANDEL
FOREST
PARK
COROMANDEL RANGE
COROMANDEL
COROMANDEL
FOREST
PARK
KAIMAI
KAIMAI-MAMAKU
FOREST
PARK
RANGE
HAURAKI
PLAINS
PACIFIC
OCEAN
Waikawau
Te Mata
Te Mata Bay
Tapu
Tapu Flat RR
Tapu-Ruamahunga Scenic Reserve
Ruamahunga
Owen Taylor Memorial SR
Waiomu
Waiomu RR
Te Puru
"Te" Puru SR
Thornton Bay SR
Thornton Bay
Ngarimu Bay
Tararu 695
Whakatete Bay
Tropical Butterfly House
Tararu
Thames North
Goldmine & Stamper Battery Experience
Thames
Parawai
Kauaeranga
Firth of Thames RAMSAR
Single Lane Bridge Traffic Delays Possible
Totara
Kopu
Orongo
Pipiroa
Kopuarahi
Matatoki
Matatoki Cheese
Puriri
Puriri SR
Turua
Piako Ostrich Farm
Horahia
Wharepoa
Omahu
Wilderness Gems
Ngatea
Ngatea Water Gardens
Hikutaia
Kerepehi
Netherton
Komata
Komata Reefs
Paeroa
L & P Bottle
Awaiti
Patetonga
Patetonga Rec Res
Te Moananui
Tirohia
Mackaytown
Karangahake
Karangahake Gorge
Karangahake 544
Waikino
Te Aroha Aerodrome
Waiti
Tahuna
Tahuna RR
Otway
Mangaiti
Mangaiti SR
Springdale
Elstow
Hangawera 302
Te Aroha
Bath Houses Soda Geyser
Te Aroha 952
Waiorongomai
Te Puninga
Mangateparu
Waihou
Te Aroha West
Wairakau
Waitoa
Tatuanui
Shaftesbury
Manawaru
Morrinsville
Kuranui
Ngarua
Motumaoho
Hungahunga
Kereone
Gordon
Tahuroa
Kiwitahi Station
Gordon Gow SR
Wardville
Matamata Aerodrome
Walton
Kiwitahi
Tamihana
Waharoa
Tauwhare
Turangaomoana
Papakai 760
Maumaupaki 822
Rapaura Watergardens
Te Kaka 577
Tanehua 659
Mt Rowe 795
Table Mountain 846
Pinnacles Hut
Trestle View
Totara Flat
Wainora
Catleys
Booms Flat
Whangaiterenga
Billy Goat Track
Hikuai
Puketui
Hotoritori
Motutapere 829
Broken Hills
Kaitarakihi 852
Shag Stream
Smith H
Fourth Branch Scenic Res
Neavesville
Coromandel FP
Wentworth Falls
Wentworth Valley
Hikurangi 693
Pukehangi 665
Maratoto
Whakamoehau 750
Golden Cross
Martha Gold & Silver Mine
Waitekauri
Puketawa 548
Goldfields Railway
Train Rides
Waihi Waterlily Gardens
Dickey Flat
Waitawheta
Daly's Clearing Hut
Mangakino Track
Waitawheta Hut
Pahiko 788
Te Rereatukahia Hut
Sapphire Springs
Sapphire Springs RR
Katikati Lavender
Motutapere Hut
Motutapere 746
Ngatamahinerua 849
Kauritatahi Hut
Wairere Falls SR
Maurihoro Scenic Res
Gordon Park SR
Wainui River SR
Tapuaetahi Scenic Res
Coromandel FP
Te Ororoa Pt
Otara Bay
Sailors Grave Historic Reserve
Pohutukawa Grove RR
Punaruku SR
Twin Kauris SR
Paku 179
Ferry
Tairua
Pauanui
Pauanui 387
Shoe Island (Motuhoa)
Slipper Island
The Aldermen Islands Nature Reserve
Ohui
Opoutere Beach Recreation Reserve
Opoutere
Wharekawa Harbour Wildlife Refuge
Wharekawa Harbour
Wharekawa
Onemana
Onemana Scenic Res
Charter Boats
Boat Cruises
Swimming with Dolphins
Whangamata
Whangamata Harbour
Whangamata Islands Sanctuary
Parakiwai
Te Karetu Pt
Waiharakeke
Waimama RR
Te Ramarama SR
Whiritoa
Otonga Pt
Mataora Bay
Golden Valley
Homunga Bay
Orokawa Scenic Reserve
Orokawa Bay
Waihi
Waihi Gold Mining Museum & Arts Centre
Waihi Beach
Waimata
Island View
Hot Springs
Athenree HR
Athenree
Pios Beach
Bowentown
Bowentown Domain RR
Katikati Entrance
Tuapiro Point RR
Tahawai
Kauri Point Hist Res
Woodlands
Murals Town
Katikati
Tauranga Harbour
Matakana Island
Matahui Pt
Aongatete
Omokoroa Beach
Gerald Crapp HR
Pahoia
Tauranga Entrance
Apata
Rangiwaea Island
Omokoroa
Fernland Spa Mineral Pools
Tauranga Suburbs See Map 94
See Map 93
Wairoa Pa
Otumoetai
Tauranga
Minden Scenic Res
Te Puna
Bethlehem
Minden
Wairoa
Gate Pa
Whakamarama
Puketoki Scenic Res
Greerton
Hairini
Welcome Bay
Tauriko
Waimapu
Tuhua (Mayor Island) Marine Res
Opuahau 355
Mayor Island (Tuhua)
Tokimataa Pt
N
0 10 km
© Hema Maps NZ Ltd

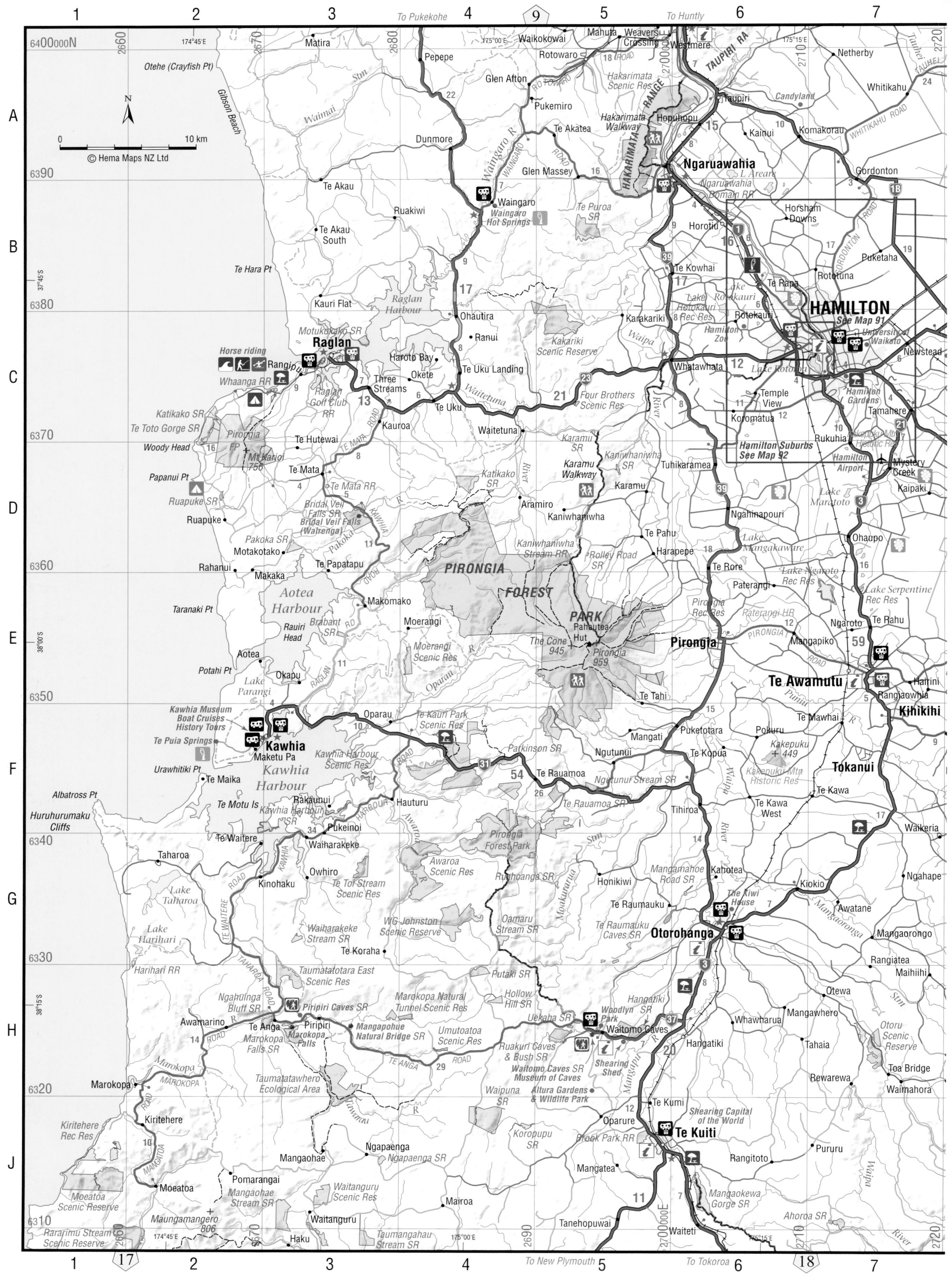

To Pukekohe
To Huntly
To New Plymouth
To Tokoroa
© Hema Maps NZ Ltd
10 km
Otehe (Crayfish Pt)
Gibson Beach
Matira
Pepepe
Waikokowai
Mahuta
Weavers Crossing
Westmere
TAUPIRI RA
Netherby
Rotowaro
Glen Afton
Pukemiro
Hakarimata Scenic Res
Taupiri
Candyland
Whitikahu
WHITIKAHU ROAD
Waimai
Dunmore
Waingaro R
Te Akatea
Hakarimata Walkway
HAKARIMATA RANGE
Hopuhopu
Kainui
Komakorau
Ngaruawahia
L Areare
Ngaruawahia Domain RR
Glen Massey
Gordonton
Te Akau
Waingaro
Waingaro Hot Springs
Ruakiwi
Te Puroa SR
Horsham Downs
Te Akau South
Horotiu
GORDONTON ROAD
Puketaha
Rototuna
Te Hara Pt
Te Kowhai
Te Rapa
Lake Rotokauri
Lake Rotokauri Rec Res
Rotokauri
Hamilton Zoo
HAMILTON
See Map 91
University of Waikato
Kauri Flat
Raglan Harbour
Ohautira
Ranui
Karakariki
Waipa
Kakariki Scenic Reserve
Motukokako SR
Raglan
Horse riding
Rangipu
Whaanga RR
Harata Bay
Okete
Te Uku Landing
Three Streams
Raglan Golf Club RR
Waitetuna
Whatawhata
Lake Rotoroa
Newstead
Temple View
Hamilton Gardens
Tamahere
Koromatua
Katikako SR
Te Toto Gorge SR
Pirongia FP
Mt Karioi 756
Woody Head
Te Uku
Kauroa
Four Brothers Scenic Res
River
Waitetuna
Karamu SR
Rukuhia
Kaniwhaniwha SR
Hamilton Suburbs See Map 92
Hamilton Airport
Mystery Creek
Te Hutewai
TE MATA ROAD
Te Mata
Te Mata RR
Papanui Pt
Karamu Walkway
Tuhikaramea
Kaipaki
Katikako SR
Karamu
Ruapuke SR
Ruapuke
Bridal Veil Falls SR
Bridal Veil Falls (Wairenga)
Aramiro
Kaniwhaniwha
Lake Maratoto
Ngahinapouri
Pakoka SR
Motakotako
Pakoka
Te Pahu
Harapepe
Ohaupo
Lake Mangakawhare
Kaniwhaniwha Stream RR
Rolley Road SR
Rahanui
Makaka
Te Papatapu
PIRONGIA
FOREST
PARK
Te Rore
Lake Ngaroto Rec Res
Paterangi
Lake Serpentine Rec Res
Aotea Harbour
Taranaki Pt
Makomako
Pirongia Rec Res
Paterangi HR
Brabant SR
Rauiri Head
Moerangi
Pahautea Hut
Ngaroto
Te Rahu
Moerangi Scenic Res
The Cone 945
Pirongia 959
Pirongia
PIRONGIA ROAD
Mangapiko
Aotea
Potahi Pt
Okapu
RAGLAN
Oparau
Te Awamutu
Hairini
Lake Parangi
Te Tahi
Rangiaowhia
Punui
Kihikihi
Kawhia Museum Boat Cruises History Tours
Te Puia Springs
Oparau
Te Kauri Park Scenic Res
Mangati
Puketotara
Te Mawhai R
Pokuru
Kakepuku + 449
Kawhia
Maketu Pa
Kawhia Harbour Scenic Res
Parkinson SR
Ngutunui
Te Kopua
Urawhitiki Pt
Te Maika
Kawhia Harbour
Te Rauamoa
Ngutunui Stream SR
Kakepuku Mtn Historic Res
Tokanui
Albatross Pt
Te Motu Is
Rakaunui
Kawhia Harbour SR
Hauturu
Te Rauamoa SR
Tihiroa
Te Kawa
Te Kawa West
Huruhurumaku Cliffs
Te Waitere
Pukeinoi
Awaroa
Pirongia Forest Park
Waikeria
Taharoa
Waiharakeke
Owhiro
Awaroa Scenic Res
Ruahoanga SR
Honikiwi
Mangamahoe Road SR
Kahotea
Ngahape
Kinohaku
Te Toi Stream Scenic Res
Kiokio
Lake Taharoa
TE WAITERE ROAD
Moakurarua
Te Raumauku
The Kiwi House
Awatane
Lake Harihari
Waiharakeke Stream SR
WG Johnston Scenic Reserve
Oamaru Stream SR
Te Raumauku Caves SR
Otorohanga
Mangaorongo
Mangaorongo
Te Koraha
Rangiatea
Harihari RR
Taumatatotara East Scenic Res
Putaki SR
Maihiihi
Ngahuinga Bluff SR
TAHAROA ROAD
Piripiri Caves SR
Marokopa Natural Tunnel Scenic Res
Hollow Hill SR
Hangatiki SR
Otewa
Stm
Awamarino
Te Anga
Piripiri
Mangapohue Natural Bridge SR
Uekaha SR
Woodlyn Park
Waitomo Caves
Whawharua
Mangawhero
Otoru Scenic Reserve
Marokopa Falls SR
Marokopa Falls
Umutoatoa Scenic Res
Hangatiki
Tahaia
Ruakuri Caves & Bush SR
Waitomo Caves SR Museum of Caves
Shearing Shed
Mangapu R
TE ANGA ROAD
Toa Bridge
Marokopa
Taumatatawhero Ecological Area
Rewarewa
Waimahora
Altura Gardens & Wildlife Park
Waipuna SR
Te Kumi
Shearing Capital of the World
Kiritehere
Kiritehere Rec Res
Oparure
Te Kuiti
Koropupu SR
Brook Park RR
Pururu
Ngapaenga
Ngapaenga SR
Rangitoto
Mangaohae
Waipa
MANGATOA
Pomarangai
Mangatea
Moeatoa
Moeatoa Scenic Reserve
Mangaohae Stream SR
Waitanguru Scenic Res
Mangaokewa Gorge SR
Mairoa
Maungamangero 806
Waitanguru
Tanehopuwai
Ahoroa SR
River
Rararimu Stream Scenic Reserve
Haku
Taumangahau Stream SR
Waiteti
174°45'E
175°00'E
175°15'E
37°45'S
38°00'S
38°15'S
6400000N
6390
6380
6370
6360
6350
6340
6330
6320
6310
2660
2670
2680
2690
2700000E
2710
2720
1
2
3
4
5
6
7
A
B
C
D
E
F
G
H
J

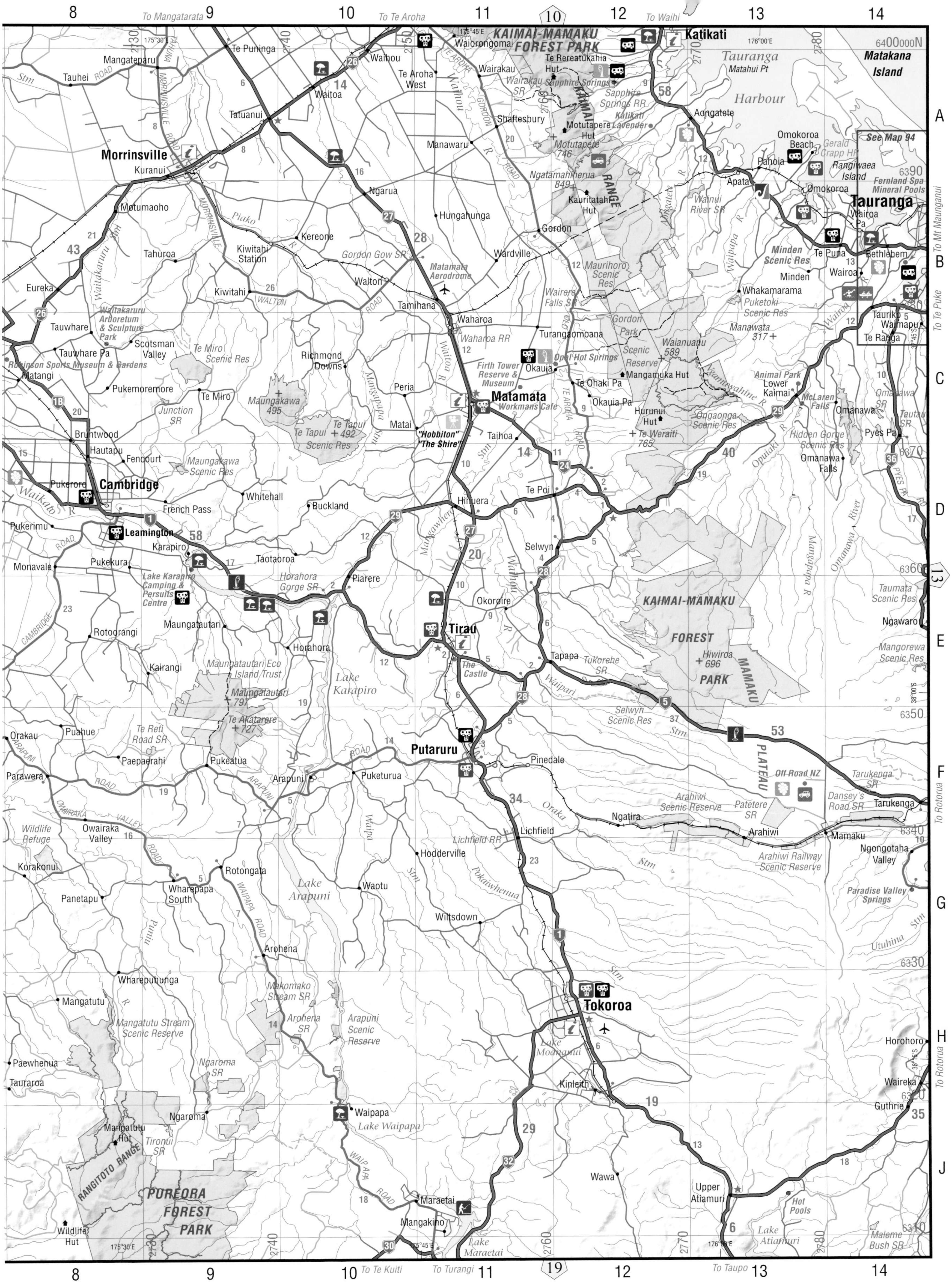

8
9
10
11
12
13
14
To Mangatarata
To Te Aroha
To Waihi
KAIMAI-MAMAKU FOREST PARK
Katikati
Tauranga Harbour
Matahui Pt
Matakana Island
Te Puninga
Mangateparu
Tauhei
Waihou
Waitoa
Te Aroha West
Waiorongomai
Wairakau
Wairakau SR
Te Rereatukahia Hut
Sapphire Springs
Sapphire Springs RR
KAIMAI RANGE
Katikati Lavender
Aongatete
Tatuanui
Shaftesbury
Motutapere Hut
Motutapere 746
Manawaru
Morrinsville
Kuranui
Omokoroa Beach
Gerald Crapp HR
Pahoia
Rangiwaea Island
Fernland Spa Mineral Pools
See Map 94
Apata
Omokoroa
Tauranga
Wairoa Pa
Ngatamahinerua 849
Kauritatahi Hut
Wainui River SR
Ngarua
Motumaoho
Hungahunga
Gordon
Piako R
Kereone
Kiwitahi Station
Tahuroa
Eureka
Gordon Gow SR
Matamata Aerodrome
Wardville
Maurihoro Scenic Res
Minden Scenic Res
Te Puna
Bethlehem
Minden
Wairoa
Whakamarama
Walton
Kiwitahi
Tamihana
Wairere Falls SR
Puketoki Scenic Res
Tauriko
Waimapu
Te Ranga
To Te Puke
To Mt Maunganui
Waitakaruru Arboretum & Sculpture Park
Tauwhare
Scotsman Valley
Tauwhare Pa
Robinson Sports Museum & Gardens
Matangi
Waharoa
Waharoa RR
Turangaomoana
Gordon Park Scenic Reserve
Waianuanu 589
Manawata 317
Te Miro Scenic Res
Richmond Downs
Firth Tower Reserve & Museum
Okauia
Opal Hot Springs
Mangamuka Hut
Animal Park
Lower Kaimai
Pukemoremore
Te Miro
Maungakawa 495
Peria
Matamata
Workmans Cafe
Te Ohaki Pa
Okauia Pa
McLaren Falls
Omanawa
Omanawa SR
Junction SR
Te Tapui 492
Te Tapui Scenic Res
Matai
"Hobbiton" "The Shire"
Taihoa
Hurunui Hut
Te Weraiti 765
Ongaonga Scenic Res
Hidden Gorge Scenic Res
Tautau SR
Pyes Pa
Bruntwood
Hautapu
Fencourt
Maungakawa Scenic Res
Omanawa Falls
Cambridge
Pukerоro
Waikato R
Whitehall
Buckland
Hinuera
Te Poi
Pukerimu
French Pass
Leamington
Karapiro
Selwyn
Monavale
Pukekura
Taotaroa
Lake Karapiro Camping & Persuits Centre
Horahora Gorge SR
Piarere
KAIMAI-MAMAKU FOREST PARK
Mangapapa R
Omanawa River
Taumata Scenic Res
Okoroire
Maungatautari
Rotoorangi
Tirau
Horahora
Ngawaro
Kairangi
Maungatautari Eco Island Trust
Tapapa
Tukorehe SR
Hiwiroa 696
MAMAKU
Mangorewa Scenic Res
The Castle
Lake Karapiro
Maungatautari 797
Te Akatarere 727
Waipari
Selwyn Scenic Res
MAMAKU PLATEAU
Orakau
Puahue
Te Reti Road SR
Putaruru
Paepaerahi
Pukeatua
Pinedale
Parawera
Arapuni
Puketurua
Off Road NZ
Tarukenga SR
Dansey's Road SR
Tarukenga
Arahiwi Scenic Reserve
Patetere SR
Wildlife Refuge
Owairaka Valley
Lichfield
Ngatira
Arahiwi
Mamaku
Ngongotaha Valley
Lichfield RR
Arahiwi Railway Scenic Reserve
To Rotorua
Korakonui
Hodderville
Rotongata
Wharepapa South
Waotu
Lake Arapuni
Paradise Valley Springs
Panetapu
Wiltsdown
Utuhina Stm
Arohena
Wharepuhunga
Mangatutu
Makomako Stream SR
Arohena SR
Arapuni Scenic Reserve
Tokoroa
Mangatutu Stream Scenic Reserve
Lake Moananui
Horohoro
Paewhenua
Ngaroma SR
Tauraroa
Kinleith
Waireka
Guthrie
Waipapa
Lake Waipapa
Ngaroma
Mangatutu Hut
Tironui SR
RANGITOTO RANGE
PUREORA FOREST PARK
Wawa
Upper Atiamuri
Hot Pools
Maraetai
Mangakino
Lake Maraetai
Lake Atiamuri
Maleme Bush SR
Wildlife Hut
To Te Kuiti
To Turangi
To Taupo
A
B
C
D
E
F
G
H
J

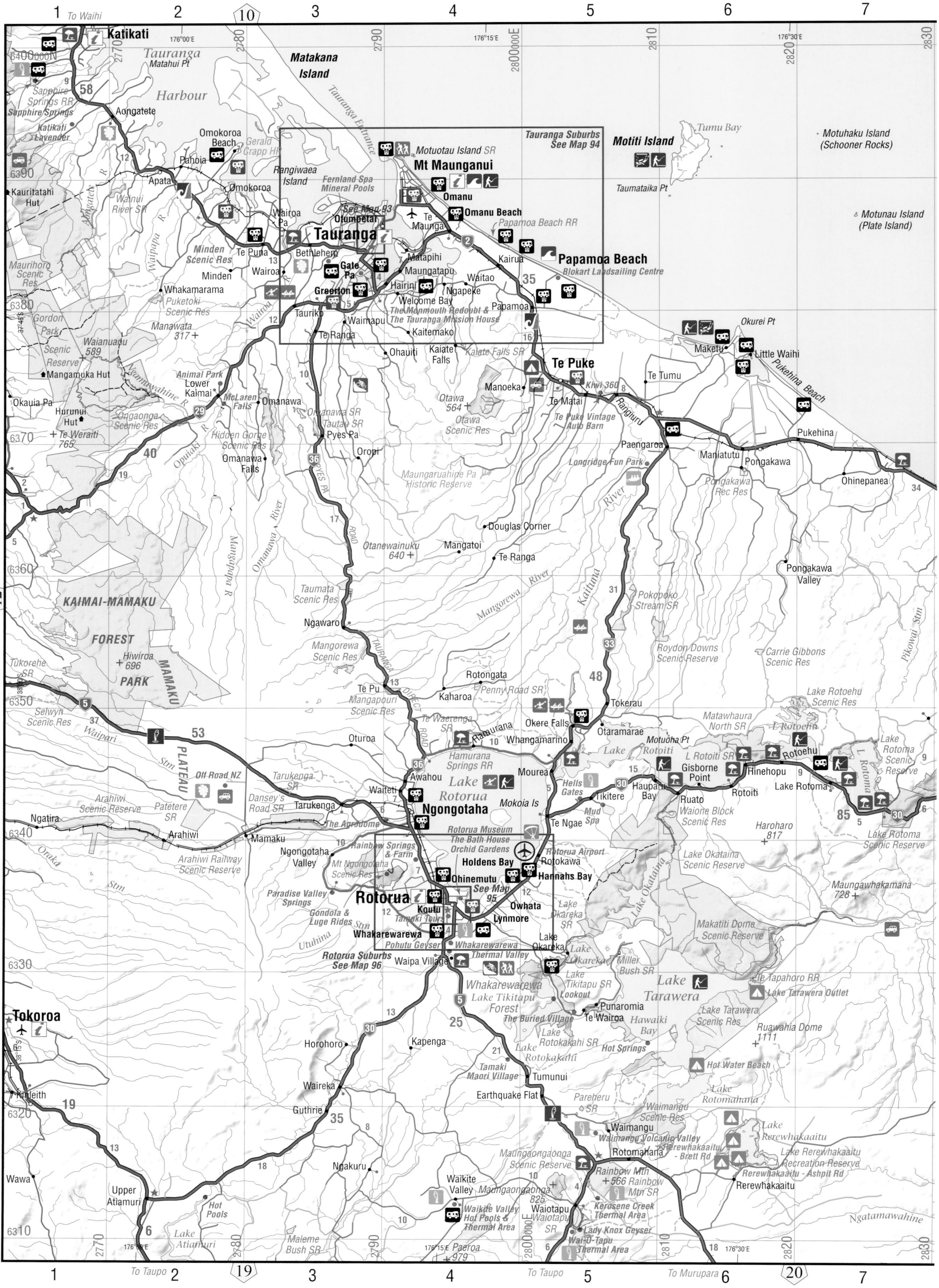

Katikati
Tauranga Harbour
Matakana Island
Aongatete
Omokoroa Beach
Pahoia
Apata
Omokoroa
Mt Maunganui
Omanu
Omanu Beach
Tauranga
Papamoa Beach
Motiti Island
Tauranga Suburbs See Map 94
Te Puna
Bethlehem
Minden
Wairoa
Whakamarama
Greerton
Gate Pa
Maungatapu
Welcome Bay
Papamoa
Tauriko
Te Ranga
Waimapu
Kaitemako
Ohauiti
Te Puke
Maketu
Little Waihi
Te Tumu
Pukehina
Paengaroa
Pongakawa
Ohinepanea
Oropi
Pyes Pa
Douglas Corner
Mangatoi
Otanewainuku 640
KAIMAI-MAMAKU FOREST PARK
Ngawaro
Te Pu
Rotongata
Kaharoa
Tokerau
Okere Falls
Hamurana
Lake Rotorua
Ngongotaha
Mokoia Is
Rotorua
Ohinemutu
Whakarewarewa
Lake Rotoiti
Lake Rotoehu
Lake Rotoma
Lake Okataina
Lake Tarawera
Rotorua Suburbs See Map 96
Mamaku
Tokoroa
Kinleith
Horohoro
Kapenga
Waireka
Guthrie
Earthquake Flat
Waimangu
Rotomahana
Ngakuru
Waikite Valley
Waiotapu
Upper Atiamuri
Wawa
Lake Atiamuri
To Waihi
To Taupo
To Murupara

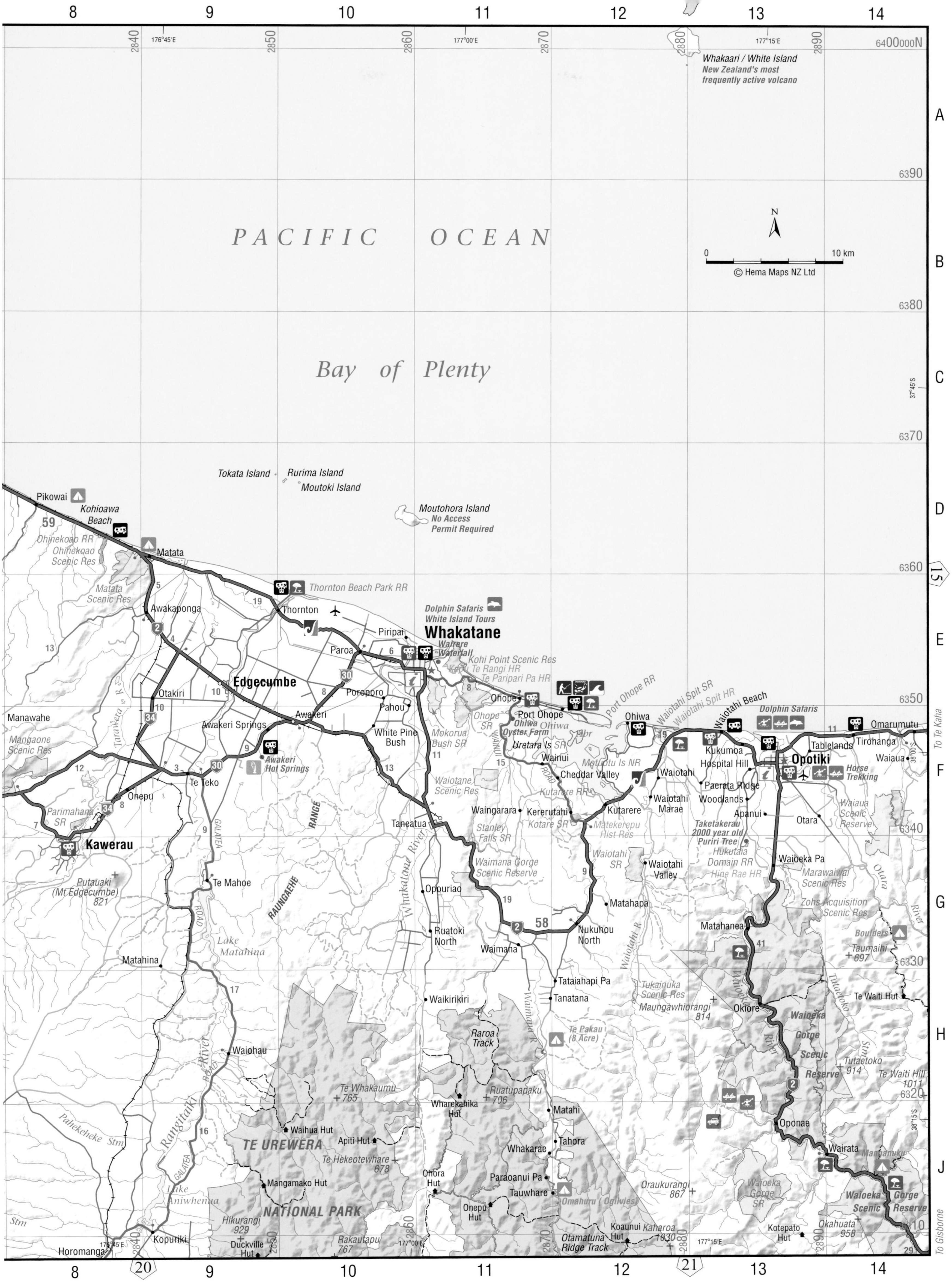
8
9
10
11
12
13
14
A
B
C
D
E
F
G
H
J
6400000N
6390
6380
6370
6360
6350
6340
6330
6320
6310
2840
2850
2860
2870
2880
2890
176°45'E
177°00'E
177°15'E
37°45'S
38°00'S
38°15'S
Whakaari / White Island
New Zealand's most frequently active volcano
PACIFIC OCEAN
N
0
10 km
© Hema Maps NZ Ltd
Bay of Plenty
Tokata Island
Rurima Island
Moutoki Island
Moutohora Island
No Access
Permit Required
Pikowai
Kohioawa Beach
Ohinekoao RR
Ohinekoao Scenic Res
Matata
Matata Scenic Res
Thornton Beach Park RR
Thornton
Awakaponga
Dolphin Safaris
White Island Tours
Piripai
Whakatane
Wairere Waterfall
Kohi Point Scenic Res
Te Rangi HR
Te Paripari Pa HR
Paroa
Edgecumbe
Otakiri
Poroporo
Pahou
Awakeri
Awakeri Springs
Awakeri Hot Springs
White Pine Bush
Mokorua Bush SR
Ohope
Ohope SR
Port Ohope
Ohiwa Oyster Farm
Uretara Is SR
Ohiwa Hbr
Port Ohope RR
Ohiwa
Waiotahi Spit SR
Waiotahi Spit HR
Waiotahi Beach
Dolphin Safaris
Omarumutu
Tirohanga
Tablelands
Kukumoa
Hospital Hill
Opotiki
Horse Trekking
Waiaua
Manawahe
Mangaone Scenic Res
Tarawera R
Te Teko
Onepu
Parimahana SR
Kawerau
Putauaki (Mt Edgecumbe) 821
Te Mahoe
GALATEA ROAD
RAUNGAEHE RANGE
Lake Matahina
Matahina
Waiohau
Rangitaiki River
Pahekeheke Stm
Lake Aniwhenua
Kopuriki
Horomanga
Stm
Taneatua
Whakatane River
Waiotane Scenic Res
Wainui
Motuotu Is NR
Cheddar Valley
Kutarere RR
Waiotahi
Waiotahi Marae
Paerata Ridge
Woodlands
Apanui
Otara
Waiaua Scenic Reserve
Waingarara
Kererutahi
Kotare SR
Kutarere
Matekerepu Hist Res
Stanley Falls SR
Taketakerau 2000 year old Puriri Tree
Hukutaia Domain RR
Hine Rae HR
Waimana Gorge Scenic Reserve
Waiotahi SR
Waiotahi Valley
Waioeka Pa
Marawaiwai Scenic Res
Zohs Acquisition Scenic Res
Otara River
Opouriao
Matahapa
Ruatoki North
Waimana
Nukuhou North
Matahanea
Boulders
Taumaihi 697
Waiotahi R
WAINUI ROAD
Tataiahapi Pa
Tanatana
Waikirikiri
Tukainuka Scenic Res
Maungawhiorangi 814
Okiore
Te Waiti Hut
Waioeka Gorge Scenic Reserve
Tutaetoko Stm
Tutaetoko 914
Te Waiti Hill 1011
Raroa Track
Te Pakau (8 Acre)
Waimana R
Te Whakaumu 765
Ruatupapaku 706
Wharekahika Hut
Waihua Hut
Matahi
Apiti Hut
TE UREWERA
Te Hekeotewhare 678
Whakarae
Tahora
Oponae
Wairata
Manganuku
Mangamako Hut
Ohora Hut
Paraoanui Pa
Tauwhare
Omahuru (Ogilvies)
Oraukurangi 867
Waioeka Gorge SR
Waioeka Gorge Scenic Reserve
NATIONAL PARK
Hikurangi 929
Onepu Hut
Duckville Hut
Rakautapu 767
Koaunui Hut
Kaharoa 1030
Otamatuna Ridge Track
Kotepato Hut
Okahuata 958
To Te Kaha
To Gisborne
15
20
21
2
30
34
58
59

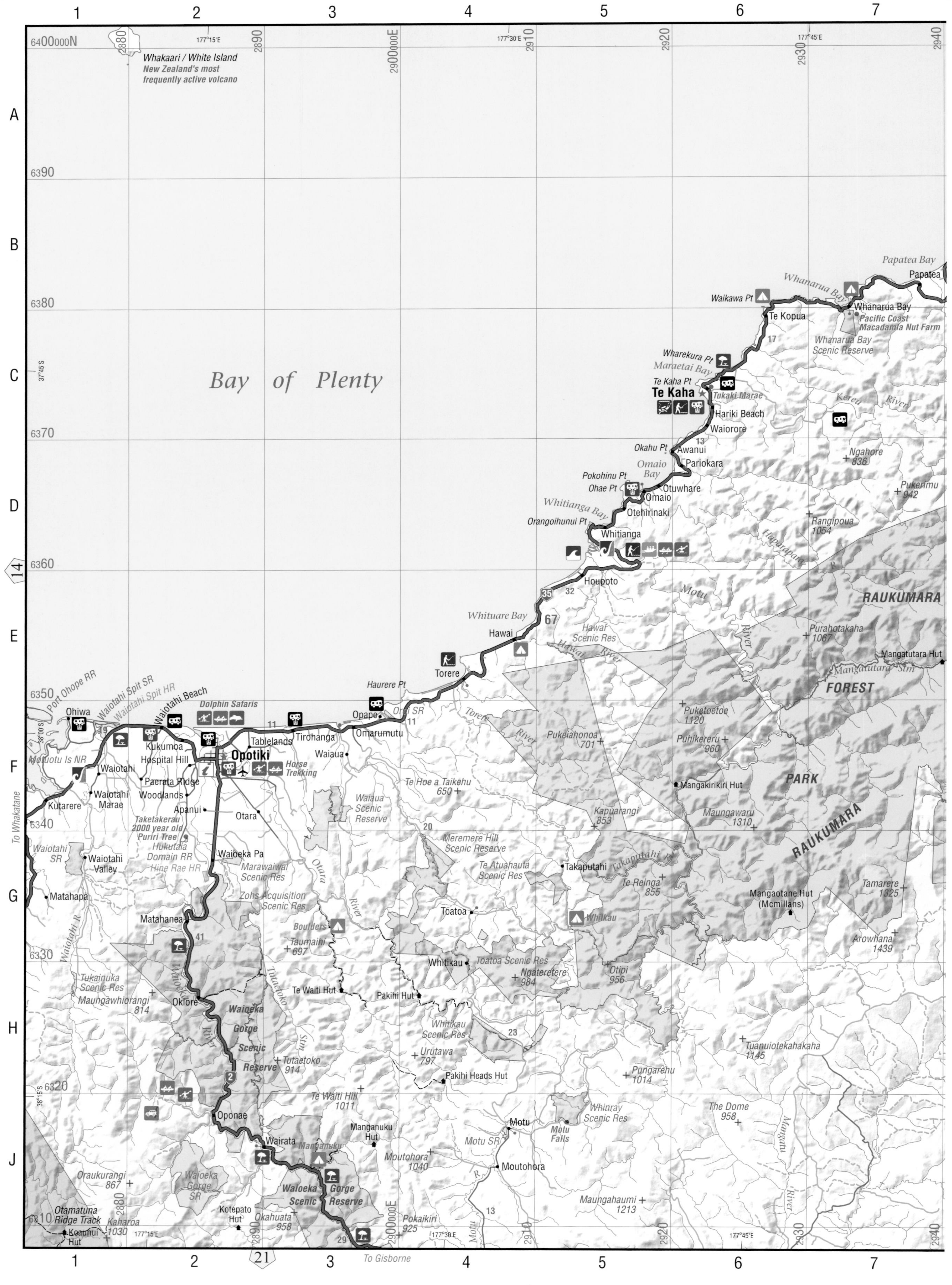

Whakaari / White Island
New Zealand's most frequently active volcano
Bay of Plenty
Papatea Bay
Papatea
Whanarua Bay
Waikawa Pt
Te Kopua
Whanarua Bay
Pacific Coast Macadamia Nut Farm
Whanarua Bay Scenic Reserve
Wharekura Pt
Maraetai Bay
Te Kaha Pt
Te Kaha
Tukaki Marae
Hariki Beach
Waiorore
Kereu River
Okahu Pt
Awanui
Pariokara
Omaio Bay
Pokohinu Pt
Ohae Pt
Otuwhare
Omaio
Otehirinaki
Whitianga Bay
Orangoihunui Pt
Whitianga
Ngahore 836
Pukerimu 942
Rangipoua 1054
Haparapara
Houpoto
Motu
RAUKUMARA
Whituare Bay
Hawai
Hawai Scenic Res
Hawai River
Purahotakaha 1067
Mangatutara Hut
Mangatutara Strm
FOREST
Torere
Haurere Pt
Port Ohope RR
Waiotahi Spit SR
Waiotahi Spit HR
Waiotahi Beach
Dolphin Safaris
Ohiwa
Opape
Oroi SR
Omarumutu
Tirohanga
Tablelands
Kukumoa
Opotiki
Hospital Hill
Waiaua
Horse Trekking
Motuotu Is NR
Waiotahi
Paerata Ridge
Waiotahi Marae
Woodlands
Kutarere
Apanui
Otara
Torere River
Pukeiahonoa 701
Puketoetoe 1120
Puhikereru 960
Mangakirikiri Hut
PARK
Te Hoe a Taikehu 650
Waiaua Scenic Reserve
Kapuarangi 853
Maungawaru 1310
RAUKUMARA
To Whakatane
Taketakerau 2000 year old Puriri Tree
Hukutaia Domain RR
Hine Rae HR
Waiotahi SR
Waiotahi Valley
Waioeka Pa
Meremere Hill Scenic Reserve
Marawaiwai Scenic Res
Te Atuahauta Scenic Res
Takaputahi
Takaputahi R
Te Reinga 855
Otara River
Zohs Acquisition Scenic Res
Matahapa
Matahanea
Boulders
Toatoa
Whitikau
Mangaotane Hut (Mcmillans)
Tamarere 1325
Taumaihi 697
Waiotahi R
Arowhana 1439
Whitikau
Toatoa Scenic Res
Ngateretere 984
Otipi 956
Tukainuka Scenic Res
Maungawhiorangi 814
Waioeka
Titiaetoko Strm
Te Waiti Hut
Pakihi Hut
Okiore
Waioeka Gorge Scenic Reserve
Whitikau Scenic Res
Tutaetoko 914
Urutawa 797
Tuanuiotekahakahaka 1145
Pakihi Heads Hut
Pungarehu 1014
Te Waiti Hill 1011
Whinray Scenic Res
The Dome 958
Mangatu
Oponae
Motu
Motu Falls
Manganuku Hut
Wairata
Manganuku
Motu SR
Moutohora 1040
Moutohora
Oraukurangi 867
Waioeka Gorge SR
Waioeka Gorge Scenic Reserve
Maungahaumi 1213
River
Otamatuna Ridge Track
Kaharoa 1030
Koauhui Hut
Kotepato Hut
Okahuata 958
Pokaikiri 925
Motu R
To Gisborne
6400000N
6390
6380
6370
6360
6350
6340
6330
6320
6310
2880
2890
2900000E
2910
2920
2930
2940
177°15'E
177°30'E
177°45'E
37°45'S
38°00'S
38°15'S
1 2 3 4 5 6 7
A B C D E F G H J
2
35
14
21

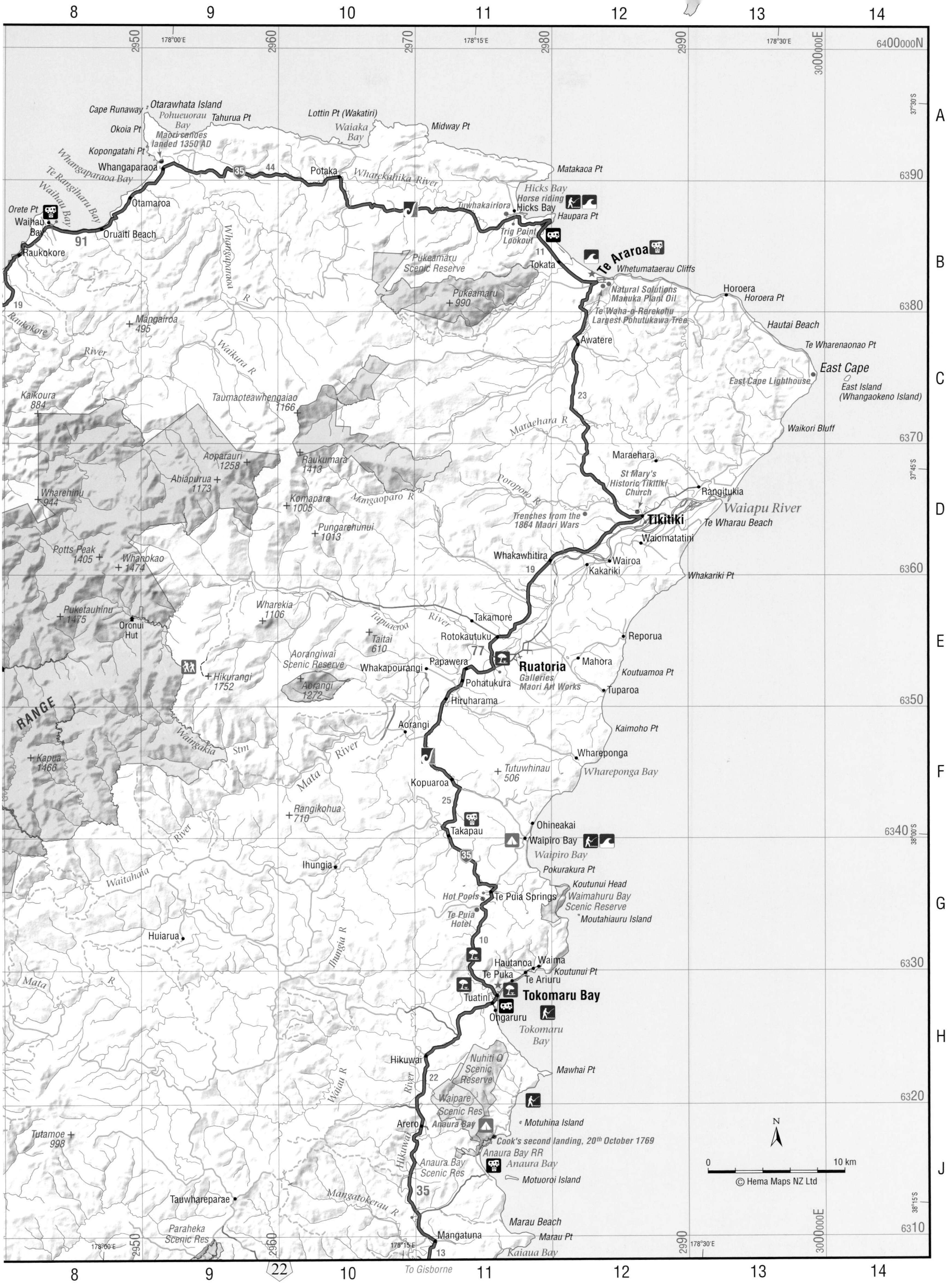

Cape Runaway
Otarawhata Island
Pohueuorau Bay
Tahurua Pt
Okoia Pt
Maori canoes landed 1350 AD
Kopongatahi Pt
Whangaparaoa
Whangaparaoa Bay
Te Rangiharu Bay
Waihau Bay
Orete Pt
Otamaroa
Oruaiti Beach
Raukokore
Lottin Pt (Wakatiri)
Waiaka Bay
Midway Pt
Potaka
Wharekahika River
Matakaoa Pt
Hicks Bay
Horse riding
Tuwhakairiora
Haupara Pt
Trig Point Lookout
Pukeamaru Scenic Reserve
Pukeamaru 990
Tokata
Te Araroa
Whetumataerau Cliffs
Natural Solutions Manuka Plant Oil
Te Waha-o-Rerekohu Largest Pohutukawa Tree
Horoera
Horoera Pt
Hautai Beach
Te Wharenaonao Pt
East Cape
East Cape Lighthouse
East Island (Whangaokeno Island)
Waikori Bluff
Awatere
Mangairoa 495
Raukokore River
Whangaparaoa R
Waikura R
Kaikoura 884
Taumaoteawhengaiao 1166
Maraehara R
Maraehara
Aoparauri 1258
Raukumara 1413
Abiapurua 1173
Wharehinu 944
Komapara 1005
Mangaoparo R
Poroporo R
St Mary's Historic Tikitiki Church
Rangitukia
Waiapu River
Te Wharau Beach
Trenches from the 1864 Maori Wars
Tikitiki
Waiomatatini
Pungarehunui 1013
Potts Peak 1405
Whanokao 1474
Whakawhitira
Wairoa
Kakariki
Whakariki Pt
Puketauhinu 1475
Oronui Hut
Wharekia 1106
Tapuaeroa River
Takamore
Rotokautuku
Reporua
Taitai 610
Aorangiwai Scenic Reserve
Papawera
Ruatoria
Galleries Maori Art Works
Mahora
Whakapourangi
Koutuamoa Pt
Hikurangi 1752
Aorangi 1272
Pohatukura
Tuparoa
Hiruharama
RANGE
Aorangi
Kaimoho Pt
Waingakia Stm
Mata River
Kapua 1466
Whareponga
Whareponga Bay
Tutuwhinau 506
Kopuaroa
Rangikohua 710
Ohineakai
Takapau
Waipiro Bay
Waitahaia River
Ihungia
Pokurakura Pt
Koutunui Head
Hot Pools
Te Puia Springs
Waimahuru Bay Scenic Reserve
Te Puia Hotel
Moutahiauru Island
Huiarua
Ihungia R
Mata R
Hautanoa
Waima
Te Puka
Koutunui Pt
Te Ariuru
Tuatini
Tokomaru Bay
Ongaruru
Hikuwai
Waiau R
Nuhiti Q Scenic Reserve
Mawhai Pt
Hikuwai River
Waipare Scenic Res
Arero
Anaura Bay
Motuhina Island
Cook's second landing, 20th October 1769
Tutamoe 998
Anaura Bay RR
Anaura Bay Scenic Res
Motuoroi Island
Mangatokerau R
Tauwhareparae
Marau Beach
Marau Pt
Paraheka Scenic Res
Mangatuna
Kaiaua Bay
To Gisborne
0 10 km
© Hema Maps NZ Ltd
N

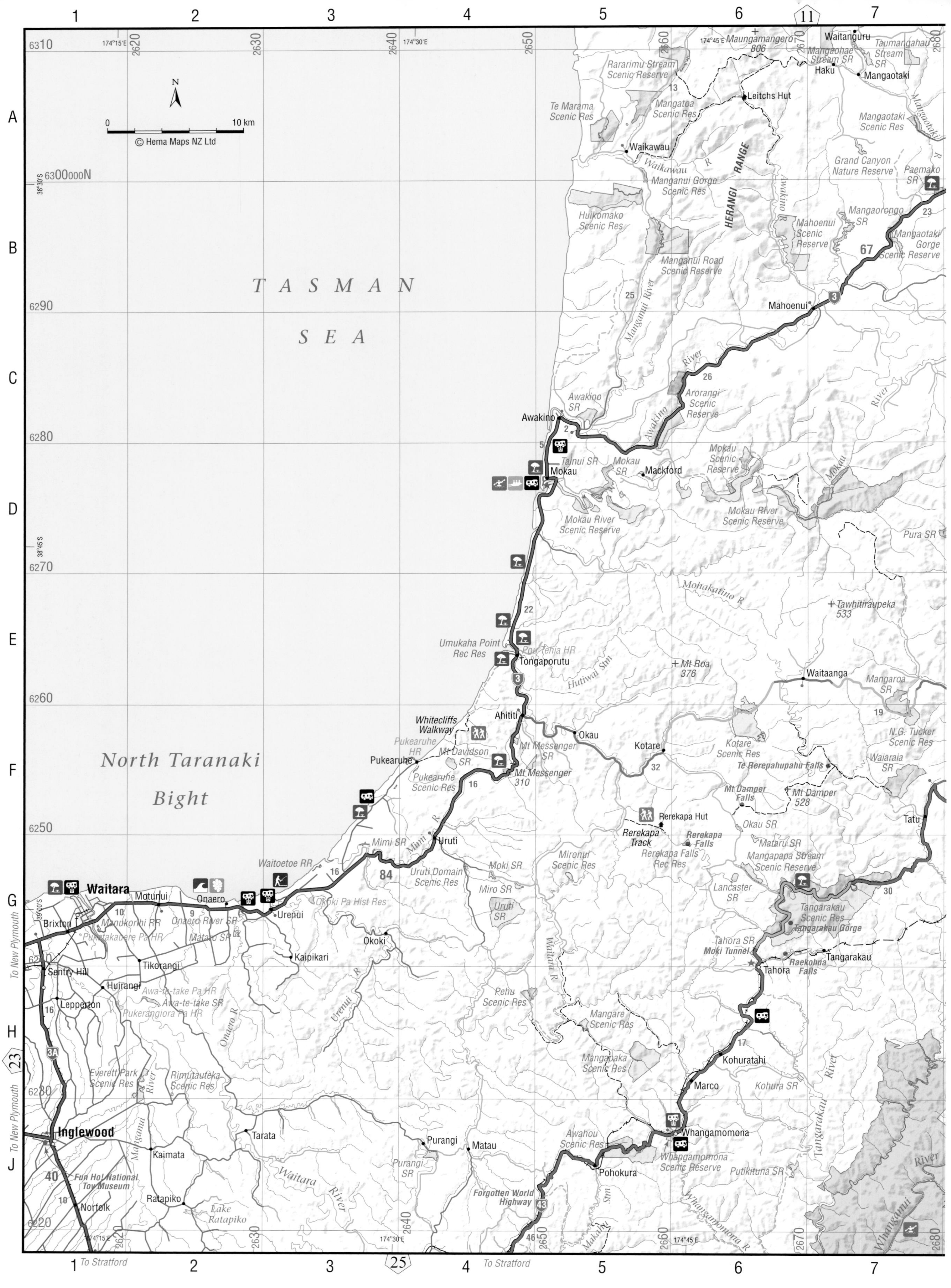
TASMAN SEA
North Taranaki Bight
© Hema Maps NZ Ltd
0
10 km
N
6300000N
6310
6290
6280
6270
6260
6250
6230
6220
2620
2630
2640
2650
2660
2670
2680
174°15'E
174°30'E
174°45'E
38°30'S
38°45'S
39°00'S
1
2
3
4
5
6
7
A
B
C
D
E
F
G
H
J
11
23
25
Maungamangero
806
Waitanguru
Taumangahau Stream SR
Mangaohae Stream SR
Haku
Mangaotaki
Rararimu Stream Scenic Reserve
Leitchs Hut
Te Marama Scenic Res
Mangatoa Scenic Res
Mangaotaki Scenic Res
Waikawau
Waikawau R
HERANGI RANGE
Grand Canyon Nature Reserve
Paemako SR
Manganui Gorge Scenic Res
Awakino R
Huikomako Scenic Res
Mahoenui Scenic Reserve
Mangaorongo SR
Mangaotaki Gorge Scenic Reserve
Manganui Road Scenic Reserve
67
Manganui River
Mahoenui
3
Awakino River
Arorangi Scenic Reserve
Awakino SR
Awakino
Tainui SR
Mokau SR
Mackford
Mokau Scenic Reserve
Mokau
Mokau River Scenic Reserve
Pura SR
Mohakatino R
Tawhitiraupeka
533
Umukaha Point Rec Res
Pou Tehia HR
Tongaporutu
Mt Roa
376
Hutiwai Stm
Waitaanga
Mangaroa SR
Ahititi
Okau
Whitecliffs Walkway
Pukearuhe HR
Mt Davidson SR
Mt Messenger SR
Kotare
Kotare Scenic Res
N.G. Tucker Scenic Res
Pukearuhe
Pukearuhe Scenic Res
Mt Messenger
310
Te Rerepahupahu Falls
Waiaraia SR
Mt Damper Falls
Mt Damper
528
Rerekapa Hut
Rerekapa Track
Rerekapa Falls
Okau SR
Tatu
Mimi SR
Mimi R
Uruti
Rerekapa Falls Rec Res
Mataru SR
Mironui Scenic Res
Mangapapa Stream Scenic Reserve
Waitoetoe RR
84
Uruti Domain Scenic Res
Moki SR
Miro SR
Lancaster SR
Tangarakau Scenic Res
Tangarakau Gorge
Waitara
Motunui
Onaero
Urenui
Okoki Pa Hist Res
Uruti SR
Brixton
Manukorihi RR
Onaero River SR
Pukitakauere Pa HR
Matai SR
Okoki
Kaipikari
Tahora SR
Moki Tunnel
Raekohua Falls
Tangarakau
Sentry Hill
Tikorangi
Tahora
Huirangi
Awa-te-take Pa HR
Awa-te-take SR
Urenui R
Waitara R
Lepperton
Pukerangiora Pa HR
Onaero R
Pehu Scenic Res
Mangare Scenic Res
Mangapaka Scenic Res
Kohuratahi
Everett Park Scenic Res
Rimutauteka Scenic Res
Marco
Kohura SR
Tangarakau River
Inglewood
Tarata
Purangi
Matau
Whangamomona
Awahou Scenic Res
Kaimata
Manganui River
Purangi SR
Pohokura
Whangamomona Scenic Reserve
Putikituna SR
Fun Ho! National Toy Museum
Waitara River
Forgotten World Highway
43
Whangamomona R
Whanganui River
Norfolk
Ratapiko
Lake Ratapiko
Makahu Stm
40
3A
16
To New Plymouth
To Stratford

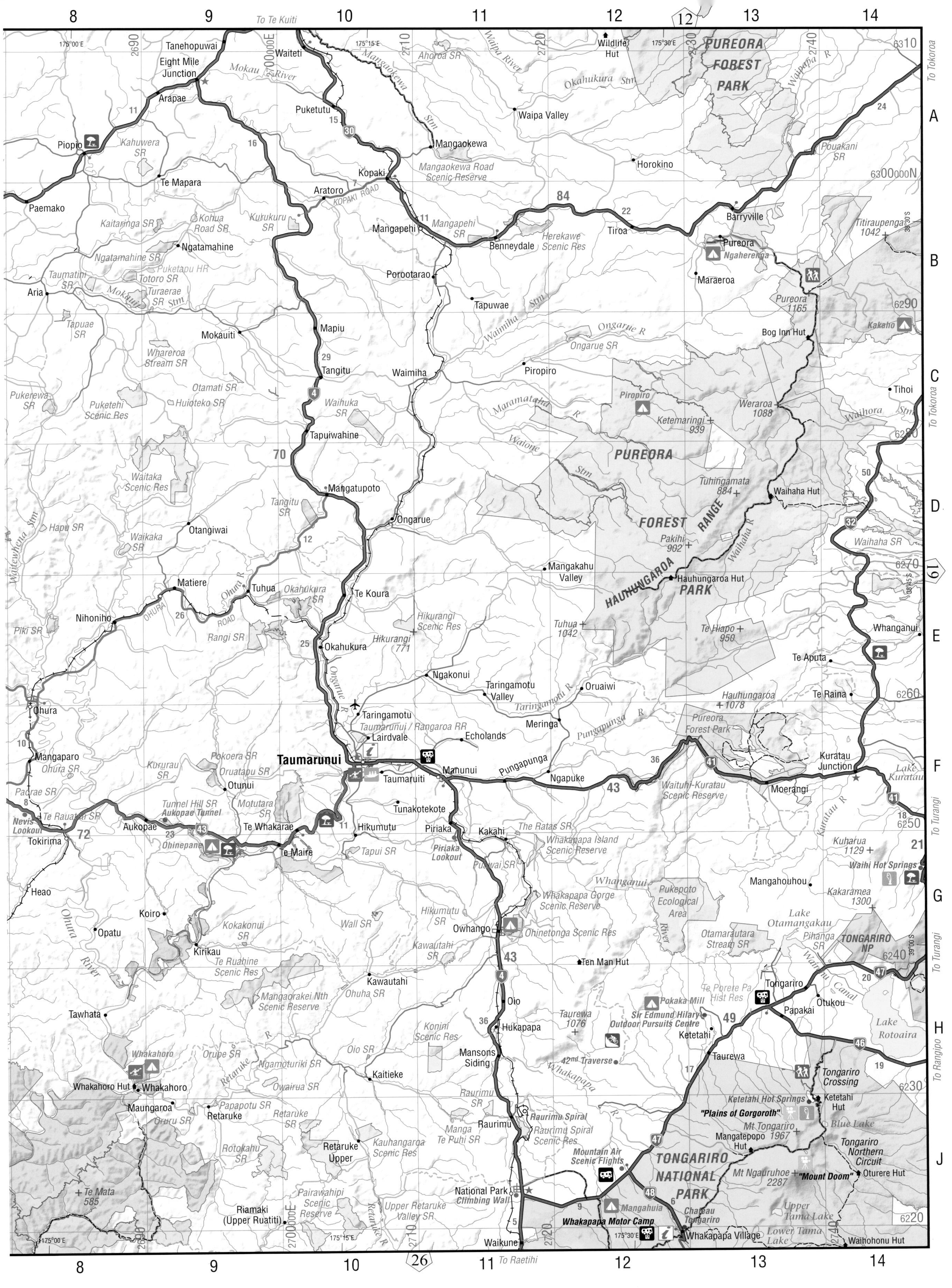

To Te Kuiti
To Tokoroa
To Turangi
To Rangipo
To Raetihi
PUREORA FOREST PARK
Wildlife Hut
Tanehopuwai
Eight Mile Junction
Waiteti
Mokau River
Ahoroa SR
Waipa River
Okahukura Stm
Waipapa R
Arapae
Puketutu
Waipa Valley
Piopio
Kahuwera SR
Mangaokewa
Mangaokewa Stm
Pouakani SR
Mangaokewa Road Scenic Reserve
Horokino
Te Mapara
Kopaki
Paemako
Aratoro
KOPAKI ROAD
84
Barryville
Tiroa
Kohua Road SR
Kurukuru SR
Mangapehi
Mangapehi SR
Herekawe Scenic Res
Titiraupenga 1042
Kaitaringa SR
Benneydale
Pureora
Ngaherenga
Ngatamahine
Ngatamahine SR
Puketapu HR
Porootarao
Taumatini SR
Totoro SR
Maraeroa
Aria
Turaerae SR
Mokauiti Stm
Tapuwae
Pureora 1165
Tapuae SR
Mapiu
Waimiha Stm
Ongarue R
Kakaho
Mokauiti
Ongarue SR
Bog Inn Hut
Whareroa Stream SR
Tangitu
Waimiha
Piropiro
Otamati SR
Huioteko SR
Tihoi
Pukerewa SR
Maramataha R
Piropiro
Weraroa 1088
Waihuka SR
Puketehi Scenic Res
Ketemaringi 939
Waihora Stm
Tapuiwahine
Waione Stm
70
PUREORA
Waitaka Scenic Res
Tuhingamata 884
Waihaha Hut
Mangatupoto
Tangitu SR
FOREST
Ongarue
HAUHUNGAROA RANGE
Hapu SR
Otangiwai
Pakihi 902
Waihaha R
Waihaha SR
Waikaka SR
Waitewhena Stm
Mangakahu Valley
Hauhungaroa Hut
PARK
Matiere
Tuhua
Okahukura SR
Ohura R
Te Koura
Nihoniho
OHURA ROAD
Hikurangi Scenic Res
Tuhua 1042
Te Hiapo 950
Whanganui
Piki SR
Rangi SR
Okahukura
Hikurangi 771
Te Aputa
Ngakonui
Ongarue R
Taringamotu Valley
Oruaiwi
Hauhungaroa 1078
Te Raina
Ohura
Taringamotu
Taringamotu R
Taumarunui / Rangaroa RR
Meringa
Pureora Forest Park
Lairdvale
Echolands
Pungapunga R
Mangaparo
Ohura SR
Pokoera SR
Kururau SR
Oruatapu SR
Taumarunui
Manunui
Pungapunga
Ngapuke
Kuratau Junction
Lake Kuratau
Pacrae SR
Otunui
Taumaruiti
43
Waituhi-Kuratau Scenic Reserve
Moerangi
Tunnel Hill SR
Aukopae Tunnel
Motutara SR
Tunakotekote
Kuratau R
Te Rauaha SR
Nevis Lookout
72
Aukopae
Te Whakarae
Hikumutu
Piriaka
Kakahi
The Ratas SR
Whakapapa Island Scenic Reserve
Tokirima
Ohinepane
Te Maire
Tapui SR
Piriaka Lookout
Kuharua 1129
Waihi Hot Springs
Puawai SR
Whanganui
Mangahouhou
Heao
Ohura River
Koiro
Hikumutu SR
Whakapapa Gorge Scenic Reserve
Pukepoto Ecological Area
Kakaramea 1300
Opatu
Kokakonui SR
Wall SR
Owhango
Ohinetonga Scenic Res
Lake Otamangakau
Kirikau
Kawautahi SR
Otamarautara Stream SR
Pihanga SR
TONGARIRO NP
Te Ruahine Scenic Res
Ten Man Hut
Kawautahi
Ohuha SR
Mangaorakei Nth Scenic Reserve
Oio
Te Porere Pa Hist Res
Tongariro
Otukou
Tawhata
Pokaka Mill
Papakai
Lake Rotoaira
Taurewa 1076
Sir Edmund Hilary Outdoor Pursuits Centre
Konini Scenic Res
Hukapapa
Ketetahi
Whakahoro
Orupe SR
Oio SR
Mansons Siding
Taurewa
Tongariro Crossing
42nd Traverse
Whakapapa
Ngamoturiki SR
Kaitieke
Whakahoro Hut
Whakahoro
Owairua SR
Raurimu SR
Ketetahi Hot Springs
Ketetahi Hut
Maungaroa
Papapotu SR
Retaruke
Retaruke SR
"Plains of Gorgoroth"
Mt Tongariro 1967
Blue Lake
Oruru SR
Raurimu
Raurimu Spiral
Raurimu Spiral Scenic Res
Mangatepopo Hut
Tongariro Northern Circuit
Rotokahu SR
Retaruke Upper
Kauhangaroa Scenic Res
Manga Te Puhi SR
Mountain Air Scenic Flights
TONGARIRO NATIONAL PARK
Mt Ngauruhoe 2287
"Mount Doom"
Oturere Hut
Te Mata 585
Pairawahipi Scenic Reserve
National Park
Climbing Wall
Mangahuia
Riamaki (Upper Ruatiti)
Upper Retaruke Valley SR
Chateau Tongariro
Upper Tama Lake
Whakapapa Motor Camp
Lower Tama Lake
Waikune
Whakapapa Village
Waihohonu Hut

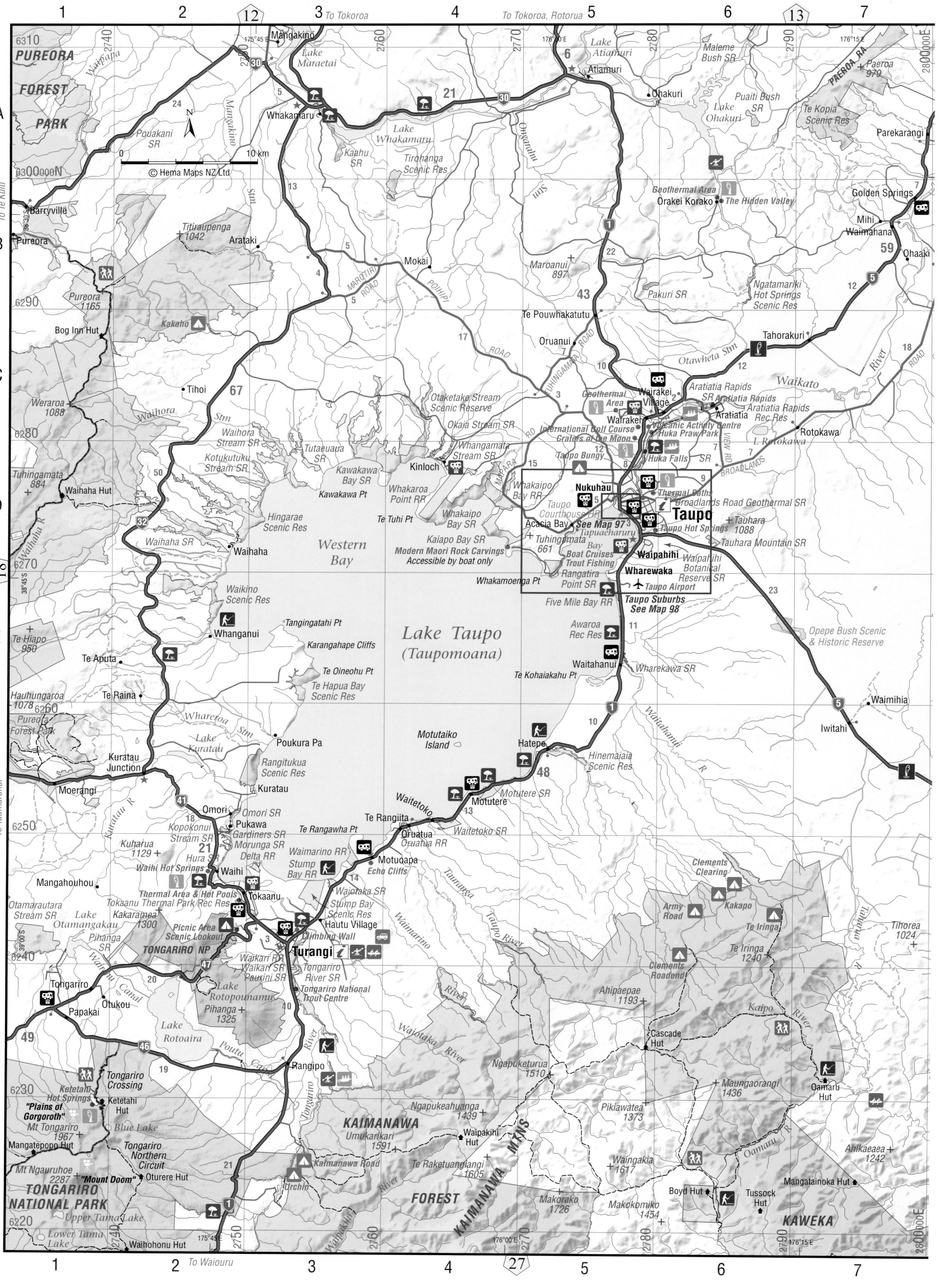

To Tokoroa
To Tokoroa, Rotorua
To Te Kuiti
To Taumarunui
To Raetihi
To Waiouru
© Hema Maps NZ Ltd
10 km
PUREORA FOREST PARK
Pouakani SR
Mangakino
Lake Maraetai
Whakamaru
Lake Whakamaru
Kaahu SR
Tirohanga Scenic Res
Atiamuri
Lake Atiamuri
Maleme Bush SR
Ohakuri
Puaiti Bush SR
Lake Ohakuri
Paeroa 979
Te Kopia Scenic Res
Parekarangi
Geothermal Area
Orakei Korako
The Hidden Valley
Golden Springs
Mihi
Waimahana
Ohaaki
Barryville
Pureora
Titiraupenga 1042
Arataki
Mokai
Maroanui 897
Pakuri SR
Ngatamariki Hot Springs Scenic Res
Pureora 1165
Kakaho
Bog Inn Hut
Te Pouwhakatutu
Oruanui
Tahorakuri
Otawheta Stm
Tihoi
Weraroa 1088
Waihora Stm
Waihora Stream SR
Kotukutuku Stream SR
Tutaeuaua SR
Otaketake Stream Scenic Reserve
Okaia Stream SR
Whangamata Stream SR
Kinloch
Wairakei Village
Wairakei
Geothermal Area
Aratiatia Rapids SR
Aratiatia Rapids
Aratiatia
Aratiatia Rapids Rec Res
Rotokawa
L Rotokawa
Waikato River
International Golf Course
Craters of the Moon
Volcanic Activity Centre
Huka Prawn Park
Huka Falls
Taupo Bungy
Tuhingamata 884
Waihaha Hut
Kawakawa Bay SR
Kawakawa Pt
Whakaroa Point RR
Whakaipo Bay SR
Whakaipo Bay RR
Nukuhau
Taupo Courthouse RR
Thermal Baths
Broadlands Road Geothermal SR
Taupo
Tauhara 1088
Tauhara Mountain SR
Hingarae Scenic Res
Te Tuhi Pt
Acacia Bay
See Map 97
Tuhingamata 661
Tapuaeharuru Bay
Taupo Hot Springs
Waihaha SR
Waihaha
Western Bay
Kaiapo Bay SR
Modern Maori Rock Carvings Accessible by boat only
Boat Cruises
Trout Fishing
Rangatira Point SR
Waipahihi
Waipahihi Botanical Reserve SR
Wharewaka
Taupo Airport
Whakamoenga Pt
Five Mile Bay RR
Taupo Suburbs See Map 98
Waikino Scenic Res
Tangingatahi Pt
Lake Taupo (Taupomoana)
Awaroa Rec Res
Opepe Bush Scenic & Historic Reserve
Te Hiapo 950
Whanganui
Karangahape Cliffs
Te Aputa
Te Oineohu Pt
Waitahanui
Te Kohaiakahu Pt
Wharekawa SR
Te Hapua Bay Scenic Res
Hauhungaroa 1078
Te Raina
Pureora Forest Park
Whareroa Stm
Lake Kuratau
Poukura Pa
Motutaiko Island
Hatepe
Waitahanui R
Waimihia
Iwitahi
Kuratau Junction
Moerangi
Rangitukua Scenic Res
Kuratau
Hinemaiaia Scenic Res
Motutere
Motutere SR
Omori
Omori SR
Pukawa
Kopokonui Stream SR
Gardiners SR
Morunga SR
Delta RR
Te Rangawha Pt
Te Rangiita
Waitetoko
Waitetoko SR
Oruatua
Oruatua RR
Kuharua 1129
Hura SR
Waimarino RR
Stump Bay RR
Motuoapa
Echo Cliffs
Waihi Hot Springs
Waihi
Mangahouhou
Thermal Area & Hot Pools
Tokaanu
Tokaanu Thermal Park Rec Res
Waiotaka SR
Stump Bay Scenic Res
Hautu Village
Otamarautara Stream SR
Lake Otamangakau
Kakaramea 1300
Picnic Area Scenic Lookout
Pihanga SR
TONGARIRO NP
Climbing Wall
Turangi
Tauranga Taupo River
Waimarino River
Clements Clearing
Kakapo
Army Road
Te Iringa
Te Iringa 1240
Tihorea 1024
Clements Roadend
Tongariro
Otukou
Papakai
Wairari SR
Waikari SR
Pauirini SR
Tongariro River SR
Tongariro National Trout Centre
Lake Rotopounamu
Pihanga 1325
Lake Rotoaira
Poutu Canal
Ahipaepae 1193
Cascade Hut
Kaipo River
Waiotaka River
Ngapuketurua 1510
Rangipo
Tongariro Crossing
Ketetahi Hot Springs
Ketetahi Hut
"Plains of Gorgoroth"
Mt Tongariro 1967
Blue Lake
Mangatepopo Hut
Tongariro Northern Circuit
Ngapukeahuanga 1439
KAIMANAWA
Umukarikari 1591
Waipakihi Hut
Maungaorangi 1436
Pikiawatea 1373
Oamaru Hut
Kaimanawa Road
Urchin
Te Raketuanganga 1605
KAIMANAWA MTNS
FOREST
Waingakia 1617
Ahikaeaea 1242
Mangatainoka Hut
Mt Ngauruhoe 2287
"Mount Doom"
Oturere Hut
TONGARIRO NATIONAL PARK
Upper Tama Lake
Lower Tama Lake
Waihohonu Hut
Makorako 1726
Makokomiko 1454
Boyd Hut
Tussock Hut
KAWEKA
Oamaru River

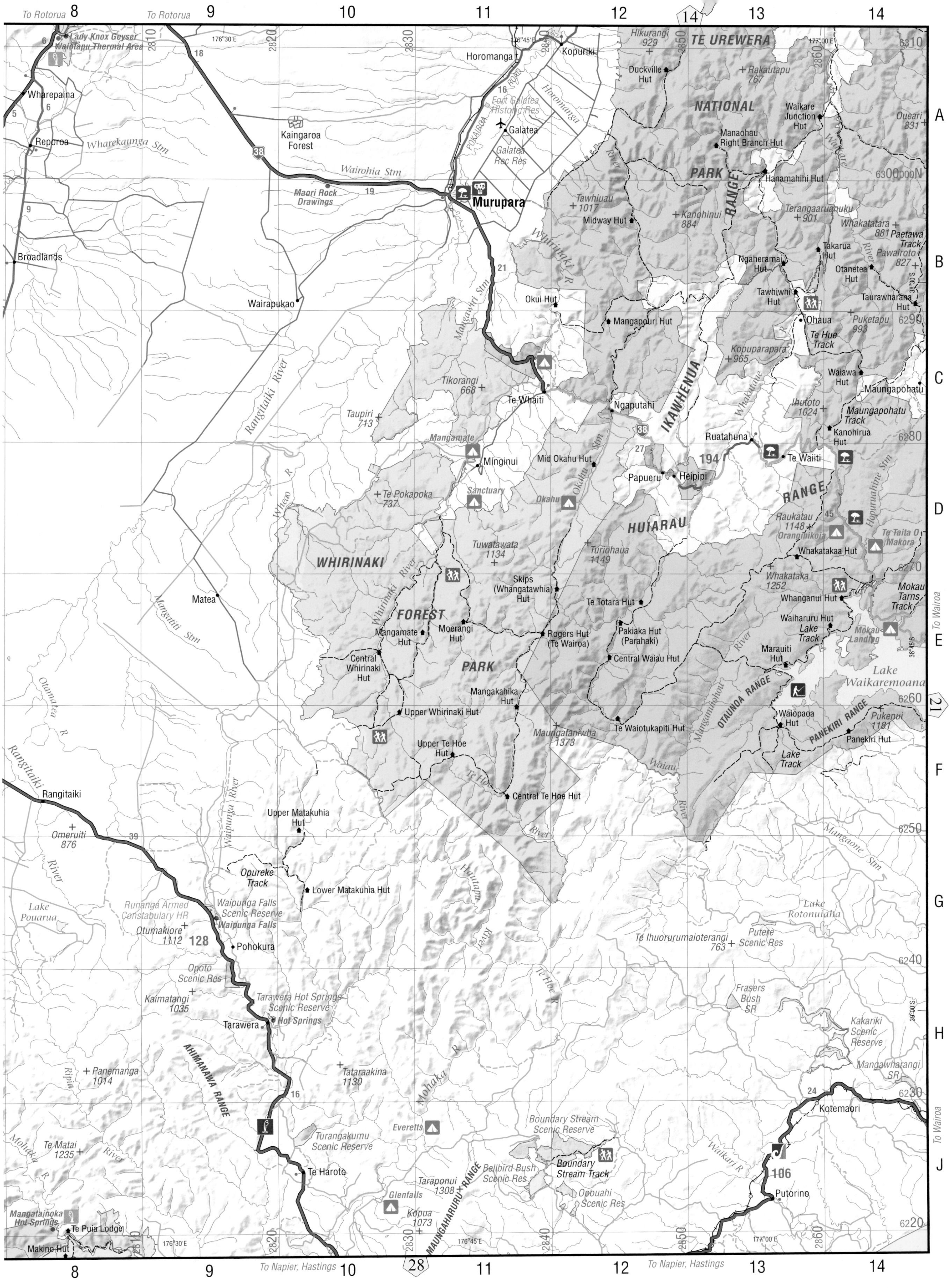

To Rotorua
To Rotorua
8
9
10
11
12
13
14
14
Lady Knox Geyser
Waiotapu Thermal Area
Wharepaina
Reporoa
Wharekaunga Stm
Broadlands
Wairapukao
Kaingaroa Forest
Wairohia Stm
Maori Rock Drawings
Murupara
Horomanga
Kopuriki
Fort Galatea Historic Res
Galatea
Galatea Rec Res
POKAIROA ROAD
Horomanga
Hikurangi 929
TE UREWERA
NATIONAL
PARK
Duckville Hut
Rakautapu 767
Waikare Junction Hut
Oueari 831
Manaohau Right Branch Hut
Hanamahihi Hut
RANGE
Tawhiuau 1017
Midway Hut
Kanohinui 884
Terangaaruanuku 901
Whakatatara 881
Paetawa Track
Takarua Hut
Pawairoto 827
Ngaheramai Hut
Otanetea Hut
Tawhiwhi Hut
Taurawharana Hut
Whirinaki R
Okui Hut
Mangapouri Hut
Ohaua
Puketapu 993
Te Hue Track
Kopuparapara 965
Waiawa Hut
Maungapohatu
Mangawiri Stm
Tikorangi 668
Te Whaiti
Ngaputahi
IKAWHENUA
Ihutoto 1024
Maungapohatu Track
Kanohirua Hut
Taupiri 713
Mangamate
Minginui
Ruatahuna
Te Waiiti
Mid Okahu Hut
Okahu Stm
Papueru
Heipipi
RANGE
Te Pokapoka 737
Sanctuary
Okahu
HUIARAU
Raukatau 1148
Orangihikoia
Te Taita O Makora
Rangitaiki River
Whirinaki River
WHIRINAKI
Tuwatawata 1134
Turiohaua 1149
Whakatakaa Hut
Whakataka 1252
Skips (Whangatawhia) Hut
Whanganui Hut
Mokau Tarns Track
Matea
Te Totara Hut
FOREST
Mangamate Hut
Moerangi Hut
Rogers Hut (Te Wairoa)
Pakiaka Hut (Parahaki)
Waiharuru Hut
Lake Track
Mokau Landing
Mangatiti Stm
Central Whirinaki Hut
PARK
Central Waiau Hut
Marauiti Hut
Lake Waikaremoana
Mangakahika Hut
OTAUNOA RANGE
Waiopaoa Hut
PANEKIRI RANGE
Pukenui 1181
Panekiri Hut
Upper Whirinaki Hut
Maungataniwha 1373
Te Waiotukapiti Hut
Upper Te Hoe Hut
Lake Track
Otamatea R
Rangitaiki
Rangitaiki
Central Te Hoe Hut
Te Hoe River
Waiau River
Omeruiti 876
River
Waipunga River
Upper Matakuhia Hut
Mangaone Stm
Opureke Track
Lower Matakuhia Hut
Hautapu
Lake Pouarua
Runanga Armed Constabulary HR
Waipunga Falls Scenic Reserve
Waipunga Falls
Otumakiore 1112
128
Pohokura
Lake Rotonuiaha
Te Ihuorurumaioterangi 763
Putere Scenic Res
Opoto Scenic Res
Kaimatangi 1035
Tarawera Hot Springs Scenic Reserve
Hot Springs
Tarawera
Te Hoe R
Frasers Bush SR
Kakariki Scenic Reserve
AHIMANAWA RANGE
Panemanga 1014
Ripia
Tataraakina 1130
Mohaka R
Mangawharangi SR
Kotemaori
Turangakumu Scenic Reserve
Everetts
Boundary Stream Scenic Reserve
Te Matai 1235
Mohaka R
River
Te Haroto
MAUNGAHARURU RANGE
Bellbird Bush Scenic Res
Boundary Stream Track
Waikari R
106
Taraponui 1308
Glenfalls
Opouahi Scenic Res
Putorino
Kopua 1073
Mangatainoka Hot Springs
Te Puia Lodge
Makino Hut
To Napier, Hastings
To Napier, Hastings
28
21
To Wairoa
To Wairoa
A
B
C
D
E
F
G
H
J

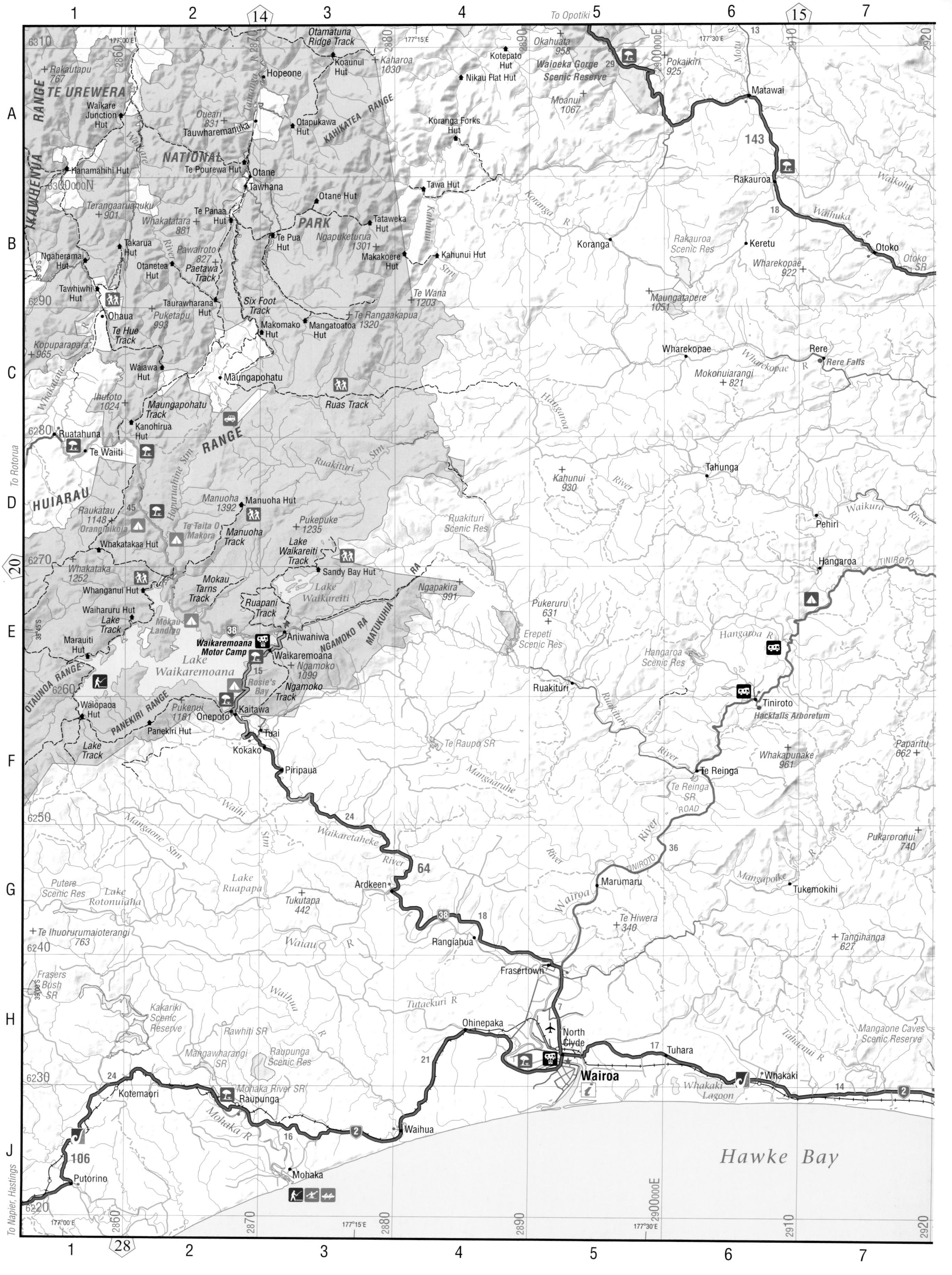

To Opotiki
Otamatuna Ridge Track
Koaunui Hut
Kaharoa 1030
Kotepato Hut
Okahuata 958
Waioeka Gorge Scenic Reserve
Pokaikiri 925
Motu
Rakautapu 767
TE UREWERA
RANGE
Hopeone
Nikau Flat Hut
Moanui 1067
Matawai
Waikare Junction Hut
Oueari 831
Tauwharemanuka
Otapukawa Hut
KAHIKATEA RANGE
Koranga Forks Hut
143
KAWHENUA
Hanamahihi Hut
NATIONAL
Te Pourewa Hut
Otane
Tawhana
Rakauroa
Waikohu
Terangaaruanuku 901
Otane Hut
Tawa Hut
Koranga R
18
Waihuka R
Te Panaa Hut
Whakatatara 881
PARK
Tataweka Hut
Kahunui
Te Pua Hut
Ngapukuterua 1301
Koranga
Rakauroa Scenic Res
Keretu
Otoko
Otoko SR
Takarua Hut
Ngaheramai Hut
Pawairoto 827
Paetawa Track
Otanetea Hut
Makakoere Hut
Kahunui Hut
Wharekopae 922
Tawhiwhi Hut
Taurawharana Hut
Six Foot Track
Te Wana 1203
Maungatapere 1051
Ohaua
Puketapu 993
Te Rangaakapua 1320
Te Hue Track
Makomako Hut
Mangatoatoa Hut
Kopuparapara 965
Wharekopae
Rere
Rere Falls
Waiawa Hut
Maungapohatu
Mokonuiarangi 821
Inutoto 1024
Maungapohatu Track
Ruas Track
Hangaroa
Ruatahuna
Kanohirua Hut
To Rotorua
Te Waiiti
RANGE
Ruakituri
Stm
Tahunga
Kahunui 930
River
HUIARAU
Raukatau 1148
Orangihikoia
Manuoha 1392
Manuoha Hut
Pukepuke 1235
Ruakituri Scenic Res
Waikura River
Pehiri
Te Taita O Makora
Manuoha Track
Whakatakaa Hut
Lake Waikareiti Track
Whakataka 1252
Sandy Bay Hut
Hangaroa
TINIROTO
Whanganui Hut
Mokau Tarns Track
Lake Waikareiti
Ngapakira 991
Ruapani Track
Pukeruru 631
Waiharuru Hut
Lake Track
Mokau Landing
Aniwaniwa
NGAMOKO RA
MATAKUHIA RA
Erepeti Scenic Res
Hangaroa R
Marauiti Hut
Waikaremoana Motor Camp
Waikaremoana
Ngamoko 1099
Hangaroa Scenic Res
Lake Waikaremoana
Rosie's Bay
Ngamoko Track
Ruakituri
Tiniroto
Hackfalls Arboretum
OTAUNOA RANGE
Waiopaoa Hut
PANEKIRI RANGE
Pukenui 1181
Onepoto
Kaitawa
Panekiri Hut
Tuai
Te Raupo SR
Whakapunake 961
Paparitu 662
Lake Track
Kokako
Piripaua
River
Te Reinga
Mangaaruhe
Te Reinga SR
ROAD
Waihi
24
Waikaretaheke
Stm
Mangaone Stm
River
Pukaroronui 740
River
64
36
Ardkeen
Mangapoike
Putere Scenic Res
Lake Rotonuiaha
Lake Ruapapa
Tukutapa 442
Marumaru
Tukemokihi
Wairoa
Te Hiwera 340
Te Ihuoruruimaioterangi 763
Rangiahua
Tangihanga 627
Waiau R
Frasertown
Frasers Bush SR
Waihua
Tutaekuri R
Kakariki Scenic Reserve
Rawhiti SR
Ohinepaka
North Clyde
Mangaone Caves Scenic Reserve
Tahaenui R
Mangawharangi SR
Raupunga Scenic Res
21
17
Tuhara
Wairoa
Whakaki
Whakaki Lagoon
24
Kotemaori
Mohaka River SR
Raupunga
14
Mohaka R
16
Waihua
Hawke Bay
106
Putorino
Mohaka
To Napier, Hastings

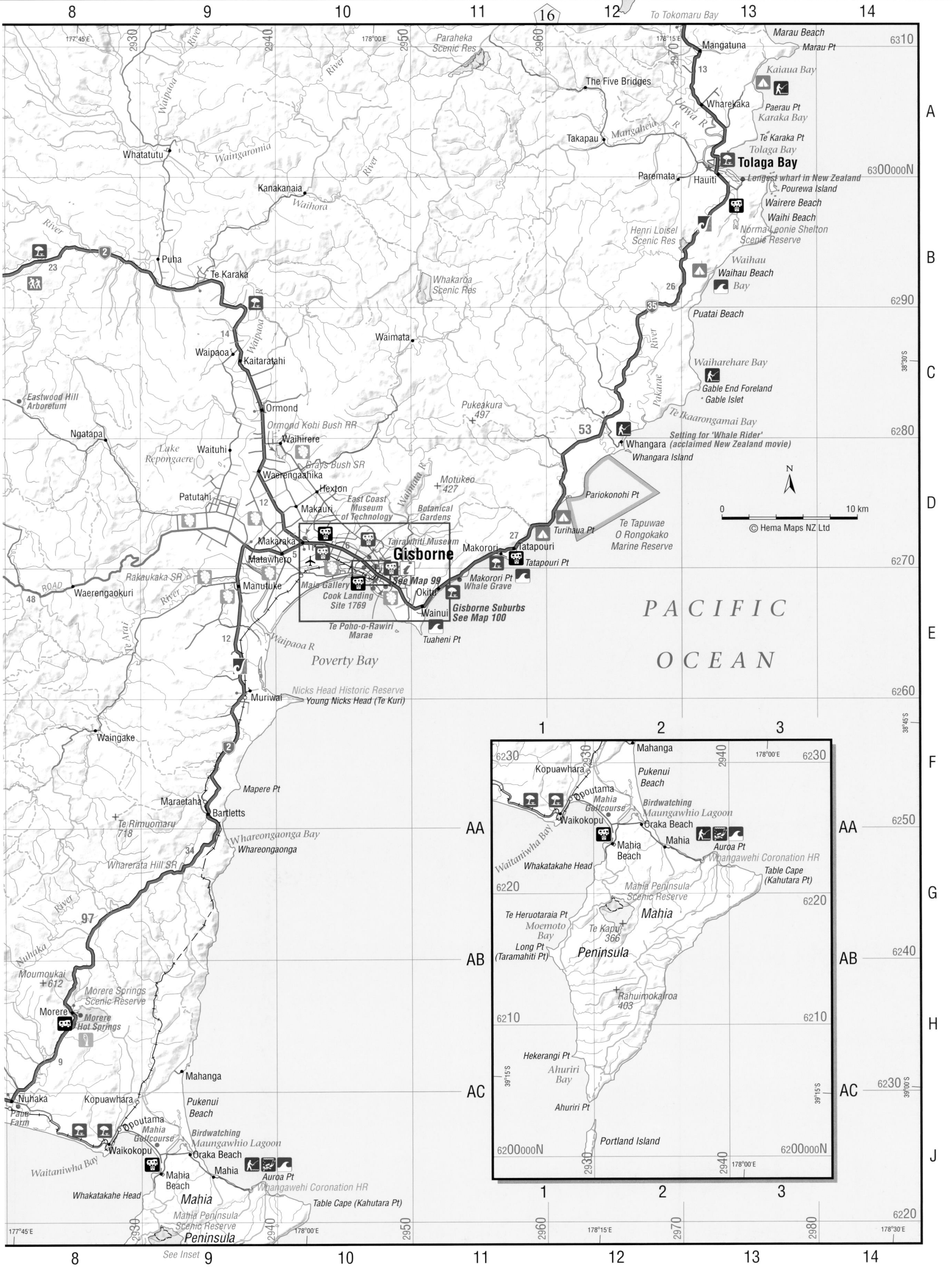
To Tokomaru Bay
16
Mangatuna
Marau Beach
Marau Pt
Paraheka Scenic Res
The Five Bridges
Kaiaua Bay
Wharekaka
Paerau Pt
Karaka Bay
Uawa R
Takapau
Mangaheia R
Te Karaka Pt
Tolaga Bay
Whatatutu
Waingaromia
Waipaoa River
Tolaga Bay
Paremata
Hauiti
Longest wharf in New Zealand
Pourewa Island
Kanakanaia
Waihora
Wairere Beach
Waihi Beach
Henri Loisel Scenic Res
Norma Leonie Shelton Scenic Reserve
Waihau
Waihau Beach
Bay
Puha
Te Karaka
Whakaroa Scenic Res
Puatai Beach
Waimata
Waipaoa
Kaitaratahi
Waiharehare Bay
Gable End Foreland
Gable Islet
Eastwood Hill Arboretum
Ormond
Pukeakura 497
Te Ikaarongamai Bay
Ormond Kohi Bush RR
Pakarae
Ngatapa
Waihirere
Whangara
Setting for 'Whale Rider' (acclaimed New Zealand movie)
Whangara Island
Waituhi
Lake Repongaere
Grays Bush SR
Waerengaahika
Hexton
Motukeo 427
Pariokonohi Pt
Patutahi
Makauri
East Coast Museum of Technology
Botanical Gardens
10 km
© Hema Maps NZ Ltd
Turihaua Pt
Te Tapuwae O Rongokako Marine Reserve
Makaraka
Tairawhiti Museum
Makorori
Tatapouri
Matawhero
Gisborne
Tatapouri Pt
Rakaukaka SR
Makorori Pt Whale Grave
Waerengaokuri
Manutuke
Maia Gallery
See Map 99
Okitu
Cook Landing Site 1769
Wainui
Gisborne Suburbs See Map 100
PACIFIC OCEAN
Te Poho-o-Rawiri Marae
Tuaheni Pt
Te Arai
Waipaoa R
Poverty Bay
Muriwai
Nicks Head Historic Reserve
Young Nicks Head (Te Kuri)
Waingake
Mapere Pt
Maraetaha
Bartletts
Te Rimuomaru 718
Whareongaonga Bay
Whareongaonga
Wharerata Hill SR
Nuhaka River
Moumoukai 612
Morere Springs Scenic Reserve
Morere
Morere Hot Springs
Mahanga
Nuhaka
Kopuawhara
Pukenui Beach
Opoutama
Mahia Golfcourse
Birdwatching Maungawhio Lagoon
Waikokopu
Oraka Beach
Waitaniwha Bay
Mahia Beach
Mahia
Auroa Pt
Whangawehi Coronation HR
Table Cape (Kahutara Pt)
Whakatakahe Head
Mahia Peninsula Scenic Reserve
Peninsula
See Inset
Mahia Peninsula
Te Heruotaraia Pt
Moemoto Bay
Te Kapu 366
Long Pt (Taramahiti Pt)
Rahuimokairoa 403
Hekerangi Pt
Ahuriri Bay
Ahuriri Pt
Portland Island

Taranaki & River Region

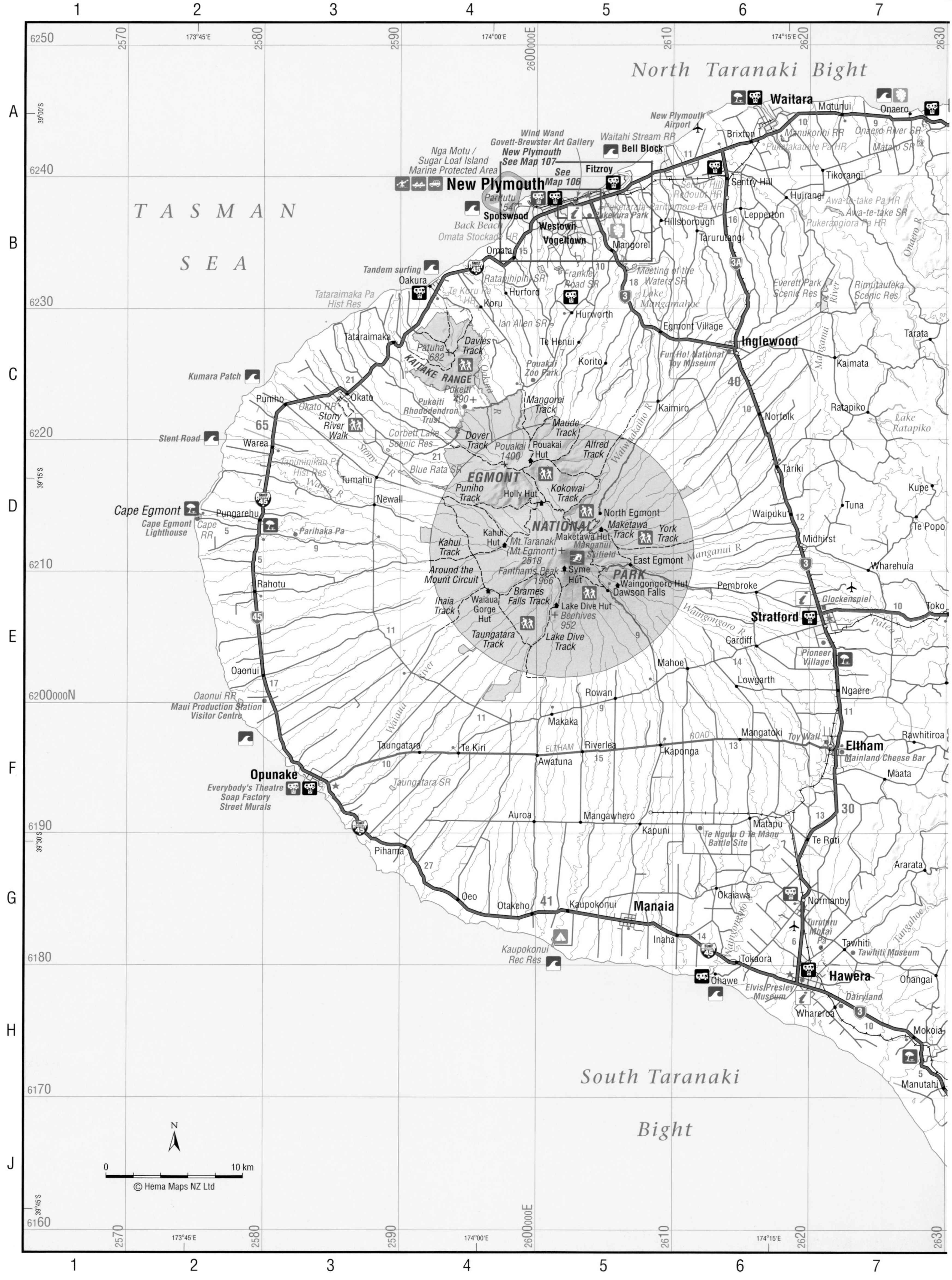

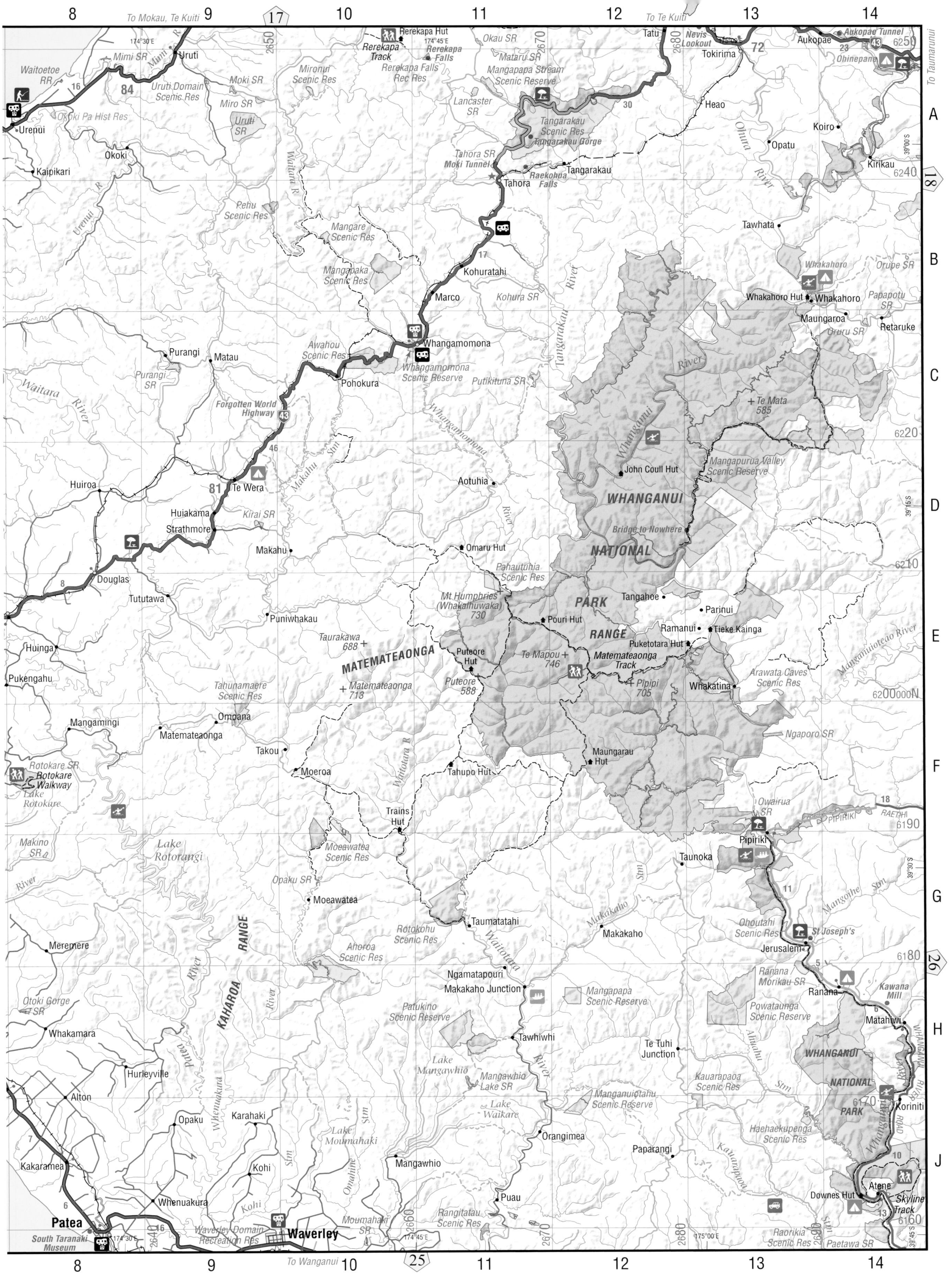

To Mokau, Te Kuiti
To Te Kuiti
To Taumarunui
To Wanganui
Uruti
Mimi SR
Waitoetoe RR
Urenui
Okoki Pa Hist Res
Okoki
Kaipikari
Uruti Domain Scenic Res
Moki SR
Miro SR
Uruti SR
Mironui Scenic Res
Rerekapa Hut
Rerekapa Track
Rerekapa Falls
Rerekapa Falls Rec Res
Okau SR
Mataru SR
Mangapapa Stream Scenic Reserve
Lancaster SR
Tangarakau Scenic Res
Tangarakau Gorge
Tahora SR
Moki Tunnel
Tahora
Raekohua Falls
Tangarakau
Tatu
Nevis Lookout
Tokirima
Heao
Aukopae
Aukopae Tunnel
Ohinepane
Koiro
Opatu
Ohura River
Kirikau
Tawhata
Whakahoro
Orupe SR
Whakahoro Hut
Papapotu SR
Maungaroa
Retaruke
Oruru SR
Pehu Scenic Res
Waitara R
Urenui R
Mangare Scenic Res
Mangapaka Scenic Res
Kohuratahi
Marco
Kohura SR
Tangarakau River
Whangamomona
Awahou Scenic Res
Whangamomona Scenic Reserve
Pohokura
Putikituna SR
Purangi
Matau
Purangi SR
Waitara River
Forgotten World Highway
Te Mata 585
Whanganui River
Mangapurua Valley Scenic Reserve
John Coull Hut
Whangamomona River
Makahu Stm
Te Wera
Huiroa
Huiakama
Strathmore
Kirai SR
Aotuhia
WHANGANUI NATIONAL PARK
Bridge to Nowhere
Makahu
Omaru Hut
Douglas
Tututawa
Pahautuhia Scenic Res
Mt Humphries (Whakaihuwaka) 730
Tangahoe
Parinui
Puniwhakau
Pouri Hut
Ramanui
Tieke Kainga
RANGE
Puketotara Hut
Taurakawa 688
Huinga
MATEMATEAONGA
Puteore Hut
Te Mapou 746
Matemateaonga Track
Pipipi 705
Whakatina
Arawata Caves Scenic Res
Mangaunuiteao River
Pukengahu
Puteore 588
Matemateaonga 713
Tahunamaere Scenic Res
Omoana
Matemateaonga
Mangamingi
Ngaporo SR
Maungarau Hut
Takou
Moeroa
Tahupo Hut
Rotokare SR
Rotokare Walkway
Lake Rotokare
Whitotara R
Owairua SR
Pipiriki
Raetihi
Trains Hut
Makino SR
Lake Rotorangi
Moeawatea Scenic Res
Taunoka
Opaku SR
Moeawatea
KAHAROA RANGE
Taumatatahi
Makakaho
Mangoihe Stm
Ohoutahi Scenic Res
St Joseph's
Jerusalem
Meremere
Rotokohu Scenic Res
Ahoroa Scenic Res
Waitotara
Ngamatapouri
Makakaho Junction
Mangapapa Scenic Reserve
Ranana / Morikau SR
Ranana
Kawana Mill
Otoki Gorge SR
Patukino Scenic Reserve
Powataunga Scenic Reserve
Matahiwi
Whakamara
Tawhiwhi
Te Tuhi Junction
Hurleyville
Lake Mangawhio
Mangawhio Lake SR
Kauarapaoa Scenic Res
Alton
Manganuiotahu Scenic Reserve
Lake Waikare
Whenuakura
Patea
Opaku
Karahaki
Orangimea
Haehaekupenga Scenic Res
Koriniti
Lake Moumahaki
Paparangi
Kakaramea
Mangawhio
Kohi
Atene
Downes Hut
Skyline Track
Puau
Whenuakura
Rangitatau Scenic Res
Moumahaki SR
Waverley Domain Recreation Res
Waverley
South Taranaki Museum
Raorikia Scenic Res
Paetawa SR
Whanganui River Road

To New Plymouth
To Taumarunui
To Opunake
Lake Ratapiko
Tariki
Kupe
Huiroa
Te Wera
Tuna
Waipuku
Te Popo
Huiakama
Strathmore
Kirai SR
Midhirst
Makahu
Wharehuia
Douglas
Tututawa
Pembroke
Glockenspiel
Toko
Puniwhakau
Stratford
Cardiff
Huinga
Pioneer Village
Lowgarth
Pukengahu
Ngaere
Mangatoki
Toy Wall
Eltham
Mainland Cheese Bar
Rawhitiroa
Mangamingi
Matemateaonga
Omoana
Takou
Moeroa
Maata
Rotokare SR
Rotokare Walkway
Lake Rotokare
Matapu
Te Roti
Makino SR
Lake Rotorangi
Ararata
River
Okaiawa
Normanby
Turuturu Mokai Pa
Tawhiti
Tawhiti Museum
Tokaora
Ohawe
Hawera
Elvis Presley Museum
Dairyland
Whareroa
Ohangai
Meremere
Otoki Gorge SR
Mokoia
Whakamara
Manutahi
Hurleyville
Alton
Opaku
Karahaki
KAHAROA RANGE
Kakaramea
Kohi
Whenuakura
Patea
South Taranaki Museum
Patea R
Waverley Domain Recreation Res
Waverley
Moumahaki
L Oturi
Lake Herengawe
L Waiau
L Okoia
Makara Scenic Res
Waitotara R
Nukumaru RR
Waiinu Beach
Nukumaru Rec Res
Lake Marahau
Waitotara
Nukumaru
Maxwell
Kai Iwi
Koatanui SR
Rapanui
Nukumaru RR
Kai Iwi Beach
4WD Beach Track
Wanganui Suburbs See Map 109
Castlecliff
Whanganui River
South Taranaki Bight
Aotuhia
Whangamomona River
John Coull Hut
WHANGANUI NATIONAL PARK
Omaru Hut
Pahautuhia Scenic Res
Mt Humphries (Whakahuwaka) 730
Tangahoe
Pouri Hut
RANGE
Taurakawa 688
MATEMATEAONGA
Puteore Hut
Puteore 588
Te Mapou 746
Matemateaonga Track
Pipipi 705
Tahunamaere Scenic Res
Matemateaonga 713
Maungarau Hut
Tahupo Hut
Waitotara R
Trains Hut
Moeawatea Scenic Res
Opaku SR
Moeawatea
Taunoka
Taumatatahi
Makakaho
Rotokohu Scenic Res
Ahoroa Scenic Res
Ngamatapouri
Makakaho Junction
Mangapapa Scenic Reserve
Patukino Scenic Reserve
Tawhiwhi
Te Tuhi Junction
Lake Mangawhio
Mangawhio Lake SR
Lake Waikare
Manganuiotahu Scenic Reserve
Lake Moumahaki
Orangimea
Paparangi
Mangawhio
Puau
Rangitatau Scenic Res
Moumahaki SR
Ngutuwera
Rangitatau
N
0
10 km
© Hema Maps NZ Ltd

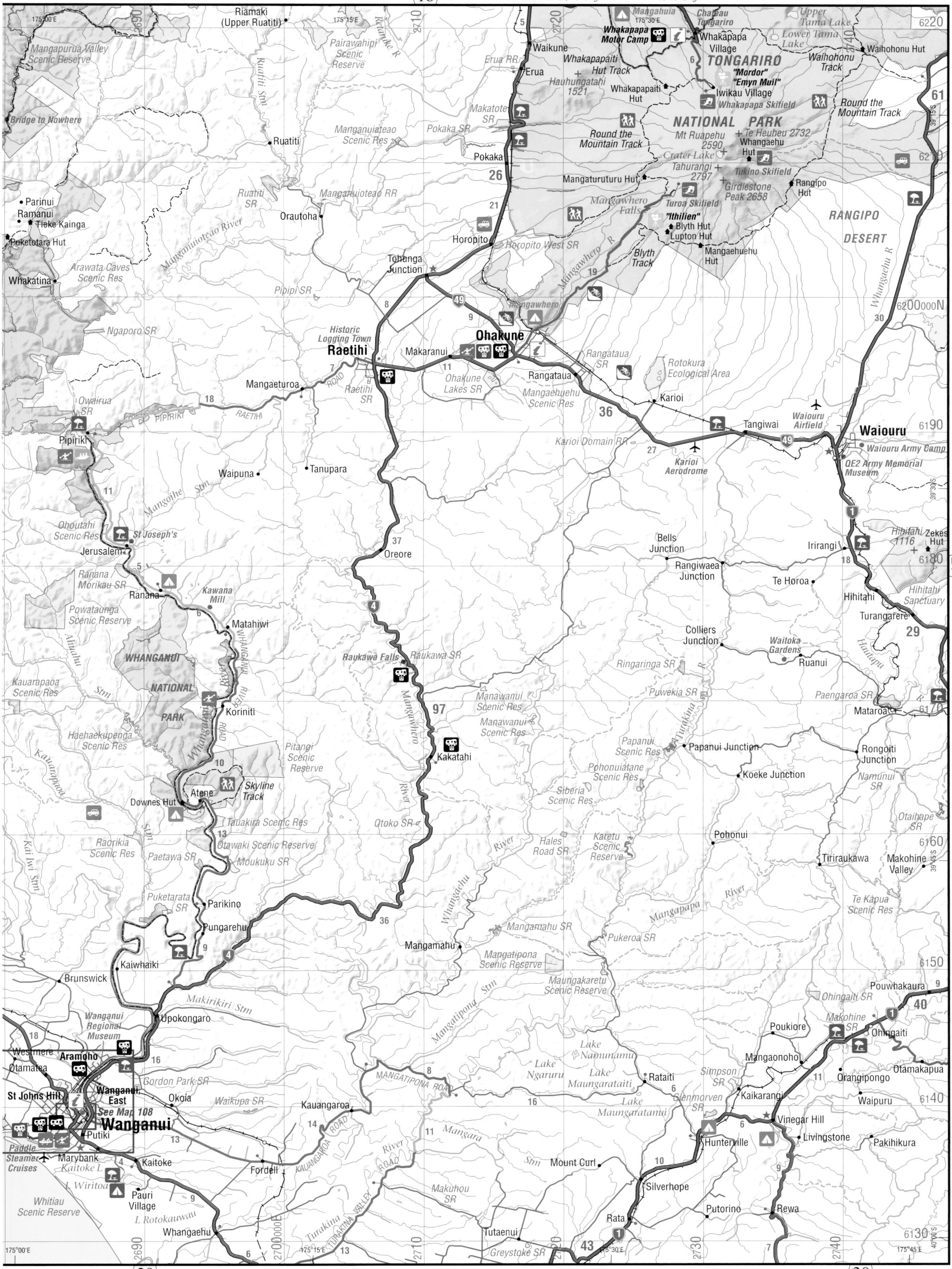

To Taumarunui, Turangi
To Turangi
To Bulls
To Feilding
To Taihape
Wanganui
Raetihi
Ohakune
Waiouru
TONGARIRO NATIONAL PARK
WHANGANUI NATIONAL PARK
RANGIPO DESERT
Mt Ruapehu 2590
Te Heuheu 2732
Tahurangi 2797
Girdlestone Peak 2658
Hauhungatahi 1521
Hihitahi 1116
Chateau Tongariro
Whakapapa Village
Whakapapa Motor Camp
Whakapapa Skifield
Turoa Skifield
Tukino Skifield
Iwikau Village
Round the Mountain Track
Skyline Track
Bridge to Nowhere
Pipiriki
Jerusalem
Ranana
Matahiwi
Koriniti
Atene
Downes Hut
Parikino
Pungarehu
Kaiwhaiki
Upokongaro
Wanganui Regional Museum
Paddle Steamer Cruises
See Map 108
Raukawa Falls
Kakatahi
Mangamahu
Hunterville
Vinegar Hill
Mangaonoho
Ohingaiti
Taihape
Karioi
Tangiwai
Waiouru Army Camp
QE2 Army Memorial Museum
Historic Logging Town
Waiouru Airfield
Karioi Aerodrome
Horopito
Tohunga Junction
Makaranui
Rangataua
Bells Junction
Rangiwaea Junction
Colliers Junction
Papanui Junction
Koeke Junction
Rongoiti Junction
Mataroa
Turangarere
Hihitahi
Irirangi
Pohonui
Tirirakawa
Makohine Valley
Silverhope
Rata
Rewa
Kaikarangi
Rataiti
Mount Curl
Fordell
Kauangaroa
Kaitoke
Marybank
Putiki
Aramoho
Westmere
Otamatea
St Johns Hill
Wanganui East
Okoia
Brunswick
Whangaehu
Pauri Village
Whitiau Scenic Reserve
Tutaenui
Putorino
Livingstone
Pakihikura
Orangipongo
Waipuru
Otamakapua
Poukiore
Pouwhakaura
Ruatiti
Orautoha
Riamaki (Upper Ruatiti)
Mangaeturoa
Waipuna
Tanupara
Oreore
Parinui
Ramanui
Tieke Kainga
Puketotara Hut
Whakatina
Erua
Waikune
Pokaka
A B C D E F G H J
8 9 10 11 12 13 14

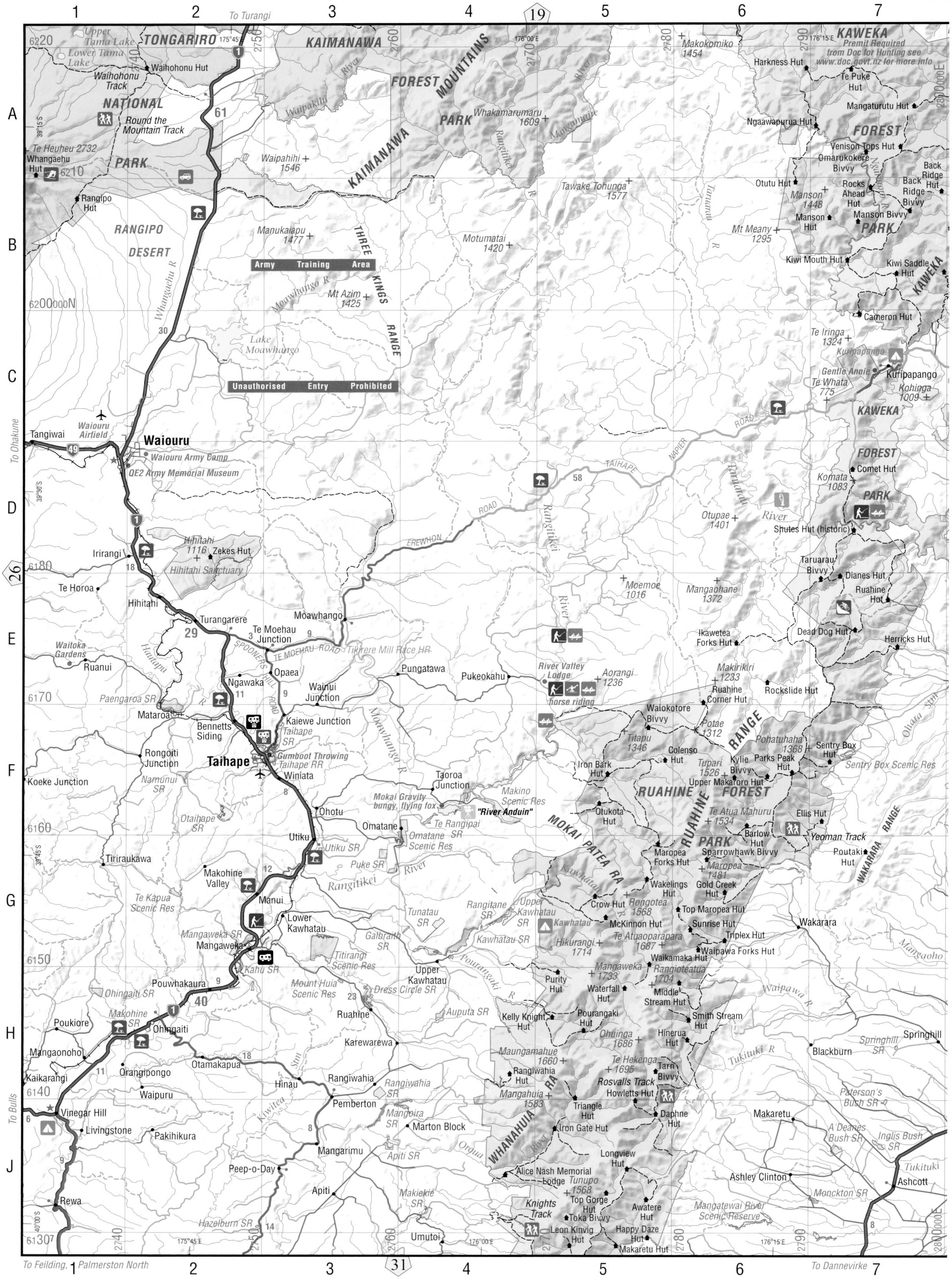

1 2 3 4 5 6 7
To Turangi
19
A B C D E F G H J
TONGARIRO
NATIONAL
PARK
Upper Tama Lake
Lower Tama Lake
Waihohonu Hut
Waihohonu Track
Round the Mountain Track
Te Heuheu 2732
Whangaehu Hut
Rangipo Hut
KAIMANAWA
FOREST
PARK
KAIMANAWA MOUNTAINS
Waipakihi River
Waipahihi 1546
Whakamarumaru 1609
Makokomiko 1454
Tawake Tohunga 1577
Motumatai 1420
RANGIPO DESERT
Whangaehu R
Manukaiapu 1477
THREE KINGS RANGE
Army Training Area
Moawhango R
Mt Azim 1425
Lake Moawhango
Unauthorised Entry Prohibited
KAWEKA
Premit Required from Doc for Hunting see www.doc.govt.nz for more info
Harkness Hut
Te Puke Hut
Mangaturutu Hut
Ngaawapurua Hut
FOREST
Venison Tops Hut
Omarukokere Bivvy
Back Ridge Hut
Back Ridge Bivvy
Rocks Ahead Hut
Otutu Hut
Manson 1448
Manson Hut
Manson Bivvy
PARK
Mt Meany 1295
Taruarau R
Kiwi Mouth Hut
Kiwi Saddle Hut
KAWEKA
Cameron Hut
Te Iringa 1324
Kuripapango
Gentle Annie
Te Whata 775
Kuripapango
Kohinga 1009
KAWEKA
FOREST
Comet Hut
Komata 1083
PARK
Shutes Hut (historic)
Otupae 1401
River
Taruarau Bivvy
Dianes Hut
Ruahine Hut
Dead Dog Hut
Herricks Hut
Mangaohane 1372
Moemoe 1016
Ikawetea Forks Hut
Makirikiri 1233
Ruahine Corner Hut
Rockslide Hut
Waiouru Airfield
Tangiwai
To Ohakune
Waiouru
Waiouru Army Camp
QE2 Army Memorial Museum
49
1
61
30
TAIHAPE NAPIER ROAD
58
ERUWHON ROAD
Rangitikei River
Hihitahi 1116
Zekes Hut
Hihitahi Sanctuary
Irirangi
18
26
Te Horoa
Hihitahi
Turangarere
29
Te Moehau Junction
Moawhango
TE MOEHAU ROAD
Tikirere Mill Race HR
Waitoka Gardens
Ruanui
Hautapu R
SPOONERS HILL ROAD
Opaea
Ngawaka
11
Wainui Junction
Pungatawa
Pukeokahu
River Valley Lodge
horse riding
Aorangi 1236
Paengaroa SR
Mataroa
Bennetts Siding
Kaiewe Junction
Taihape SR
Gumboot Throwing
Taihape RR
Rongoiti Junction
Taihape
Winiata
Koeke Junction
Namunui SR
Moawhango R
Taoroa Junction
Makino Scenic Res
Mokai Gravity bungy, flying fox
"River Anduin"
Te Rangipai SR
Ohotu
Omatane
Omatane Scenic Res
Otaihape SR
Utiku
Utiku SR
Tiriraukawa
Puke SR
Rangitikei River
Makohine Valley
12
Te Kapua Scenic Res
Manui
Lower Kawhatau
Tunatau SR
Rangitane SR
Upper Kawhatau SR
Kawhatau
Kawhatau SR
Mangaweka SR
Mangaweka
Galbraith SR
Titirangi Scenic Res
Kahu SR
Upper Kawhatau
Pourangaki R
Pouwhakaura
9
40
Ohingaiti SR
Mount Huia Scenic Res
23
Dress Circle SR
Ruahine
Aupuka SR
Makohine SR
Ohingaiti
Poukiore
Karewarewa
Mangaonoho
Otamakapua
18
11
Orangipongo
Kaikarangi
Waipuru
Hinau
Rangiwahia
Rangiwahia SR
Pemberton
Kiwitea Stm
To Bulls
6
Vinegar Hill
Livingstone
Pakihikura
Mangoira SR
Marton Block
Mangarimu
Apiti SR
Oroua
Peep-o-Day
Apiti
Makiekie SR
Rewa
Hazelburn SR
14
Umutoi
To Feilding, Palmerston North
31
RUAHINE RANGE
Waiokotore Bivvy
Potae 1312
Titapu 1346
Colenso Hut
Pohatuhaha 1368
Sentry Box Hut
Iron Bark Hut
Tupari 1526
Kylie Bivvy
Parks Peak Hut
Sentry Box Scenic Res
Upper Makaroro Hut
RUAHINE FOREST PARK
Otukota Hut
Te Atua Mahuru 1534
Ellis Hut
MOKAI PATEA RA
Barlow Hut
Yeoman Track
WAKARARA RANGE
Maropea Forks Hut
Sparrowhawk Bivvy
Poutaki Hut
Maropea 1481
Wakelings Hut
Gold Creek Hut
Kawhatau R
Crow Hut
Rongotea 1568
Top Maropea Hut
McKinnon Hut
Sunrise Hut
Wakarara
Te Atuaoparapara 1687
Hikurangi 1714
Triplex Hut
Waipawa Forks Hut
Mangaohu
Waikamaka Hut
Mangaweka 1733
Rangioteatua 1704
Purity Hut
Waterfall Hut
Middle Stream Hut
Waipawa R
Kelly Knight Hut
Pourangaki Hut
Smith Stream Hut
Ohuinga 1686
Hinerua Hut
Springhill
Springhill SR
Blackburn
Maungamahue 1660
Tukituki R
Te Hekenga 1695
Tarn Bivvy
Rangiwahia Hut
Rosvalls Track
Howletts Hut
Mangahuia 1583
Paterson's Bush SR
WHANAHUIA RA
Triangle Hut
Daphne Hut
Makaretu
Iron Gate Hut
A Deanes Bush SR
Inglis Bush SR
Longview Hut
Alice Nash Memorial Lodge
Tunupo 1568
Ashley Clinton
Tukituki
Ashcott
Top Gorge Hut
Awatere Hut
Monckton SR
Knights Track
Toka Bivvy
Mangatewai River Scenic Reserve
Leon Kinvig Hut
Happy Daze Hut
Makaretu Hut
8
To Dannevirke

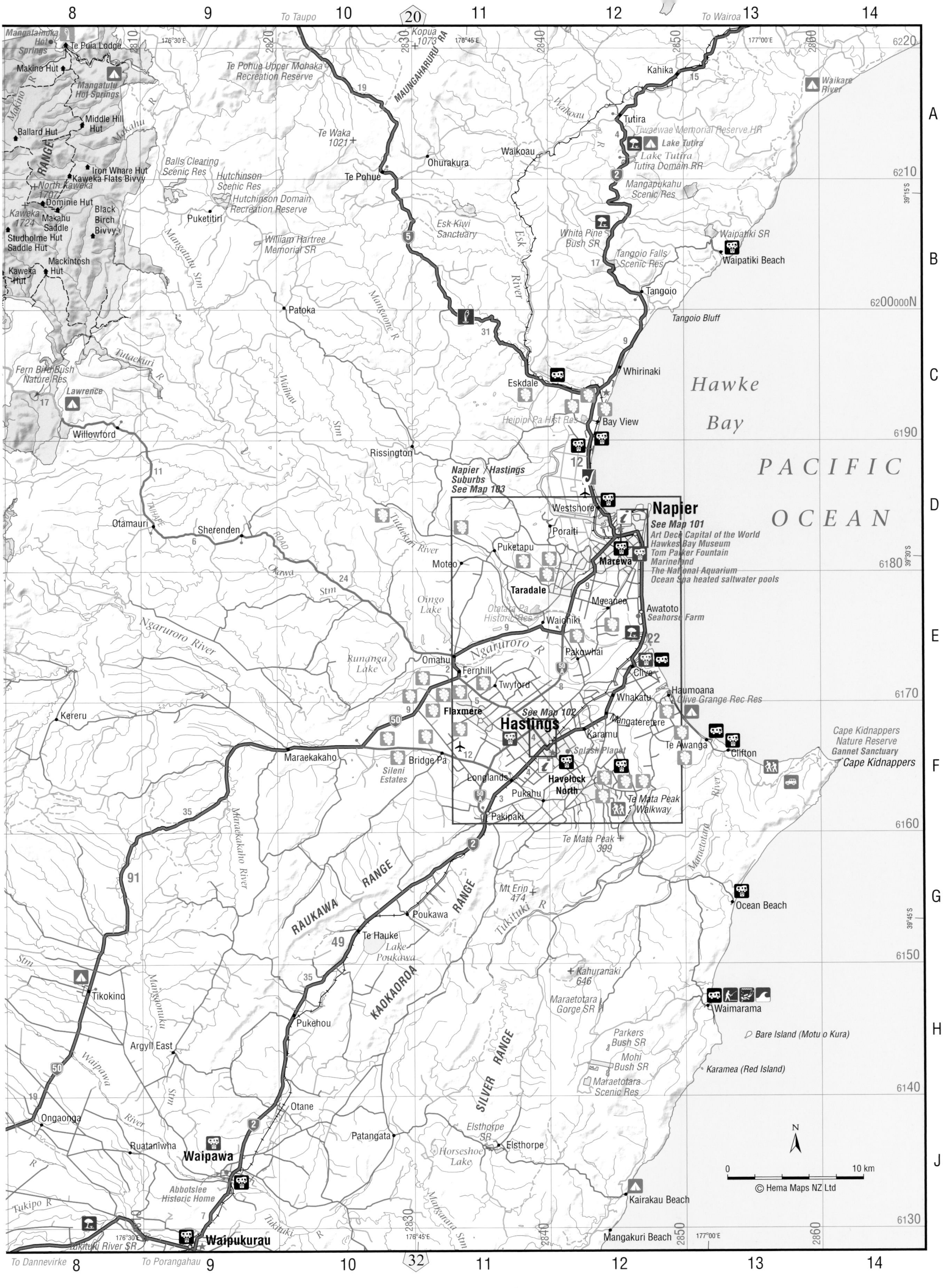
To Taupo
To Wairoa
20
32
To Dannevirke
To Porangahau
Hawke Bay
PACIFIC OCEAN
Napier
See Map 101
Art Deco Capital of the World
Hawkes Bay Museum
Tom Parker Fountain
Marineland
The National Aquarium
Ocean Spa heated saltwater pools
Napier / Hastings Suburbs See Map 103
Hastings
See Map 102
Havelock North
Taradale
Marewa
Westshore
Poraiti
Puketapu
Meeanee
Awatoto
Seahorse Farm
Waiohiki
Otatara Pa Historic Res
Pakowhai
Clive
Haumoana
Clive Grange Rec Res
Whakatu
Mangateretere
Karamu
Te Awanga
Clifton
Cape Kidnappers Nature Reserve Gannet Sanctuary
Cape Kidnappers
Splash Planet
Te Mata Peak Walkway
Te Mata Peak 399
Pukahu
Pakipaki
Longlands
Flaxmere
Twyford
Fernhill
Omahu
Bridge Pa
Sileni Estates
Maraekakaho
Kereru
Moteo
Oingo Lake
Runanga Lake
Ngaruroro River
Tutaekuri River
Rissington
Otamauri
Sherenden
Taihape Road
Willowford
Lawrence
Fern Bird Bush Nature Res
Patoka
Puketitiri
Te Pohue
Ohurakura
Waikoau
Tutira
Lake Tutira
Tutira Domain RR
Tiwaewae Memorial Reserve HR
Mangapukahu Scenic Res
White Pine Bush SR
Tangoio Falls Scenic Res
Tangoio
Tangoio Bluff
Waipatiki SR
Waipatiki Beach
Kahika
Waikare River
Whirinaki
Eskdale
Bay View
Heipipi Pa Hist Res
Esk Kiwi Sanctuary
Esk River
Te Waka 1021
Kopua 1073
Maungaharuru Ra
Te Pohue Upper Mohaka Recreation Reserve
Balls Clearing Scenic Res
Hutchinson Scenic Res
Hutchinson Domain Recreation Reserve
William Hartree Memorial SR
Mangatainoka Hot Springs
Te Puia Lodge
Makino Hut
Mangatutu Hot Springs
Middle Hill Hut
Ballard Hut
Iron Whare Hut
Kaweka Flats Bivvy
North Kaweka 1707
Dominie Hut
Kaweka 1724
Makahu Saddle
Black Birch Bivvy
Studholme Hut Saddle Hut
Mackintosh Hut
Kaweka Hut
Range
Raukawa Range
Kaokaoroa
Silver Range
Poukawa
Te Hauke
Lake Poukawa
Pukehou
Argyll East
Tikokino
Otane
Patangata
Elsthorpe
Elsthorpe SR
Horseshoe Lake
Waipawa
Ruataniwha
Ongaonga
Abbotsleee Historic Home
Waipukurau
Tukituki River SR
Tukipo R
Waipawa River
Maraekakaho River
Mt Erin 474
Tukituki R
Kahuranaki 646
Maraetotara Gorge SR
Parkers Bush SR
Mohi Bush SR
Maraetotara Scenic Res
Maraetotara River
Ocean Beach
Waimarama
Bare Island (Motu o Kura)
Karamea (Red Island)
Kairakau Beach
Mangakuri Beach
0 10 km
© Hema Maps NZ Ltd
N
176°30'E
176°45'E
177°00'E
39°15'S
39°30'S
39°45'S
6200000N
8 9 10 11 12 13 14
A B C D E F G H J

Manawatu & Horowhenua

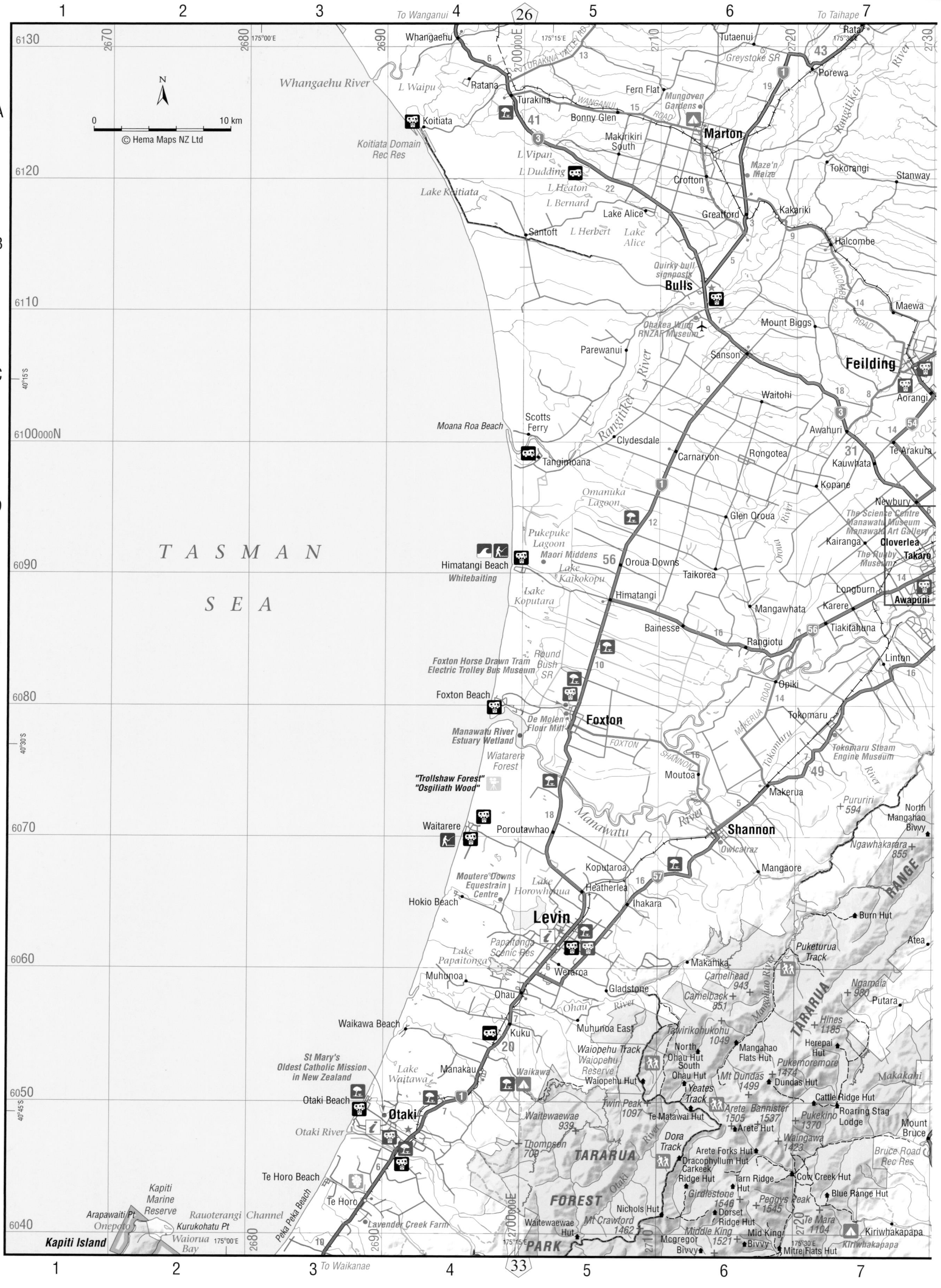

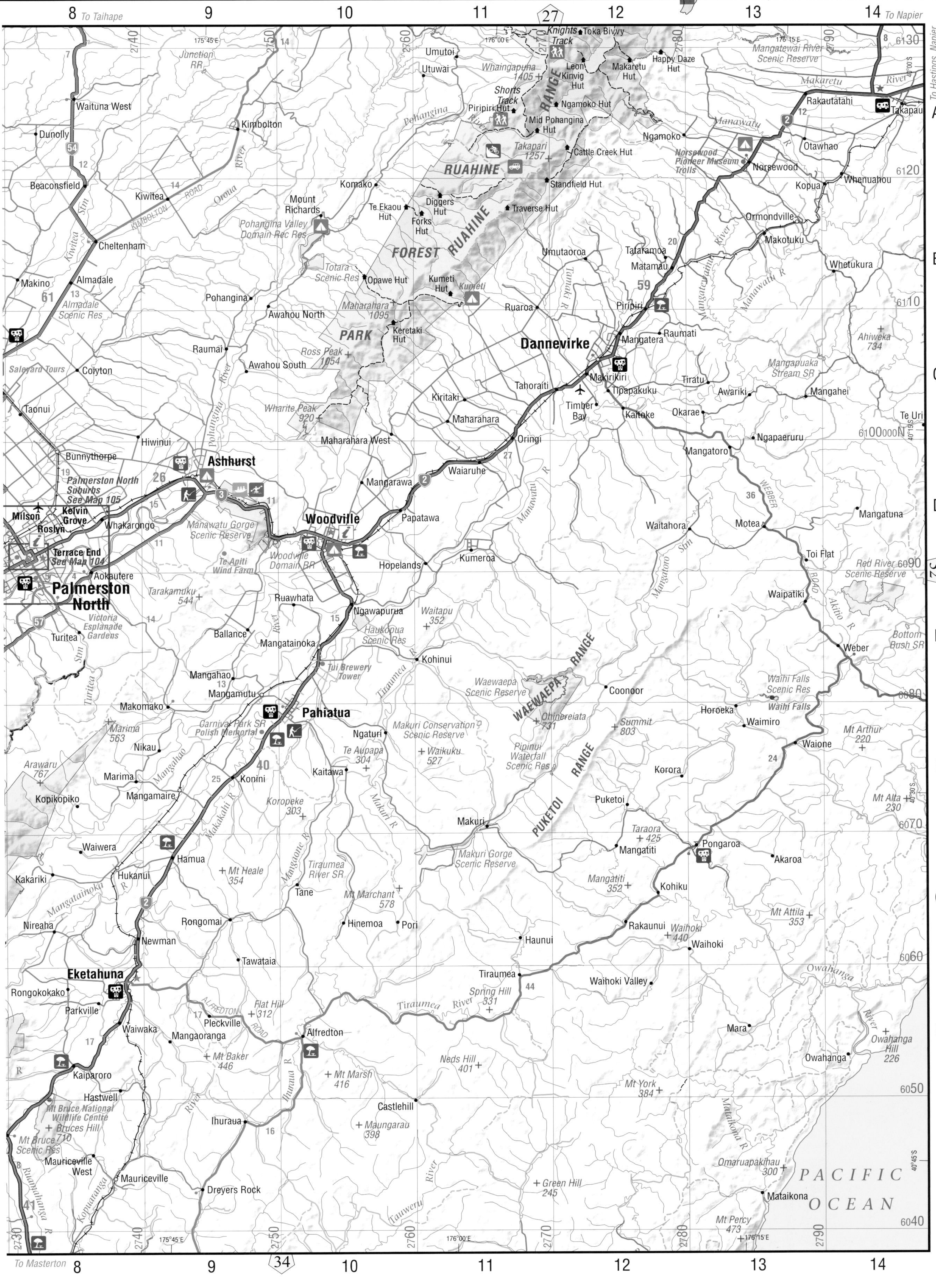
To Taihape
To Napier
To Hastings, Napier
To Masterton
Knights Track
Toka Bivvy
Happy Daze Hut
Makaretu Hut
Leon Kinvig Hut
Whaingapuna 1405
Umutoi
Utuwai
Junction RR
Waituna West
Dunolly
Kimbolton
Shorts Track
Piripiri Hut
Ngamoko Hut
Mid Pohangina Hut
RUAHINE RANGE
Takapari 1257
Cattle Creek Hut
Standfield Hut
Traverse Hut
Diggers Hut
Te Ekaou Hut
Forks Hut
RUAHINE FOREST PARK
Kumeti Hut
Opawe Hut
Keretaki Hut
Maharahara 1095
Ross Peak 1054
Wharite Peak 920
Mangatewai River Scenic Reserve
Makaretu River
Rakautatahi
Takapau
Manawatu R
Ngamoko
Norsewood Pioneer Museum
Trolls
Norsewood
Otawhao
Kopua
Whenuahou
Beaconsfield
Kiwitea
KIMBOLTON ROAD
Oroua River
Mount Richards
Komako
Pohangina Valley Domain Rec Res
Cheltenham
Ormondville
Makotuku
Umutaoroa
Tataramoa
Matamau
Whetukura
Makino
Almadale
Almadale Scenic Res
Totara Scenic Res
Pohangina
Awahou North
Ruaroa
Piripiri
Raumati
Mangatera
Dannevirke
Ahiweka 734
Raumai
Saleyard Tours
Colyton
Awahou South
Tahoraiti
Makirikiri
Tipapakuku
Mangapuaka Stream SR
Tiratu
Awariki
Mangahei
Taonui
Kiritaki
Maharahara
Timber Bay
Kaitoke
Okarae
Te Uri
Hiwinui
Maharahara West
Oringi
Ngapaeruru
Mangatoro
Bunnythorpe
Ashhurst
Palmerston North Suburbs See Map 105
Waiaruhe
Mangarawa
Milson
Kelvin Grove
Roslyn
Whakarongo
Manawatu Gorge Scenic Reserve
Woodville
Papatawa
Waitahora
Motea
Mangatuna
WEBBER ROAD
Terrace End See Map 104
Te Apiti Wind Farm
Woodville Domain BR
Hopelands
Kumeroa
Toi Flat
Red River Scenic Reserve
Aokautere
Palmerston North
Tarakamuku 544
Ruawhata
Waipatiki
Akitio R
Victoria Esplanade Gardens
Turitea
Ballance
Ngawapurua
Waitapu 352
Haukopua Scenic Res
Mangatainoka
Weber
Bottom Bush SR
Kohinui
Tui Brewery Tower
Waewaepa Scenic Reserve
WAEWAEPA RANGE
Coonoor
Mangahao
Mangamutu
Pahiatua
Makomako
Carnival Park SR
Polish Memorial
Ngaturi
Makuri Conservation Scenic Reserve
Ohinereiata 731
Summit 803
Waihi Falls Scenic Res
Waihi Falls
Horoeka
Waimiro
Waione
Mt Arthur 220
Marima 563
Nikau
Te Aupapa 304
Waikuku 527
Pipinui Waterfall Scenic Res
PUKETOI RANGE
Arawaru 767
Marima
Konini
Kaitawa
Korora
Mangamaire
Kopikopiko
Koropeke 303
Makuri
Puketoi
Mt Alta 230
Waiwera
Hamua
Taraora 425
Mangatiti
Pongaroa
Akaroa
Makuri Gorge Scenic Reserve
Kakariki
Hukanui
Mt Heale 354
Tiraumea River SR
Tane
Mangatiti 352
Kohiku
Mt Marchant 578
Mt Attila 353
Nireaha
Rongomai
Hinemoa
Pori
Rakaunui
Waihoki 440
Waihoki
Haunui
Newman
Tawataia
Eketahuna
Tiraumea
Waihoki Valley
Owahanga
Rongokokako
Parkville
Spring Hill 331
Tiraumea River
Flat Hill 312
ALFREDTON ROAD
Pleckville
Alfredton
Waiwaka
Mangaoranga
Mara
Owahanga Hill 226
Mt Baker 446
Neds Hill 401
Owahanga
Kaiparoro
Mt Marsh 416
Mt York 384
Hastwell
Castlehill
Mt Bruce National Wildlife Centre
Bruces Hill 710
Mt Bruce Scenic Res
Ihuraua
Maungarau 398
Mataikona R
Omaruapakihau 300
Mauriceville West
Mauriceville
Dreyers Rock
Green Hill 245
PACIFIC OCEAN
Mataikona
Mt Percy 473
Ruamahanga R
Kopuaranga
Tauweru

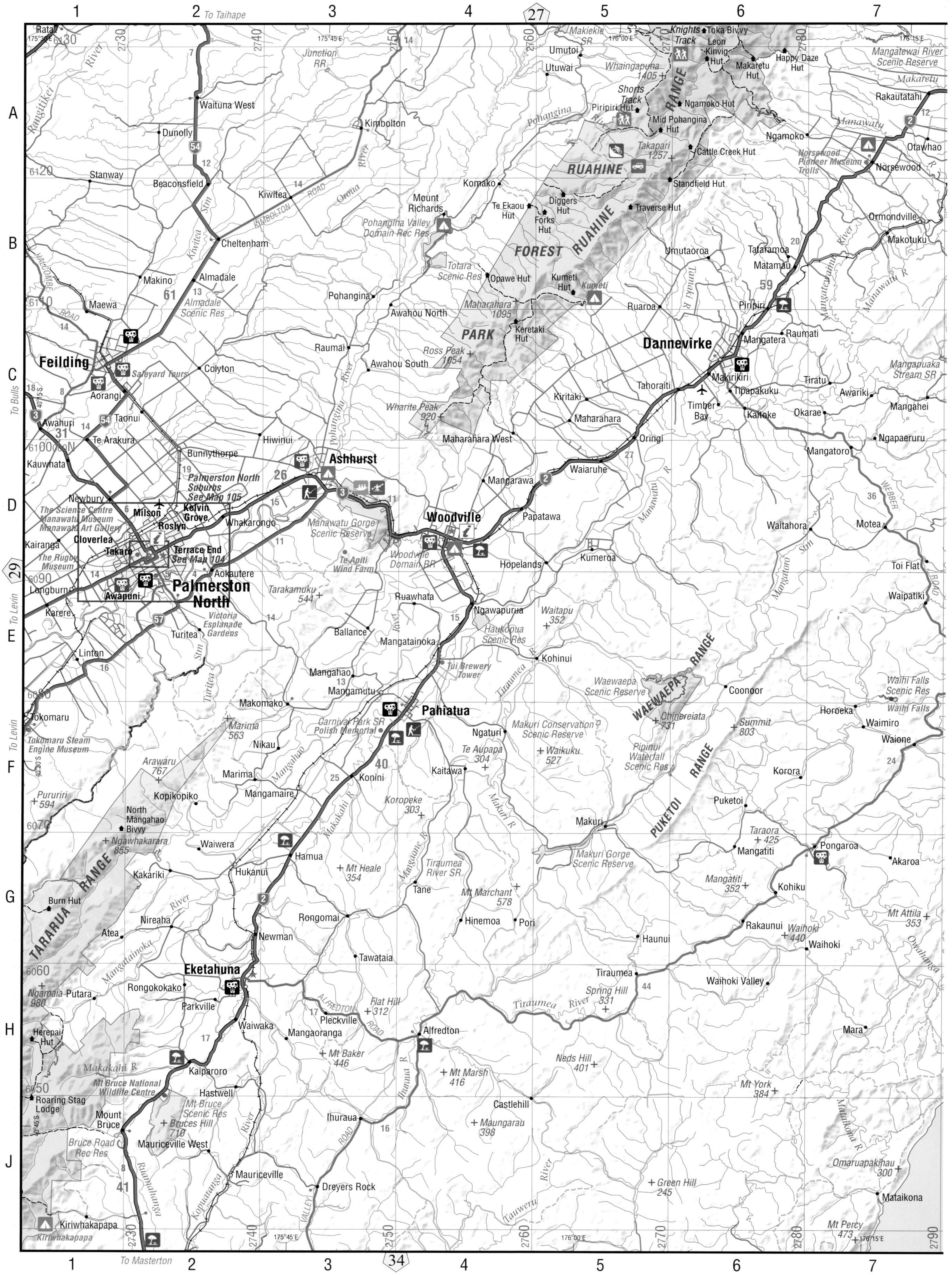

1
2 To Taihape
3
4
27
5
6
7
A
B
C
D
E
F
G
H
J
To Bulls
To Levin
To Levin
29
To Masterton
34
Rata
Rangitikei River
Waituna West
Dunolly
Stanway
Beaconsfield
Kiwitea
Kimbolton
Kimbolton Road
Cheltenham
Junction RR
Oroua River
Pohangina River
Mount Richards
Pohangina Valley Domain Rec Res
Komako
Umutoi
Utuwai
Makiekie SR
Whaingapuna 1405
Knights Track
Toka Bivvy
Leon Kinvig Hut
Makaretu Hut
Happy Daze Hut
Shorts Track
Piripiri Hut
Ngamoko Hut
Mid Pohangina Hut
Cattle Creek Hut
Takapari 1257
Ruahine
Ruahine Range
Standfield Hut
Te Ekaou Hut
Diggers Hut
Forks Hut
Traverse Hut
Ruahine Forest Park
Totara Scenic Res
Opawe Hut
Kumeti Hut
Kumeti
Maharahara 1095
Keretaki Hut
Ross Peak 1054
Wharite Peak 920
Mangatewai River Scenic Reserve
Makaretu
Rakautatahi
Ngamoko
Otawhao
Manawatu
Norsewood Pioneer Museum Trolls
Norsewood
Ormondville
Makotuku
Tataramoa
Matamau
Umutaoroa
Piripiri
Ruaroa
Raumati
Mangatera
Dannevirke
Makirikiri
Tipapakuku
Timber Bay
Kaitoke
Tiratu
Awariki
Mangahei
Mangapuaka Stream SR
Okarae
Ngapaeruru
Mangatoro
Tahoraiti
Kiritaki
Maharahara
Maharahara West
Oringi
Waiaruhe
Mangarawa
Papatawa
Hopelands
Kumeroa
Manawatu R
Waitahora
Motea
Mangatoro Stm
Toi Flat
Waipatiki
Webber Road
Makino
Almadale
Almadale Scenic Res
Maewa
Halcombe Road
Pohangina
Awahou North
Raumai
Awahou South
Feilding
Saleyard Tours
Colyton
Aorangi
Taonui
Awahuri
Te Arakura
Kauwhata
Bunnythorpe
Hiwinui
Ashhurst
Palmerston North Suburbs See Map 105
Newbury
Milson
Kelvin Grove
Roslyn
Whakarongo
The Science Centre Manawatu Museum Manawatu Art Gallery
Cloverlea
Kairanga
Takaro
Terrace End See Map 104
The Rugby Museum
Aokautere
Longburn
Awapuni
Palmerston North
Karere
Victoria Esplanade Gardens
Turitea
Linton
Manawatu Gorge Scenic Reserve
Te Apiti Wind Farm
Woodville
Woodville Domain BR
Tarakamuku 544
Ruawhata
Ngawapurua
Ballance
Mangatainoka
Haukopua Scenic Res
Waitapu 352
Kohinui
Tiraumea R
Tui Brewery Tower
Mangahao
Mangamutu
Makomako
Turitea Stm
Tokomaru
Tokomaru Steam Engine Museum
Marima 563
Nikau
Carnival Park SR
Polish Memorial
Pahiatua
Ngaturi
Makuri Conservation Scenic Reserve
Waewaepa Scenic Reserve
Waewaepa Range
Ohinereiata 731
Coonoor
Waihi Falls Scenic Res
Waihi Falls
Horoeka
Waimiro
Summit 803
Waione
Arawaru 767
Marima
Mangahao
Konini
Te Aupapa 304
Waikuku 527
Pipinui Waterfall Scenic Res
Puketoi Range
Kaitawa
Korora
Pururiri 594
Kopikopiko
Mangamaire
Koropeke 303
Makuri R
North Mangahao Bivvy
Ngawhakarara 855
Waiwera
Hamua
Makakahi R
Mangaone R
Makuri
Puketoi
Taraora 425
Mangatiti
Pongaroa
Akaroa
Makuri Gorge Scenic Reserve
Tiraumea River SR
Kakariki
Hukanui
Mt Heale 354
Tane
Mt Marchant 578
Mangatiti 352
Kohiku
Burn Hut
Tararua Range
Nireaha
Rongomai
Hinemoa
Pori
Rakaunui
Waihoki 440
Waihoki
Mt Attila 353
Atea
Newman
Haunui
Owahanga
Tawataia
Eketahuna
Tiraumea
Waihoki Valley
Ngamaia 980
Putara
Rongokokako
Parkville
Mangatainoka River
Alfredton Road
Flat Hill 312
Spring Hill 331
Tiraumea River
Pleckville
Herepai Hut
Waiwaka
Mangaoranga
Alfredton
Mara
Makakahi R
Kaiparoro
Mt Baker 446
Mt Marsh 416
Neds Hill 401
Mt Bruce National Wildlife Centre
Hastwell
Roaring Stag Lodge
Mt Bruce Scenic Res
Bruces Hill 710
Mount Bruce
Castlehill
Mt York 384
Ihuraua
Ihuraua R
Maungarau 398
Bruce Road Rec Res
Mauriceville West
Mauriceville
Kopuaranga River
Ruamahanga
Dreyers Rock
Valley
Green Hill 245
Tauweru River
Matakona R
Omaruapakihau 300
Mataikona
Kiriwhakapapa
Mt Percy 473
175°30'E
175°45'E
176°00'E
176°15'E
40°15'S
40°30'S
40°45'S

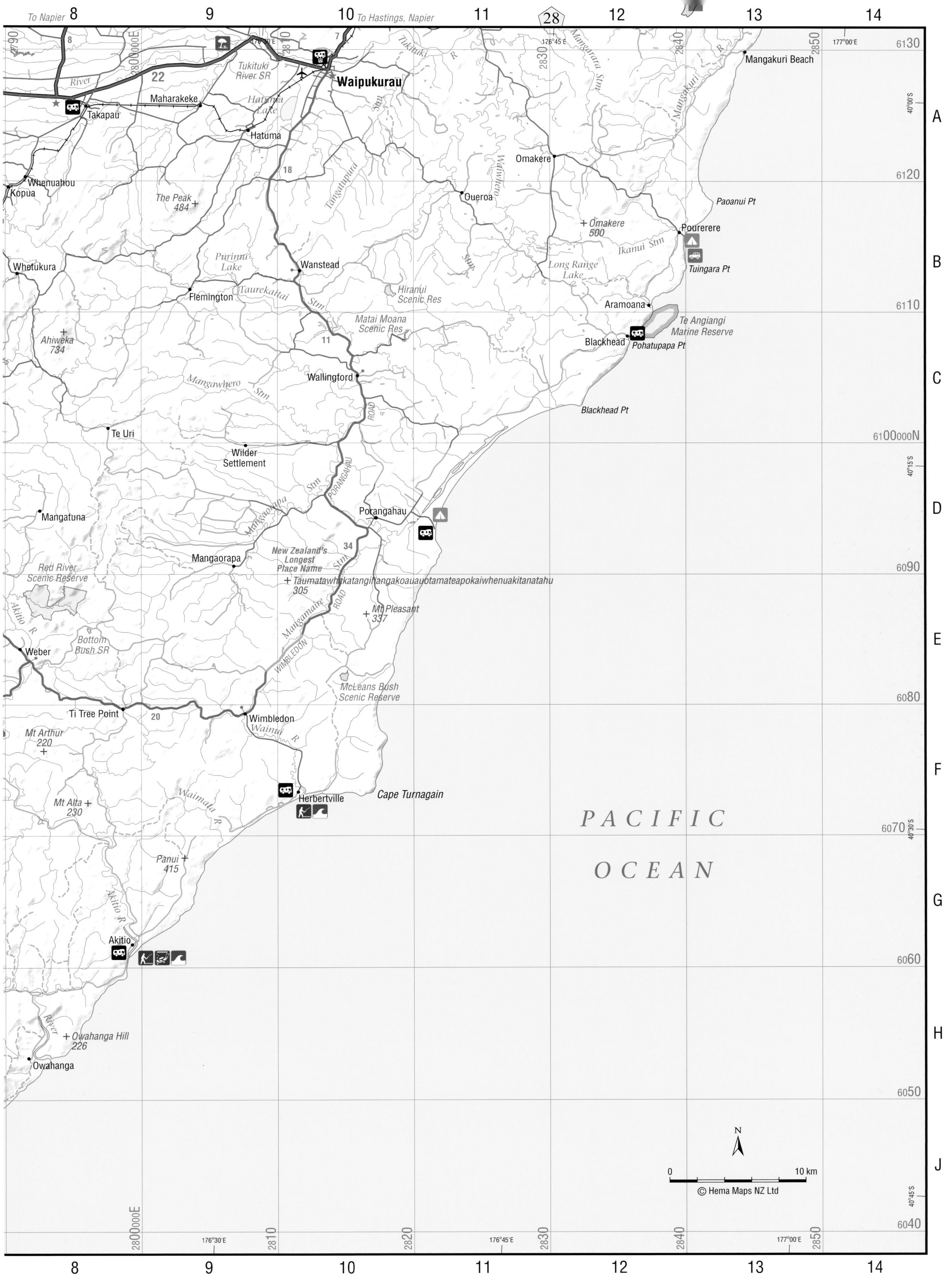

To Napier
To Hastings, Napier
28
8
9
10
11
12
13
14
A
B
C
D
E
F
G
H
J
Waipukurau
Tukituki River SR
22
Takapau
Maharakeke
Hatuma Lake
Hatuma
Whenuahou
Kopua
The Peak 484
Whetukura
Purimu Lake
Flemington
Taurekaitai Stm
Wanstead
Tangatupura
18
Omakere
Oueroa
Omakere 500
Pourerere
Paoanui Pt
Tuingara Pt
Ikanui Stm
Long Range Lake
Hiranui Scenic Res
Matai Moana Scenic Res
Aramoana
Te Angiangi Marine Reserve
Blackhead
Pohatupapa Pt
Blackhead Pt
Mangakuri Beach
Mangarara Stm
Mangakuri
Tukituki R
Ahiweka 734
11
Wallingford
Mangawhero Stm
Te Uri
Wilder Settlement
ROAD
PORANGAHAU
Porangahau
Mangatuna
Mangaorapa
34
New Zealand's Longest Place Name
Taumatawhakatangihangakoauauotamateapokaiwhenuakitanatahu 305
Mt Pleasant 337
Red River Scenic Reserve
Akitio R
Bottom Bush SR
Weber
Mangamaire
WIMBLEDON
McLeans Bush Scenic Reserve
Ti Tree Point
20
Wimbledon
Wainui R
Mt Arthur 220
Mt Alta 230
Waimata R
Herbertville
Cape Turnagain
PACIFIC OCEAN
Panui 415
Akitio R
Akitio
River
Owahanga Hill 226
Owahanga
6130
6120
6110
6100000N
6090
6080
6070
6060
6050
6040
2800000E
2810
2820
2830
2840
2850
176°30'E
176°45'E
177°00'E
40°00'S
40°15'S
40°30'S
40°45'S
N
0
10 km
© Hema Maps NZ Ltd

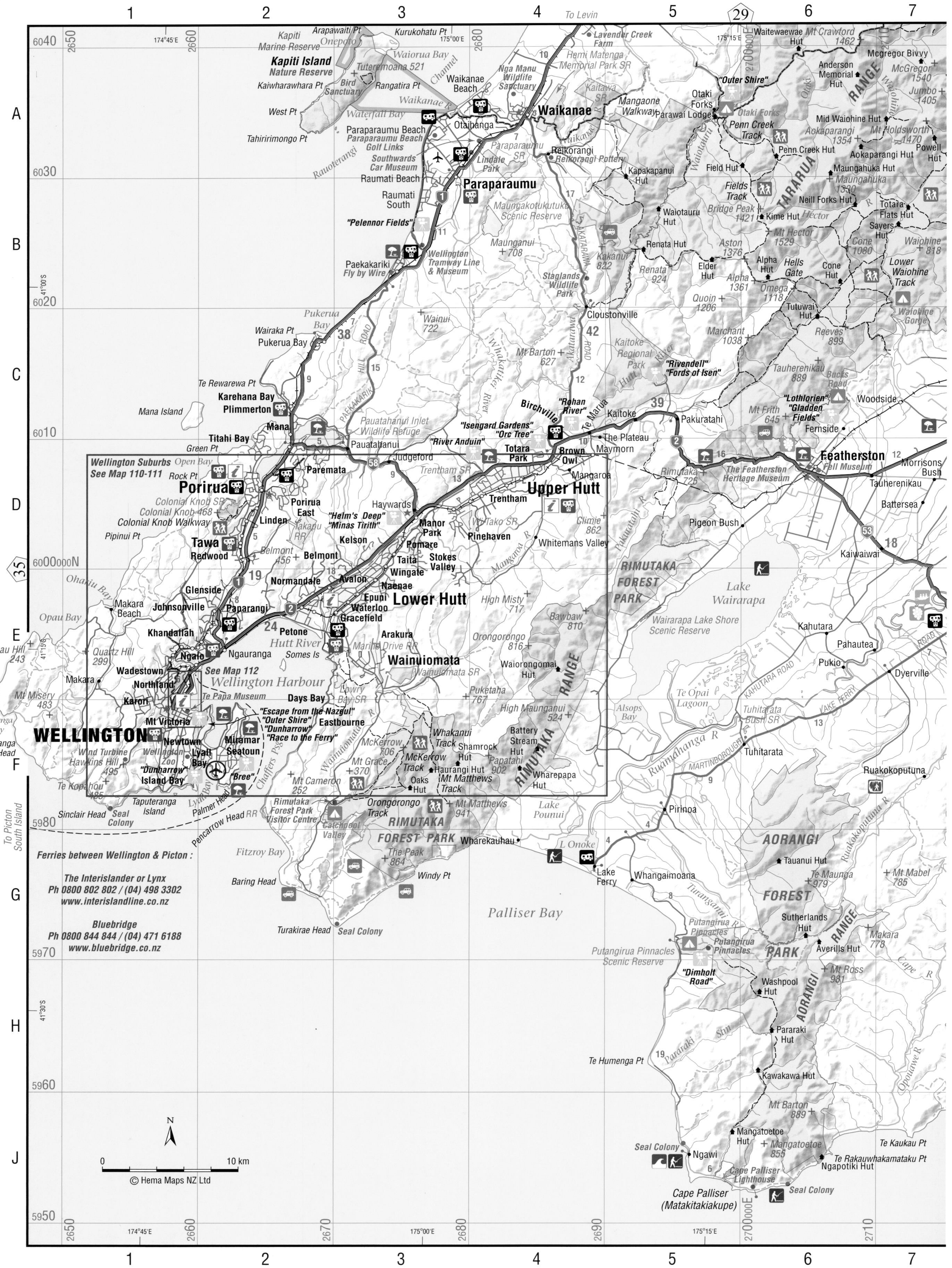
To Levin
Kapiti Marine Reserve
Kapiti Island Nature Reserve
Arapawaiti Pt
Onepoto
Kurukohatu Pt
Waiorua Bay
Tuteremoana 521
Bird Sanctuary
Rangatira Pt
Kaiwharawhara Pt
West Pt
Waterfall Bay
Tahiririmongo Pt
Waikanae Beach
Waikanae
Otaihanga
Nga Manu Wildlife Sanctuary
Lavender Creek Farm
Hemi Matenga Memorial Park SR
Mangaone Walkway
Paraparaumu Beach
Paraparaumu Beach Golf Links
Southwards Car Museum
Raumati Beach
Raumati South
Lindale Park
Paraparaumu
Reikorangi
Reikorangi Pottery
"Pelennor Fields"
Wellington Tramway Line & Museum
Paekakariki
Fly by Wire
Maungakotukutuku Scenic Reserve
Maunganui 708
Staglands Wildlife Park
Kakanui 822
Cloustonville
Pukerua Bay
Wairaka Pt
Wainui 722
Mt Barton 627
Kaitoke Regional Park
"Rivendell" "Fords of Isen"
"Rohan River"
Birchville
Te Rewarewa Pt
Karehana Bay
Plimmerton
Mana Island
Mana
Titahi Bay
Green Pt
Pauatahanui Inlet Wildlife Refuge
Pauatahanui
"Isengard Gardens" "Orc Tree"
"River Anduin"
Totara Park
Te Marua
Kaitoke
The Plateau
Maymorn
Pakuratahi
Brown Owl
Mangaroa
Wellington Suburbs See Map 110-111
Open Bay
Rock Pt
Porirua
Paremata
Judgeford
Trentham SR
Trentham
Upper Hutt
Colonial Knob SR
Colonial Knob 468
Colonial Knob Walkway
Porirua East
Haywards
"Helm's Deep" "Minas Tirith"
Linden
Pipinui Pt
Tawa
Redwood
Manor Park
Kelson
Pinehaven
Whitemans Valley
Climie 862
Belmont 456
Belmont
Pomare
Taita
Stokes Valley
Wingate
Glenside
Normandale
Avalon
Naenae
Makara Beach
Johnsonville
Paparangi
Epuni
Waterloo
Gracefield
Lower Hutt
High Misty 717
Opau Bay
Ohariu Bay
Khandallah
Petone
Hutt River
Somes Is
Arakura
Marine Drive RR
Orongorongo 816
Bawbaw 810
Ohau Hill 243
Quartz Hill 299
Ngaio
Ngauranga
Wadestown
Northland
See Map 112
Wellington Harbour
Wainuiomata
Wainuiomata SR
Waiorongomai Hut
Makara
Mt Misery 483
Karori
Te Papa Museum
Days Bay
Lowry Bay SR
Puketaha 767
High Maunganui 524
Otaranga Bay
Otaranga Head
Mt Victoria
WELLINGTON
Newtown
Wellington Zoo
"Escape from the Nazgul" "Outer Shire" "Dunharrow" "Race to the Ferry"
Eastbourne
Miramar
Seatoun
Wind Turbine
Hawkins Hill 495
Lyall Bay
"Dunharrow"
Island Bay
"Bree"
Te Kopahou 485
McKerrow 706
Mt Grace 370
Whakanui Track
McKerrow Track
Shamrock Hut
Haurangi Hut
Mt Matthews Track
Papatahi 902
Battery Stream Hut
Wharepapa Hut
Oaks Hut
Mt Cameron 252
RIMUTAKA RANGE
Sinclair Head
Seal Colony
Taputeranga Island
Palmer Head
Lyall Bay
Chaffers Pass
Pencarrow Head RR
Rimutaka Forest Park Visitor Centre
Orongorongo Track
Mt Matthews 941
Catchpool Valley
RIMUTAKA FOREST PARK
The Peak 864
Lake Pounui
Wharekauhau
Fitzroy Bay
Windy Pt
Baring Head
Turakirae Head
Seal Colony
Palliser Bay
To Picton South Island
Ferries between Wellington & Picton :
The Interislander or Lynx
Ph 0800 802 802 / (04) 498 3302
www.interislandline.co.nz
Bluebridge
Ph 0800 844 844 / (04) 471 6188
www.bluebridge.co.nz
Otaki Forks
Parawai Lodge
"Outer Shire"
Penn Creek Track
Penn Creek Hut
Kapakapanui Hut
Field Hut
Fields Track
Waiotauru Hut
Renata Hut
Renata 924
Elder Hut
Bridge Peak 1421
Kime Hut
Aston 1376
Alpha Hut
Alpha 1361
Hells Gate
Quoin 1206
Marchant 1038
Omega 1118
Tutuwai Hut
Waitewaewae Hut
Mt Crawford 1462
Anderson Memorial Hut
Mcgregor Bivvy
McGregor 1540
Jumbo 1405
Mid Waiohine Hut
Mt Holdsworth 1470
Powell Hut
Aokaparangi 1354
Aokaparangi Hut
Maungahuka Hut
Maungahuka 1330
Neill Forks Hut
TARARUA RANGE
Totara Flats Hut
Sayers Hut
Mt Hector 1529
Cone 1080
Waiohine 818
Cone Hut
Lower Waiohine Track
Waiohine Gorge
Reeves 899
Tauherenikau 889
Bucks Road
"Lothlorien" "Gladden Fields"
Mt Frith 645
Woodside
Fernside
Featherston
The Featherston Heritage Museum
Fell Museum
Rimutaka 725
Morrisons Bush
Tauherenikau
Battersea
Pigeon Bush
Kaiwaiwai
RIMUTAKA FOREST PARK
Lake Wairarapa
Wairarapa Lake Shore Scenic Reserve
Kahutara
Pahautea
Pukio
Dyerville
Te Opai Lagoon
Alsops Bay
Tuhitarata Bush SR
Ruamahanga R
Tuhitarata
Ruakokoputuna
Pirinoa
L Onoke
Lake Ferry
Whangaimoana
AORANGI FOREST PARK
Tauanui Hut
Te Maunga 979
Mt Mabel 785
Sutherlands Hut
Averills Hut
Makara 778
Putangirua Pinnacles
Putangirua Pinnacles Scenic Reserve
"Dimholt Road"
Washpool Hut
Mt Ross 981
AORANGI RANGE
Pararaki Hut
Te Humenga Pt
Kawakawa Hut
Mt Barton 889
Mangatoetoe Hut
Mangatoetoe 855
Seal Colony
Ngawi
Te Kaukau Pt
Te Rakauwhakamataku Pt
Ngapotiki Hut
Cape Palliser Lighthouse
Seal Colony
Cape Palliser (Matakitakiakupe)
0 10 km
© Hema Maps NZ Ltd

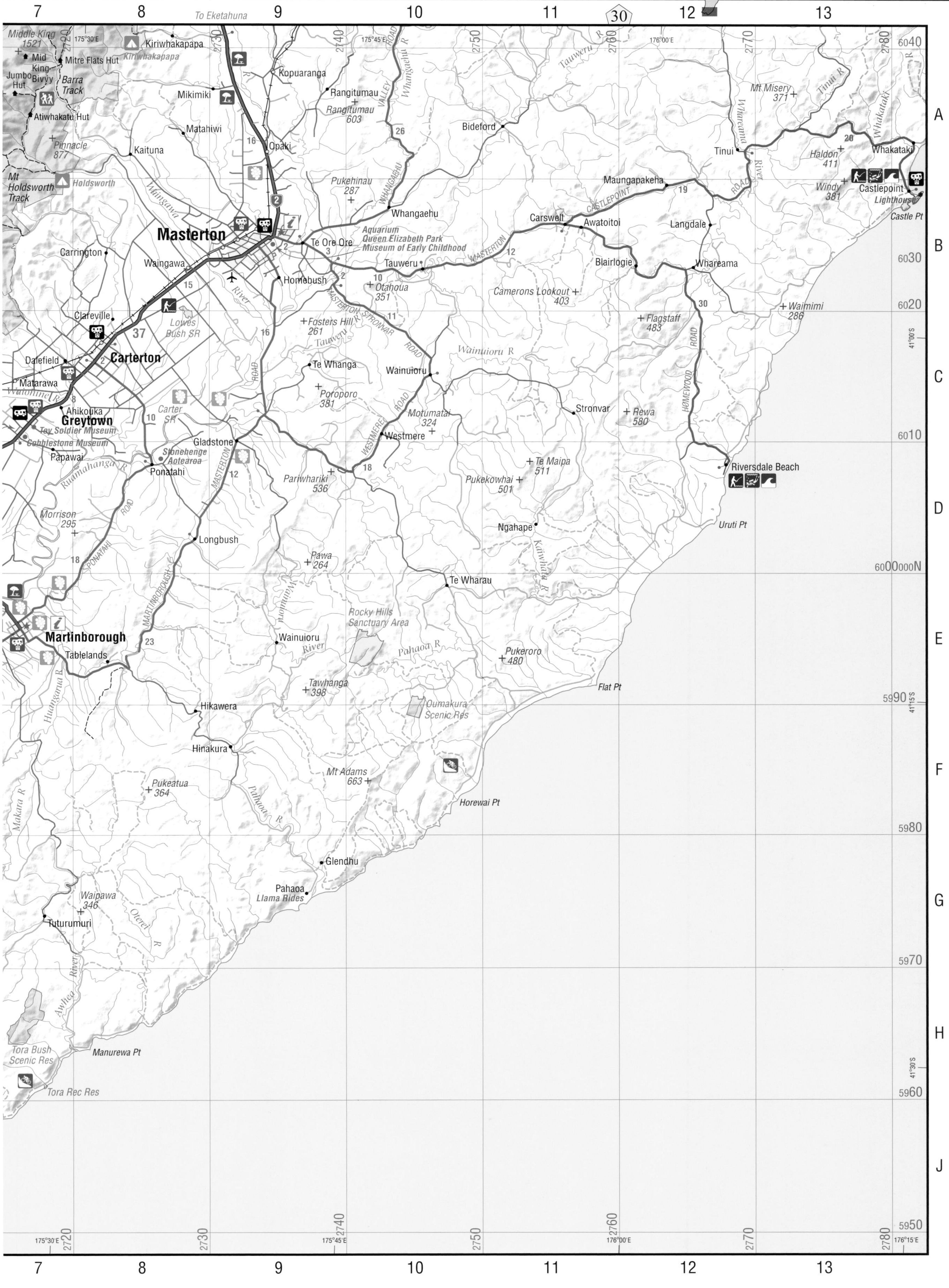
To Eketahuna
30
Middle King 1521
Mid King Bivvy
Jumbo Hut
Mitre Flats Hut
Barra Track
Atiwhakatu Hut
Pinnacle 877
Mt Holdsworth Track
Holdsworth
Kiriwhakapapa
Mikimiki
Matahiwi
Kaituna
Opaki
Kopuaranga
Rangitumau
Rangitumau 603
VALLEY ROAD
Whangaehu R
Bideford
Pukehinau 287
Whangaehu
Masterton
Waingawa
Carrington
Te Ore Ore
Aquarium
Queen Elizabeth Park
Museum of Early Childhood
Homebush
Tauweru
Otahoua 351
Fosters Hill 261
MASTERTON STRONVAR ROAD
Te Whanga
Poroporo 381
Wainuioru
Wainuioru R
Motumatai 324
Westmere
WESTMERE ROAD
Clareville
Lowes Bush SR
Carterton
Dalefield
Matarawa
Ahikouka
Greytown
Toy Soldier Museum
Cobblestone Museum
Papawai
Carter SR
Gladstone
Stonehenge Aotearoa
Ponatahi
Ruamahanga R
Morrison 295
PONATAHI ROAD
MASTERTON
Longbush
Pariwhariki 536
Pawa 264
MARTINBOROUGH
Martinborough
Tablelands
Huangarua R
Wainuioru River
Rocky Hills Sanctuary Area
Pahaoa R
Tawhanga 398
Oumakura Scenic Res
Hikawera
Hinakura
Pukeatua 364
Mt Adams 663
Horewai Pt
Glendhu
Pahaoa
Llama Rides
Waipawa 346
Tuturumuri
Oterei R
Makara R
Awhea River
Tora Bush Scenic Res
Manurewa Pt
Tora Rec Res
Te Wharau
Pukeroro 480
Flat Pt
Ngahape
Kaiwhata R
Pukekowhai 501
Te Maipa 511
Stronvar
Rewa 580
Camerons Lookout 403
Carswell
Awatoitoi
CASTLEPOINT
Maungapakeha
Langdale
Blairlogie
Whareama
Flagstaff 483
HOMEWOOD ROAD
Riversdale Beach
Uruti Pt
Waimimi 286
Tauweru R
Mt Misery 371
Whareama River
Tinui
Tinui R
Haldon 411
Whakataki
Windy 381
Castlepoint
Lighthouse
Castle Pt
175°30'E
175°45'E
176°00'E
176°15'E
41°00'S
41°15'S
41°30'S
6040
6030
6020
6010
6000000N
5990
5980
5970
5960
5950
2720
2730
2740
2750
2760
2770
2780
7
8
9
10
11
12
13
A
B
C
D
E
F
G
H
J

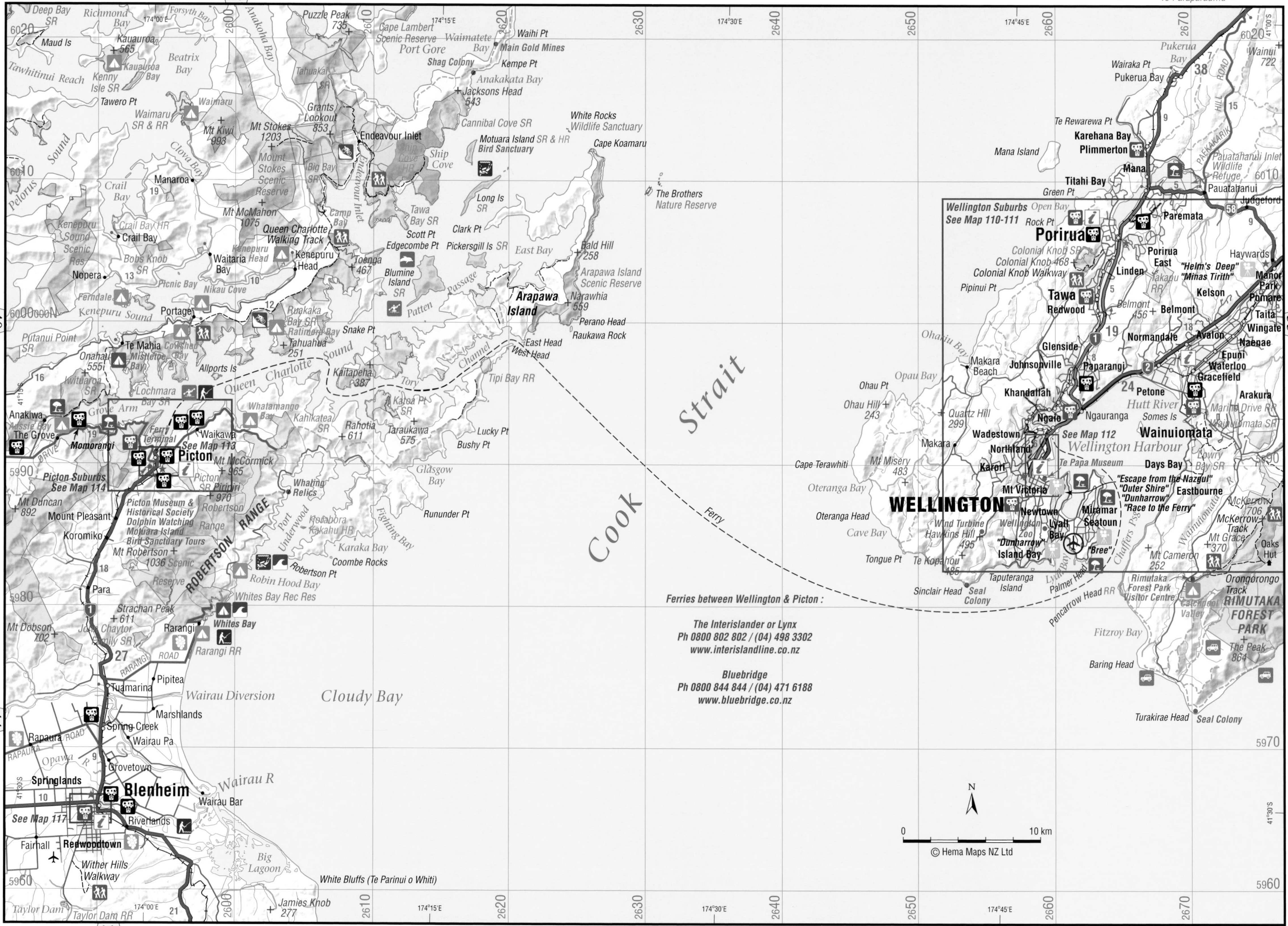
Cook Strait
Cloudy Bay
WELLINGTON
Porirua
Picton
Blenheim
Wellington Harbour
Ferries between Wellington & Picton :
The Interislander or Lynx
Ph 0800 802 802 / (04) 498 3302
www.interislandline.co.nz
Bluebridge
Ph 0800 844 844 / (04) 471 6188
www.bluebridge.co.nz
Ferry
Wellington Suburbs
See Map 110-111
See Map 112
See Map 113
Picton Suburbs
See Map 114
See Map 117
Arapawa Island
Queen Charlotte Sound
Tory Channel
Queen Charlotte Walking Track
Robertson Range
Wairau Diversion
Wairau R
Big Lagoon
White Bluffs (Te Parinui o Whiti)
The Brothers
Nature Reserve
RIMUTAKA FOREST PARK
Picton Museum & Historical Society
Dolphin Watching
Motuara Island Bird Sanctuary Tours
"Escape from the Nazgul"
"Outer Shire"
"Dunharrow"
"Race to the Ferry"
"Helm's Deep"
"Minas Tirith"
"Bree"
To Paraparaumu
To Upper Hutt
To Renwick
To Kaikoura
© Hema Maps NZ Ltd
0
10 km

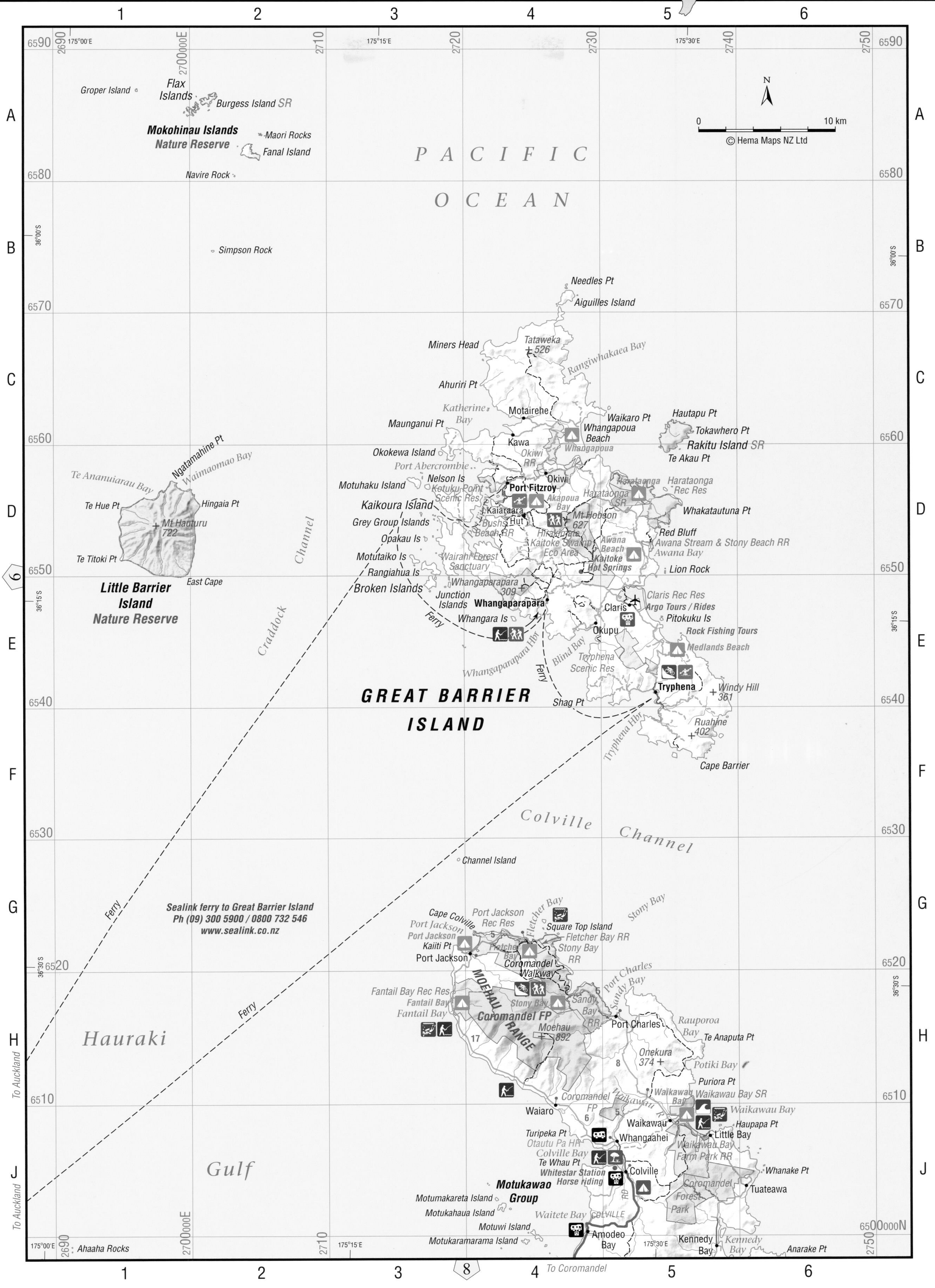
PACIFIC OCEAN
N
0 10 km
© Hema Maps NZ Ltd
Groper Island
Flax Islands
Burgess Island SR
Mokohinau Islands Nature Reserve
Maori Rocks
Fanal Island
Navire Rock
Simpson Rock
Needles Pt
Aiguilles Island
Miners Head
Tataweka 526
Rangiwhakaea Bay
Ahuriri Pt
Katherine Bay
Motairehe
Maunganui Pt
Waikaro Pt
Whangapoua Beach
Whangapoua
Hautapu Pt
Tokawhero Pt
Rakitu Island SR
Te Akau Pt
Kawa
Okiwi RR
Okokewa Island
Port Abercrombie
Okiwi
Nelson Is
Kotuku Point Scenic Res
Motuhaku Island
Port Fitzroy
Harataonga
Harataonga Rec Res
Harataonga SR
Kaikoura Island
Akapoua Bay
Kaiaraara Hut
Grey Group Islands
Bushs Beach RR
Mt Hobson 627
Whakatautuna Pt
Opakau Is
Hirakimata
Kaitoke Swamp Eco Area
Red Bluff
Awana Stream & Stony Beach RR
Awana Bay
Awana Beach
Motutaiko Is
Wairahi Forest Sanctuary
Kaitoke Hot Springs
Rangiahua Is
Lion Rock
Broken Islands
Whangaparapara 309
Junction Islands
Whangaparapara
Claris Rec Res
Claris
Argo Tours / Rides
Whangara Is
Pitokuku Is
Okupu
Rock Fishing Tours
Ferry
Medlands Beach
Whangaparapara Hbr
Blind Bay
Tryphena Scenic Res
Tryphena
Windy Hill 361
Shag Pt
Ruahine 402
Tryphena Hbr
Cape Barrier
GREAT BARRIER ISLAND
Te Ananuiarau Bay
Ngatamahine Pt
Waimaomao Bay
Te Hue Pt
Hingaia Pt
Mt Hauturu 722
Te Titoki Pt
East Cape
Little Barrier Island Nature Reserve
Channel
Craddock
Colville Channel
Channel Island
Sealink ferry to Great Barrier Island
Ph (09) 300 5900 / 0800 732 546
www.sealink.co.nz
Ferry
Cape Colville
Port Jackson Rec Res
Fletcher Bay
Square Top Island
Stony Bay
Fletcher Bay RR
Stony Bay RR
Port Jackson
Kaiiti Pt
Coromandel Walkway
Port Charles
Sandy Bay
Fantail Bay Rec Res
Fantail Bay
Stony Bay
Coromandel FP
MOEHAU RANGE
Moehau 892
Sandy Bay RR
Rauporoa Bay
Te Anaputa Pt
Hauraki
Onekura 374
Potiki Bay
Puriora Pt
Waikawau Bay
Waikawau Bay SR
Coromandel FP
Wairo
Waikawau
Haupapa Pt
Whangaahei
Little Bay
Turipeka Pt
Otautu Pa HR
Colville Bay
Te Whau Pt
Whitestar Station Horse riding
Waikawau Bay Farm Park RR
Whanake Pt
Colville
Tuateawa
Coromandel Forest Park
Gulf
Motukawao Group
Motumakareta Island
Motukahaua Island
Waitete Bay
Colville Rd
Motuwi Island
Motukaramarama Island
Amodeo Bay
Kennedy Bay
Anarake Pt
Ahaaha Rocks
To Auckland
To Auckland
To Coromandel
175°00'E
175°15'E
175°30'E
36°00'S
36°15'S
36°30'S
2700000E
6500000N
1 2 3 4 5 6
A B C D E F G H J

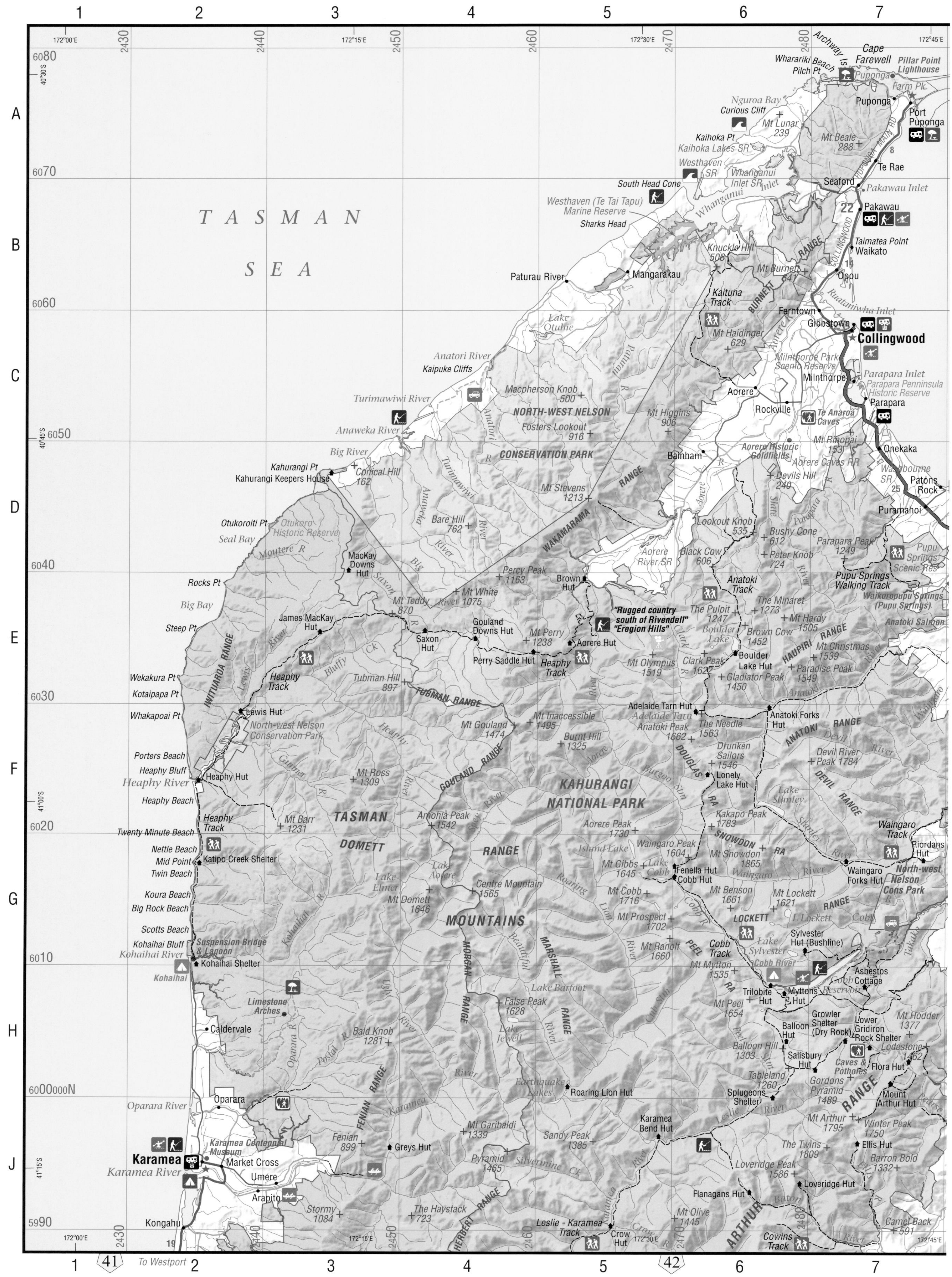

TASMAN SEA
Cape Farewell
Pillar Point Lighthouse
Wharariki Beach
Pilch Pt
Archway Is
Puponga
Farm Pk
Port Puponga
Nguroa Bay
Curious Cliff
Mt Lunar 239
Kaihoka Pt
Kaihoka Lakes SR
Mt Beale 288
Te Rae
Westhaven SR
Whanganui Inlet SR
Seaford
Pakawau Inlet
South Head Cone
Westhaven (Te Tai Tapu) Marine Reserve
Sharks Head
Whanganui Inlet
Pakawau
Taimatea Point
Waikato
Knuckle Hill 506
Mt Burnett 641
Paturau River
Mangarakau
Opou
Kaitune Track
Ruataniwha Inlet
Ferntown
Gibbstown
Collingwood
Lake Otuhie
Mt Haidinger 629
Milnthorpe Park Scenic Reserve
Milnthorpe
Parapara Inlet
Parapara Peninsula Historic Reserve
Anatori River
Kaipuke Cliffs
Macpherson Knob 500
Aorere
Parapara
Turimawiwi River
NORTH-WEST NELSON
Mt Higgins 906
Rockville
Te Anaroa Caves
Anaweka River
Fosters Lookout 916
CONSERVATION PARK
Bainham
Aorere Historic Goldfields
Mt Rimopai 153
Onekaka
Big River
Aorere Caves RR
Kahurangi Pt
Kahurangi Keepers House
Conical Hill 162
Devils Hill 240
Washbourne SR
Patons Rock
Mt Stevens 1213
RANGE
Puramahoi
Otukoroiti Pt
Otukoroiti Historic Reserve
Seal Bay
Bare Hill 762
WAKAMARAMA
Lookout Knob 535
Bushy Cone 612
Parapara Peak 1249
Moutere R
MacKay Downs Hut
Aorere River SR
Black Cow 606
Peter Knob 724
Pupu Springs Scenic Res
Percy Peak 1163
Brown Hut
Anatoki Track
Pupu Springs Walking Track
Rocks Pt
Big Bay
Mt White 1075
Mt Teddy 870
Waikoropupu Springs (Pupu Springs)
The Minaret 1273
The Pulpit 1247
James MacKay Hut
Steep Pt
Gouland Downs Hut
"Rugged country south of Rivendell" "Eregion Hills"
Boulder Lake
Mt Hardy 1505
Anatoki Salmon
Saxon Hut
Mt Perry 1238
Aorere Hut
Brown Cow 1452
HAUPIRI RANGE
Mt Christmas 1539
Perry Saddle Hut
Heaphy Track
Mt Olympus 1519
Clark Peak 1622
Boulder Lake Hut
Paradise Peak 1549
Wekakura Pt
Heaphy Track
Tubman Hill 897
Gladiator Peak 1450
Kotaipapa Pt
TUBMAN RANGE
IWITUAROA RANGE
Lewis Hut
Adelaide Tarn Hut
Adelaide Tarn
Anatoki Forks Hut
Whakapoai Pt
North-west Nelson Conservation Park
Mt Gouland 1474
Mt Inaccessible 1495
Anatoki Peak 1662
The Needle 1563
ANATOKI RANGE
Burnt Hill 1325
Drunken Sailors 1546
Porters Beach
GOULAND RANGE
DOUGLAS RA
Devil River Peak 1784
Heaphy Bluff
Heaphy Hut
Heaphy River
Mt Ross 1309
KAHURANGI NATIONAL PARK
Lonely Lake Hut
DEVIL RANGE
Heaphy Beach
Lake Stanley
Heaphy Track
Twenty Minute Beach
Mt Barr 1231
TASMAN
Amohia Peak 1542
Aorere Peak 1730
Kakapo Peak 1783
Waingaro Track
Nettle Beach
Mid Point
Katipo Creek Shelter
DOMETT
RANGE
Island Lake
Waingaro Peak 1604
SNOWDON RA
Riordans Hut
Twin Beach
Mt Gibbs 1645
Lake Cobb
Fenella Hut
Cobb Hut
Mt Snowdon 1865
Waingaro Forks Hut
North-west Nelson Cons Park
Lake Aorere
Lake Elmer
Centre Mountain 1565
Koura Beach
Big Rock Beach
Mt Domett 1646
Mt Cobb 1716
Mt Benson 1661
Mt Lockett 1621
MOUNTAINS
Mt Prospect 1702
LOCKETT RANGE
L Lockett
Scotts Beach
Kohaihai Bluff
Suspension Bridge & Lagoon
MORGAN RANGE
MARSHALL RANGE
Mt Ranolf 1660
Sylvester Hut (Bushline)
Kohaihai River
Kohaihai Shelter
PEEL RA
Cobb Track
Lake Sylvester
Mt Mytton 1535
Cobb River
Asbestos Cottage
Kohaihai
Lake Barfoot
Trilobite Hut
Myttons Hut
Cobb Reservoir
Limestone Arches
False Peak 1628
Mt Peel 1654
Growler Shelter (Dry Rock)
Lower Gridiron
Rock Shelter
Mt Hodder 1377
Caldervale
Bald Knob 1281
Lake Jewell
Balloon Hut
Balloon Hill 1303
Salisbury Hut
Lodestone 1462
Caves & Pothores
Flora Hut
FENIAN RANGE
Earthquake Lakes
Roaring Lion Hut
Tableland 1260
Gordons Pyramid 1489
RANGE
Mount Arthur Hut
Oparara
Oparara River
Spulgeons Shelter
Mt Garibaldi 1339
Karamea Bend Hut
Mt Arthur 1795
Winter Peak 1750
Fenian 899
Greys Hut
Sandy Peak 1385
The Twins 1809
Ellis Hut
Karamea Centennial Museum
Karamea
Market Cross
Karamea River
Pyramid 1465
Silvermine Ck
Loveridge Peak 1586
Barron Bold 1332
Umere
Loveridge Hut
Arapito
Flanagans Hut
Stormy 1084
The Haystack 723
HERBERT RANGE
ARTHUR
Mt Olive 1445
Kongahu
Leslie - Karamea Track
Crow Hut
Camel Back 591
Cowins Track
To Westport
41
42

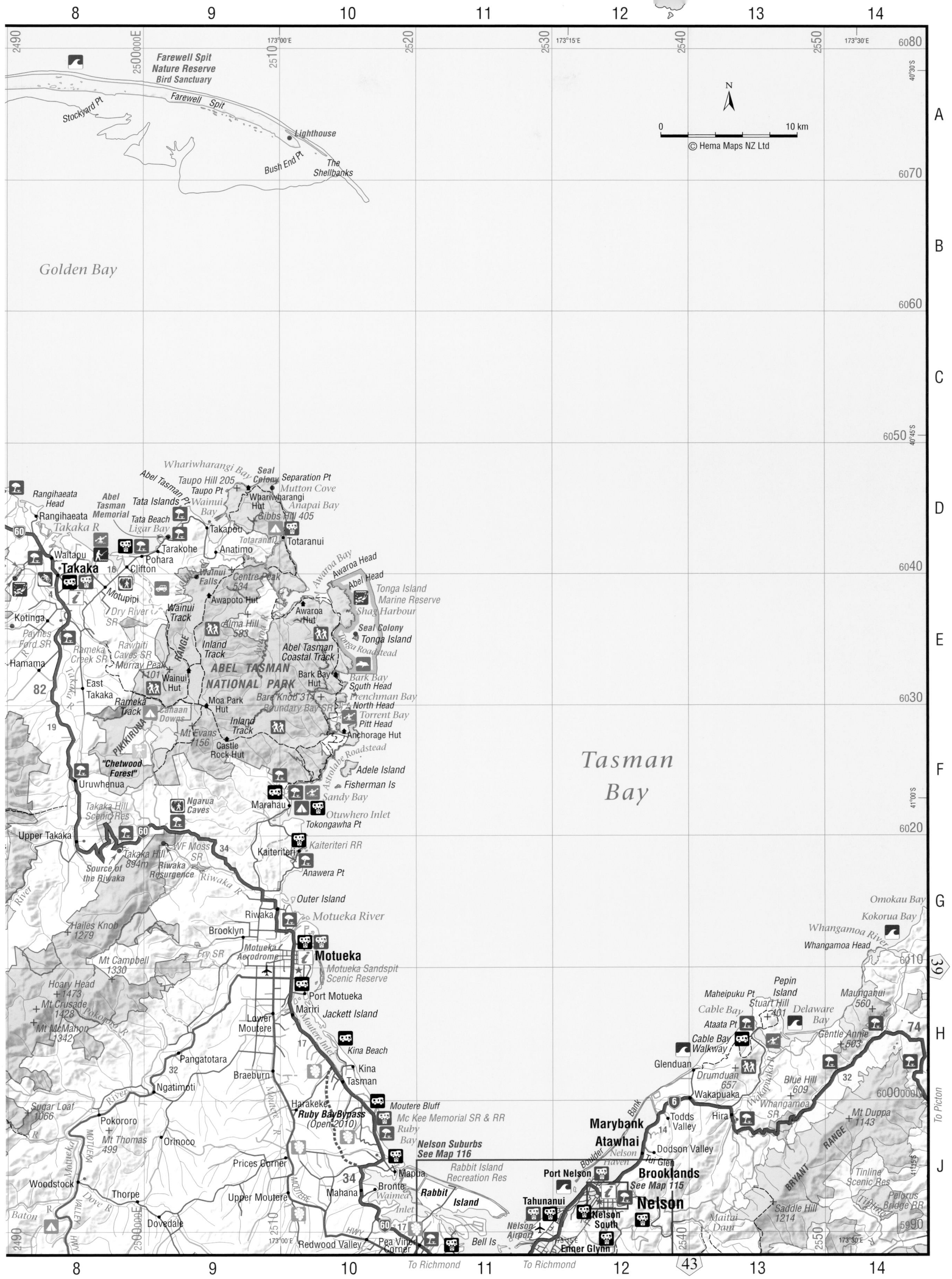

Farewell Spit
Nature Reserve
Bird Sanctuary
Farewell Spit
Stockyard Pt
Lighthouse
Bush End Pt
The Shellbanks
0
10 km
© Hema Maps NZ Ltd
Golden Bay
Tasman
Bay
Whariwharangi Bay
Seal Colony
Separation Pt
Mutton Cove
Abel Tasman Pt
Taupo Hill 205
Taupo Pt
Whariwharangi Hut
Anapai Bay
Rangihaeata Head
Abel Tasman Memorial
Tata Islands
Wainui Bay
Gibbs Hill 405
Rangihaeata
Takaka R
Tata Beach
Ligar Bay
Takapou
Totaranui
Tarakohe
Anatimo
Waitapu
Takaka
Pohara
Clifton
Awaroa Bay
Awaroa Head
Abel Head
Wainui Falls
Centre Peak 534
Tonga Island Marine Reserve
Motupipi
Awapoto Hut
Dry River SR
Kotinga
Wainui Track
Alma Hill 583
Awaroa Hut
Shag Harbour
Seal Colony
Tonga Island
Payne's Ford SR
Rawhiti Caves SR
Inland Track
Abel Tasman Coastal Track
Tonga Roadstead
Rameka Creek SR
Hamama
Murray Peak 1101
ABEL TASMAN NATIONAL PARK
Bark Bay Hut
Bark Bay
South Head
East Takaka
Wainui Hut
Bare Knob 314
Frenchman Bay
Boundary Bay SR
North Head
Moa Park Hut
Rameka Track
Canaan Downs
Torrent Bay
Pitt Head
Anchorage Hut
Mt Evans 1156
Inland Track
PIKIKIRUNA
Castle Rock Hut
Astrolabe Roadstead
"Chetwood Forest"
Adele Island
Uruwhenua
Fisherman Is
Marahau
Sandy Bay
Takaka Hill Scenic Res
Ngarua Caves
Otuwhero Inlet
Tokongawha Pt
Upper Takaka
WF Moss SR
Kaiteriteri RR
Takaka Hill 894m
Kaiteriteri
Source of the Riwaka
Riwaka Resurgence
Anawera Pt
Riwaka R
Outer Island
Riwaka
Motueka River
Hailes Knob 1279
Brooklyn
Motueka Aerodrome
Motueka
Mt Campbell 1330
Fry SR
Motueka Sandspit Scenic Reserve
Hoary Head 1473
Port Motueka
Mt Crusade 1428
Mariri
Jackett Island
Mt McMahon 1342
Lower Moutere
Moutere Inlet
Kina Beach
Pangatotara
Kina
Braeburn
Tasman
Ngatimoti
Sugar Loaf 1066
Harakeke
Moutere Bluff
Ruby Bay Bypass (Open 2010)
Mc Kee Memorial SR & RR
Ruby Bay
Pokororo
Mt Thomas 499
Orinoco
Nelson Suburbs See Map 116
Prices Corner
Rabbit Island Recreation Res
Mapua
Woodstock
Thorpe
Upper Moutere
Mahana
Bronte
Waimea Inlet
Rabbit Island
Dovedale
Redwood Valley
Pea Viner Corner
Bell Is
To Richmond
To Richmond
Omokau Bay
Kokorua Bay
Whangamoa River
Whangamoa Head
Pepin Island
Maheipuku Pt
Stuart Hill 401
Maungahui 560
Cable Bay
Delaware Bay
Ataata Pt
Cable Bay Walkway
Gentle Annie 503
Glenduan
Drumduan 657
Blue Hill 609
Wakapuaka
Whangamoa SR
Hira
Mt Duppa 1143
Marybank
Todds Valley
Atawhai
Dodson Valley
Boulder Bank
Nelson Haven
Port Nelson
Brooklands
See Map 115
Tahunanui
Nelson
Nelson South
Nelson Airport
Enner Glynn
Maitai Dam
BRYANT RANGE
Tinline Scenic Res
Saddle Hill 1214
Pelorus Bridge RR
To Picton

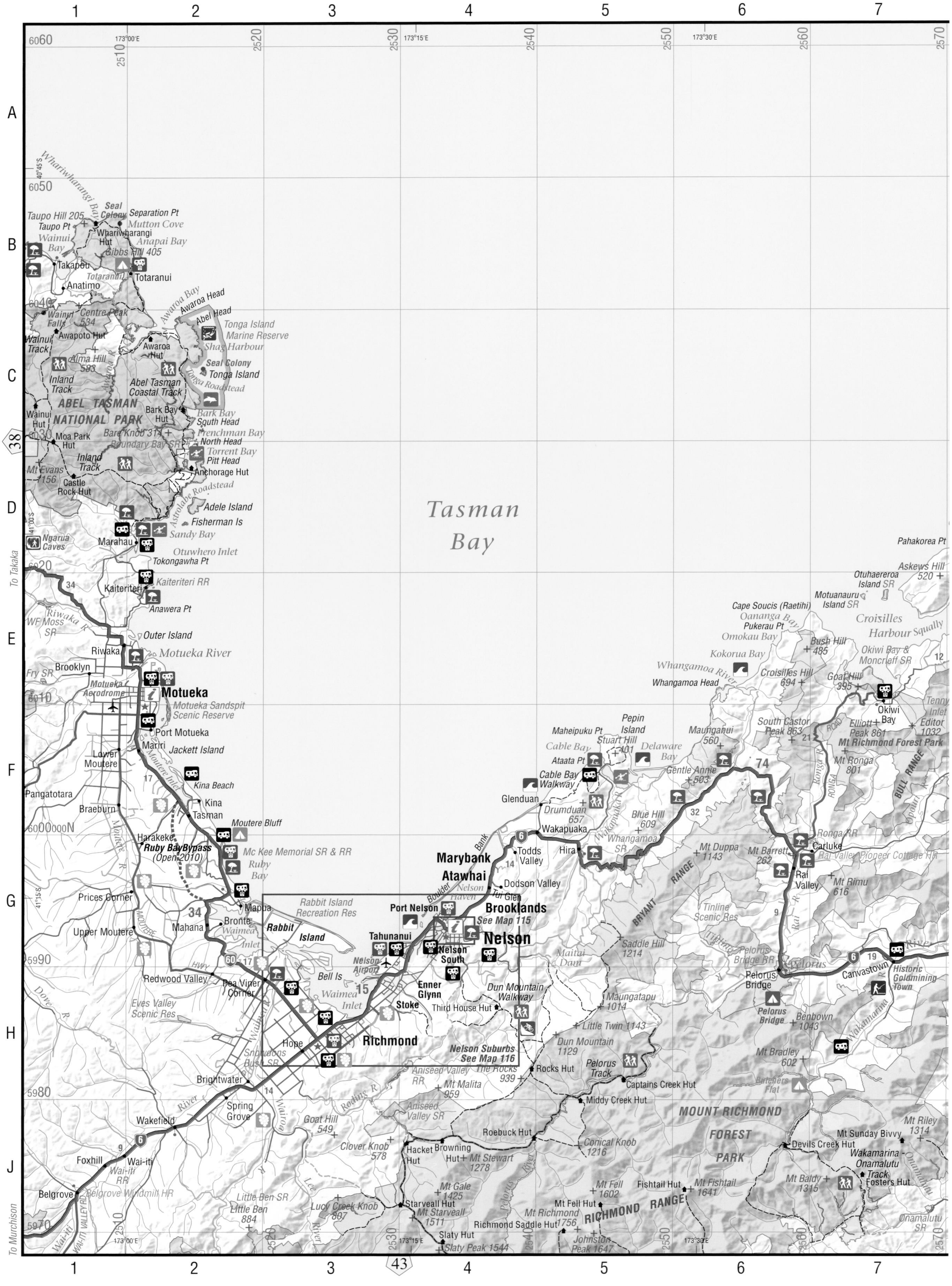
Tasman Bay
ABEL TASMAN NATIONAL PARK
Abel Tasman Coastal Track
Inland Track
Seal Colony
Separation Pt
Mutton Cove
Anapai Bay
Whariwharangi Bay
Whariwharangi Hut
Taupo Hill 205
Taupo Pt
Wainui Bay
Gibbs Hill 405
Takapou
Totaranui
Anatimo
Awaroa Bay
Awaroa Head
Abel Head
Tonga Island Marine Reserve
Shag Harbour
Seal Colony
Tonga Island
Tonga Roadstead
Centre Peak 534
Wainui Falls
Awapoto Hut
Wainui Track
Awaroa Hut
Alma Hill 593
Bark Bay Hut
Bark Bay
South Head
Frenchman Bay
North Head
Torrent Bay
Pitt Head
Anchorage Hut
Wainui Hut
Moa Park Hut
Bare Knob 314
Boundary Bay SR
Mt Evans 1156
Castle Rock Hut
Astrolabe Roadstead
Adele Island
Fisherman Is
Sandy Bay
Ngarua Caves
Marahau
Otuwhero Inlet
Tokongawha Pt
Kaiteriteri
Kaiteriteri RR
Anawera Pt
Riwaka R
WF Moss SR
Outer Island
Riwaka
Motueka River
Brooklyn
Fry SR
Motueka Aerodrome
Motueka
Motueka Sandspit Scenic Reserve
Port Motueka
Jackett Island
Lower Moutere
Marriri
Moutere Inlet
Kina Beach
Kina
Tasman
Pangatotara
Braeburn
Moutere Bluff
Harakeke
Ruby Bay Bypass (Open 2010)
Mc Kee Memorial SR & RR
Ruby Bay
Prices Corner
Mapua
Mahana
Bronte
Upper Moutere
Rabbit Island Recreation Res
Rabbit Island
Waimea Inlet
Redwood Valley
Pea Viner Corner
Bell Is
Nelson Airport
Eves Valley Scenic Res
Hope
Snowdons Bush SR
Brightwater
Spring Grove
Wakefield
Foxhill
Wai-iti
Wai-iti RR
Belgrove
Belgrove Windmill HR
Tahunanui
Port Nelson
Nelson Haven
Boulder Bank
Brooklands
See Map 115
Nelson
Nelson South
Enner Glynn
Stoke
Richmond
Third House Hut
Dun Mountain Walkway
Nelson Suburbs See Map 116
Marybank
Atawhai
Todds Valley
Dodson Valley
Tui Glen
Glenduan
Wakapuaka
Drumduan 657
Hira
Whangamoa SR
Blue Hill 609
Cable Bay
Cable Bay Walkway
Ataata Pt
Maheipuku Pt
Pepin Island
Stuart Hill 401
Delaware Bay
Maungahui 560
Gentle Annie 503
Whangamoa Head
Whangamoa River
Kokorua Bay
Omokau Bay
Pukerau Pt
Oananga Bay
Cape Soucis (Raetihi)
Croisilles Hill 694
Bush Hill 485
Croisilles Harbour
Motuanauru Island SR
Otuhaereroa Island SR
Askews Hill 520
Pahakorea Pt
Okiwi Bay & Moncrieff SR
Goat Hill 395
Okiwi Bay
South Castor Peak 863
Elliott Peak 861
Editor 1032
Mt Richmond Forest Park
Mt Ronga 801
BULL RANGE
Rongo RR
Rai Valley Pioneer Cottage HR
Carluke
Mt Barrett 262
Rai Valley
Mt Rimu 616
Mt Duppa 1143
BRYANT RANGE
Tinline Scenic Res
Saddle Hill 1214
Maitai Dam
Pelorus Bridge RR
Pelorus Bridge
Pelorus River
Canvastown
Historic Goldmining Town
Maungatapu 1014
Little Twin 1143
Dun Mountain 1129
Pelorus Track
Benbown 1043
Mt Bradley 602
Rocks Hut
The Rocks 939
Aniseed Valley RR
Mt Malita 959
Captains Creek Hut
Middy Creek Hut
Aniseed Valley SR
Goat Hill 549
Roding R
MOUNT RICHMOND FOREST PARK
Roebuck Hut
Conical Knob 1216
Clover Knob 578
Hacket Hut
Browning Hut
Mt Stewart 1278
Devils Creek Hut
Mt Sunday Bivvy
Mt Riley 1314
Wakamarina - Onamalutu Track
Fosters Hut
Mt Baldy 1315
Mt Gale 1425
Starveall Hut
Mt Starveall 1511
Mt Fell 1602
Mt Fell Hut
Fishtail Hut
Mt Fishtail 1641
Mt Richmond 1756
Richmond Saddle Hut
RICHMOND RANGE
Little Ben SR
Little Ben 884
Lucy Creek Knob 807
Slaty Hut
Slaty Peak 1544
Johnston Peak 1647
Onamalutu SR
To Takaka
To Murchison
173°00'E
173°15'E
173°30'E
41°00'S
41°15'S
40°45'S
6000000N
1 2 3 4 5 6 7
A B C D E F G H J

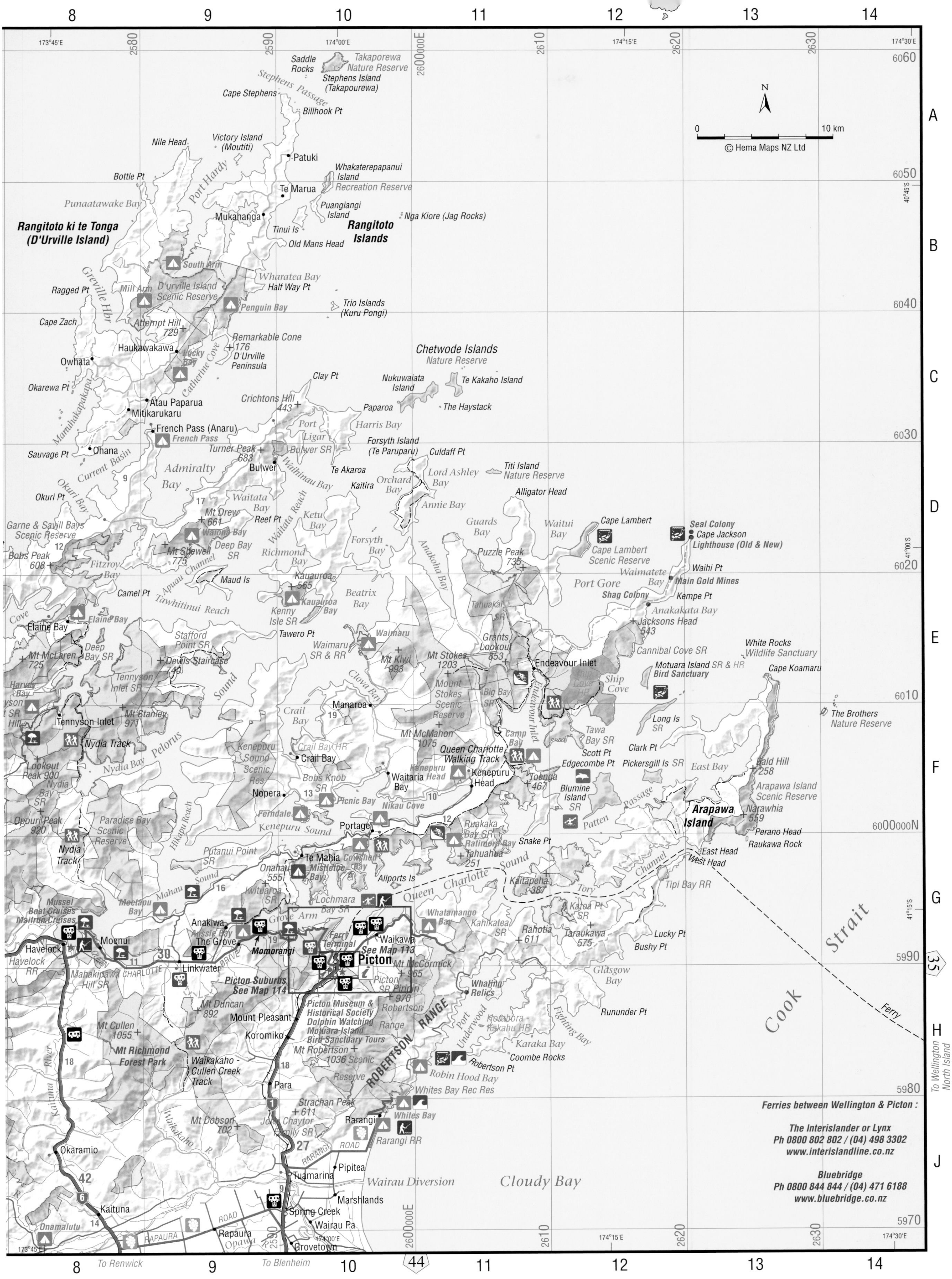

8
9
10
11
12
13
14
A
B
C
D
E
F
G
H
J
© Hema Maps NZ Ltd
0
10 km
N
Saddle Rocks
Takaporewa Nature Reserve
Stephens Island (Takapourewa)
Stephens Passage
Cape Stephens
Billhook Pt
Nile Head
Victory Island (Moutiti)
Patuki
Bottle Pt
Port Hardy
Whakaterepapanui Island Recreation Reserve
Te Marua
Punaatawake Bay
Mukahanga
Puangiangi Island
Nga Kiore (Jag Rocks)
Tinui Is
Rangitoto Islands
Rangitoto ki te Tonga (D'Urville Island)
Old Mans Head
South Arm
Wharatea Bay
Half Way Pt
Ragged Pt
Greville Hbr
Mill Arm
D'urville Island Scenic Reserve
Trio Islands (Kuru Pongi)
Penguin Bay
Cape Zach
Attempt Hill 729
Remarkable Cone 176
Haukawakawa
Chetwode Islands Nature Reserve
Owhata
D'Urville Peninsula
Lucky Bay
Catherine Cove
Clay Pt
Okarewa Pt
Nukuwaiata Island
Te Kakaho Island
Atau Paparua
Crichtons Hill 443
Mitikarukaru
Paparoa
The Haystack
French Pass (Anaru)
Port Ligar
Harris Bay
French Pass
Forsyth Island (Te Paruparu)
Sauvage Pt
Ohana
Turner Peak 683
Bulwer SR
Culdaff Pt
Current Basin
Admiralty Bay
Bulwer
Te Akaroa
Lord Ashley Bay
Titi Island Nature Reserve
Kaitira
Orchard Bay
Okuri Pt
Okuri Bay
Waitata Bay
Annie Bay
Alligator Head
Mt Drew 661
Reef Pt
Waitata Reach
Ketu Bay
Guards Bay
Waitui Bay
Cape Lambert
Seal Colony
Cape Jackson
Lighthouse (Old & New)
Garne & Savill Bays Scenic Reserve
Waiona Bay
Forsyth Bay
Bobs Peak 608
Mt Shewell 775
Deep Bay SR
Richmond Bay
Puzzle Peak 735
Cape Lambert Scenic Reserve
Waihi Pt
Fitzroy Bay
Apuau Channel
Maud Is
Kauauroa 565
Waimatete Bay
Port Gore
Main Gold Mines
Camel Pt
Tawhitinui Reach
Kauauroa Bay
Beatrix Bay
Shag Colony
Kempe Pt
Kenny Isle SR
Tahuakai SR
Anakakata Bay
Elaine Bay
Jacksons Head 543
Cove
Tawero Pt
Waimaru
Grants Lookout 853
Stafford Point SR
Cannibal Cove SR
White Rocks Wildlife Sanctuary
Mt McLaren 725
Deep Bay SR
Devils Staircase 740
Waimaru SR & RR
Mt Kiwi 993
Mt Stokes 1203
Endeavour Inlet
Motuara Island SR & HR
Bird Sanctuary
Cape Koamaru
Tennyson Inlet SR
Clova Bay
Mount Stokes Scenic Reserve
Big Bay SR
Ship Cove
Harvey Bay
Mt Stanley 971
Manaroa
Tennyson Inlet
Crail Bay
Pelorus Sound
Endeavour Inlet
The Brothers Nature Reserve
Nydia Track
Long Is SR
Mt McMahon 1075
Camp Bay
Tawa Bay SR
Crail Bay HR
Crail Bay
Kenepuru Sound Scenic Res
Queen Charlotte Walking Track
Scott Pt
Clark Pt
Bald Hill 258
Lookout Peak 900
Nydia Bay SR
Nydia Bay
Bobs Knob SR
Waitaria Bay
Kenepuru Head
Toenga 467
Edgecombe Pt
Pickersgill Is SR
East Bay
Nopera
Blumine Island SR
Arapawa Island Scenic Reserve
Opouri Peak 920
Paradise Bay Scenic Reserve
Hikapu Reach
Picnic Bay
Nikau Cove
Ferndale
Patten Passage
Arapawa Island
Narawhia 559
Kenepuru Sound
Portage
Ruakaka Bay SR
Ratimera Bay
Snake Pt
Perano Head
Raukawa Rock
Nydia Track
Putanui Point SR
Te Mahia
Cowshed Bay
Tahuahua 251
East Head
West Head
Onahau 555
Mistletoe Bay
Allports Is
Queen Charlotte Sound
Kaitapeha 387
Channel
Tory
Tipi Bay RR
Mahau Sound
Iwituaroa SR
Mussel Boat Cruises
Mail Run Cruises
Moetapu Bay
Lochmara Bay SR
Grove Arm
Whatamango Bay
Kahikatea SR
Karaka Pt SR
Cook Strait
Anakiwa
Aussie Bay
The Grove
Ferry Terminal
Waikawa
Rahotia 611
Tarakawa 575
Lucky Pt
Bushy Pt
Havelock
Moenui
30
Momorangi
See Map 113
Picton
Havelock RR
Linkwater
Mt McCormick 965
Glasgow Bay
Mahakipawa Hill SR
Queen Charlotte Drive
Picton Suburbs See Map 114
Picton SR
Piripiri 970
Whaling Relics
Mt Duncan 892
Picton Museum & Historical Society
Dolphin Watching
Motuara Island Bird Sanctuary Tours
Robertson Range
Robertson Range
Port Underwood
Rununder Pt
Ferry
Mt Cullen 1055
Mount Pleasant
Koromiko
Kakahu HR
Fighting Bay
Karaka Bay
Mt Richmond Forest Park
Waikakaho - Cullen Creek Track
Mt Robertson 1036
Scenic Reserve
Coombe Rocks
Robertson Pt
Robin Hood Bay
Kaituna River
Para
Whites Bay Rec Res
To Wellington North Island
Strachan Peak 611
Mt Dobson 702
John Chaytor Family SR
Rarangi
Whites Bay
Rarangi RR
Rarangi Road
Ferries between Wellington & Picton :
The Interislander or Lynx
Ph 0800 802 802 / (04) 498 3302
www.interislandline.co.nz
Okaramio
Tuamarina
Pipitea
Wairau Diversion
Cloudy Bay
Bluebridge
Ph 0800 844 844 / (04) 471 6188
www.bluebridge.co.nz
42
Kaituna
Marshlands
Spring Creek
Wairau Pa
Onamalutu
Rapaura Road
Rapaura
Opawa
Grovetown
To Renwick
To Blenheim
44

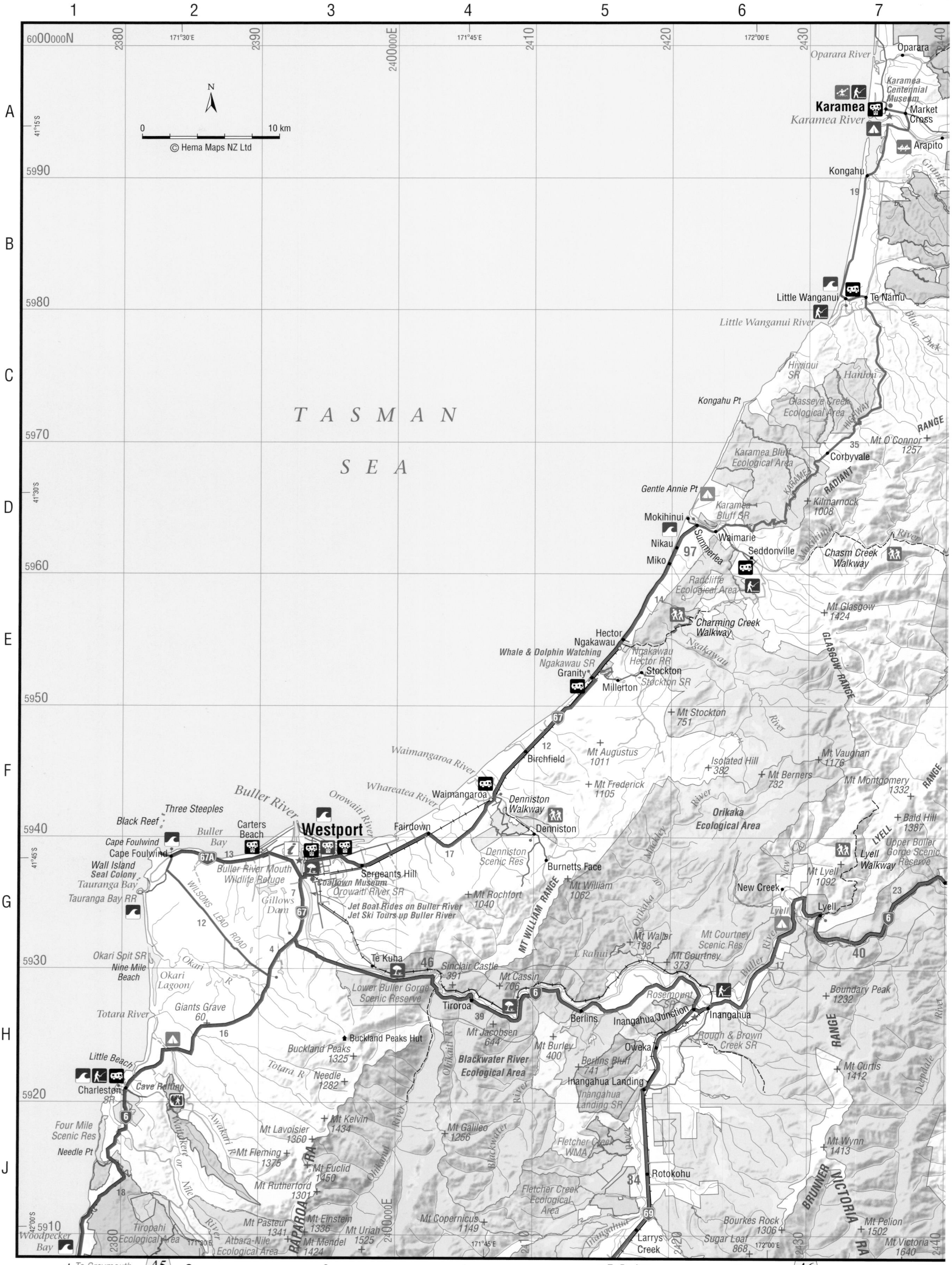

TASMAN SEA
© Hema Maps NZ Ltd
0
10 km
N
Oparara
Oparara River
Karamea Centennial Museum
Karamea
Market Cross
Karamea River
Arapito
Kongahu
Little Wanganui
Te Namu
Little Wanganui River
Hiwinui SR
Kongahu Pt
Glasseye Creek Ecological Area
Mt O'Connor 1257
Corbyvale
Karamea Bluff Ecological Area
Gentle Annie Pt
Karamea Bluff SR
RADIANT RANGE
Kilmarnock 1008
Mokihinui
Nikau
Miko
Waimarie
Summerlea
Seddonville
Chasm Creek Walkway
Radcliffe Ecological Area
Mt Glasgow 1424
Charming Creek Walkway
Hector
Ngakawau
Whale & Dolphin Watching
Ngakawau SR
Ngakawau Hector RR
Granity
Stockton
Millerton
Stockton SR
GLASGOW RANGE
Mt Stockton 751
Birchfield
Mt Augustus 1011
Waimangaroa River
Isolated Hill 382
Mt Vaughan 1176
Mt Berners 732
Mt Montgomery 1332
Whareatea River
Waimangaroa
Mt Frederick 1105
Denniston Walkway
Orikaka Ecological Area
Buller River
Orowaiti River
Three Steeples
Black Reef
Buller Bay
Carters Beach
Westport
Fairdown
Denniston
Bald Hill 1387
Upper Buller Gorge Scenic Reserve
Lyell Walkway
LYELL RANGE
Cape Foulwind
Wall Island Seal Colony
Tauranga Bay
Tauranga Bay RR
Buller River Mouth Wildlife Refuge
Coaltown Museum
Orowaiti River SR
Sergeants Hill
Denniston Scenic Res
Burnetts Face
Mt William 1062
Mt Lyell 1092
New Creek
WILSONS LEAD ROAD
Gillows Dam
Jet Boat Rides on Buller River
Jet Ski Tours up Buller River
Mt Rochfort 1040
MT WILLIAM RANGE
Lyell
Mt Waller 798
Mt Courtney Scenic Res
Mt Courtney 373
Okari Spit SR
Nine Mile Beach
Okari Lagoon
Te Kuha
Sinclair Castle 391
Mt Cassin 706
Lower Buller Gorge Scenic Reserve
Tiroroa
Berlins
Inangahua Junction
Inangahua
Rosemount SR
Boundary Peak 1232
Totara River
Giants Grave 60
Buckland Peaks Hut
Mt Jacobsen 644
Mt Burley 400
Rough & Brown Creek SR
Buckland Peaks 1325
Oweka
Berlins Bluff 741
Mt Curtis 1412
Little Beach
Blackwater River Ecological Area
Needle 1282
Inangahua Landing
Inangahua Landing SR
Charleston
Cave Rafting
Four Mile Scenic Res
Needle Pt
Mt Kelvin 1434
Mt Lavoisier 1360
Mt Galileo 1256
Mt Fleming 1375
Fletcher Creek WMA
Mt Wynn 1413
Mt Euclid 1450
Rotokohu
Mt Rutherford 1301
Fletcher Creek Ecological Area
BRUNNER RANGE
VICTORIA RA
Mt Pasteur 1341
Mt Einstein 1336
Mt Copernicus 1149
Bourkes Rock 1306
Mt Pelion 1502
Woodpecker Bay
Tiropahi Ecological Area
Atbara-Nile Ecological Area
Mt Mendel 1424
Mt Uriah 1525
PAPAROA RA
Larrys Creek
Sugar Loaf 868
Mt Victoria 1640
To Greymouth
To Reefton

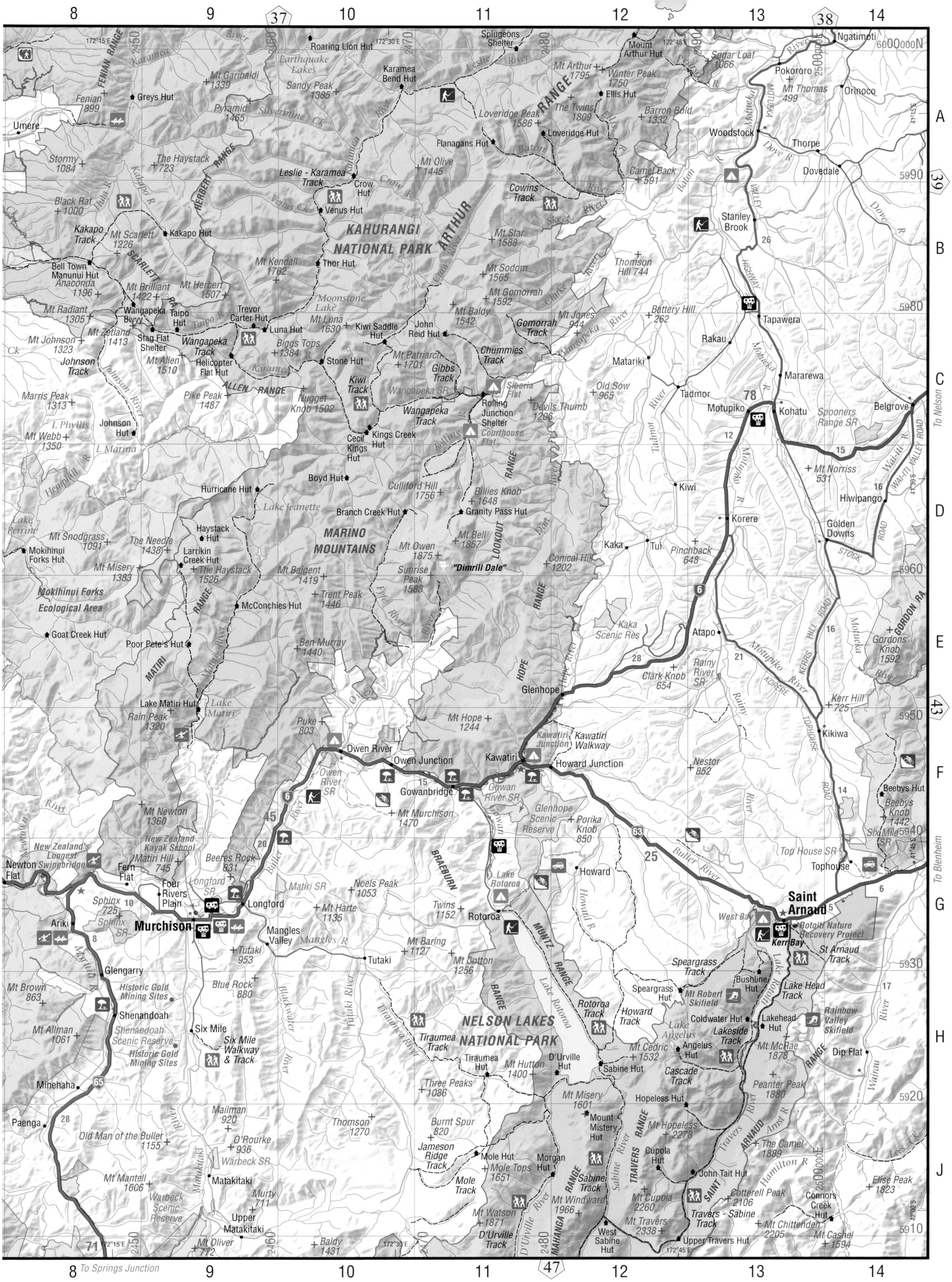

8
9
10
11
12
13
14
37
38
39
43
47
A
B
C
D
E
F
G
H
J
Roaring Lion Hut
Splugeons Shelter
Mount Arthur Hut
Ngatimoti
Sugar Loaf 1066
FENIAN RANGE
Karamea River
Earthquake Lakes
Mt Garibaldi 1339
Sandy Peak 1385
Karamea Bend Hut
Mt Arthur 1795
Winter Peak 1750
Pokororo
Mt Thomas 499
Orinoco
Fenian 899
Greys Hut
Pyramid 1465
Silvermine Ck
Ellis Hut
Barron Bold 1332
Umere
Loveridge Peak 1586
The Twins 1809
ARTHUR RANGE
Loveridge Hut
Woodstock
Thorpe
Flanagans Hut
Baton
Stormy 1084
The Haystack 723
Mt Olive 1445
Camel Back 591
Dovedale
Dove R
HERBERT RANGE
Leslie - Karamea Track
Crow Hut
Cowins Track
Black Rat 1000
Venus Hut
Stanley Brook
Kakapo Track
Mt Scarlett 1226
Kakapo Hut
KAHURANGI NATIONAL PARK
Mt Star 1588
Thomson Hill 744
Bell Town Manunui Hut
Anaconda 1196
Mt Kendall 1762
Thor Hut
SCARLETT RA
Mt Brilliant 1422
Mt Herbert 1507
Mt Sodom 1565
Mt Gomorrah 1592
Moonstone Lake
Battery Hill 262
Tapawera
Mt Radiant 1305
Wangapeka Bivvy
Taipo Hut
Trevor Carter Hut
Mt Luna 1630
Kiwi Saddle Hut
John Reid Hut
Mt Baldy 1542
Gomorrah Track
Mt Jones 944
Rakau
Mt Johnson 1323
Mt Zetland 1413
Stag Flat Shelter
Luna Hut
Wangapeka Track
Biggs Tops 1384
Mt Patriarch 1701
Chummies Track
Matariki
Johnson Track
Mt Allen 1510
Helicopter Flat Hut
Stone Hut
Gibbs Track
Mararewa
ALLEN RANGE
Kiwi Track
Wangapeka SR
Siberia Flat
Old Sow 965
Tadmor
Marris Peak 1313
Pike Peak 1487
Nugget Knob 1502
Rolling Junction Shelter
Devils Thumb 1206
Motupiko
Kohatu
Spooners Range SR
Belgrove
To Nelson
L Phyllis
Johnson Hut
Wangapeka Track
Kings Creek Hut
Cecil Kings Hut
Courthouse Flat
Mt Webb 1350
L Marina
Mt Norriss 531
WAI-ITI VALLEY ROAD
Boyd Hut
Hurricane Hut
Culliford Hill 1756
Billies Knob 1648
Kiwi
Hiwipango
Lake Jeanette
Branch Creek Hut
Granity Pass Hut
Korere
Lake Rerrine
Mt Snodgrass 1091
Haystack Hut
MARINO MOUNTAINS
Golden Downs
Mokihinui Forks Hut
The Needle 1438
Larrikin Creek Hut
Mt Owen 1875
Mt Bell 1857
LOOKOUT RANGE
Kaka
Tui
Pinchback 648
Mt Misery 1383
The Haystack 1526
Mt Baigent 1419
Sunrise Peak 1583
"Dimrill Dale"
Conical Hill 1202
Mokihinui Forks Ecological Area
Trent Peak 1446
McConchies Hut
Fyfe River
GORDON RA
Kaka Scenic Res
Atapo
Goat Creek Hut
Poor Pete's Hut
Ben Murray 1440
Gordons Knob 1592
MATIRI
Clark Knob 654
Rainy River SR
Motupiko River
KERRS HILL ROAD
Glenhope
HOPE RANGE
Kerr Hill 725
Lake Matiri Hut
Lake Matiri
Rain Peak 1320
Puke 803
Mt Hope 1244
Kikiwa
Owen River
Kawatiri Junction
Kawatiri Walkway
Owen Junction
Kawatiri
Howard Junction
Nestor 852
Beebys Hut
Owen River SR
Gowanbridge
Gowan River SR
Beebys Knob 1442
Mt Newton 1360
Mt Murchison 1470
Glenhope Scenic Reserve
Porika Knob 850
Six Mile SR
New Zealand's Longest Swingbridge
New Zealand Kayak School
Matiri Hill 745
Beeres Rock 631
BRAEBURN
Top House SR
Newton Flat
Fern Flat
Howard
Tophouse
To Blenheim
Four Rivers Plain
Longford SR
Matiri SR
Noels Peak 1053
Lake Rotoroa
Buller River
Saint Arnaud
Sphinx 725
Sphinx SR
Longford
Mt Harte 1135
Twins 1152
West Bay
Rotoiti Nature Recovery Project
Ariki
Murchison
Mangles Valley
Rotoroa
Kerr Bay
Mt Baring 1127
Mangles R
Tutaki
Mt Cotton 1256
St Arnaud Track
Tutaki 953
Glengarry
Speargrass Track
Bushline Hut
Lake Head Track
Historic Gold Mining Sites
Blue Rock 880
MONTZ RANGE
Speargrass Hut
Mt Robert Skifield
Mt Brown 863
Shenandoah
Rotoroa Track
Howard Track
Lakehead Hut
Rainbow Valley Skifield
Lake Rotoroa
Coldwater Hut
Lakeside Track
Mt Allman 1061
Six Mile
NELSON LAKES NATIONAL PARK
Lake Angelus
Shenandoah Scenic Reserve
Six Mile Walkway & Track
Tiraumea Track
Mt Cedric 1532
Angelus Hut
Mt McRae 1878
Dip Flat
Historic Gold Mining Sites
Tiraumea Hut
Mt Hutton 1400
D'Urville Hut
Sabine Hut
Cascade Track
Minehaha
Three Peaks 1086
Peanter Peak 1880
Mt Misery 1601
Hopeless Hut
Mailman 920
Thomson 1270
Mount Mistery Hut
TRAVERS RANGE
Mt Hopeless 2278
Paenga
Burnt Spur 820
Old Man of the Buller 1155
O'Rourke 936
Warbeck SR
Jameson Ridge Track
Cupola Hut
The Camel 1889
Mole Hut
Mole Tops 1651
Morgan Hut
Hamilton R
Lees Ck
Mt Mantell 1606
Matakitaki
Mole Track
Sabine Track
John Tait Hut
Elise Peak 1823
Warbeck Scenic Reserve
Murty 711
Mt Cupola 2260
Cotterell Peak 2106
Connors Creek Hut
Mt Watson 1871
Mt Windward 1966
MAHANGA RANGE
SAINT ARNAUD
Travers - Sabine Track
Upper Matakitaki
D'Urville Track
Mt Travers 2338
Mt Chittenden 2205
Mt Cashel 1594
Mt Oliver 772
Baldy 1431
West Sabine Hut
Upper Travers Hut
To Springs Junction

1 2 3 4 5 6 7

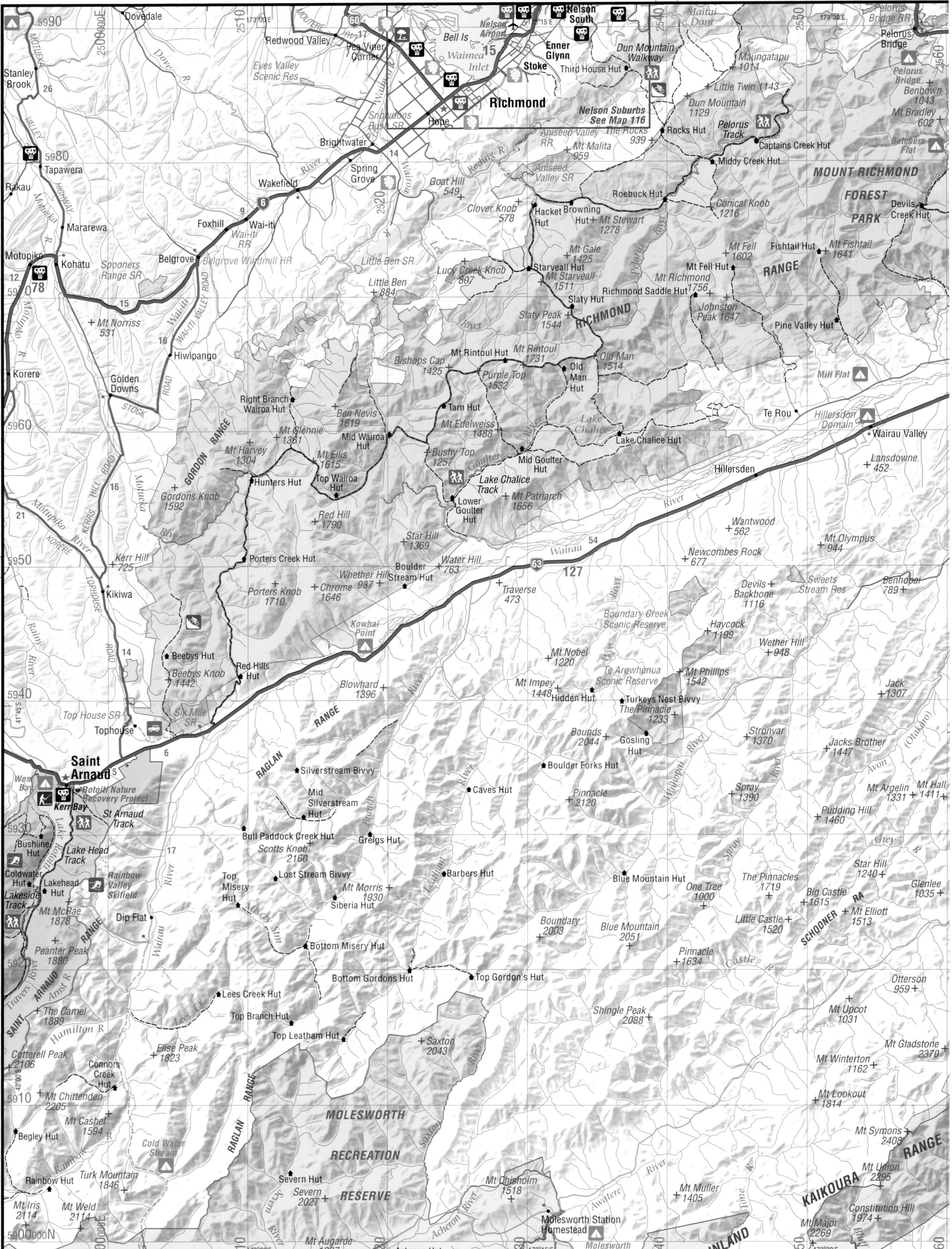

1 2 3 4 5 6 7

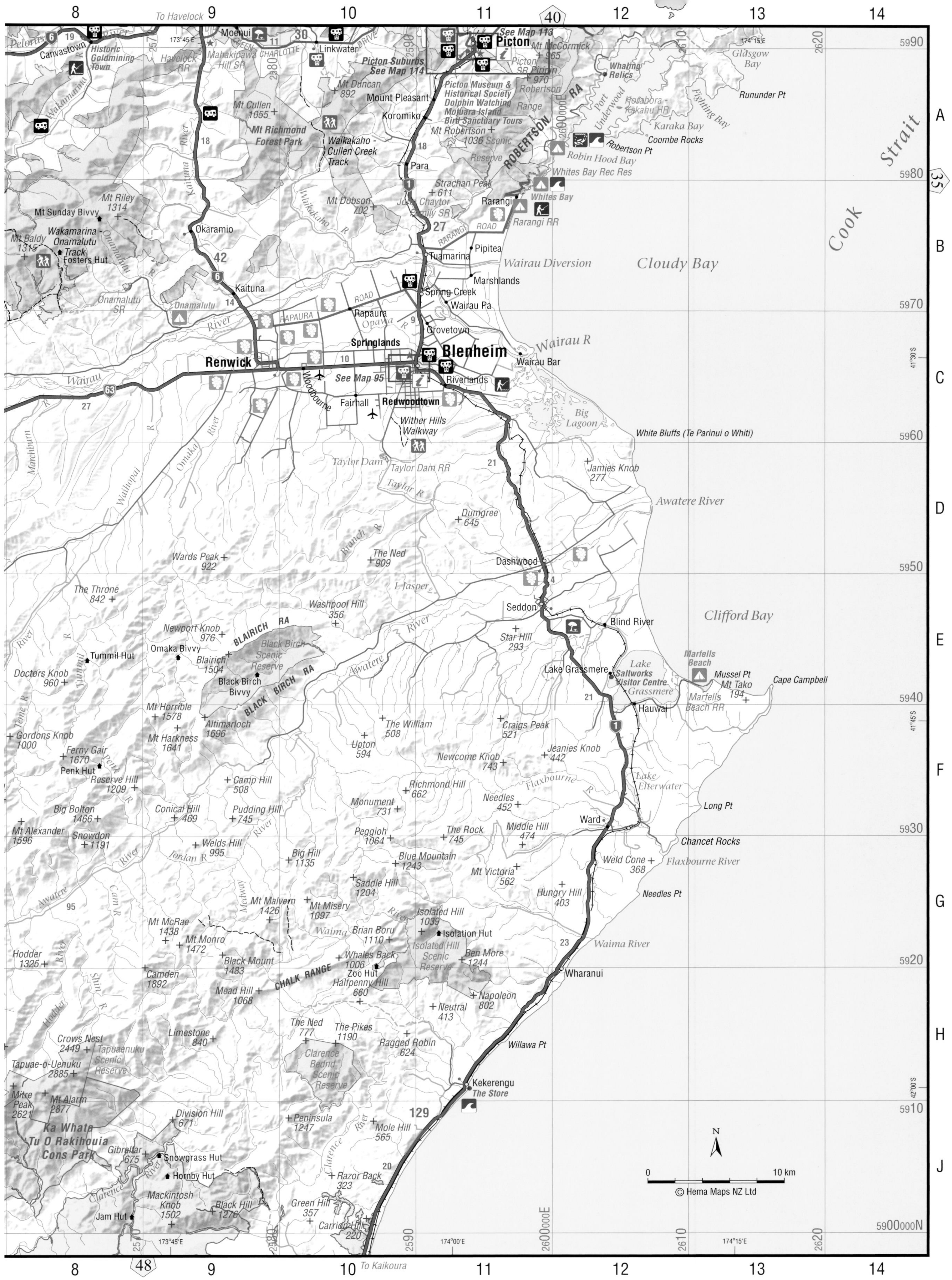

To Havelock
To Kaikoura
See Map 113
Picton
Picton Suburbs See Map 114
Picton Museum & Historical Society
Dolphin Watching
Motuara Island Bird Sanctuary Tours
Canvastown
Historic Goldmining Town
Havelock RR
Mahakipawa Hill SR
Moenui
Linkwater
Mt McCormick 965
Picton SR Pirini 970
Robertson Range
ROBERTSON RA
Whaling Relics
Port Underwood
Glasgow Bay
Rununder Pt
Fighting Bay
Karaka Bay
Coombe Rocks
Robertson Pt
Robin Hood Bay
Whites Bay Rec Res
Whites Bay
Rarangi
Rarangi RR
Mt Duncan 892
Mount Pleasant
Koromiko
Mt Robertson 1036
Mt Cullen 1055
Mt Richmond Forest Park
Waikakaho - Cullen Creek Track
Para
Strachan Peak 611
Mt Dobson 702
John Chaytor Family SR
Mt Riley 1314
Mt Sunday Bivvy
Mt Baldy 1315
Wakamarina Onamalutu Track
Fosters Hut
Okaramio
Kaituna
Onamalutu
Onamalutu SR
Tuamarina
Pipitea
Wairau Diversion
Cloudy Bay
Cook Strait
Marshlands
Spring Creek
Wairau Pa
Rapaura
Grovetown
Springlands
Blenheim
Wairau R
Wairau Bar
Renwick
See Map 95
Riverlands
Woodbourne
Fairhall
Redwoodtown
Wither Hills Walkway
Big Lagoon
White Bluffs (Te Parinui o Whiti)
Taylor Dam
Taylor Dam RR
James Knob 277
Awatere River
Dumgree 645
Wards Peak 922
The Ned 909
Dashwood
The Throne 842
Washpool Hill 356
Seddon
Blind River
Clifford Bay
Newport Knob 976
BLAIRICH RA
Black Birch Scenic Reserve
Star Hill 293
Omaka Bivvy
Blairich 1504
Tummil Hut
Doctors Knob 960
Black Birch Bivvy
BLACK BIRCH RA
Lake Grassmere
Saltworks Visitor Centre
Marfells Beach
Mussel Pt
Mt Tako 194
Cape Campbell
Marfells Beach RR
Hauwai
Mt Horrible 1578
Altimarloch 1696
The William 508
Craigs Peak 521
Gordons Knob 1000
Mt Harkness 1641
Upton 594
Jeanies Knob 442
Ferny Gair 1670
Newcome Knob 743
Penk Hut
Camp Hill 508
Reserve Hill 1209
Richmond Hill 662
Lake Elterwater
Needles 452
Long Pt
Big Bolton 1466
Conical Hill 469
Pudding Hill 745
Monument 731
Middle Hill 474
Ward
Mt Alexander 1596
Snowdon 1191
Peggioh 1064
The Rock 745
Chancet Rocks
Welds Hill 995
Big Hill 1135
Blue Mountain 1243
Weld Cone 368
Flaxbourne River
Mt Victoria 562
Saddle Hill 1204
Hungry Hill 403
Needles Pt
Mt Malvern 1426
Mt Misery 1097
Isolated Hill 1039
Isolation Hut
Mt McRae 1438
Brian Boru 1110
Waima River
Mt Monro 1472
Isolated Hill Scenic Reserve
Hodder 1325
Black Mount 1483
Whales Back 1006
Ben More 1244
CHALK RANGE
Zoo Hut
Camden 1892
Halfpenny Hill 660
Wharanui
Mead Hill 1068
Napoleon 802
Neutral 413
Limestone 840
The Ned 777
The Pikes 1190
Crows Nest 2449
Tapuaenuku Scenic Reserve
Ragged Robin 624
Willawa Pt
Tapuae-o-Uenuku 2885
Clarence Bend Scenic Reserve
Kekerengu
The Store
Mitre Peak 2621
Mt Alarm 2877
Ka Whata Tu O Rakihouia Cons Park
Division Hill 671
Peninsula 1247
Mole Hill 565
Gibraltar 675
Snowgrass Hut
Hornby Hut
Razor Back 323
Mackintosh Knob 1502
Black Hill 1276
Green Hill 357
Jam Hut
Carrion Hill 220
0
10 km
© Hema Maps NZ Ltd

Central West Coast

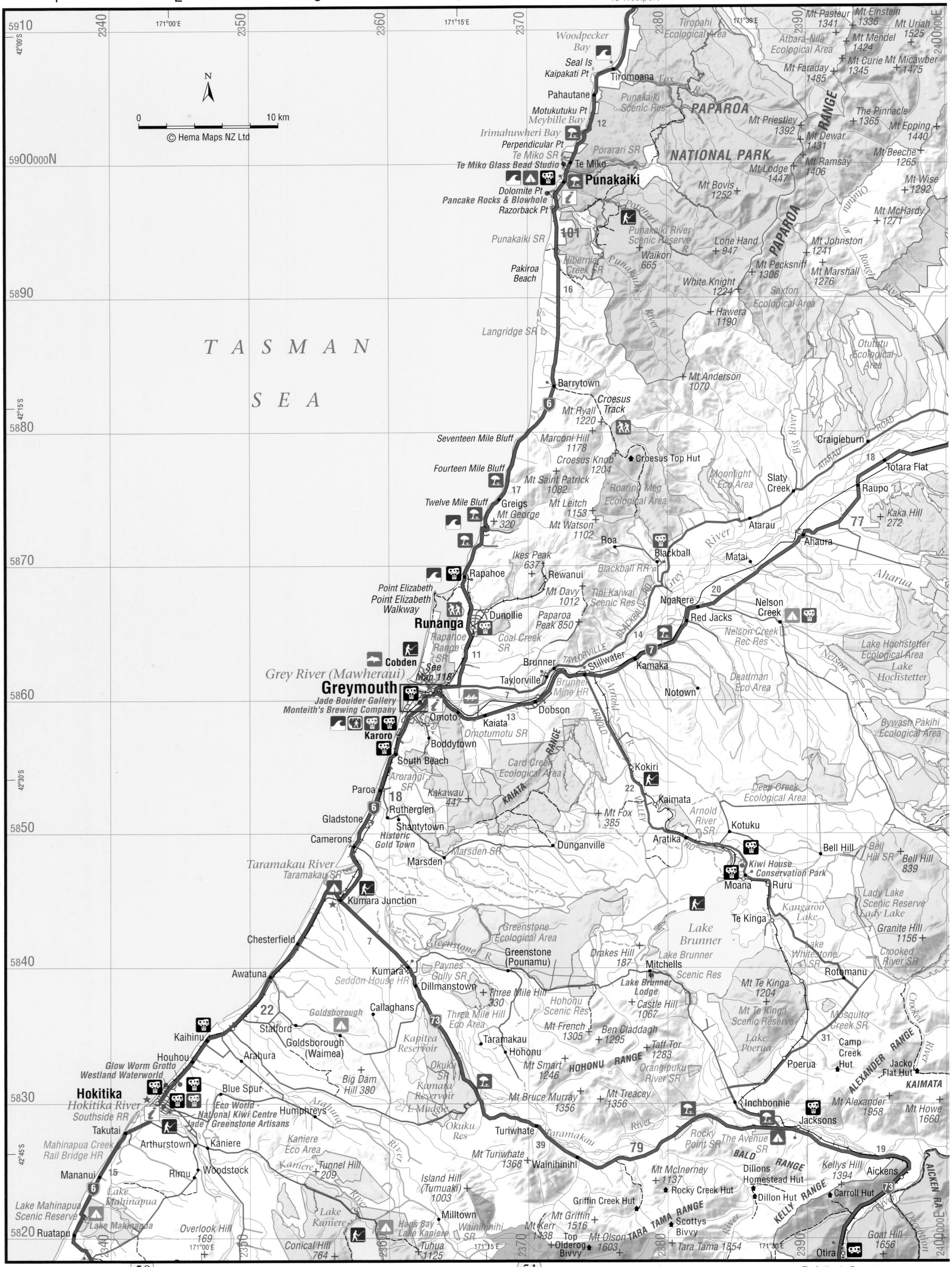

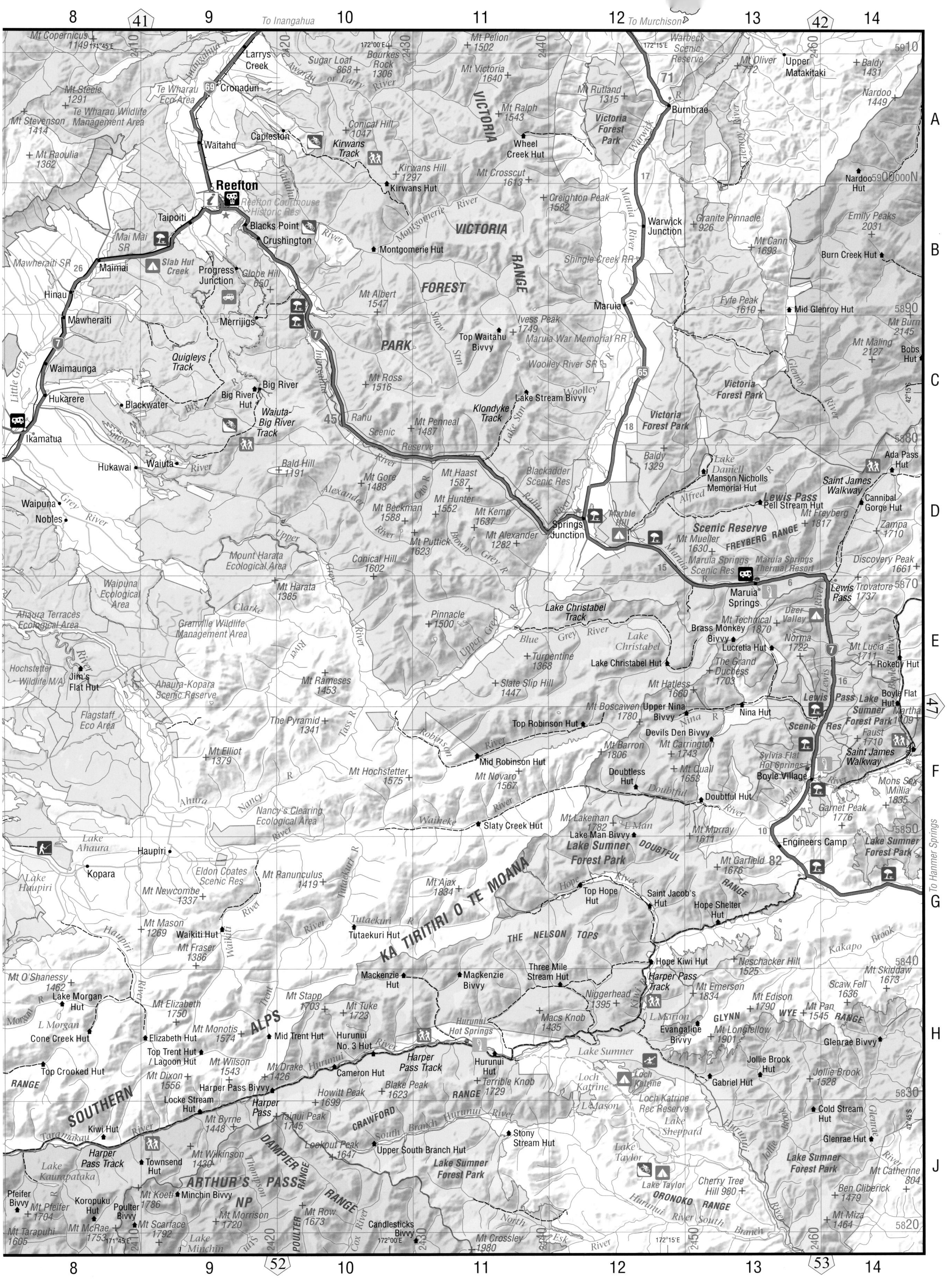
8
9
10
11
12
13
14
41
42
47
52
53
A
B
C
D
E
F
G
H
J
To Inangahua
To Murchison
To Hanmer Springs
172°00'E
172°15'E
171°45'E
42°15'S
42°45'S
5910
5900000N
5890
5880
5870
5850
5840
5830
5820
2410
2420
2430
2440
2450
2460
Mt Copernicus 1149
Larrys Creek
Sugar Loaf 868
Bourkes Rock 1306
Mt Pelion 1502
Mt Victoria 1640
Warbeck Scenic Reserve
Mt Oliver 772
Upper Matakitaki
Baldy 1431
Mt Steele 1291
Te Wharau Eco Area
Te Wharau Wildlife Management Area
Cronadun
Awarau or Larry River
Mt Rutland 1315
Nardoo 1449
Mt Stevenson 1414
Waitahu
Capleston
Conical Hill 1047
Kirwans Track
VICTORIA
Mt Ralph 1543
Victoria Forest Park
Wheel Creek Hut
Burnbrae
Warwick
Glenroy River
Mt Raoulia 1362
Reefton
Reefton Courthouse Historic Res
Kirwans Hill 1297
Kirwans Hut
Mt Crosscut 1613
Creighton Peak 1582
Nardoo Hut
Taipoiti
Blacks Point
Crushington
Montgomerie River
VICTORIA
Warwick Junction
Granite Pinnacle 926
Emily Peaks 2031
Mai Mai SR
Maruia River
Mawheraiti SR
Slab Hut Creek
Maimai
Progress Junction
Globe Hill 650
Montgomerie Hut
Shingle Creek RR
RANGE
Mt Cann 1693
Burn Creek Hut
Hinau
FOREST
Mt Albert 1547
Maruia
Fyfe Peak 1610
Mid Glenroy Hut
Mt Burn 2145
Mawheraiti
Merrijigs
Ivess Peak 1749
Top Waitahu Bivvy
Maruia War Memorial RR
Mt Maling 2127
Bobs Hut
Little Grey R
Waimaunga
Quigleys Track
PARK
Shaw Stm
Woolley River SR
Hukarere
Blackwater
Big River
Big River Hut
Mt Ross 1516
Lake Stream Bivvy
Woolley
Victoria Forest Park
Waiuta-Big River Track
Klondyke Track
Lake Stm
Victoria Forest Park
Glenroy River
Ikamatua
Rahu Scenic Reserve
Mt Penneal 1487
Inangahua
Snowy
Baldy 1329
Lake Daniell
Manson Nicholls Memorial Hut
Ada Pass Hut
Hukawai
Waiuta
River
Bald Hill 1191
Mt Gore 1488
Mt Haast 1587
Blackadder Scenic Res
Alfred R
Lewis Pass
Saint James Walkway
Cannibal Gorge Hut
Waipuna
Grey River
Nobles
Alexander
Mt Beckman 1588
Mt Hunter 1552
Mt Kemp 1637
Otto R
Rahu River
Springs Junction
Marble Hill
Pell Stream Hut
Mt Freyberg 1817
Zampa 1710
Upper
Mt Puttick 1623
Brown
Mt Alexander 1282
Grey R
Scenic Reserve
FREYBERG RANGE
Mt Mueller 1630
Maruia Springs Scenic Res
Maruia Springs Thermal Resort
Discovery Peak 1661
Mount Harata Ecological Area
Conical Hill 1602
Waipuna Ecological Area
Mt Harata 1385
Maruia Springs
Lewis Pass
Trovatore 1737
Ahaura Terraces Ecological Area
Clarke
Granville Wildlife Management Area
Pinnacle 1500
Lake Christabel Track
Deer Valley
Mt Technical 1870
Brass Monkey Bivvy
Upper Grey
Blue Grey River
Lake Christabel
Norma 1722
Lucretia Hut
Mt Lucia 1711
Turpentine 1368
Lake Christabel Hut
The Grand Duchess 1703
Rokeby Hut
Hochstetter Wildlife M/A
Jim's Flat Hut
Ahaura-Kopara Scenic Reserve
Mt Rameses 1453
Slate Slip Hill 1447
Mt Hatless 1660
Lewis R
Boyle Flat Hut
Flagstaff Eco Area
The Pyramid 1341
Tass R
Mt Boscawen 1780
Upper Nina Bivvy
Nina R
Nina Hut
Lewis Pass Lake Sumner Forest Park
Martha 1709
Top Robinson Hut
Robinson River
Devils Den Bivvy
Scenic Res
Faust 1710
Mt Elliot 1379
Mid Robinson Hut
Mt Barron 1806
Mt Carrington 1743
Sylvia Flat Hot Springs
Saint James Walkway
Mt Hochstetter 1575
Mt Novaro 1567
Doubtless Hut
Mt Cuall 1653
Boyle Village
Doubtful Hut
Doubtful River
Boyle River
Mons Sex Millia 1835
Ahura
Nancy
Nancy's Clearing Ecological Area
Waiheke
Slaty Creek Hut
Mt Lakeman 1782
L Man
Mt Murray 1611
Garnet Peak 1776
Lake Ahaura
Haupiri
Lake Man Bivvy
Lake Sumner Forest Park
DOUBTFUL
Engineers Camp
Lake Sumner Forest Park
Kopara
Eldon Coates Scenic Res
Mt Ranunculus 1419
Tutaekuri R
Mt Garfield 1676
Lake Haupiri
Mt Newcombe 1337
Mt Ajax 1834
KA TIRITIRI O TE MOANA
Hope River
Top Hope Hut
Saint Jacob's Hut
RANGE
Mt Mason 1269
Waikiti Hut
Waikiti
Tutaekuri R
Tutaekuri Hut
Hope Shelter Hut
Mt Fraser 1386
THE NELSON TOPS
Kakapo Brook
Haupiri
Hope Kiwi Hut
Neschacker Hill 1525
Mt O'Shanessy 1462
Mackenzie Hut
Mackenzie Bivvy
Three Mile Stream Hut
Harper Pass Track
Mt Skiddaw 1673
Lake Morgan Hut
Mt Stapp 1703
Mt Tuke 1723
Niggerhead 1395
Mt Emerson 1834
Scaw Fell 1636
Morgan R
Mt Elizabeth 1750
Trent
Kiwi R
L Marion
Mt Edison 1790
Mt Pan 1545
L Morgan
ALPS
Macs Knob 1435
GLYNN
WYE RANGE
Cone Creek Hut
Elizabeth Hut
Mt Monotis 1574
Mid Trent Hut
Hurunui No. 3 Hut
Hurunui Hot Springs
Evangaline Bivvy
Mt Longfellow 1901
Glenrae Bivvy
Top Trent Hut / Lagoon Hut
Mt Wilson 1543
River
Harper Pass Track
Hurunui Hut
Lake Sumner
Jollie Brook Hut
Top Crooked Hut
Mt Drake 1426
Hurunui
Cameron Hut
Terrible Knob 1729
Loch Katrine
Gabriel Hut
Jollie Brook 1528
RANGE
Mt Dixon 1556
Harper Pass Bivvy
Blake Peak 1623
RANGE
Loch Katrine Rec Reserve
SOUTHERN
Locke Stream Hut
Harper Pass
Howitt Peak 1699
L Mason
Cold Stream Hut
Mt Byrne 1448
Tainui Peak 1745
CRAWFORD
South Branch Hurunui River
Lake Sheppard
Glenrae River
Kiwi Hut
Taramakau River
Stony Stream Hut
Harper Pass Track
Lookout Peak 1647
Upper South Branch Hut
Glenrae Hut
Lake Kaurapataka
Townsend Hut
Mt Wilkinson 1430
Thompson
DAMPIER RANGE
Lake Sumner Forest Park
Lake Taylor
Lake Sumner Forest Park
Jollie Brook
Mt Catherine 804
Pfeifer Bivvy
Mt Pfeifer 1704
Koropuku Hut
Poulter Bivvy
Mt Koeti 1786
Minchin Bivvy
ARTHUR'S PASS NP
RANGE
Lake Taylor
Cherry Tree Hill 980
ORONOKO RANGE
Ben Cliberick 1479
Mt Morrison 1720
Mt Row 1673
Hurunui River South Branch
Mt Miza 1464
Mt Tarapuhi 1605
Mt McRae 1753
Mt Scarface 1792
POULTER
Cox River
Candlesticks Bivvy
North
Mt Crossley 1980
Esk River
Lake Minchin
15
16
17
18
26
45
65
69
71
82
7
6
10

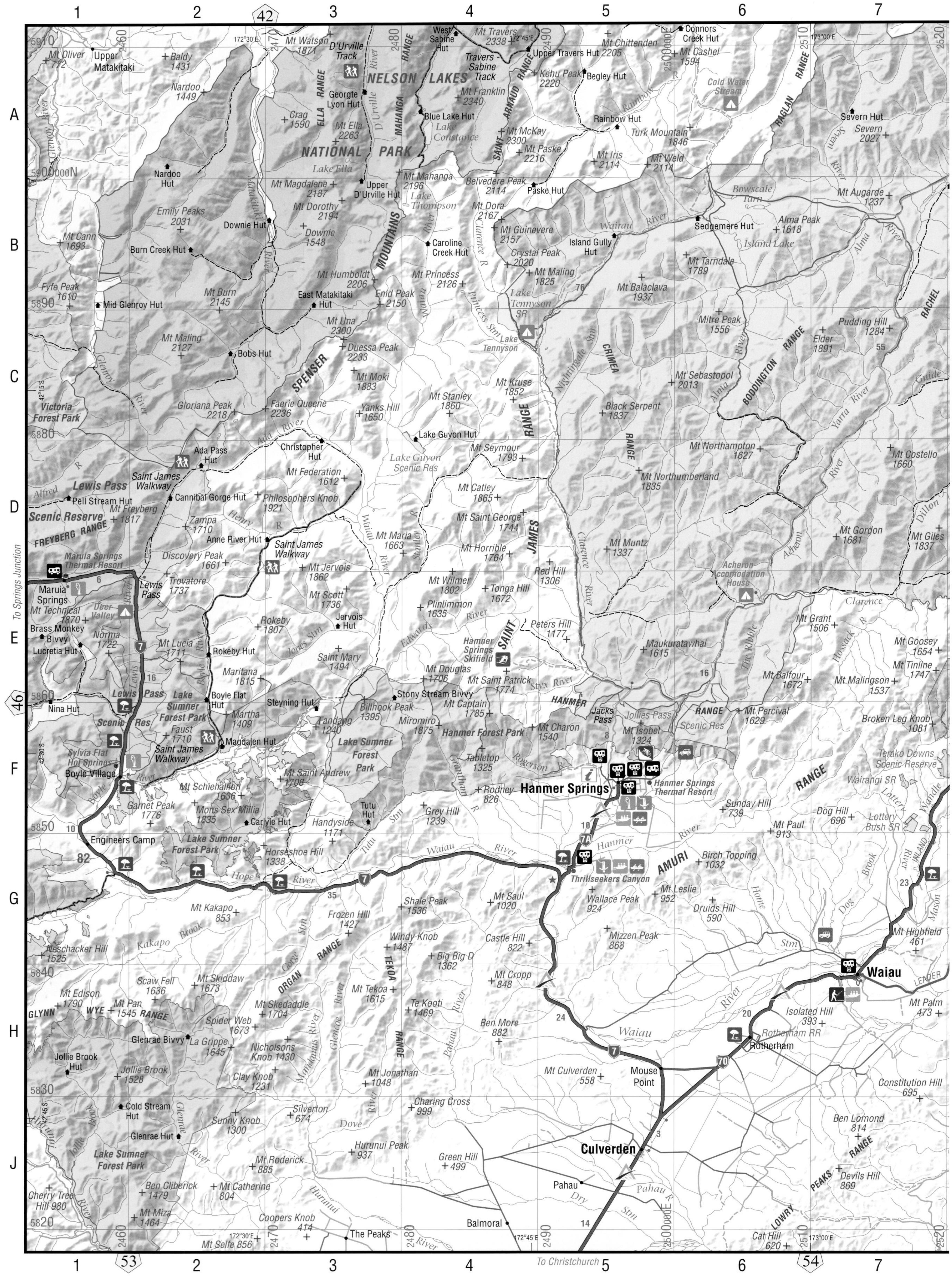

1
2
3
4
5
6
7
A
B
C
D
E
F
G
H
J
42
46
53
54
Mt Oliver 772
Upper Matakitaki
Baldy 1431
Mt Watson 1871
D'Urville Track
NELSON LAKES
NATIONAL PARK
West Sabine Hut
Mt Travers 2338
Travers Sabine Track
Upper Travers Hut 2205
Mt Chittenden
Connors Creek Hut
Mt Cashel 1594
Nardoo 1449
ELLA RANGE
Georgte Lyon Hut
MAHANGA RANGE
Mt Franklin 2340
Kehu Peak 2220
Begley Hut
Cold Water Stream
RAGLAN RANGE
Crag 1590
Mt Ella 2263
Blue Lake Hut
Lake Constance
SAINT ARNAUD RANGE
Rainbow
Rainbow Hut
Turk Mountain 1846
Severn Hut
Severn 2027
Mt McKay 2300
Mt Paske 2216
Mt Iris 2114
Mt Weld 2114
Nardoo Hut
Lake Ella
Mt Magdalene 2187
Upper D'Urville Hut
Mt Mahanga 2196
Lake Thompson
Belvedere Peak 2114
Paske Hut
Bowscale Tarn
Mt Augarde 1237
Emily Peaks 2031
Mt Dorothy 2194
Mt Dora 2167
Mt Guinevere 2157
Waiau River
Sedgemere Hut
Alma Peak 1618
Downie Hut
Downie 1548
MOUNTAINS
Caroline Creek Hut
Clarence R
Island Gully Hut
Island Lake
Alma River
Mt Cann 1693
Burn Creek Hut
Crystal Peak 2020
Mt Maling 1825
Mt Tarndale 1789
Mt Humboldt 2206
Mt Princess 2126
Fyfe Peak 1610
Mid Glenroy Hut
Mt Burn 2145
East Matakitaki Hut
Enid Peak 2150
Lake Tennyson SR
Mt Balaclava 1937
Mt Una 2300
Princess Stm
Mitre Peak 1556
Pudding Hill 1284
RACHEL
Mt Maling 2127
Bobs Hut
Duessa Peak 2233
Lake Tennyson
Elder 1891
BODDINGTON RANGE
SPENSER
Mt Moki 1883
Mt Kruse 1852
CRIMEA
Mt Sebastopol 2013
Glenroy River
Mt Stanley 1860
Victoria Forest Park
Gloriana Peak 2218
Faerie Queene 2236
Yanks Hill 1650
RANGE
Black Serpent 1837
Yarra River
Guide
Ada River
Lake Guyon Hut
Christopher Hut
Mt Seymour 1793
Mt Northampton 1627
Mt Costello 1660
Ada Pass Hut
Lake Guyon Scenic Res
Mt Federation 1612
Mt Northumberland 1835
Alfred R
Lewis Pass
Saint James Walkway
Cannibal Gorge Hut
Pell Stream Hut
Philosophers Knob 1921
Mt Catley 1865
Scenic Reserve
Mt Freyberg 1817
FREYBERG RANGE
Zampa 1710
Henry R
Mt Saint George 1744
JAMES
Mt Gordon 1681
Dillon
Mt Giles 1837
Anne River Hut
Mt Maria 1663
Mt Muntz 1337
Acheron
Maruia Springs Thermal Resort
Discovery Peak 1661
Saint James Walkway
Mt Horrible 1764
Red Hill 1306
Clarence River
Acheron Accomodation House
To Springs Junction
Maruia Springs
Lewis Pass
Trovatore 1737
Mt Jervois 1862
Mt Wilmer 1802
Tonga Hill 1672
Mt Technical 1870
Deer Valley
Mt Scott 1736
Plinlimmon 1635
Clarence
Brass Monkey Bivvy
Rokeby 1807
Jervois Hut
SAINT
Peters Hill 1177
Mt Grant 1506
Norma 1722
Lucretia Hut
Mt Lucia 1711
Rokeby Hut
Jones Stm
Edwards
Hanmer Springs Skifield
Maukuratawhai 1615
The Ribble
Hossack R
Mt Goosey 1654
Saint Mary 1494
Mt Tinline 1747
Maritana 1815
Mt Douglas 1706
Mt Saint Patrick 1774
Styx River
Mt Balfour 1672
Mt Malingson 1537
Nina Hut
Lewis Pass
Lake Sumner Forest Park
Boyle Flat Hut
Steyning Hut
Stony Stream Bivvy
Billhook Peak 1395
Mt Captain 1785
HANMER
Jacks Pass
Jollies Pass
RANGE
Mt Percival 1629
Broken Leg Knob 1081
Scenic Res
Martha 1409
Fandang 1240
Miromiro 1875
Hanmer Forest Park
Mt Charon 1540
Mt Isobel 1324
Scenic Res
Faust 1710
Magdalen Hut
Lake Sumner Forest Park
Tabletop 1325
Rogerson R
Terako Downs Scenic Reserve
Sylvia Flat Hot Springs
Boyle Village
Mt Saint Andrew 1708
Hanmer Springs
Hanmer Springs Thermal Resort
RANGE
Wairangi SR
Mt Schiehallion 1636
Rodney 826
Sunday Hill 739
Lottery
Dog Hill 696
Lottery Bush SR
Garnet Peak 1776
Mons Sex Millia 1835
Carlyle Hut
Tutu Hut
Grey Hill 1239
Handyside 1171
Mt Paul 913
Engineers Camp
Lake Sumner Forest Park
Horseshoe Hill 1338
Waiau River
Hanmer River
AMURI
Birch Topping 1032
INLAND
82
Hope River
Thrillseekers Canyon
Mt Kakapo 853
Shale Peak 1536
Mt Saul 1020
Wallace Peak 924
Mt Leslie 952
Druids Hill 590
Frozen Hill 1427
Kakapo Brook
Gorge Stm
RANGE
Windy Knob 1487
Castle Hill 822
Mizzen Peak 868
Neschacker Hill 1525
TEKOA
Big Big D 1362
Mt Highfield 461
Mt Skiddaw 1673
Scaw Fell 1636
ORGAN
Mt Cropp 848
Waiau
Mt Edison 1790
Mt Pan 1545
WYE RANGE
Mt Tekoa 1615
Te Kooti 1469
Mt Skedaddle 1704
Isolated Hill 393
Mt Palm 473
GLYNN
Spider Web 1673
Ben More 882
Waiau
Rotherham RR
Rotherham
Glenrae Bivvy
La Gripps 1645
Nicholsons Knob 1430
Jollie Brook Hut
Jollie Brook 1528
Clay Knob 1231
Mt Jonathan 1048
Mt Culverden 558
Mouse Point
Constitution Hill 695
Cold Stream Hut
Charing Cross 999
Silverton 674
Sunny Knob 1300
Dove
Ben Lomond 814
Glenrae Hut
Lake Sumner Forest Park
Hurunui Peak 937
Green Hill 499
Culverden
Mt Roderick 885
Pahau
Pahau R
PEAKS RANGE
Devils Hill 869
Ben Cliberick 1479
Mt Catherine 804
Cherry Tree Hill 980
Mt Miza 1464
Hurunui
Coopers Knob 414
Balmoral
LOWRY
The Peaks
Mt Selfe 856
Cat Hill 620
To Christchurch

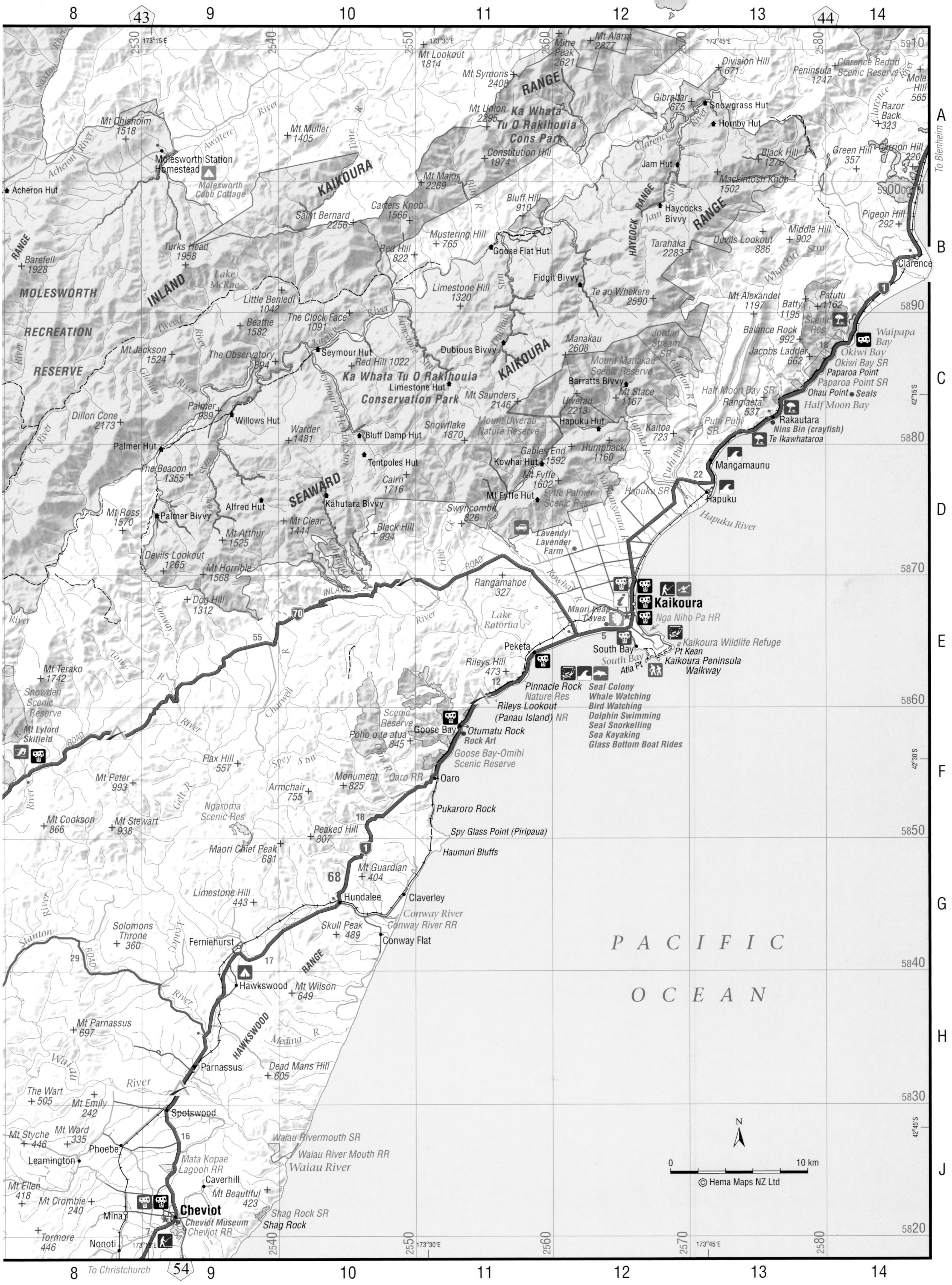

8
9
10
11
12
13
14
43
44
54
A
B
C
D
E
F
G
H
J
To Blenheim
To Christchurch
Mt Alarm 2877
Mitre Peak 2621
Mt Lookout 1814
Mt Symons 2408
RANGE
Ka Whata Tu O Rakihouia Cons Park
Mt Union 2295
Constitution Hill 1974
Division Hill 671
Peninsula 1247
Clarence Bedrd Scenic Reserve
Mole Hill 565
Gibraltar 675
Snowgrass Hut
Hornby Hut
Razor Back 323
Green Hill 357
Carrion Hill 220
Black Hill 1276
Jam Hut
Mackintosh Knob 1502
Mt Chisholm 1518
Mt Muller 1405
Molesworth Station Homestead
Molesworth Cobb Cottage
Acheron Hut
Acheron River
Awatere River
KAIKOURA
Mt Major 2269
Bluff Hill 910
Carters Knob 1566
Saint Bernard 2256
Haycocks Bivvy
HAYCOCK RANGE
RANGE
Pigeon Hill 292
Middle Hill 902
Devils Lookout 886
Tarahaka 2283
Mustering Hill 765
Red Hill 822
Goose Flat Hut
Clarence
Turks Head 1958
Barefell 1928
RANGE
MOLESWORTH
RECREATION
RESERVE
INLAND
Lake McRae
Little Benledi 1042
Beattie 1582
The Clock Face 1091
Limestone Hill 1320
Fidgit Bivvy
Te ao Whekere 2590
Mt Alexander 1197
Batty 1195
Patutu 1162
Waipapa Bay
Balance Rock 992
Scenic Res
Okiwi Bay
Okiwi Bay SR
Jacobs Ladder 662
Paparoa Point
Paparoa Point SR
Ohau Point
Seals
Half Moon Bay SR
Half Moon Bay
Rangiaeta 537
Rakautara
Nins Bin (crayfish)
Te Ikawhataroa
Puhi Puhi SR
Mangamaunu
Hapuku
Hapuku SR
Hapuku River
Mt Jackson 1524
The Observatory 894
Seymour Hut
Red Hill 1022
Ka Whata Tu O Rakihouia Conservation Park
Limestone Hut
Dubious Bivvy
KAIKOURA
Manakau 2608
Mount Manakau Scenic Reserve
Jordan Stream SR
Barratts Bivvy
Mt Stace 1167
Uwerau 2213
Mt Saunders 2146
Mount Uwerau Nature Reserve
Hapuku Hut
Kaitoa 723
Dillon Cone 2173
Palmer 989
Willows Hut
Warder 1481
Bluff Damp Hut
Snowflake 1870
Palmer Hut
Tentpoles Hut
Gables End 1592
Humpback 1160
Kowhai Hut
The Beacon 1355
Cairn 1716
Mt Fyffe 1602
Mt Fyffe Hut
Fyffe Palmer Scenic Res
SEAWARD
Kahutara Bivvy
Alfred Hut
Palmer Bivvy
Mt Ross 1570
Mt Clear 1444
Black Hill 994
Swyncombe 826
Mt Arthur 1525
Lavendyl Lavender Farm
Devils Lookout 1265
Mt Horrible 1568
Rangamahoe 327
Kaikoura
Maori Leap Caves
Nga Niho Pa HR
Dog Hill 1312
INLAND ROAD
70
55
Lake Rotorua
Kaikoura Wildlife Refuge
Pt Kean
Kaikoura Peninsula Walkway
Peketa
South Bay
Atia Pt
Rileys Hill 473
Pinnacle Rock
Nature Res
Seal Colony
Whale Watching
Bird Watching
Dolphin Swimming
Seal Snorkelling
Sea Kayaking
Glass Bottom Boat Rides
Rileys Lookout (Panau Island) NR
Mt Terako 1742
Snowden Scenic Reserve
Mt Lyford Skifield
Scenic Reserve
Goose Bay
Otumatu Rock
Rock Art
Poho o te atua 845
Goose Bay-Omihi Scenic Reserve
Flax Hill 557
Mt Peter 993
Monument 825
Oaro RR
Oaro
Armchair 755
Ngaroma Scenic Res
Pukaroro Rock
Mt Cookson 866
Mt Stewart 938
Peaked Hill 807
Spy Glass Point (Piripaua)
Maori Chief Peak 681
Haumuri Bluffs
Mt Guardian 404
68
Limestone Hill 443
Hundalee
Claverley
Conway River
Conway River RR
Solomons Throne 360
Skull Peak 489
Conway Flat
Ferniehurst
Stanton ROAD
29
17
RANGE
PACIFIC
OCEAN
Hawkswood
Mt Wilson 649
Mt Parnassus 697
HAWKSWOOD
Medina R
Waiau River
Parnassus
Dead Mans Hill 605
The Wart 505
Mt Emily 242
Spotswood
Mt Styche 446
Mt Ward 335
Phoebe
16
Waiau Rivermouth SR
Waiau River Mouth RR
Waiau River
Leamington
Mata Kopae Lagoon RR
Caverhill
Mt Beautiful 423
Mt Ellen 418
Mt Crombie 240
Mina
Cheviot
Cheviot Museum
Cheviot RR
Shag Rock SR
Shag Rock
Tormore 446
Nonoti
N
0
10 km
© Hema Maps NZ Ltd
173°15'E
173°30'E
173°45'E
42°15'S
42°30'S
42°45'S
5910
5900
5890
5880
5870
5860
5850
5840
5830
5820
2530
2540
2550
2560
2570
2580

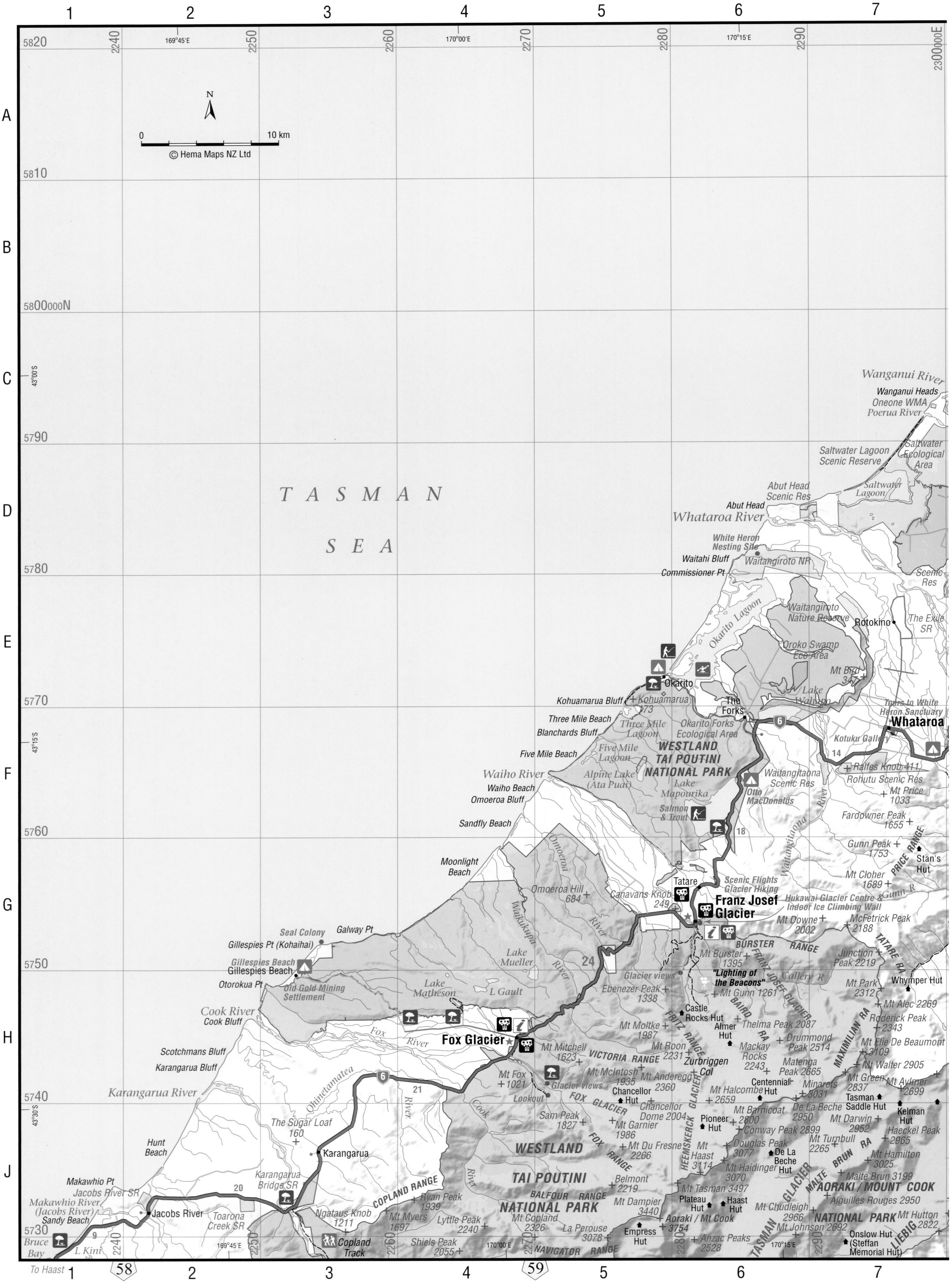

© Hema Maps NZ Ltd
0
10 km
N
TASMAN SEA
Wanganui River
Wanganui Heads
Oneone WMA
Poerua River
Saltwater Lagoon Scenic Reserve
Saltwater Ecological Area
Saltwater Lagoon
Abut Head Scenic Res
Abut Head
Whataroa River
White Heron Nesting Site
Waitahi Bluff
Waitangiroto NR
Commissioner Pt
Scenic Res
Okarito Lagoon
Waitangiroto Nature Reserve
Rotokino
The Exile SR
Oroko Swamp Eco Area
Mt Bird 347
Okarito
Lake Wahapo
Kohuamarua Bluff
Kohuamarua 373
The Forks
Tours to White Heron Sanctuary
Whataroa
Three Mile Beach
Three Mile Lagoon
Okarito Forks Ecological Area
Blanchards Bluff
Kotuku Gallery
WESTLAND TAI POUTINI NATIONAL PARK
Five Mile Beach
Five Mile Lagoon
Ralfes Knob 411
Rohutu Scenic Res
Waiho River
Alpine Lake (Ata Puai)
Waitangitaona Scenic Res
Waiho Beach
Lake Mapourika
Okarito MacDonalds
Mt Price 1033
Omoeroa Bluff
Salmon & Trout
Waitangitaona River
Fardowner Peak 1655
Sandfly Beach
Gunn Peak 1753
PRICE RANGE
Stan's Hut
Moonlight Beach
Omoeroa River
Tatare
Scenic Flights Glacier Hiking
Mt Cloher 1689
Gunn R
Omoeroa Hill 684
Canavans Knob 249
Franz Josef Glacier
Hukawai Glacier Centre & Indoor Ice Climbing Wall
Mt Downe 2002
McFetrick Peak 2188
Waikukupa River
Seal Colony
Galway Pt
Gillespies Pt (Kohaihai)
Lake Mueller
BURSTER RANGE
TATARE RA
Junction Peak 2219
Gillespies Beach
Mt Burster 1395
FRANZ JOSEF GLACIER
Otorokua Pt
Old Gold Mining Settlement
Glacier views
"Lighting of the Beacons"
Callery R
Lake Matheson
L Gault
Mt Gunn 1261
Ebenezer Peak 1338
Mt Park 2312
Whymper Hut
Cook River
Cook Bluff
Castle Rocks Hut
Mt Alec 2269
Roderick Peak 2343
Almer Hut
BAIRD RA
Thelma Peak 2087
Mt Moltke 1987
FRITZ RANGE
Fox River
Fox Glacier
Mackay Rocks 2243
Drummond Peak 2514
Scotchmans Bluff
Mt Mitchell 1623
VICTORIA RANGE
Mt Roon 2231
Zurbriggen Col
Mt Elie De Beaumont 3109
MAXIMILIAN RA
Karangarua Bluff
Mt McIntosh 1935
Mt Anderegg 2360
Matenga Peak 2665
Mt Walter 2905
Mt Fox 1021
Glacier views
Lookout
Centennial Hut
Minarets 3031
Mt Green 2837
Mt Aylmer 2699
Karangarua River
Ohinetamatea River
Chancellor Hut
Mt Halcombe 2659
Tasman Saddle Hut
FOX GLACIER
Chancellor Dome 2004
Mt Barnicoat 2800
De La Beche 2950
Kelman Hut
The Sugar Loaf 160
Sam Peak 1827
Mt Garnier 1986
Pioneer Hut
Conway Peak 2899
Mt Darwin 2952
Haeckel Peak 2965
Cook River
WESTLAND
FOX RANGE
HEEMSKERCK GLACIER
Mt Turnbull 2265
Hunt Beach
Karangarua
Mt Du Fresne 2266
Mt Haast 3114
Douglas Peak 3077
De La Beche Hut
Mt Hamilton 3025
Mt Haidinger 3070
Makawhio Pt
Jacobs River SR
Karangarua Bridge SR
COPLAND RANGE
TAI POUTINI
Belmont 2219
Mt Tasman 3497
TASMAN GLACIER
MALTE BRUN RA
Malte Brun 3199
AORAKI / MOUNT COOK
Makawhio River (Jacobs River)
Sandy Beach
Jacobs River
Toarona Creek SR
Ryan Peak 1939
BALFOUR RANGE
Mt Dampier 3440
Plateau Hut
Haast Hut
Aiguilles Rouges 2950
Ngataus Knob 1211
Mt Myers 1697
Lyttle Peak 2240
NATIONAL PARK
Mt Copland 2326
Aoraki / Mt Cook 3754
Mt Chudleigh 2966
NATIONAL PARK
Mt Hutton 2822
Bruce Bay
L Kini
Copland Track
Shiels Peak 2055
La Perouse 3078
Empress Hut
Anzac Peaks 2528
Mt Johnson 2692
Onslow Hut (Steffan Memorial Hut)
LIEBIG
NAVIGATOR RANGE
To Haast
58
59

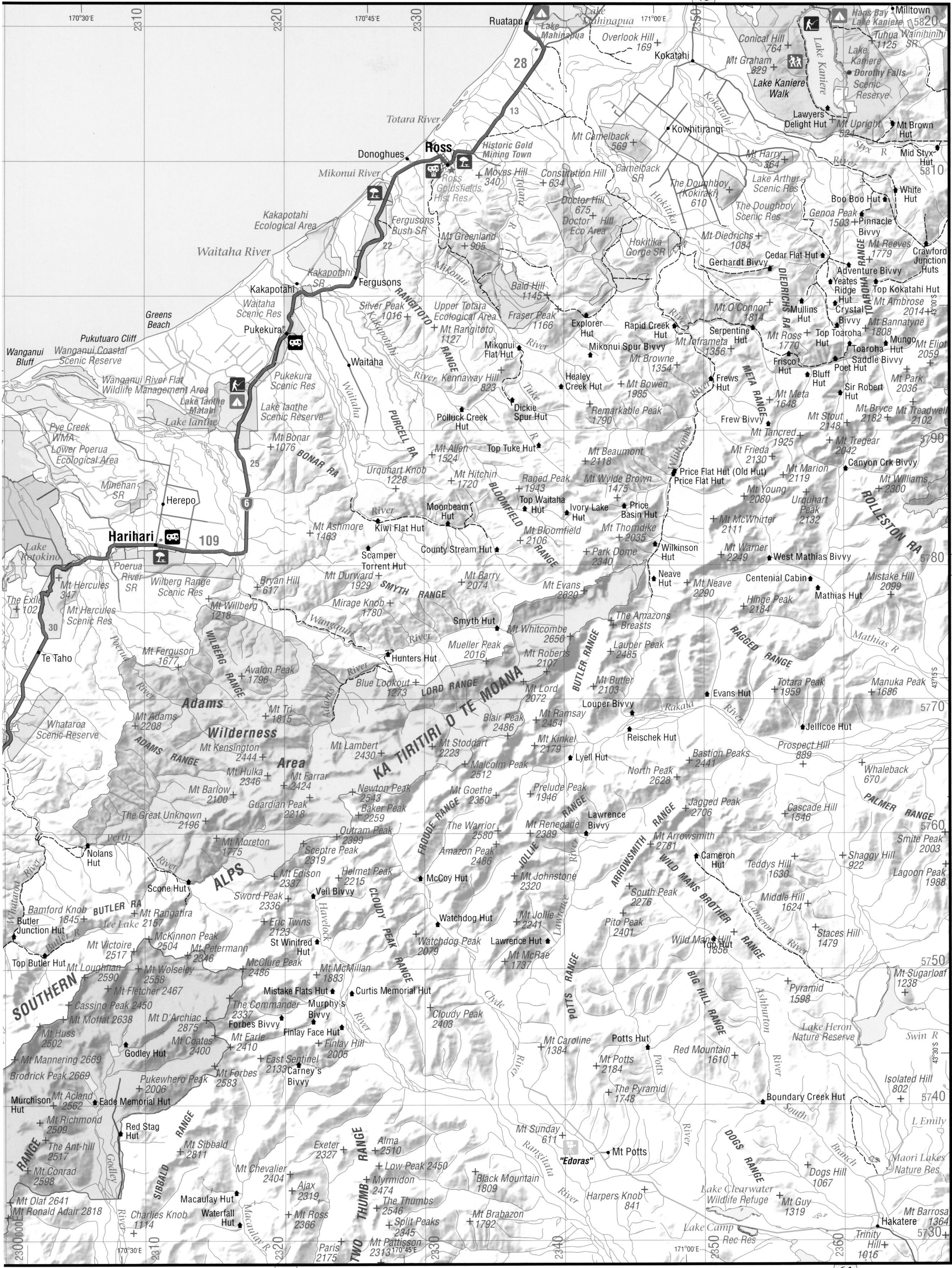

To Hokitika, Greymouth
Ross
Historic Gold Mining Town
Donoghues
Ruatapu
Lake Mahinapua
Kokatahi
Kowhitirangi
Lake Kaniere Walk
Lake Kaniere
Hans Bay
Milltown
Dorothy Falls Scenic Reserve
Lawyers Delight Hut
Mt Upright 524
Mt Brown Hut
Mid Styx Hut
Totara River
Mikonui River
Waitaha River
Kakapotahi Ecological Area
Kakapotahi
Fergusons
Pukekura
Waitaha
Greens Beach
Pukutuaro Cliff
Wanganui Bluff
Wanganui Coastal Scenic Reserve
Wanganui River Flat Wildlife Management Area
Lake Ianthe Matahi
Lake Ianthe
Lake Ianthe Scenic Reserve
Pye Creek WMA
Lower Poerua Ecological Area
Minehan SR
Herepo
Harihari
Lake Rotokino
Poerua River SR
Wilberg Range Scenic Res
Mt Hercules 347
The Exile 102
Mt Hercules Scenic Res
Te Taho
Whataroa Scenic Reserve
Adams Wilderness Area
KA TIRITIRI O TE MOANA
SOUTHERN ALPS
Mt Whitcombe 2650
Mt Evans 2620
Price Flat Hut
Mt Arrowsmith 2781
Lake Heron Nature Reserve
"Edoras"
Mt Potts
Rangitata River
Lake Clearwater Wildlife Refuge
Lake Camp Rec Res
Hakatere
Maori Lakes Nature Res
L Emily
Mt Sunday 611
Harpers Knob 841
Boundary Creek Hut
Potts Hut
Mt Caroline 1384
Red Mountain 1610
Mt Sugarloaf 1238
Isolated Hill 802
Dogs Hill 1067
Mt Guy 1319
Trinity Hill 1016
Mt Barrosa 1364

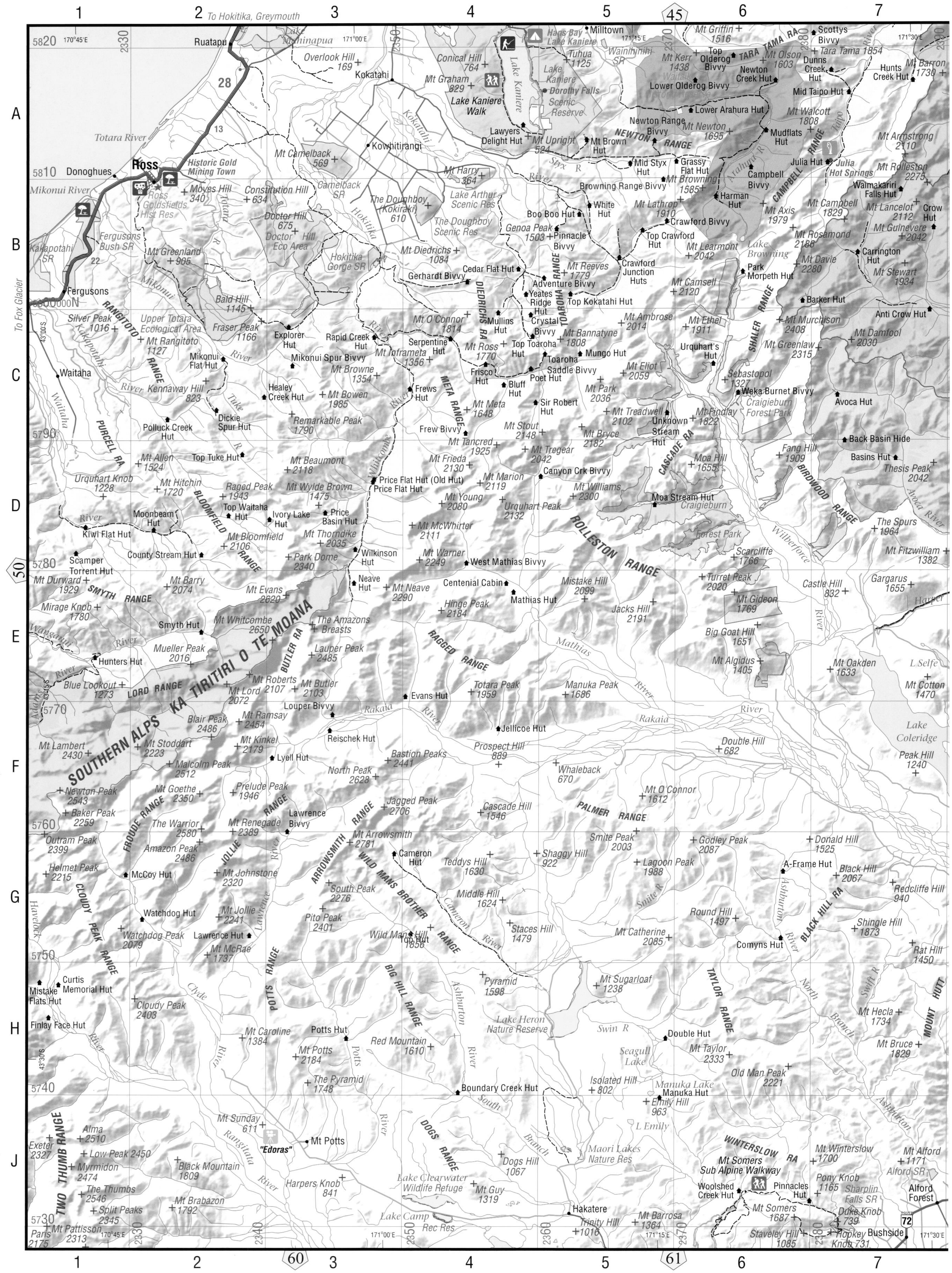

1 2 3 4 5 6 7
To Hokitika, Greymouth
45
5820 170°45'E 2330 171°00'E 2350 2370 2380 171°30'E 2390
Ruatapu
Lake Mahinapua
Overlook Hill 169
Kokatahi
Conical Hill 764
Mt Graham 829
Lake Kaniere Walk
Lake Kaniere
Hans Bay Lake Kaniere
Milltown
Tuhua 1125
Lake Kaniere Scenic Reserve
Dorothy Falls
Wainihinihi SR
Mt Griffin 1516
Top Olderog Bivvy
TARA TAMA RA
Scottys Bivvy
Tara Tama 1854
Mt Kerr 1438
Mt Olson 1603
Dunns Creek Hut
Newton Creek Hut
Hunts Creek Hut
Mt Barron 1730
Lower Olderog Bivvy
Mid Taipo Hut
Lower Arahura Hut
28
13
Totara River
A
Kowhitirangi
Kokatahi
Lawyers Delight Hut
Mt Upright 524
Mt Brown Hut
NEWTON RANGE
Newton Range Bivvy
Mt Newton 1695
Mt Walcott 1808
Mudflats Hut
CAMPBELL RANGE
Mt Armstrong 2110
Mt Camelback 569
Styx R
Mid Styx Hut
Grassy Flat Hut
Arahura R
Julia Hut
Julia Hot Springs
5810 Donoghues
Ross
Historic Gold Mining Town
Mikonui River
Ross Goldsfields Hist Res
Moyes Hill 340
Constitution Hill 634
Camelback SR
Mt Harry 364
Lake Arthur Scenic Res
River
Browning Range Bivvy
Mt Browning 1585
Campbell Bivvy
Harman Hut
Mt Rolleston 2275
Waimakariri Falls Hut
The Doughboy (Kokiraki) 610
The Doughboy Scenic Res
White Hut
Mt Lathrop 1910
Mt Axis 1979
Mt Campbell 1829
Mt Lancelot 2112
Crow Hut
Doctor Hill 675
Doctor Hill Eco Area
Totara R
Hokitika
Boo Boo Hut
Genoa Peak 1503
Pinnacle Bivvy
Crawford Bivvy
Mt Guinevere 2042
B
Fergusons Bush SR
Kakapotahi SR
22
Mt Greenland 905
Hokitika Gorge SR
Mt Diedrichs 1084
Top Crawford Hut
Mt Learmont 2042
Lake Browning
Mt Rosamond 2186
Carrington Hut
Fergusons
Mikonui
Cedar Flat Hut
Gerhardt Bivvy
TOAROHA RANGE
Mt Reeves 1779
Crawford Junction Huts
Park Morpeth Hut
Mt Davie 2280
Mt Stewart 1934
To Fox Glacier
5800000N
RANGITOTO
Bald Hill 1145
DIEDRICHS RA
Adventure Bivvy
Yeates Ridge Hut
Top Kokatahi Hut
Mt Camsell 2120
SHALER RANGE
Barker Hut
43°00'S
Silver Peak 1016
Kakapotahi
Upper Totara Ecological Area
Fraser Peak 1166
Explorer Hut
Rapid Creek Hut
River
Mt O'Connor 1814
Mullins Hut
Crystal Bivvy
Mt Ambrose 2014
Mt Ethel 1911
Mt Murchison 2408
Anti Crow Hut
Mt Rangitoto 1127
Serpentine Hut
Mt Ross 1770
Top Hut
Top Toaroha
Mt Bannatyne 1808
Mungo Hut
Urquhart's Hut
Mt Greenlaw 2315
Mt Damfool 2030
Waitaha
RANGE
Mikonui Flat Hut
River
Mikonui Spur Bivvy
Mt Inframeta 1356
Frisco Hut
Toaroha Saddle Bivvy
Poet Hut
Mt Eliot 2059
Sebastopol 327
C
Kennaway Hill 823
Tuke
Healey Creek Hut
Mt Browne 1354
Mt Bowen 1985
Frews Hut
META RANGE
Bluff Hut
Mt Park 2036
Weka Burnet Bivvy
Craigieburn Forest Park
Avoca Hut
Waitaha
River
PURCELL RA
Pollock Creek Hut
Dickie Spur Hut
Remarkable Peak 1790
Mt Meta 1648
Sir Robert Hut
Mt Treadwell 2102
Unknown Stream Hut
Mt Findlay 1822
5790
Frew Bivvy
Mt Stout 2148
Mt Bryce 2182
CASCADE RA
Back Basin Hide
Mt Tancred 1925
Mt Tregear 2042
Fang Hill 1909
Basins Hut
Mt Allen 1524
Top Tuke Hut
Mt Beaumont 2118
Whitcombe
Mt Frieda 2130
Moa Hill 1655
Thesis Peak 2042
BIRDWOOD RANGE
Urquhart Knob 1228
Mt Hitchin 1720
Raged Peak 1943
Mt Wylde Brown 1475
Price Flat Hut (Old Hut)
Price Flat Hut
Mt Marion 2119
Canyon Crk Bivvy
BLOOMFIELD
Top Waitaha Hut
Mt Young 2080
Mt Williams 2300
Moa Stream Hut
Craigieburn
D
Urquhart Peak 2132
Avoca River
River
Moonbeam Hut
Ivory Lake Hut
Price Basin Hut
ROLLESTON RANGE
Forest Park
The Spurs 1964
Kiwi Flat Hut
Mt Bloomfield 2106
Mt Thorndike 2035
Mt McWhirter 2111
RANGE
Wilberforce
Mt Fitzwilliam 1382
Scamper Torrent Hut
County Stream Hut
Park Dome 2340
Wilkinson Hut
Mt Warner 2249
West Mathias Bivvy
Scarcliffe 1766
50
5780
Mt Durward 1929
Mt Barry 2074
SMYTH RANGE
Neave Hut
Mt Neave 2290
Centenial Cabin
Mathias Hut
Mistake Hill 2099
Turret Peak 2020
Castle Hill 832
Gargarus 1655
Mirage Knob 1780
Mt Evans 2620
Hinge Peak 2184
Jacks Hill 2191
Mt Gideon 1769
Harper
Smyth Hut
Mt Whitcombe 2650
The Amazons Breasts
River
E
Wanganui
River
KA TIRITIRI O TE MOANA
Mueller Peak 2016
RAGGED RANGE
Big Goat Hill 1651
River
Mathias
Lauper Peak 2485
Hunters Hut
BUTLER RA
Mt Algidus 1405
Mt Oakden 1633
L Selfe
River
Blue Lookout 1273
LORD RANGE
Mt Roberts 2107
Mt Butler 2103
Totara Peak 1959
Manuka Peak 1686
River
Mt Cotton 1470
43°45'S
Mt Lord 2072
Evans Hut
5770
Adams
Louper Bivvy
Rakaia
River
Rakaia
River
Blair Peak 2486
Mt Ramsay 2454
Jellicoe Hut
Lake Coleridge
Mt Lambert 2430
Mt Stoddart 2223
Mt Kinkel 2179
Reischek Hut
Prospect Hill 889
Double Hill 682
SOUTHERN ALPS
Malcolm Peak 2512
Lyell Hut
Bastion Peaks 2441
Peak Hill 1240
F
North Peak 2628
Whaleback 670
Newton Peak 2543
Mt Goethe 2350
Prelude Peak 1946
Mt O'Connor 1612
Baker Peak 2259
FROUDE RANGE
RANGE
Jagged Peak 2706
Cascade Hill 1546
PALMER RANGE
5760
The Warrior 2580
Mt Renegade 2389
Lawrence Bivvy
RANGE
Outram Peak 2399
Amazon Peak 2486
JOLLIE
River
Mt Arrowsmith 2781
Smite Peak 2003
Godley Peak 2087
Donald Hill 1525
ARROWSMITH
Cameron Hut
Teddys Hill 1630
Shaggy Hill 922
Lagoon Peak 1988
A-Frame Hut
Helmet Peak 2215
McCoy Hut
Mt Johnstone 2320
WILD MANS BROTHER
Black Hill 2067
G
CLOUDY
South Peak 2276
Middle Hill 1624
Smite R
Ashburton
Redcliffe Hill 940
Havelock
Watchdog Hut
Mt Jollie 2241
Cameron
Round Hill 1497
BLACK HILL RA
Shingle Hill 1873
Lawrence
Pito Peak 2401
Staces Hill 1479
Mt Catherine 2085
PEAK
Watchdog Peak 2079
Lawrence Hut
Wild Mans Top Hut 1656
RANGE
River
Comyns Hut
River
Rat Hill 1450
5750
RANGE
Mt McRae 1737
POTTS RANGE
BIG HILL RANGE
Pyramid 1598
Mt Sugarloaf 1238
TAYLOR RANGE
North Branch
Swift R
MOUNT HUTT
Curtis Memorial Hut
Mistake Flats Hut
Clyde
Ashburton
Cloudy Peak 2403
Lake Heron Nature Reserve
Mt Hecla 1734
H
Finlay Face Hut
Swin R
Mt Caroline 1384
Potts Hut
Red Mountain 1610
River
Double Hut
Mt Bruce 1829
River
Seagull Lake
Mt Potts 2184
Potts
Mt Taylor 2333
43°30'S
River
The Pyramid 1748
Isolated Hill 802
Manuka Lake
Old Man Peak 2221
5740
Boundary Creek Hut
South
Manuka Hut
Emily Hill 963
Ashburton
Mt Sunday 611
River
L Emily
TWO THUMB RANGE
Alma 2510
Rangitata
"Edoras"
Mt Potts
DOGS RANGE
Branch
Maori Lakes Nature Res
WINTERSLOW RA
Mt Winterslow 1700
Mt Alford 1171
J
Exeter 2327
Low Peak 2450
Black Mountain 1809
Dogs Hill 1067
Mt Somers Sub Alpine Walkway
Myrmidon 2474
River
Harpers Knob 841
Lake Clearwater Wildlife Refuge
Woolshed Creek Hut
Pinnacles Hut
Pony Knob 1165
Alford SR
Sharplin Falls SR
The Thumbs 2546
Mt Guy 1319
Alford Forest
Split Peaks 2345
Mt Brabazon 1792
Hakatere
Mt Barrosa 1364
Mt Somers 1687
Duke Knob 739
5730
Mt Pattison 2313
Lake Camp Rec Res
Trinity Hill 1016
72
Paris 2175
170°45'E 2330 2340 171°00'E 2350 2360 171°15'E 2370
Staveley Hill 1085
Flopkey Knob 731
Bushside
171°30'E
1 2 60 3 4 5 61 6 7

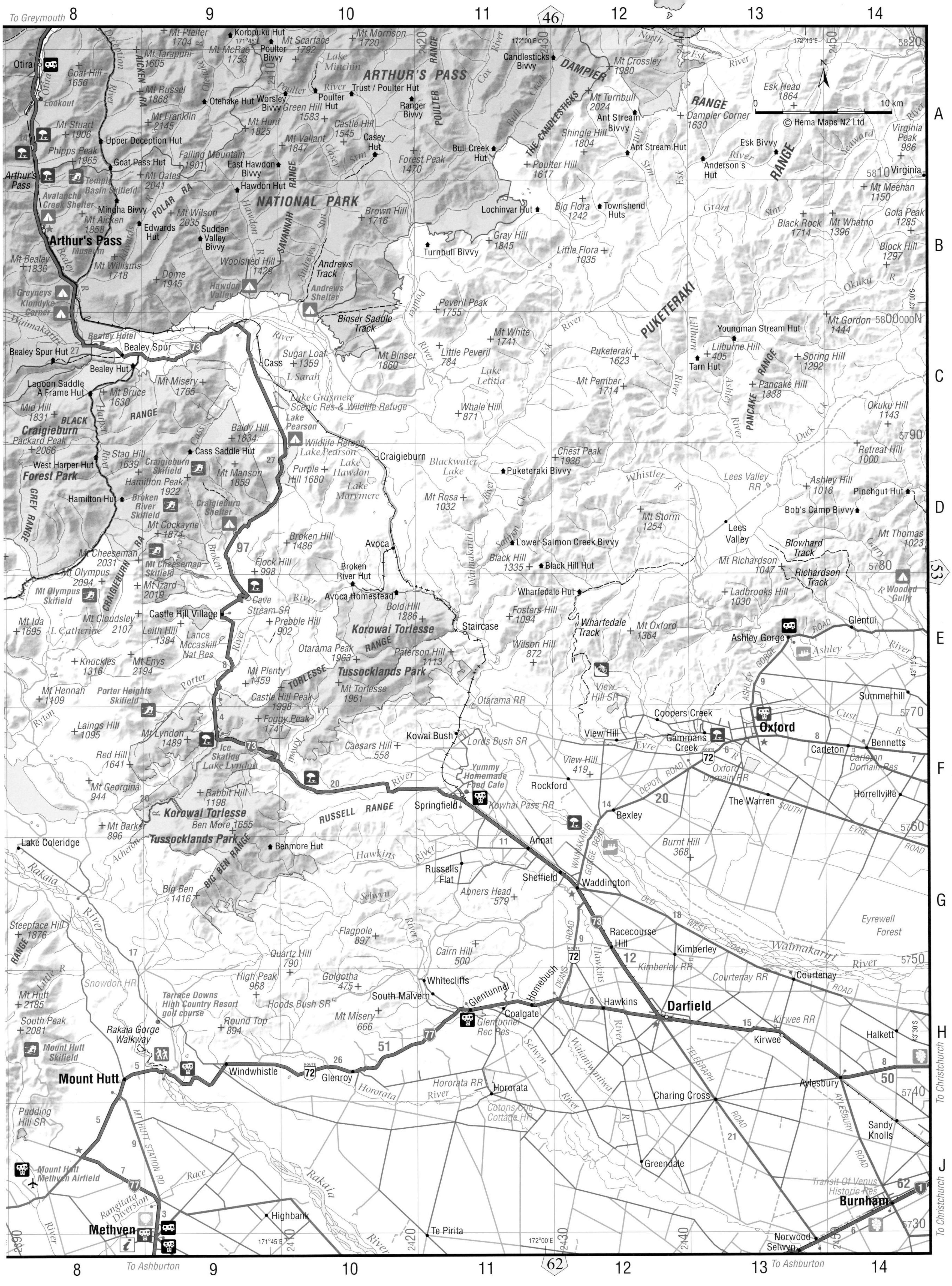

To Greymouth
8
9
10
11
46
12
13
14
A
B
C
D
E
F
G
H
J
53
62
To Ashburton
To Christchurch
© Hema Maps NZ Ltd
0
10 km
N
172°15'E
171°45'E
172°00'E
43°00'S
43°15'S
43°30'S
Otira
Goat Hill 1656
Lookout
Mt Stuart 1906
Phipps Peak 1965
Arthur's Pass
Avalanche Creek Shelter
Temple Basin Skifield
Mt Aicken 1858
Museum
Mt Bealey 1836
Greyneys
Klondyke Corner
Waimakariri
Bealey Hotel
Bealey Spur Hut
Bealey Spur
Bealey Hut
Lagoon Saddle A Frame Hut
Mid Hill 1831
BLACK
Craigieburn
Packard Peak 2066
West Harper Hut
Forest Park
Hamilton Hut
GREY RANGE
Mt Cheeseman 2031
Mt Olympus 2094
Mt Olympus Skifield
Mt Ida 1695
L Catherine
Mt Hennah 1109
Ryton
Laings Hill 1095
Red Hill 1641
Mt Georgina 944
Mt Barker 896
Lake Coleridge
Rakaia
Steepface Hill 1876
RANGE
Mt Hutt 2185
South Peak 2081
Mount Hutt Skifield
Mount Hutt
Pudding Hill SR
Mount Hutt Methven Airfield
Rangitata Diversion
Methven
Mt Pfeifer 1704
Mt Tarapuhi 1605
Mt McRae 1753
Mt Russel 1868
Mt Franklin 2145
Upper Deception Hut
Goat Pass Hut
Mt Oates 2041
Mingha Bivvy
Edwards Hut
POLAR RA
Mt Williams 1718
Dome 1945
Mt Wilson 2035
Sudden Valley Bivvy
Falling Mountain 1901
Otehake Hut
Koropuku Hut
Poulter Bivvy
Worsley Bivvy
Mt Hunt 1825
East Hawdon Bivvy
Hawdon Hut
Woolshed Hill 1429
Hawdon Valley
NATIONAL PARK
ARTHUR'S PASS
Mt Scarface 1792
Lake Minchin
Green Hill 1583
Poulter Hut
Trust / Poulter Hut
Castle Hill 1545
Mt Valiant 1847
Casey Hut
Mt Morrison 1720
Forest Peak 1470
Brown Hill 1716
Andrews Track
Andrews Shelter
Binser Saddle Track
Ranger Bivvy
POULTER RANGE
Candlesticks Bivvy
DAMPIER
THE CANDLESTICKS
Bull Creek Hut
Mt Crossley 1980
Mt Turnbull 2024
Ant Stream Bivvy
Ant Stream Hut
Shingle Hill 1804
Poulter Hill 1617
Lochinvar Hut
Big Flora 1242
Townshend Huts
Turnbull Bivvy
Gray Hill 1845
Little Flora 1035
Esk Head 1864
RANGE
Dampier Corner 1630
Esk Bivvy
Anderson's Hut
Virginia Peak 986
Virginia
Mt Meehan 1150
Gola Peak 1285
Black Rock 1714
Mt Whatno 1396
Block Hill 1297
Okuku
Mt Gordon 1444
PUKETERAKI
Peveril Peak 1755
Mt White 1741
Little Peveril 784
Mt Binser 1860
Sugar Loaf 1359
Cass
L Sarah
Lake Grasmere Scenic Res & Wildlife Refuge
Lake Pearson
Wildlife Refuge Lake Pearson
Lake Letitia
Whale Hill 871
Puketeraki 1623
Mt Pember 1714
Youngman Stream Hut
Lilburne Hill 405
Tarn Hut
Spring Hill 1292
PANCAKE RANGE
Pancake Hill 1338
Okuku Hill 1143
Retreat Hill 1000
Mt Misery 1765
Mt Bruce 1630
RANGE
Baldy Hill 1834
Cass Saddle Hut
Stag Hill 1639
Craigieburn Skifield
Hamilton Peak 1922
Mt Manson 1859
Broken River Skifield
Craigieburn Shelter
Mt Cockayne 1874
Mt Cheeseman Skifield
Mt Izard 2019
CRAIGIEBURN RA
Purple Hill 1680
Lake Hawdon
Lake Marymere
Craigieburn
Blackwater Lake
Chest Peak 1936
Puketeraki Bivvy
Mt Rosa 1032
Lees Valley RR
Ashley Hill 1018
Pinchgut Hut
Bob's Camp Bivvy
Mt Storm 1254
Lees Valley
Blowhard Track
Mt Thomas 1023
Broken Hill 1486
Avoca
Flock Hill 998
Broken River Hut
Lower Salmon Creek Bivvy
Black Hill 1335
Black Hill Hut
Mt Richardson 1047
Richardson Track
Wooded Gully
Cave Stream SR
Castle Hill Village
Avoca Homestead
Bold Hill 1286
Wharfedale Hut
Ladbrooks Hill 1030
Prebble Hill 902
Korowai Torlesse
Staircase
Fosters Hill 1094
Wharfedale Track
Mt Oxford 1364
Ashley Gorge
Glentui
Mt Cloudsley 2107
Leith Hill 1384
Lance Mccaskill Nat Res
Knuckles 1316
Mt Enys 2194
Porter Heights Skifield
Porter
Otarama Peak 1963
RANGE
Paterson Hill 1113
Wilson Hill 872
Ashley
Mt Plenty 1459
TORLESSE
Tussocklands Park
Mt Torlesse 1961
Castle Hill Peak 1998
Foggy Peak 1741
Otarama RR
View Hill SR
Summerhill
Mt Lyndon 1489
Kowai Bush
Lords Bush SR
Coopers Creek
Oxford
View Hill
Gammans Creek
Bennetts
Carleton
Carleton Domain Res
Ice Skating Lake Lyndon
Caesars Hill 558
View Hill 419
Oxford Domain RR
Rabbit Hill 1198
Yummy Homemade Food Cafe
Rockford
DEPOT ROAD
Horrellville
Springfield
Kowhai Pass RR
RUSSELL RANGE
Bexley
The Warren
SOUTH EYRE ROAD
Korowai Torlesse
Ben More 1655
Tussocklands Park
BIG BEN RANGE
Benmore Hut
Hawkins
Annat
Burnt Hill 368
Russells Flat
Sheffield
Waddington
WAIMAKARIRI GORGE ROAD
Big Ben 1416
Abners Head 579
Selwyn
OLD WEST COAST
Eyrewell Forest
Flagpole 897
Racecourse Hill
Kimberley
Cairn Hill 500
Quartz Hill 790
Kimberley RR
Waimakariri River
Courtenay RR
Courtenay
ROAD
Snowdon HR
High Peak 968
Golgotha 475
Whitecliffs
South Malvern
Glentunnel
Homebush
Hawkins
Darfield
Terrace Downs High Country Resort golf course
Hoods Bush SR
Mt Misery 666
Coalgate
Glentunnel Rec Res
Kirwee RR
Kirwee
Halkett
Round Top 894
Rakaia Gorge Walkway
Windwhistle
Glenroy
Hororata RR
Hororata
Aylesbury
Charing Cross
TELEGRAPH ROAD
AYLESBURY ROAD
Cotons Cob Cottage HR
Sandy Knolls
MT HUTT STATION RD
Race
Greendale
Transit Of Venus Historic Res
Burnham
Highbank
Te Pirita
Norwood
Selwyn
73
97
72
77
20
51
50
12

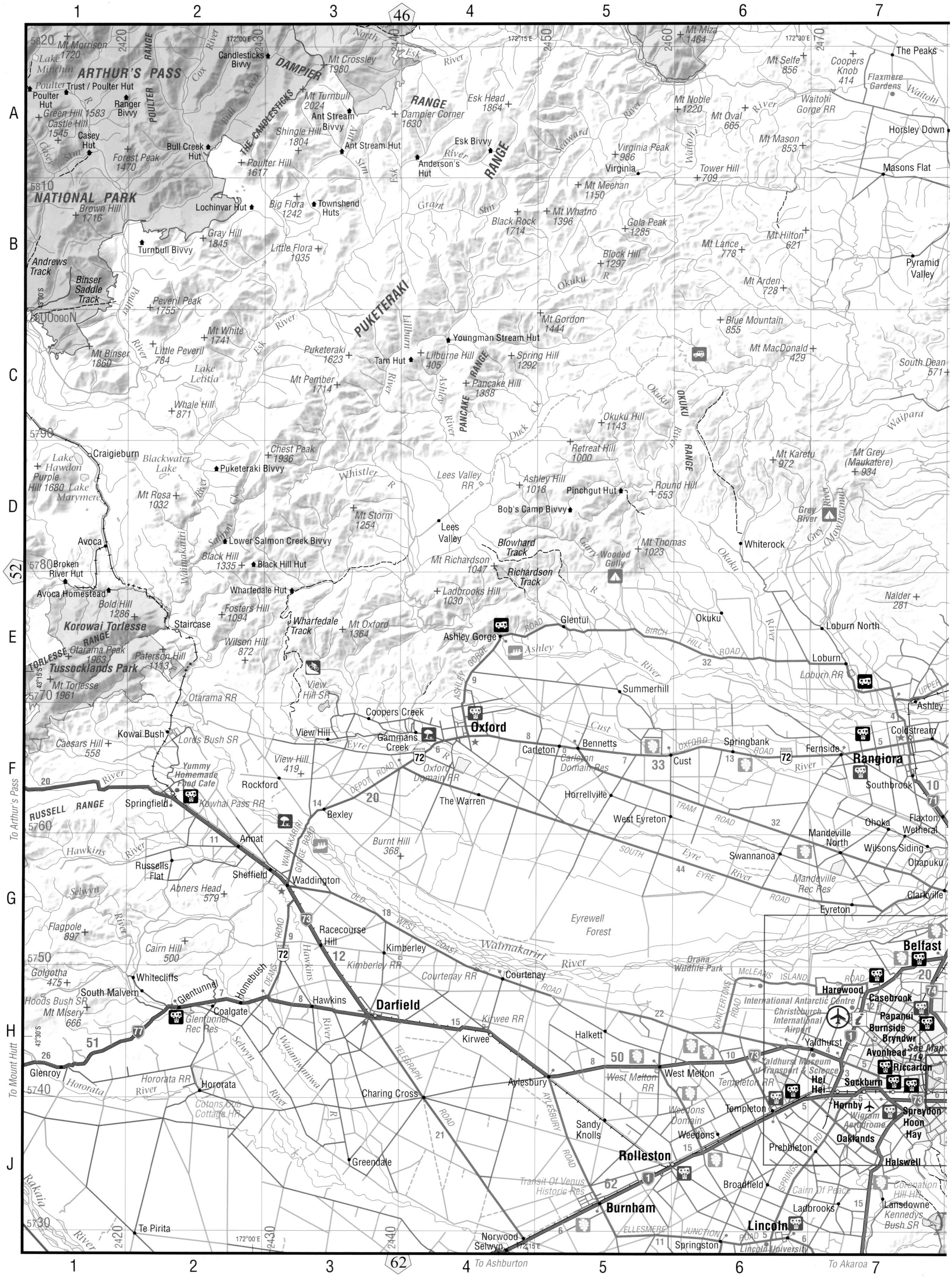

ARTHUR'S PASS
NATIONAL PARK
Mt Morrison 1720
Lake Minchin
Poulter Hut
Trust / Poulter Hut
Ranger Bivvy
Green Hill 1583
Castle Hill 1545
Casey Hut
Forest Peak 1470
POULTER RANGE
Candlesticks Bivvy
DAMPIER
THE CANDLESTICKS
Mt Crossley 1980
Mt Turnbull 2024
Ant Stream Bivvy
Shingle Hill 1804
Ant Stream Hut
Bull Creek Hut
Poulter Hill 1617
Lochinvar Hut
Big Flora 1242
Townshend Huts
Brown Hill 1716
Gray Hill 1845
Turnbull Bivvy
Little Flora 1035
Andrews Track
Binser Saddle Track
Peveril Peak 1755
Mt White 1741
Little Peveril 784
Mt Binser 1860
Lake Letitia
Whale Hill 871
PUKETERAKI
Puketeraki 1623
Mt Pember 1714
Tarn Hut
Lilburne Hill 405
Youngman Stream Hut
Spring Hill 1292
PANCAKE RANGE
Pancake Hill 1338
RANGE
Dampier Corner 1630
Esk Head 1864
Esk Bivvy
Anderson's Hut
Mt Miza 1464
Mt Noble 1220
Mt Oval 665
Mt Selfe 856
Coopers Knob 414
The Peaks
Flaxmere Gardens
Waitohi Gorge RR
Horsley Down
Mt Mason 853
Virginia Peak 986
Virginia
Tower Hill 709
Masons Flat
Mt Meehan 1150
Black Rock 1714
Mt Whatno 1396
Gola Peak 1285
Block Hill 1297
Mt Hilton 621
Mt Lance 778
Pyramid Valley
Mt Arden 728
Mt Gordon 1444
Blue Mountain 855
Mt MacDonald 429
South Dean 571
OKUKU RANGE
Okuku Hill 1143
Retreat Hill 1000
Mt Karetu 972
Mt Grey (Maukatere) 934
Craigieburn
Lake Hawdon
Purple Hill 1680
Lake Marymere
Blackwater Lake
Puketeraki Bivvy
Chest Peak 1936
Mt Rosa 1032
Lees Valley RR
Ashley Hill 1018
Pinchgut Hut
Round Hill 553
Bob's Camp Bivvy
Grey River
Mt Storm 1254
Lees Valley
Whiterock
Avoca
Lower Salmon Creek Bivvy
Blowhard Track
Mt Thomas 1023
Broken River Hut
Black Hill 1335
Black Hill Hut
Mt Richardson 1047
Richardson Track
Wooded Gully
Avoca Homestead
Wharfedale Hut
Ladbrooks Hill 1030
Nalder 281
Bold Hill 1286
Fosters Hill 1094
Korowai Torlesse
Staircase
Wharfedale Track
Mt Oxford 1364
Ashley Gorge
Glentui
Okuku
Loburn North
Otarama Peak 1963
TORLESSE RANGE
Tussocklands Park
Paterson Hill 1113
Wilson Hill 872
Loburn
Loburn RR
Mt Torlesse 1961
Otarama RR
View Hill SR
Summerhill
Ashley
Kowai Bush
Lords Bush SR
Coopers Creek
View Hill
Gammans Creek
Oxford
Carleton
Bennetts
Cust
Springbank
Fernside
Coldstream
Rangiora
Caesars Hill 558
View Hill 419
Oxford Domain RR
Carleton Domain Res
Southbrook
Yummy Homemade Food Cafe
Rockford
Springfield
Kowhai Pass RR
RUSSELL RANGE
Bexley
The Warren
Horrellville
West Eyreton
Flaxton
Ohoka
Wetheral
Annat
Burnt Hill 368
Mandeville North
Wilsons Siding
Russells Flat
Sheffield
Waddington
Swannanoa
Ohapuku
Abners Head 579
Mandeville Rec Res
Clarkville
Eyreton
Eyrewell Forest
Flagpole 897
Racecourse Hill
Kimberley
Cairn Hill 500
Kimberley RR
Courtenay RR
Courtenay
Orana Wildlife Park
Belfast
Golgotha 475
Whitecliffs
South Malvern
Glentunnel
Homebush
Hawkins
Darfield
Harewood
Casebrook
International Antarctic Centre
Christchurch International Airport
Papanui
Hoods Bush SR
Mt Misery 666
Glentunnel Rec Res
Coalgate
Kirwee RR
Kirwee
Halkett
Burnside
Bryndwr
See Map 119
Avonhead
Yaldhurst
Yaldhurst Museum of Transport & Science
Riccarton
Glenroy
Hororata RR
Hororata
Charing Cross
Aylesbury
West Melton
West Melton RR
Templeton RR
Hei Hei
Sockburn
Cotons Cob Cottage HR
Templeton
Hornby
Wigram Aerodrome
Spreydon
Hoon Hay
Sandy Knolls
Weedons Domain
Weedons
Oaklands
Prebbleton
Greendale
Rolleston
Halswell
Transit Of Venus Historic Res
Burnham
Broadfield
Cairn Of Peace
Coronation Hill HR
Lansdowne
Kennedys Bush SR
Ladbrooks
Te Pirita
Norwood
Selwyn
Springston
Lincoln
Lincoln University
To Arthur's Pass
To Mount Hutt
To Ashburton
To Akaroa

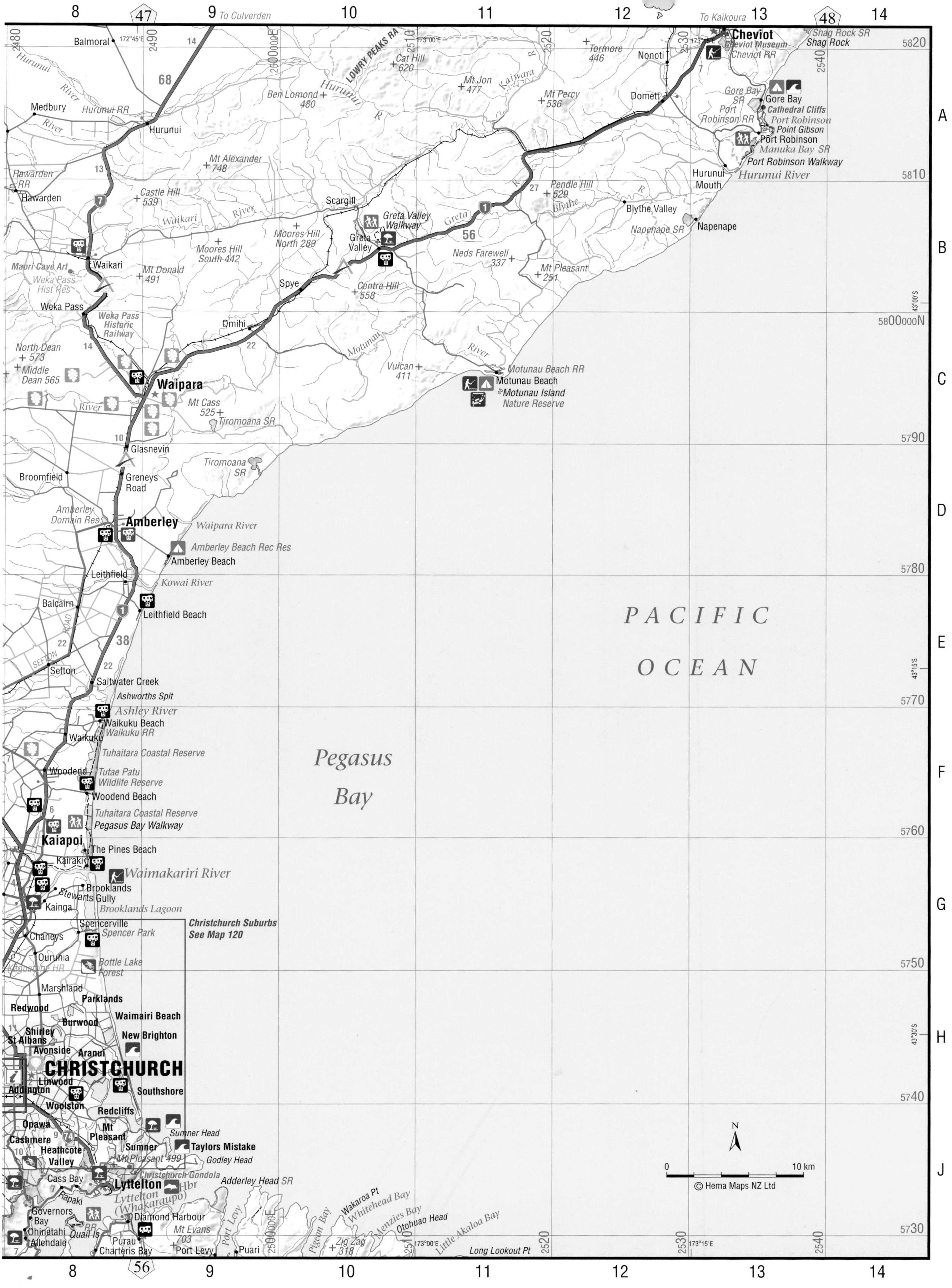

To Culverden
To Kaikoura
Cheviot
Cheviot Museum
Cheviot RR
Shag Rock SR
Shag Rock
Balmoral
LOWRY PEAKS RA
Cat Hill 620
Mt Jon 477
Kaiwara
Tormore 446
Nonoti
Hurunui River
Hurunui RR
Medbury
Hurunui
Ben Lomond 480
Mt Percy 536
Domett
Gore Bay SR
Gore Bay
Cathedral Cliffs
Port Robinson RR
Port Robinson
Point Gibson
Manuka Bay SR
Port Robinson Walkway
Mt Alexander 748
Hawarden RR
Hawarden
Castle Hill 539
Scargill
Pendle Hill 529
Blythe
Blythe Valley
Hurunui Mouth
Hurunui River
Waikari River
Greta Valley Walkway
Greta Valley
Moores Hill North 289
Moores Hill South 442
Napenape SR
Napenape
Maori Cave Art
Waikari
Weka Pass Hist Res
Mt Donald 491
Neds Farewell 337
Mt Pleasant 251
Spye
Centre Hill 558
Weka Pass
Weka Pass Historic Railway
Omihi
North Dean 573
Middle Dean 565
Motunau River
Vulcan 411
Motunau Beach RR
Motunau Beach
Motunau Island Nature Reserve
Waipara
Mt Cass 525
Tiromoana SR
Glasnevin
Broomfield
Greneys Road
Amberley Domain Res
Amberley
Waipara River
Amberley Beach Rec Res
Amberley Beach
Leithfield
Kowai River
Balcairn
Leithfield Beach
Sefton
Saltwater Creek
Ashworths Spit
Ashley River
Waikuku Beach
Waikuku RR
Waikuku
Tuhaitara Coastal Reserve
Woodend
Tutae Patu Wildlife Reserve
Woodend Beach
Pegasus Bay Walkway
Kaiapoi
The Pines Beach
Kairaki
Waimakariri River
Brooklands
Stewarts Gully
Kainga
Brooklands Lagoon
Spencerville
Spencer Park
Christchurch Suburbs See Map 120
Chaneys
Ouruhia
Bottle Lake Forest
Marshland
Parklands
Redwood
Waimairi Beach
Burwood
Shirley
St Albans
New Brighton
Avonside
Aranui
CHRISTCHURCH
Linwood
Addington
Southshore
Woolston
Redcliffs
Opawa
Mt Pleasant
Sumner Head
Cashmere
Sumner
Taylors Mistake
Heathcote Valley
Mt Pleasant 499
Godley Head
Christchurch Gondola
Cass Bay
Adderley Head SR
Lyttelton
Lyttelton Hbr (Whakaraupo)
Rapaki
Governors Bay
Diamond Harbour
Ohinetahi
Quail Is
Mt Evans 703
Allendale
Purau
Charteris Bay
Port Levy
Puari
Pigeon Bay
Wakaroa Pt
Whitehead Bay
Menzies Bay
Otohuao Head
Little Akaloa Bay
Zig Zag 318
Long Lookout Pt
Pegasus Bay
PACIFIC OCEAN
© Hema Maps NZ Ltd

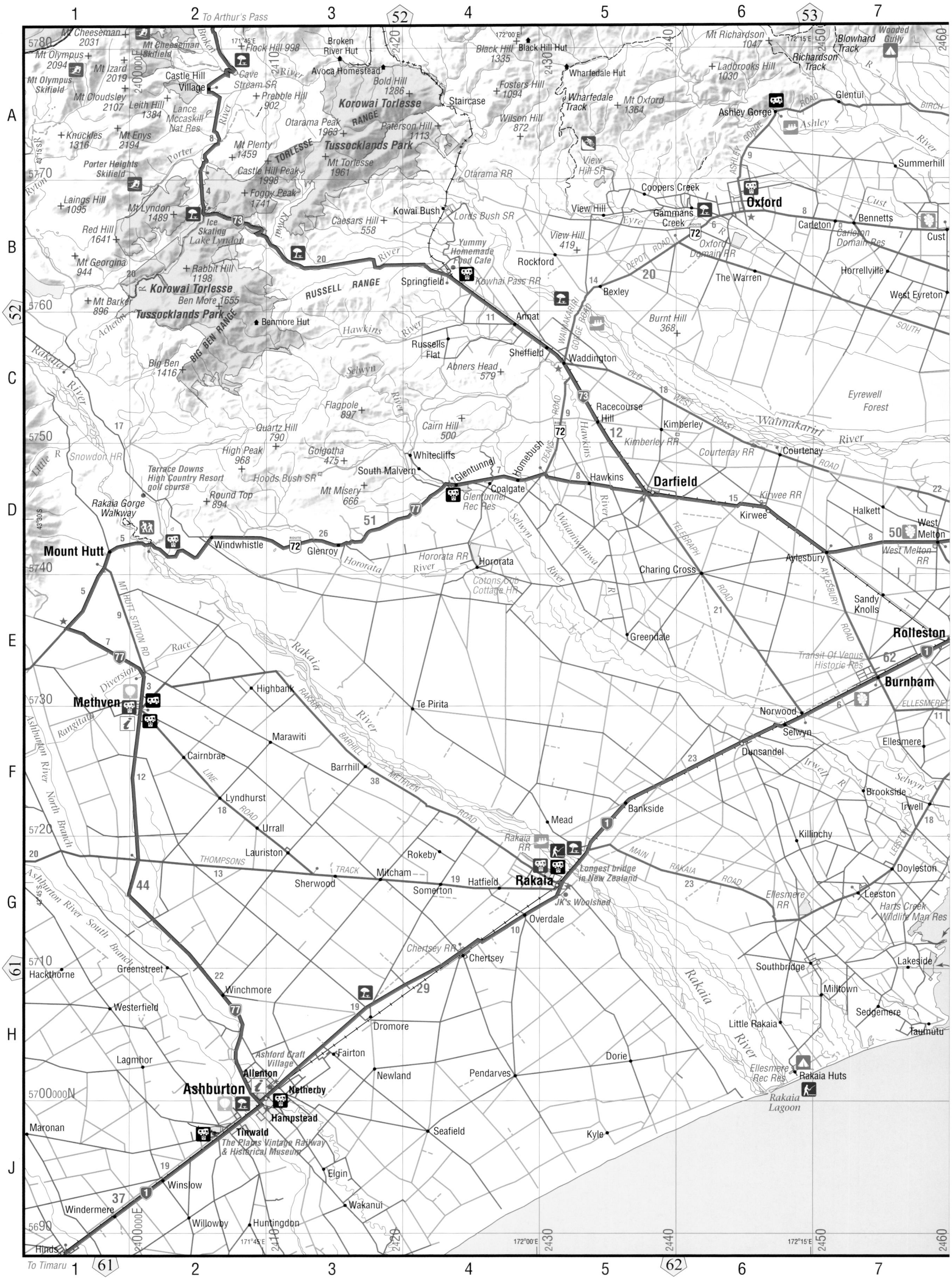

To Arthur's Pass
To Timaru
Mt Cheeseman 2031
Mt Cheeseman Skifield
Mt Olympus 2094
Mt Olympus Skifield
Mt Izard 2019
Mt Cloudsley 2107
Castle Hill Village
Leith Hill 1384
Lance Mccaskill Nat Res
Knuckles 1316
Mt Enys 2194
Porter Heights Skifield
Laings Hill 1095
Mt Lyndon 1489
Red Hill 1641
Ice Skating Lake Lyndon
Mt Georgina 944
Rabbit Hill 1198
Korowai Torlesse Tussocklands Park
Ben More 1655
Mt Barker 896
Benmore Hut
Big Ben 1416
BIG BEN RANGE
Flock Hill 998
Cave Stream SR
Prebble Hill 902
Broken River Hut
Avoca Homestead
Bold Hill 1286
Korowai Torlesse
TORLESSE RANGE
Tussocklands Park
Otarama Peak 1963
Paterson Hill 1113
Mt Plenty 1459
Castle Hill Peak 1998
Mt Torlesse 1961
Foggy Peak 1741
Caesars Hill 558
Staircase
Otarama RR
Kowai Bush
Lords Bush SR
Yummy Homemade Food Cafe
Springfield
Kowhai Pass RR
RUSSELL RANGE
Black Hill 1335
Black Hill Hut
Fosters Hill 1094
Wilson Hill 872
Wharfedale Hut
Wharfedale Track
Mt Oxford 1364
View Hill SR
View Hill
View Hill 419
Rockford
Mt Richardson 1047
Ladbrooks Hill 1030
Blowhard Track
Richardson Track
Wooded Gully
Glentui
Ashley Gorge
Ashley River
Summerhill
Coopers Creek
Oxford
Gammans Creek
Oxford Domain RR
Bennetts
Carleton
Carleton Domain Res
Cust
Horrellville
The Warren
West Eyreton
Bexley
Burnt Hill 368
Amat
Sheffield
Waddington
Russells Flat
Hawkins River
Abners Head 579
Selwyn River
Flagpole 897
Cairn Hill 500
Quartz Hill 790
High Peak 968
Golgotha 475
Whitecliffs
South Malvern
Glentunnel
Glentunnel Rec Res
Coalgate
Homebush
Hoods Bush SR
Mt Misery 666
Round Top 894
Terrace Downs High Country Resort golf course
Rakaia Gorge Walkway
Snowdon HR
Racecourse Hill
Kimberley
Kimberley RR
Courtenay
Courtenay RR
Eyrewell Forest
Waimakariri River
Hawkins
Darfield
Kirwee
Kirwee RR
Halkett
West Melton
West Melton RR
Mount Hutt
Windwhistle
Glenroy
Hororata
Hororata RR
Cotons Cob Cottage HR
Charing Cross
Aylesbury
Sandy Knolls
Greendale
Rolleston
Transit Of Venus Historic Res
Burnham
Norwood
Selwyn
Dunsandel
Ellesmere
Brookside
Irwell
Methven
Highbank
Te Pirita
Marawiti
Cairnbrae
Barrhill
Lyndhurst
Urrall
Lauriston
Rokeby
Mead
Bankside
Killinchy
Doyleston
Mitcham
Sherwood
Somerton
Hatfield
Rakaia
Rakaia RR
Longest bridge in New Zealand
JK's Woolshed
Overdale
Ellesmere RR
Leeston
Harts Creek Wildlife Man Res
Chertsey
Chertsey RR
Southbridge
Lakeside
Milltown
Sedgemere
Taumutu
Little Rakaia
Ellesmere Rec Res
Rakaia Huts
Rakaia Lagoon
Rakaia River
Hackthorne
Greenstreet
Winchmore
Westerfield
Dromore
Lagmhor
Fairton
Ashford Craft Village
Allenton
Ashburton
Netherby
Hampstead
Newland
Pendarves
Dorie
Seafield
Kyle
Maronan
Tinwald
The Plains Vintage Railway & Historical Museum
Elgin
Winslow
Wakanui
Windermere
Willowby
Huntingdon
Hinds
Ashburton River North Branch
Ashburton River South Branch

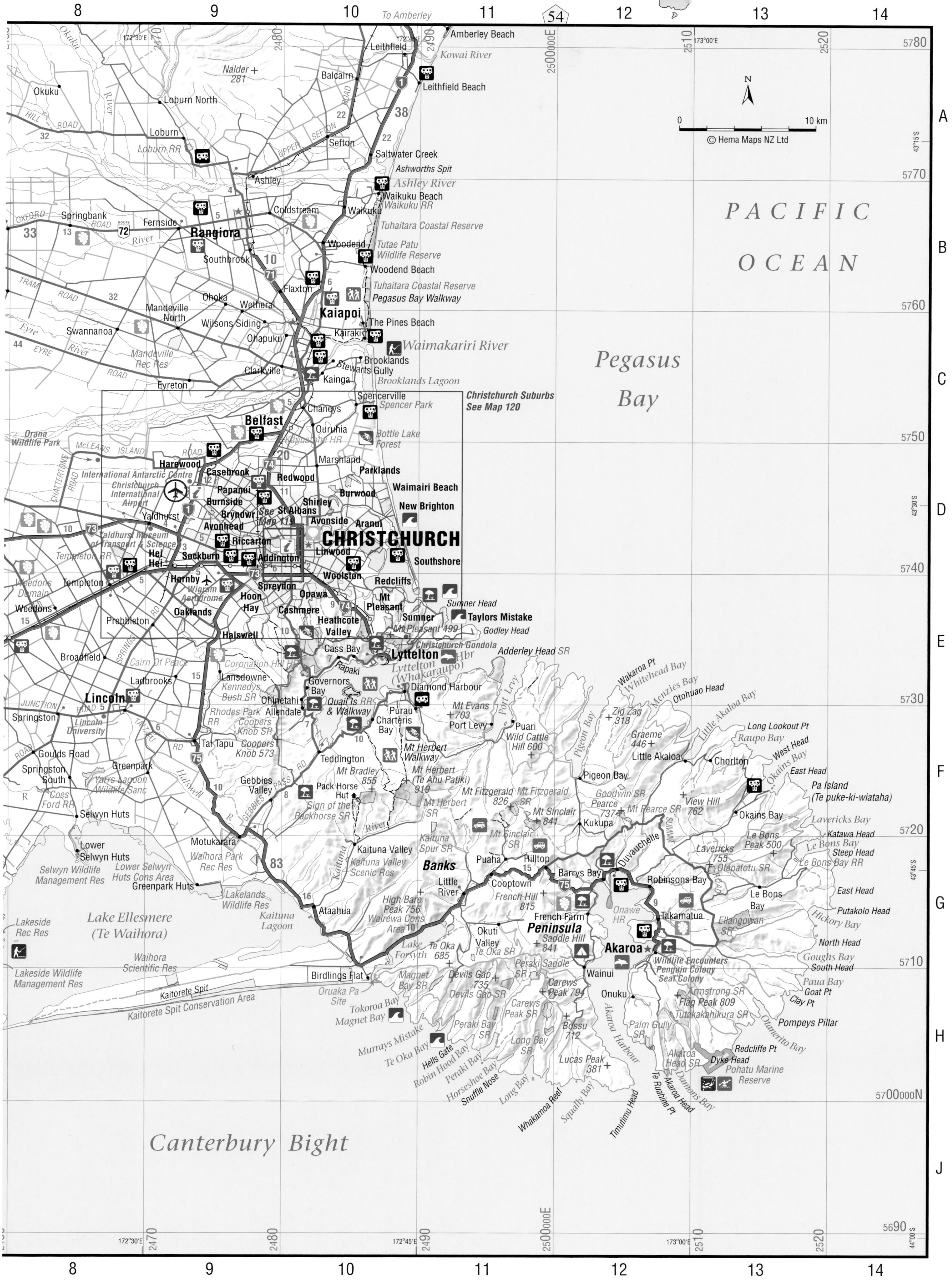

To Amberley
54
Amberley Beach
Leithfield
Kowai River
Leithfield Beach
Balcairn
Nalder 281
Okuku
Loburn North
Loburn
Loburn RR
Hill Road
Upper Sefton Road
Sefton
Saltwater Creek
Ashworths Spit
Ashley
Ashley River
Waikuku Beach
Waikuku RR
Waikuku
Coldstream
Springbank
Oxford Road
Fernside
Rangiora
River
Southbrook
Tuhaitara Coastal Reserve
Tutae Patu Wildlife Reserve
Woodend
Woodend Beach
Flaxton
Tram Road
Ohoka
Wetheral
Tuhaitara Coastal Reserve
Pegasus Bay Walkway
Kaiapoi
Mandeville North
Wilsons Siding
Swannanoa
The Pines Beach
Kairaki
Waimakariri River
Ohapuku
Eyre River
Mandeville Rec Res
Brooklands
Stewarts Gully
Clarkville
Kainga
Brooklands Lagoon
Eyreton
Spencerville
Spencer Park
Christchurch Suburbs See Map 120
Chaneys
Belfast
Ouruhia
Bottle Lake Forest
Orana Wildlife Park
McLeans Island Road
Marshland
Harewood
Casebrook
Parklands
International Antarctic Centre
Christchurch International Airport
Redwood
Papanui
Waimairi Beach
Burnside
Shirley
Burwood
New Brighton
Bryndwr
St Albans
Yaldhurst
Avonside
Aranui
Avonhead
CHRISTCHURCH
Yaldhurst Museum of Transport & Science
Riccarton
Linwood
Templeton RR
Hei Hei
Sockburn
Addington
Southshore
Weedons Domain
Templeton
Hornby
Wigram Aerodrome
Woolston
Redcliffs
Spreydon
Opawa
Weedons
Hoon Hay
Mt Pleasant
Sumner Head
Oaklands
Cashmere
Taylors Mistake
Sumner
Prebbleton
Heathcote Valley
Godley Head
Halswell
Mt Pleasant 499
Broadfield
Cass Bay
Christchurch Gondola
Lyttelton
Adderley Head SR
Cairn Of Peace
Coronation Hill
Rapaki
Lyttelton Hbr (Whakaraupo)
Lansdowne
Ladbrooks
Kennedys Bush SR
Governors Bay
Diamond Harbour
Lincoln
Ohinetahi
Quail Is & Walkway
Junction Road
Allendale
Purau
Springston
Rhodes Park RR
Mt Evans 703
Port Levy
Port Levy
Lincoln University
Coopers Knob SR
Charteris Bay
Puari
Wild Cattle Hill 600
Wakaroa Pt
Whitehead Bay
Menzies Bay
Otohuao Head
Little Akaloa Bay
Zig Zag 318
Pigeon Bay
Long Lookout Pt
Raupo Bay
Tai Tapu
Coopers Knob 573
Graeme 446
West Head
Goulds Road
Mt Herbert Walkway
Teddington
Little Akaloa
Chorlton
Okains Bay
Springston South
Greenpark
Yarrs Lagoon Wildlife Sanc
Mt Bradley 855
Mt Herbert (Te Ahu Patiki) 919
Pigeon Bay
East Head
Pa Island (Te puke-ki-wiataha)
Coes Ford RR
Gebbies Valley
Gebbies Pass
Pack Horse Hut
Mt Fitzgerald 826
Mt Fitzgerald SR
Goodwin SR
Pearce 737
Mt Pearce SR
View Hill 762
Halswell
Mt Herbert SR
Sign of the Packhorse SR
Mt Sinclair 841
Kukupa
Okains Bay
Lavericks Bay
Selwyn Huts
River
Summit Road
Katawa Head
Motukarara
Mt Sinclair SR
Le Bons Peak 500
Le Bons Bay
Lower Selwyn Huts
Waihora Park Rec Res
Kaituna Valley
Kaituna Spur SR
Hilltop
Lavericks 755
Steep Head
Kaituna Valley Scenic Res
Duvauchelle
Otepatotu SR
Le Bons Bay RR
Selwyn Wildlife Management Res
Lower Selwyn Huts Cons Area
Kaituna
Banks
Puaha
Barrys Bay
Robinsons Bay
Greenpark Huts
Little River
Cooptown
Le Bons Bay
East Head
Lakelands Wildlife Res
Ataahua
High Bare Peak 756
French Hill 815
Onawe HR
Putakolo Head
Lakeside Rec Res
Lake Ellesmere (Te Waihora)
Kaituna Lagoon
Wairewa Cons Area
French Farm
Takamatua
Ellangowan SR
Hickory Bay
Okuti Valley
Peninsula
Saddle Hill 841
North Head
Lake Forsyth
Te Oka 685
Te Oka SR
Akaroa
Goughs Bay
South Head
Waihora Scientific Res
Peraki Saddle SR
Wainui
Wildlife Encounters Penguin Colony Seal Colony
Lakeside Wildlife Management Res
Birdlings Flat
Magnet Bay SR
Devils Gap 735
Devils Gap SR
Carews Peak 794
Paua Bay
Goat Pt
Clay Pt
Armstrong SR
Kaitorete Spit
Oruaka Pa Site
Onuku
Flag Peak 809
Kaitorete Spit Conservation Area
Tokoroa Bay
Carews Peak SR
Tutakakahikura SR
Pompeys Pillar
Magnet Bay
Peraki Bay SR
Palm Gully SR
Otanerito Bay
Murrays Mistake
Long Bay SR
Bossu 712
Akaroa Harbour
Redcliffe Pt
Te Oka Bay
Hells Gate
Robin Hood Bay
Peraki Bay
Akaroa Head SR
Dyke Head
Lucas Peak 381
Pohatu Marine Reserve
Horseshoe Bay
Snuffle Nose
Long Bay
Damons Bay
Whakamoa Reef
Squally Bay
Timutimu Head
Te Ruahine Pt
Akaroa Head
PACIFIC OCEAN
Pegasus Bay
Canterbury Bight
0 10 km
© Hema Maps NZ Ltd
N

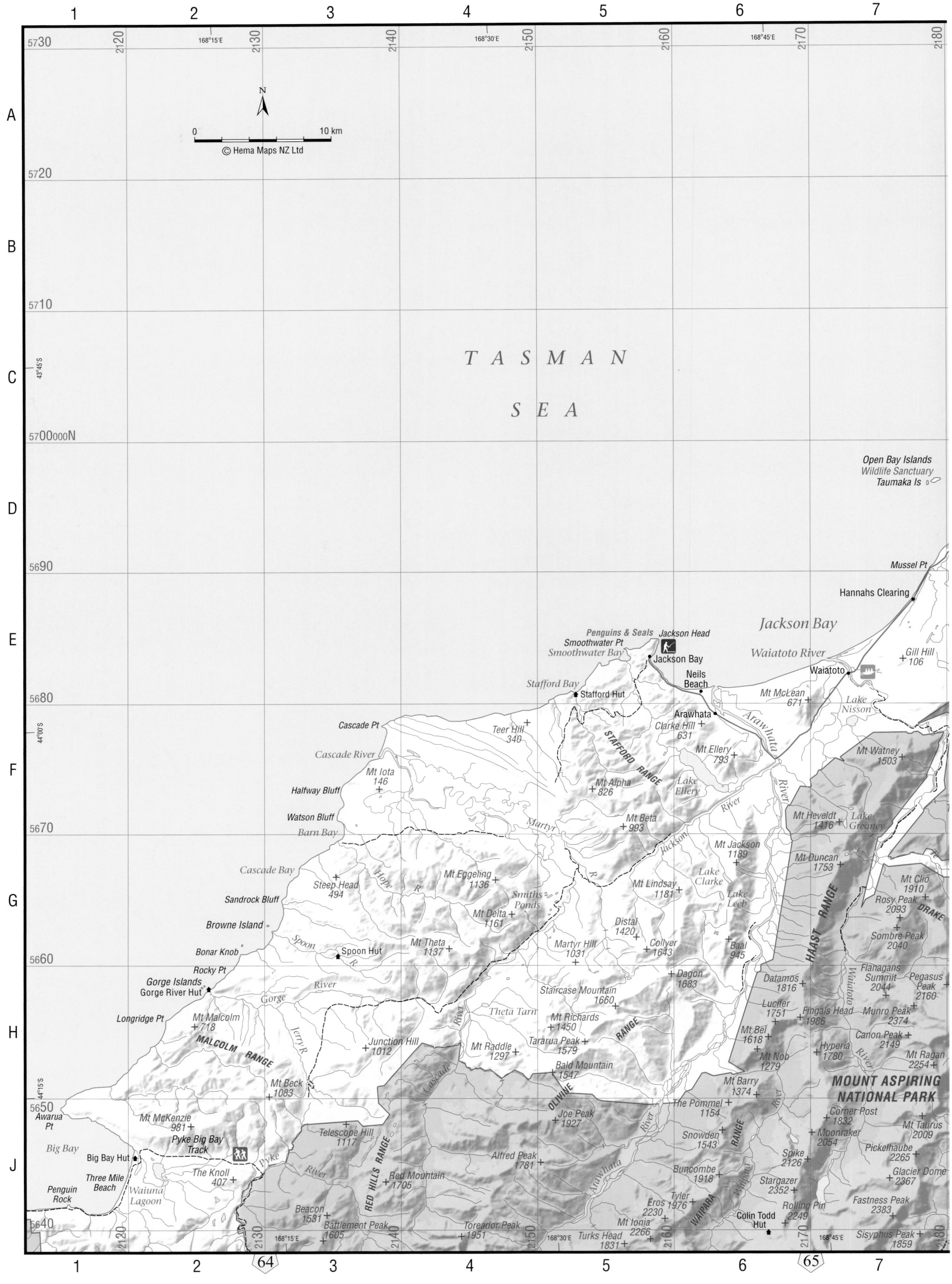

1
2
3
4
5
6
7
A
B
C
D
E
F
G
H
J
5730
5720
5710
5700000N
5690
5680
5670
5660
5650
5640
2120
2130
2140
2150
2160
2170
2180
168°15'E
168°30'E
168°45'E
43°45'S
44°00'S
44°15'S
N
0
10 km
© Hema Maps NZ Ltd
T A S M A N
S E A
Open Bay Islands
Wildlife Sanctuary
Taumaka Is
Mussel Pt
Hannahs Clearing
Jackson Bay
Waiatoto River
Gill Hill
106
Waiatoto
Penguins & Seals
Jackson Head
Smoothwater Pt
Smoothwater Bay
Jackson Bay
Neils
Beach
Stafford Bay
Stafford Hut
Mt McLean
671
Lake
Nisson
Arawhata
Clarke Hill
631
Arawhata
Teer Hill
340
Cascade Pt
STAFFORD RANGE
Mt Ellery
793
Cascade River
Mt Iota
146
Mt Watney
1503
Halfway Bluff
Mt Alpha
826
Lake
Ellery
River
Watson Bluff
Barn Bay
Martyr
Mt Beta
993
Jackson
River
Mt Heveldt
1416
Lake
Greaney
Mt Jackson
1189
Mt Duncan
1753
Cascade Bay
Hope
R
Mt Eggeling
1136
R
Lake
Clarke
Mt Clio
1910
Steep Head
494
Smiths
Ponds
Mt Lindsay
1181
Lake
Leeb
HAAST RANGE
Rosy Peak
2093
DRAKE
Sandrock Bluff
Mt Delta
1161
Browne Island
Distal
1420
Sombre Peak
2040
Spoon
Mt Theta
1137
Martyr Hill
1031
Collyer
1643
Baal
945
Bonar Knob
Spoon Hut
R
Flanagans
Summit
2044
Pegasus
Peak
2160
Rocky Pt
Dagon
1683
Datamos
1816
Gorge Islands
Gorge River Hut
River
Staircase Mountain
1660
Waiatoto
Gorge
Lucifer
1751
Fingals Head
1986
Munro Peak
2374
Longridge Pt
Mt Malcolm
718
Theta Tarn
Mt Richards
1450
Jerry R
River
RANGE
Mt Bel
1618
Hyperia
1780
Canon Peak
2149
MALCOLM RANGE
Junction Hill
1012
Mt Raddle
1297
Tararua Peak
1579
Mt Nob
1279
River
Mt Ragan
2254
Bald Mountain
1547
Cascade
Mt Beck
1083
OLIVINE
Mt Barry
1374
MOUNT ASPIRING
NATIONAL PARK
Awarua
Pt
Mt McKenzie
981
Joe Peak
1927
The Pommel
1154
River
Corner Post
1832
Mt Taurus
2009
Big Bay
Pyke Big Bay
Track
Telescope Hill
1117
River
Snowden
1543
RANGE
Moonraker
2054
Pickelhaube
2265
Big Bay Hut
Pyke
Alfred Peak
1781
Spike
2126
Glacier Dome
2367
Three Mile
Beach
The Knoll
407
River
RED HILLS RANGE
Red Mountain
1705
Arawhata
Buncombe
1918
Stargazer
2352
Penguin
Rock
Waiuna
Lagoon
Tyler
1976
Fastness Peak
2383
Beacon
1581
Eros
2230
WAIPARA
Rolling Pin
2249
Battlement Peak
1605
Toreador Peak
1951
Mt Ionia
2266
Colin Todd
Hut
Turks Head
1831
Sisyphus Peak
1859

64
65

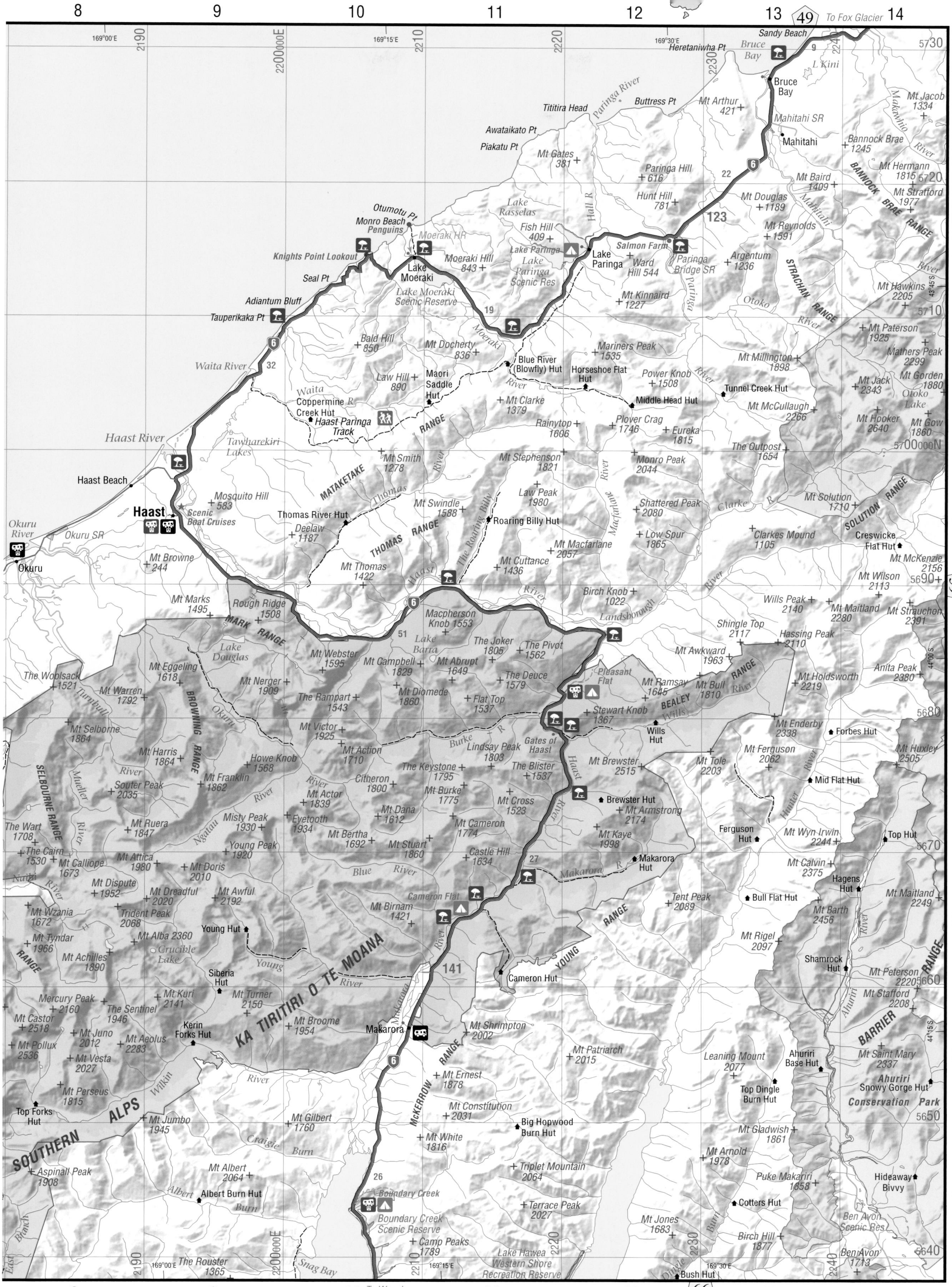
Haast
Bruce Bay
Mahitahi
Lake Moeraki
Lake Paringa
Haast Beach
Okuru
Makarora
Knights Point Lookout
Haast Paringa Track
MATAKETAKE RANGE
THOMAS RANGE
MARK RANGE
BROWNING RANGE
SELBOURNE RANGE
BEALEY RANGE
YOUNG RANGE
McKERROW RANGE
STRACHAN RANGE
SOLUTION RANGE
BARRIER RANGE
BANNOCK BRAE RANGE
KA TIRITIRI O TE MOANA
SOUTHERN ALPS
Ahuriri Conservation Park
Gates of Haast
Cameron Flat
Boundary Creek
Lake Hawea Western Shore Recreation Reserve
To Fox Glacier
To Wanaka
49
59
66

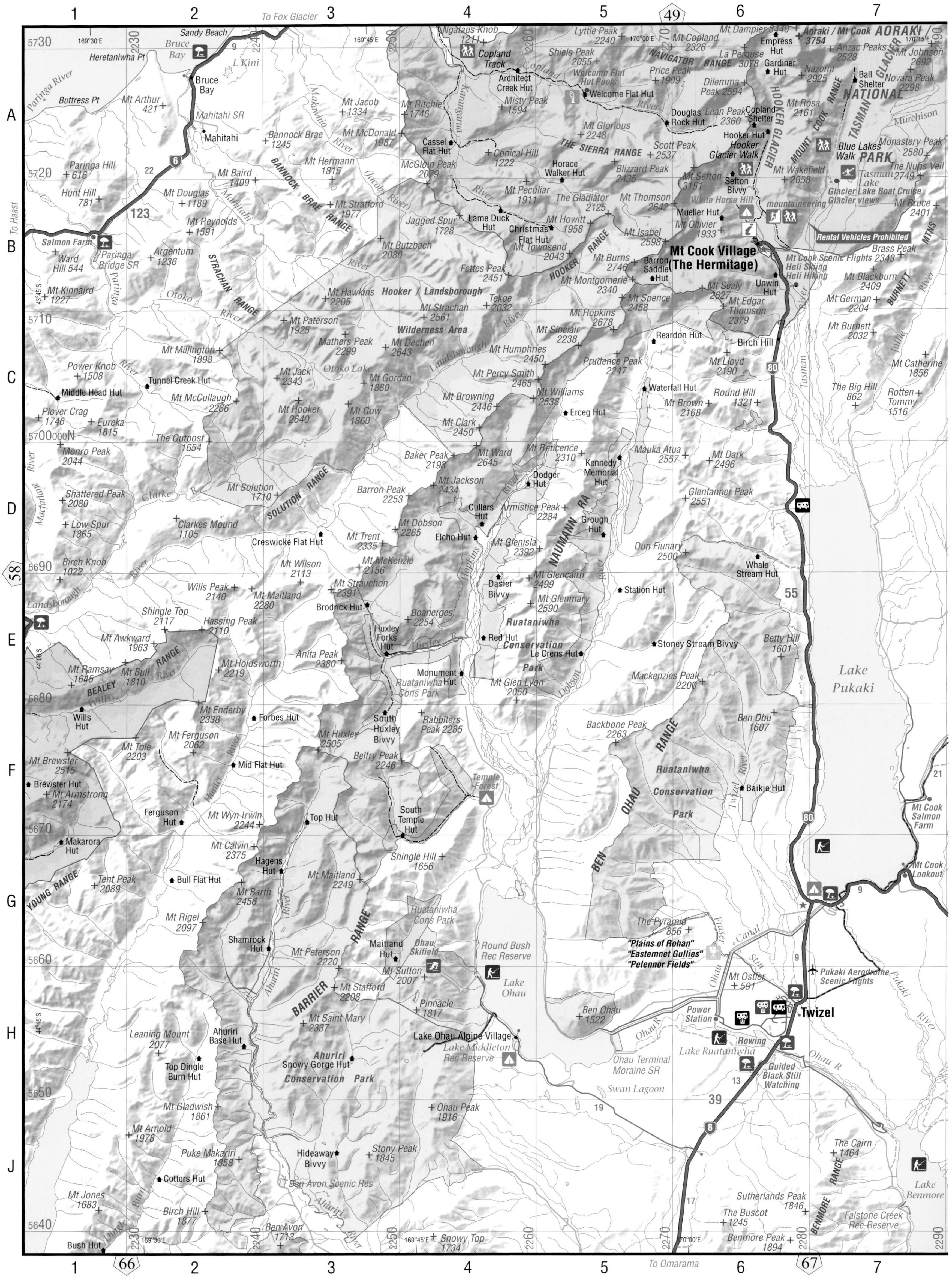

To Fox Glacier
49
To Haast
58
66
67
To Omarama
Sandy Beach
Bruce Bay
Heretaniwha Pt
L Kini
Paringa River
Buttress Pt
Mt Arthur 421
Mahitahi SR
Mahitahi
Paringa Hill 616
Hunt Hill 781
Salmon Farm
Ward Hill 544
Paringa Bridge SR
Mt Kinnaird 1227
Mt Baird 1409
Mt Douglas 1189
Mt Reynolds 1591
Argentum 1236
STRACHAN RANGE
Otoko River
Mt Jacob 1334
Bannock Brae 1245
BANNOCK BRAE RANGE
Mt Hermann 1815
Mt Stratford 1977
Jacobs River
Mt McDonald 1987
Mt Ritchie 1746
Makawhio River
Ngataus Knob 1211
Copland Track
Architect Creek Hut
Karangarua
Cassel Flat Hut
McGloin Peak 2079
Jagged Spur 1728
Mt Butzbach 2080
Lame Duck Hut
Christmas Flat Hut
Conical Hill 1222
Misty Peak 1594
Copland River
Welcome Flat Hot Pools
Welcome Flat Hut
Shiels Peak 2055
Lyttle Peak 2240
Mt Copland 2326
NAVIGATOR RANGE
Price Peak 1909
La Perouse 3078
Mt Dampier 3440
Aoraki / Mt Cook 3754
Empress Hut
Anzac Peaks 2528
Gardiner Hut
Dilemma Peak 2594
Lean Peak 2360
Douglas Rock Hut
Copland Shelter
Hooker Hut
Hooker Glacier Walk
HOOKER GLACIER
Nazomi 2925
Mt Rosa 2161
MOUNT COOK RANGE
TASMAN GLACIER
AORAKI / MOUNT COOK NATIONAL PARK
Mt Johnson 2692
Ball Shelter
Novara Peak 2298
Murchison
Blue Lakes Walk
Monastery Peak 2580
The Nuns Veil 2749
Tasman Lake
Glacier Lake Boat Cruise
Glacier views
Mt Bruce 2401
Mt Wakefield 2058
mountaineering
Mt Sefton 3151
Sefton Bivvy
White Horse Hill
Mueller Hut
Mt Ollivier 1933
Rental Vehicles Prohibited
Mt Glorious 2248
THE SIERRA RANGE
Scott Peak 2537
Horace Walker Hut
Blizzard Peak 2435
Mt Peculiar 1911
The Gladiator 2125
Mt Thomson 2642
Mt Howitt 1958
Mt Townsend 2043
HOOKER RANGE
Mt Isabel 2598
Mt Cook Village (The Hermitage)
Mt Burns 2746
Barron Saddle Hut
Mt Montgomerie 2340
Mt Cook Scenic Flights
Heli Skiing
Heli Hiking
Brass Peak 2343
Unwin Hut
Mt Sealy 2627
Mt Edgar Thomson 2379
Mt Blackburn 2409
BURNETT MTNS
Mt German 2204
Mt Burnett 2032
Jollie
Mt Spence 2458
Mt Hopkins 2678
Fettes Peak 2451
Tekoe 2032
Mt Hawkins 2205
Hooker / Landsborough Wilderness Area
Mt Strachan 2561
Mt Paterson 1925
Mathers Peak 2299
Mt Dechen 2643
Otoko Lake
Mt Jack 2343
Mt Gorden 1880
Landsborough
Mt Sinclair 2238
Reardon Hut
Birch Hill
Tasman River
Mt Catherine 1856
Mt Humphries 2450
Prudence Peak 2247
Mt Lloyd 2190
Mt Percy Smith 2465
Mt Williams 2538
Waterfall Hut
Round Hill 1321
The Big Hill 862
Rotten Tommy 1516
Mt Browning 2446
Erceg Hut
Mt Brown 2168
Mt Clark 2450
Power Knob 1508
Tunnel Creek Hut
Middle Head Hut
Mt McCullaugh 2266
Mt Millington 1898
Plover Crag 1746
Eureka 1815
Mt Hooker 2640
Mt Gow 1860
The Outpost 1654
Monro Peak 2044
Macfarlane River
Shattered Peak 2080
Clarke R
Mt Solution 1710
SOLUTION RANGE
Low Spur 1865
Clarkes Mound 1105
Birch Knob 1022
Landsborough
Baker Peak 2193
Mt Ward 2645
Mt Reticence 2310
Kennedy Memorial Hut
Mauka Atua 2557
Mt Dark 2496
Mt Jackson 2434
Dodger Hut
Barron Peak 2253
Glentanner Peak 2551
Cullers Hut
Armistice Peak 2284
NAUMANN RA
Grough Hut
Mt Dobson 2265
Elcho Hut
Creswicke Flat Hut
Mt Trent 2335
Mt Glenisla 2392
Dun Fiunary 2500
Whale Stream Hut
Mt McKenzie 2156
Mt Wilson 2113
Hopkins
Dasler Bivvy
Mt Glencairn 2499
Station Hut
55
Mt Strauchon 2391
Wills Peak 2140
Mt Maitland 2280
Brodrick Hut
Mt Glenmary 2590
Boanerges 2254
Shingle Top 2117
Hassing Peak 2110
Ruataniwha Conservation Park
Red Hut
Le Crens Hut
Stoney Stream Bivvy
Betty Hill 1601
Mt Awkward 1963
Huxley Forks Hut
Huxley R
Anita Peak 2380
Monument Hut
Ruataniwha Cons Park
Mt Glen Lyon 2050
Dobson
Mackenzies Peak 2200
Lake Pukaki
BEALEY RANGE
Mt Ramsay 1645
Mt Bull 1810
Wills River
Mt Holdsworth 2219
Wills Hut
Mt Enderby 2338
Forbes Hut
South Huxley Bivvy
Rabbiters Peak 2285
Backbone Peak 2263
Ben Dhu 1607
Mt Ferguson 2062
Mt Tole 2203
Mt Huxley 2505
Belfry Peak 2246
Mt Brewster 2515
Brewster Hut
Mt Armstrong 2174
Mid Flat Hut
Hunter River
Temple Forest
BEN OHAU RANGE
Ruataniwha Conservation Park
Twizel River
Baikie Hut
21
Mt Cook Salmon Farm
Ferguson Hut
Mt Wyn Irwin 2244
Top Hut
South Temple Hut
Makarora Hut
Mt Calvin 2375
Hagens Hut
Shingle Hill 1656
Mt Cook Lookout
YOUNG RANGE
Tent Peak 2089
Bull Flat Hut
Mt Maitland 2249
Mt Barth 2456
9
Mt Rigel 2097
Ruataniwha Cons Park
BARRIER RANGE
The Pyramid 856
Fraser
Canal
Shamrock Hut
Maitland Hut
Ohau Skifield
Round Bush Rec Reserve
"Plains of Rohan"
"Eastemnet Gullies"
"Pelennor Fields"
Mt Peterson 2220
Mt Sutton 2007
Lake Ohau
Mt Ostler 591
Pukaki Aerodrome Scenic Flights
Pukaki River
Mt Stafford 2208
Pinnacle 1817
Ohau
Ahuriri
Mt Saint Mary 2337
Ben Ohau 1522
Power Station
Twizel
Leaning Mount 2077
Ahuriri Base Hut
Lake Ohau Alpine Village
Lake Middleton Rec Reserve
Ohau R
Rowing
Lake Ruataniwha
Top Dingle Burn Hut
Ahuriri Snowy Gorge Hut
Conservation Park
Ohau Terminal Moraine SR
Guided Black Stilt Watching
13
Swan Lagoon
Mt Gladwish 1861
Ohau Peak 1916
19
39
8
Mt Arnold 1978
The Cairn 1464
Puke Makariri 1858
Hideaway Bivvy
Stony Peak 1845
Cotters Hut
Ben Avon Scenic Res
Ahuriri River
Lake Benmore
Mt Jones 1683
Dingle Burn
Birch Hill 1877
Sutherlands Peak 1846
BENMORE RANGE
17
The Buscot 1245
Falstone Creek Rec Reserve
Ben Avon 1713
Snowy Top 1734
Benmore Peak 1894
Bush Hut

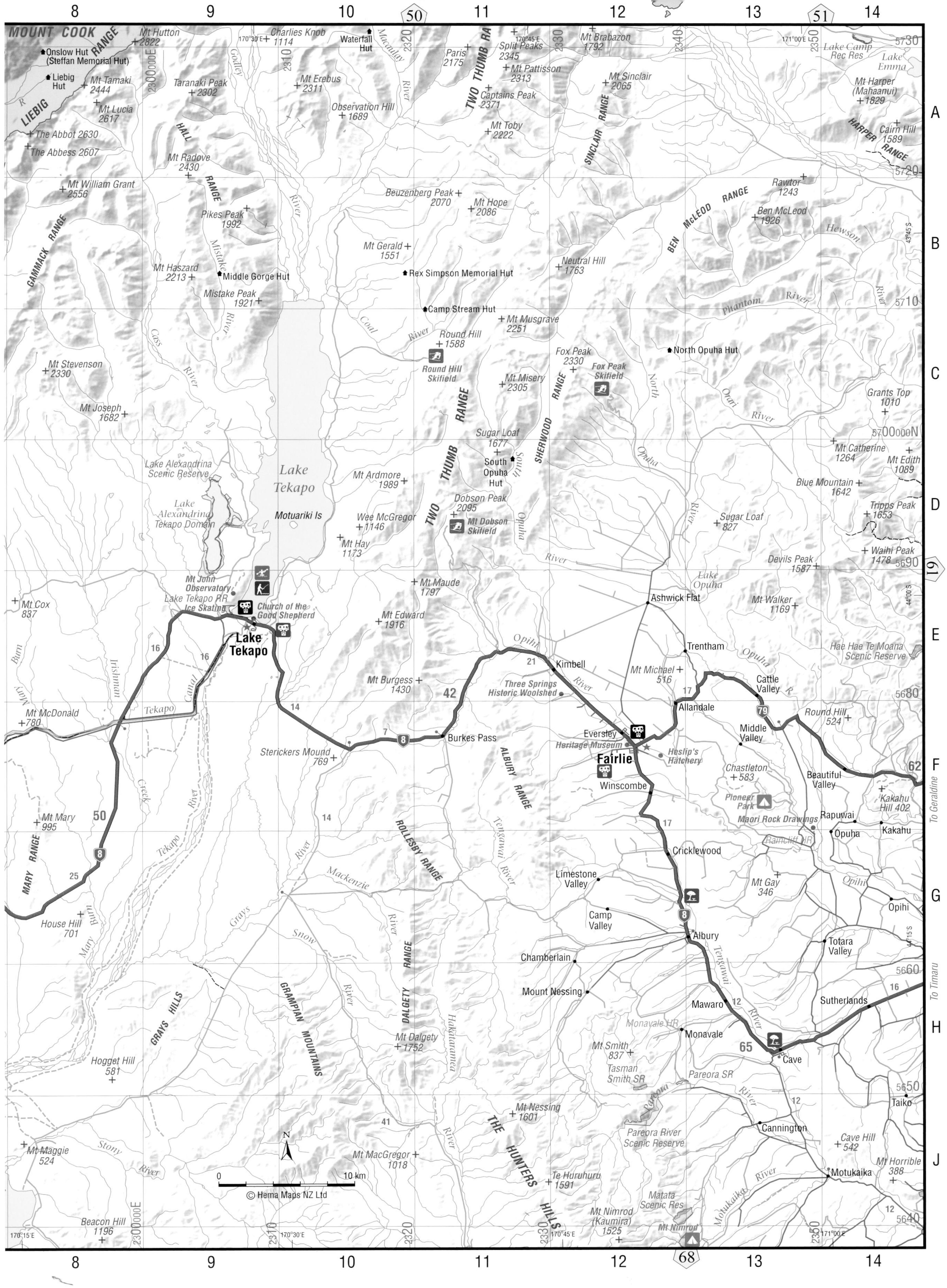

8
9
10
50
11
12
13
51
14
MOUNT COOK
Onslow Hut (Steffan Memorial Hut)
Liebig Hut
LIEBIG
RANGE
Mt Hutton 2822
Mt Tamaki 2444
Mt Lucia 2617
The Abbot 2630
The Abbess 2607
Charlies Knob 1114
170°30'E
Waterfall Hut
Godley
Macaulay
River
Paris 2175
TWO THUMB RA
170°45'E
Split Peaks 2345
Mt Pattisson 2313
Captains Peak 2371
Mt Toby 2222
Mt Brabazon 1792
Mt Sinclair 2065
SINCLAIR RANGE
171°00'E
Lake Camp Rec Res
Lake Emma
Mt Harper (Mahaanui) 1829
Cairn Hill 1589
HARPER RANGE
Taranaki Peak 2302
Mt Erebus 2311
Observation Hill 1689
HALL
RANGE
Mt Radove 2430
Mt William Grant 2556
Beuzenberg Peak 2070
Mt Hope 2086
Rawtor 1243
BEN McLEOD RANGE
Ben McLeod 1926
Hewson
Pikes Peak 1992
GAMMACK RANGE
Mt Gerald 1551
Mt Haszard 2213
Middle Gorge Hut
Mistake
Rex Simpson Memorial Hut
Neutral Hill 1763
43°45'S
Mistake Peak 1921
Camp Stream Hut
Phantom
River
Coal
River
Mt Musgrave 2251
Round Hill 1588
Round Hill Skifield
North Opuha Hut
Cass
River
Fox Peak 2330
Fox Peak Skifield
Mt Stevenson 2330
Mt Misery 2305
RANGE
SHERWOOD
North
Grants Top 1010
Otari
River
Mt Joseph 1682
RANGE
Sugar Loaf 1677
South Opuha Hut
Mt Catherine 1264
Mt Edith 1089
Lake Alexandrina Scenic Reserve
Lake Tekapo
TWO THUMB
Mt Ardmore 1989
Opuha
Blue Mountain 1642
Lake Alexandrina Tekapo Domain
Motuariki Is
Wee McGregor 1146
Dobson Peak 2095
Mt Dobson Skifield
Sugar Loaf 827
Tripps Peak 1653
Mt Hay 1173
River
Waihi Peak 1478
Devils Peak 1587
Mt John Observatory
Lake Tekapo RR
Ice Skating
Church of the Good Shepherd
Mt Maude 1797
Lake Opuha
Ashwick Flat
Mt Cox 837
Mt Walker 1169
44°00'S
Mt Edward 1916
Lake Tekapo
Trentham
Hae Hae Te Moana Scenic Reserve
Opihi
Kimbell
Burn
Irishman
16
21
Mt Michael 516
Opuha
Three Springs Historic Woolshed
Mt Burgess 1430
River
17
Cattle Valley
42
Canal
Allandale
Mt McDonald 780
Tekapo
14
79
Round Hill 524
Burkes Pass
Eversley
Heritage Museum
Middle Valley
Stericker's Mound 769
Heslip's Hatchery
Fairlie
Chastleton 583
Beautiful Valley
62
ALBURY RANGE
Winscombe
Kakahu Hill 402
To Geraldine
Pioneer Park
Maori Rock Drawings
Rapuwai
Mt Mary 995
50
14
17
Opuha
Kakahu
Creek
River
Tengawai
Ramcliff HR
MARY RANGE
ROLLESBY RANGE
Cricklewood
River
River
25
Tekapo
Limestone Valley
Mt Gay 346
Mackenzie
Opihi
Camp Valley
Opihi
House Hill 701
Grays
Snow
River
Albury
Mary
Burn
Totara Valley
44°15'S
Chamberlain
RANGE
Tengawai
Mount Nessing
To Timaru
GRAYS HILLS
GRAMPIAN MOUNTAINS
River
DALGETY
Hakataramea
Mawaro
12
Sutherlands
16
Monavale HR
Monavale
Mt Dalgety 1752
Mt Smith 837
River
Hogget Hill 581
Tasman Smith SR
65
Cave
Pareora SR
Pareora
River
12
Taiko
Mt Nessing 1601
THE HUNTERS HILLS
41
Cannington
Pareora River Scenic Reserve
Mt Maggie 524
Stony
River
Mt MacGregor 1018
River
Cave Hill 542
Mt Horrible 388
0
10 km
© Hema Maps NZ Ltd
Te Huruhuru 1591
Motukaika
Motukaika
River
Matata Scenic Res
12
Beacon Hill 1196
Mt Nimrod (Kaumira) 1525
Mt Nimrod
170°15'E
170°30'E
170°45'E
171°00'E
68
A
B
C
D
E
F
G
H
J
19

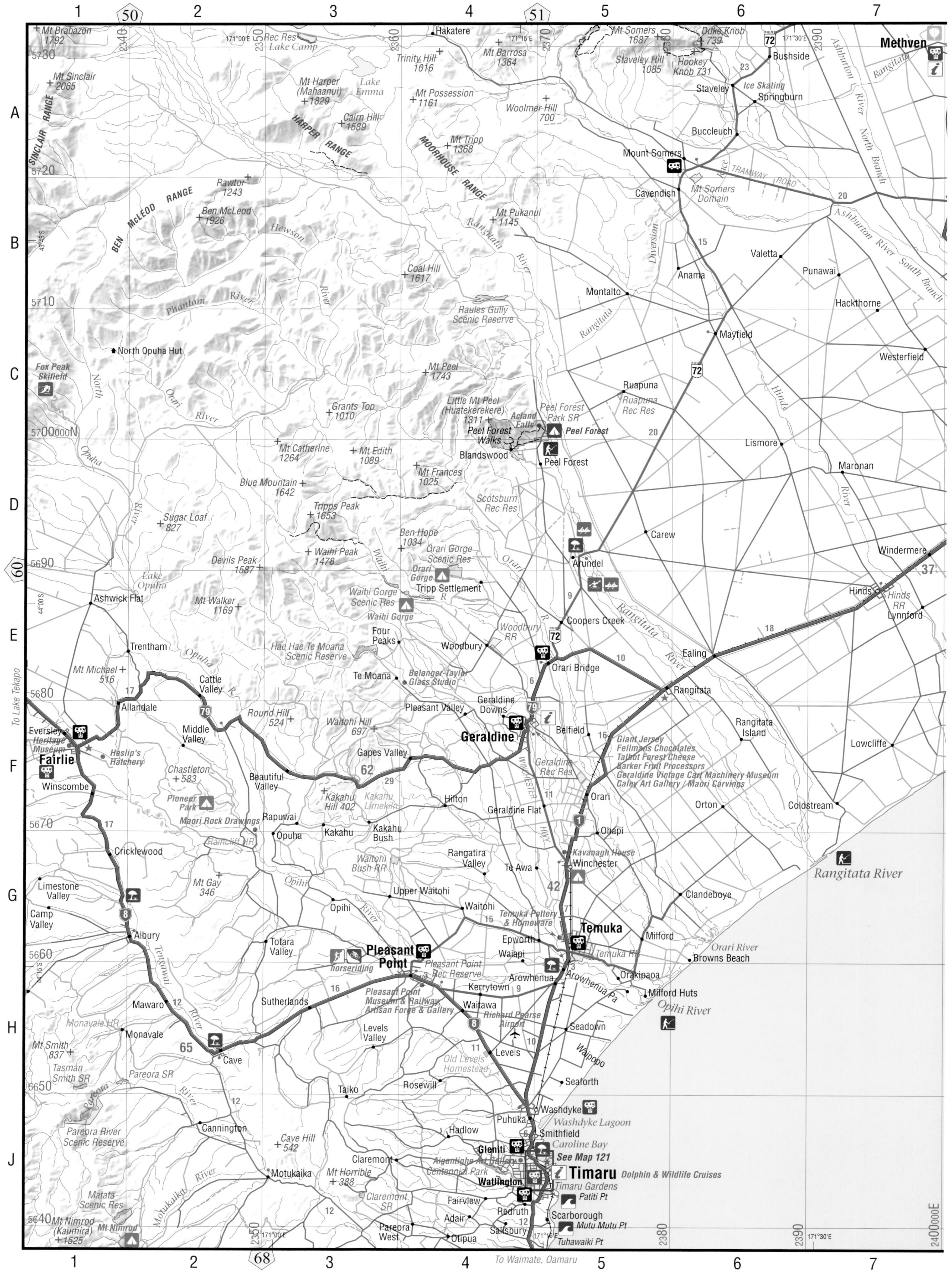

Methven
Bushside
Staveley
Ice Skating
Springburn
Buccleuch
Mount Somers
Cavendish
Mt Somers Domain
TRAMWAY ROAD
Ashburton River North Branch
Ashburton River South Branch
Anama
Valetta
Punawai
Hackthorne
Montalto
Mayfield
Westerfield
Ruapuna
Ruapuna Rec Res
Lismore
Maronan
Carew
Arundel
Windermere
Hinds
Hinds RR
Lynnford
Coopers Creek
Ealing
Rangitata
Rangitata Island
Lowcliffe
Coldstream
Orton
Rangitata River
Clandeboye
Milford
Orari River
Browns Beach
Orakipaoa
Milford Huts
Opihi River
Hakatere
Mt Brabazon 1792
Rec Res
Lake Camp
Trinity Hill 1016
Mt Barrosa 1364
Mt Somers 1687
Staveley Hill 1085
Duke Knob 739
Hookey Knob 731
Mt Sinclair 2065
SINCLAIR RANGE
Mt Harper (Mahaanui) 1829
Lake Emma
Mt Possession 1161
Woolmer Hill 700
Cairn Hill 1589
HARPER RANGE
Mt Tripp 1368
MOORHOUSE RANGE
Rawtor 1243
BEN McLEOD RANGE
Ben McLeod 1926
Hewson
Mt Pukanui 1145
Rangitata River
Diversion
Coal Hill 1617
Phantom River
Raules Gully Scenic Reserve
North Opuha Hut
Fox Peak Skifield
North Opuha River
Orari River
Mt Peel 1743
Grants Top 1010
Little Mt Peel (Huatekerekere) 1311
Acland Falls
Peel Forest Park SR
Peel Forest
Peel Forest Walks
Blandswood
Mt Catherine 1264
Mt Edith 1089
Mt Frances 1025
Blue Mountain 1642
Scotsburn Rec Res
Tripps Peak 1653
Sugar Loaf 827
Ben Hope 1034
Waihi Peak 1478
Orari Gorge Scenic Res
Orari Gorge
Tripp Settlement
Devils Peak 1587
Lake Opuha
Waihi Gorge Scenic Res
Waihi Gorge
Ashwick Flat
Mt Walker 1169
Woodbury RR
Trentham
Hae Hae Te Moana Scenic Reserve
Four Peaks
Woodbury
Orari Bridge
Opuha R
Mt Michael 516
Te Moana
Belanger-Taylor Glass Studio
Cattle Valley
Allandale
To Lake Tekapo
Round Hill 524
Waitohi Hill 697
Pleasant Valley
Geraldine Downs
Belfield
Eversley
Heritage Museum
Middle Valley
Fairlie
Heslip's Hatchery
Geraldine
Giant Jersey
Fellmans Chocolates
Talbot Forest Cheese
Barker Fruit Processors
Geraldine Vintage Car Machinery Museum
Caley Art Gallery / Maori Carvings
Chastleton 583
Gapes Valley
Geraldine Rec Res
Winscombe
Beautiful Valley
Kakahu Hill 402
Kakahu Limekiln
Hilton
Orari
Pioneer Park
Geraldine Flat
WINCHESTER HWY
Maori Rock Drawings
Rapuwai
Opuha
Kakahu
Kakahu Bush
Ohapi
Raincliff HR
Cricklewood
Waitohi Bush RR
Rangatira Valley
Kavanagh House
Winchester
Te Awa
Mt Gay 346
Limestone Valley
Opihi
Upper Waitohi
Camp Valley
Opihi River
Waitohi
Temuka Pottery & Homeware
Temuka
Albury
Tengawai River
Totara Valley
Epworth
Waiapi
Temuka RR
Pleasant Point
horseriding
Pleasant Point Rec Reserve
Arowhenua
Arowhenua Pa
Kerrytown
Sutherlands
Pleasant Point Museum & Railway
Artisan Forge & Gallery
Waitawa
Richard Pearse Airport
Mawaro
Monavale HR
Monavale
Levels Valley
Seadown
Mt Smith 837
Cave
Levels
Waipopo
Tasman Smith SR
Pareora SR
Old Levels Homestead
Seaforth
Taiko
Rosewill
Pareora River
Washdyke
Puhuka
Washdyke Lagoon
Cannington
Pareora River Scenic Reserve
Hadlow
Smithfield
Caroline Bay
Cave Hill 542
Glentti
See Map 121
Claremont
Aigantighe Art Gallery
Centennial Park
Timaru
Dolphin & Wildlife Cruises
Motukaika
Mt Horrible 388
Watlington
Timaru Gardens
Matata Scenic Res
Motukaika River
Claremont SR
Fairview
Patiti Pt
Redruth
Scarborough
Mt Nimrod (Kaumira) 1525
Mt Nimrod
Pareora West
Adair
Mutu Mutu Pt
Otipua
Salisbury
Tuhawaiki Pt
To Waimate, Oamaru
43°45'S
44°00'S
44°15'S
171°00'E
171°15'E
171°30'E
5700000N
2400000E

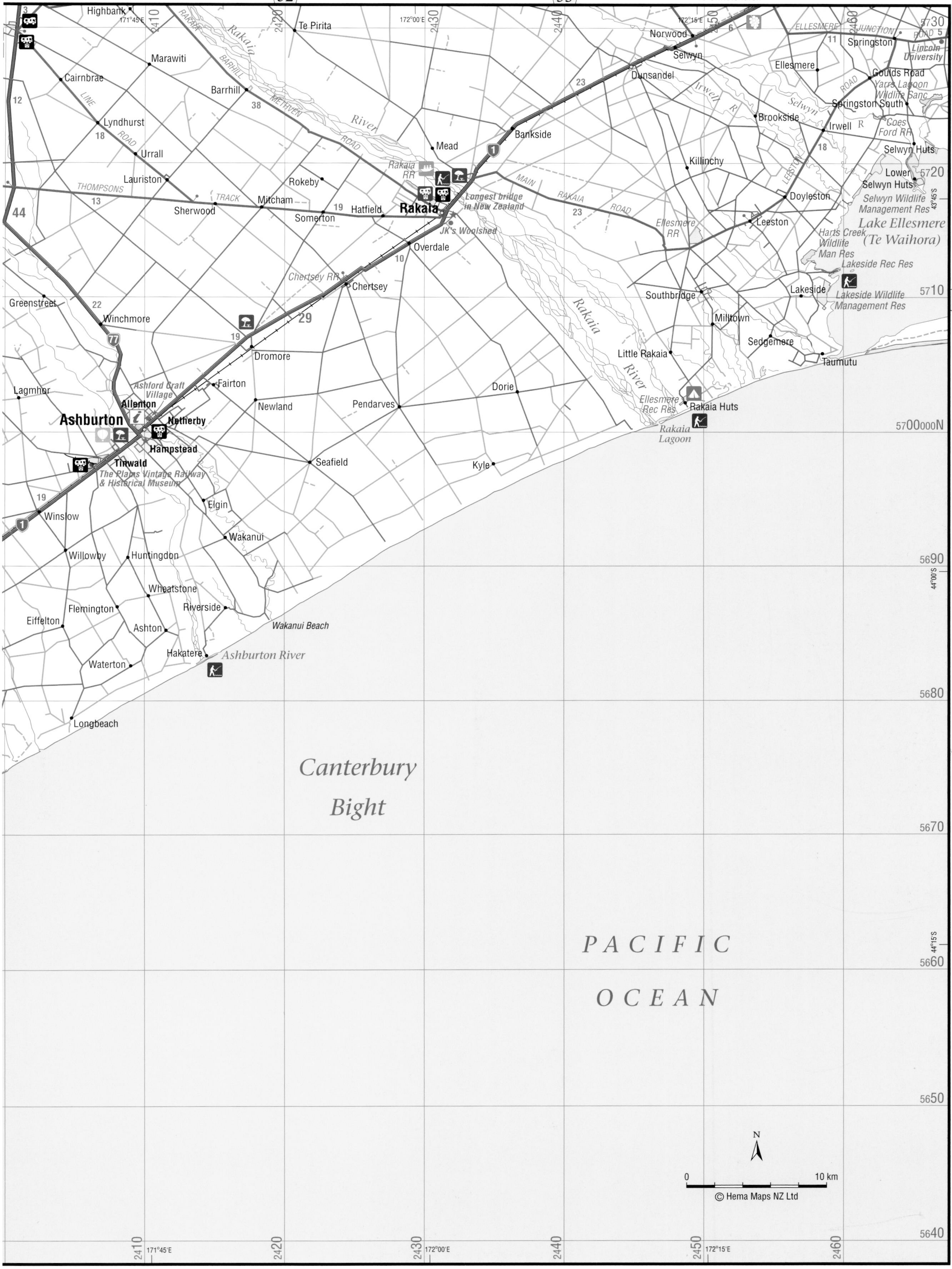

To Mount Hutt
To Christchurch
52
53
56
Highbank
Te Pirita
Marawiti
Cairnbrae
Barrhill
Lyndhurst
Urrall
Lauriston
Rakaia River
Mead
Bankside
Norwood
Selwyn
Dunsandel
Ellesmere
Springston
Lincoln University
Goulds Road
Yarrs Lagoon Wildlife Sanc
Springston South
Brookside
Irwell
Coes Ford RR
Selwyn Huts
Lower Selwyn Huts
Killinchy
Doyleston
Leeston
Selwyn Wildlife Management Res
Lake Ellesmere (Te Waihora)
Harts Creek Wildlife Man Res
Lakeside Rec Res
Lakeside
Lakeside Wildlife Management Res
Rokeby
Mitcham
Sherwood
Somerton
Hatfield
Rakaia
Rakaia RR
Longest bridge in New Zealand
JK's Woolshed
Overdale
Ellesmere RR
Southbridge
Milltown
Sedgemere
Taumutu
Little Rakaia
Chertsey RR
Chertsey
Greenstreet
Winchmore
Dromore
Fairton
Ashford Craft Village
Allenton
Ashburton
Netherby
Hampstead
Tinwald
The Plains Vintage Railway & Historical Museum
Lagmhor
Newland
Pendarves
Dorie
Ellesmere Rec Res
Rakaia Huts
Rakaia Lagoon
Seafield
Kyle
Elgin
Winslow
Wakanui
Willowby
Huntingdon
Wheatstone
Riverside
Flemington
Eiffelton
Ashton
Wakanui Beach
Hakatere
Ashburton River
Waterton
Longbeach
Canterbury Bight
PACIFIC OCEAN
10 km
© Hema Maps NZ Ltd

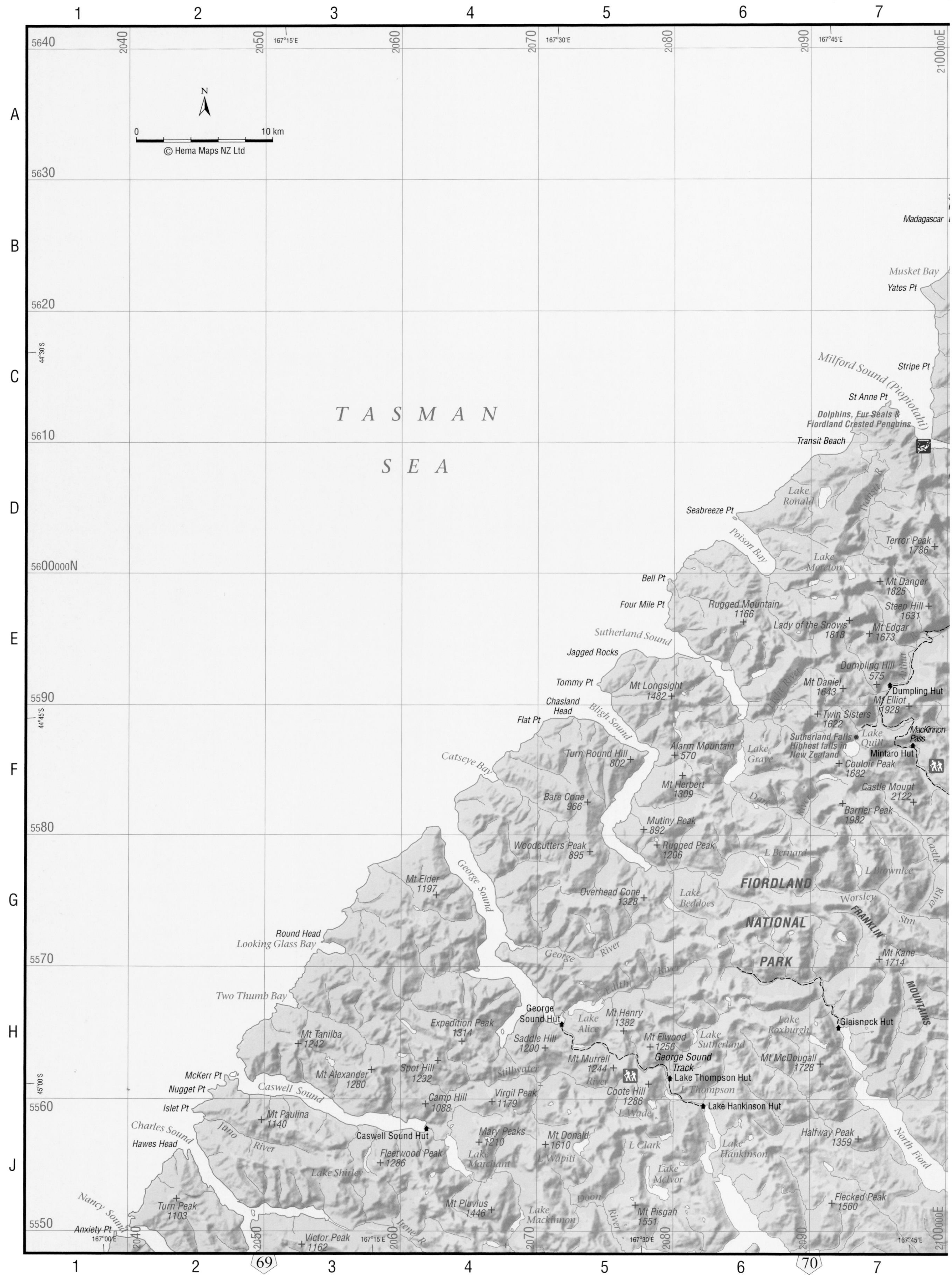

1 2 3 4 5 6 7
A B C D E F G H J
167°15'E
167°30'E
167°45'E
167°00'E
44°30'S
44°45'S
45°00'S
5640
5630
5620
5610
5600000N
5590
5580
5570
5560
5550
2040
2050
2060
2070
2080
2090
2100000E
N
0
10 km
© Hema Maps NZ Ltd
TASMAN
SEA
Madagascar
Musket Bay
Yates Pt
Milford Sound (Piopiotahi)
Stripe Pt
St Anne Pt
Dolphins, Fur Seals & Fiordland Crested Penguins
Transit Beach
Lake Ronald
Seabreeze Pt
Poison Bay
Terror Peak 1786
Lake Moreton
Mt Danger 1825
Bell Pt
Four Mile Pt
Rugged Mountain 1166
Steep Hill 1631
Lady of the Snows 1818
Mt Edgar 1673
Sutherland Sound
Jagged Rocks
Dumpling Hill 575
Tommy Pt
Mt Longsight 1482
Mt Daniel 1643
Dumpling Hut
Chasland Head
Bligh Sound
Mt Elliot 1928
Flat Pt
Twin Sisters 1622
Sutherland Falls Highest falls in New Zealand
Lake Quill
MacKinnon Pass
Alarm Mountain 570
Lake Grave
Mintaro Hut
Turn Round Hill 802
Catseye Bay
Couloir Peak 1682
Mt Herbert 1309
Castle Mount 2122
Bare Cone 966
Barrier Peak 1982
Mutiny Peak 892
Woodcutters Peak 895
Rugged Peak 1206
L Bernard
L Brownlee
Mt Elder 1197
George Sound
Overhead Cone 1328
Lake Beddoes
FIORDLAND
NATIONAL
PARK
Worsley
Stm
FRANKLIN
MOUNTAINS
Round Head
Looking Glass Bay
George River
Edith River
Mt Kane 1714
Two Thumb Bay
George Sound Hut
Lake Alice
Mt Henry 1382
Expedition Peak 1314
Lake Roxburgh
Glaisnock Hut
Mt Tanilba 1242
Saddle Hill 1200
Mt Elwood 1256
Lake Sutherland
George Sound Track
Mt Murrell 1244
Mt McDougall 1728
McKerr Pt
Mt Alexander 1280
Spot Hill 1232
Stillwater River
Lake Thompson Hut
Nugget Pt
Caswell Sound
Coote Hill 1286
L Thompson
Islet Pt
Camp Hill 1088
Virgil Peak 1179
Lake Hankinson Hut
Mt Paulina 1140
L Wade
Charles Sound
Juno River
Caswell Sound Hut
Mary Peaks 1210
Mt Donald 1610
Halfway Peak 1359
Hawes Head
Fleetwood Peak 1286
Lake Marchant
L Wapiti
L Clark
Lake Hankinson
North Fiord
Lake Shirley
Lake McIvor
Nancy Sound
Turn Peak 1103
Mt Pluvius 1446
Doon River
Mt Pisgah 1551
Flecked Peak 1560
Lake Mackinnon
Anxiety Pt
Victor Peak 1162
Irene R
Transit R
Arthur R
Clinton R
Castle River
Dark River

69
70

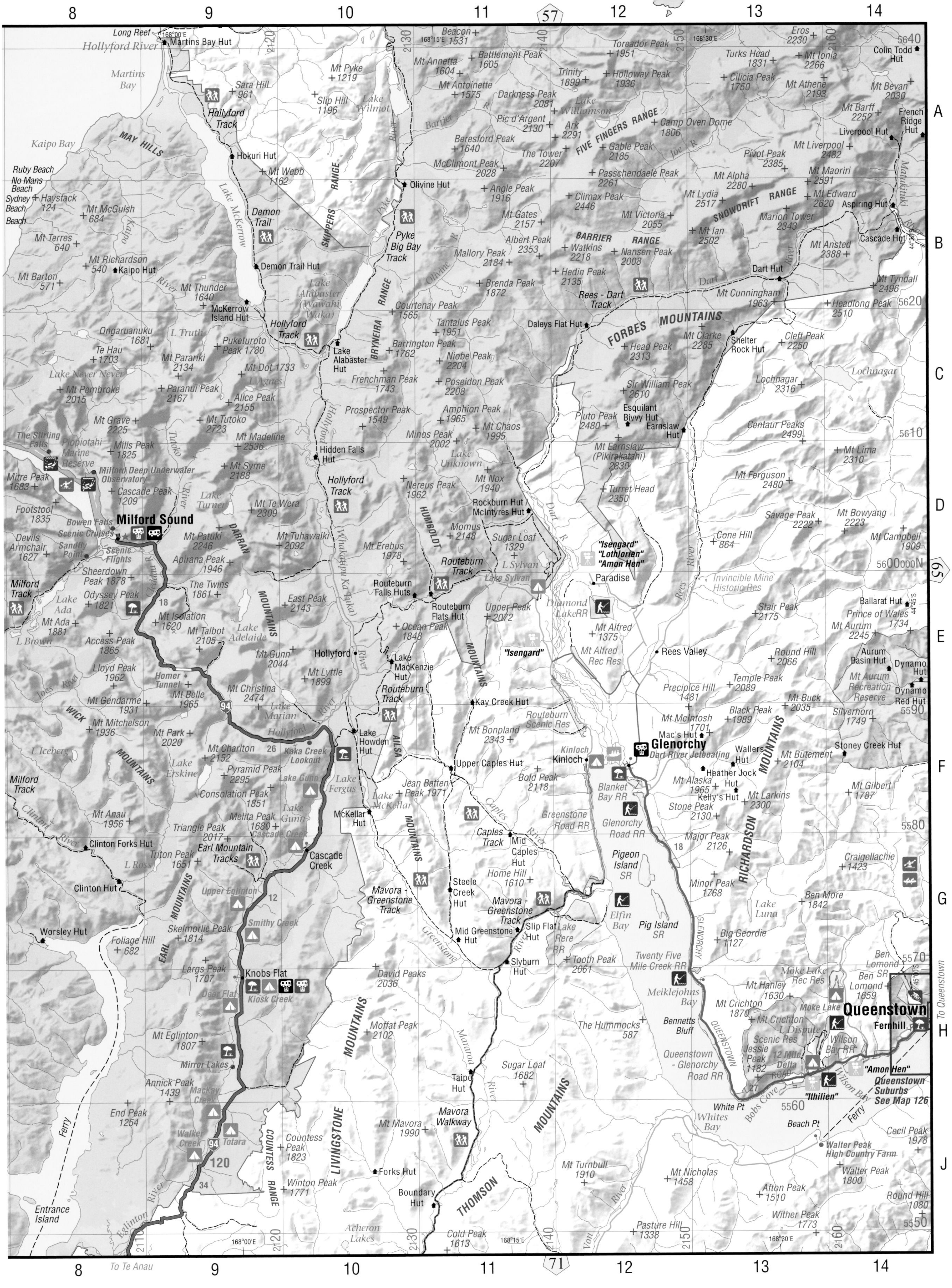

57
71
65
8
9
10
11
12
13
14
A
B
C
D
E
F
G
H
J
Long Reef
Martins Bay Hut
Hollyford River
Martins Bay
Kaipo Bay
MAY HILLS
Ruby Beach
No Mans Beach
Sydney Beach
Beach
Haystack 124
Mt McGulsh 684
Mt Terres 640
Mt Richardson 540
Kaipo Hut
Mt Barton 571
Sara Hill 961
Hollyford Track
Hokuri Hut
Mt Webb 1162
Lake McKerrow
Demon Trail
Demon Trail Hut
Mt Thunder 1640
McKerrow Island Hut
Mt Pyke 1219
Slip Hill 1196
Lake Wilmot
SKIPPERS RANGE
Olivine Hut
Pyke Big Bay Track
Lake Alabaster (Wawahi Waka)
Lake Alabaster Hut
BRYNEIRA RANGE
Beacon 1531
Mt Annetta 1604
Battlement Peak 1605
Mt Antoinette 1575
Darkness Peak 2081
Pic d'Argent 2130
Beresford Peak 1640
McClimont Peak 2028
Angle Peak 1916
Mt Gates 2157
Albert Peak 2353
Mallory Peak 2184
Brenda Peak 1872
Courtenay Peak 1565
Tantalus Peak 1951
Barrington Peak 1762
Niobe Peak 2204
Frenchman Peak 1743
Poseidon Peak 2208
Prospector Peak 1549
Amphion Peak 1965
Minos Peak 2002
Mt Chaos 1995
Lake Unknown
Mt Nox 1940
Nereus Peak 1962
Rockburn Hut / McIntyres Hut
Toreador Peak 1951
Trinity 1899
Holloway Peak 1936
Lake Williamson
Ark 2291
The Tower 2207
FIVE FINGERS RANGE
Camp Oven Dome 1806
Gable Peak 2185
Passchendaele Peak 2261
Climax Peak 2446
Mt Victoria 2055
BARRIER RANGE
Watkins 2218
Nansen Peak 2008
Hedin Peak 2135
Rees - Dart Track
Daleys Flat Hut
FORBES MOUNTAINS
Head Peak 2313
Sir William Peak 2610
Pluto Peak 2480
Esquilant Bivvy Hut
Earnslaw Hut
Mt Earnslaw (Pikirakatahi) 2830
Turret Head 2350
Eros 2230
Turks Head 1831
Mt Ionia 2266
Colin Todd Hut
Cilicia Peak 1750
Mt Athene 2193
Mt Bevan 2030
Mt Barff 2252
French Ridge Hut
Liverpool Hut
Mt Liverpool 2482
Pivot Peak 2385
Mt Alpha 2280
Mt Maoriri 2591
Mt Lydia 2517
SNOWDRIFT RANGE
Mt Edward 2620
Aspiring Hut
Marion Tower 2343
Mt Ian 2502
Cascade Hut
Mt Ansted 2388
Dart Hut
Mt Cunningham 1963
Mt Tyndall 2496
Headlong Peak 2510
Mt Clarke 2285
Shelter Rock Hut
Cleft Peak 2250
Lochnagar 2316
Lochnagar
Centaur Peaks 2499
Mt Lima 2310
Mt Ferguson 2480
Savage Peak 2222
Mt Bowyang 2223
Mt Campbell 1909
Cone Hill 864
Ongaruanuku 1681
L Truth
Puketuroto Peak 1780
Te Hau 1703
Mt Parariki 2134
Mt Dot 1733
L Agnes
Lake Never Never
Mt Pembroke 2015
Paranui Peak 2167
Alice Peak 2155
Mt Grave 2225
Mt Tutoko 2723
Mt Madeline 2536
The Stirling Falls
Piopiotahi Marine Reserve
Mills Peak 1825
Milford Deep Underwater Observatory
Mt Syme 2188
Mitre Peak 1683
Cascade Peak 1209
Lake Turner
Mt Te Wera 2309
Footstool 1835
Milford Sound
Bowen Falls
Scenic Cruises
Devils Armchair 1627
Sandfly Point
Scenic Flights
Mt Patuki 2246
DARRAN
Mt Tuhawaiki 2092
Apirana Peak 1946
Sheerdown Peak 1878
Milford Track
Lake Ada
Odyssey Peak 1821
The Twins 1861
MOUNTAINS
East Peak 2143
Mt Ada 1881
Mt Isolation 1620
Mt Talbot 2105
Lake Adelaide
L Brown
Access Peak 1865
Lloyd Peak 1962
Homer Tunnel
Mt Gunn 2044
Mt Belle 1965
Mt Christina 2474
Joes River
Mt Gendarme 1931
WICK MOUNTAINS
Mt Mitchelson 1936
Lake Marian
Hollyford
Hidden Falls Hut
Hollyford Track
Mt Erebus 1978
HUMBOLDT
Momus 2148
Sugar Loaf 1329
L Sylvan
Lake Sylvan
Routeburn Track
Routeburn Falls Huts
Routeburn Flats Hut
Upper Peak 2072
Ocean Peak 1848
Lake MacKenzie Hut
Routeburn Track
Kay Creek Hut
"Isengard"
"Lothlorien"
"Amon Hen"
Paradise
Diamond Lake RR
Mt Alfred 1375
Mt Alfred Rec Res
Rees Valley
Invincible Mine Historic Res
Stair Peak 2175
Ballarat Hut
Prince of Wales 1734
Mt Aurum 2245
Aurum Basin Hut
Round Hill 2066
Mt Aurum Recreation Reserve
Dynamo Hut
Dynamo Red Hut
Temple Peak 2089
Precipice Hill 1481
Black Peak 1989
Mt Buck 2035
Silverhorn 1749
Mt McIntosh 1701
Mac's Hut
Stoney Creek Hut
Glenorchy
Dart River Jetboating
Wallers Hut
Mt Butement 2104
RICHARDSON MOUNTAINS
Heather Jock Hut
Mt Alaska 1965
Kelly's Hut
Mt Larkins 2300
Mt Gilbert 1787
Stone Peak 2130
Routeburn Scenic Res
Mt Bonpland 2343
Upper Caples Hut
Kinloch
Blanket Bay RR
Glenorchy Road RR
Bold Peak 2118
Greenstone Road RR
Mt Park 2020
Mt Charlton 2152
Lake Howden Hut
Kaka Creek Lookout
L Iceberg
Pyramid Peak 2295
Lake Erskine
Lake Fergus
AILSA
Consolation Peak 1851
Lake Gunn
Lake Gunn
Milford Track
Mt Anau 1956
Melita Peak 1680
Triangle Peak 2017
Cascade Creek
Clinton River
Clinton Forks Hut
Triton Peak 1651
Earl Mountain Tracks
Cascade Creek
L Ross
Jean Batten Peak 1971
Lake McKellar
McKellar Hut
MOUNTAINS
Caples Track
Mid Caples Hut
Home Hill 1610
Steele Creek Hut
Mavora - Greenstone Track
Mavora - Greenstone Track
Mid Greenstone Hut
Slip Flat Hut
Lake Rere RR
Pigeon Island SR
Elfin Bay
Pig Island SR
Major Peak 2126
Minor Peak 1768
Craigellachie 1423
Ben More 1842
Lake Luna
Big Geordie 1127
Clinton Hut
Upper Eglinton
EARL MOUNTAINS
Smithy Creek
Worsley Hut
Foliage Hill 682
Skelmorlie Peak 1814
Largs Peak 1707
Knobs Flat
Kiosk Creek
Deer Flat
Greenstone
Slyburn Hut
Tooth Peak 2061
Twenty Five Mile Creek RR
Meiklejohns Bay
Ben Lomond SR
Moke Lake Rec Res
Ben Lomond 1659
Mt Hanley 1630
Mt Crichton 1870
Moke Lake
Queenstown
Fernhill
To Queenstown
David Peaks 2036
MOUNTAINS
Moffat Peak 2102
The Hummocks 587
Bennetts Bluff
Mt Crichton
L Dispute
Scenic Res
Wilson Bay RR
Jessie Peak 1182
12 Mile Delta
"Amon Hen"
"Ithilien"
Queenstown Suburbs See Map 126
Queenstown - Glenorchy Road RR
GLENORCHY - QUEENSTOWN ROAD
Mt Eglinton 1807
Mirror Lakes
Annick Peak 1439
MacKay Creek
End Peak 1254
Walker Creek
Totara
Ferry
Entrance Island
Eglinton River
COUNTESS RANGE
Countess Peak 1823
LIVINGSTONE
Mt Mavora 1990
Mavora Walkway
Taipo Hut
Sugar Loaf 1682
Mararoa River
MOUNTAINS
THOMSON
Forks Hut
Winton Peak 1771
Boundary Hut
Acheron Lakes
Cold Peak 1613
Mt Turnbull 1910
Von River
Mt Nicholas 1458
Pasture Hill 1338
White Pt
Whites Bay
Bobs Cove
Beach Pt
Wilson Bay
Ferry
Walter Peak High Country Farm
Cecil Peak 1978
Walter Peak 1800
Afton Peak 1510
Round Hill 1080
Wither Peak 1773
To Te Anau
168°00'E
168°15'E
168°30'E
44°45'S
5600000N

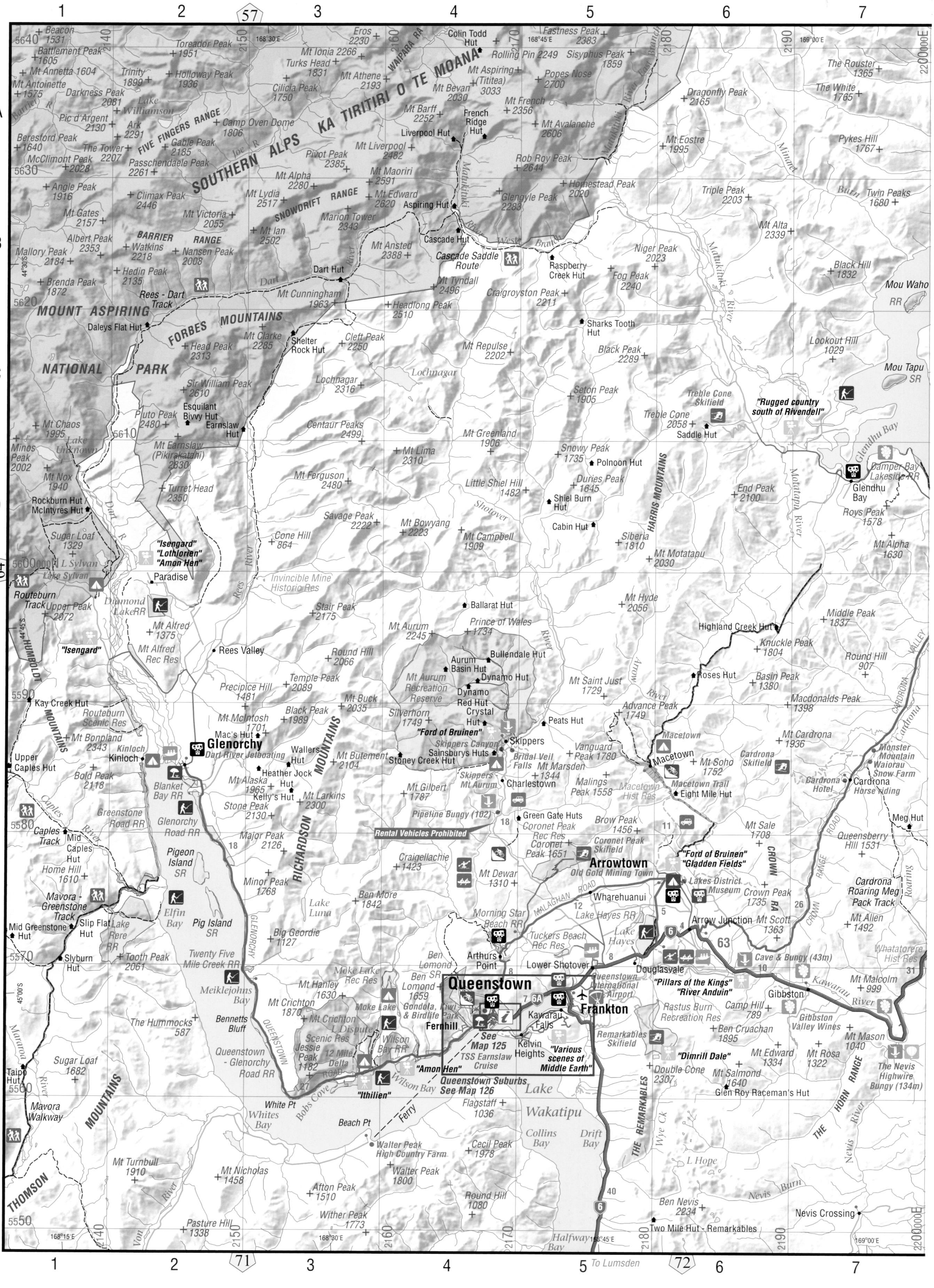
SOUTHERN ALPS KA TIRITIRI O TE MOANA
MOUNT ASPIRING NATIONAL PARK
FIVE FINGERS RANGE
SNOWDRIFT RANGE
BARRIER RANGE
FORBES MOUNTAINS
WAIPARA RA
HARRIS MOUNTAINS
RICHARDSON MOUNTAINS
HUMBOLDT MOUNTAINS
THOMSON MOUNTAINS
THE REMARKABLES
CROWN RA
THE HORN RANGE
Beacon 1531
Battlement Peak 1605
Mt Annetta 1604
Mt Antoinette 1575
Toreador Peak 1951
Trinity 1899
Holloway Peak 1936
Darkness Peak 2081
Lake Williamson
Pic d'Argent 2130
Ark 2291
Camp Oven Dome 1806
Beresford Peak 1640
The Tower 2207
Gable Peak 2185
McClimont Peak 2028
Passchendaele Peak 2261
Angle Peak 1916
Climax Peak 2446
Mt Gates 2157
Mt Victoria 2055
Albert Peak 2353
Watkins 2218
Nansen Peak 2008
Mallory Peak 2184
Hedin Peak 2135
Brenda Peak 1872
Rees - Dart Track
Daleys Flat Hut
Head Peak 2313
Mt Clarke 2285
Sir William Peak 2610
Pluto Peak 2480
Esquilant Bivvy Hut
Earnslaw Hut
Mt Earnslaw (Pikirakatahi) 2830
Mt Chaos 1995
Lake Unknown
Minos Peak 2002
Mt Nox 1940
Turret Head 2350
Rockburn Hut / McIntyres Hut
Sugar Loaf 1329
L Sylvan
Lake Sylvan
"Isengard" "Lothlorien" "Amon Hen"
Paradise
Routeburn Track
Upper Peak 2072
Diamond Lake RR
Mt Alfred 1375
Mt Alfred Rec Res
"Isengard"
Rees Valley
Kay Creek Hut
Routeburn Scenic Res
Mt Bonpland 2343
Kinloch
Upper Caples Hut
Bold Peak 2118
Glenorchy
Dart River Jetboating
Blanket Bay RR
Glenorchy Road RR
Greenstone Road RR
Caples Track
Mid Caples Hut
Home Hill 1610
Mavora - Greenstone Track
Slip Flat Hut
Mid Greenstone Hut
Lake Rere RR
Slyburn Hut
Tooth Peak 2061
Pigeon Island SR
Elfin Bay
Pig Island SR
Twenty Five Mile Creek RR
Meiklejohns Bay
Bennetts Bluff
The Hummocks 587
Queenstown - Glenorchy Road RR
Sugar Loaf 1682
Taipo Hut
Mavora Walkway
Mt Turnbull 1910
Mt Nicholas 1458
Pasture Hill 1338
Eros 2230
Mt Ionia 2266
Turks Head 1831
Mt Athene 2193
Cilicia Peak 1750
Colin Todd Hut
Mt Aspiring (Tititea) 3033
Mt Bevan 2030
Rolling Pin 2249
Fastness Peak 2383
Sisyphus Peak 1859
Popes Nose 2700
Mt French 2356
Mt Barff 2252
French Ridge Hut
Liverpool Hut
Mt Avalanche 2606
Mt Liverpool 2482
Pivot Peak 2385
Rob Roy Peak 2644
Mt Alpha 2280
Mt Maoriri 2591
Mt Lydia 2517
Mt Edward 2620
Homestead Peak 2020
Aspiring Hut
Glengyle Peak 2283
Marion Tower 2343
Mt Ian 2502
Cascade Hut
Mt Ansted 2388
Cascade Saddle Route
Raspberry Creek Hut
Dart Hut
Mt Tyndall 2496
Mt Cunningham 1963
Headlong Peak 2510
Craigroyston Peak 2211
Shelter Rock Hut
Cleft Peak 2250
Mt Repulse 2202
Lochnagar 2316
Centaur Peaks 2499
Mt Lima 2310
Mt Greenland 1906
Mt Ferguson 2480
Little Shiel Hill 1482
Savage Peak 2222
Mt Bowyang 2223
Mt Campbell 1909
Cone Hill 864
Invincible Mine Historic Res
Stair Peak 2175
Ballarat Hut
Prince of Wales 1734
Mt Aurum 2245
Bullendale Hut
Aurum Basin Hut
Dynamo Hut
Mt Aurum Recreation Reserve
Dynamo Red Hut
Round Hill 2066
Temple Peak 2089
Precipice Hill 1481
Black Peak 1989
Mt Buck 2035
Mt McIntosh 1701
Mac's Hut
Silverhorn 1749
Crystal Hut
"Ford of Bruinen"
Skippers
Skippers Canyon
Sainsburys Huts
Wallers Hut
Mt Butement 2104
Stoney Creek Hut
Heather Jock Hut
Mt Alaska 1965
Kelly's Hut
Mt Larkins 2300
Stone Peak 2130
Major Peak 2126
Mt Gilbert 1787
Pipeline Bungy (102)
Rental Vehicles Prohibited
Craigellachie 1423
Minor Peak 1768
Ben More 1842
Lake Luna
Big Geordie 1127
Mt Dewar 1310
Morning Star Beach RR
Arthurs Point
Ben Lomond SR
Moke Lake Rec Res
Ben Lomond 1659
Mt Hanley 1630
Moke Lake
Gondola, Luge & Birdlife Park
Mt Crichton 1870
Mt Crichton
L Dispute
Scenic Res
Jessie Peak 1182
12 Mile Delta
Wilson Bay RR
"Amon Hen"
"Ithilien"
Bobs Cove
Wilson Bay
White Pt
Whites Bay
Beach Pt
Ferry
Walter Peak High Country Farm
Walter Peak 1800
Afton Peak 1510
Wither Peak 1773
Queenstown
Fernhill
See Map 125
TSS Earnslaw Cruise
Queenstown Suburbs See Map 126
Kelvin Heights
Kawarau Falls
"Various scenes of Middle Earth"
Frankton
Queenstown International Airport
Lake Wakatipu
Flagstaff 1036
Cecil Peak 1978
Collins Bay
Drift Bay
Round Hill 1080
Halfway Bay
Mt Aspiring
Dragonfly Peak 2165
Mt Eostre 1995
The Rouster 1365
The White 1765
Pykes Hill 1767
Triple Peak 2203
Twin Peaks 1680
Mt Alta 2339
Niger Peak 2023
Fog Peak 2240
Black Hill 1832
Mou Waho
Sharks Tooth Hut
Black Peak 2289
Lookout Hill 1029
Mou Tapu SR
Seton Peak 1905
Treble Cone Skifield
Treble Cone 2058
Saddle Hut
"Rugged country south of Rivendell"
Glendhu Bay
Damper Bay Lakeside RR
Snowy Peak 1735
Polnoon Hut
Duries Peak 1645
Shiel Burn Hut
End Peak 2100
Roys Peak 1578
Cabin Hut
Siberia 1810
Mt Motatapu 2030
Mt Alpha 1630
Mt Hyde 2056
Middle Peak 1837
Highland Creek Hut
Knuckle Peak 1804
Round Hill 907
Roses Hut
Basin Peak 1380
Mt Saint Just 1729
Advance Peak 1749
Macdonalds Peak 1398
Peats Hut
Bridal Veil Falls
Vanguard Peak 1780
Mt Cardrona 1936
Macetown
Mt Soho 1752
Cardrona Skifield
Monster Mountain Waiorau Snow Farm
Cardrona Hotel
Cardrona Horse Riding
Mt Marsden 1344
Charlestown
Malings Peak 1558
Macetown Hist Res
Macetown Trail
Eight Mile Hut
Green Gate Huts
Coronet Peak Rec Res
Coronet Peak 1651
Coronet Peak Skifield
Brow Peak 1456
Mt Sale 1708
Meg Hut
Queensberry Hill 1531
Arrowtown
Old Gold Mining Town
"Ford of Bruinen" "Gladden Fields"
Lakes District Museum
Cardrona Roaring Meg Pack Track
Wharehuanui
Malaghan Road
Lake Hayes RR
Lake Hayes
Crown Peak 1735
Arrow Junction
Mt Scott 1363
Mt Allen 1492
Tuckers Beach Rec Res
Lower Shotover
Douglasvale
Cave & Bungy (43m)
Whatatorere Hist Res
"Pillars of the Kings" "River Anduin"
Gibbston
Mt Malcolm 999
Rastus Burn Recreation Res
Camp Hill 789
Gibbston Valley Wines
Remarkables Skifield
Ben Cruachan 1895
Mt Mason 1040
"Dimrill Dale"
Mt Edward 1334
Mt Rosa 1322
The Nevis Highwire Bungy (134m)
Double Cone 2307
Mt Salmond 1640
Glen Roy Raceman's Hut
L Hope
Ben Nevis 2234
Two Mile Hut - Remarkables
Nevis Crossing
Kawarau River
Shotover River
Arrow River
Matukituki River
Motatapu River
Dart R
Rees River
Caples River
Nevis River
Nevis Burn
Wye Ck
Minaret Burn
Cardrona River
Mararoa River
Von River
To Lumsden
168°15'E
168°30'E
168°45'E
169°00'E
44°30'S
44°45'S
45°00'S

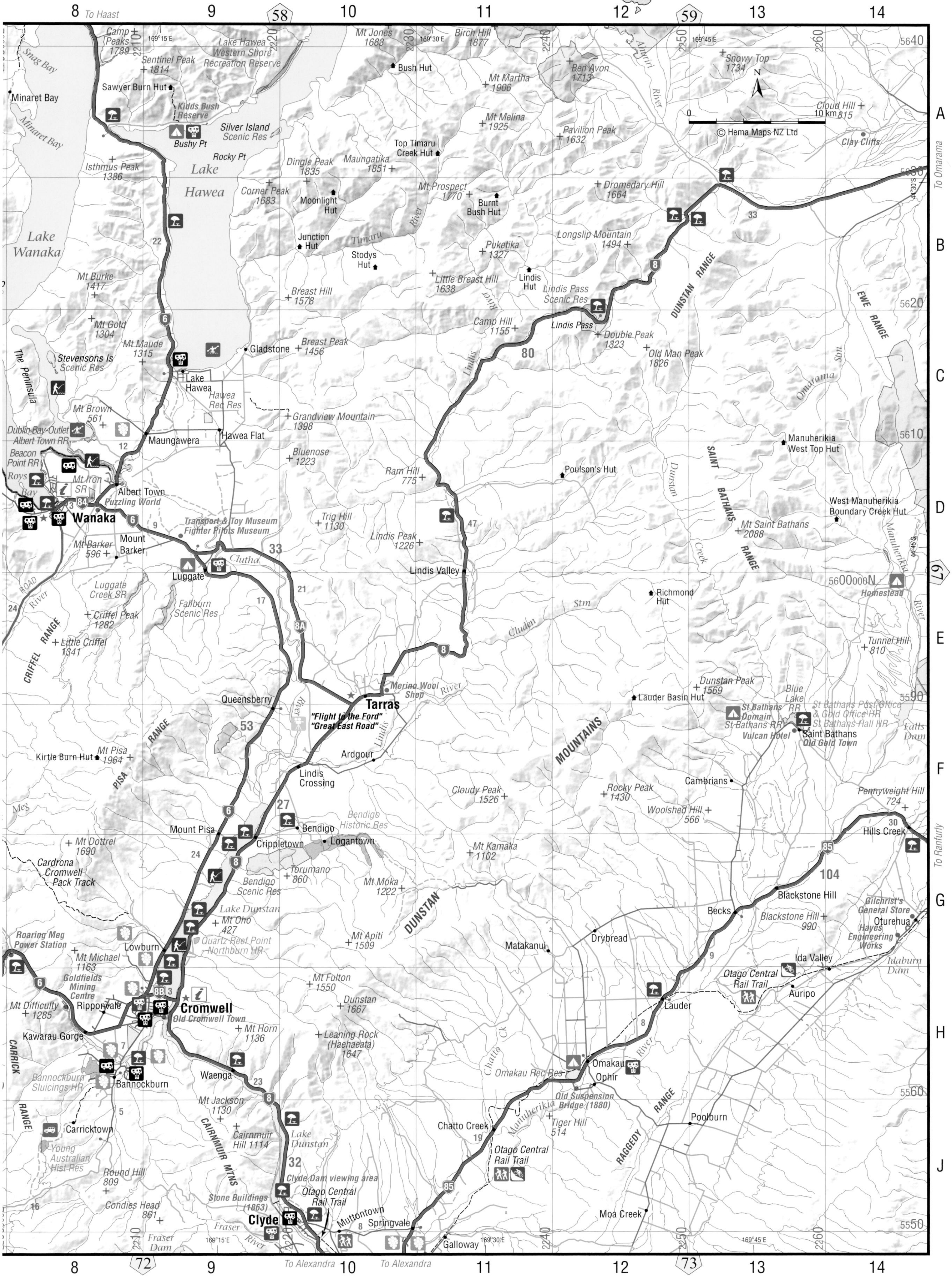

To Haast
Lake Hawea
Lake Wanaka
Camp Peaks 1789
Sentinel Peak 1814
Lake Hawea Western Shore Recreation Reserve
Sawyer Burn Hut
Minaret Bay
Snag Bay
Kidds Bush Reserve
Bushy Pt
Silver Island Scenic Res
Rocky Pt
Isthmus Peak 1386
Mt Jones 1688
Bush Hut
Birch Hill 1877
Mt Martha 1906
Ben Avon 1713
Snowy Top 1734
Mt Melina 1925
Pavilion Peak 1632
Cloud Hill 815
Clay Cliffs
© Hema Maps NZ Ltd
10 km
Top Timaru Creek Hut
Dingle Peak 1835
Maungatika 1851
Corner Peak 1683
Moonlight Hut
Mt Prospect 1770
Burnt Bush Hut
Dromedary Hill 1664
To Omarama
Junction Hut
Timaru River
Stodys Hut
Puketika 1327
Longslip Mountain 1494
Mt Burke 1417
Breast Hill 1578
Little Breast Hill 1638
Lindis Hut
Lindis Pass Scenic Res
Lindis Pass
DUNSTAN RANGE
EWE RANGE
Mt Gold 1304
Camp Hill 1155
Double Peak 1323
Old Man Peak 1826
Mt Maude 1315
Gladstone
Breast Peak 1456
The Peninsula
Stevensons Is Scenic Res
Lake Hawea
Hawea Rec Res
Omarama Stm
Mt Brown 561
Grandview Mountain 1398
Dublin Bay-Outlet
Albert Town RR
Maungawera
Hawea Flat
Manuherikia West Top Hut
Beacon Point RR
Bluenose 1223
SAINT BATHANS RANGE
Roys Bay
Mt Iron SR
Albert Town
Puzzling World
Ram Hill 775
Poulson's Hut
Dunstan Creek
West Manuherikia Boundary Creek Hut
Wanaka
Transport & Toy Museum
Fighter Pilots Museum
Trig Hill 1130
Mt Saint Bathans 2088
Mt Barker 596
Mount Barker
Lindis Peak 1226
Clutha
Luggate
Lindis Valley
Homestead
Luggate Creek SR
Richmond Hut
Fallburn Scenic Res
Criffel Peak 1282
Cluden Stm
CRIFFEL RANGE
Little Criffel 1341
Tunnel Hill 810
Merino Wool Shop
Dunstan Peak 1569
Queensberry
Tarras
Lauder Basin Hut
Blue Lake RR
St Bathans Post Office & Gold Office HR
St Bathans Hall HR
St Bathans Domain
St Bathans RR
Vulcan Hotel
Saint Bathans
Old Gold Town
Falls Dam
"Flight to the Ford"
"Great East Road"
PISA RANGE
Kirtle Burn Hut
Mt Pisa 1964
Ardgour
Lindis Crossing
MOUNTAINS
Cambrians
Cloudy Peak 1526
Rocky Peak 1430
Pennyweight Hill 724
Woolshed Hill 566
Bendigo
Bendigo Historic Res
Mount Pisa
Crippletown
Logantown
Hills Creek
To Ranfurly
Mt Dottrel 1690
Cardrona Cromwell Pack Track
Mt Kamaka 1102
Torumano 860
Bendigo Scenic Res
Mt Moka 1222
Blackstone Hill
Lake Dunstan
Mt Oho 427
DUNSTAN
Becks
Blackstone Hill 990
Gilchrist's General Store
Oturehua
Hayes Engineering Works
Roaring Meg Power Station
Quartz Reef Point Northburn HR
Lowburn
Mt Apiti 1509
Matakanui
Drybread
Ida Valley
Idaburn Dam
Mt Michael 1163
Goldfields Mining Centre
Mt Fulton 1550
Otago Central Rail Trail
Auripo
Mt Difficulty 1285
Ripponvale
Cromwell
Old Cromwell Town
Dunstan 1667
Lauder
Kawarau Gorge
Mt Horn 1136
Leaning Rock (Haehaeata) 1647
CARRICK RANGE
Chatto Ck
Manuherikia River
Bannockburn Sluicings HR
Bannockburn
Waenga
Omakau Rec Res
Omakau
Ophir
Old Suspension Bridge (1880)
Mt Jackson 1130
CAIRNMUIR MTNS
RAGGEDY RANGE
Carricktown
Cairnmuir Hill 1114
Lake Dunstan
Chatto Creek
Tiger Hill 514
Poolburn
Young Australian Hist Res
Round Hill 809
Clyde Dam viewing area
Otago Central Rail Trail
Stone Buildings (1863)
Condies Head 861
Clyde
Muttontown
Springvale
Moa Creek
Fraser River
Fraser Dam
Galloway
To Alexandra
To Alexandra

Southern Canterbury & Northern Otago

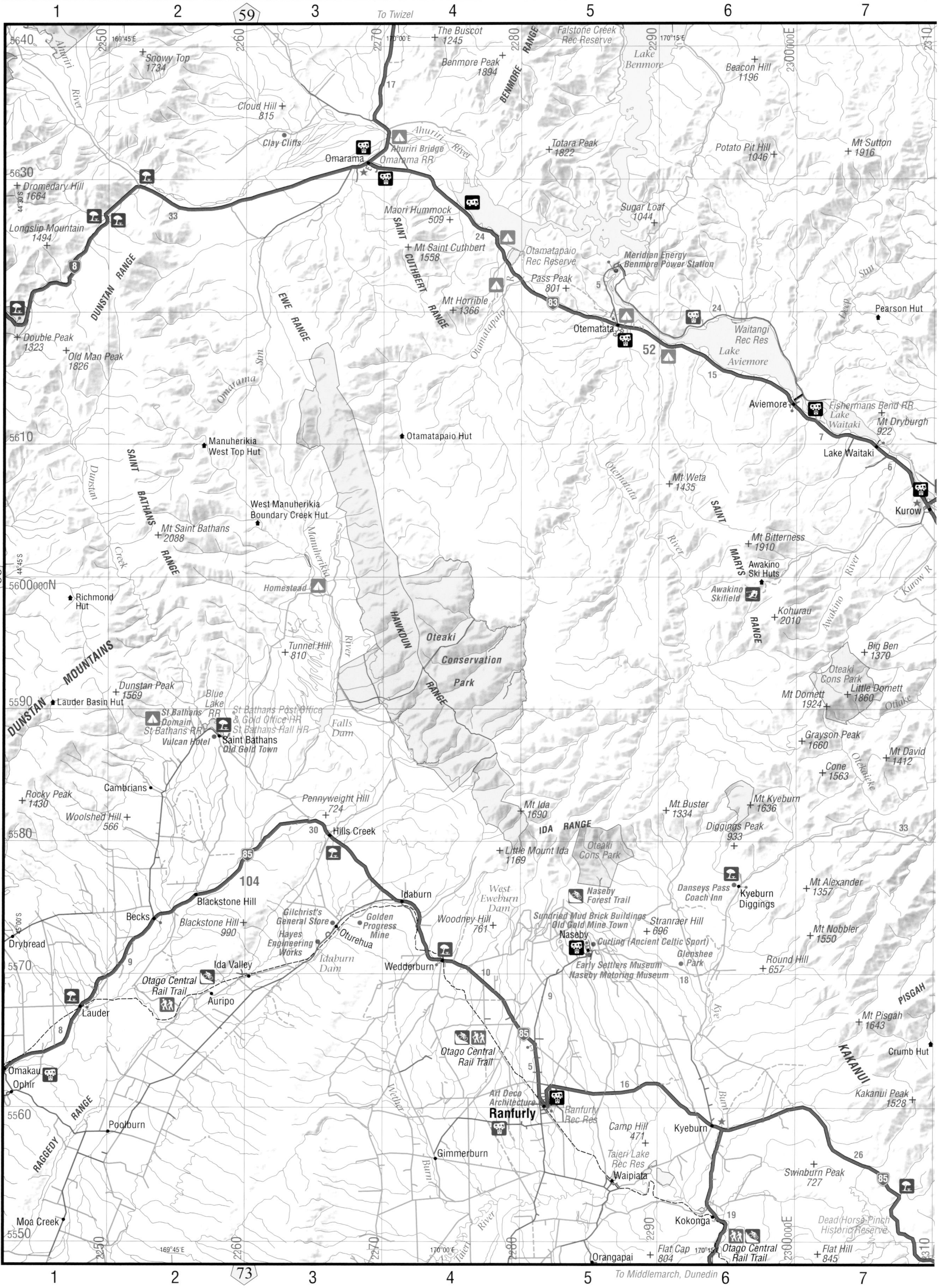

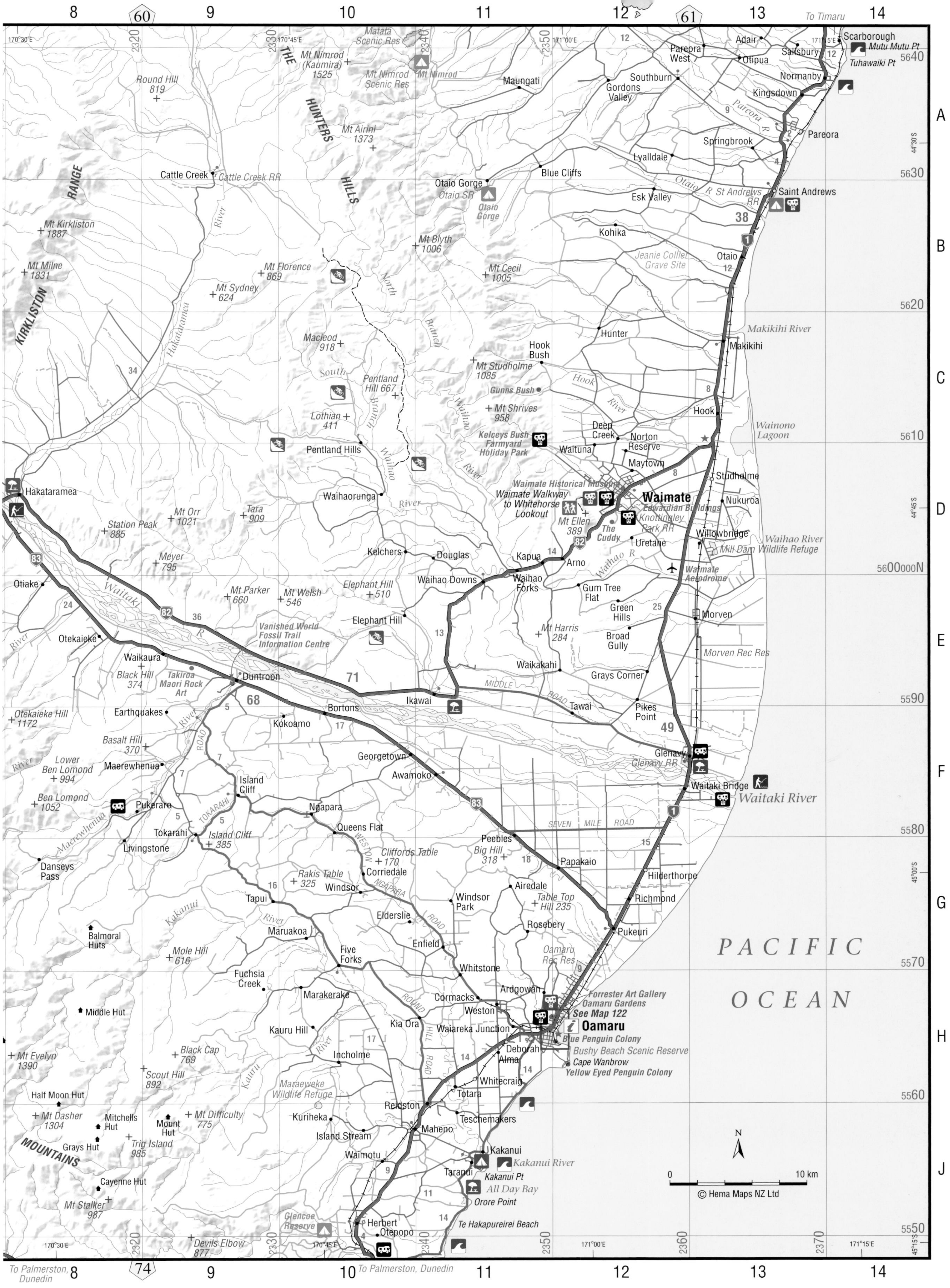
8
9
10
11
12
13
14
To Timaru
A
B
C
D
E
F
G
H
J
Scarborough
Mutu Mutu Pt
Tuhawaiki Pt
Adair
Saltsbury
Otipua
Pareora West
Southburn
Normanby
Kingsdown
Gordons Valley
Maungati
Pareora
Springbrook
Lyalldale
Blue Cliffs
Otaio Gorge
Otaio SR
Saint Andrews
St Andrews RR
Esk Valley
Kohika
Jeanie Collier Grave Site
Otaio
Matata Scenic Res
Mt Nimrod (Kaumira) 1525
Mt Nimrod Scenic Res
Mt Nimrod
THE HUNTERS HILLS
Mt Airini 1373
Round Hill 819
Cattle Creek
Cattle Creek RR
KIRKLISTON RANGE
Mt Kirkliston 1887
Mt Milne 1831
Mt Florence 869
Mt Sydney 624
Mt Blyth 1006
Mt Cecil 1005
Hunter
Makikihi
Makikihi River
Hook Bush
Mt Studholme 1085
Macleod 918
Pentland Hill 667
Gunns Bush
Mt Shrives 958
Hook
Wainono Lagoon
Lothian 411
Pentland Hills
Kelceys Bush Farmyard Holiday Park
Deep Creek
Waituna
Norton Reserve
Maytown
Studholme
Hakataramea
Waihaorunga
Waimate Historical Museum
Waimate Walkway to Whitehorse Lookout
Waimate
Edwardian Buildings
Knottingley Park RR
Nukuroa
Mt Ellen 389
The Cuddy
Uretane
Willowbridge
Waihao River
Mill Dam Wildlife Refuge
Mt Orr 1021
Tara 909
Station Peak 885
Meyer 795
Kelchers
Douglas
Kapua
Arno
Waimate Aerodrome
Waihao Downs
Waihao Forks
Gum Tree Flat
Green Hills
Otiake
Waitaki R
Mt Parker 660
Mt Welsh 546
Elephant Hill 510
Elephant Hill
Morven
Mt Harris 284
Broad Gully
Morven Rec Res
Otekaieke
Vanished World Fossil Trail Information Centre
Waikaura
Black Hill 374
Takiroa Maori Rock Art
Duntroon
Waikakahi
Grays Corner
MIDDLE ROAD
Ikawai
Tawai
Pikes Point
Otekaieke Hill 1172
Earthquakes
Kokoamo
Bortons
Basalt Hill 370
Lower Ben Lomond 994
Maerewhenua
Georgetown
Awamoko
Glenavy
Glenavy RR
Waitaki Bridge
Waitaki River
Island Cliff
Ben Lomond 1052
Pukeraro
Ngapara
Tokarahi
Island Cliff 385
Livingstone
Queens Flat
SEVEN MILE ROAD
Peebles
Danseys Pass
Cliffords Table 170
Big Hill 318
Papakaio
Corriedale
Rakis Table 325
Windsor
Hilderthorpe
Tapui
Airedale
Windsor Park
Table Top Hill 235
Richmond
Elderslie
Balmoral Huts
Maruakoa
Rosebery
Pukeuri
Enfield
Mole Hill 616
Five Forks
Whitstone
Oamaru Rec Res
PACIFIC OCEAN
Fuchsia Creek
Ardgowan
Marakerake
Cormacks
Forrester Art Gallery
Oamaru Gardens
See Map 122
Middle Hut
Weston
Oamaru
Kia Ora
Waiareka Junction
Blue Penguin Colony
Kauru Hill
Bushy Beach Scenic Reserve
Deborah
Mt Evelyn 1390
Black Cap 769
Incholme
Alma
Cape Wanbrow
Yellow Eyed Penguin Colony
Scout Hill 892
Whitecraig
Maraeweke Wildlife Refuge
Totara
Half Moon Hut
Mt Dasher 1304
Mitchells Hut
Mount Hut
Mt Difficulty 775
Kuriheka
Reidston
Teschemakers
Grays Hut
Trig Island 985
Island Stream
Maheno
MOUNTAINS
Kakanui
Waimotu
Kakanui River
Cayenne Hut
Taranui
Kakanui Pt
0
10 km
© Hema Maps NZ Ltd
All Day Bay
Mt Stalker 987
Orore Point
Glencoe Reserve
Herbert
Otepopo
Te Hakapureirei Beach
Devils Elbow 877
To Palmerston, Dunedin
To Palmerston, Dunedin

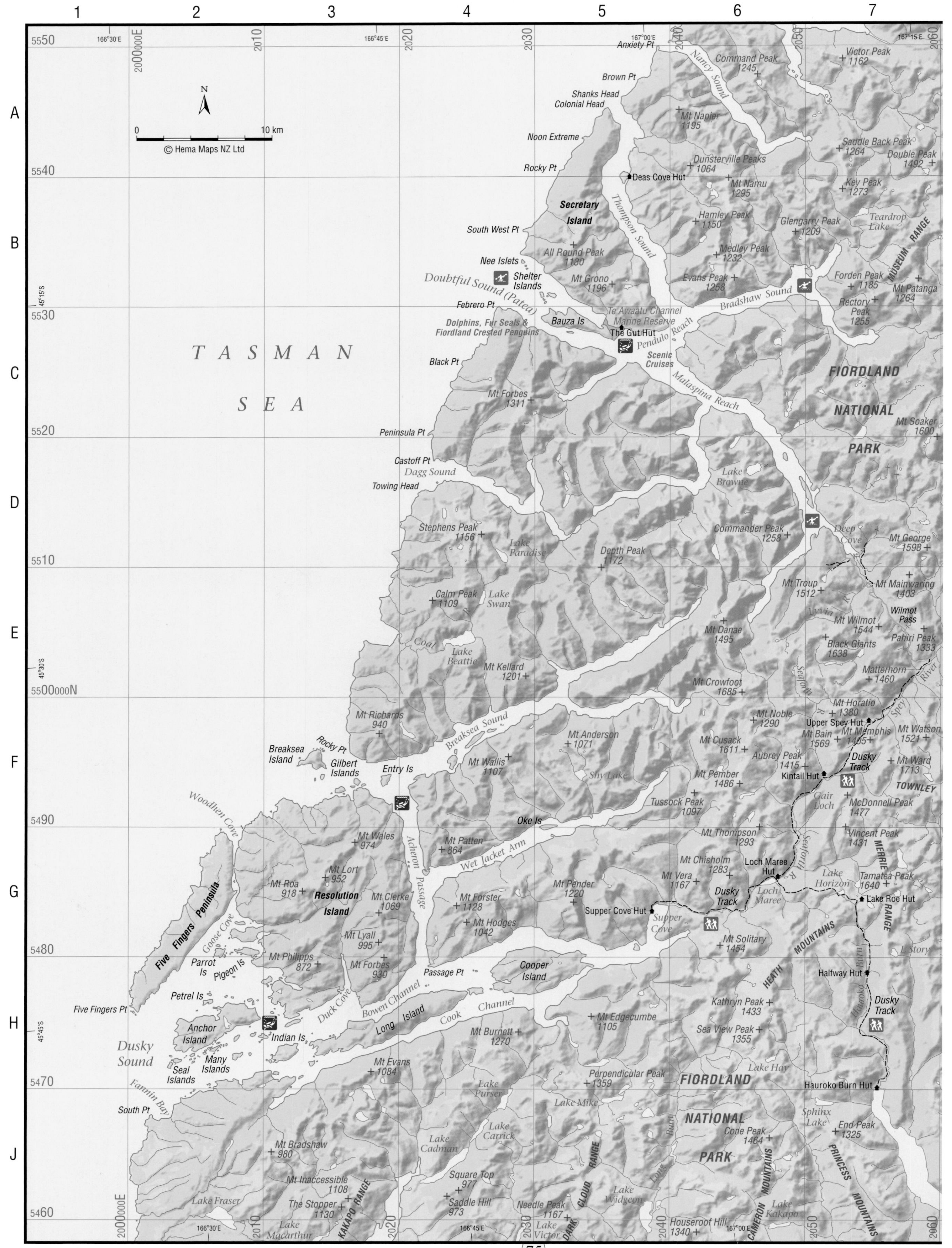

TASMAN SEA
© Hema Maps NZ Ltd
0
10 km
N
Anxiety Pt
Brown Pt
Shanks Head
Colonial Head
Noon Extreme
Rocky Pt
Secretary Island
South West Pt
All Round Peak 1130
Nee Islets
Shelter Islands
Mt Grono 1196
Doubtful Sound (Patea)
Febrero Pt
Dolphins, Fur Seals & Fiordland Crested Penguins
Bauza Is
Te Awaatu Channel Marine Reserve
The Gut Hut
Scenic Cruises
Pendulo Reach
Black Pt
Nancy Sound
Command Peak 1245
Mt Napier 1195
Dunsterville Peaks 1064
Deas Cove Hut
Mt Namu 1295
Thompson Sound
Hamley Peak 1150
Medley Peak 1232
Evans Peak 1258
Glengarry Peak 1209
Bradshaw Sound
Victor Peak 1162
Saddle Back Peak 1264
Double Peak 1492
Key Peak 1273
Teardrop Lake
MUSEUM RANGE
Forden Peak 1185
Mt Patanga 1264
Rectory Peak 1255
FIORDLAND NATIONAL PARK
Malaspina Reach
Mt Forbes 1311
Peninsula Pt
Mt Soaker 1600
Castoff Pt
Dagg Sound
Towing Head
Lake Browne
Stephens Peak 1156
Lake Paradise
Depth Peak 1172
Commander Peak 1258
Deep Cove
Mt George 1598
Mt Troup 1512
Mt Mainwaring 1403
Calm Peak 1109
Lake Swan
Lyvia R
Mt Danae 1495
Mt Wilmot 1544
Wilmot Pass
Pahiri Peak 1333
Black Giants 1638
Coal
Lake Beattie
Mt Kellard 1201
Mt Crowfoot 1685
Seaforth
Matterhorn 1460
Spey River
Mt Horatio 1380
Upper Spey Hut
Mt Noble 1290
Mt Richards 940
Breaksea Sound
Mt Anderson 1071
Mt Cusack 1611
Mt Bain 1569
Mt Memphis 1405
Mt Watson 1521
Breaksea Island
Rocky Pt
Gilbert Islands
Entry Is
Mt Wallis 1107
Shy Lake
Aubrey Peak 1415
Kintail Hut
Dusky Track
Mt Ward 1713
Mt Pember 1486
Gair Loch
TOWNLEY
McDonnell Peak 1477
Woodhen Cove
Tussock Peak 1097
Oke Is
Mt Wales 974
Mt Patten 864
Acheron Passage
Wet Jacket Arm
Mt Thompson 1293
Vincent Peak 1431
MERRIE RANGE
Mt Lort 952
Mt Chisholm 1283
Loch Maree Hut
Seaforth R
Mt Roa 918
Resolution Island
Mt Clerke 1069
Mt Pender 1220
Mt Vera 1167
Dusky Track
Loch Maree
Lake Horizon
Tamatea Peak 1640
Five Fingers Peninsula
Mt Forster 1128
Supper Cove Hut
Lake Roe Hut
Goose Cove
Mt Hodges 1042
Supper Cove
Mt Lyall 995
Mt Solitary 1454
HEATH MOUNTAINS
L Story
Parrot Is
Pigeon Is
Mt Philipps 872
Mt Forbes 930
Cooper Island
Passage Pt
Halfway Hut
Hauroko Burn
Petrel Is
Duck Cove
Bowen Channel
Kathryn Peak 1433
Five Fingers Pt
Long Island
Cook Channel
Mt Edgecumbe 1105
Dusky Track
Anchor Island
Indian Is
Mt Burnett 1270
Sea View Peak 1355
Dusky Sound
Seal Islands
Many Islands
Mt Evans 1084
Lake Hay
Perpendicular Peak 1359
FIORDLAND
Hauroko Burn Hut
Fannin Bay
Lake Purser
Lake Mike
South Pt
Lake Carrick
NATIONAL PARK
Sphinx Lake
Cone Peak 1464
End Peak 1325
Mt Bradshaw 980
Lake Cadman
CLOUD RANGE
Burn
PARK
PRINCESS MOUNTAINS
Mt Inaccessible 1108
Square Top 977
Lake Widgeon
Lous
CAMERON MOUNTAINS
Lake Fraser
The Stopper 1130
KAKAPO RANGE
Saddle Hill 973
Needle Peak 1167
DARK
Lake Kakapo
Lake Macarthur
Lake Victor
Houseroof Hill 1340
1 2 3 4 5 6 7
A B C D E F G H J
166°30'E
166°45'E
167°00'E
167°15'E
45°15'S
45°30'S
45°45'S
5550
5540
5530
5520
5510
5500000N
5490
5480
5470
5460
2000000E
2010
2020
2030
2040
2050
2060

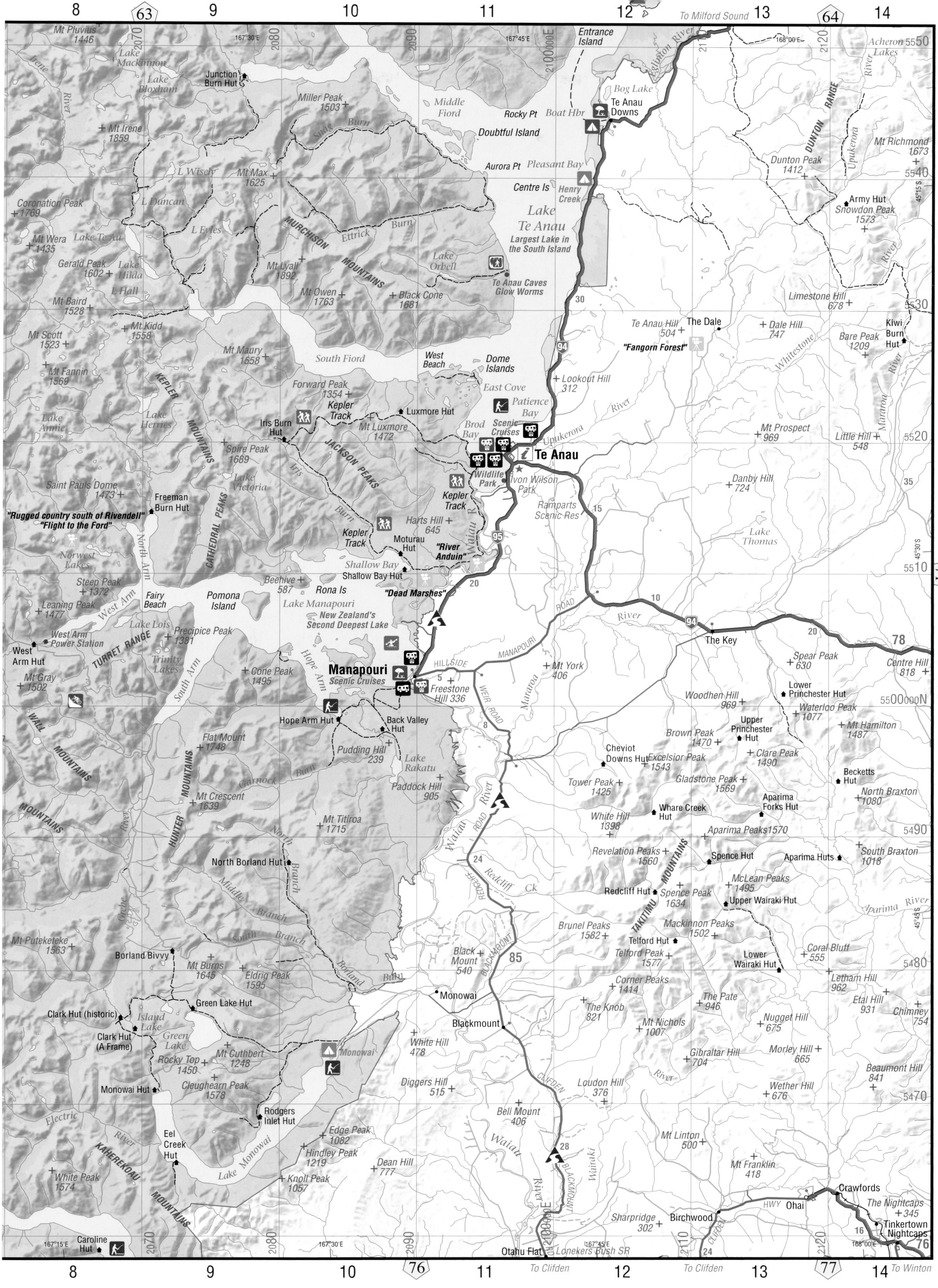
Lake Te Anau
Largest Lake in the South Island
Te Anau
Manapouri
Lake Manapouri
New Zealand's Second Deepest Lake
Te Anau Downs
Doubtful Island
Te Anau Caves Glow Worms
MURCHISON MOUNTAINS
KEPLER MOUNTAINS
JACKSON PEAKS
CATHEDRAL PEAKS
TURRET RANGE
WALL MOUNTAINS
HUNTER MOUNTAINS
TAKITIMU MOUNTAINS
KAHEREKOAU MOUNTAINS
DUNTON RANGE
"Fangorn Forest"
"Rugged country south of Rivendell"
"Flight to the Ford"
"River Anduin"
"Dead Marshes"
Kepler Track
Luxmore Hut
Iris Burn Hut
Moturau Hut
Shallow Bay Hut
West Arm Power Station
West Arm Hut
Hope Arm Hut
Back Valley Hut
North Borland Hut
Borland Bivvy
Green Lake Hut
Clark Hut (historic)
Clark Hut (A Frame)
Monowai Hut
Rodgers Inlet Hut
Eel Creek Hut
Caroline Hut
Lake Monowai
Monowai
Blackmount
The Key
Birchwood
Ohai
Crawfords
Tinkertown Nightcaps
Otahu Flat
To Milford Sound
To Lumsden
To Clifden
To Winton

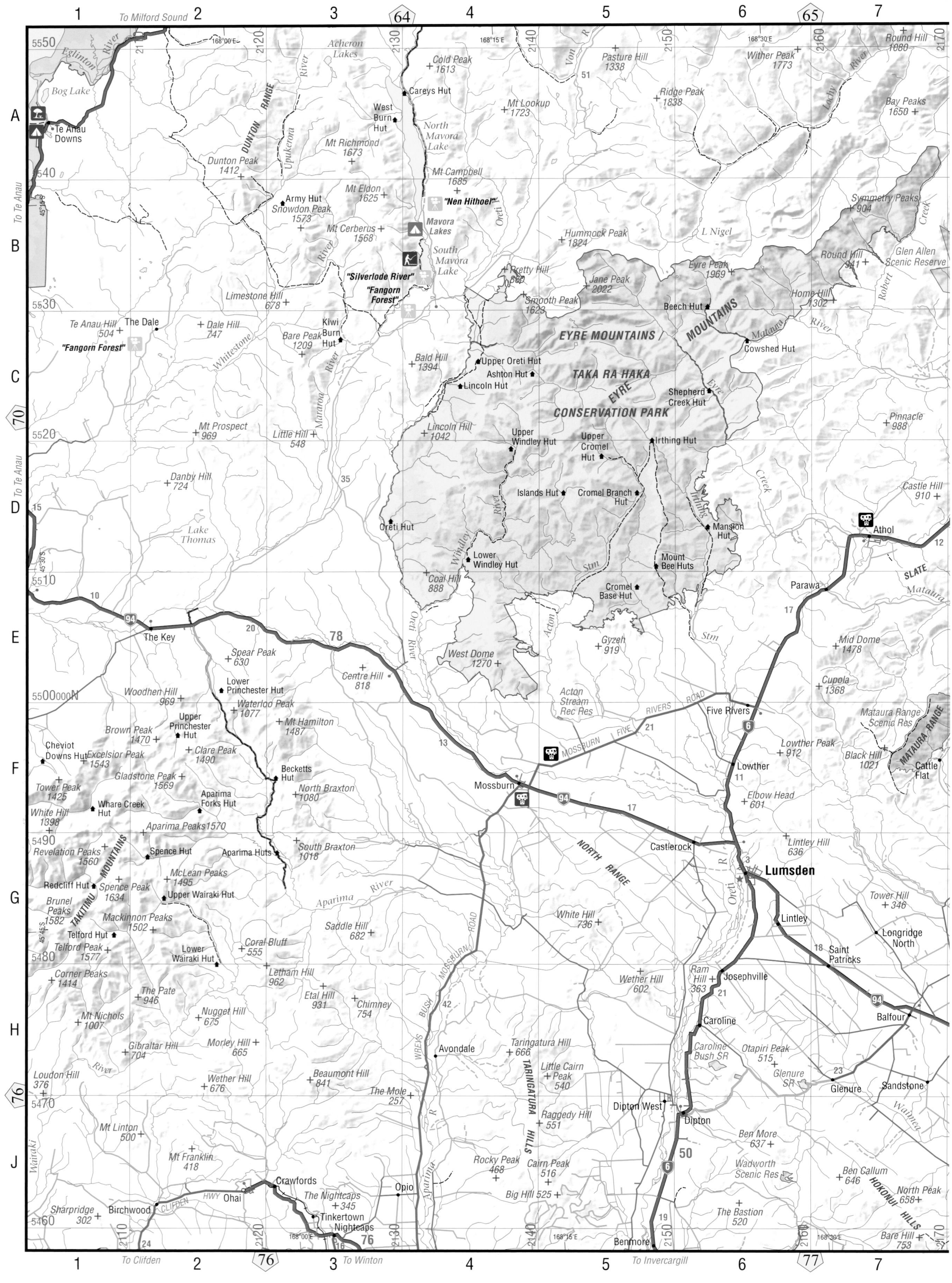
1
2
3
4
5
6
7
A
B
C
D
E
F
G
H
J
To Milford Sound
To Te Anau
To Clifden
To Winton
To Invercargill
64
65
70
76
77
Eglinton
River
Bog Lake
Te Anau Downs
DUNTON RANGE
Dunton Peak 1412
Upukerora
Acheron Lakes
Careys Hut
West Burn Hut
North Mavora Lake
Mt Richmond 1673
Cold Peak 1613
Mt Campbell 1685
"Nen Hithoel"
Mt Eldon 1625
Army Hut
Snowdon Peak 1573
Mt Cerberus 1568
Mavora Lakes
South Mavora Lake
"Silverlode River"
"Fangorn Forest"
Limestone Hill 678
Kiwi Burn Hut
Bare Peak 1209
Te Anau Hill 504
The Dale
Dale Hill 747
"Fangorn Forest"
Whitestone
Mararoa River
Mt Prospect 969
Little Hill 548
Danby Hill 724
Lake Thomas
Pasture Hill 1338
Mt Lookup 1723
Ridge Peak 1838
Oreti
Von R
Wither Peak 1773
Round Hill 1080
Bay Peaks 1650
Lochy River
Hummock Peak 1824
L Nigel
Symmetry Peaks 904
Round Hill 941
Glen Allen Scenic Reserve
Creek
Robert
Pretty Hill 800
Jane Peak 2022
Smooth Peak 1623
Eyre Peak 1969
Beech Hut
Home Hill 1302
Mataura River
Cowshed Hut
EYRE MOUNTAINS / TAKA RA HAKA CONSERVATION PARK
EYRE MOUNTAINS
Bald Hill 1394
Upper Oreti Hut
Ashton Hut
Lincoln Hut
Shepherd Creek Hut
Eyre
Lincoln Hill 1042
Upper Windley Hut
Upper Cromel Hut
Irthing Hut
Pinnacle 988
Islands Hut
Cromel Branch Hut
Irthing
Mansion Hut
Castle Hill 910
Athol
Oreti Hut
Windley River
Lower Windley Hut
Mount Bee Huts
Coal Hill 888
Stm
Cromel Base Hut
Parawa
SLATE
Mataura
West Dome 1270
Acton
Gyzeh 919
Mid Dome 1478
Cupola 1368
The Key
Spear Peak 630
Centre Hill 818
Oreti River
Woodhen Hill 969
Lower Princhester Hut
Waterloo Peak 1077
Mt Hamilton 1487
Acton Stream Rec Res
FIVE RIVERS ROAD
Five Rivers
Mataura Range Scenic Res
MATAURA RANGE
Brown Peak 1470
Upper Princhester Hut
Clare Peak 1490
Cheviot Downs Hut
Excelsior Peak 1543
Gladstone Peak 1569
Becketts Hut
MOSSBURN FIVE RIVERS
Mossburn
Lowther Peak 912
Lowther
Black Hill 1021
Cattle Flat
Tower Peak 1425
White Hill 1398
Whare Creek Hut
Aparima Forks Hut
North Braxton 1080
Elbow Head 601
Aparima Peaks 1570
Revelation Peaks 1560
Spence Hut
Aparima Huts
South Braxton 1018
NORTH RANGE
Castlerock
Lintley Hill 636
Lumsden
TAKITIMU MOUNTAINS
Redcliff Hut
Spence Peak 1634
McLean Peaks 1495
Upper Wairaki Hut
Brunel Peaks 1582
Mackinnon Peaks 1502
Aparima River
White Hill 736
Tower Hill 346
Lintley
Longridge North
Telford Hut
Telford Peak 1577
Coral Bluff 555
Saddle Hill 682
Saint Patricks
Lower Wairaki Hut
Corner Peaks 1414
Letham Hill 962
Wether Hill 602
Ram Hill 363
Josephville
The Pate 946
Etal Hill 931
Chimney 754
Mt Nichols 1007
Nugget Hill 675
Caroline
Balfour
Morley Hill 665
Gibraltar Hill 704
River
WREYS BUSH MOSSBURN ROAD
Avondale
Taringatura Hill 666
TARINGATURA HILLS
Caroline Bush SR
Otapiri Peak 515
Glenure SR
Glenure
Sandstone
Loudon Hill 376
Wether Hill 676
Beaumont Hill 841
The Mole 257
Little Cairn Peak 540
Dipton West
Dipton
Waimea
Mt Linton 500
Raggedy Hill 551
Ben More 637
Mt Franklin 418
Rocky Peak 468
Cairn Peak 516
Wadworth Scenic Res
Ben Callum 646
HOKONUI HILLS
Wairaki
Crawfords
Ohai
CLIFDEN HWY
Opio
Aparima
The Nightcaps 345
Big Hill 525
The Bastion 520
North Peak 658
Sharpridge 302
Birchwood
Tinkertown
Nightcaps
Benmore
Bare Hill 753
168°00'E
168°15'E
168°30'E
45°15'S
45°30'S
45°45'S
5550
5540
5530
5520
5510
5500000N
5490
5480
5470
5460
2110
2120
2130
2140
2150
2160
2170
94
78
6
50

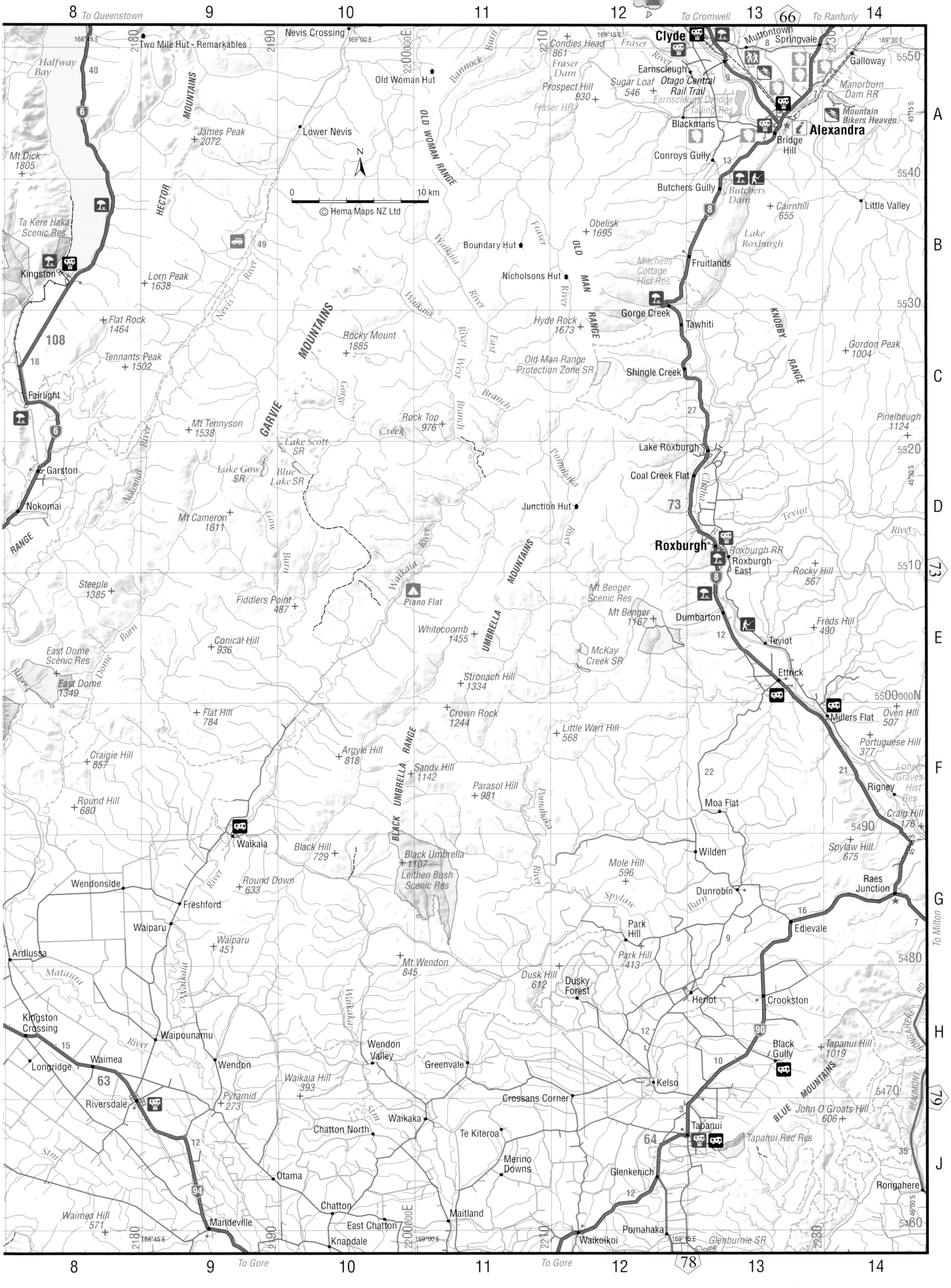
To Queenstown
To Cromwell
To Ranfurly
To Gore
To Milton
Two Mile Hut - Remarkables
Nevis Crossing
Clyde
Muttontown
Springvale
Galloway
Halfway Bay
Condies Head 861
Fraser Dam
Earnscleugh
Otago Central Rail Trail
Old Woman Hut
Prospect Hill 930
Sugar Loaf 546
Manorburn Dam RR
Fraser HR
Earnscleugh Dredge Tailing Res
Mountain Bikers Heaven
Blackmans
Alexandra
Bridge Hill
James Peak 2072
Lower Nevis
OLD WOMAN RANGE
MOUNTAINS
Mt Dick 1805
Conroys Gully
HECTOR
Butchers Gully
Butchers Dam
Cairnhill 655
Little Valley
© Hema Maps NZ Ltd
Ta Kere Haka Scenic Res
Obelisk 1695
Lake Roxburgh
Boundary Hut
Mitchells Cottage Hist Res
Fruitlands
Kingston
Nicholsons Hut
OLD MAN RANGE
Lorn Peak 1638
Gorge Creek
Tawhiti
Flat Rock 1464
GARVIE MOUNTAINS
Hyde Rock 1673
Rocky Mount 1885
KNOBBY RANGE
Gordon Peak 1004
Tennants Peak 1502
Old Man Range Protection Zone SR
Shingle Creek
Fairlight
Rock Top 976
Pinelbeugh 1124
Mt Tennyson 1538
Lake Scott SR
Lake Roxburgh
Garston
Lake Gow SR
Blue Lake SR
Coal Creek Flat
Nokomai
Junction Hut
Mt Cameron 1611
Teviot
RANGE
Roxburgh
Roxburgh RR
Roxburgh East
Rocky Hill 567
Steeple 1385
UMBRELLA MOUNTAINS
Fiddlers Point 487
Piano Flat
Mt Benger Scenic Res
Mt Benger 1167
Dumbarton
Freds Hill 490
Whitecoomb 1455
Conical Hill 936
East Dome Scenic Res
East Dome 1349
McKay Creek SR
Teviot
Stronach Hill 1334
Ettrick
Crown Rock 1244
Millers Flat
Oven Hill 507
Flat Hill 784
Little Wart Hill 568
Portuguese Hill 377
Craigie Hill 857
Argyle Hill 818
Sandy Hill 1142
BLACK UMBRELLA RANGE
Loney Graves Hist Res
Round Hill 680
Parasol Hill 981
Rigney
Moa Flat
Craig Hill 176
Waikaia
Black Hill 729
Black Umbrella 1107
Leithen Bush Scenic Res
Mole Hill 596
Wilden
Spylaw Hill 675
Wendonside
Round Down 633
Dunrobin
Raes Junction
Freshford
Edievale
Waiparu
Park Hill
Waiparu 451
Park Hill 413
Ardlussa
Mt Wendon 845
Dusk Hill 612
Dusky Forest
Heriot
Crookston
Kingston Crossing
Waipounamu
Wendon Valley
Black Gully
Tapanui Hill 1019
Longridge
Waimea
Wendon
Greenvale
Kelso
BLUE MOUNTAINS
Waikaia Hill 393
Riversdale
Pyramid 273
Crossans Corner
John O'Groats Hill 606
Chatton North
Waikaka
Te Kiteroa
Tapanui
Tapanui Rec Res
Merino Downs
Glenkenich
Otama
Rongahere
Waimea Hill 571
Chatton
Maitland
East Chatton
Mandeville
Pomahaka
Knapdale
Waikoikoi
Glenburnie SR
Mataura River
Waikaia River
Nevis River
Nokomai River
Pomahaka River
Spylaw Burn
Clutha
Teviot River
Fraser River
Bannock Burn
Gow Burn
Gorge Creek
Dome Burn
Waikaka Stm
BEAUMONT
RONGAHERE RD
A
B
C
D
E
F
G
H
J
8
9
10
11
12
13
14

Central Otago & Dunedin

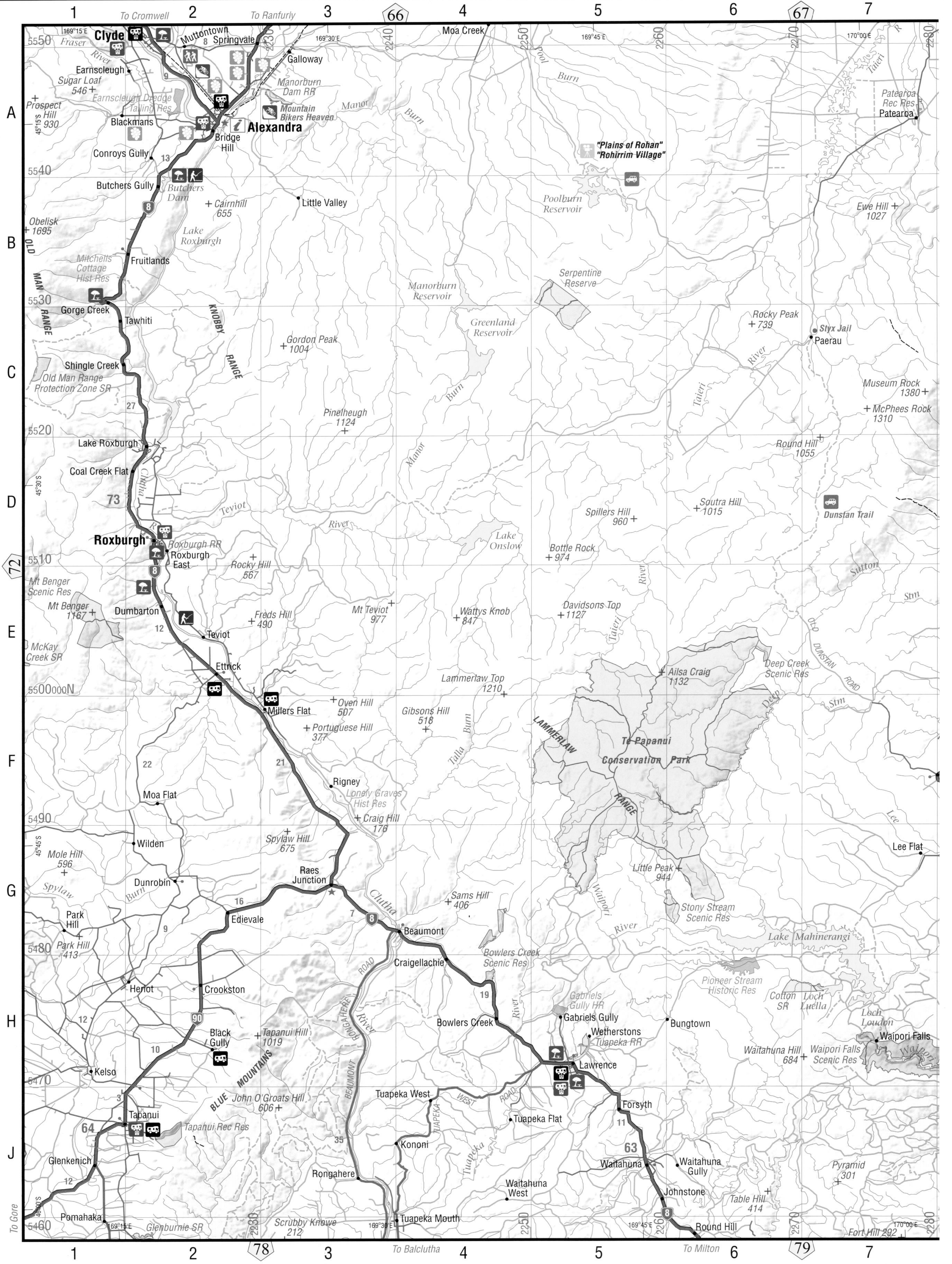

To Ranfurly
To Oamaru
To Milton
68
Otago Central Rail Trail
Orangapai
Flat Cap 804
Flat Hill 845
Morrisons
Green Valley
HORSE RANGE
Devils Elbow 877
Conical Peak 945
Table Hill 594
Prominent Peak 581
Waianakarua Scenic Reserve
Staircase Hut
Mt Fortune 789
Glencoe Reserve
Herbert
Otepopo
Te Hakapureirei Beach
Waianakarua
Lookout Bluff
The Bluff 116
Tiroiti
Taieri
Hyde
Hyde RR
ROCK AND PILLAR RANGE
Sister Peaks 737
Golden Point Historic Res
Waihemo
Shag River
Waianakarua Scenic Res
Hampden
Hampden Beach
Moeraki Boulders SR
Moeraki Pt
Moeraki
Hillgrove
Kaik
MACRAES ROAD
Brother Peaks 715
Macraes Flat
Mt Hellene 529
Waynes
Razorback 604
Pigeon Bush SR
Makareao
Dunback
Rock and Pillar Scenic Res
Rock and Pillar
Stag Hill 600
Moonlight
Dunback Hill 599
Inch Valley
Trotters Gorge Scenic Reserve
Katiki
Katiki Pt Historic Res
Harrys Peak 220
Trotters Gorge
Katiki Beach
Leaning Lodge
Summit Rock 1450
Big Hut
Redbank Scenic Res
Bog Pine SR
Stoneburn
Glenpark
Pukehiwitahi 227
Shag Point
Matakaea RR
Meadowbank
Bushey
Shag Pt
Shag River Onewhenua Hist Res
Ngapuna
The Sisters 661
Sheepwash Ck
Nenthorn
Lots Wife 714
North Branch
Taieri Peak 308
Palmerston Butterfly & Bird Haven
Palmerston
Goldfields Heritage Trail
Otago Central Rail Trail
Black Rock 526
Deighton Creek Nature Reserve
Slip Hill 502
MOONLIGHT
Middlemarch
Swampy Hill 733
Mt Trotter 587
Mt Pleasant 418
Wairunga
Mt Royal 319
Goodwood SR
Tavora Reserve
Bobbys Head
Mt Royal 709
Bald Hill 476
Waikouaiti River
Goodwood
Flag Swamp
Hummock 736
Mt Watkin (Hikaroroa) 616
Hawksbury Bush
Tumai
Pleasant River
Derdan Hill (Pahatea) 444
Mt Watkin Rec Res
Mt Scott 664
Sutton
Waikouaiti
Mt Ross 340
Mount Stoker
Mt Stoker 435
Mt Paul 544
Bucklands Crossing
Cornish Head
Matarae
Little Peak 655
Merton
Karitane
Waikouaiti River
Pukerangi
Puketeraki
Green Pt
Brinns Pt
Taieri Gorge Scenic Railway
Shannon
Mt Misery 714
Seacliff
Omimi
Deep Stm
Lamb Hill 661
Yellow Hut
Jubilee Hut
Silverpeaks Scenic Res
Possum Hut
Warrington
Evansdale
Blueskin Bay
Purakanui Bay
Potato Pt
Purakanui
Long Beach
Heyward Pt
Hindon
Mt John 678
Mt Allan 715
Mount Allan
Pulpit Rock 760
Clarks Junction
GEORGE KING MEMORIAL
Waitati
Michies Crossing
Orokonui
Osborne
Heyward Point SR
Upper Waitati
Silver Peaks Route
Fortification Peak 515
Mihiwakai
Te Ngaru
Aramoana
Taiaroa Head NR
Royal Albatross Centre / Albatross Colony
Rerewahine Pt
Penguin Place
Natures Wonders (seals, penguins)
Lee Stream
Boulder Hill 557
Chalkies SR
Whare Flat
Swampy Summit 739
Pigeon Flat
Deborah Bay
Mt Cargill
Mt Cargill SR
Sawyers Bay
Port Chalmers
Careys Bay
Aramoana Cons Area
Harington Point
Pipikaretu Pt
Otakou
Te Whakarekaiwi
Mt Hyde 443
Round Ridge Hill 452
Tara Hills
North Taieri
Flagstaff SR
Upper Junction
Roseneath
Harwood
Lower Portobello
Wickliffe Bay
Papanui Inlet
Leith Valley
Glenleith
St Leonards
Otago Harbour
Portobello
Otago Peninsula
Harveys Flat
Taieri Gorge / Outram Glen SR
North East Valley
Broad Bay
Hoopers Inlet
Mt Charles (Poatiri) 408
Maukaatua Range Scenic Reserve
Woodside
Outram
Wyllies Crossing
Janefield
Wakari
Dunedin
See Map 123
Macandrew Bay
Maungatua 895
Mosgiel
Wingatui
Mornington
The Cove
Ravensbourne
Sandymount
Cape Saunders
Matakitaki Pt
Wharekakahu Is NR
Fairfield
Green Island
Waverley
Highcliff
Pukehiki
Lovers Leap
Allans Beach RR
Hoopers Inlet
Maungatua
Owhiro
St Kilda
St Clair
Ocean Grove
Maori Head
Highcliff
Boulder Beach
Seal Pt
Sandfly Bay
Harakeke Pt
Sandymount Rec Res
Mill Creek Scenic Res
Momona
Allanton
East Taieri
Saddle Hill
Scroggs Hill
Blackhead
Black Head
St Clair Beach
St Kilda Beach
Glenfalloch Woodland Gardens
Dunedin Airport
Hope Hill SR
Westwood
Waldronville
Kaikorai Lagoon
Dunedin Suburbs See Map 124
Berwick
Otokia
Otokia Hill 174
Ocean View
Westwood RR
Green Is NR
Brighton
Bruce Rocks
L Waipori
Henley
Henley SR
Sinclair Wetlands
Waihola Hill 184
Ferry Hill 216
Puke Kuri 196
Taieri River Scenic Res
Kuri Bush
Kiri Bush RR
L Waihola
Waihola
0
10 km
© Hema Maps NZ Ltd
N
170°15'E
170°30'E
170°45'E
45°15'S
45°30'S
45°45'S
46°00'S
2290
2300000E
2310
2320
2330
2340
5540
5530
5520
5510
5500000N
5490
5480
5470
5460
8
9
10
11
12
13
14
A
B
C
D
E
F
G
H
J

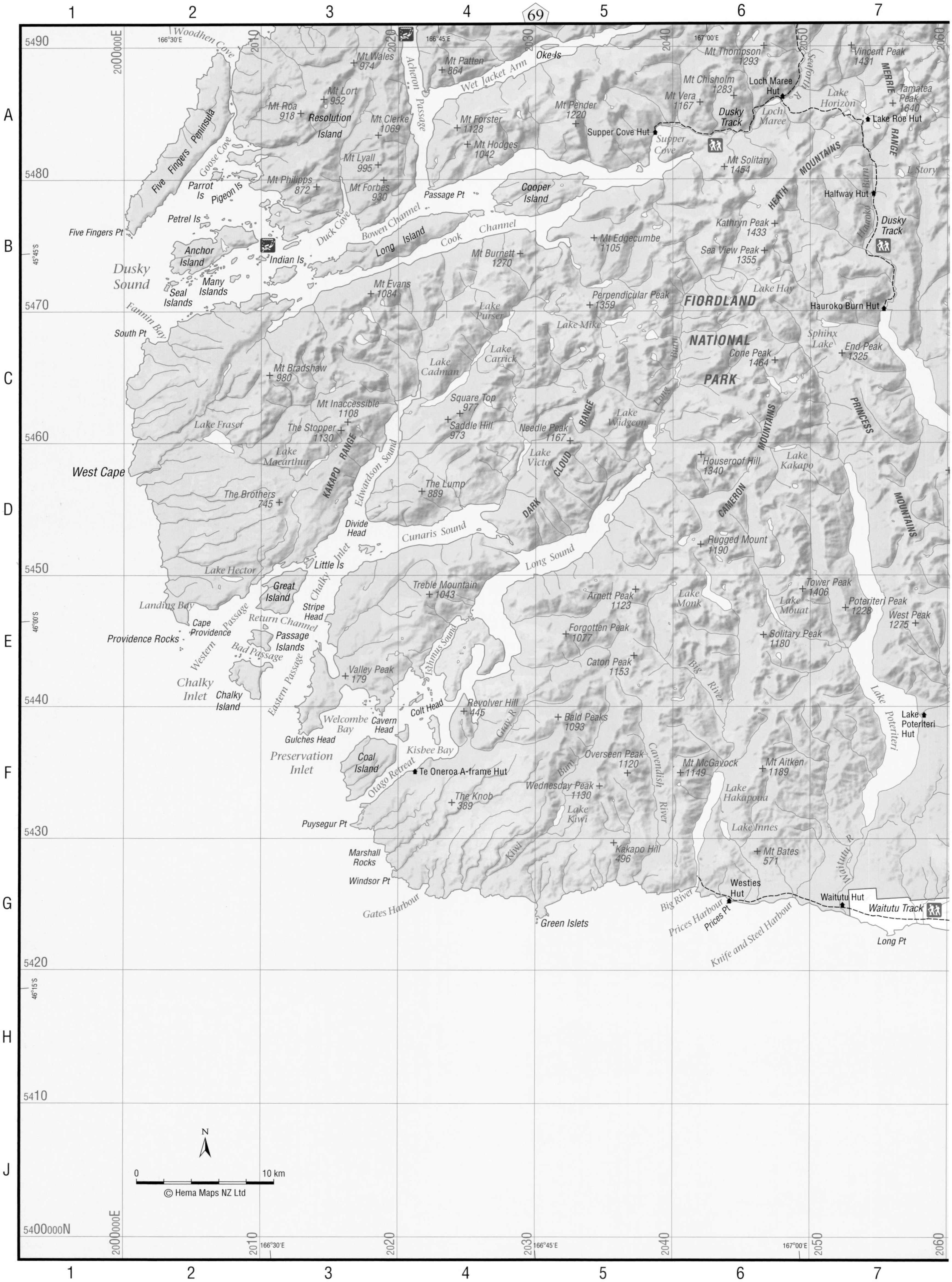

69
Woodhen Cove
Five Fingers Peninsula
Goose Cove
Parrot Is
Pigeon Is
Petrel Is
Five Fingers Pt
Anchor Island
Dusky Sound
Seal Islands
Many Islands
Indian Is
Fannin Bay
South Pt
Mt Wales 974
Mt Lort 952
Mt Roa 918
Resolution Island
Mt Clerke 1069
Mt Lyall 995
Mt Philipps 872
Mt Forbes 930
Duck Cove
Acheron Passage
Mt Patten 864
Wet Jacket Arm
Oke Is
Mt Forster 1128
Mt Hodges 1042
Passage Pt
Bowen Channel
Long Island
Cook Channel
Cooper Island
Mt Pender 1220
Supper Cove Hut
Supper Cove
Mt Thompson 1293
Mt Chisholm 1283
Mt Vera 1167
Dusky Track
Loch Maree Hut
Loch Maree
Seaforth R
Mt Solitary 1454
Vincent Peak 1431
Lake Horizon
Tamatea Peak 1640
Lake Roe Hut
MERRIE RANGE
HEATH MOUNTAINS
L Story
Halfway Hut
Hauroko Burn
Dusky Track
Kathryn Peak 1433
Sea View Peak 1355
Mt Edgecumbe 1105
Mt Burnett 1270
Mt Evans 1084
Perpendicular Peak 1359
Lake Hay
Hauroko Burn Hut
FIORDLAND NATIONAL PARK
Lake Purser
Lake Mike
Lake Carrick
Lake Cadman
Mt Bradshaw 980
Sphinx Lake
End Peak 1325
Cone Peak 1464
Mt Inaccessible 1108
The Stopper 1130
Square Top 977
Saddle Hill 973
Needle Peak 1167
Lake Widgeon
Lake Fraser
Lake Macarthur
KAKAPO RANGE
Edwardson Sound
Lake Victor
CLOUD RANGE
DARK
Houseroof Hill 1340
Lake Kakapo
PRINCESS MOUNTAINS
CAMERON MOUNTAINS
West Cape
The Brothers 745
The Lump 889
Divide Head
Cunaris Sound
Rugged Mount 1190
Little Is
Long Sound
Lake Hector
Great Island
Chalky Inlet
Treble Mountain 1043
Arnett Peak 1123
Lake Monk
Lake Mouat
Tower Peak 1406
Poteriteri Peak 1228
West Peak 1275
Landing Bay
Cape Providence
Western Passage
Return Channel
Stripe Head
Passage Islands
Bad Passage
Providence Rocks
Isthmus Sound
Forgotten Peak 1077
Solitary Peak 1180
Caton Peak 1153
Big River
Chalky Inlet
Chalky Island
Eastern Passage
Valley Peak 179
Colt Head
Revolver Hill 445
Gray R
Bald Peaks 1093
Lake Poteriteri
Lake Poteriteri Hut
Welcombe Bay
Cavern Head
Gulches Head
Preservation Inlet
Coal Island
Kisbee Bay
Otago Retreat
Te Oneroa A-frame Hut
Overseen Peak 1120
Cavendish River
Mt McGavock 1149
Mt Aitken 1189
Wednesday Peak 1130
Lake Hakapoua
The Knob 389
Lake Kiwi
Lake Innes
Puysegur Pt
Kiwi Burn
Kakapo Hill 496
Mt Bates 571
Waitutu R
Marshall Rocks
Windsor Pt
Westies Hut
Big River
Gates Harbour
Green Islets
Prices Harbour
Prices Pt
Waitutu Hut
Waitutu Track
Knife and Steel Harbour
Long Pt
166°30'E
166°45'E
167°00'E
45°45'S
46°00'S
46°15'S
5490
5480
5470
5460
5450
5440
5430
5420
5410
5400000N
2000000E
2010
2020
2030
2040
2050
2060
1 2 3 4 5 6 7
A B C D E F G H J
N
0 10 km
© Hema Maps NZ Ltd

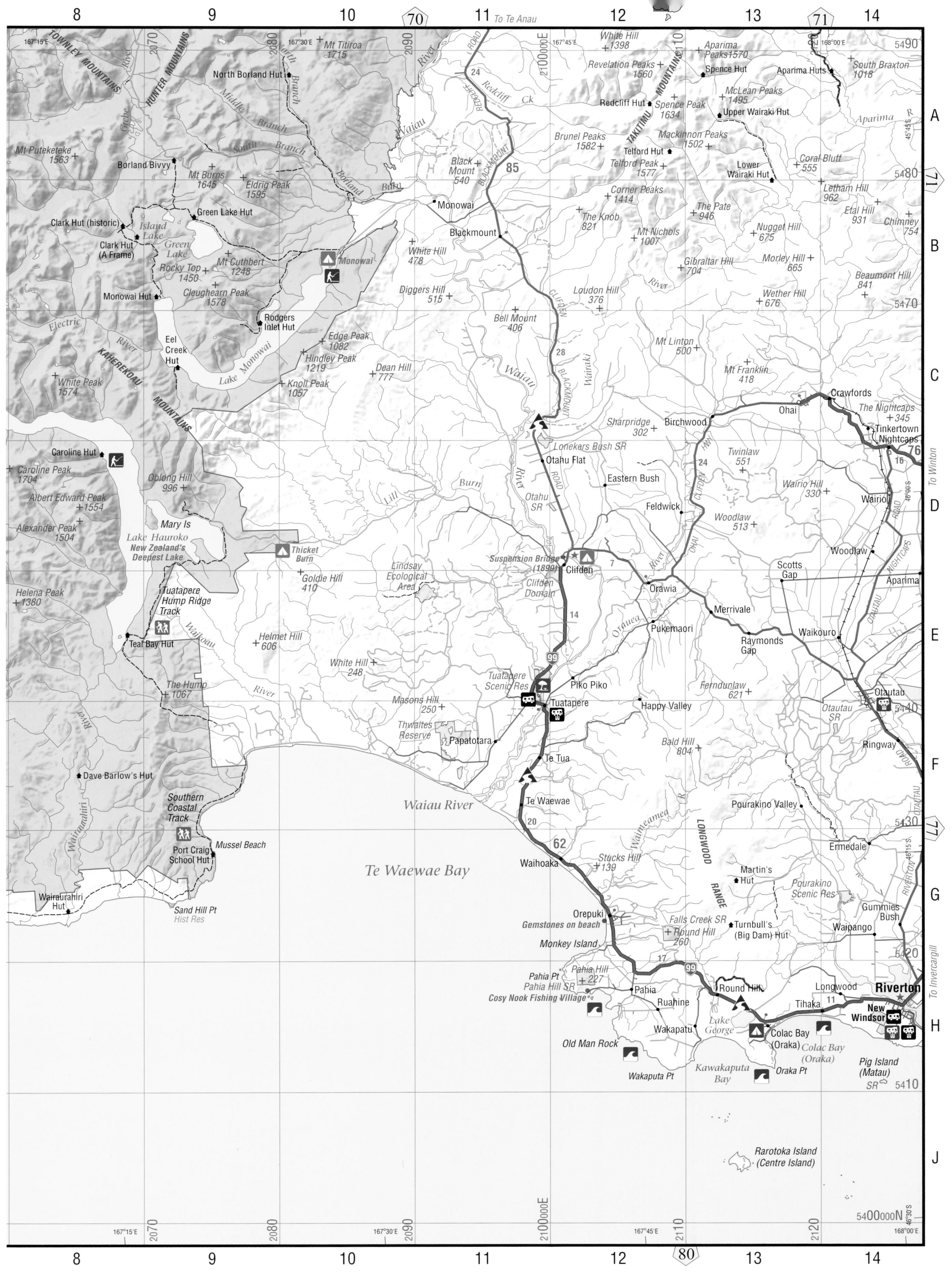
8
9
10
11
12
13
14
70
71
To Te Anau
TOWNLEY MOUNTAINS
HUNTER MOUNTAINS
Mt Titiroa
1715
North Borland Hut
North Branch
Middle Branch
South Branch
Borland
Grebe River
Mt Puteketeke
1563
Borland Bivvy
Mt Burns
1645
Eldrig Peak
1595
Clark Hut (historic)
Island Lake
Green Lake Hut
Clark Hut
(A Frame)
Green Lake
Mt Cuthbert
1248
Rocky Top
1450
Cleughearn Peak
1578
Monowai Hut
Monowai
Rodgers
Inlet Hut
Electric River
Eel
Creek
Hut
Lake Monowai
KAHEREKOAU MOUNTAINS
White Peak
1574
Edge Peak
1082
Hindley Peak
1219
Knoll Peak
1057
Dean Hill
777
Caroline Hut
Caroline Peak
1704
Oblong Hill
996
Albert Edward Peak
1554
Alexander Peak
1504
Mary Is
Lake Hauroko
New Zealand's
Deepest Lake
Thicket
Burn
Helena Peak
1380
Goldie Hill
410
Tuatapere
Hump Ridge
Track
Teal Bay Hut
Waiau River
Helmet Hill
606
White Hill
248
The Hump
1067
Dave Barlow's Hut
Southern
Coastal
Track
Mussel Beach
Port Craig
School Hut
Wairaurahiri River
Wairaurahiri
Hut
Sand Hill Pt
Hist Res
Waiau
Redcliff Ck
REDCLIFF ROAD
24
Black
Mount
540
BLACKMOUNT
85
Monowai
Blackmount
White Hill
478
Diggers Hill
515
Bell Mount
406
CLIFDEN
28
Waiau
BLACKMOUNT
Lill Burn
Otahu Flat
Otahu
SR
Lindsay
Ecological
Area
Suspension Bridge
(1899)
Clifden
Clifden
Domain
14
99
Tuatapere
Scenic Res
Piko Piko
Tuatapere
Masons Hill
250
Thwaites
Reserve
Papatotara
Te Tua
Te Waewae
Waiau River
Te Waewae Bay
20
62
Waihoaka
White Hill
1398
Revelation Peaks
1560
Aparima
Peaks1570
Spence Hut
Aparima Huts
South Braxton
1018
TAKITIMU MOUNTAINS
Redcliff Hut
Spence Peak
1634
McLean Peaks
1495
Upper Wairaki Hut
Aparima R
Brunel Peaks
1582
Mackinnon Peaks
1502
Telford Hut
Telford Peak
1577
Lower
Wairaki Hut
Coral Bluff
555
Corner Peaks
1414
Letham Hill
962
The Knob
821
The Pate
946
Etal Hill
931
Chimney
754
Mt Nichols
1007
Nugget Hill
675
Gibraltar Hill
704
Morley Hill
665
Beaumont Hill
841
Loudon Hill
376
River
Wether Hill
676
Mt Linton
500
Mt Franklin
418
Wairaki
Crawfords
Ohai
The Nightcaps
345
Tinkertown
Nightcaps
76
16
Sharpridge
302
Birchwood
Lonekers Bush SR
Twinlaw
551
24
CLIFDEN HWY
Eastern Bush
Wairio Hill
330
Wairio
Feldwick
Woodlaw
513
Woodlaw
NIGHTCAPS
7
Ohai River
Orawia
Scotts
Gap
Aparima
Merrivale
Pukemaori
Orauea
Raymonds
Gap
Waikouro
Ferndunlaw
621
Happy Valley
Otautau
Otautau
SR
Bald Hill
804
Ringway
Pourakino Valley
Waimeamea R
LONGWOOD RANGE
Stucks Hill
139
Ermedale
Martin's
Hut
Pourakino
Scenic Res
Gummies
Bush
Orepuki
Gemstones on beach
Falls Creek SR
Round Hill
260
Turnbull's
(Big Dam) Hut
Waipango
Monkey Island
17
99
Pahia Pt
Pahia Hill
227
Pahia Hill SR
Cosy Nook Fishing Village
Pahia
Round Hill
Ruahine
Longwood
Riverton
Tihaka
11
New
Windsor
Wakapatu
Lake
George
Colac Bay
(Oraka)
Colac Bay
(Oraka)
Old Man Rock
Kawakaputa
Bay
Oraka Pt
Wakaputa Pt
Pig Island
(Matau)
SR
Rarotoka Island
(Centre Island)
To Winton
To Invercargill
OTAUTAU
RIVERTON
A
B
C
D
E
F
G
H
J
2070
2080
2090
2100000E
2110
2120
5490
5480
5470
5440
5430
5420
5410
5400000N
167°15'E
167°30'E
167°45'E
168°00'E
45°45'S
46°00'S
46°15'S
46°30'S
80
77
71

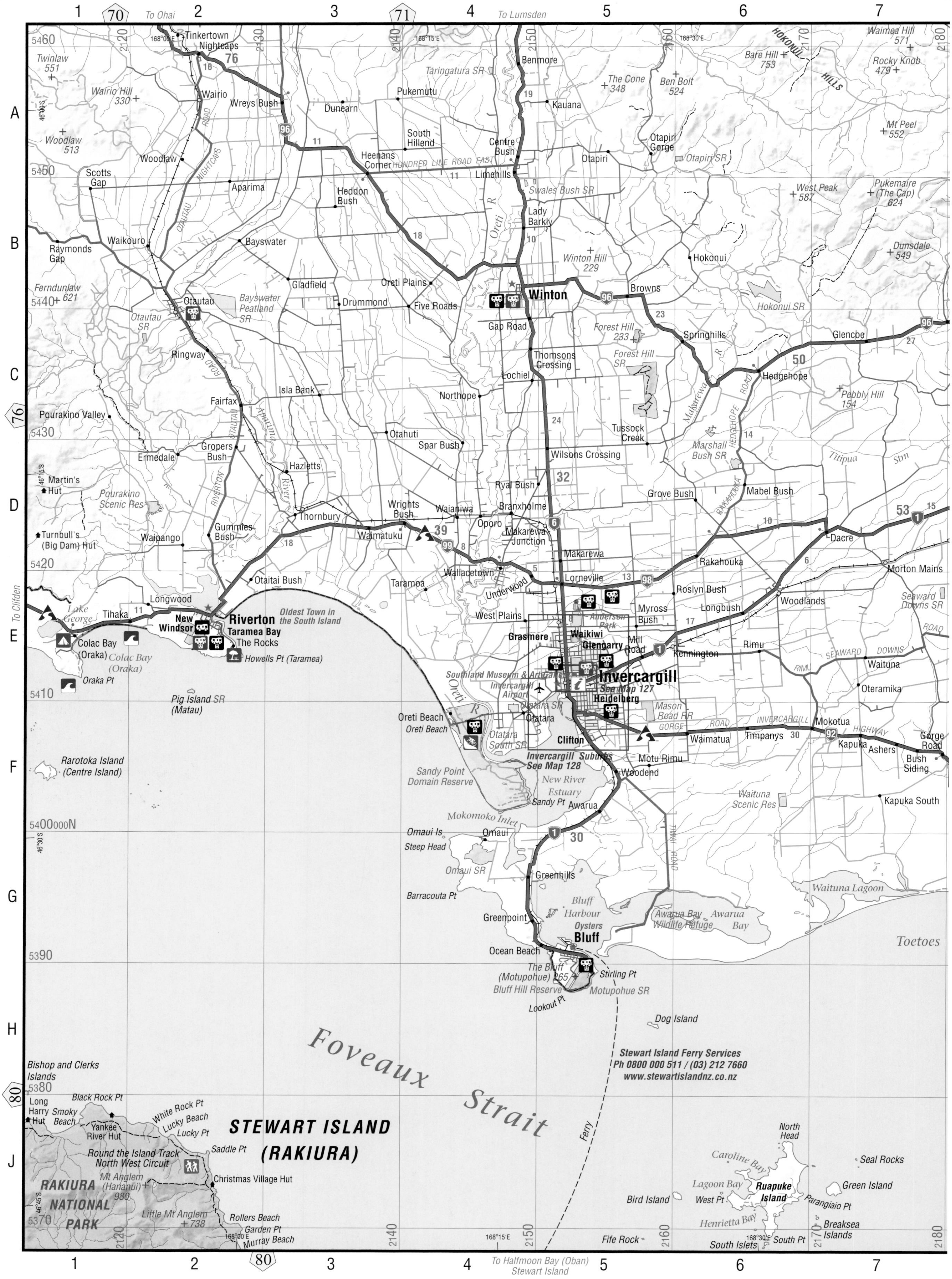

1
2
3
4
5
6
7
70
71
76
80
To Ohai
To Lumsden
To Clifden
To Halfmoon Bay (Oban)
Stewart Island
A
B
C
D
E
F
G
H
J
168°00'E
168°15'E
168°30'E
46°00'S
46°15'S
46°30'S
46°45'S
5460
5450
5440
5430
5420
5410
5400000N
5390
5380
5370
2120
2130
2140
2150
2160
2170
2180
Tinkertown
Nightcaps
Twinlaw 551
Wairio Hill 330
Wairio
Wreys Bush
Woodlaw 513
Woodlaw
Scotts Gap
Aparima
Otautau
Nightcaps Road
Raymonds Gap
Waikouro
Bayswater
Ferndunlaw 621
Otautau
Bayswater Peatland SR
Otautau SR
Ringway
Pourakino Valley
Fairfax
Ermedale
Gropers Bush
Aparima
Hazletts
Martin's Hut
Pourakino Scenic Res
Riverton
Thornbury
Turnbull's (Big Dam) Hut
Waipango
Gummies Bush
Otaitai Bush
Longwood
Lake George
Tihaka
New Windsor
Riverton
Taramea Bay
The Rocks
Oldest Town in the South Island
Colac Bay (Oraka)
Colac Bay (Oraka)
Howells Pt (Taramea)
Oraka Pt
Pig Island SR (Matau)
Rarotoka Island (Centre Island)
Dunearn
Pukemutu
Taringatura SR
South Hillend
Heenans Corner
Hundred Line Road East
Heddon Bush
Centre Bush
Limehills
Benmore
Kauana
Swales Bush SR
Oreti R
Lady Barkly
Gladfield
Oreti Plains
Drummond
Five Roads
Winton
Winton Hill 229
Gap Road
Thomsons Crossing
Lochiel
Isla Bank
Northope
Otahuti
Spar Bush
Ryal Bush
Wilsons Crossing
Wrights Bush
Waianiwa
Branxholme
Oporo
Makarewa Junction
Makarewa
Waimatuku
Wallacetown
Taramoa
Underwood
Lorneville
West Plains
Grasmere
Waikiwi
Glengarry
Anderson Park
Mill Road
Myross Bush
Roslyn Bush
Longbush
Invercargill
See Map 127
Heidelberg
Southland Museum & Art Gallery
Invercargill Airport
Otatara SR
Otatara
Oreti Beach
Oreti Beach
Oreti R
Otatara South SR
Clifton
Invercargill Suburbs
See Map 128
Mason Road RR
Gorge Road
Waimatua
Motu Rimu
Woodend
Sandy Point Domain Reserve
New River Estuary
Sandy Pt
Awarua
Mokomoko Inlet
Omaui Is
Omaui
Steep Head
Omaui SR
Greenhills
Barracouta Pt
Greenpoint
Bluff Harbour
Oysters
Bluff
Ocean Beach
The Bluff (Motupohue) 265
Bluff Hill Reserve
Stirling Pt
Motupohue SR
Lookout Pt
Awarua Bay Wildlife Refuge
Awarua Bay
Tiwai Road
Dog Island
Foveaux Strait
Stewart Island Ferry Services
Ph 0800 000 511 / (03) 212 7660
www.stewartislandnz.co.nz
Ferry
The Cone 348
Ben Bolt 524
Bare Hill 753
Hokonui Hills
Waimea Hill 571
Rocky Knob 479
Mt Peel 552
Otapiri Gorge
Otapiri
Otapiri SR
West Peak 587
Pukemaire (The Cap) 624
Hokonui
Dunsdale 549
Browns
Hokonui SR
Forest Hill 233
Forest Hill SR
Springhills
Glencoe
Makarewa R
Hedgehope Road
Hedgehope
Pebbly Hill 154
Tussock Creek
Marshall Bush SR
Titipua Stm
Grove Bush
Mabel Bush
Rakahouka
Dacre
Morton Mains
Woodlands
Seaward Downs SR
Kennington
Rimu
Seaward Downs Road
Waituna
Oteramika
Mokotua
Invercargill Highway
Timpanys
Kapuka
Ashers
Gorge Road
Bush Siding
Waituna Scenic Res
Kapuka South
Waituna Lagoon
Toetoes
Bishop and Clerks Islands
Black Rock Pt
Long Harry Hut
Smoky Beach
White Rock Pt
Lucky Beach
Lucky Pt
Yankee River Hut
Saddle Pt
Round the Island Track
North West Circuit
Christmas Village Hut
Mt Anglem (Hananui) 980
Rakiura National Park
Little Mt Anglem 738
Rollers Beach
Garden Pt
Murray Beach
Stewart Island (Rakiura)
North Head
Caroline Bay
Lagoon Bay
West Pt
Ruapuke Island
Henrietta Bay
Seal Rocks
Green Island
Parangiaio Pt
Breaksea Islands
Bird Island
Fife Rock
South Islets
South Pt

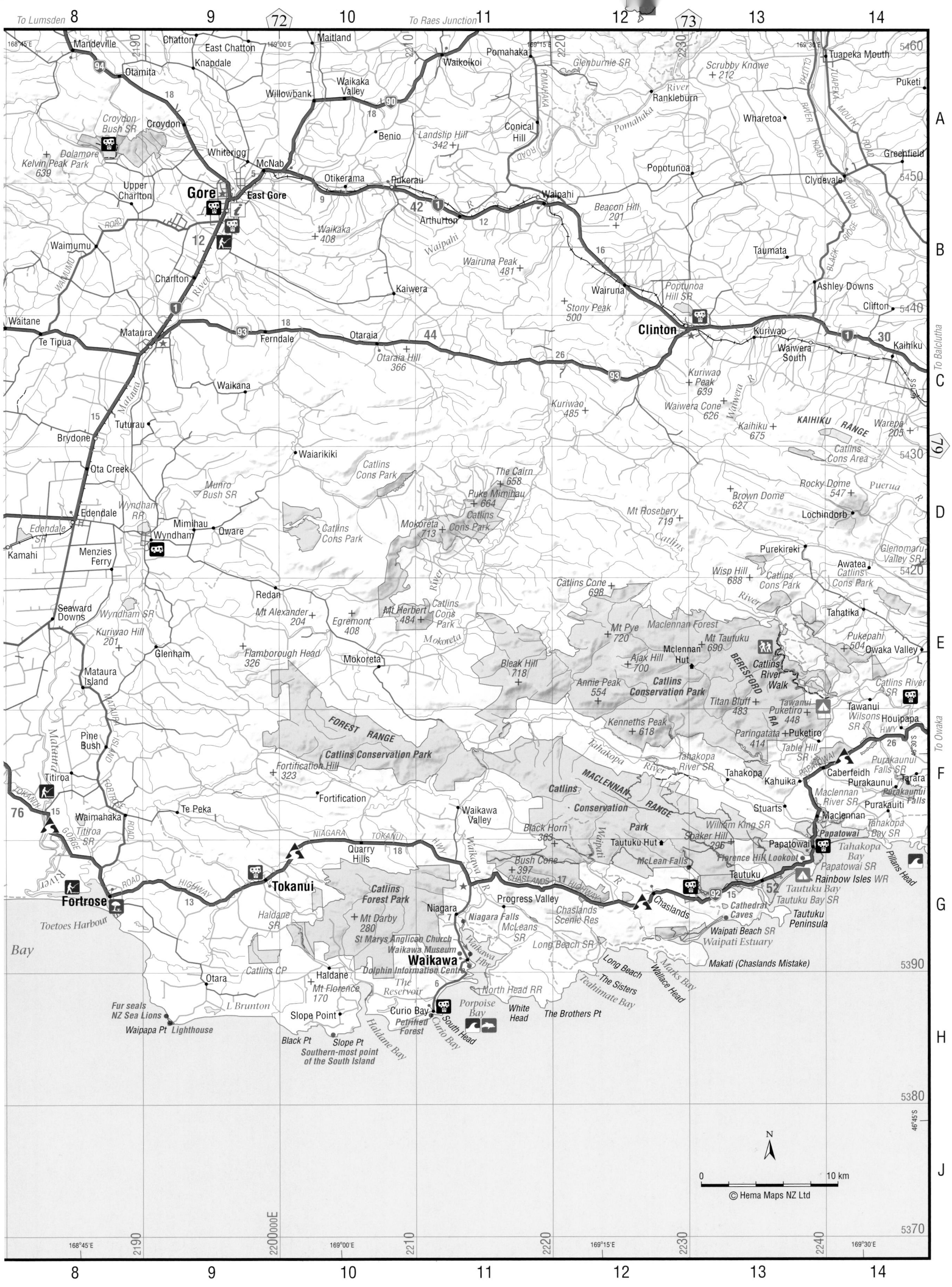
To Lumsden
To Raes Junction
To Balclutha
To Owaka
8
9
10
11
12
13
14
A
B
C
D
E
F
G
H
J
72
73
79
94
90
1
93
92
Mandeville
Chatton
East Chatton
Maitland
Waikoikoi
Pomahaka
Glenburnie SR
Scrubby Knowe 212
Tuapeka Mouth
Puketi
Otamita
Knapdale
Waikaka Valley
Willowbank
Rankleburn
Wharetoa
Croydon Bush SR
Croydon
Benio
Landslip Hill 342
Conical Hill
Pomahaka
Dolamore
Kelvin Peak Park 639
Whiterigg
McNab
Otikerama
Pukerau
Popotunoa
Greenfield
Clydevale
Gore
East Gore
Upper Charlton
Waipahi
Beacon Hill 201
Arthurton
Waikaka 408
Waipahi
Wairuna Peak 481
Taumata
Waimumu
Charlton
Kaiwera
Wairuna
Poptunoa Hill SR
Ashley Downs
Clifton
Stony Peak 500
Waitane
Te Tipua
Mataura
Ferndale
Otaraia
Otaraia Hill 366
Clinton
Kuriwao
Waiwera South
Kaihiku
Waikana
Kuriwao Peak 639
Kuriwao 485
Waiwera Cone 626
Tuturau
Brydone
Kaihiku 675
KAIHIKU RANGE
Warepa 205
Waiarikiki
Catlins Cons Area
Ota Creek
Catlins Cons Park
The Cairn 658
Rocky Dome 547
Puerua
Munro Bush SR
Brown Dome 627
Puke Mimihau 664
Edendale
Wyndham RR
Catlins Cons Park
Mt Rosebery 719
Lochindorb
Edendale SR
Mimihau
Oware
Mokoreta 713
Wyndham
Catlins
Kamahi
Menzies Ferry
Purekireki
Glenomaru Valley SR
Awatea
Wisp Hill 688
Catlins Cons Park
Catlins Cone 698
Redan
Seaward Downs
Mt Alexander 204
Egremont 408
Mt Herbert 484
Tahatika
Wyndham SR
Maclennan Forest
Mt Pye 720
Mt Tautuku 690
Pukepahi 504
Owaka Valley
Kuriwao Hill 201
Glenham
Mokoreta
Flamborough Head 326
Mclennan Hut
Ajax Hill 700
Mataura Island
Mokoreta
Bleak Hill 718
Annie Peak 554
Catlins Conservation Park
BERESFORD RA
Catlins River Walk
Catlins River SR
Titan Bluff 483
Tawanui
Tawanui Puketiro 448
Wilsons SR
Houipapa
FOREST RANGE
Kenneths Peak 618
Paringatata 414
Puketiro
Pine Bush
Catlins Conservation Park
Tahakopa
Table Hill SR
Fortification Hill 323
Tahakopa River SR
Tahakopa
Kahuika
Caberfeidh
Purakaunui Falls SR
Tarara
Purakaunui
Titiroa
MACLENNAN RANGE
Catlins Conservation Park
Fortification
Maclennan River SR
Purakaunui Falls
Purakauiti
Te Peka
Waikawa Valley
Stuarts
Maclennan
Waimahaka
Tahakopa Bay SR
Titiroa SR
Black Horn 363
William King SR
Tautuku Hut
Soaker Hill 296
Papatowai
Tahakopa Bay
Papatowai SR
Quarry Hills
Bush Cone 397
McLean Falls
Florence Hill Lookout
Tautuku
Rainbow Isles WR
Pillans Head
Fortrose
Tokanui
Catlins Forest Park
Progress Valley
Chaslands
Tautuku Bay
Tautuku Bay SR
Cathedral Caves
Tautuku Peninsula
Niagara
Niagara Falls
Chaslands Scenic Res
Mt Darby 280
McLeans SR
Waipati Beach SR
Waipati Estuary
Toetoes Harbour
Haldane SR
St Marys Anglican Church
Waikawa Museum
Long Beach SR
Bay
Waikawa
Dolphin Information Centre
Long Beach
Wallace Head
Marks Bay
Makati (Chaslands Mistake)
Catlins CP
Haldane
The Sisters
Teahimate Bay
Otara
Mt Florence 170
The Reservoir
North Head RR
L Brunton
Porpoise Bay
White Head
The Brothers Pt
Fur seals NZ Sea Lions
Curio Bay
Slope Point
Waipapa Pt Lighthouse
Petrified Forest
South Head
Curio Bay
Black Pt
Slope Pt
Haldane Bay
Southern-most point of the South Island
0
10 km
© Hema Maps NZ Ltd
N
168°45'E
169°00'E
169°15'E
169°30'E
46°15'S
46°30'S
46°45'S
2200000E

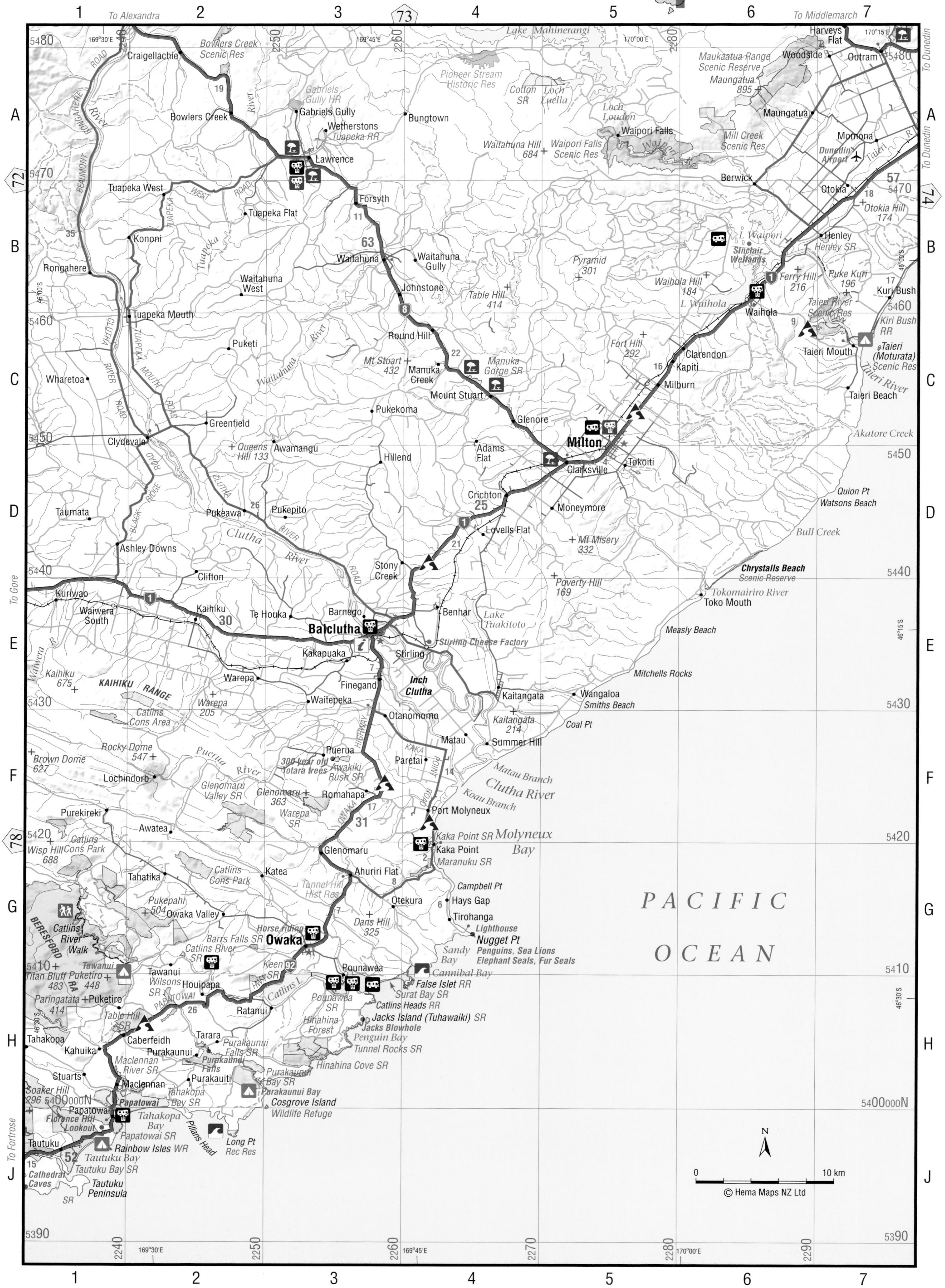

To Alexandra
To Middlemarch
To Dunedin
To Gore
To Fortrose
73
72
74
78
Lake Mahinerangi
Craigellachie
Bowlers Creek Scenic Res
Bowlers Creek
Gabriels Gully HR
Gabriels Gully
Wetherstons
Tuapeka RR
Bungtown
Pioneer Stream Historic Res
Cotton SR
Loch Luella
Loch Loudon
Waipori Falls
Waitahuna Hill 684
Waipori Falls Scenic Res
Maukaatua Range Scenic Reserve
Maungatua 895
Harveys Flat
Woodside
Outram
Maungatua
Mill Creek Scenic Res
Momona
Dunedin Airport
Taieri River
Berwick
Otokia
Otokia Hill 174
Henley
Henley SR
L Waipori
Sinclair Wetlands
Lawrence
Forsyth
Tuapeka West
Tuapeka Flat
Kononi
Beaumont River
Rongahere Road
Rongahere
Waitahuna
Waitahuna Gully
Waitahuna West
Johnstone
Table Hill 414
Pyramid 301
Waihola Hill 184
L Waihola
Waihola
Ferry Hill 216
Puke Kuri 196
Taieri River Scenic Res
Kuri Bush
Kiri Bush RR
Taieri Mouth
Taieri (Moturata) Scenic Res
Tuapeka Mouth
Tuapeka Mouth Road
Clutha River Road
Puketi
Round Hill
Mt Stuart 432
Manuka Creek
Manuka Gorge SR
Mount Stuart
Fort Hill 292
Clarendon
Kapiti
Milburn
Taieri Beach
Wharetoa
Greenfield
Pukekoma
Glenore
Milton
Akatore Creek
Clydevale
Queens Hill 133
Awamangu
Hillend
Adams Flat
Clarksville
Tokoiti
Crichton
Moneymore
Quion Pt
Watsons Beach
Black Ridge Road
Taumata
Pukeawa
Pukepito
Lovells Flat
Mt Misery 332
Bull Creek
Clutha River
Ashley Downs
Clifton
Stony Creek
Poverty Hill 169
Chrystalls Beach Scenic Reserve
Tokomairiro River
Toko Mouth
Kuriwao
Waiwera South
Kaihiku
Te Houka
Barnego
Benhar
Lake Tuakitoto
Balclutha
Stirling Cheese Factory
Measly Beach
Kakapuaka
Stirling
Waiwera R
Kaihiku 675
Kaihiku Range
Warepa
Finegand
Inch Clutha
Mitchells Rocks
Waitepeka
Kaitangata
Wangaloa
Smiths Beach
Warepa 205
Catlins Cons Area
Otanomomo
Kaitangata 214
Coal Pt
Rocky Dome 547
Matau
Summer Hill
Brown Dome 627
Puerua River
Pueruа
Paretai
Kaka Point Road
300 year old Totara trees
Awakiki Bush SR
Matau Branch
Lochindorb
Clutha River
Glenomaru Valley SR
Glenomaru 363
Romahapa
Koau Branch
Owaka Highway
Port Molyneux
Purekireki
Warepa SR
Awatea
Molyneux Bay
Kaka Point SR
Kaka Point
Wisp Hill 688
Catlins Cons Park
Glenomaru
Maranuku SR
Tahatika
Catlins Cons Park
Katea
Ahuriri Flat
Tunnel Hill Hist Res
Campbell Pt
Hays Gap
Otekura
PACIFIC OCEAN
Beresford Ra
Catlins River Walk
Pukepahi 504
Owaka Valley
Dans Hill 325
Tirohanga
Lighthouse
Nugget Pt
Penguins, Sea Lions
Elephant Seals, Fur Seals
Sandy Bay
Barrs Falls SR
Horse riding
Owaka
Catlins River SR
Tawanui
Titan Bluff 483
Puketiro 448
Keen SR
Pounawea
Cannibal Bay
Tawanui
Wilsons SR
Houipapa
Papatowai Road
Catlins L
False Islet RR
Surat Bay SR
Pounawea SR
Catlins Heads RR
Paringatata 414
Puketiro
Ratanui
Jacks Island (Tuhawaiki) SR
Table Hill SR
Hinahina Forest
Jacks Blowhole
Penguin Bay
Tahakopa
Caberfeidh
Tarara
Purakaunui Falls SR
Tunnel Rocks SR
Kahuika
Purakaunui
Purakaunui Falls
Maclennan River SR
Hinahina Cove SR
Stuarts
Purakauiti
Purakaunui Bay SR
Soaker Hill 296
Maclennan
Tahakopa Bay SR
Purakaunui Bay
Cosgrove Island Wildlife Refuge
Papatowai
Papatowai
Florence Hill Lookout
Tahakopa Bay
Papatowai SR
Pillans Head
Long Pt Rec Res
Tautuku
Rainbow Isles WR
Tautuku Bay
Tautuku Bay SR
Cathedral Caves
Tautuku Peninsula
SR
0
10 km
N
© Hema Maps NZ Ltd
169°30'E
169°45'E
170°00'E
170°15'E
46°00'S
46°15'S
46°30'S
5480
5470
5460
5450
5440
5430
5420
5410
5400000N
5390
2240
2250
2260
2270
2280
2290
1
2
3
4
5
6
7
A
B
C
D
E
F
G
H
J

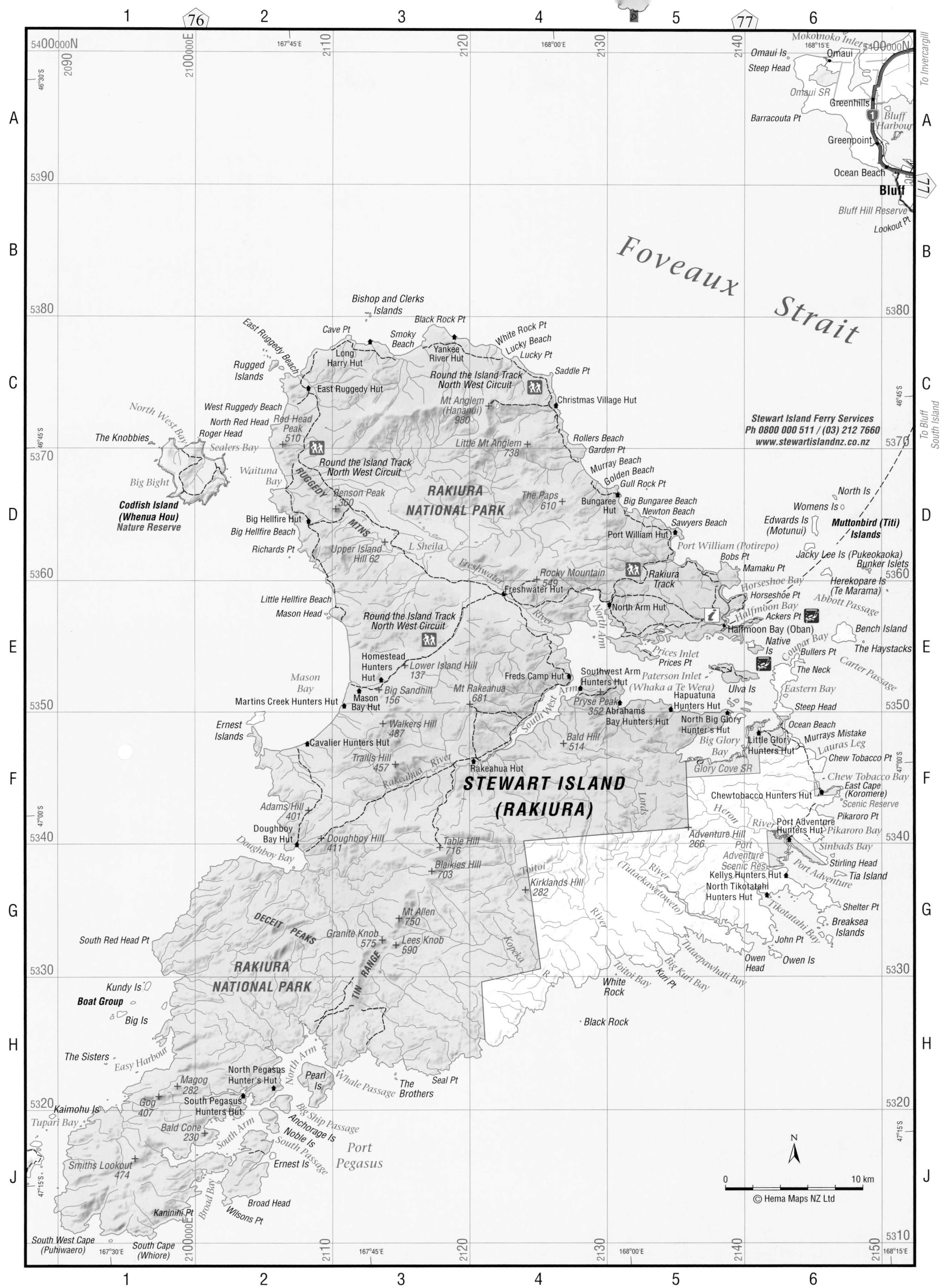
76
77
Foveaux Strait
To Invercargill
Mokomoko Inlet
Omaui Is
Omaui
Steep Head
Omaui SR
Greenhills
Barracouta Pt
Bluff Harbour
Greenpoint
Ocean Beach
Bluff
Bluff Hill Reserve
Lookout Pt
To Bluff South Island
Stewart Island Ferry Services
Ph 0800 000 511 / (03) 212 7660
www.stewartislandnz.co.nz
Bishop and Clerks Islands
Black Rock Pt
Cave Pt
Smoky Beach
White Rock Pt
Lucky Beach
Lucky Pt
Yankee River Hut
Long Harry Hut
East Ruggedy Beach
Rugged Islands
East Ruggedy Hut
Saddle Pt
Round the Island Track North West Circuit
Christmas Village Hut
Mt Anglem (Hananui) 980
West Ruggedy Beach
North West Bay
North Red Head
Red Head Peak 510
Roger Head
Sealers Bay
The Knobbies
Little Mt Anglem 738
Rollers Beach
Garden Pt
Murray Beach
Golden Beach
Gull Rock Pt
Big Bight
Waituna Bay
Codfish Island (Whenua Hou) Nature Reserve
RUGGEDY MTNS
Benson Peak 360
RAKIURA NATIONAL PARK
The Paps 610
Bungaree Hut
Big Bungaree Beach
Newton Beach
Sawyers Beach
North Is
Womens Is
Edwards Is (Motunui)
Muttonbird (Titi) Islands
Big Hellfire Hut
Big Hellfire Beach
L Sheila
Upper Island Hill 62
Richards Pt
Port William Hut
Port William (Potirepo)
Bobs Pt
Jacky Lee Is (Pukeokaoka)
Bunker Islets
Mamaku Pt
Freshwater
Rocky Mountain 549
Rakiura Track
Horseshoe Bay
Herekopare Is (Te Marama)
Horseshoe Pt
Abbott Passage
Little Hellfire Beach
Freshwater Hut
North Arm Hut
Halfmoon Bay
Ackers Pt
Mason Head
River
North Arm
Halfmoon Bay (Oban)
Bench Island
Native Is
Couper Bay
The Haystacks
Prices Inlet
Prices Pt
Bullers Pt
Homestead Hunters Hut
Lower Island Hill 137
The Neck
Carter Passage
Mason Bay
Freds Camp Hut
Southwest Arm Hunters Hut
Paterson Inlet (Whaka a Te Wera)
Ulva Is
Eastern Bay
Mason Bay Hut
Big Sandhill 156
Mt Rakeahua 681
Prysé Peak 352
Abrahams Bay Hunters Hut
Hapuatuna Hunters Hut
Steep Head
Martins Creek Hunters Hut
South West Arm
Walkers Hill 487
North Big Glory Hunter's Hut
Ocean Beach
Ernest Islands
Bald Hill 514
Little Glory Hunters Hut
Murrays Mistake
Lauras Leg
Big Glory Bay
Cavalier Hunters Hut
Trails Hill 457
Chew Tobacco Pt
Glory Cove SR
Rakeahua River
Rakeahua Hut
Chew Tobacco Bay
STEWART ISLAND (RAKIURA)
East Cape (Koromere)
Chewtobacco Hunters Hut
Scenic Reserve
Lords
Adams Hill 401
Heron
River
Pikaroro Pt
Port Adventure Hunters Hut
Pikaroro Bay
Doughboy Bay Hut
Doughboy Hill 411
Adventure Hill 266
Doughboy Bay
Table Hill 716
Port Adventure Scenic Res
Sinbads Bay
Stirling Head
Blaikies Hill 703
Toitoi
River (Tutaekawetoweto)
Kellys Hunters Hut
Tia Island
Port Adventure
Kirklands Hill 282
North Tikotatahi Hunters Hut
Tikotatahi Bay
Shelter Pt
DECEIT PEAKS
Mt Allen 750
Breaksea Islands
Granite Knob 575
Lees Knob 590
River
John Pt
South Red Head Pt
Kopeka
Tutaepawhati Bay
Owen Head
Owen Is
RAKIURA NATIONAL PARK
TIN RANGE
Toitoi Bay
Big Kuri Bay
Kuri Pt
White Rock
Kundy Is
Boat Group
Big Is
Black Rock
The Sisters
Easy Harbour
North Arm
North Pegasus Hunter's Hut
Pearl Is
Whale Passage
Seal Pt
The Brothers
Magog 282
Gog 407
Kaimohu Is
South Pegasus Hunters Hut
Tupari Bay
Big Ship Passage
Anchorage Is
Noble Is
Bald Cone 230
South Arm
South Passage
Port Pegasus
Smiths Lookout 474
Ernest Is
Broad Bay
Broad Head
Kaninihi Pt
Wilsons Pt
South West Cape (Puhiwaero)
South Cape (Whiore)
0
10 km
© Hema Maps NZ Ltd

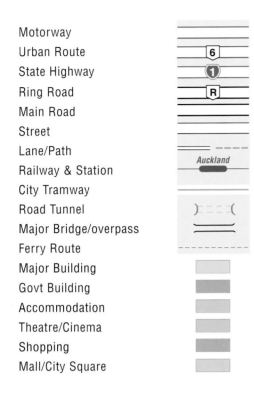

Motorway	
Urban Route	6
State Highway	1
Ring Road	R
Main Road	
Street	
Lane/Path	
Railway & Station	Auckland
City Tramway	
Road Tunnel	
Major Bridge/overpass	
Ferry Route	
Major Building	
Govt Building	
Accommodation	
Theatre/Cinema	
Shopping	
Mall/City Square	

School/Educational	
Park/Reserve	
Cemetery	
Hospital	
Postal Service	
Police Station	POLICE
Church	
One Way Street	
Place of Interest	Tui Brewery
Information Centre	i
To Airport	
Alpine Pacific Triangle Tourist Route	
Inland Scenic Tourist Route	ROUTE 72
Southern Scenic Tourist Route	
Twin Coast Tourist Route	
Thermal Explorer Tourist Route	
Pacific Coast Tourist Route	

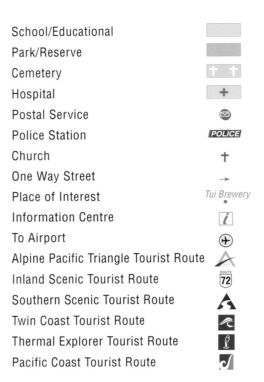

Suburbs Legend

Motorway	
Motorway (proposed)	
Urban Ring Road	R
State Highway/Number	1
Main Rd/Regional Number	72
Secondary Road	
Minor Road	
Railway and Station	Rolleston
Busway	
Park, Reserve, Golf Course	Harewood
Special Use	Hospital
Mountain	Mt Herbert
Ferry Route	
Tourist Point of Interest	Christchurch Gondola
Major Shopping Centre	The Palms Mall
Information Centre	i

map 81 Bay of Islands

For touring map see map 4

map 82 Russell

map 83 Paihia (below)

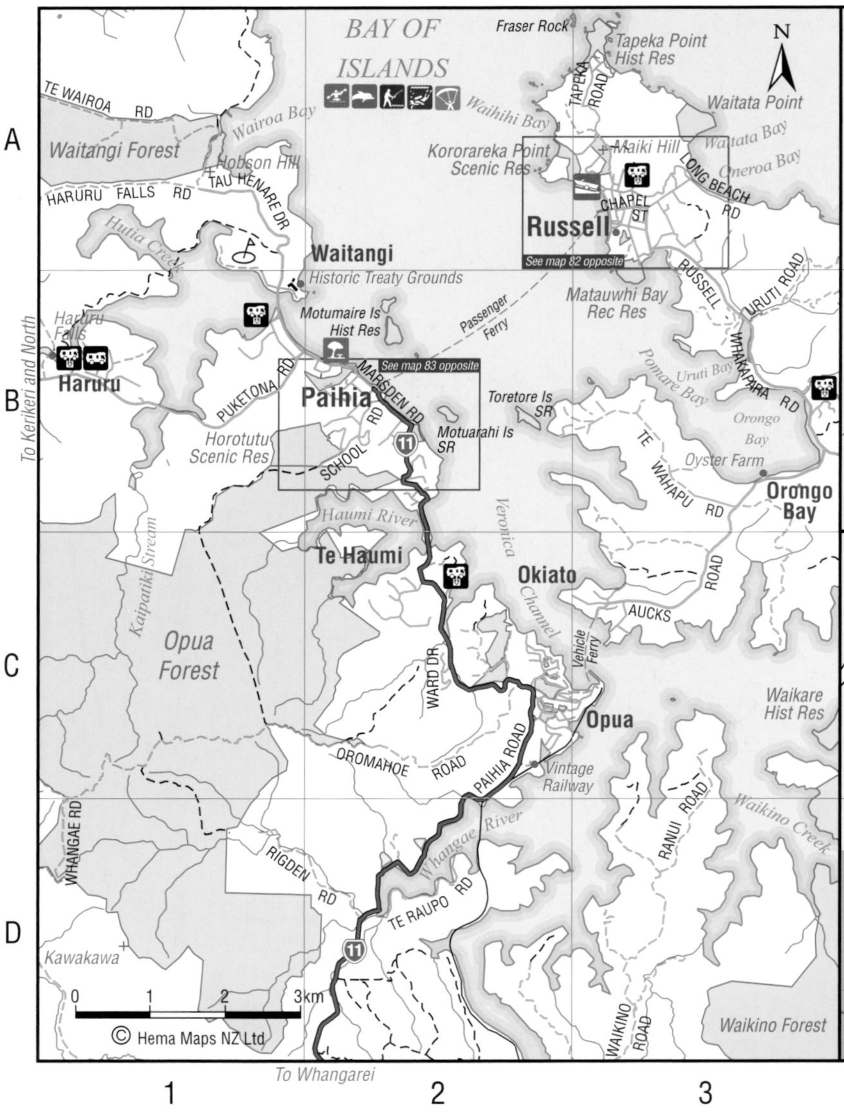

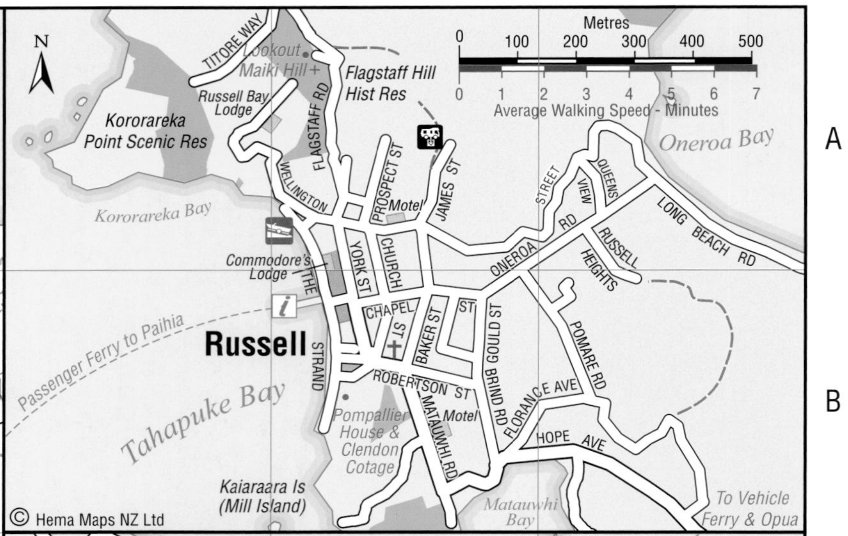

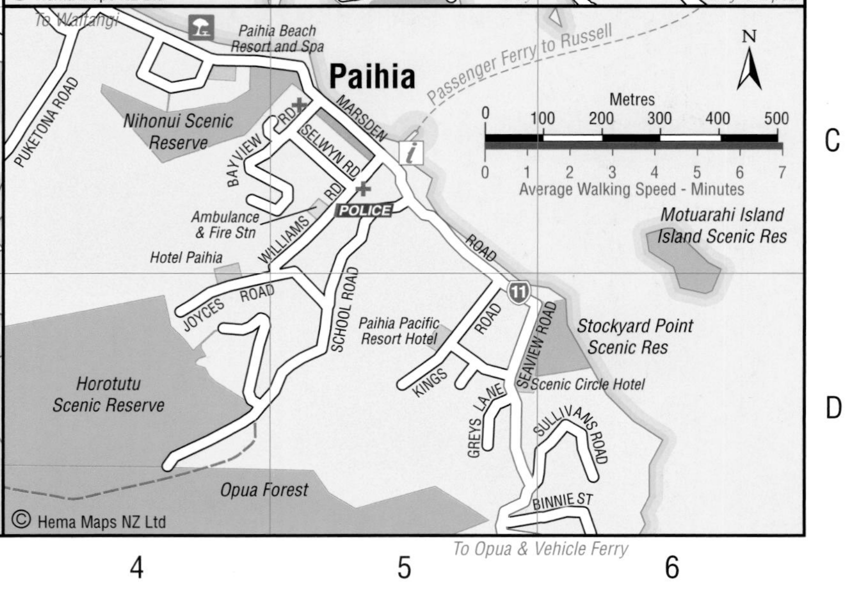

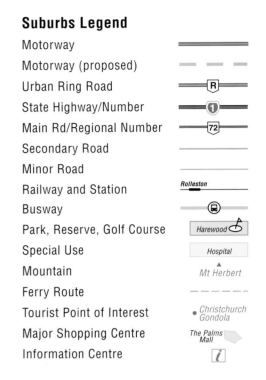

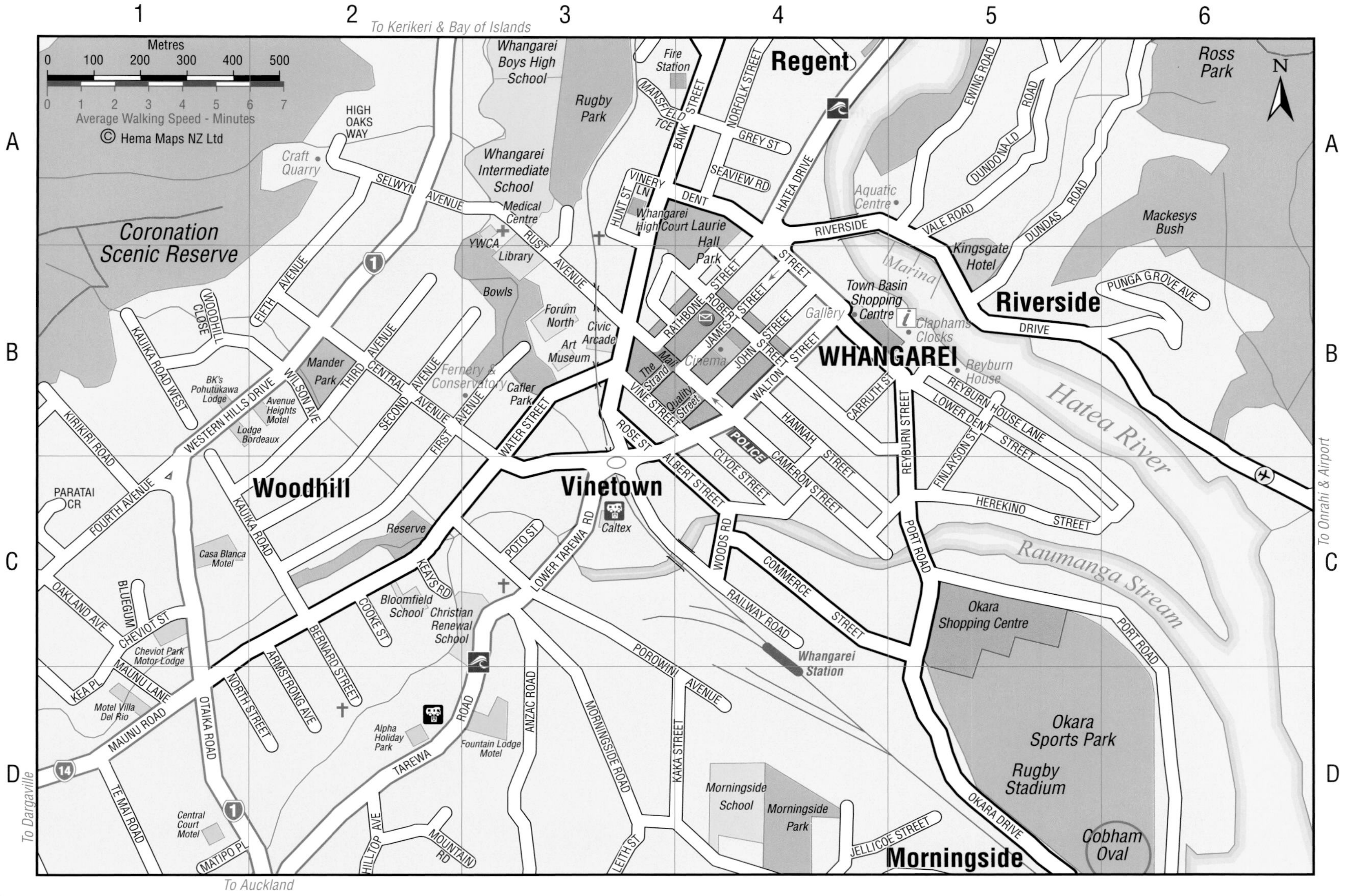

For touring map see map 4 **Whangarei Suburbs** map 85 **Kerikeri CBD** map 86

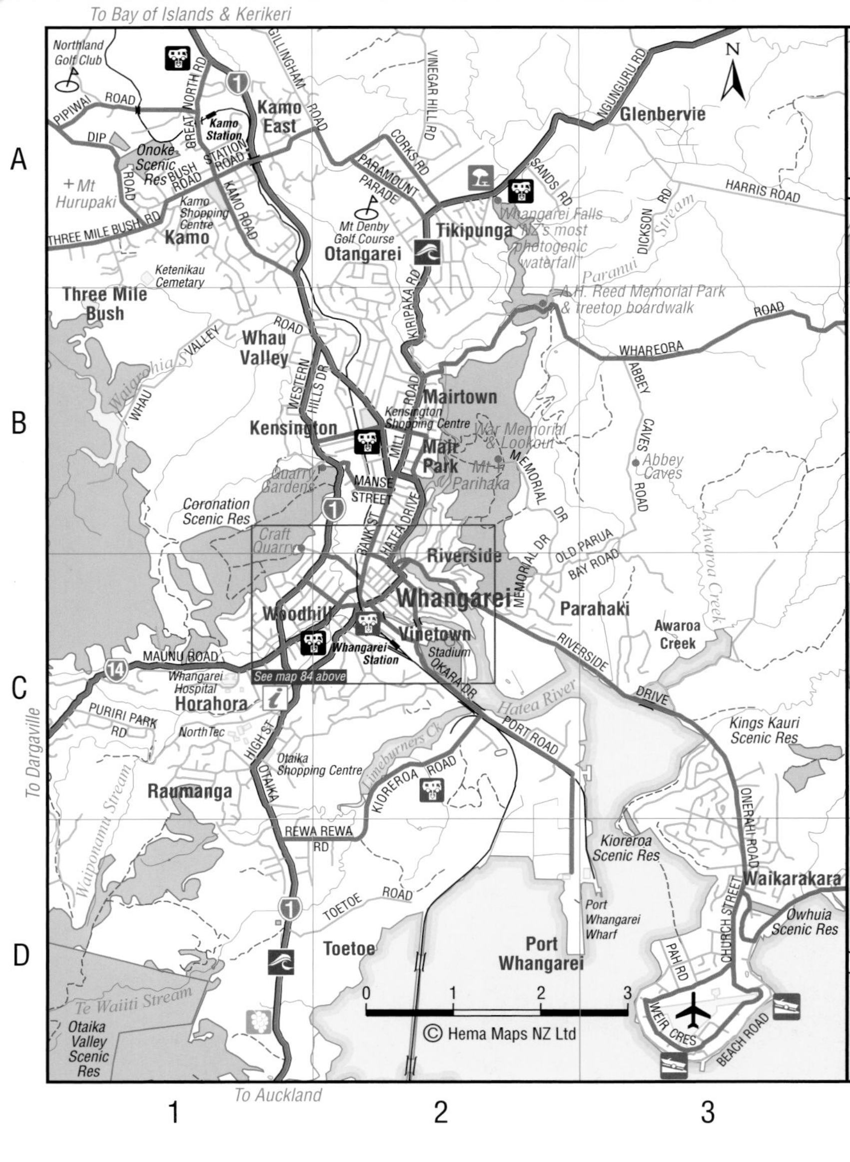

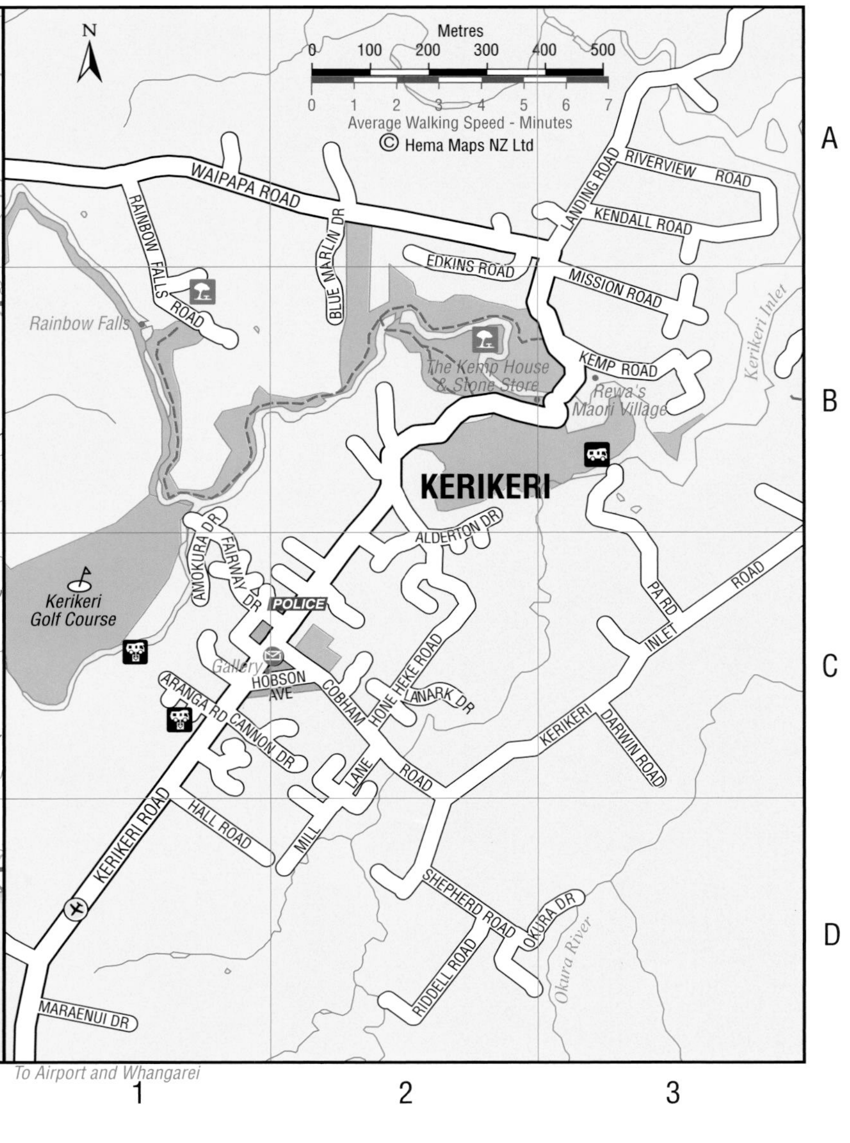

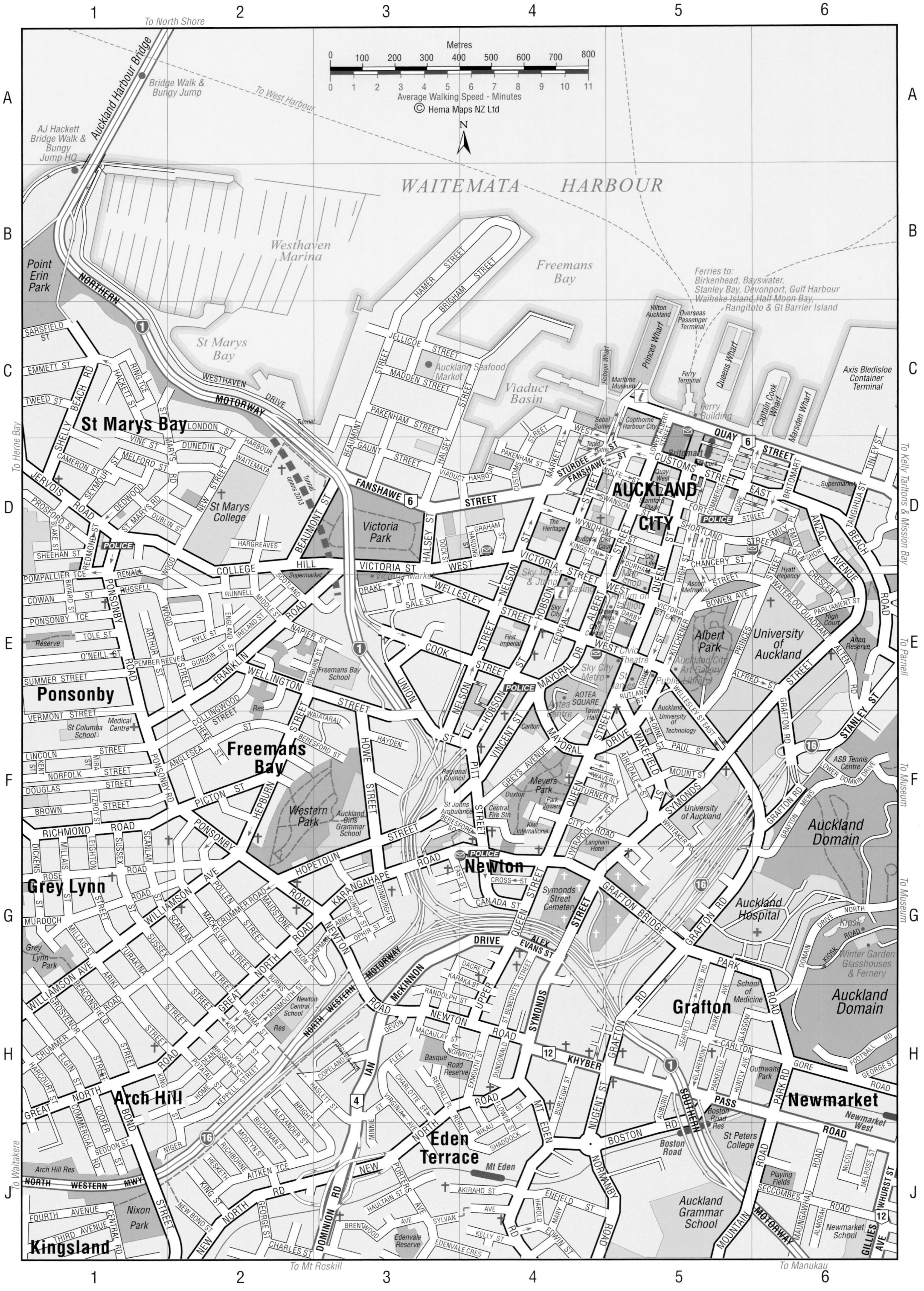
To North Shore
Metres
0 100 200 300 400 500 600 700 800
0 1 2 3 4 5 6 7 8 9 10 11
Average Walking Speed - Minutes
© Hema Maps NZ Ltd
N
Auckland Harbour Bridge
Bridge Walk & Bungy Jump
To West Harbour
AJ Hackett Bridge Walk & Bungy Jump HQ
WAITEMATA HARBOUR
Westhaven Marina
Freemans Bay
Ferries to:
Birkenhead, Bayswater, Stanley Bay, Devonport, Gulf Harbour
Waiheke Island, Half Moon Bay, Rangitoto & Gt Barrier Island
Point Erin Park
St Marys Bay
Viaduct Basin
Auckland Seafood Market
Hilton Auckland
Overseas Passenger Terminal
Princes Wharf
Queens Wharf
Ferry Terminal
Ferry Building
Captain Cook Wharf
Marsden Wharf
Axis Bledisloe Container Terminal
Maritime Museum
Hobson Wharf
St Marys Bay
St Marys College
Victoria Park
AUCKLAND CITY
POLICE
Sky Tower & Jump
Casino
Albert Park
University of Auckland
Auckland City Art Gallery
Public Library
Civic Theatre
AOTEA SQUARE
Town Hall
Aotea Centre
Freemans Bay School
Ponsonby
Freemans Bay
Western Park
Auckland Girls Grammar School
St Columba School
Medical Centre
Regional Council
St Johns Ambulance
Central Fire Stn
Myers Park
Newton
Symonds Street Cemetery
Grey Lynn
Grey Lynn Park
Auckland Domain
Auckland Hospital
Winter Garden Glasshouses & Fernery
Grafton
School of Medicine
Newton Central School
Arch Hill
Basque Road Reserve
Eden Terrace
Mt Eden
Newmarket
Newmarket West
Boston Road
St Peters College
Auckland Grammar School
Playing Fields
Newmarket School
Edenvale Reserve
Nixon Park
Arch Hill Res
Kingsland
Outhwaite Park
ASB Tennis Centre
Alten Reserve
University of Technology
Hyatt Regency
High Court
NORTHERN MOTORWAY
WESTHAVEN DRIVE
NORTH WESTERN MOTORWAY
SOUTHERN MOTORWAY
NORTH WESTERN MWY
FANSHAWE STREET
QUAY STREET
CUSTOMS STREET
VICTORIA ST WEST
WELLESLEY STREET
COLLEGE HILL
PONSONBY ROAD
KARANGAHAPE ROAD
GREAT NORTH ROAD
NEW NORTH RD
SYMONDS STREET
KHYBER PASS ROAD
GRAFTON BRIDGE
PARK ROAD
BROADWAY
MT EDEN ROAD
DOMINION RD
SANDRINGHAM
To Herne Bay
To Kelly Tarltons & Mission Bay
To Parnell
To Museum
To Waitakere
To Mt Roskill
To Manukau
1 2 3 4 5 6
A B C D E F G H J

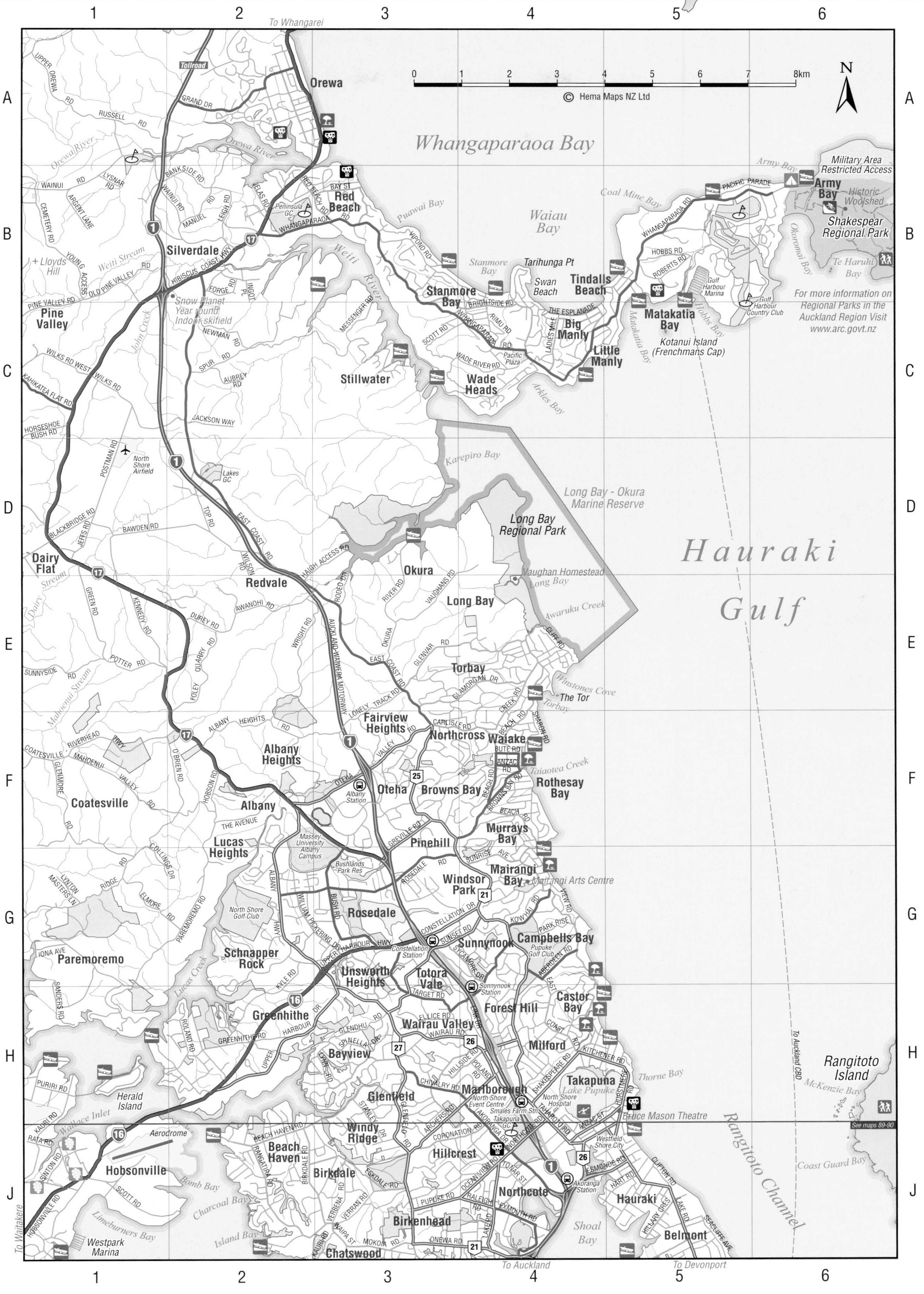
To Whangarei
0 1 2 3 4 5 6 7 8km
© Hema Maps NZ Ltd
N
Orewa
Whangaparaoa Bay
Red Beach
Silverdale
Tollroad
Puawai Bay
Waiau Bay
Coal Mine Bay
Army Bay
Military Area Restricted Access
Historic Woolshed
Shakespear Regional Park
Te Haruhi Bay
Okoromai Bay
Weiti River
Stanmore Bay
Tarihunga Pt
Swan Beach
Tindalls Beach
Big Manly
Little Manly
Matakatia Bay
Gulf Harbour Marina
Gulf Harbour Country Club
Kotanui Island (Frenchmans Cap)
For more information on Regional Parks in the Auckland Region Visit www.arc.govt.nz
Lloyds Hill
Pine Valley
Snow Planet Year round Indoor skifield
Stillwater
Wade Heads
Arkles Bay
North Shore Airfield
Lakes GC
Karepiro Bay
Long Bay - Okura Marine Reserve
Long Bay Regional Park
Hauraki Gulf
Dairy Flat
Redvale
Okura
Long Bay
Vaughan Homestead
Awaruku Creek
Torbay
Winstones Cove
The Tor
Fairview Heights
Northcross
Waiake
Albany Heights
Coatesville
Albany
Albany Station
Oteha
Browns Bay
Rothesay Bay
Taiaotea Creek
Massey University Albany Campus
Lucas Heights
Pinehill
Murrays Bay
Windsor Park
Mairangi Bay
Mairangi Arts Centre
North Shore Golf Club
Rosedale
Campbells Bay
Pupuke Golf Club
Paremoremo
Schnapper Rock
Constellation Station
Sunnynook
Sunnynook Station
Unsworth Heights
Totara Vale
Castor Bay
Forest Hill
Greenhithe
Wairau Valley
Milford
Bayview
Takapuna
Lake Pupuke
Thorne Bay
Rangitoto Island
McKenzie Bay
Herald Island
Wallace Inlet
Glenfield
Marlborough
North Shore Event Centre
Smales Farm Stn
North Shore Hospital
Bruce Mason Theatre
Aerodrome
Hobsonville
Beach Haven
Windy Ridge
Hillcrest
Westfield Shore City
Rangitoto Channel
To Auckland CBD
Coast Guard Bay
Bomb Bay
Birkdale
Northcote
Akoranga Station
Hauraki
Charcoal Bay
Limeburners Bay
Birkenhead
Shoal Bay
Belmont
Island Bay
Westpark Marina
Chatswood
To Waitakere
To Auckland
To Devonport
See maps 89-90

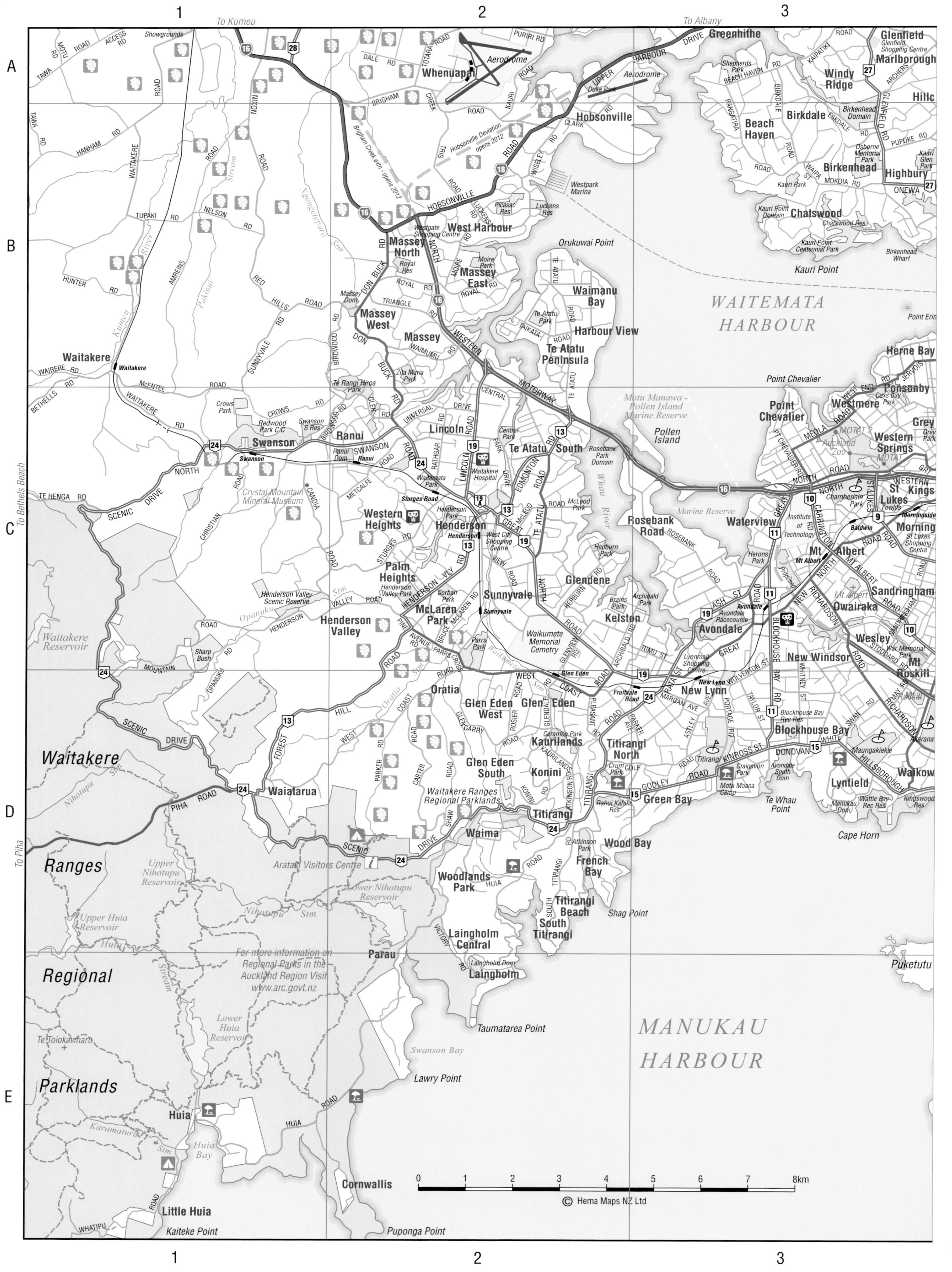

1
2
3
A
B
C
D
E
To Kumeu
To Albany
To Bethells Beach
To Piha
Greenhithe
Glenfield
Glenfield Shopping Centre
Marlborough
Whenuapai
Aerodrome
Hobsonville
Windy Ridge
Beach Haven
Birkdale
Birkenhead
Highbury
Hillcrest
Chatswood
Kauri Point
West Harbour
Westgate Shopping Centre
Westpark Marina
Orukuwai Point
Massey North
Massey East
Massey West
Massey
Waimanu Bay
Harbour View
Te Atatu Peninsula
WAITEMATA HARBOUR
Herne Bay
Ponsonby
Point Chevalier
Westmere
Grey Lynn
Western Springs
Auckland Zoo
Motu Manawa - Pollen Island Marine Reserve
Pollen Island
Marine Reserve
Waitakere
Waitakere
Swanson
Swanson
Ranui
Redwood Park C/C
Crows Park
Lincoln
Te Atatu South
Waitakere Hospital
Crystal Mountain Mineral Museum
Western Heights
Henderson
West City Shopping Centre
Rosebank Road
Waterview
Institute of Technology
St Lukes
Kingsland
Morningside
Mt Albert
Palm Heights
Henderson Valley Scenic Reserve
Glendene
Sunnyvale
McLaren Park
Henderson Valley
Kelston
Avondale
Avondale Racecourse
Owairaka
Sandringham
Mt Roskill
Wesley
New Windsor
Waitakere Reservoir
Waikumete Memorial Cemetery
Glen Eden
New Lynn
Lynnmall Shopping Centre
Fruitvale Road
Oratia
Glen Eden West
Blockhouse Bay
Kaurilands
Titirangi North
Glen Eden South
Konini
Waitakere Ranges Regional Parklands
Waiatarua
Green Bay
Lynfield
Te Whau Point
Cape Horn
Titirangi
Waima
Wood Bay
French Bay
Arataki Visitors Centre
Woodlands Park
Titirangi Beach
South Titirangi
Shag Point
Laingholm Central
Laingholm
Parau
Waitakere
Ranges
Regional
Parklands
Upper Nihotupu Reservoir
Lower Nihotupu Reservoir
Upper Huia Reservoir
Lower Huia Reservoir
For more information on Regional Parks in the Auckland Region Visit www.arc.govt.nz
Te Toiokawharu
Taumatarea Point
Swanson Bay
Lawry Point
MANUKAU HARBOUR
Puketutu
Huia
Huia Bay
Little Huia
Kaiteke Point
Cornwallis
Puponga Point
0 1 2 3 4 5 6 7 8km
© Hema Maps NZ Ltd

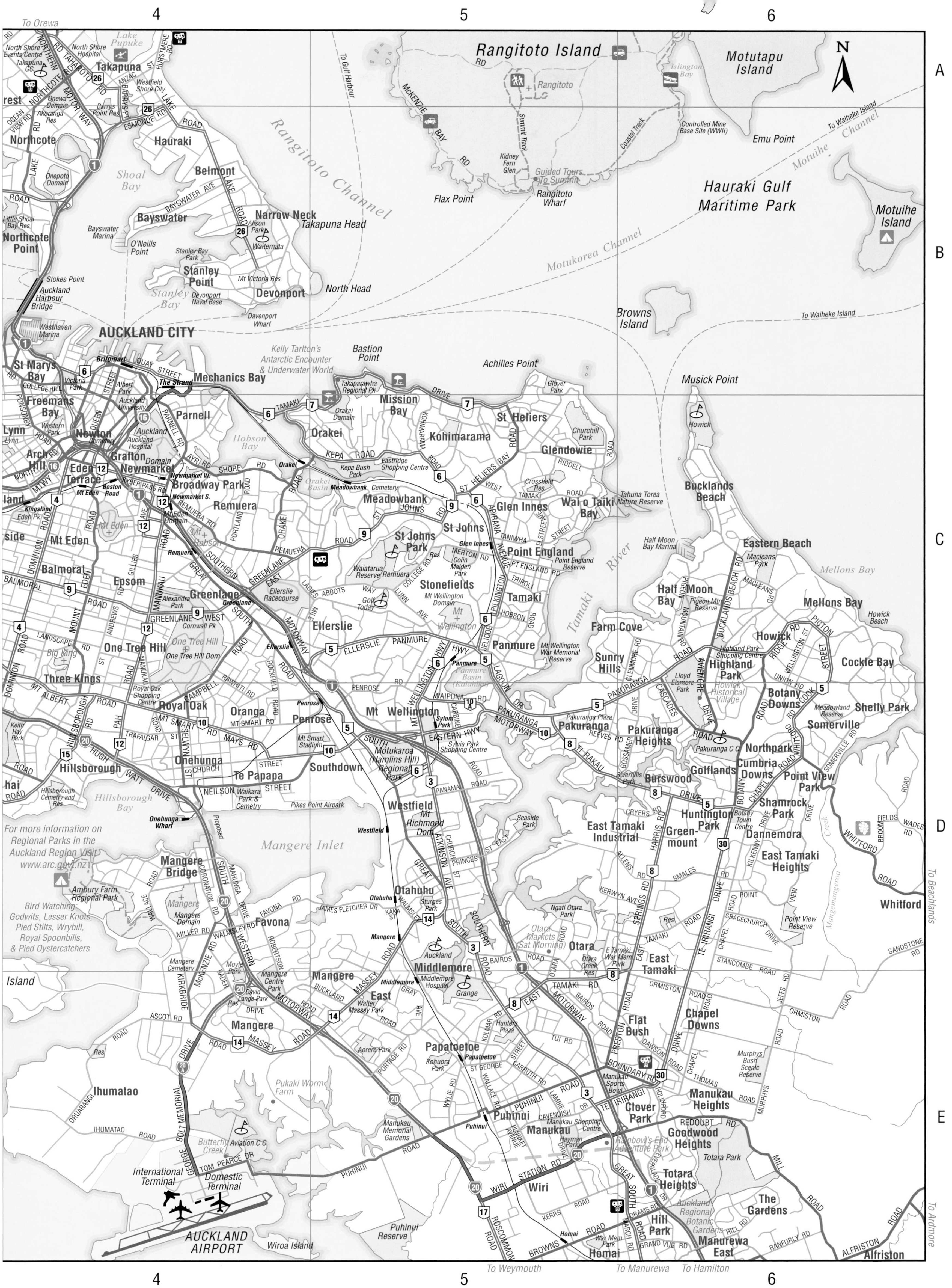

4
5
6
A
B
C
D
E
To Orewa
Rangitoto Island
Motutapu Island
Islington Bay
Rangitoto
Summit Track
Coastal Track
Controlled Mine Base Site (WWII)
Emu Point
To Waiheke Island
Motuihe Channel
Kidney Fern Glen
Guided Tours To Summit
Rangitoto Wharf
Flax Point
Hauraki Gulf Maritime Park
Motuihe Island
Motukorea Channel
Rangitoto Channel
To Gulf Harbour
North Shore Events Centre
North Shore Hospital
Lake Pupuke
Takapuna
Takapuna GC
Westfield Shore City
Onewa Domain
Akoranga Res
Barrys Point Res
Northcote
Hauraki
Belmont
Onepoto Domain
Shoal Bay
Bayswater
Bayswater Marina
Little Shoal Bay Res
Northcote Point
O'Neills Point
Narrow Neck
Alison Park
Waitemata
Takapuna Head
Stanley Bay Park
Stanley Point
Stanley Bay
Mt Victoria Res
Devonport
Devonport Naval Base
Devonport Wharf
North Head
Stokes Point
Auckland Harbour Bridge
Westhaven Marina
Browns Island
AUCKLAND CITY
Bastion Point
Kelly Tarlton's Antarctic Encounter & Underwater World
Achilles Point
Musick Point
St Marys Bay
Britomart
Quay Street
The Strand
Mechanics Bay
Victoria Park
Albert Park
Auckland University
Freemans Bay
Parnell
Hobson Bay
Takaparawha Regional Pk
Mission Bay
Glover Park
Orakei Domain
Orakei
Kohimarama
St Heliers
Churchill Park
Glendowie
Howick
Lynn
Western Park
Newton
Auckland Domain
Auckland Hospital
Arch Hill
Grafton
Eden Terrace
Newmarket
Broadway Park
Kepa Road
Eastridge Shopping Centre
Kepa Bush Park
Orakei Basin
Meadowbank
Cemetery
Meadowbank
Crossfield Res
Tahuna Torea Nature Reserve
Bucklands Beach
Mt Eden
Boston Road
Kingsland
Eden Pk
Remuera
Glen Innes
Wai o Taiki Bay
Mt Eden
Mt Hobson
St Johns
St Johns Park
Glen Innes
Half Moon Bay Marina
Eastern Beach
Macleans Park
Mellons Bay
Balmoral
Waiatarua Reserve
Remuera
Colin Maiden Park
Point England
Point England Reserve
Tamaki River
Epsom
Greenlane
Alexandra Park
Ellerslie Racecourse
Golf Today
Stonefields
Mt Wellington Domain
Tamaki
Half Moon Bay
Pigeon Mtn Reserve
Mellons Bay
Howick Beach
Ellerslie
Cornwall Pk
One Tree Hill
One Tree Hill Dom
One Tree Hill
Big King
Mt Wellington
Panmure
Mt Wellington War Memorial Reserve
Farm Cove
Sunny Hills
Howick
Highland Park Shopping Centre
Highland Park
Cockle Bay
Lloyd Elsmore Park
Howick Historical Village
Three Kings
Panmure Basin (Kalandra)
Botany Downs
Meadowland Reserve
Shelly Park
Royal Oak
Royal Oak Shopping Centre
Oranga
Penrose
Mt Wellington
Sylvia Park
Pakuranga Plaza
Pakuranga
Somerville
Keith Hay Park
Mt Smart Stadium
Sylvia Park Shopping Centre
Pakuranga Heights
Pakuranga C C
Northpark
Hillsborough
Onehunga
Te Papapa
Southdown
Motukaroa (Hamlins Hill) Regional Park
Cumbria Downs
Golflands
Point View Park
Hillsborough Cemetery and Res
Waikara Park & Cemetery
Pikes Point Airpark
Riverhills Park
Burswood
Huntington Park
Shamrock Park
Botany Town Centre
Hillsborough Bay
Westfield
Mt Richmond Dom
Seaside Park
East Tamaki Industrial
Greenmount
Dannemora
Onehunga Wharf
Mangere Inlet
East Tamaki Heights
Whitford
For more information on Regional Parks in the Auckland Region Visit www.arc.govt.nz
Mangere Bridge
Otahuhu
Sturges Park
Ngati Otara Park
Point View Reserve
Ambury Farm Regional Park
Bird Watching: Godwits, Lesser Knots, Pied Stilts, Wrybill, Royal Spoonbills, & Pied Oystercatchers
Mangere
Mangere Domain
Favona
Otara Markets (Sat Morning)
Otara
E Tamaki War Mem Park
Otara Creek Res
East Tamaki
Mangere Cemetery
Moyle Park
Mangere Centre Park
Auckland
Middlemore
Middlemore Hospital
Grange
Island
Mangere East
Walter Massey Park
David Lange Park
Hunters Plaza
Flat Bush
Chapel Downs
Mangere
Papatoetoe
Aorere Park
Kohuora Park
Murphys Bush Scenic Reserve
Manukau Sports Bowl
Boundary Rd
Ihumatao
Pukaki Worm Farm
Puhinui
Manukau
Manukau Shopping Centre
Clover Park
Manukau Heights
Manukau Memorial Gardens
Hayman Park
Rainbow's End Adventure Park
Goodwood Heights
Totara Park
Butterfly Creek
Aviation C C
International Terminal
Domestic Terminal
Wiri
Totara Heights
The Gardens
AUCKLAND AIRPORT
Puhinui Reserve
Wiroa Island
Homai
War Mem Park
Hill Park
Auckland Regional Botanic Gardens
Manurewa East
Alfriston
To Weymouth
To Manurewa
To Hamilton
To Ardmore
To Beachlands

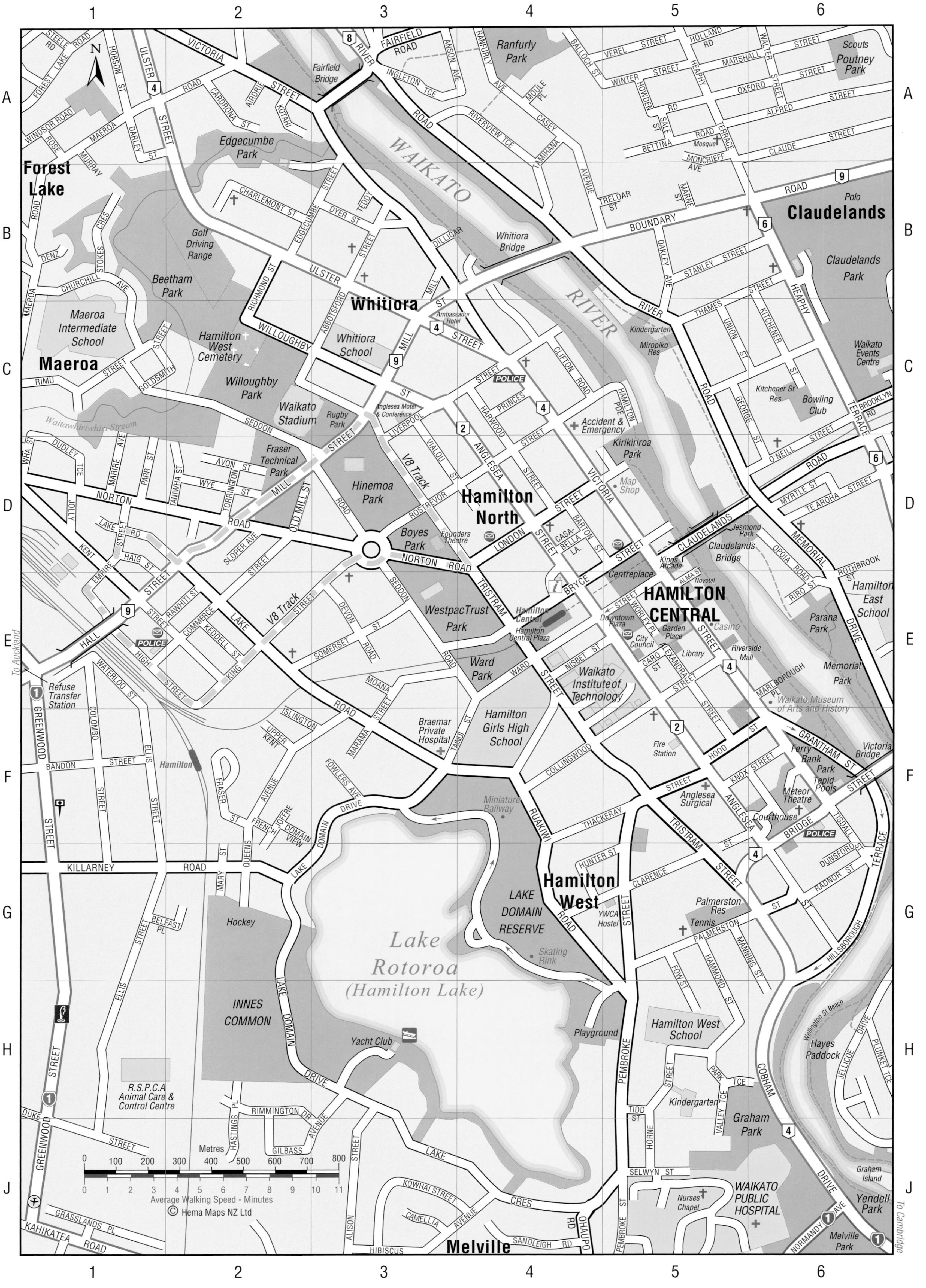

1
2
3
4
5
6
A
B
C
D
E
F
G
H
J
N
Forest Lake
Maeroa
Whitiora
Hamilton North
HAMILTON CENTRAL
Claudelands
Hamilton West
Melville
WAIKATO RIVER
Lake Rotoroa (Hamilton Lake)
LAKE DOMAIN RESERVE
INNES COMMON
Fairfield Bridge
Whitiora Bridge
Claudelands Bridge
Victoria Bridge
Ranfurly Park
Poutney Park
Scouts
Edgecumbe Park
Golf Driving Range
Beetham Park
Maeroa Intermediate School
Hamilton West Cemetery
Willoughby Park
Whitiora School
Waikato Stadium
Rugby Park
Fraser Technical Park
Hinemoa Park
Boyes Park
Founders Theatre
WestpacTrust Park
Ward Park
Waikato Institute of Technology
Hamilton Girls High School
Braemar Private Hospital
Miniature Railway
Skating Rink
Playground
Yacht Club
Hockey
R.S.P.C.A Animal Care & Control Centre
Refuse Transfer Station
Hamilton
Ambassador Hotel
Anglesea Motel & Conference
Accident & Emergency
Kirikiriroa Park
Map Shop
Kindergarten
Miropiko Res
Kitchener St Res
Bowling Club
Claudelands Park
Polo
Waikato Events Centre
Jesmond Park
Kings Arcade
Novotel
Centreplace
Hamilton Central
Hamilton Central Plaza
Downtown Plaza
City Council
Garden Place
Casino
Library
Riverside Mall
Hamilton East School
Parana Park
Memorial Park
Waikato Museum of Arts and History
Fire Station
Ferry Bank Park
Tapid Pools
Meteor Theatre
Courthouse
Anglesea Surgical
Palmerston Res
Tennis
YWCA Hostel
Hamilton West School
Kindergarten
Graham Park
Wellington St Beach
Hayes Paddock
Graham Island
Yendell Park
Melville Park
Nurses Chapel
WAIKATO PUBLIC HOSPITAL
Mosque
POLICE
V8 Track
Waitawhiriwhiri Stream
To Auckland
To Cambridge
VICTORIA STREET
RIVER ROAD
FAIRFIELD ROAD
ULSTER STREET
BOUNDARY ROAD
NORTON ROAD
MILL STREET
LAKE ROAD
KILLARNEY ROAD
GREENWOOD STREET
TRISTRAM STREET
ANGLESEA STREET
PEMBROKE STREET
COBHAM DRIVE
MEMORIAL DRIVE
GRANTHAM ST
CLAUDELANDS ROAD
LAKE DOMAIN DRIVE
RUAKIWI ROAD
SEDDON ROAD
WILLOUGHBY ST
Metres
0 100 200 300 400 500 600 700 800
Average Walking Speed - Minutes
0 1 2 3 4 5 6 7 8 9 10 11
© Hema Maps NZ Ltd

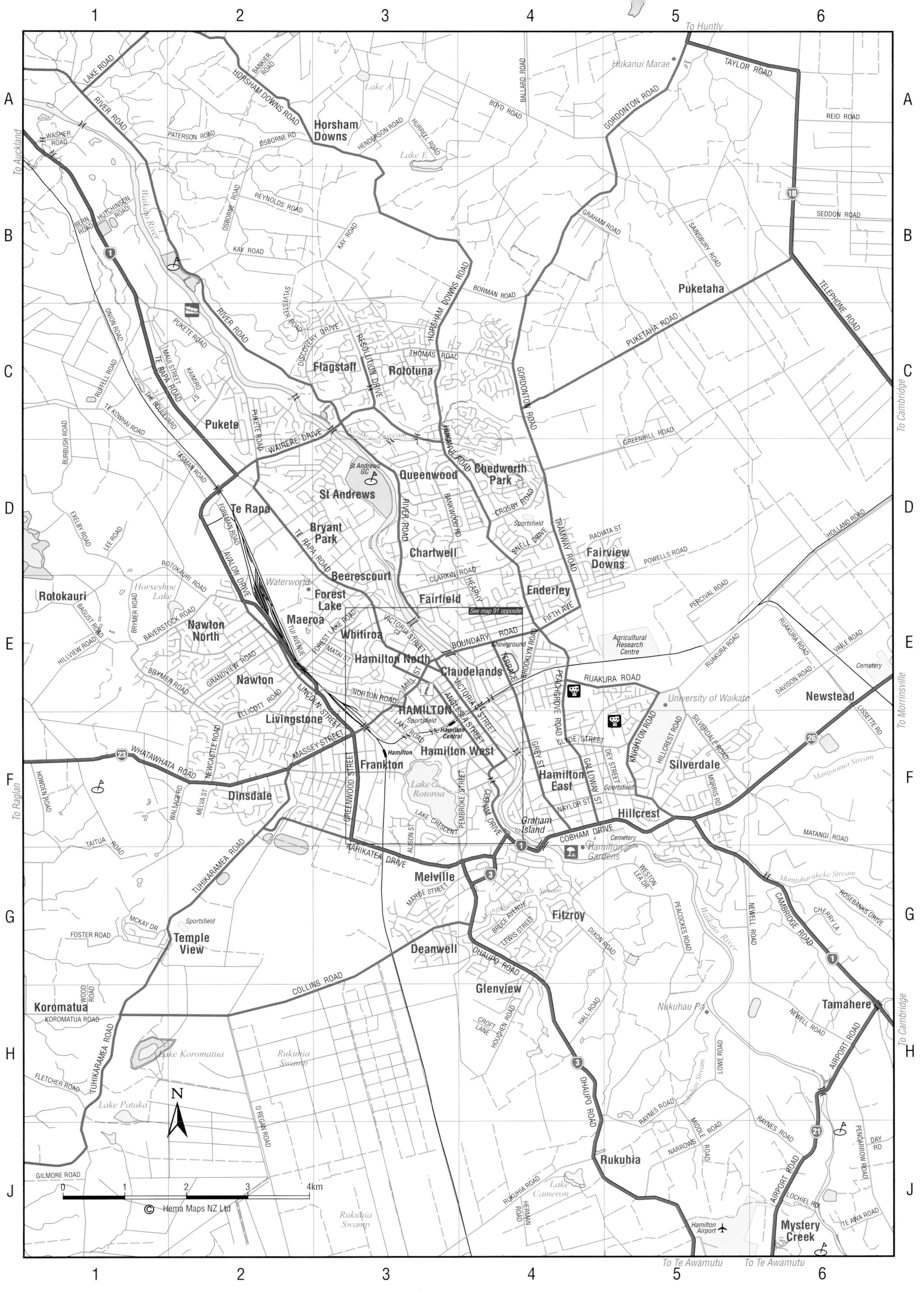

To Huntly
To Auckland
To Raglan
To Cambridge
To Morrinsville
To Te Awamutu
To Te Awamutu
Horsham Downs
Flagstaff
Rototuna
Pukete
Puketaha
Queenwood
Chedworth Park
St Andrews
Te Rapa
Bryant Park
Chartwell
Fairview Downs
Rotokauri
Beerescourt
Forest Lake
Fairfield
Enderley
Maeroa
Nawton North
Whitiroa
Hamilton North
Claudelands
Nawton
Livingstone
HAMILTON
Hamilton West
Frankton
Hamilton East
Silverdale
Newstead
Dinsdale
Hillcrest
Graham Island
Melville
Fitzroy
Temple View
Deanwell
Glenview
Koromatua
Tamahere
Rukuhia
Mystery Creek
Hukanui Marae
Lake A
Lake E
Horseshoe Lake
Waterworld
Lake Rotoroa
Lake Koromatua
Lake Pataka
Lake Cameron
Rukuhia Swamp
Nukuhau Pa
Hamilton Airport
Hamilton Gardens
University of Waikato
Agricultural Research Centre
Waikato River
Kirikiriroa Stream
Mangaonua Stream
Mangaharakeke Stream
Mangakotukutuku Stream
St Andrews GC
Sportsfield
Showground
Cemetery
Hamilton Central
See map 91 opposite
LAKE ROAD
RIVER ROAD
HORSHAM DOWNS ROAD
BANKIER ROAD
TAYLOR ROAD
GORDONTON ROAD
REID ROAD
SEDDON ROAD
TELEPHONE ROAD
PUKETAHA ROAD
GRAHAM ROAD
SAINSBURY ROAD
BORMAN ROAD
THOMAS ROAD
DISCOVERY DRIVE
RESOLUTION DRIVE
HUKANUI ROAD
WAIRERE DRIVE
TE RAPA ROAD
PUKETE ROAD
THE BOULEVARD
TASMAN ROAD
TE KOWHAI ROAD
BURBUSH ROAD
RUFFELL ROAD
ONION ROAD
EXELBY ROAD
LEE ROAD
ROTOKAURI ROAD
BAVERSTOCK ROAD
BAGUST ROAD
HILLVIEW ROAD
BRYMER ROAD
GRANDVIEW ROAD
ELLICOTT ROAD
NEWCASTLE ROAD
WHATAWHATA ROAD
HOWDEN ROAD
TAITUA ROAD
TUHIKARAMEA ROAD
MCKAY DR
FOSTER ROAD
KOROMATUA ROAD
FLETCHER ROAD
GILMORE ROAD
COLLINS ROAD
O'REGAN ROAD
KAHIKATEA DRIVE
GREENWOOD STREET
MASSEY STREET
LINCOLN STREET
AVALON DRIVE
FOREST LAKE ROAD
VICTORIA STREET
BOUNDARY ROAD
ANGLESEA STREET
NORTON ROAD
COBHAM DRIVE
GREY ST
GALLOWAY ST
PEACHGROVE ROAD
RUAKURA ROAD
KNIGHTON ROAD
HILLCREST ROAD
SILVERDALE ROAD
MORRIS RD
MATANGI ROAD
CAMBRIDGE ROAD
NEWELL ROAD
AIRPORT ROAD
OHAUPO ROAD
PEACOCKES ROAD
DIXON ROAD
HALL ROAD
HOUCHEN ROAD
RAYNES ROAD
MIDDLE ROAD
NARROWS ROAD
LOWE ROAD
RUKUHIA ROAD
HERMAN ROAD
PENCARROW ROAD
LOCHIEL RD
TE AWA ROAD
DAY RD
HOLLAND ROAD
POWELLS ROAD
PERCIVAL ROAD
VAILE ROAD
DAVISON ROAD
LISSETTE RD
TRAMWAY ROAD
FIFTH AVE
CROSBY ROAD
RIVER ROAD
GREENHILL ROAD
0 1 2 3 4km
© Hema Maps NZ Ltd

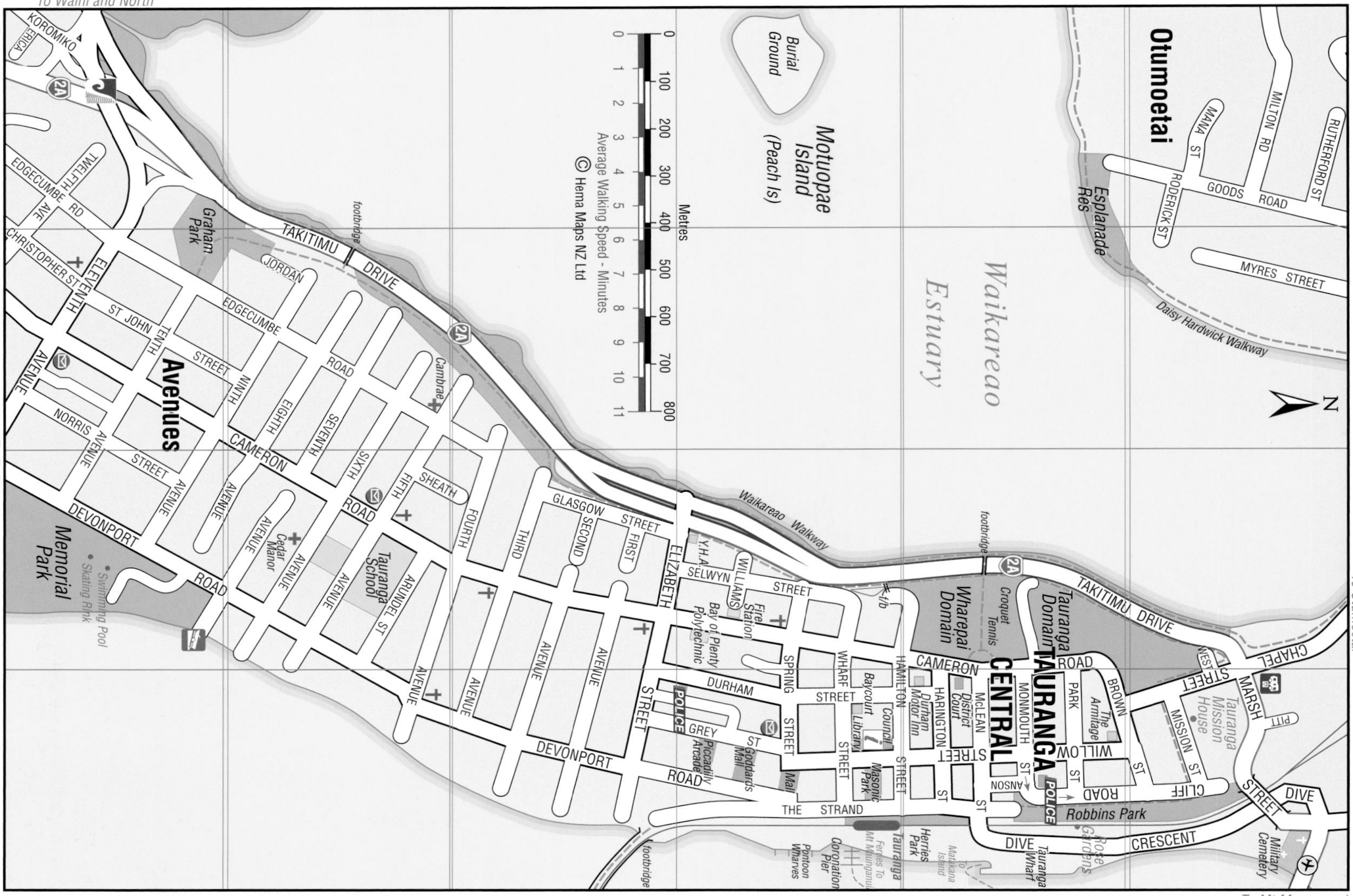

Tauranga Suburbs

For touring map see map 13

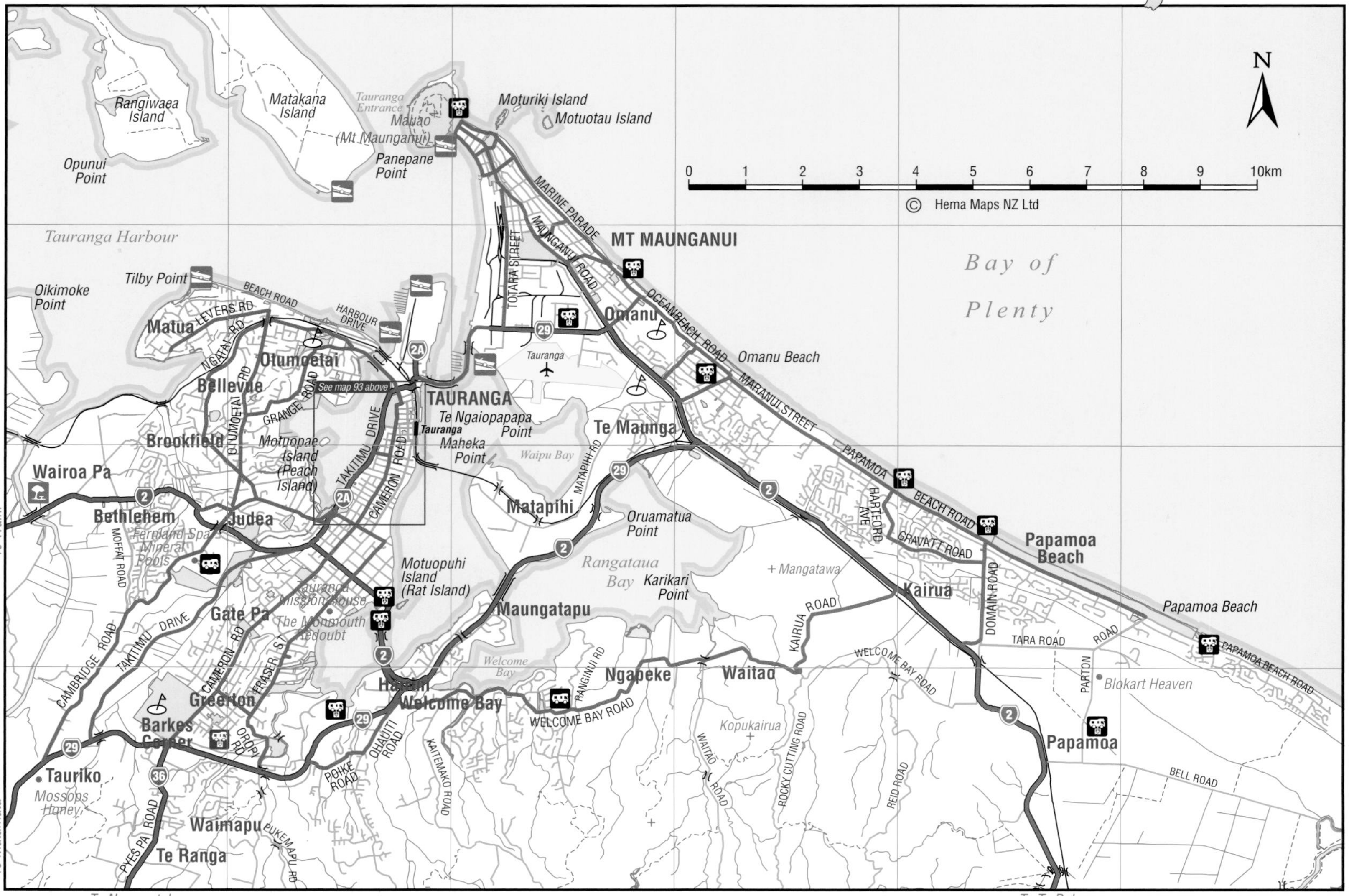

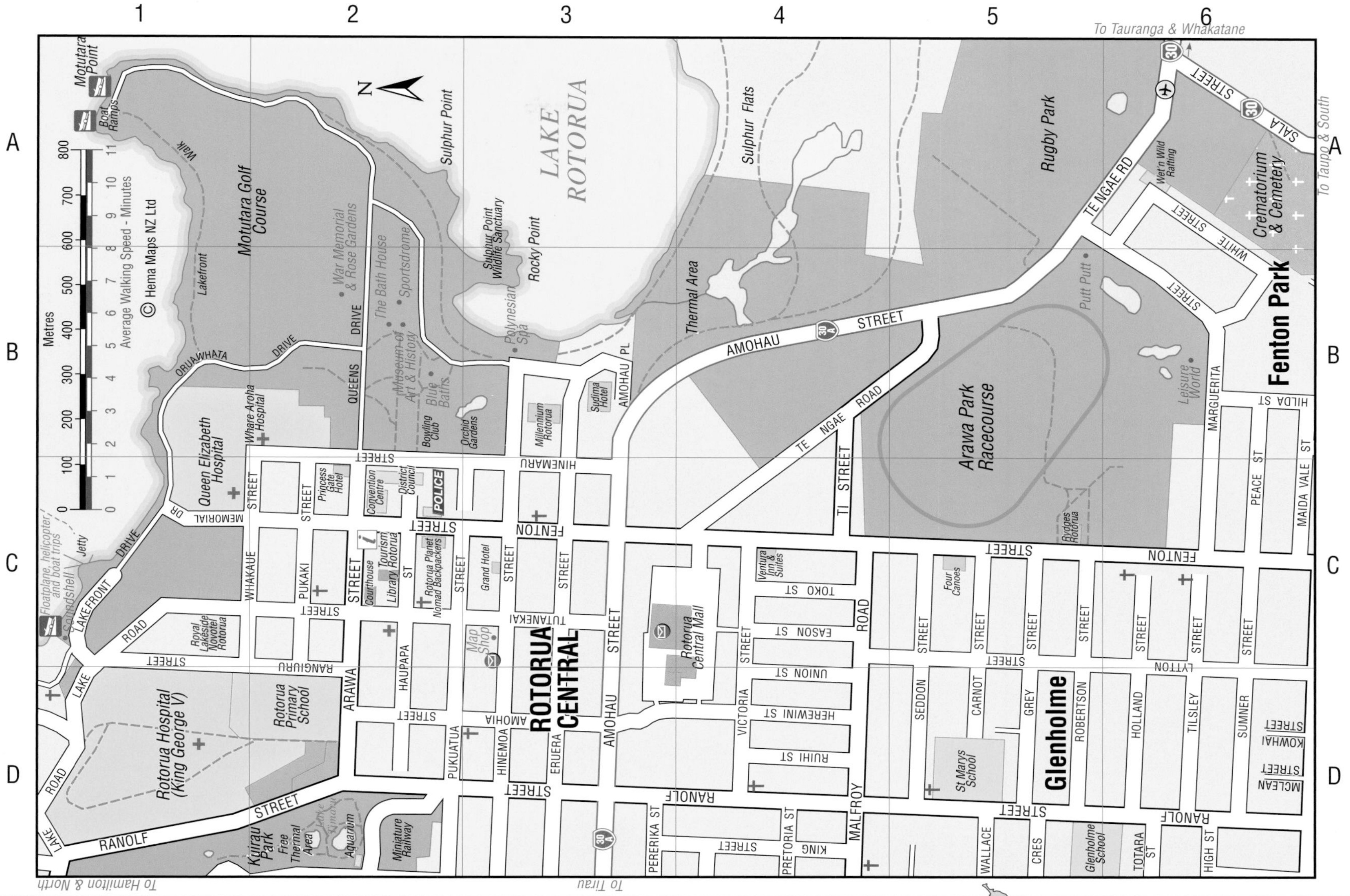

For touring map see map 13

Rotorua Suburbs

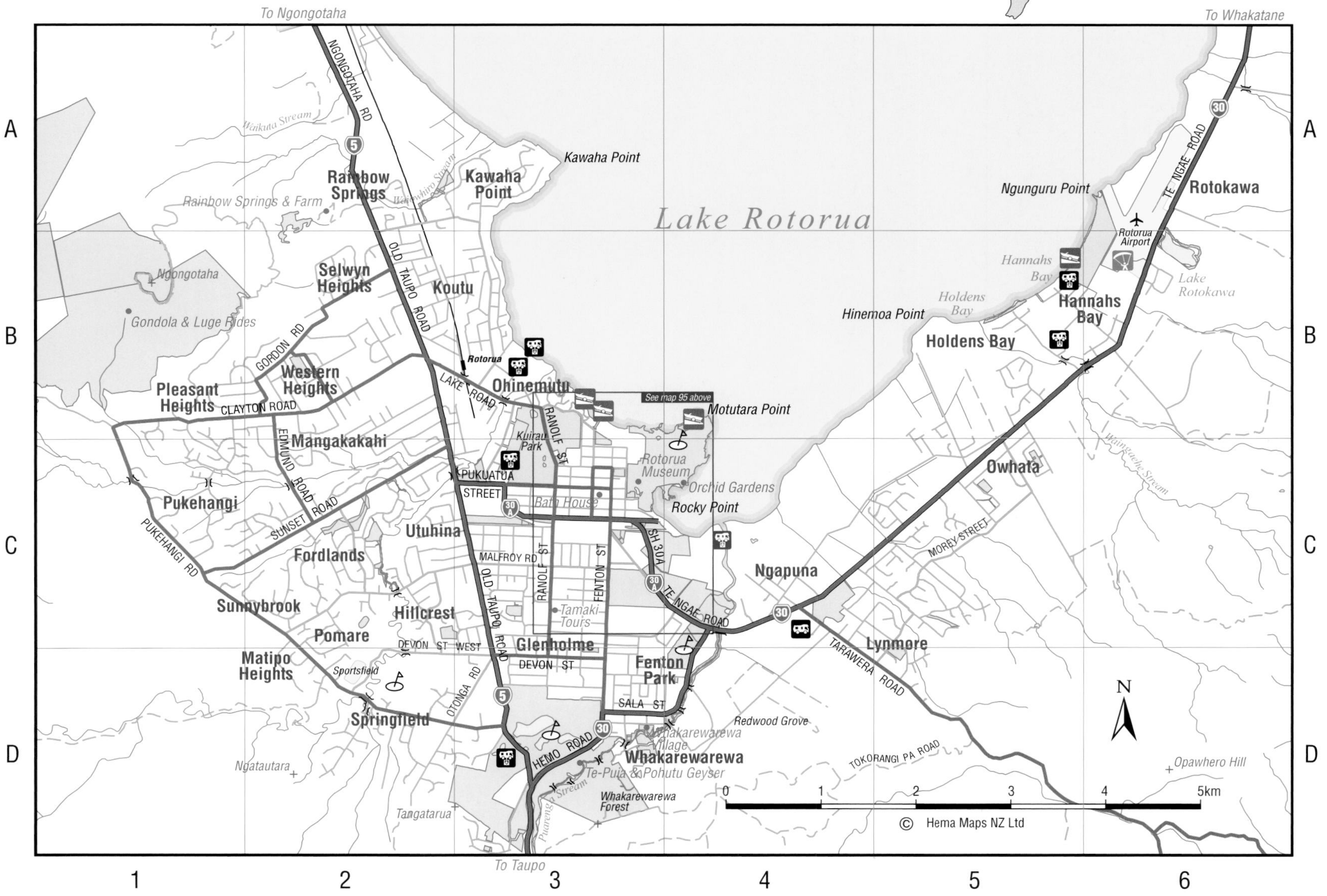

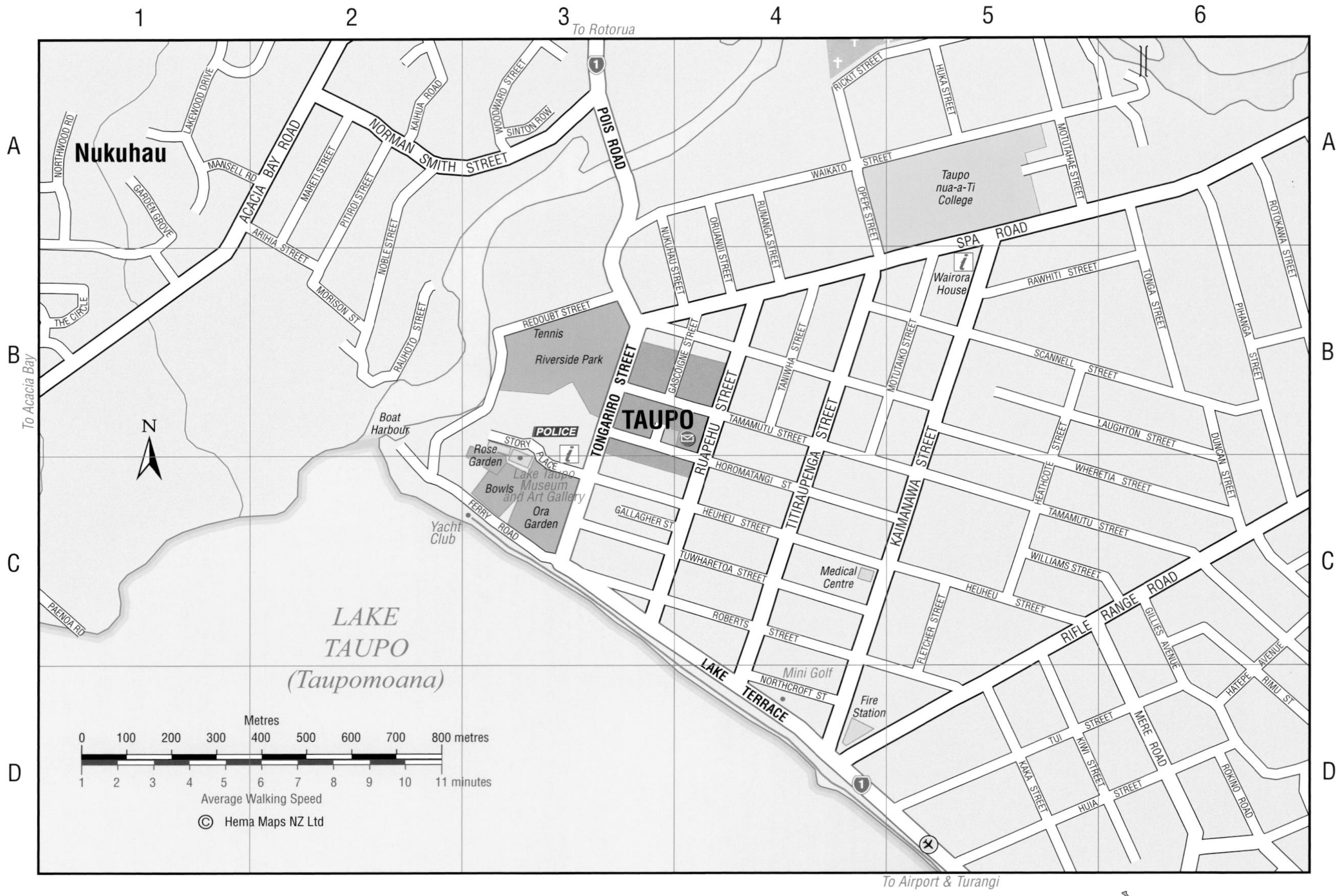

map 98

Taupo Suburbs

For touring map see map 19

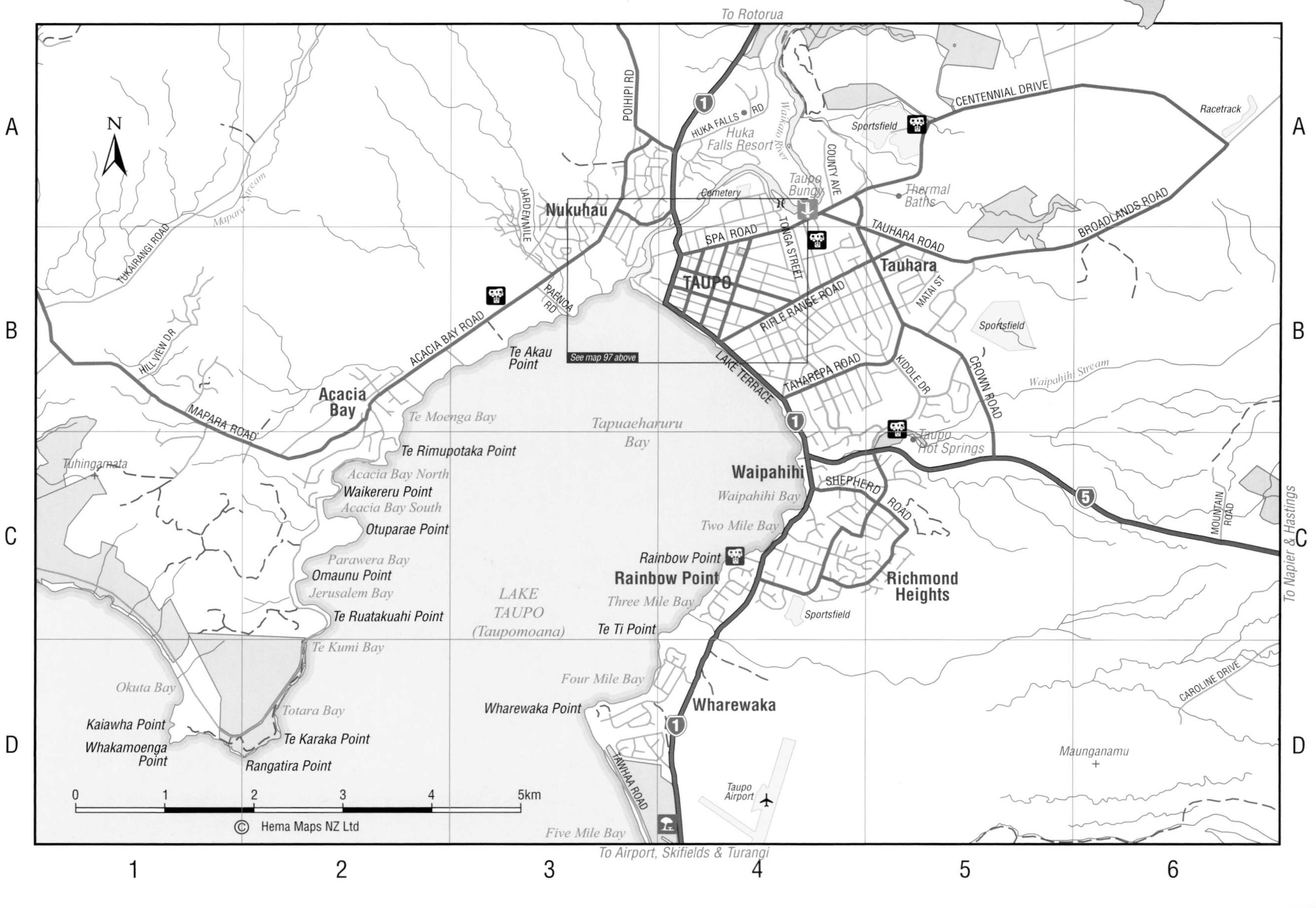

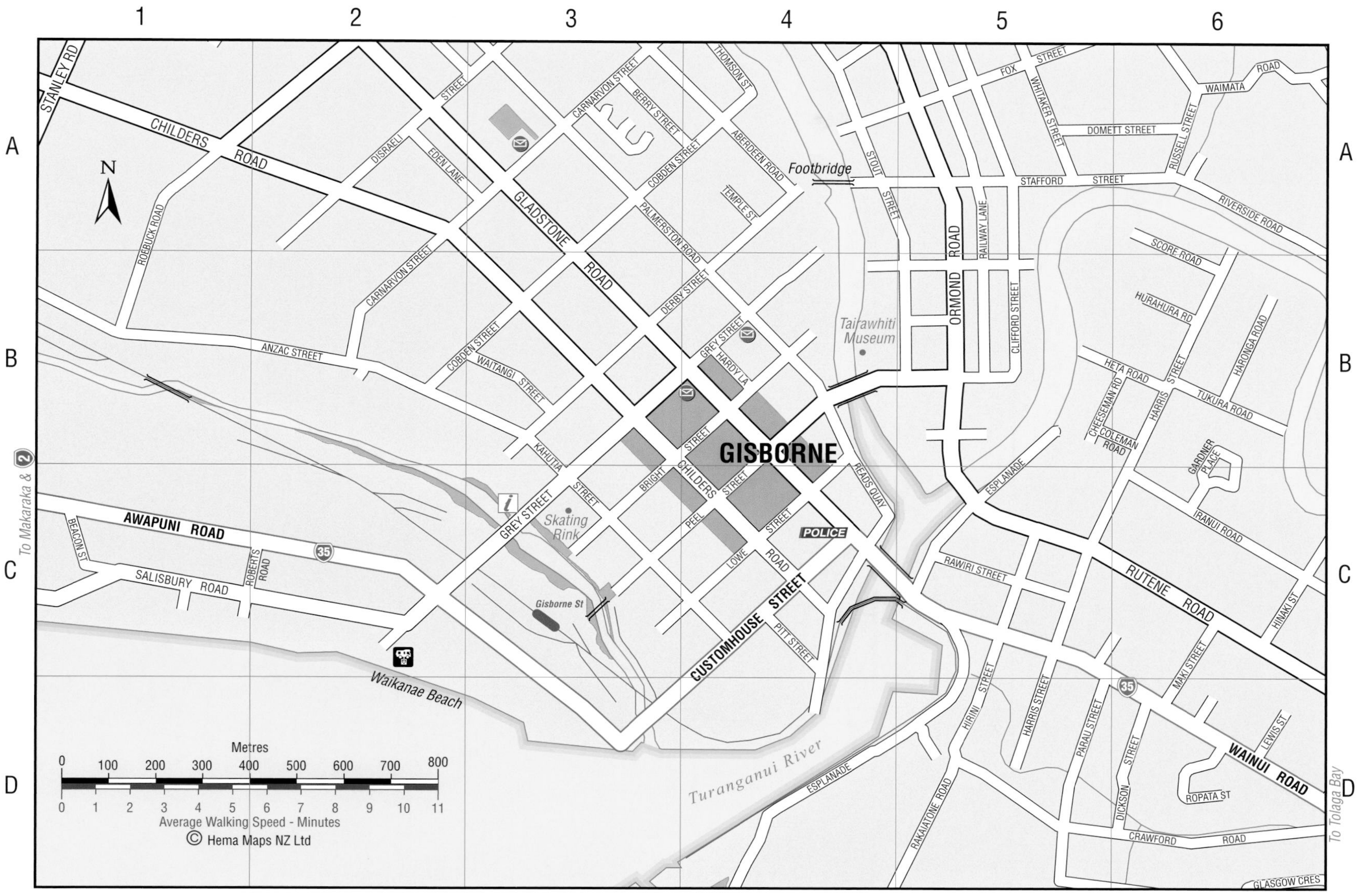

For touring map see map 22

Gisborne Suburbs

map 100

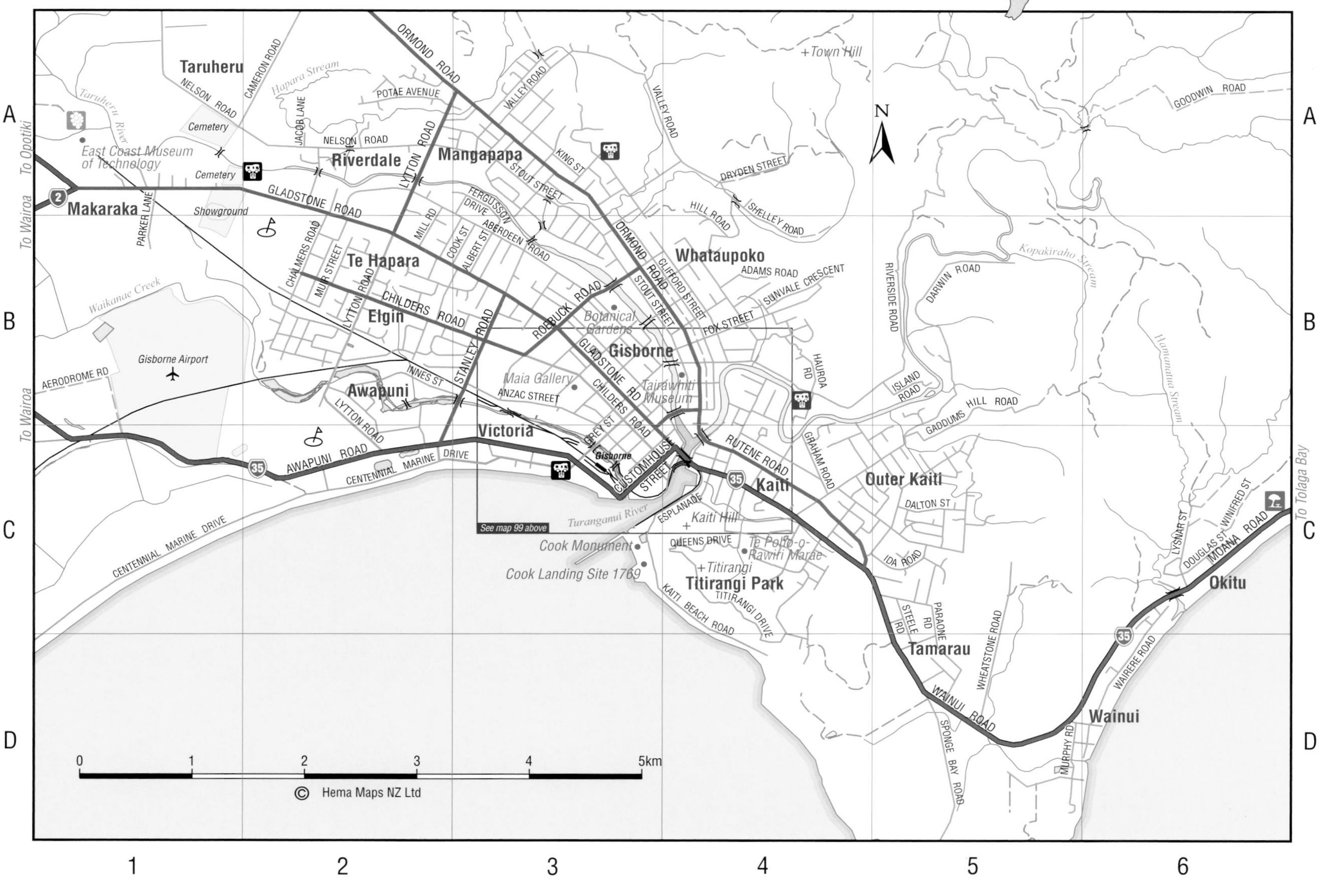

Napier CBD

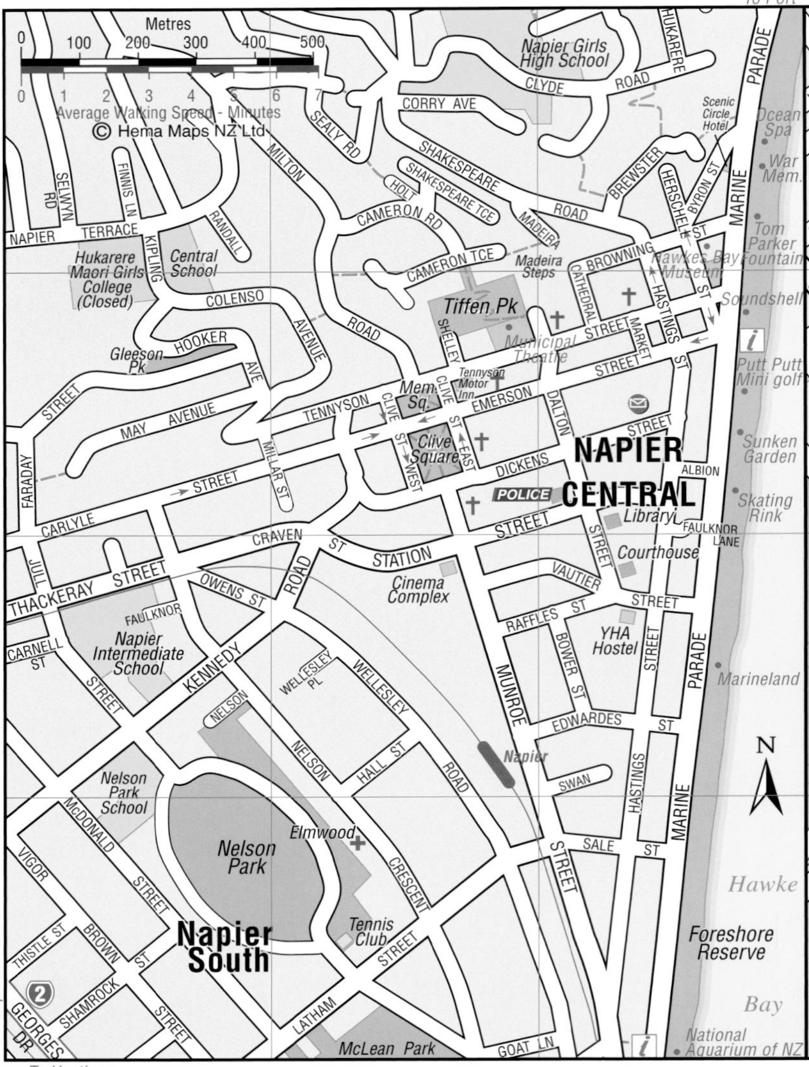

Hastings CBD

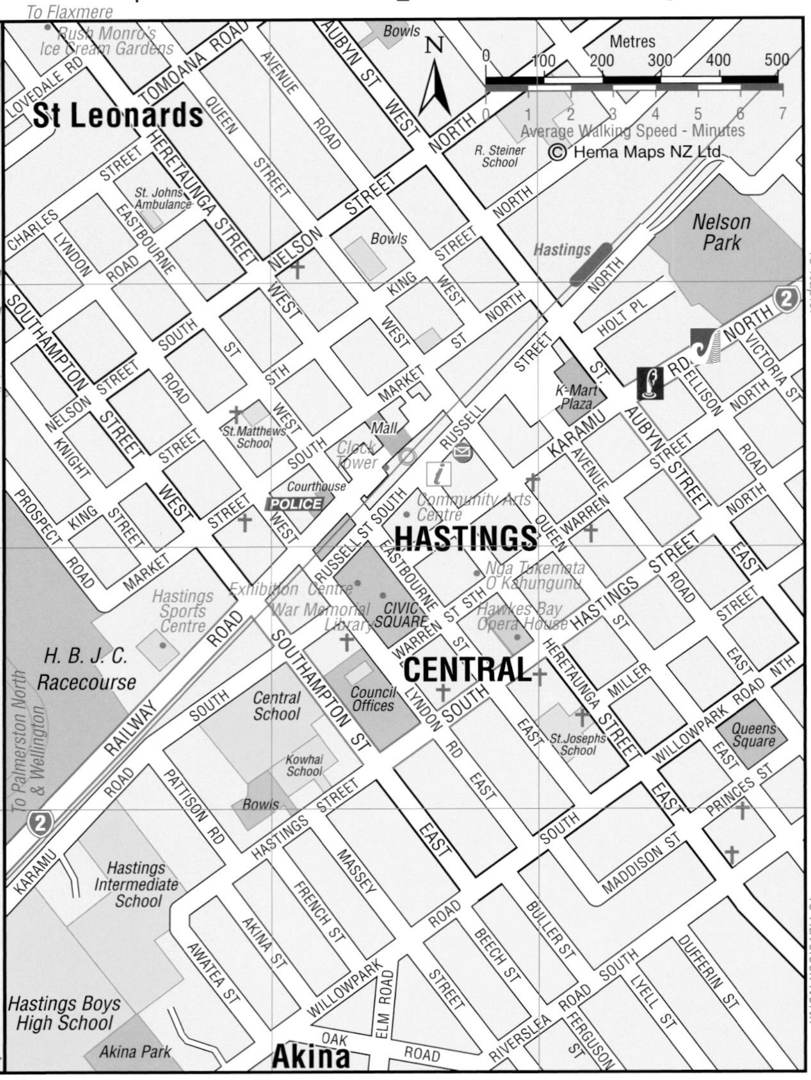

map 103 Napier / Hastings Suburbs

For touring map see map 28

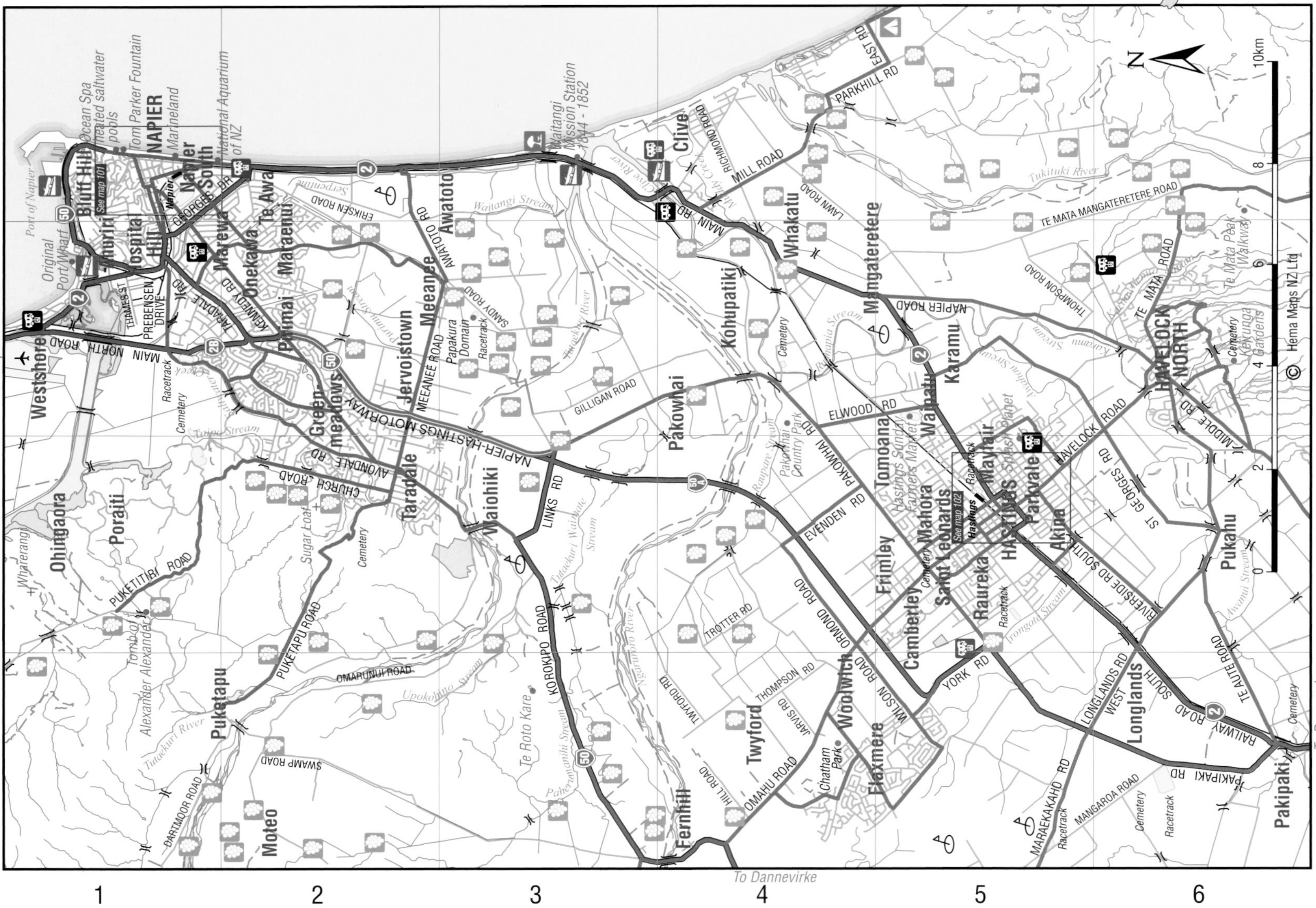

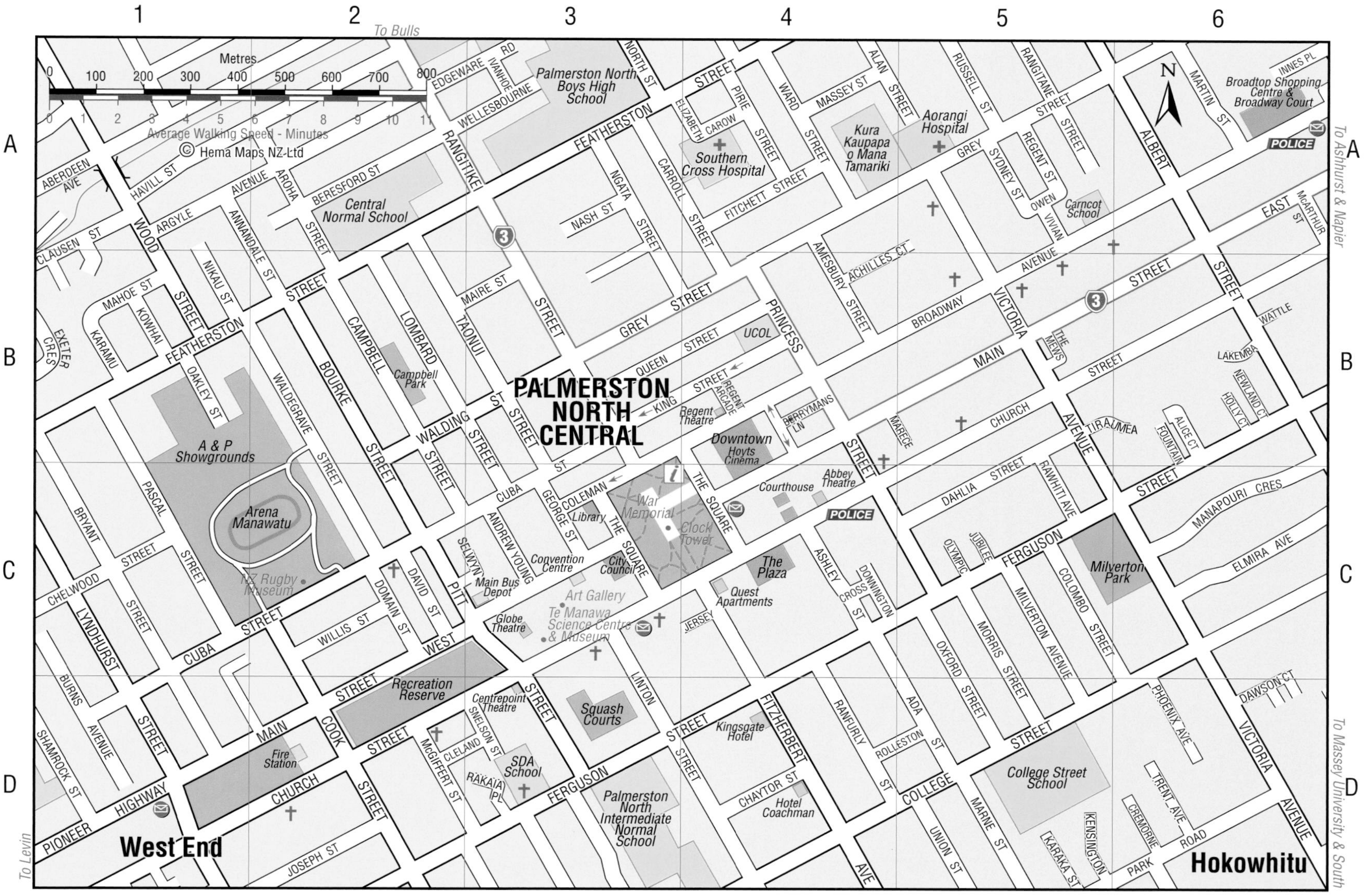

Palmerston North Suburbs

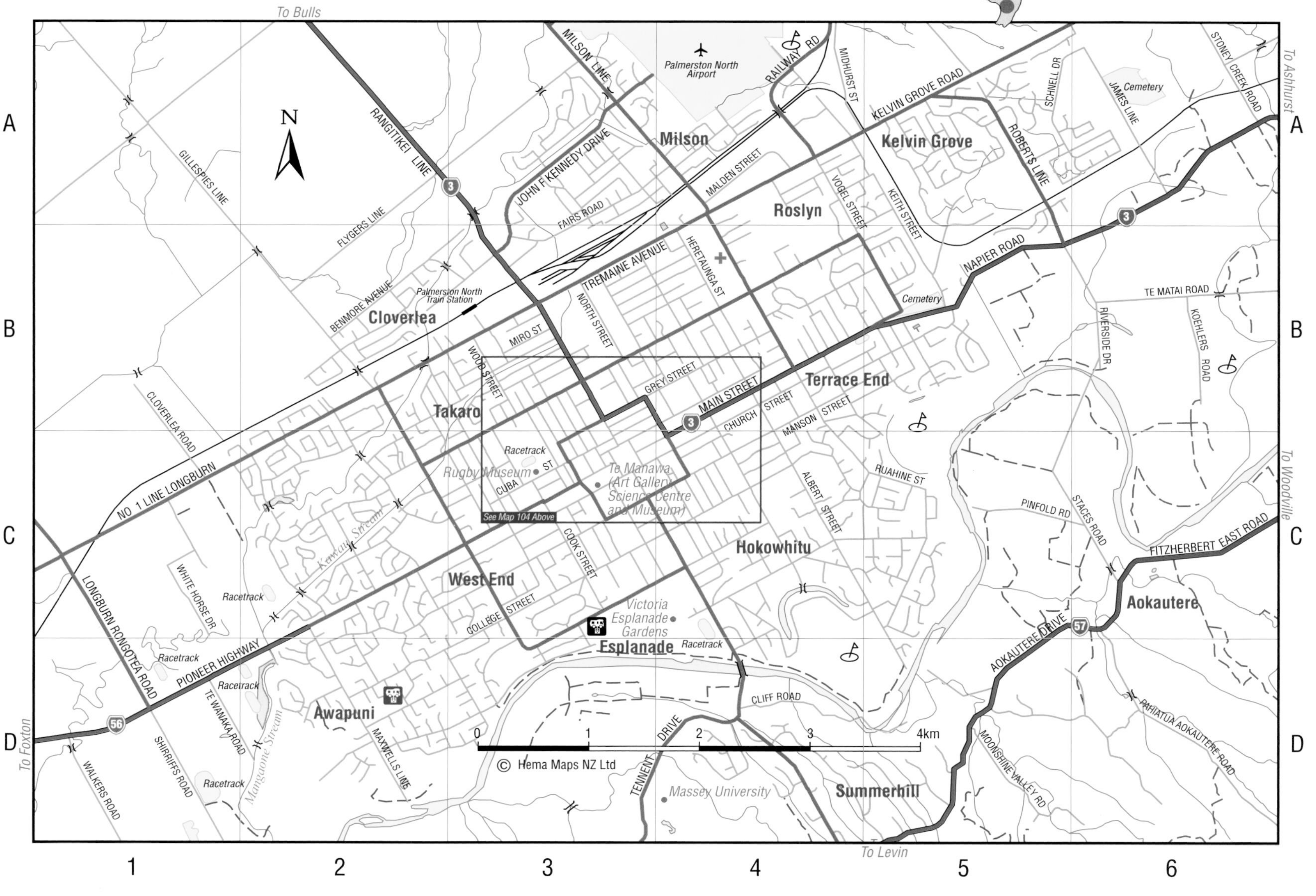

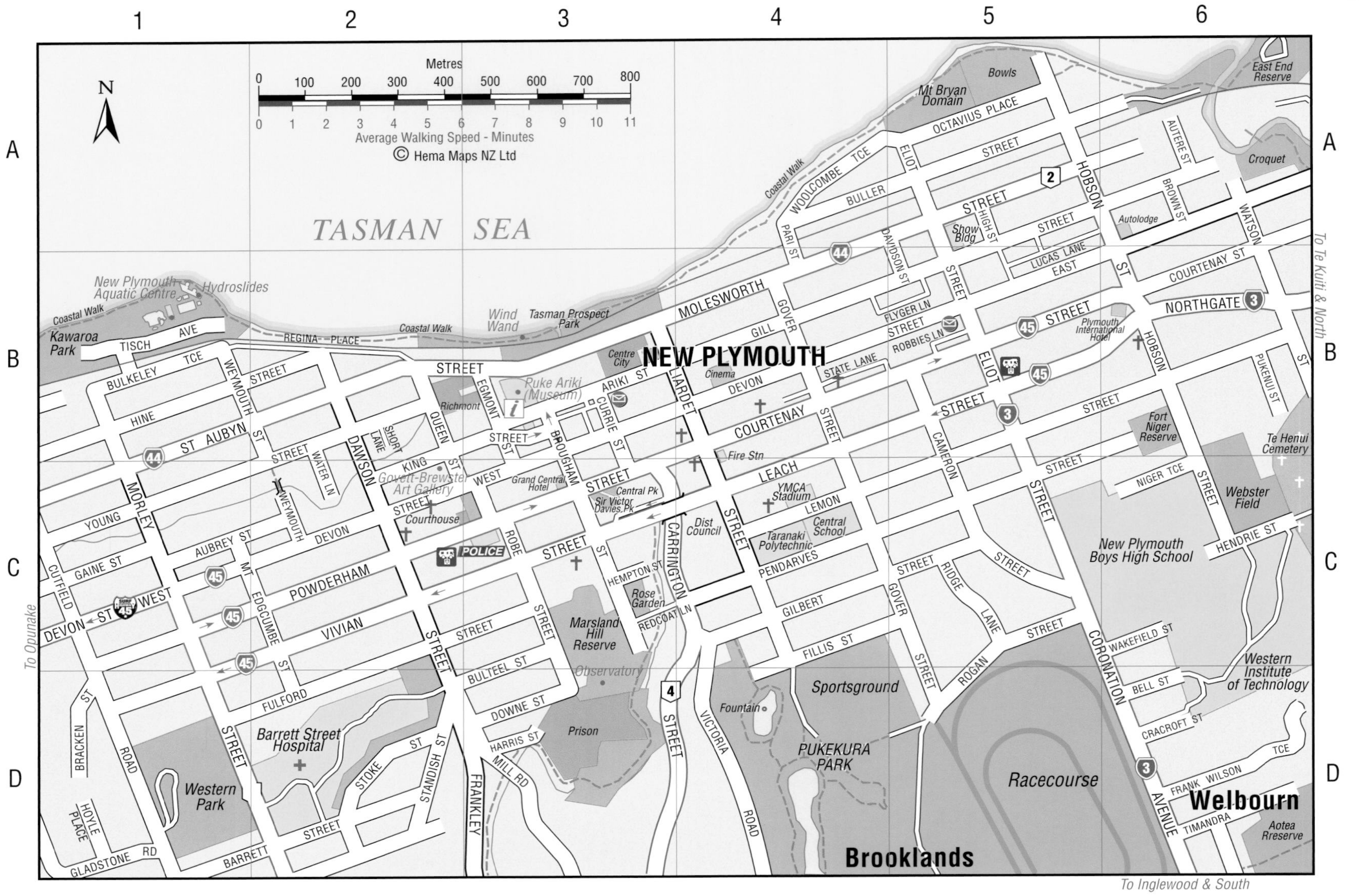

For touring map see map 23

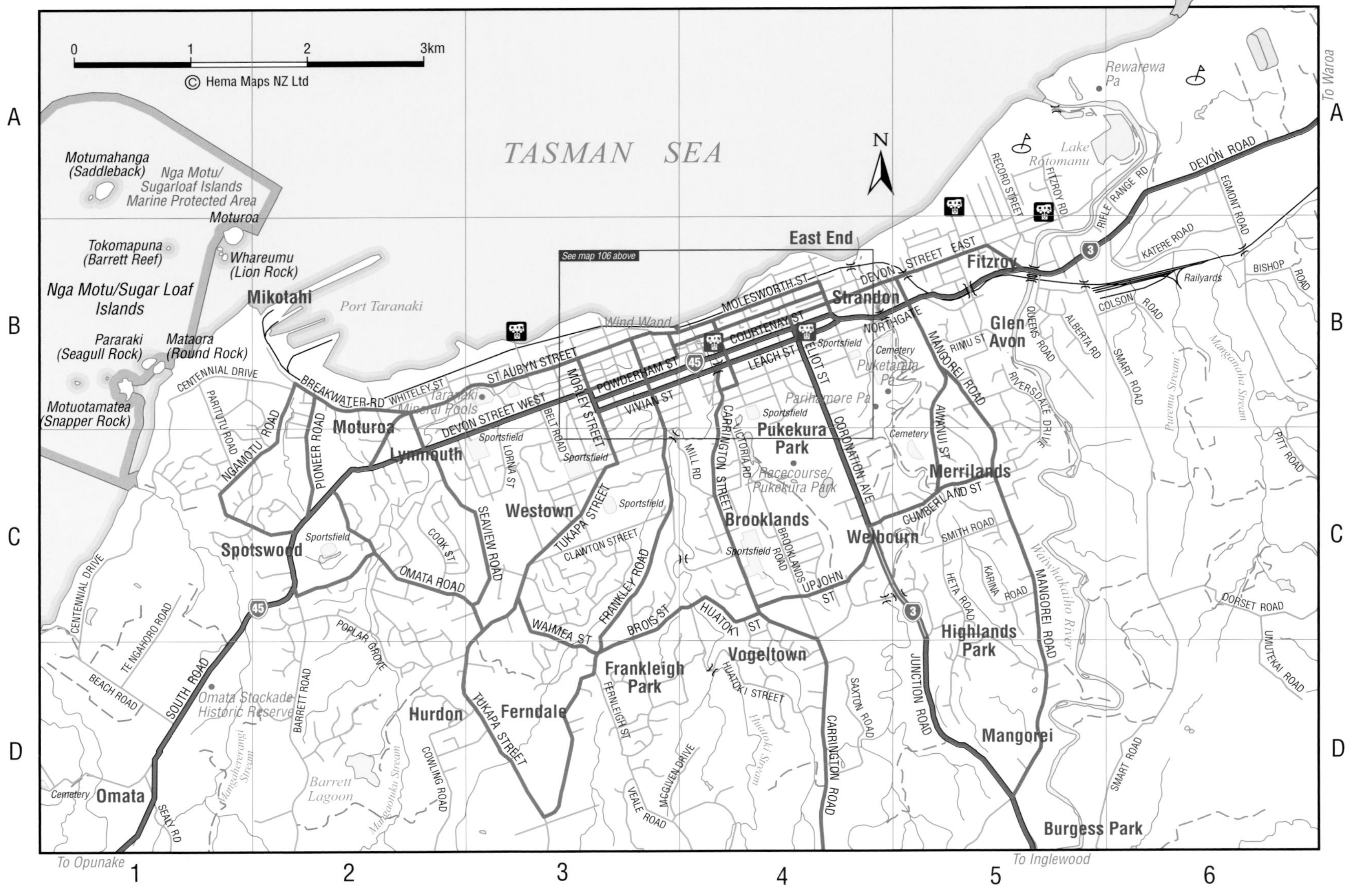

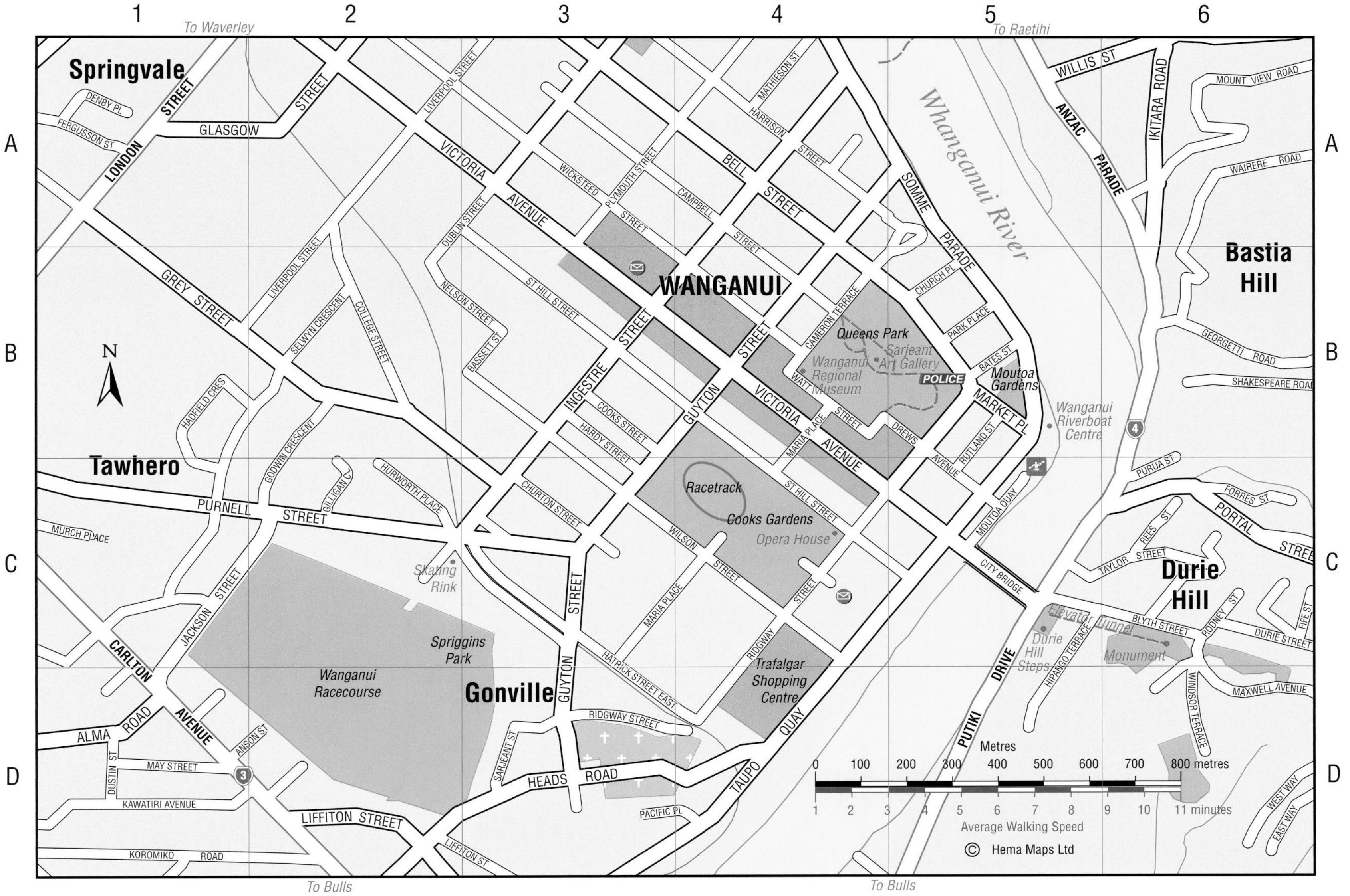

For touring map see map 26

Wanganui Suburbs

map 109

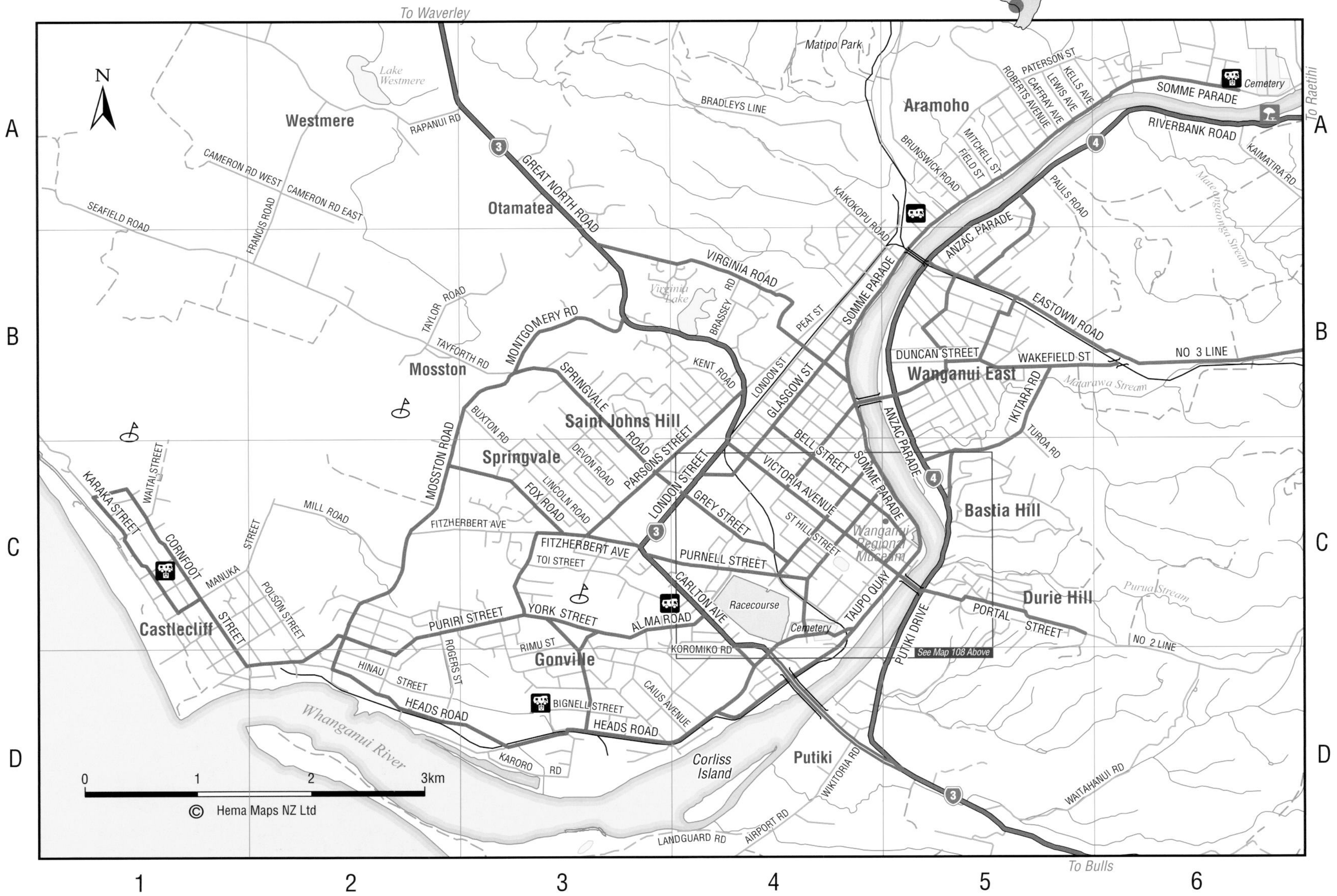

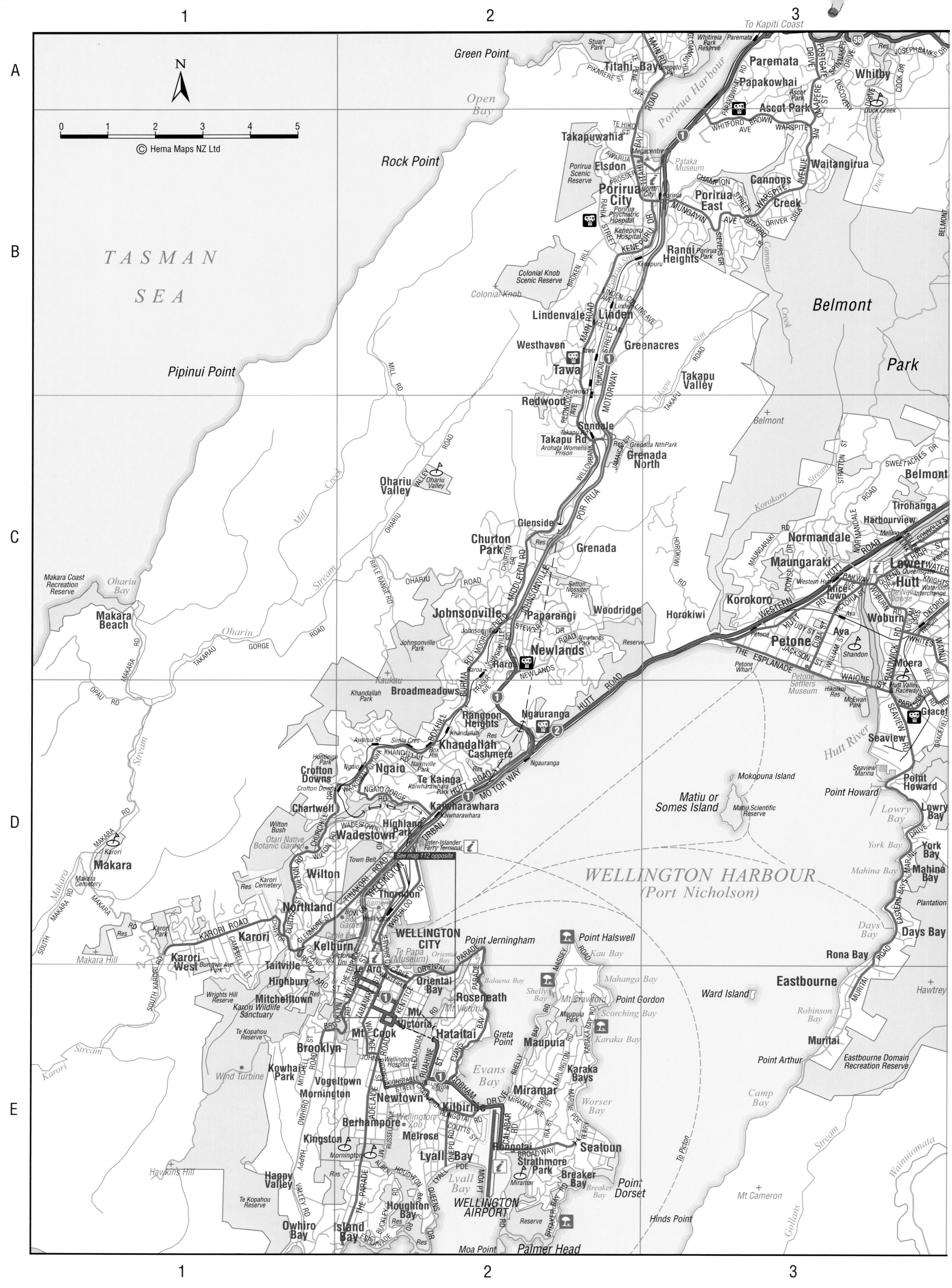

1
2
3
A
B
C
D
E
To Kapiti Coast
TASMAN SEA
Hema Maps NZ Ltd
0 1 2 3 4 5
N
Green Point
Open Bay
Rock Point
Pipinui Point
Stuart Park
Titahi Bay
Whitireia Park Reserve
Paremata
Papakowhai
Ascot Park
Whitby
Duck Creek
Porirua Harbour
Takapuwahia
Elsdon
Porirua Scenic Reserve
Porirua City
Porirua Psychiatric Hospital
Kenepuru Hospital
Pataka Museum
Porirua East
Cannons Creek
Waitangirua
Ranui Heights
Colonial Knob Scenic Reserve
Colonial Knob
Lindenvale
Linden
Westhaven
Greenacres
Tawa
Redwood
Takapu Valley
Belmont Park
Belmont
Sundale
Takapu Rd
Arohata Womens Prison
Grenada North
Ohariu Valley
Glenside
Churton Park
Grenada
Johnsonville
Paparangi
Woodridge
Horokiwi
Newlands
Tirohanga
Harbourview
Normandale
Maungaraki
Korokoro
Lower Hutt
Alicetown
Woburn
Petone
Ava
Moera
Gracefield
Seaview
Makara Coast Recreation Reserve
Ohariu Bay
Makara Beach
Broadmeadows
Khandallah Park
Rangoon Heights
Ngauranga
Khandallah
Cashmere
Crofton Downs
Ngaio
Te Kainga
Kaiwharawhara
Chartwell
Wilton Bush
Highland Park
Wadestown
Otari Native Botanic Garden
Inter-Islander Ferry Terminal
Mokopuna Island
Matiu or Somes Island
Matiu Scientific Reserve
Point Howard
Lowry Bay
York Bay
Mahina Bay
Makara
Wilton
Karori Cemetery
WELLINGTON HARBOUR (Port Nicholson)
See map 112 opposite
Thorndon
Northland
Plantation
Days Bay
Karori
Karori West
Kelburn
WELLINGTON CITY
Te Papa (Museum)
Point Jerningham
Point Halswell
Kau Bay
Makara Hill
Taitville
Te Aro
Oriental Bay
Rona Bay
Highbury
Balaena Bay
Mahanga Bay
Eastbourne
Hawtrey
Wrights Hill Reserve
Karori Wildlife Sanctuary
Mitchelltown
Roseneath
Mt Crawford
Point Gordon
Ward Island
Mt Victoria
Hataitai
Scorching Bay
Robinson Bay
Te Kopahou Reserve
Mt Cook
Greta Point
Maupuia
Karaka Bay
Muritai
Brooklyn
Wellington Hospital
Karaka Bays
Point Arthur
Eastbourne Domain Recreation Reserve
Wind Turbine
Kowhai Park
Vogeltown
Evans Bay
Miramar
Worser Bay
Mornington
Newtown
Kilbirnie
Camp Bay
Berhampore
Wellington Zoo
Kingston
Melrose
Rongotai
Seatoun
To Picton
Hawkins Hill
Lyall Bay
Strathmore Park
Breaker Bay
Point Dorset
Mt Cameron
Happy Valley
WELLINGTON AIRPORT
Houghton Bay
Owhiro Bay
Island Bay
Hinds Point
Moa Point
Palmer Head
Reserve

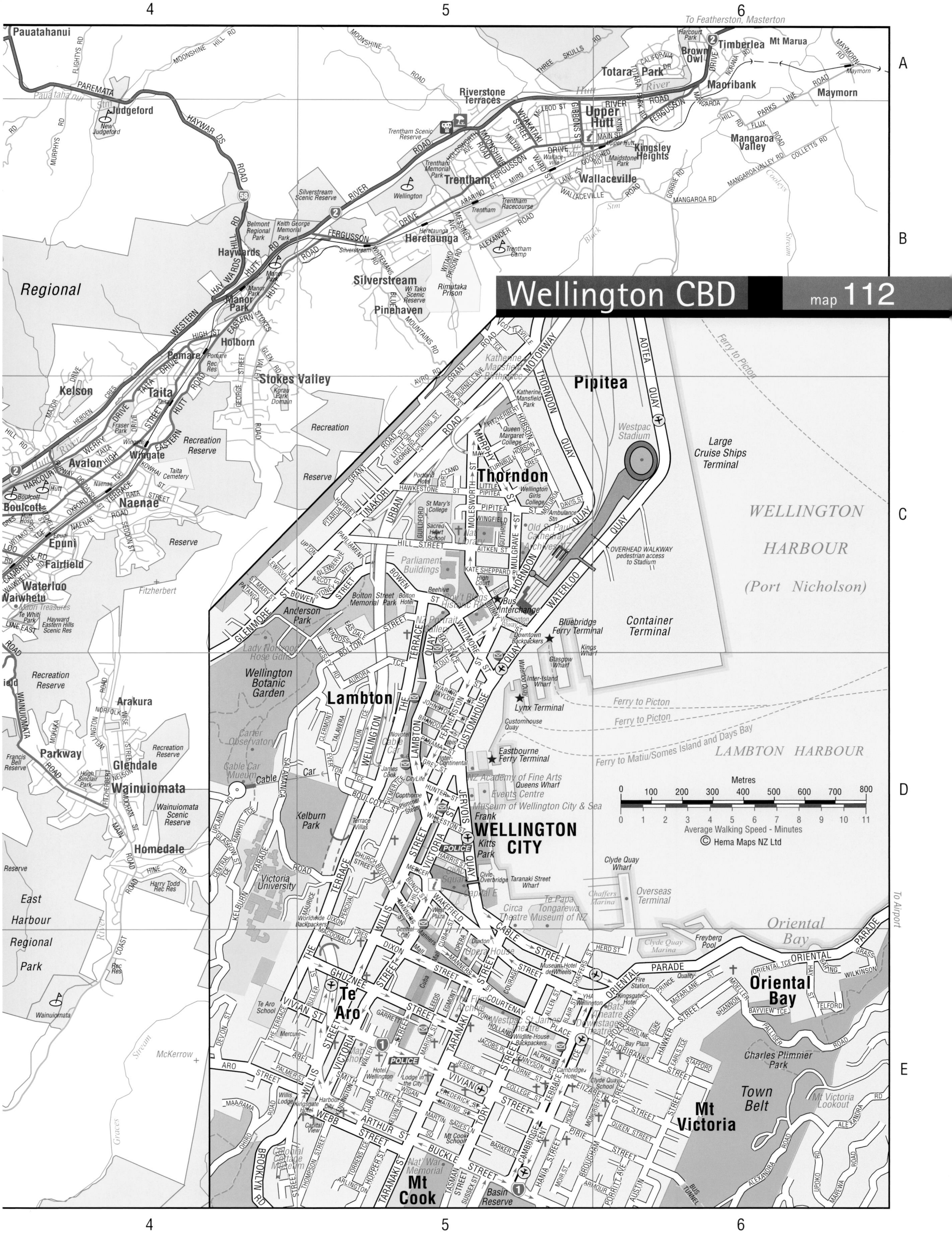
Wellington CBD
map 112
4
5
6
A
B
C
D
E
To Featherston, Masterton
To Airport
Pauatahanui
Judgeford
Timberlea
Mt Marua
Brown Owl
Totara Park
Maoribank
Maymorn
Riverstone Terraces
Upper Hutt
Mangaroa Valley
Kingsley Heights
Trentham
Wallaceville
Heretaunga
Silverstream
Pinehaven
Haywards
Manor Park
Holborn
Pomare
Stokes Valley
Kelson
Taita
Avalon
Wingate
Naenae
Boulcott
Epuni
Fairfield
Waterloo
Waiwhetu
Arakura
Parkway
Glendale
Wainuiomata
Homedale
Regional
Recreation Reserve
Recreation
Reserve
East Harbour Regional Park
Rimutaka Prison
Trentham Racecourse
Trentham Camp
Pipitea
Thorndon
Lambton
Te Aro
WELLINGTON CITY
Oriental Bay
Mt Victoria
Mt Cook
Kelburn Park
Wellington Botanic Garden
Victoria University
Parliament Buildings
Westpac Stadium
Large Cruise Ships Terminal
WELLINGTON HARBOUR
(Port Nicholson)
Container Terminal
Bluebridge Ferry Terminal
Lynx Terminal
Eastbourne Ferry Terminal
Ferry to Picton
Ferry to Matiu/Somes Island and Days Bay
LAMBTON HARBOUR
Te Papa Tongarewa Museum of NZ
Overseas Terminal
Oriental Bay
Town Belt
Charles Plimmer Park
Mt Victoria Lookout
Basin Reserve
Nat' War Memorial
Frank Kitts Park
Civic Square
Metres
0 100 200 300 400 500 600 700 800
0 1 2 3 4 5 6 7 8 9 10 11
Average Walking Speed - Minutes
© Hema Maps NZ Ltd

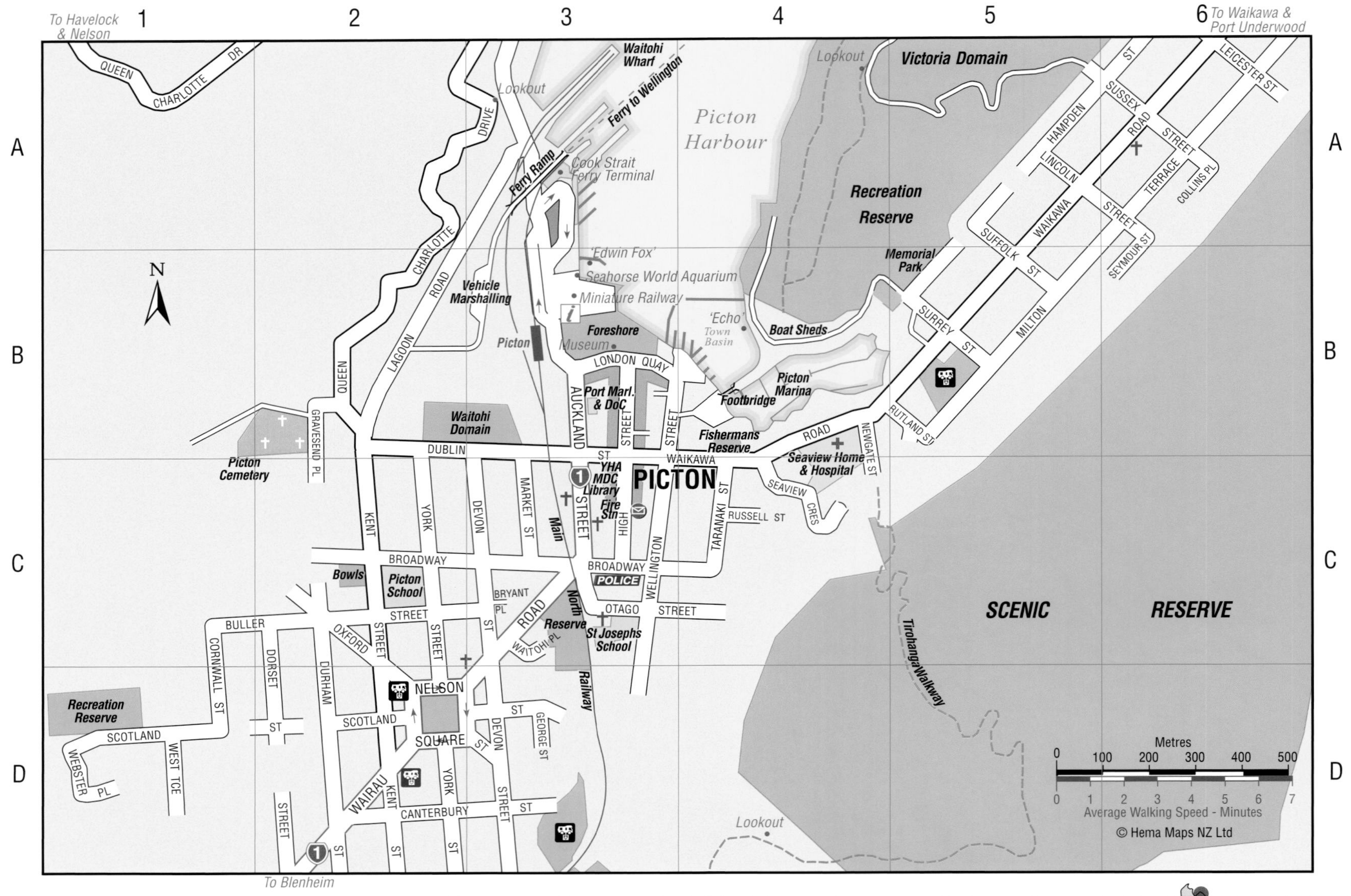

map 114 Picton Suburbs

For touring map see map 40

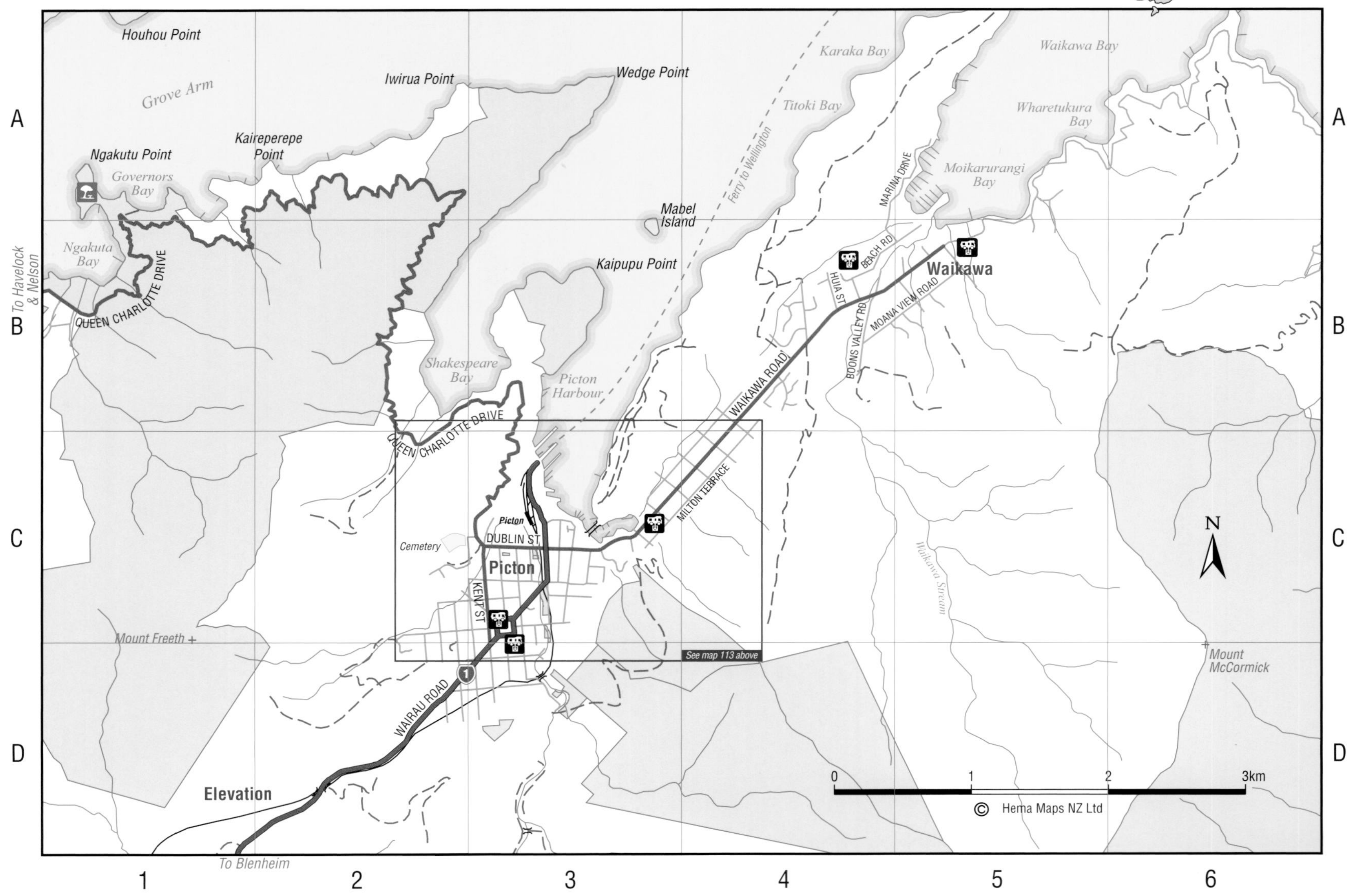

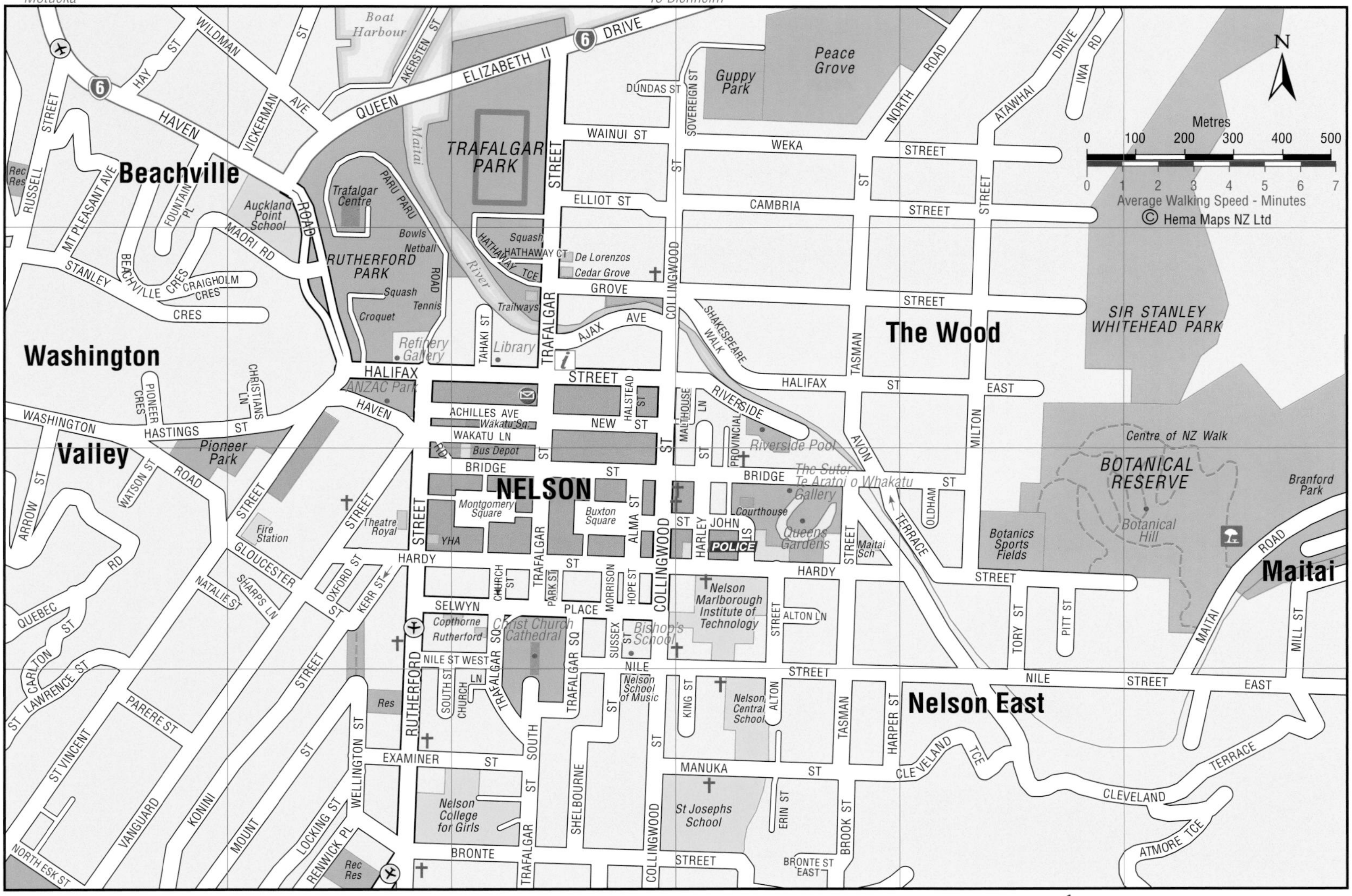

For touring map
see map 39

Nelson Suburbs

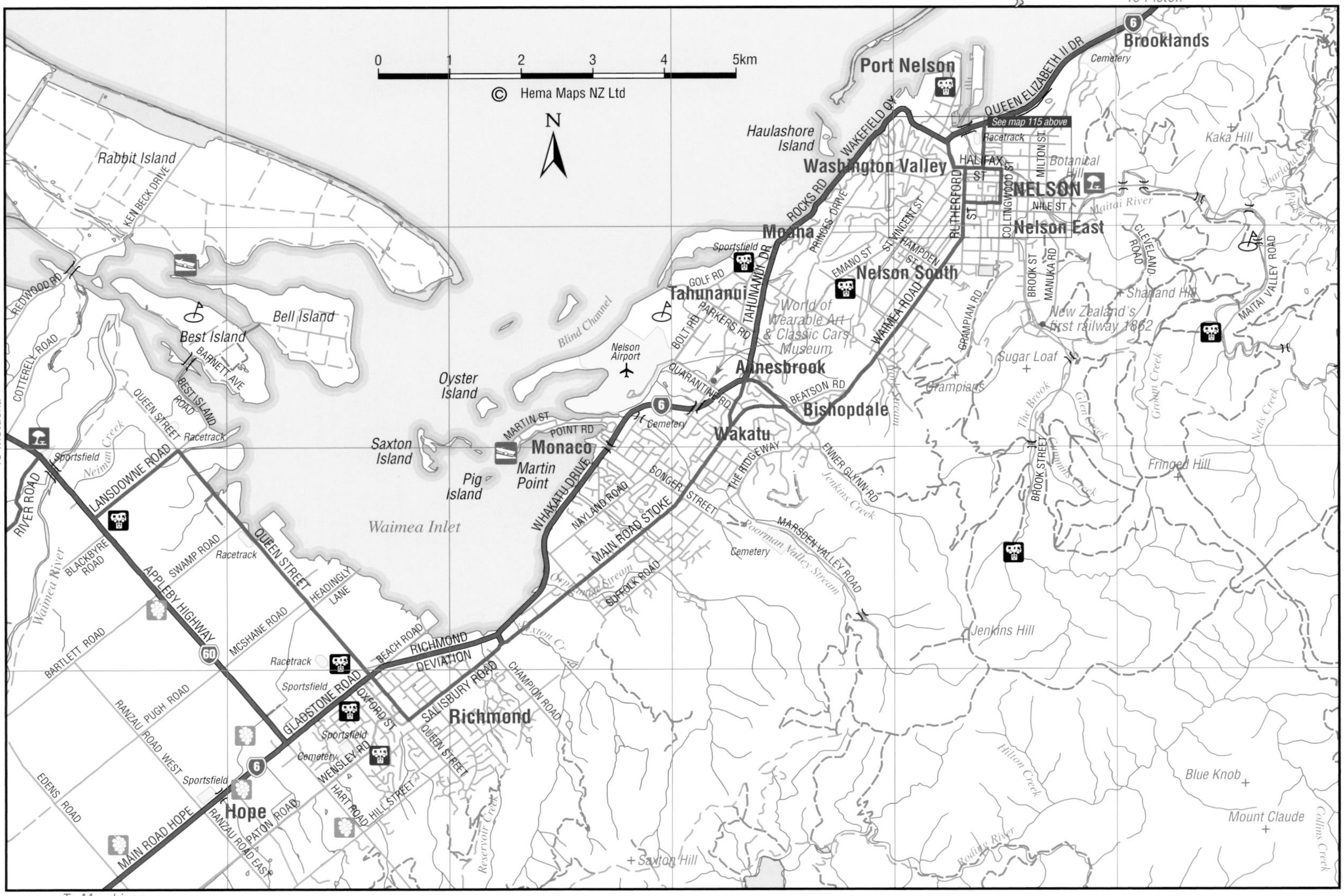

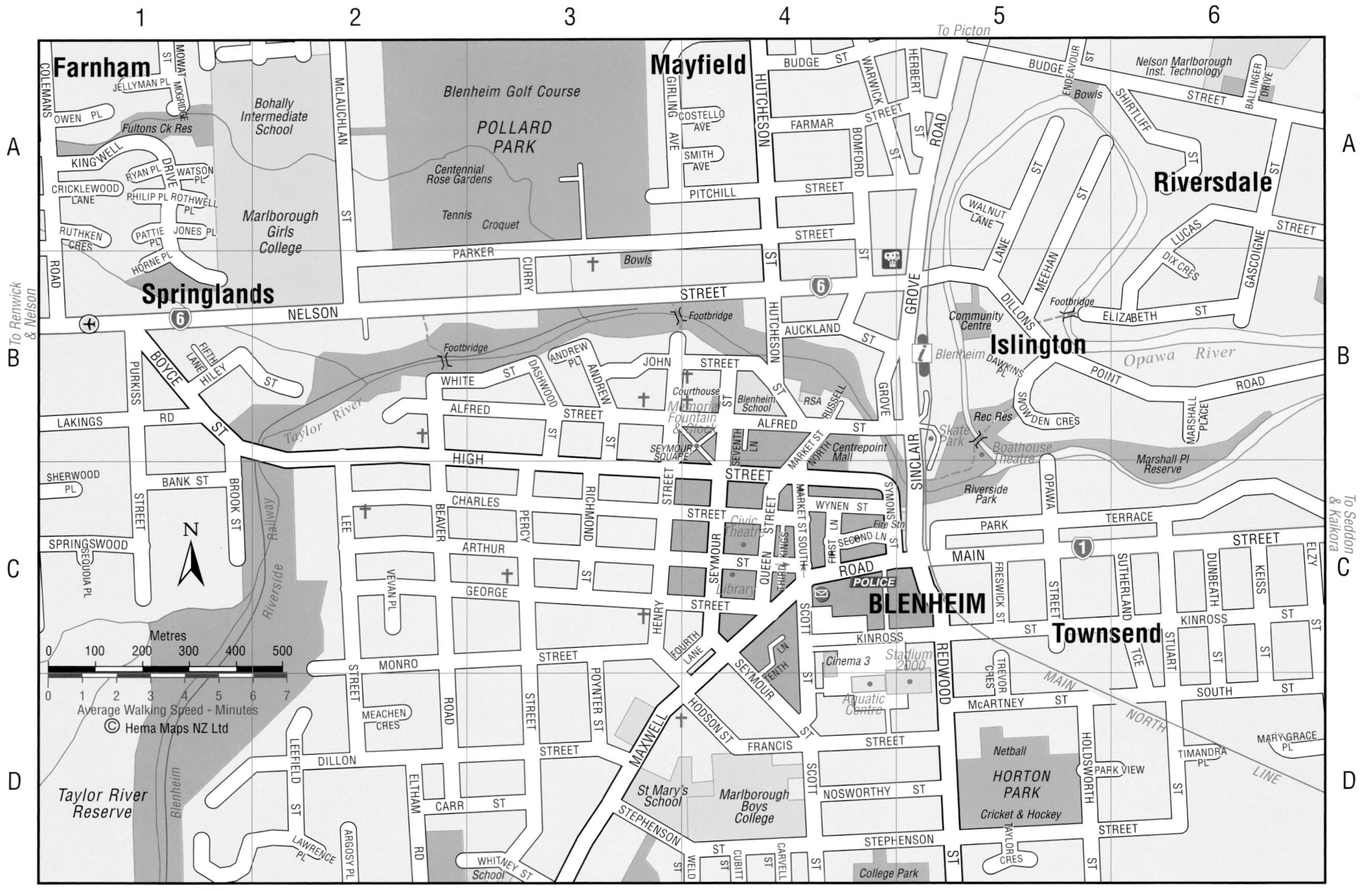

map 118 Greymouth CBD

For touring map see map 45

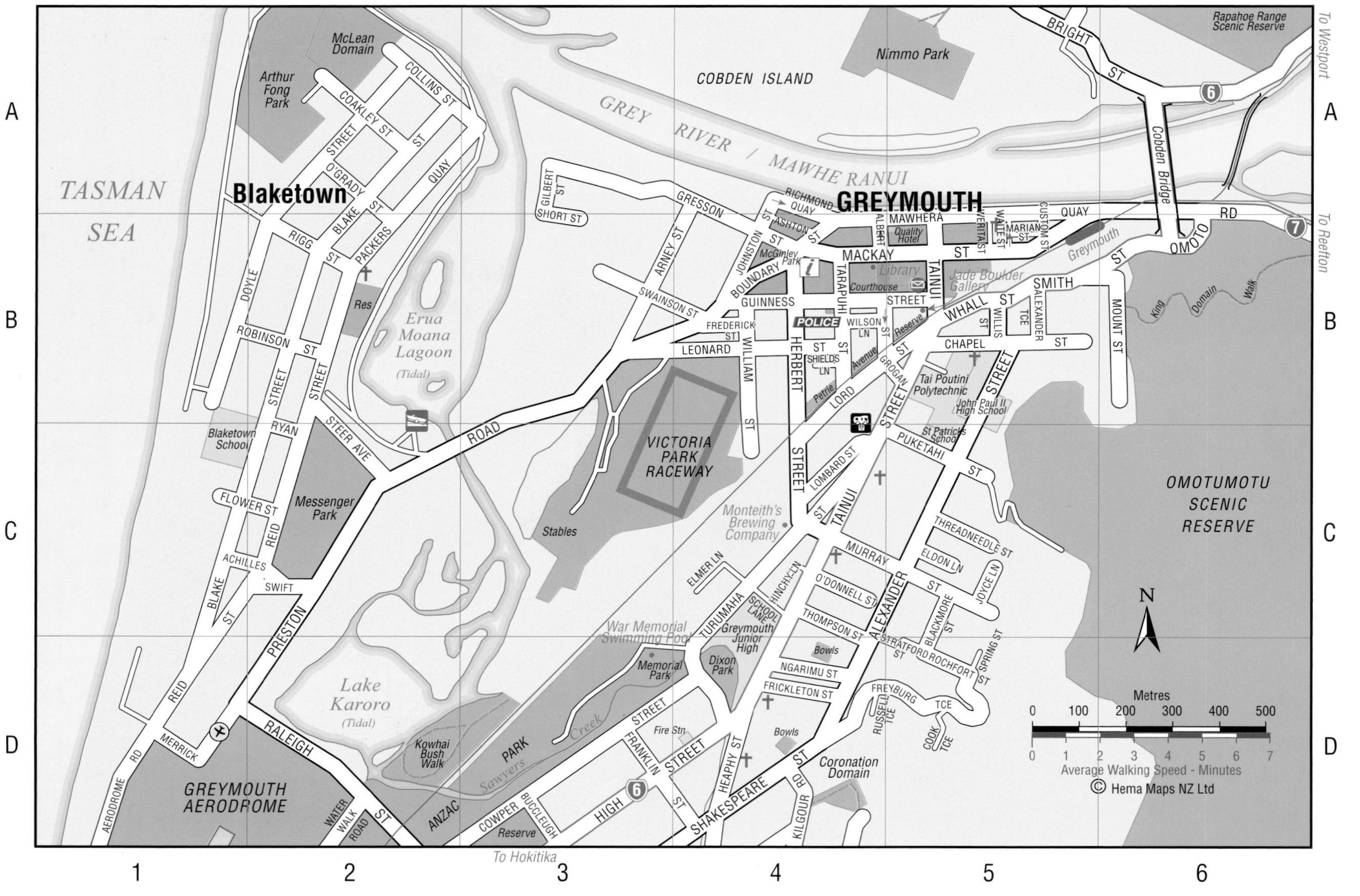

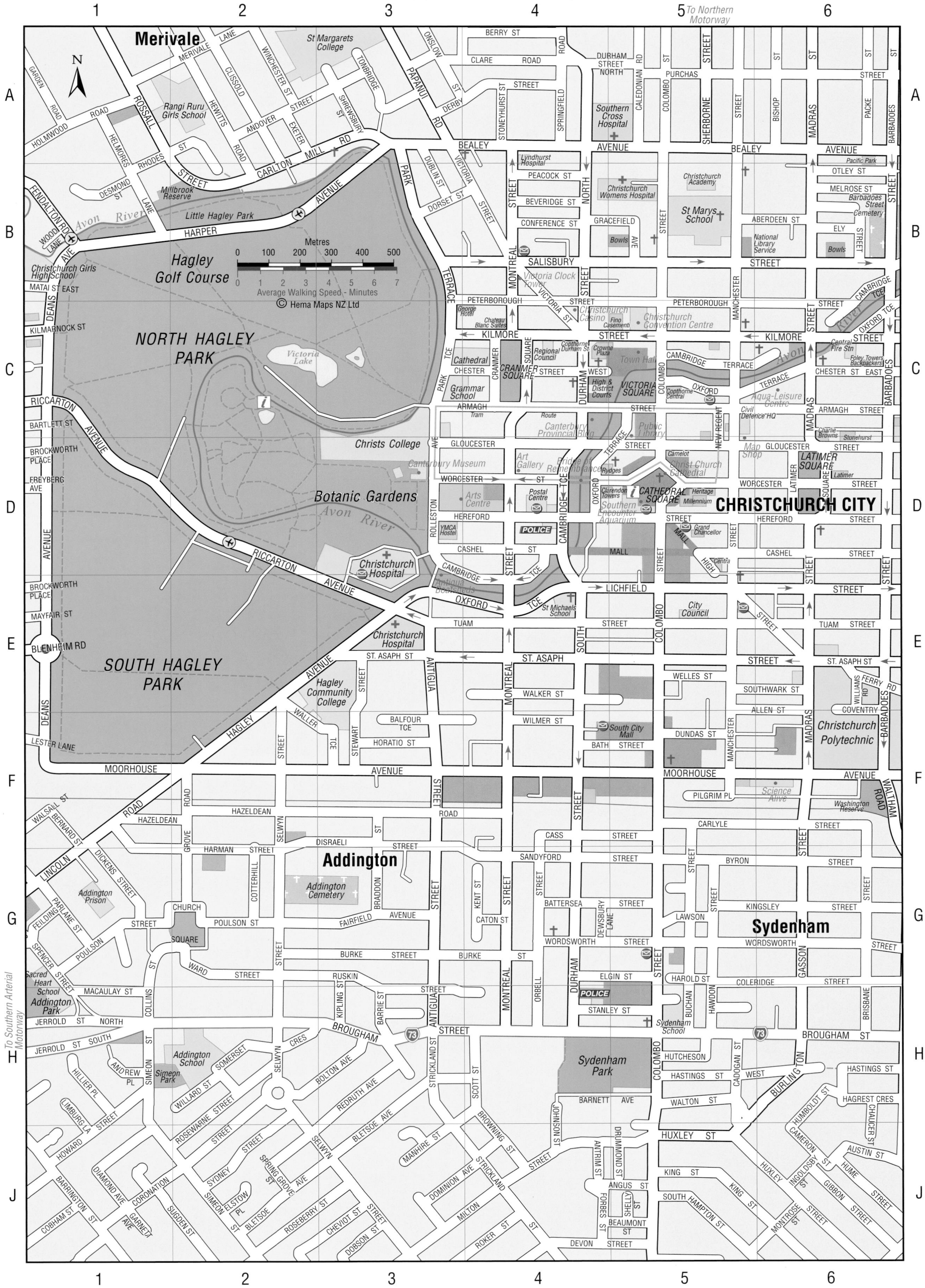
1
2
3
4
5
6
A
B
C
D
E
F
G
H
J
To Northern Motorway
To Southern Arterial Motorway
Merivale
N
Metres
0 100 200 300 400 500
0 1 2 3 4 5 6 7
Average Walking Speed - Minutes
© Hema Maps NZ Ltd
St Margarets College
Rangi Ruru Girls School
Millbrook Reserve
Little Hagley Park
Avon River
Hagley Golf Course
NORTH HAGLEY PARK
Victoria Lake
Christs College
Canterbury Museum
Botanic Gardens
Christchurch Hospital
SOUTH HAGLEY PARK
Christchurch Girls High School
Hagley Community College
Christchurch Hospital
Southern Cross Hospital
Lyndhurst Hospital
Christchurch Womens Hospital
Christchurch Academy
St Marys School
National Library Service
Bowls
Barbadoes Street Cemetery
Pacific Park
Victoria Clock Tower
George Hotel
Chateau Blanc Suites
Christchurch Casino
Fino Casementi
Christchurch Convention Centre
Cathedral Grammar School
CRANMER SQUARE
Regional Council
Copthorne Durham St
Crowne Plaza
Town Hall
High & District Courts
VICTORIA SQUARE
Copthorne Central
Aqua-Leisure Centre
Central Fire Stn
Foley Towers Backpackers
Tram Route
Canterbury Provincial Bldg
Public Library
Civil Defence HQ
Charlie Browns
Stonehurst
Art Gallery
Bridge of Remembrance
Rydges
Camelot
Christ Church Cathedral
Map Shop
LATIMER SQUARE
Latimer
Arts Centre
Postal Centre
Clarendon Towers
Southern Encounter Aquarium
CATHEDRAL SQUARE
Heritage
Millennium
CHRISTCHURCH CITY
YMCA Hostel
POLICE
Grand Chancellor
Centra
Antigua Boatsheds
St Michaels School
City Council
Christchurch Polytechnic
South City Mall
Science Alive
Washington Reserve
Addington
Addington Cemetery
Addington Prison
SQUARE
Sacred Heart School
Addington Park
Addington School
Simeon Park
Sydenham
POLICE
Sydenham School
Sydenham Park
73
BERRY ST
CLARE ROAD
DURHAM STREET NORTH
CALEDONIAN RD
PURCHAS
COLOMBO ST
SHERBORNE STREET
BISHOP ST
MADRAS ST
PACKE ST
BARBADOES ST
GARDEN ROAD
HOLMWOOD ROAD
ROSSALL ST
MERIVALE LANE
HEWITTS ROAD
CLISSOLD ST
WINCHESTER ST
ANDOVER STREET
EXETER ST
SHREWSBURY ST
TONBRIDGE ST
ONSLOW ST
PAPANUI RD
DERBY ST
STONEYHURST ST
SPRINGFIELD ROAD
HELMORES LANE
RHODES ST
CARLTON MILL RD
DESMOND ST
FENDALTON RD
WOOD LANE
HARPER AVENUE
BEALEY AVENUE
DUBLIN ST
VICTORIA STREET
DORSET ST
PARK TERRACE
PEACOCK ST
BEVERIDGE ST
CONFERENCE ST
GRACEFIELD AVE
NORTH STREET
ABERDEEN ST
OTLEY ST
MELROSE ST
ELY
MONTREAL STREET
SALISBURY STREET
PETERBOROUGH STREET
MANCHESTER STREET
CAMBRIDGE TCE
OXFORD TCE
KILMORE STREET
CAMBRIDGE TERRACE
CHESTER STREET
CHESTER ST EAST
CRAMMER SQUARE
DURHAM ST
OXFORD TCE
ARMAGH STREET
NEW REGENT ST
GLOUCESTER STREET
WORCESTER ST
WORCESTER STREET
HEREFORD STREET
ROLLESTON AVE
CASHEL STREET
MALL
HIGH ST
LICHFIELD STREET
TUAM STREET
ST. ASAPH ST
ANTIGUA ST
SOUTH ST
WELLES ST
SOUTHWARK ST
ALLEN ST
WILLIAMS ST
FERRY RD
COVENTRY
WALKER ST
WILMER ST
BALFOUR TCE
WALLER TCE
STEWART ST
HORATIO ST
DUNDAS ST
BATH STREET
MOORHOUSE AVENUE
PILGRIM PL
WALTHAM ROAD
MATAI ST EAST
KILMARNOCK ST
DEANS AVE
RICCARTON AVENUE
BARTLETT ST
BROCKWORTH PLACE
FREYBERG AVE
MAYFAIR ST
BLENHEIM RD
LESTER LANE
HAGLEY AVENUE
WALSALL ST
BERNARD ST
HAZELDEAN ROAD
LINCOLN ROAD
GROVE ROAD
HARMAN STREET
SELWYN ST
DISRAELI STREET
STRICKLAND STREET
CASS STREET
CARLYLE STREET
SANDYFORD STREET
BYRON STREET
DICKENS STREET
COTTERHILL
BRADDON
KENT ST
CATON ST
BATTERSEA STREET
DEWSBURY LANE
LAWSON
KINGSLEY STREET
PARLANE ST
FEILDING
CHURCH SQUARE
POULSON ST
FAIRFIELD AVENUE
WORDSWORTH STREET
GASSON STREET
SPENCER STREET
WARD STREET
BURKE STREET
RUSKIN STREET
ORBELL
HAROLD ST
ELGIN ST
HAWDON
BUCHAN
COLERIDGE STREET
BRISBANE
MACAULAY ST
COLLINS ST
KIPLING ST
BARRIE ST
STANLEY ST
BROUGHAM STREET
BROUGHAM ST
JERROLD ST NORTH
JERROLD ST SOUTH
ANDREW PL
HILLIER PL
SOMERSET
SELWYN CRES
BOLTON AVE
WILLARD ST
REDRUTH AVE
SCOTT ST
HUTCHESON
HASTINGS ST WEST
CADOGAN ST
BURLINGTON ST
HASTINGS ST
HAGREST CRES
HUMBOLDT ST
CHAUCER ST
BARNETT AVE
WALTON ST
JOHNSON ST
LIMBURG LA
HOWARD STREET
ROSEWARNE STREET
BLETSOE AVE
BROWNING ST
HUXLEY ST
CAMERON
AUSTIN ST
BARRINGTON ST
DIAMOND AVE
CORONATION
SYDNEY STREET
SPRING GROVE ST
MANHIRE ST
DOMINION AVE
ANTRIM ST
DRUMMOND ST
KING ST
INGOLDSBY ST
HUME
ANGUS ST
SOUTH HAMPTON ST
GIBBON STREET
COBHAM ST
GARNETT AVE
SUGDEN ST
SIMEON ST
ELSTOW PL
ROSEBERRY ST
CHEVIOT ST
MILTON
FORBES ST
SHELLY ST
MONTROSE ST
DOBSON ST
ROKER ST
BEAUMONT ST
DEVON STREET

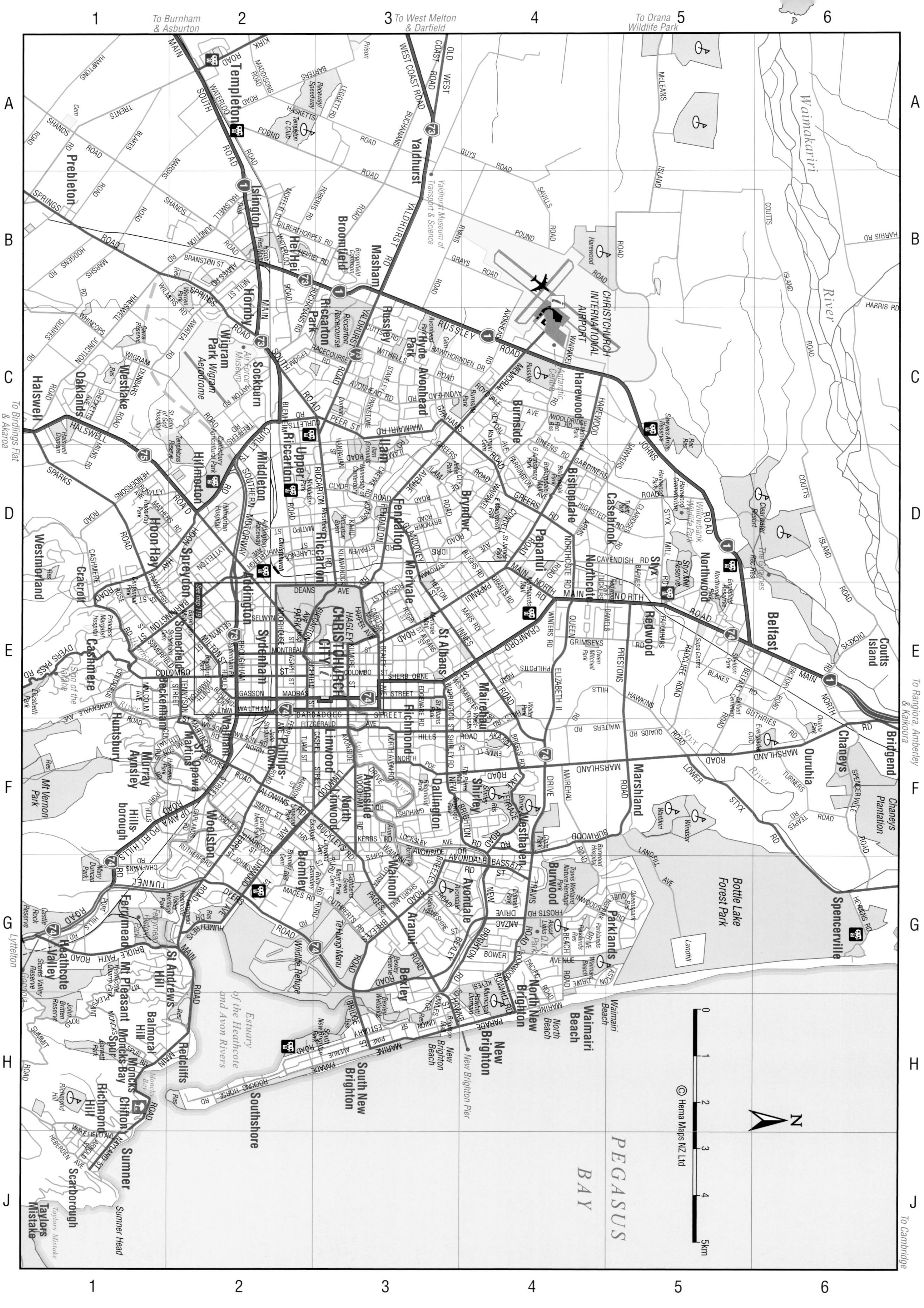

To Burnham & Asburton
To West Melton & Darfield
To Orana Wildlife Park
To Birdlings Flat & Akaroa
To Rangiora, Amberley & Kaikoura
To Cambridge
Lyttelton
Templeton
Prebleton
Islington
Yaldhurst
Yaldhurst Museum of Transport & Science
Broomfield
Hei Hei
Masham
Hornby
Riccarton Park
Russley
Hyde Park
Avonhead
Wigram
Park Wigram Aerodrome
Air Force Museum
Sockburn
Halswell
Oaklands
Westlake
Hillmorton
Middleton
Upper Riccarton
Ilam
Burnside
Harewood
CHRISTCHURCH INTERNATIONAL AIRPORT
Bishopdale
Casebrook
Bryndwr
Fendalton
Papanui
Northcote
Styx
Northwood
Belfast
Coutts Island
Westmorland
Cracroft
Hoon Hay
Spreydon
Addington
Riccarton
Merivale
St Albans
Redwood
Cashmere
Somerfield
Sydenham
CHRISTCHURCH CITY
Hagley Park
Beckenham
Huntsbury
Waltham
Phillipstown
Linwood
Richmond
Mairehau
Shirley
Marshland
Chaneys
Bridgend
Ouruhia
Murray Aynsley
St Martins
Opawa
Woolston
Avonside
North Linwood
Dallington
Westhaven
Burwood
Spencerville
Chaneys Plantation
Mt Vernon Park
Hillsborough
Wainoni
Avondale
Aranui
Parklands
Bottle Lake Forest Park
Landfill
Ferrymead
Heathcote Valley
St Andrews Hill
Bromley
Bexley
North New Brighton
Waimairi Beach
Mt Pleasant
Balmoral Hill
Redcliffs
Moncks Spur
Moncks Bay
Clifton
Richmond Hill
Estuary of the Heathcote and Avon Rivers
Wildlife Refuge
South New Brighton
New Brighton
New Brighton Pier
Southshore
Sumner
Scarborough
Taylors Mistake
Sumner Head
Waimakariri River
Styx River
PEGASUS BAY
© Hema Maps NZ Ltd
0 1 2 3 4 5km
N
See map 119
1 2 3 4 5 6
A B C D E F G H J

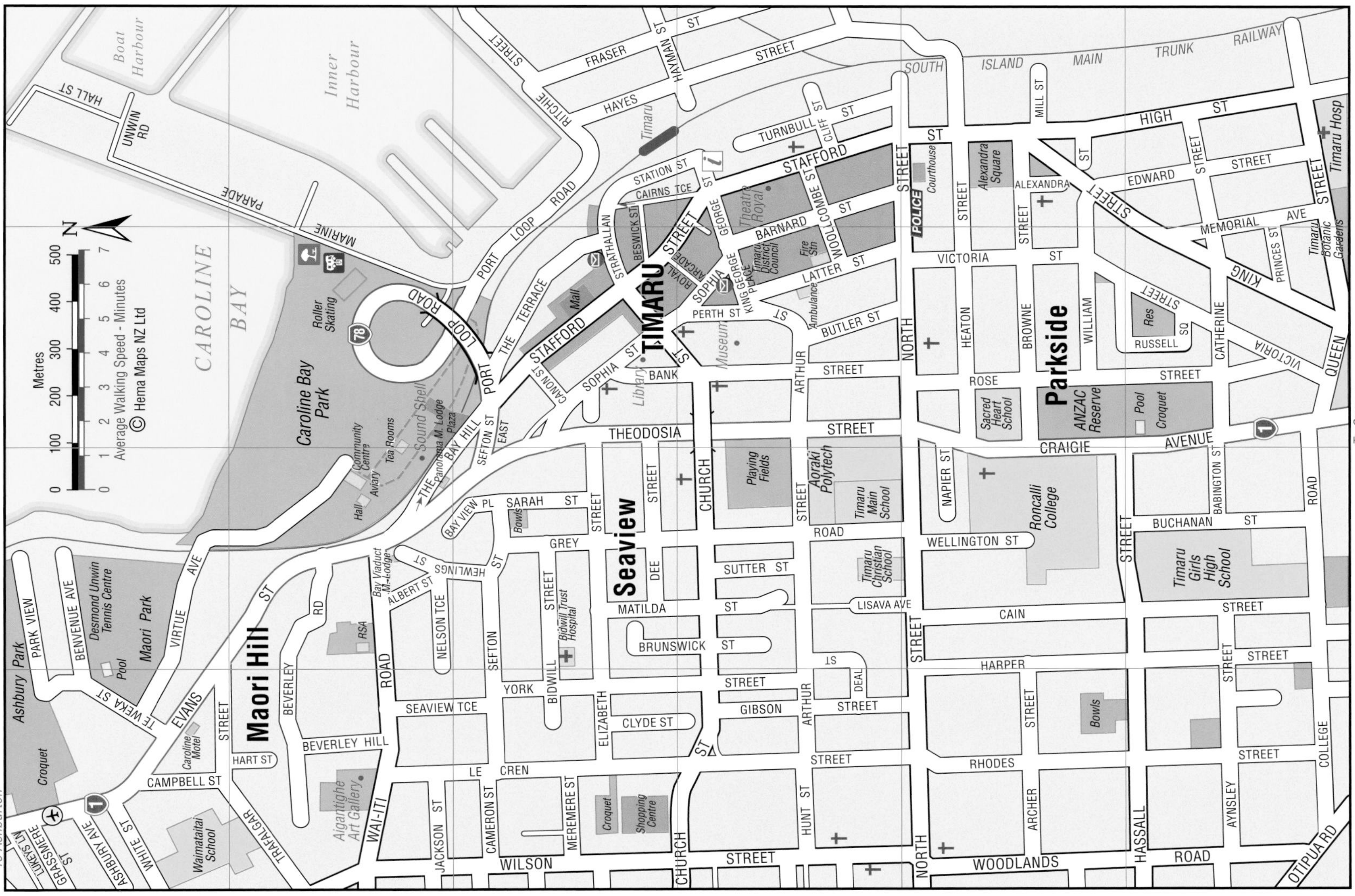
CAROLINE BAY
Caroline Bay Park
Inner Harbour
Boat Harbour
MARINE PARADE
TIMARU
Seaview
Maori Hill
Parkside
Maori Park
Ashbury Park
Roncalli College
Timaru Girls High School
Aoraki Polytech
Timaru Main School
Timaru Christian School
Sacred Heart School
ANZAC Reserve
Alexandra Square
Courthouse
Theatre Royal
Timaru District Council
Museum
Library
Aigantighe Art Gallery
Waimataitai School
Desmond Unwin Tennis Centre
Bidwill Trust Hospital
Timaru Hosp
Timaru Botanic Gardens
STAFFORD STREET
THEODOSIA STREET
CRAIGIE AVENUE
NORTH STREET
CHURCH STREET
WAI-ITI ROAD
WILSON STREET
WOODLANDS ROAD
HIGH ST
To Ashburton
To Oamaru
Metres
Average Walking Speed - Minutes
© Hema Maps NZ Ltd

Oamaru CBD

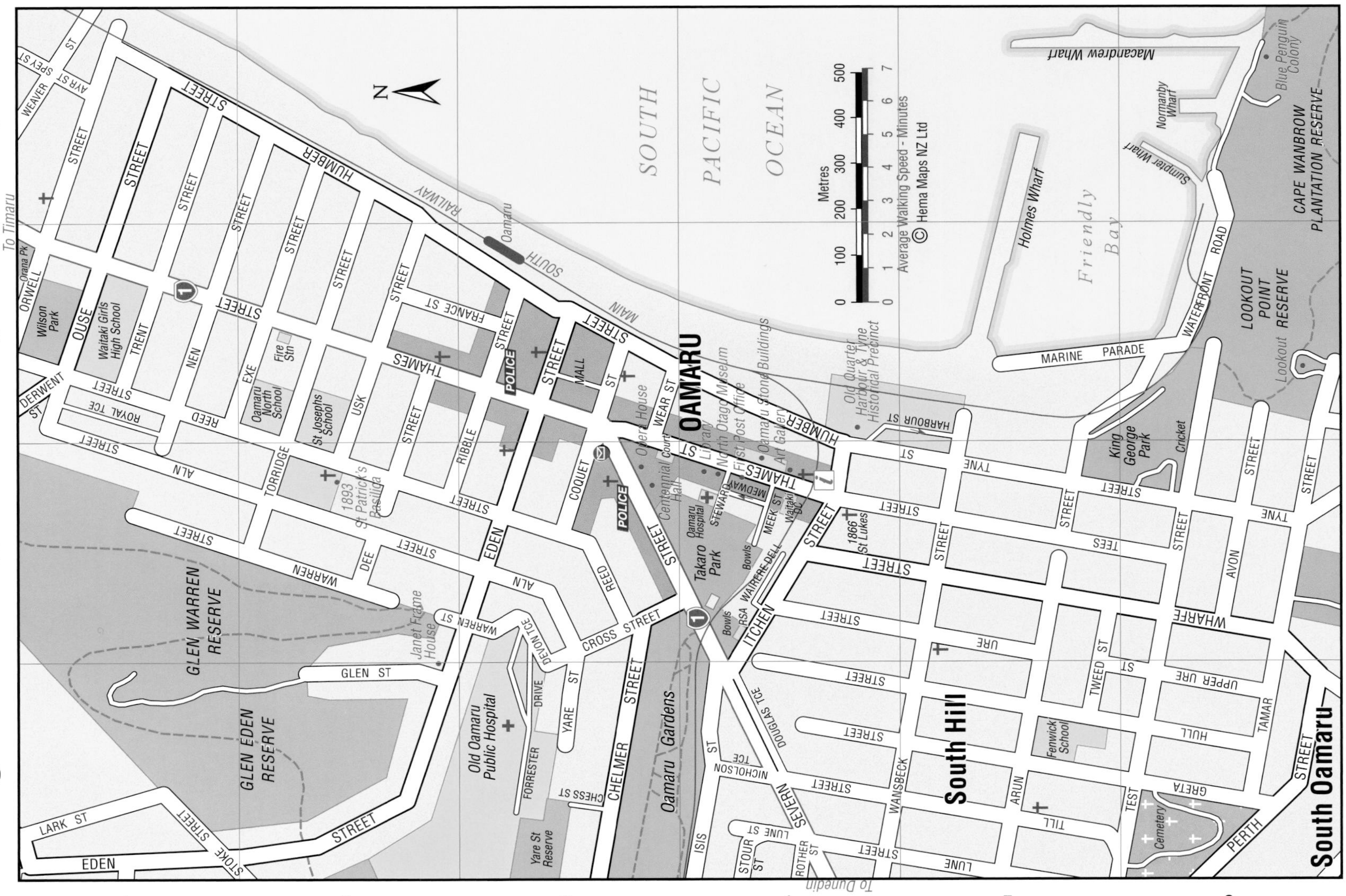
SOUTH PACIFIC OCEAN
Friendly Bay
Holmes Wharf
Macandrew Wharf
Normanby Wharf
Sumpter Wharf
OAMARU
South Hill
South Oamaru
THAMES STREET
HUMBER STREET
Wilson Park
Waitaki Girls High School
Oamaru North School
St Josephs School
1893 St Patrick's Basilica
Opera House
Centennial Court
Takaro Park
Oamaru Gardens
Old Oamaru Public Hospital
Yare St Reserve
GLEN WARREN RESERVE
GLEN EDEN RESERVE
Janet Frame House
North Otago Museum
First Post Office
Oamaru Stone Buildings
Old Quarter Harbour & Tyne Historical Precinct
King George Park
LOOKOUT POINT RESERVE
CAPE WANBROW PLANTATION RESERVE
Blue Penguin Colony
1866 St Lukes
Fenwick School
Cemetery
To Timaru
To Dunedin
Metres
Average Walking Speed - Minutes
© Hema Maps NZ Ltd

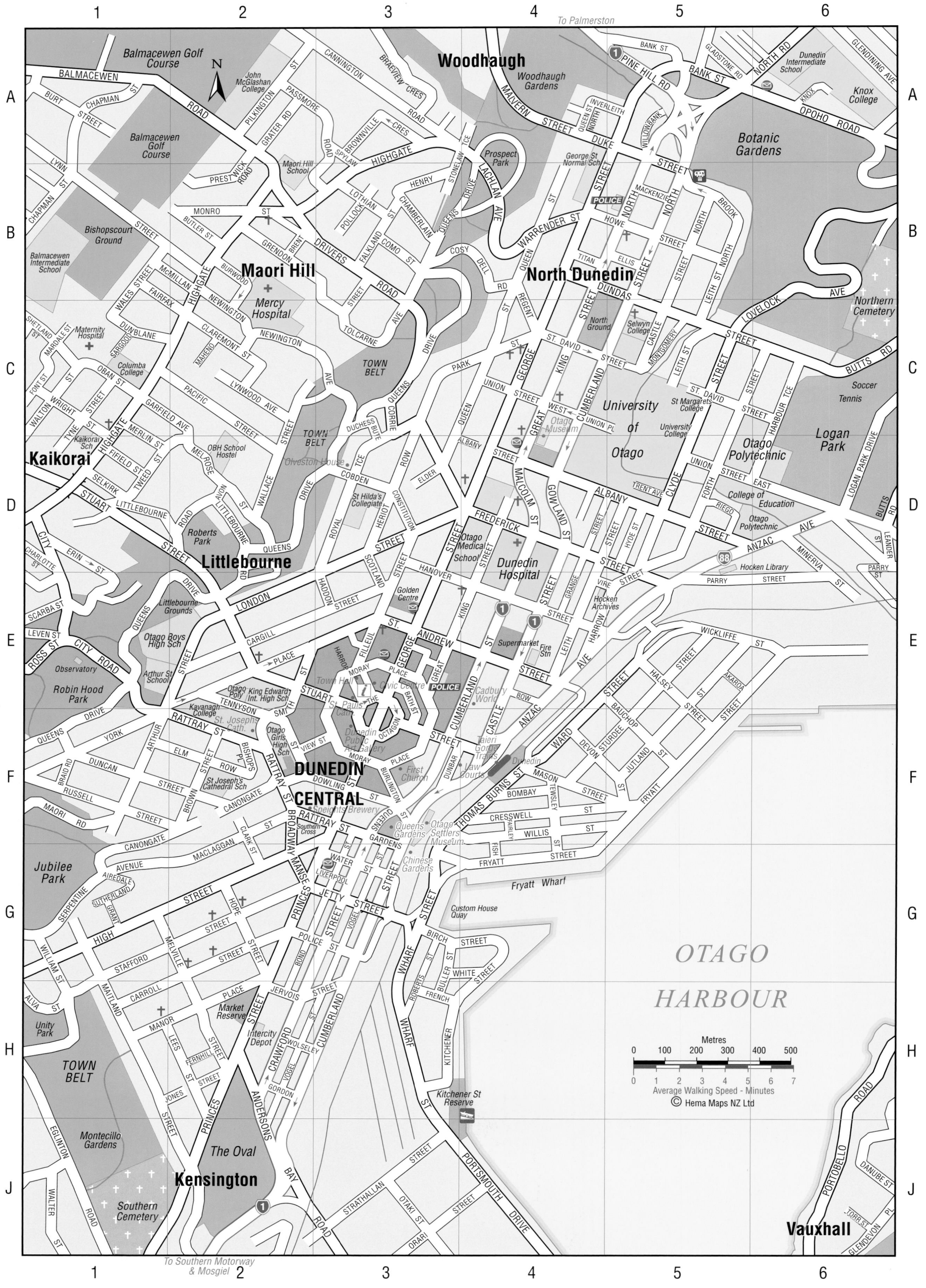

To Palmerston
Woodhaugh
Woodhaugh Gardens
Balmacewen Golf Course
John McGlashan College
Maori Hill
Mercy Hospital
Maori Hill School
Prospect Park
North Dunedin
George St Normal Sch
POLICE
Botanic Gardens
Dunedin Intermediate School
Knox College
Northern Cemetery
Bishopscourt Ground
Balmacewen Intermediate School
Maternity Hospital
Columba College
TOWN BELT
North Ground
Selwyn College
University of Otago
St Margarets College
University College
Otago Museum
Otago Polytechnic
Logan Park
Soccer
Tennis
College of Education
Kaikorai
Kaikorai Sch
OBH School Hostel
Olveston House
St Hilda's Collegiate
Otago Medical School
Dunedin Hospital
Hocken Library
Hocken Archives
Roberts Park
Littlebourne
Littlebourne Grounds
Otago Boys High Sch
Observatory
Robin Hood Park
Arthur St School
Golden Centre
Supermarket
Fire Stn
Town Hall
Civic Centre
Cadbury World
Otago Poly
King Edward Int. High Sch
Kavanagh College
St. Joseph's Cath.
St. Paul's Cath.
Otago Girls High Sch
Dunedin Public Art Gallery
First Church
Law Courts
Taieri Gorge Trains
Dunedin
DUNEDIN CENTRAL
St Joseph's Cathedral Sch
Speights Brewery
Southern Cross
Queens Gardens
Otago Settlers Museum
Chinese Gardens
Jubilee Park
Fryatt Wharf
Custom House Quay
OTAGO HARBOUR
Market Reserve
Intercity Depot
Unity Park
TOWN BELT
Montecillo Gardens
The Oval
Kensington
Southern Cemetery
Kitchener St Reserve
Vauxhall
Metres
0 100 200 300 400 500
0 1 2 3 4 5 6 7
Average Walking Speed - Minutes
© Hema Maps NZ Ltd
To Southern Motorway & Mosgiel
1 2 3 4 5 6
A B C D E F G H J

For touring map
see map 74

Dunedin Suburbs

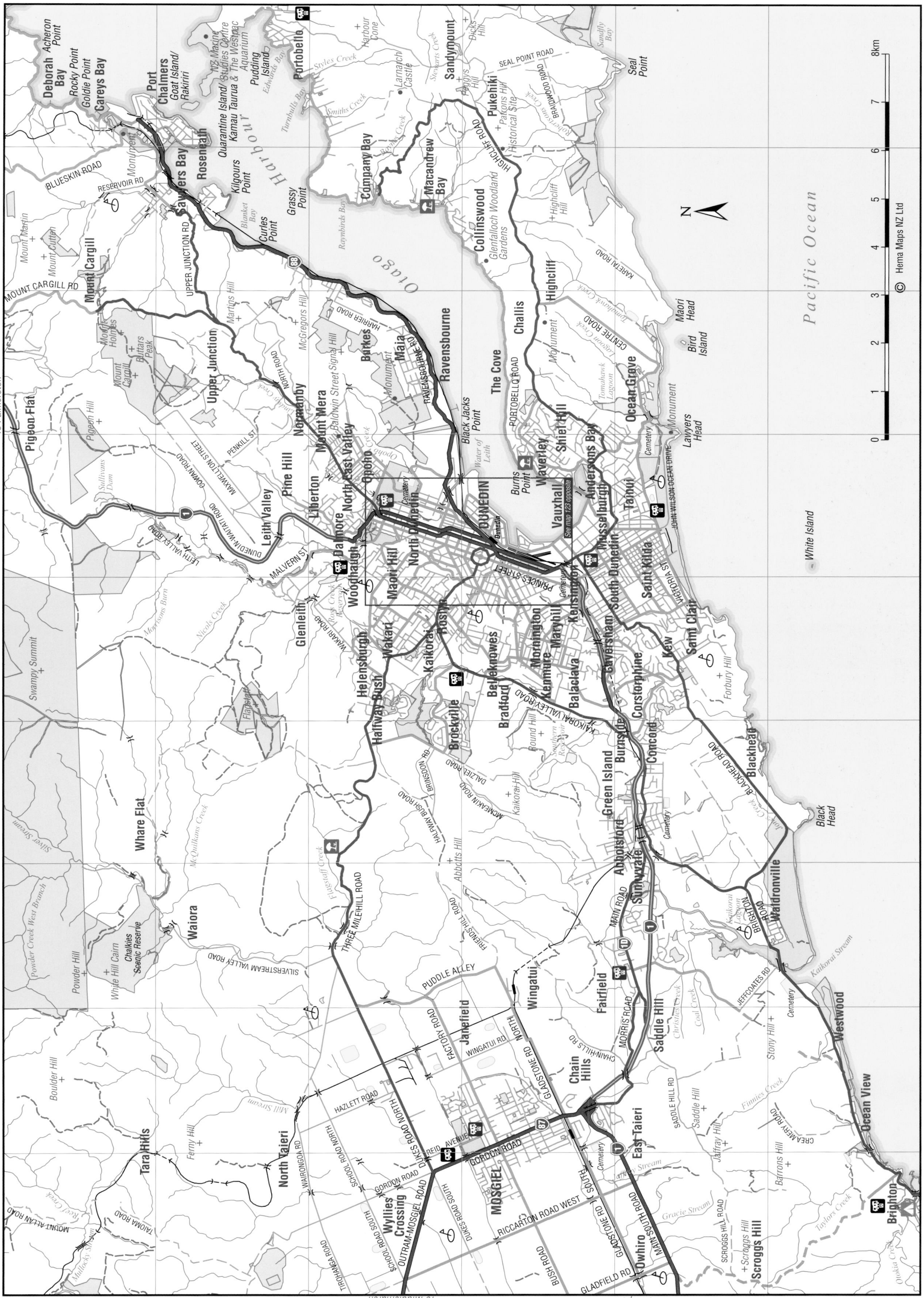

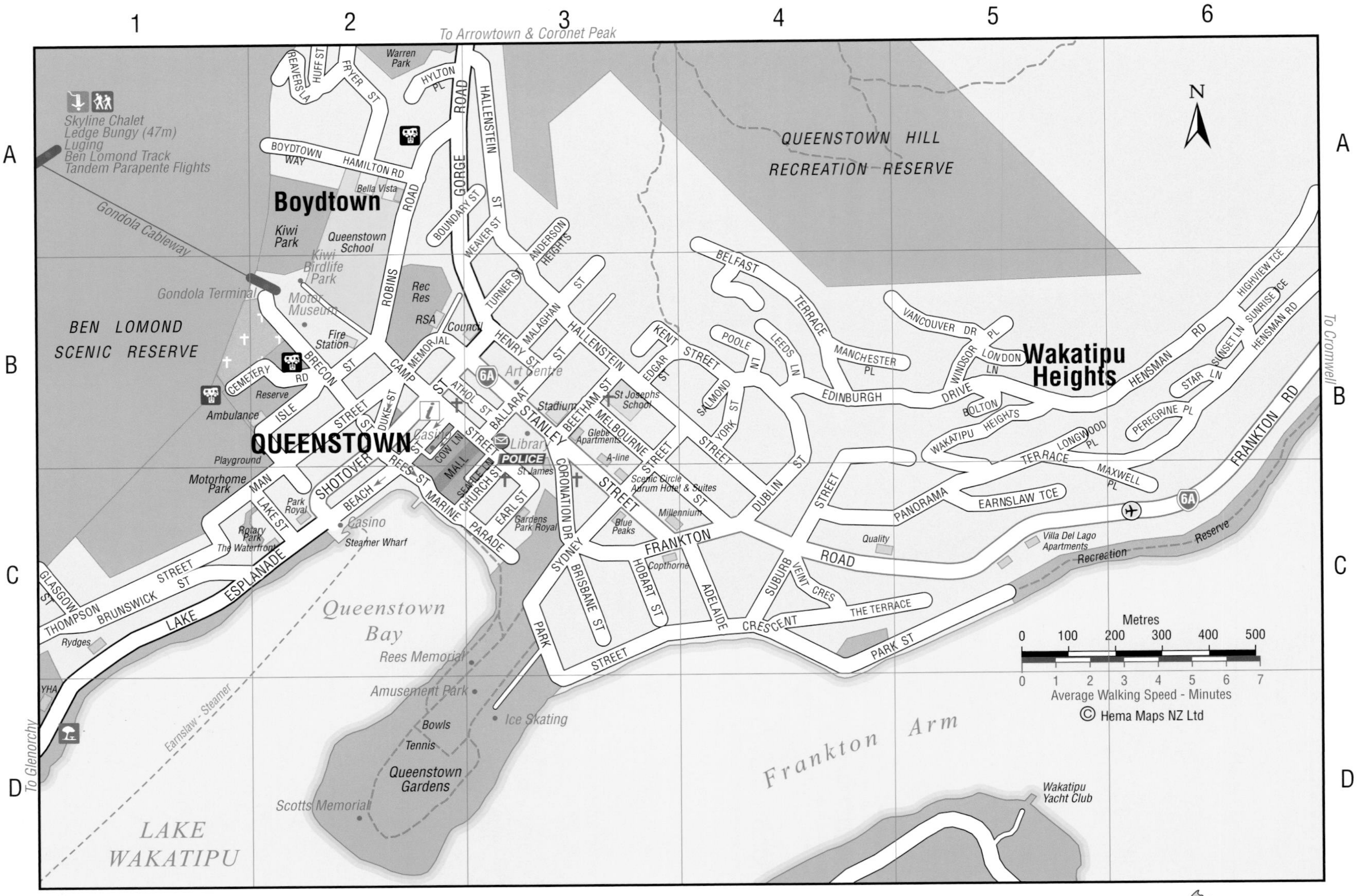

Queenstown Suburbs

For touring map see map 65

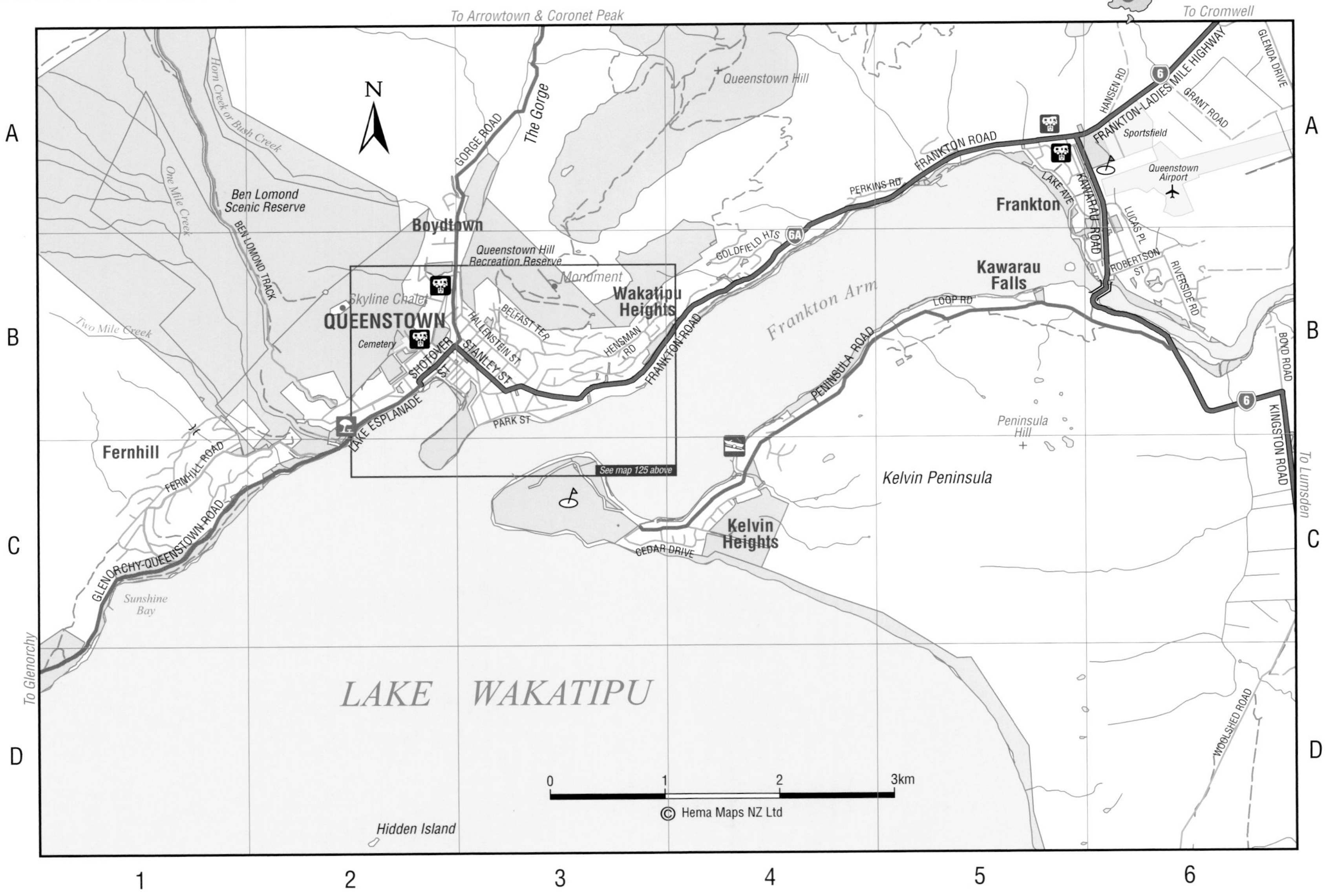

Invercargill CBD

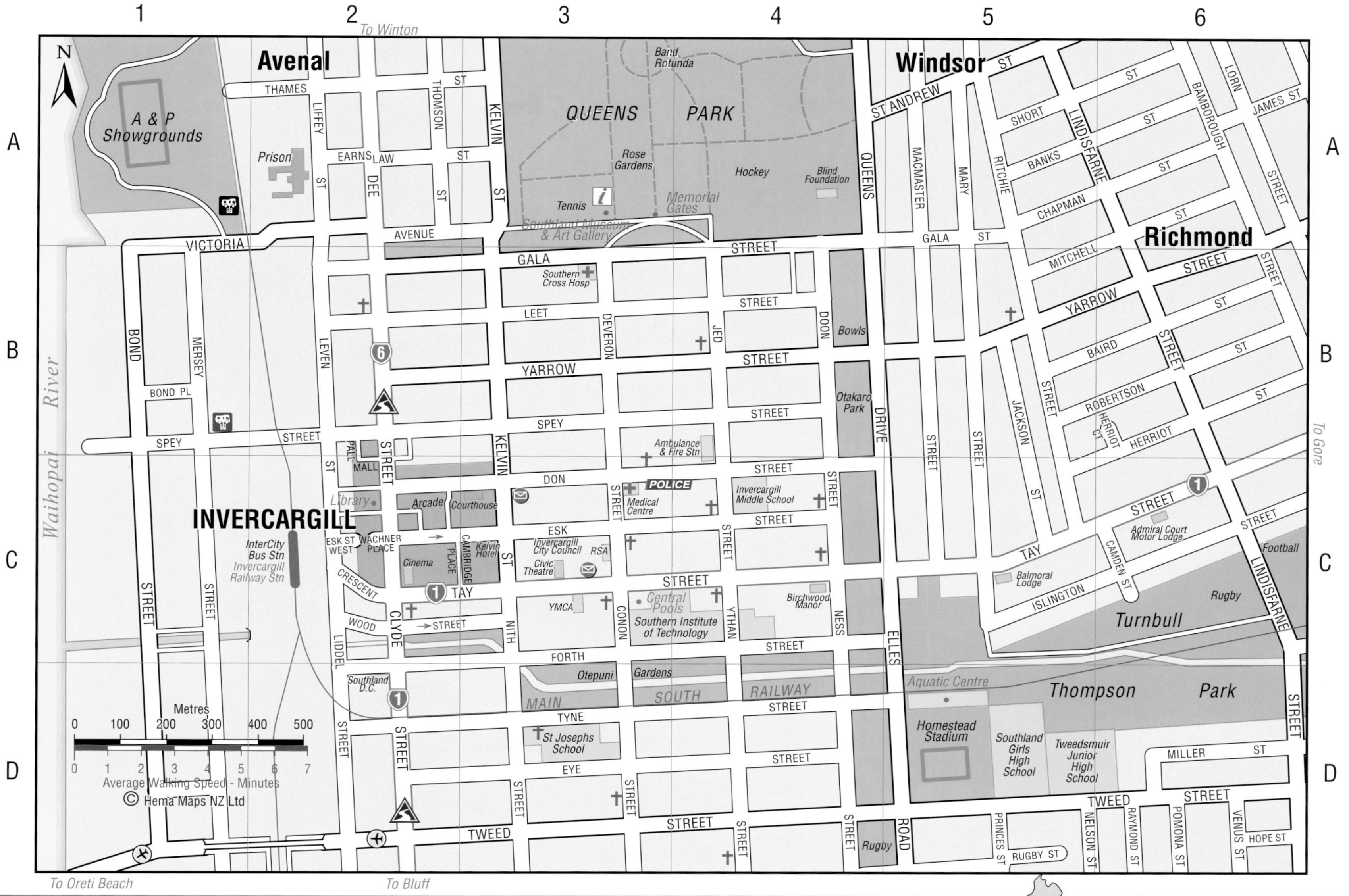

For touring map see map 77

Invercargill Suburbs

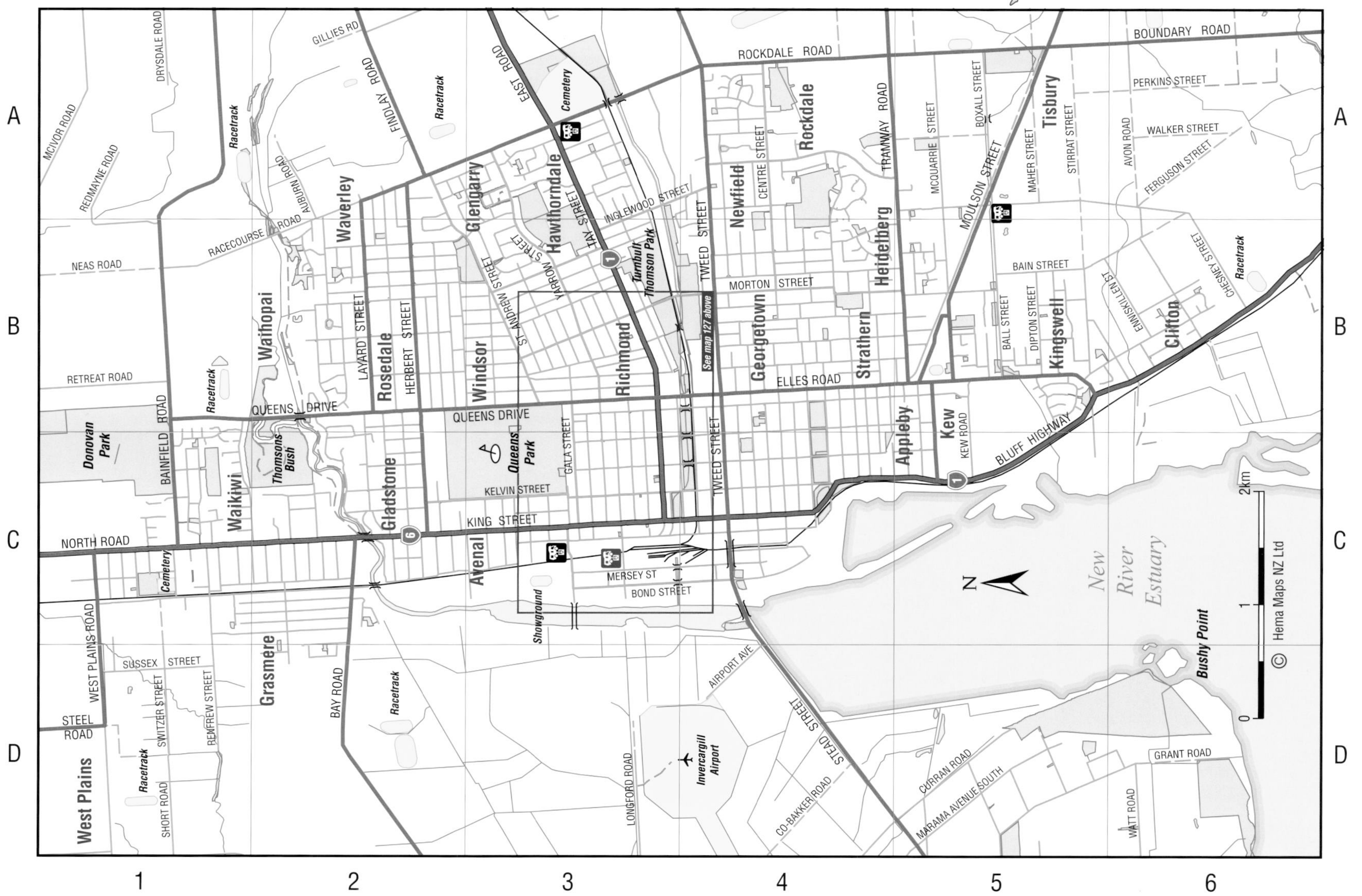

Kingston, South Island Photo: Michelle Bignell

International dump station/waste disposal signs for black and grey waste water.

Motorhome Park / Caravan Park with Dump Station (Wastewater Disposal Site)

Motorhome Dump Station (Wastewater Disposal Site)

The disposal of waste from the sink, shower (grey) and toilet (black) is to be made at dump station/waste disposal sites. The locations listed here refer to most of the symbols shown on the maps. There may be a charge for using a dump station at some camping grounds, unless you are staying there. Some dump stations on septic tanks may limit their availability during peak times.
Under no circumstances is it acceptable to dispose of wastewater in rubbish disposal facilities.
For more information see Ministry of Tourism brochure: Finding a dump station in NZ

For more information on campsites, caravan parks and motorhome parks see Hema Maps' **NZ Motorhome & Camping Atlas**.

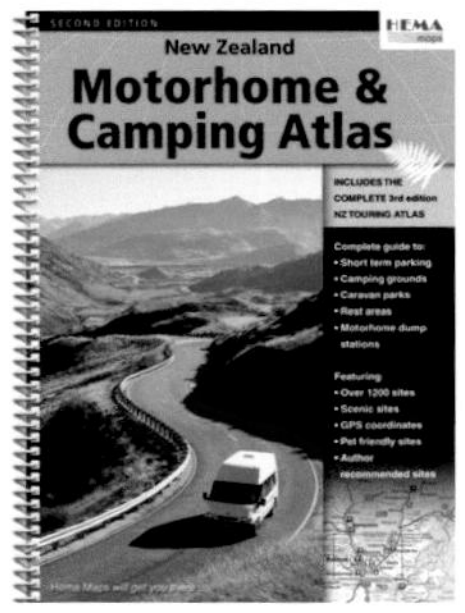

Motorhome Park/Caravan Park with dump station (wastewater disposal site)

NORTH ISLAND

Far North

Pukenui Holiday Park (1 F5) – Lamb Rd, Pukenui; 45km north of Kaitaia; Opposite Pukenui School: (09) 409 8803
Wagener Holiday Motor Camp (Houhora Heads Motor Camp) (1 F5) – On Houhora Heads Rd, Houhora; Opposite Wagener Museum: (09) 409 8564
Norfolk Campervan Park (1 H6) – Cnr SH1 & SH10; 300m from Awanui: (09) 406 7515
The Park Top 10 Ninety Mile Beach (1 H4) – West Coast Rd, Waipapakauri;18km north of Kaitaia: (09) 406 7298
Kaitaia Holiday Park (1 J6) – Adjacent SH1 at the south end of Kaitaia: (09) 408 1212
Ahipara Backpackers & Motor Camp (1 J5) – Takahe St, Ahipara: (09) 409 4864
Whatuwhiwhi Top 10 Holiday Park (2 F7) – 17 Whatuwhiwhi Rd, Karikari Peninsula; RD 3, Kaitaia: (09) 408 7202
Hihi Beach Holiday Camp (2 G9) – 58 Hihi Rd, Mangonui: (09) 406 0307
Whangaroa Harbour Holiday Park (2 H10) – Whangaroa Harbour, Kaeo: (09) 405 0306
Matauri Bay Holiday Park (2 H12) – Matauri Bay, Whangaroa: (09) 405 0525
Tauranga Bay Holiday Park (2 H11) – Tauranga Bay, Whangaroa; 17.5km from Kaeo: (09) 405 0436
Kerikeri Top 10 Holiday Park (4 A8) – Aranga Drive, 500m south of town centre; Opposite BP Service Station, Kerikeri: (09) 407 9326
Hideaway Lodge (4 A8) – Wiroa Rd, Kerikeri: (09) 407 9773
Gibby's Place (4 A8) – 331 Kerikeri Rd, Kerikeri: (09) 407 9024
Wagon Train RV Park (4 A9) – SH10, Kerikeri: (09) 407 7889
Waitangi Holiday Park (4 B9) – 21 Tahuna Rd, Waitangi: (09) 402 7866
Beachside Holiday Park (4 B10) – Opua-Paihia Rd, 2.5km south of Paihia: (09) 402 7678
Bay of Islands Holiday Park (4 B9) – Puketona Rd, Paihia: (09) 402 7646
Haruru Falls Resort, 'Panorama' (4 B9) – Old Wharf Rd, Haruru Falls; 5 min from Paihia: (09) 402 7525
Twin Pines Holiday Park (4 B9) – Puketona Rd, RD 1, Paihia: (09) 402 7322
Russell Top 10 Holiday Park (4 B10) – Long Beach Rd, Russell: (09) 403 7826
Orongo Bay Holiday Park (4 B10) – 5960 Russell Rd: (09) 403 7704
Taupo Bay Camping Ground (2 G10) – 1070 Taupo Bay Rd: (09) 406 0315
Millenium Nocturnal Glowworm & Ostrich Park (2J7) – Fairburn Road, Katia: (027) 896 816

Northland

Dargaville Holiday Park (3 J7) – 10 Onslow St, Dargaville: (09) 439 8296
Dargaville Campervan Park (3 J7) – 18 Gladstone St, Dargaville: (09) 439 8479
Kauri Coast Top 10 Holiday Park (3 G6) – Trounson Park Rd, Kaihu: (09) 439 0621
Baylys Beach Holiday Park (3 J6) – 22-24 Seaview Rd; 800m from beach: (09) 439 6349
Matakohe Top 10 Holiday Park (5 B5) – Church Rd, Matakohe: (09) 431 6431
Paparoa Motor Camp (5 B6) – Cnr SH12 & Pahi Rd, Paparoa: (09) 431 6515
Pahi Beach Motor Camp (5 B6) **–** Enter Pahi Domain and drive through to public toilets on right of wharf, Pahi: (09) 431 7322
Kellys Bay Reserve (5 D5) – Dale Rd, Kellys Bay, Pouto Peninsula: (09) 439 4204
Pakiri Beach Holiday Park (6 D10) – Pakiri River Rd, RD 2 Wellsford, Pakiri: (09) 422 6199
Tutukaka Holiday Park (4 E13) – Matapour Rd, Tutukaka: (09) 434 3938
Kamo Springs Holiday Park (4 F11) – On SH1, Whangarei: (09) 435 1208
Whangarei Top 10 Holiday Park (4 G11) – 24 Mair St, Kensington, Whangarei: (09) 437 6856
Whangarei Falls Holiday Park (85 A2) – 12 Ngunguru Rd Glenbervie: (09) 437 0609
Alpha Motel & Holiday Park (4 F11) – 34 Tarewa Rd, Whangarei: (09) 438 6600
Blue Heron Holiday Park (4 G12) – 85-87 Scott Rd, off Whangarei Heads Rd; Heading towards Parua Bay: (09) 436 2293
Treasure Island Trailer Park (4 G13) – Pataua South: (09) 436 2390
Ruakaka Reserve Motor Camp (4 J13) – 21 Beach Rd, Ruakaka: (09) 432 7590
Camp Waipu Cove (6 A8) – Cove Rd, Waipu Cove: (09) 432 0410
Waipu Cove Cottages & Camp (6 A8) – 685 Cove Rd, Waipu Cove: (09) 432 0851
Whangateau Holiday Park (6 D10) – 559 Leigh Rd, Whangateau: (09) 422 6305
Sheepworld Caravan Park (6 E9) – SH1, Warkworth: (09) 425 9962
Martin's Bay Holiday Park (6 E10) – 287 Martins Bay Rd, Sandspit/Warkworth: (09) 425 5655

Hibiscus Coast

Pinewoods Motor Park Ltd (7 B4) – 23 Marie Ave, Red Beach: (09) 426 4526
Waiwera Holiday Park (7 A4) – 37 Waiwera Place, outside the main ablution block, Waiwera: (09) 426 5270

Auckland

Auckland North Shore Holiday Park (7 D4) – 52 Northcote Rd, Takapuna; Entrance next to Pizza Hut: (09) 418 2578
Takapuna Beach Holiday Park (7 D4) – 22 The Promenade, Takapuna: (09) 489 7909
Aquatic Park Holiday Camp (5 H7) – Cnr Parkhurst & Springs Rd, Parakai; D/S is 7m from kerb: (09) 420 8998
Avondale Motor Park (7 E4) – 46 Bollard Ave, Avondale: (09) 828 7228
Manukau Top 10 Holiday Park (7 F5) **–** 902 Great South Rd, Manukau: (09) 266 8016
Orewa Beach Top 10 Holiday Park (7 A4) – 265 Hibiscus Coast Hwy, S end of Orewa Beach: (09) 426 5832
Pakiri Beach Holiday Park (6 D10) – 261 Pakiri River Rd, Pakiri: (09) 422 6199
Piha Domain Motor Camp (7 E2) – 21 Seaview Rd, Piha: (09) 812 8815

Counties

South Auckland Caravan Park (7 H6) – Ararimu Rd, Ramarama: (09) 294 8903
Orere Point Top 10 Holiday Park (8 F9) – 2 Orere Point Rd, Clevedon: (09) 292 2774
Miranda Holiday Park (8 H9) – Miranda Rd, Thames: (07) 867 3205
Clarks Beach Holiday Park (7 H4) – Torkar Rd, Clarks Beach: (09) 232 1685
Sandspit Motor Camp (7 J4) – 15 Rangiwhea Rd, Waiuku; Jane Gifford Reserve: (09) 235 9913

Hauraki/Coromandel

Dickson Holiday Park (8 G11) – 3km north of Thames on Coromandel Rd: (07) 868 7308
Te Puru Holiday Park (10 B8) – 473 Thames Coast Rd, Te Puru: (07) 868 2879
The Glade Holiday Park (8 G14) – 58 Vista Paku, Pauanui Beach: (07) 864 8559
Tapu Motor Camp (8 F11) – SH25, Thames Coast: (07) 868 4837
Tapu Creek Campervan Park (8 F11) – Tapu-Coroglen Rd, Tapu: (07) 868 4560
Riverglen Holiday Park (8 F12) – Tapu Rd, Coroglen; 3.5km from Coroglen Tavern: (07) 866 3130
Papa Aroha Holiday Park (8 C10) – Colville Rd, Coromandel: (07) 866 8818
Long Bay Motor Camp (8 C11) – 3200 Long Bay Rd, Coromandel: (07) 866 8720
Shelly Beach Top 10 Holiday Park (8 C11) – 243 Colville Rd, Coromandel: (07) 866 8988
Oamaru Bay Motor Camp (8 C11) – 440 Colville Rd, Coromandel: (07) 866 8735
Colville Bay Motel & Motor Camp (8 B11) – Wharf Rd, Colville, Coromandel: (07) 866 6814
Anglers Lodge Motels & Holiday Park (8 B10) – 1446 Colville Rd, Amodeo Bay: (07) 866 8584
Coromandel Motels & Holiday Park (8 C11) – 636 Rings Rd, Coromandel: (07) 866 8830
Kuaotunu Motor Camp (8 C13) – 33 Bluff Rd, Kuaotunu: (07) 866 5628
Otama Beach Camping Ground (8 C13) – 400 Blackjack Rd, RD 2, Whitianga: (07) 866 2872
Flaxmill Bay Hideaway Camp & Cabins (8 D13) – 1031 Purangi Rd, Flaxmill Bay, Whitianga: (07) 866 2386
Mercury Bay Holiday Park (8 D13) – 121 Albert St, Whitianga: (07) 866 5579
Harbourside Holiday Park (8 D13) – 135 Albert St, Whitianga: (07) 866 5746
Mill Creek Bird & Campervan Park (8 E12) – 365 Mill Creek Rd, Whitianga: (07) 866 0166
Seabreeze Tourist Park (8 E13) – 1043 Tairua/Whitianga Rd, Whenuakite: (07) 866 3050
Hahei Holiday Resort (8 D14) – Harsant Ave, Hahei, Whitianga: (07) 866 3889
Whangamata Motor Camp (8 J14) – 104 Barbara Ave, Whangamata: (07) 865 9128
Settler's Motor Camp (8 J14) – 101 Leander Rd, Whangamata: (07) 865 8181

Waikato

Port Waikato Motor Camp (9 E1) – Maunsell Rd, Port Waikato: (09) 232 9857
Te Aroha Holiday Park (10 G10) – 217 Stanley Rd, Te Aroha: (07) 884 9567
Waihi Motor Camp (10 F10) – 6 Waitete Rd, Waihi: (07) 863 7654
Opal Hot Springs Holiday Park (12 F11) – 257 Okauia Springs Rd, Matamata: (07) 888 8198
Waingaro Hot Springs Caravan Park (9 J3) – At Ngaruawahia turn west for 24km, Waingaro: (07) 825 4761
Hamilton City Holiday Park (11 C7) – 14 Ruakura Rd, Hamilton: (07) 855 8255
Hamilton East Motor Camp (11 C7) – 61 Cameron Rd, Hamilton East: (07) 856 6220
Roadrunner Motel and Holiday Park (11 E7) – 141 Bond Rd, Te Awamutu: (07) 871 7420
Cambridge Motor Park (12 D8) – 32 Scott St, Leamington, Cambridge: (07) 827 5649
Lake Karapiro Camping & Pursuits Centre (12 D9) – Access from SH1, cross low level bridge at south end of Cambridge: (07) 827 4178
Raglan Kopua Holiday Park (11 C3) – Camp signposted from town centre: (07) 825 8283
Kawhia Beachside S-Cape (11 F3) – 225 Pouewe St, Kawhia: (07) 871 0727
Otorohanga Kiwi Town Holiday Park (11 G6) – 7 Domain Dr, Otorohanga; Adjacent to Kiwi & Native Bird Park: (07) 873 8279
Otorohanga Holiday Park (11 G6) – 20 Huiputea Drive, Otorohanga: (07) 873 7253
Kiwitown Holiday Park (11 G6) – Domain Drive, Otorohanga: (07) 837 8279
Waitomo Top 10 Holiday Park (11 H5) – Waitomo Caves Rd, Waitomo Village: (07) 878 7639
Te Kuiti Domain Motor Camp (11 J5) – Hinerangi St, Te Kuiti; Opposite Primary School: (07) 878 8966

Rotorua

Rotorua Top 10 Holiday Park (13 G4) – 1495 Pukuatua St, Rotorua: (07) 348 1886
Holdens Bay Top 10 Holiday Park & Conference Centre (13 G4) – 5-7 Stonebridge Park Drive, off Robinson Ave, Rotorua: (07) 345 9925
All Seasons Holiday Park (13 G5) – 50-58 Lee Rd, Hannahs Bay, Rotorua: 0800 422 674
Blue Lake Top 10 Holiday Park (13 H5) – 723 Tarawera Rd, On shores of Blue Lake, Rotorua: (07) 362 8120
Rotorua Lakeside Thermal Holiday Park (13 G4) – 54 Whittaker Rd, Rotorua: (07) 348 1693
Cosy Cottage International Holiday Park (13 G4) – 67 Whittaker Rd, Rotorua: (07) 348 3793
Rotorua Family Holiday Park (13 F4) – 22 Beaumonts Rd, Rotorua; Near lake shore Ngongotaha: (07) 357 4289
Affordable Willowhaven Holiday Park (13 F4) – 31 Beaumonts Rd, Ngongotaha, Rotorua: (07) 357 4092
Waiteti Trout Stream Holiday Park (13 F4) – 14 Okona Cres, Ngongotaha, Rotorua: (07) 357 5255
Rotorua Thermal Holiday Park (13 G4) – 463 Old Taupo Rd (south end), Rotorua; Adjacent to golf course: (07) 346 3140
Lake Rotoiti Lakeside Holiday Park (13 F5) – On SH33, Okere Falls: (07) 362 4860
Kea Motel & Holiday Park (12 F11) – 95 Tirau St, SH1, Putaruru: (07) 882 1590
Tokoroa Motor Camp & Backpackers (12 H12) – 22 Sloss Rd, Tokoroa: (07) 886 6642
Tongariro Holiday Park (Eivins Lodge) (19 H1) – SH47, Tongariro: (07) 386 8062

De Bretts Thermal Resort (19 D5) – 1.5km from Lake Taupo; SH5 Napier/Taupo Rd: (07) 378 8559
Lake Taupo Top 10 Holiday Resort (19 D5) – 28 Centennial Dr (off Spa Rd), Taupo: (07) 378 6860
Great Lake Holiday Park (19 D5) – 406 Acacia Bay Rd, Taupo: (07) 378 5159
Taupo All Seasons Holiday Park (19 D5) – 16 Rangatira St, Taupo: (07) 378 4272
Oasis Motel & Holiday Park (19 G2) – SH41 Tokaanu: (07) 386 8569
Parklands Motor Lodge (19 G3) – Cnr Arahori St & SH1, Turangi: (07) 386 7515
Club Habitat Hotels (19 G3) – 25 Ohuanga Rd, Turangi: (07) 386 7492
Turangi Cabins & Holiday Park (19 G3) – Ohuanga Rd off SH41, Turangi: (07) 386 8754
Motutere Bay Holiday Park (19 F4) – On SH1, Motutere: (07) 386 8963
Whakapapa Holiday Park (18 J13) – Tongariro National Park, Mt Ruapehu: (07) 892 3897

Bay of Plenty

Waihi Beach Holiday Park (10 F12) – 15 Beach Rd, Waihi Beach; Adjacent to Ocean Beach: (07) 863 5504
Beachhaven Motel & Holiday Park (10 F12) – 21 Leo St, Waihi Beach: (07) 863 5505
Sea-Air Motel & Holiday Park (10 F12) – Emerton Rd, Waihi Beach South: (07) 863 5655
Athenree Hot Srpings & Holiday Park (10 F12) – 1 Athenree Rd, Athenree: (07) 863 5600
Bowentown Beach Holiday Park (10 F12) – South end of Seaforth Rd, Bowentown: (07) 863 5381
Acccommodation at Te Puna (10 J13) – Cnr Waihi Rd (SH2) & Minden Rd, Te Puna, Tauranga: (07) 552 5621
Tauranga Park (10 J13) – 9 Mayfair St, Tauranga: (07) 578 3323
Sanctuary Point (10 J13) – Between Poike Rd & Welcome Bay roundabouts, on Hamilton/Mt Maunganui; SH29 bypass, Tauranga: (07) 544 0700
Silver Birch Family Holiday Park (10 J13) – 101 Turret Rd, Tauranga: (07) 578 4603
Golden Grove Holiday Park (13 B4) – 73 Girven Rd, Mt Maunganui: (07) 575 5821
Cosy Corner Holiday Park (13 B4) – 40 Ocean Beach Rd, Mt Maunganui: (07) 575 5899
Mount Maunganui Beachside Holiday Park (13 A4) – 1 Adams Ave, Mt Maunganui; at the base of the mountain: (07) 575 4471
Papamoa Village Park (13 B5) – 267 Parton Rd, Papamoa: (07) 542 1890
Papamoa Beach Top 10 Holiday Resort (13 B5) – 535 Papamoa Beach Rd, Papamoa: (07) 572 0816
Beach Grove Holiday Park (13 B5) – 386 Papamoa Beach Rd, Papamoa: (07) 572 1337
Pacific Park Christian Holiday Camp (13 B5) – 1110 Papamoa Beach Rd, Papamoa: (07) 542 0018
Bay Views Holiday Park (13 C6) – 195 Arawa Ave, Maketu: (07) 533 2222

Eastern Bay of Plenty

Awakeri Hot Springs (14 F9) – On SH30, 16km south of Whakatane: (07) 304 9117
Whakatane Holiday Park (14 E11) – McGarvey Rd, Whakatane: (07) 308 8694
Thornton Beach Holiday Park (14 E110) – 163 Thornton Beach Rd off SH2; 14km NW of Whakatane: (07) 304 8296
Opotiki Holiday Park (14 F13) – Cnr of Grey St & Potts Ave, Opotiki: (07) 315 6050
Ohope Beach Top 10 Holiday Park (14 E12) – 367 Harbour Rd, east of Ohope: 0800 264 673
Ohiwa Holiday Park (14 F12) – 380 Ohiwa Harbour Rd, Opotiki: (07) 315 4741
Tirohanga Beach Motor Camp (15 F3) – On SH35, 7km past Opotiki: (07) 315 7942
Waihau Bay Holiday Park (16 B8) – On SH35, 3km east of Waihau Bay: (07) 325 3844

Eastland

Anaura Bay Motor Camp (16 J11) – Anaura Bay Rd, Anaura Bay: (06) 862 6380
Tolaga Bay Holiday Park (22 A13) – 167 Wharf Rd, Tolaga Bay: (06) 862 6716
Tatapouri By The Sea (22 D11) – Alongside SH35, Tatapouri: (06) 868 3269
Gisborne Showgrounds Park Motorcamp (22 D10) – 20 Main Rd, Gisborne: (06) 867 5299
Waikanae Beach Holiday Park (22 E10) – Grey St, Gisborne: (06) 867 5634
Mahia Beach Motel & Holiday Camp (22 J9) – 43 Moana Dr, Mahia Beach: (06) 837 5830
Riverside Motor Camp (21 H5) – 19 Marine Pde, Wairoa: (06) 838 6301
Waikaremoana Motor Camp (21 E2) – SH38, Lake Waikaremoana: (06) 837 3803

Hawkes Bay

Waipatiki Beach Farm Park (28 B13) – 498 Waipatiki Beach Rd, Napier: (06) 836 6075
Bay View Snapper Holiday Park (28 D12) – 8 Gill Rd, Bayview: (06) 836 7084
Affordable Westshore Holiday Park (28 D12) – 88 Meeanee Quay, Westshore, Napier: (06) 835 9456
Kennedy Park Top 10 Resort (28 D12) – Storkey St, Napier: (06) 843 9126
Bay View Van Park (28 C12) – 10 Gill Rd, Bay View: (06) 836 7084
Hastings Top 10 Holiday Park (28 F12) – 610 Windsor Ave, Hastings: (06) 878 6692
Arataki Holiday Park (28 F12) – 139 Arataki Rd, Havelock North: (06) 877 7479
Ocean Beach Camping Ground (28 G13) – Ocean Beach Rd, RD 12, Havelock North: (06) 874 7894
Clifton Beach Reserve Motor Camp (28 F13) – 495 Clifton Rd, R D 2 Hastings on east coast: (06) 875 0263
River's Edge Holiday Park (28 J9) – Harker St, Waipawa; Go to town clock, turn right travelling north: (06) 857 8976
Waipukurau Holiday Park (32 A10) – River Tce, Waipukurau off SH2, adjacent Tuki Tuki River: (06) 858 8184
Warpukurau Holiday Park (32 A10) – River Tce, Waipukurau: (06) 858 8184
Dannevirke Holiday Park (31 C6) – 29 George St, Dannevirke: (06) 374 7625

Taranaki

Seaview Holiday Park (17 D5) – SH3, between Awakino and Mokau: (06) 752 9708
Taumarunui Holiday Park (18 F11) – SH4, Manunui: (07) 895 9345
Urenui Beach Camp Ground (17 G3) – 148 Beach Rd, Urenui: (06) 752 3838
Onaero Bay Holiday Park (17 G2) – SH3, North Taranaki: (06) 752 3643
Belt Rd Seaside Holiday Park (23 B5) – 2 Belt Rd, New Plymouth: (06) 758 0228
Hookner Motor Camp Park (23 B5) – 885 Carrington Rd, New Plymouth: (06) 753 9506
New Plymouth Top 10 Holiday Park (23 B5) – 29 Princes St, New Plymouth: (06) 758 2566
Marine Park Motor Camp (17 G1) – Centennial Ave, Waitara: (06) 754 7121
Fitzroy Beach Holiday Park (23 B5) – 1D Beach St, New Plymouth: (06) 758 2870
Sentry Hill Motel & Roadhouse (23 A6) – 56 Mountain Rd (SH3A): (06) 752 0696
Oakura Beach Holiday Park (23 B4) – 2 Jans Tce, Oakura: (06) 752 7861
Opunake Beach Holiday Park (23 F3) – Beach Rd, Opunake: (06) 761 7525
Stratford Holiday Park (25 B1) – 10 Page St, Stratford: (06) 765 6440
King Edward Park Motor Camp (25 E2) – 70 Waihi Rd, Hawera; SH3, adjacent to Park & gardens: (06) 278 8544
Carlyle Beach Motor Camp (25 G3) – 9 Beach Rd, Patea: (06) 273 8620

Wanganui

Raetihi Holiday Park (26 C10) – 10 Parapara Rd, Raetihi: (06) 385 4176
Ohakune Top 10 Holiday Park (26 C11) – 5 Moore St, Ohakune: (06) 385 8561
Ruakawa Falls & YMCA Raukawa Adventure Centre (26 F11) – Parapara SH4, Kakatahi; 30km south of Raetihi & 60km north of Wanganui: (06) 342 8518
Mowhanau Camp (25 H7) – Kai Iwi Beach: (06) 342 9658
Whanganui River Top 10 Holiday Park (26 H8) – 460 Somme Pde, Aramoho, Wanganui: (06) 343 8402
Castlecliff Seaside Holiday Park (25 J7) – Cnr Karaka & Rangiora St, Wanganui; Adjacent to beach: (06) 344 2227
Bignell St Motel & Caravan Park (26 J8) – 86 Bignell St, Wanganui: (06) 344 2012
Taihape Riverview Holiday Park (27 F2) – Old Abbattoir Rd, Taihape: (06) 388 0718

Manawatu

Bridge Motor Lodge (29 B6) – 2 Bridge St, Bulls: (06) 322 0894
Feilding Holiday Park (29 C7) – 5 Arnott St, Feilding: (06) 323 5623
Koitiata Camping Ground (29 A4) – Turakina Beach Rd, Koitiata: (06) 327 3770
Palmerston North Holiday Park (30 E8) – 133 Dittmer Dr, Palmerston North; Follow southern by-pass route to or from Woodville adjacent to swimming complex: (06) 358 0349
Foxton Beach Motor Camp (29 F4) – Holben Pde, Foxton: (06) 363 8211
Waitarere Beach Motor Camp (29 F4) – 133 Park Ave, Waitarere Beach: (06) 368 8732
Hydrabad Holiday Park (29 G4) – Forest Rd, Waitarere Beach: (06) 368 4941
Levin Motor Camp (29 G5) – 38 Parker Ave, Levin: (06) 368 3549
Byron's Resort (29 J3) – 20 Tasman Rd, Otaki Beach; D/S at rear of camp: (06) 364 8119
Bridge Lodge (29 J4) – 3 Otaki Gorge Rd, Otaki: (06) 364 6667

Wairarapa

Carnival Park Campground (30 F9) – Glasgow St, Pahiatua: (06) 376 6340
Eketahuna Camping (31 H2) – Standly St, Eketahuna: (06) 375 8587
Mawley Park Motor Camp (34 B9) – 15 Oxford St, Masterton: (06) 378 6454
Castlepoint Holiday Park & Motel (34 A13) – Jetty Road. D/S on roadway into camp: (06) 372 6705
Carterton Holiday Park (34 C8) – 196-8 Belvedere Rd, Carterton; 700m from main road, SH2: (06) 379 8267
Martinborough Village Camping (34 E7) – Cnr Princess & Dublin Sts, Martinborough: (06) 306 8919

Wellington

Waikanae Christian Holiday Park (33 A4) – (aka El Rancho), 1199 Kauri Rd, Waikanae: (04) 902 6287
Lindale Motor Park (33 A3) – Ventnor Dr, Paraparaumu: (04) 298 8046
Paekakariki Holiday Park (33 B3) – 180 Wellington Rd, Paekakariki: (04) 292 8292
Camp Elsdon (33 D2) – 18 Raiha St, Porirua: (04) 237 8987
Aotea Camping Ground (33 D2) – 3 Whitford Brown Ave, Porirua: (04) 235 9599
Harcourt Holiday Park (33 C4) – 45 Akatarawa Rd, Upper Hutt; turn off SH2 just north of Caltex Service Station: (04) 526 7400
Capital Gateway Motor Lodge & Caravan Park (33 E2) – 1 Newlands Rd, Newlands: (04) 478 7812
Wellington Top 10 Holiday Park (33 E3) – 95 Hutt Park Rd, Lower Hutt: (04) 568 5913
Catchpool Valley DOC Camp Site (33 F2) – On the coast road, Wainuiomata: (04) 472 7356

SOUTH ISLAND

Marlborough

Okiwi Bay Holiday Park (39 E7) – 15 Renata Rd, Rai Valley, Okiwi Bay: (03) 576 5006
Smiths Farm Holiday Park (40 G9) – 1419 Queen Charlotte Dr, Linkwater, Picton: (03) 574 2806
Havelock Motor Camp (40 G8) – 24 Inglis St, Havelock: (03) 574 2339
Alexanders Holiday Park (40 G10) – Canterbury St, Picton: (03) 573 6378
Picton Top 10 Holiday Park (40 G10) – 70-78 Waikawa Rd, Picton: (03) 573 7212
Picton Campervan Park (40 G10) – 42 Kent St, Nelson Square, Picton: (03) 573 8875
Parklands Marina Holiday Park (40 G10) – 10 Beach Rd, Waikawa Marina, Picton: (03) 573 6343
Waikawa Bay Holiday Park (40 G10) – 5 Waimarama St, Waikawa Bay: (03) 573 7434
Momorangi Bay Holiday Park (40 G9) – Momorangi Bay, Grove Arm, Queen Charlotte Sound: (03) 520 3113
Spring Creek Holiday Park (44 B10) – Rapaura Rd: (03) 570 5893
Blenheim Bridge Top 10 Holiday Park (44 C11) – 78 Grove Rd, Blenheim: (03) 578 3667
Duncannon Holiday Park (44 C11) – St Andrews, SH1; 2km south of Blenheim: (03) 578 8193
A1 Kaikoura Motels & Caravan Park (48 E12) – 11 Beach Rd, Kaikoura; on SH1: (03) 319 5999
Kaikoura Top 10 Holiday Park (48 E12) – 34 Beach Rd, Kaikoura: (03) 319 5362
Alpine-Pacific Holiday Park (48 E12) – 69 Beach Rd, Kaikoura: 0800 692 322
Kaikoura Peketa Beach Holiday Park (48 E11) – Main South Rd, Kaikoura: (03) 319 6299
Kaikoura Coastal Campgrounds, Goose Bay (48 F11) – SH1, Kaikoura: (03) 319 5348
Cheviot Motels & Holiday Park (48 J9) – 44 Ward Rd, Cheviot: (03) 319 8607

Nelson/Tasman

Pohara Beach Top 10 Holiday Park (38 D8) – Abel Tasman Dr, Takaka, Pohara: (03) 525 9500
Totaranui DOC camping ground (38 D10) – Totaranui Rd, Abel Tasman National Park: (03) 528 8083
Abel Tasman Marahau Beach Camp (39 D2) – Franklin St, Marahau: (03) 527 8176
Kaiteriteri Beach Motor Camp (39 E2) – Sandy Bay Rd, Kaiteriteri: (03) 527 8010
Motueka Top 10 Holiday Park (39 E2) – 10 Fearon St, Motueka; north end of town: (03) 528 7189
Mapua Leisure Park (39 G2) – 33 Toru St, Mapua: (03) 540 2666
Greenwood Park (39 H3) – Cnr Lansdowne Rd & Coastal Hwy, Appleby, Richmond: (03) 544 4685
Richmond Motel & Top 10 Holiday Park (39 H3) – 29 Gladstone Rd, SH6, Richmond: (03) 544 7323
Club Waimea (39 H3) – 345 Lower Queens St, Richmond: (03) 543 9179
Maitai Valley Motor Camp (39 G4) – Maitai Valley, Nelson: (03) 548 7729
Brook Valley Holiday Park (39 H4) – Brook St, Brook Valley: (03) 548 0399
Nelson City Holiday Park (39 G4) – 230 Vanguard St, Nelson: (03) 548 1445
Tahuna Beach Holiday Park (39 G3) – 70 Beach Rd, Tahunanui, Nelson: (03) 548 5159
Quinney's Bush Camp & Caravan Park (42 C13) – SH6, Motupiko: (03) 522 4249
Gowan River Holiday Camp (42 G11) – Gowan Valley Rd: (03) 523 9921
Tapawera Settle (42 B13) – Tadmore-Motupiko Rd, Tapawera/Motueka Valley: (03) 522 4334
Kerr Bay DOC camp (42 G13) – St Arnaud; opposite kitchen shelter: (03) 521 1806
Kiwi Park Motel & Holiday Park (42 G9) – 170 Fairfax St, Murchison: (03) 523 9248

West Coast

Karamea Holiday Park (41 A7) – SH67; 3km south of Karamea: (03) 782 6758
Westport Holiday Park & Motel (41 G3) – 31-37 Domett St, Westport: (03) 789 7043
Seal Colony Top 10 Tourist Park (41 G2) – Marine Pde, Carters Beach, Westport; adjacent to beach: (03) 789 8002
The Happy Wanderer (41 G3) – 56 Russell St, Westport; by RSA carpark: (03) 789 8627
Punakaiki Beach Camp (45 B5) – SH6, Owen St, Punakaiki: (03) 731 1894
Rapahoe Beach Motor Camp (45 E4) – 10 Hawken St, Rapahoe: (03) 762 7025
Reefton Domain Camp (46 B9) – Main St, Reefton; on SH7: (03) 732 8477
Nelson Creek Domain (45 E6) – Nelson Creek; camp run jointly by DOC and local community
Central Motor Home Park (45 E4) – 117 Tainui St, Greymouth: (03) 768 4924
Jacquie Grant's Place (45 H2) – Greyhound Rd, Hokitika: 0277 556 550
Greymouth Seaside Top 10 Holiday Park (45 F4) – 2 Chesterfield St, Greymouth: 0800 867 104
South Beach Motel & Motorpark (45 F3) – 318 Main South Rd, SH6, Greymouth: (03) 762 6768
Lake Brunner Motor Camp (45 G6) – 86 Ahau St, Moana: (03) 738 0600
Lake Brunner Country Motel & Holiday Park (45 G6) – 2014 Arnold Valley Rd, Moana: (03) 738 0144
Hokitika Holiday Park (45 H2) – cnr Stafford St & Livingstone St, Hokitika: (03) 755 8172
Shining Star Beachfront Accommodation (45 H2) – SH6; north end of Hokitika: (03) 755 8921
252 Beachside Motels & Holiday Park (45 H2) – 252 Revell St, Hokitika: (03) 755 8773
Jacksons Retreat (45 J6) – SH73, Great Alpine Hwy
Rainforest Holiday Park (49 G6) – 46 Cron St, Franz Josef: (03) 752 0220
Franz Josef Mountain View Top 10 Holiday Park (49 G6) – 2902 Franz Josef Hwy, SH6, Franz Josef: (03) 752 0735
Fox Glacier Holiday Park (49 H4) – Kerrs Rd, Fox Glacier: (03) 751 0821
Fox Glacier Campervan Park (49 H4) – Sullivan Rd, Fox Glacier: (03) 751 0888
Haast Lodge (58 D9) – Marks Rd, Haast; 3km east of Haast Visitor Centre: (03) 750 0703
Haast Beach Holiday Park (58 D8) – Jackson Bay/Haast Beach Rd, Haast: 0800 843 226

Canterbury

Mountain View Top 10 Holiday Park (47 F5) – Cnr Bath St and Main St, Hanmer Springs: (03) 315 7113
Alpine Adventure Holiday Park 47 F5) – 200 Jacks Pass Rd, Hanmer Springs; 2km from village: (03) 315 7112
Hanmer River Holiday Park (47 G5) – 26 Medway Rd, Hanmer Springs: (03) 315 7111
Alpine Apartments & Campground (47 G5) – 9 Fowlers Lane, Hanmer Springs: (03) 315 7478
Pines Holiday Park (47 F5) – Jacks Pass Rd, Hanmer Springs: (03) 315 7152

Waiau Motor Camp (47 H7) – 9 Highfield St, Waiau: (03) 315 6672
Waipara Sleepers Motor Camp (54 C8) – 200m from junction of SH1 & SH7, Waipara: (03) 314 6003
Mt Lyford Lodge (48 F8) – 10 Mt Lyford Forrest Drive, RDI, Waiau: (03) 315 6446
Greta Valley Camping Ground (54 B10) – 7 Valley Rd, Greta Valley, SH1; halfway between Amberley and Cheviot: (03) 314 3340
Delhaven Motels & Caravan Park (54 D8) – 124 Carters Rd, Amberley; SH1: (03) 314 8550
Woodend Beach Holiday Park (56 B10) – 14 Beach Rd, Woodend Beach: (03) 312 7643
Waikuku Beach Holiday Park (56 B10) – 1 Domain Tce, Waikuku Beach; on SH1: (03) 312 7600
Leithfield Beach Motor Camp (56 A11) – 18 Lucas Dr, Leithfield Beach: (03) 314 8518
Rangiora Holiday Park (56 B9) – 337 Lehmans Rd, Rangiora: (03) 313 5759
Pineacres Holiday Park (56 B10) – 740 Main North Rd, Kaiapoi; on SH1: (03) 327 5022
Blue Skies (56 C10) – 12 Williams St, Kaiapoi; southern end of Old Main Rd: (03) 327 8007
Kairaki Beach Holiday Park (56 C10) – Featherstone Ave, Kaiapoi; at mouth of Waimakariri River: (03) 327 7335
Riverlands Holiday Park (56 C10) – 45 Doubledays Rd, Kaiapoi: (03) 327 5511
219 On Johns Motel & Holiday Park (56 C9) – 219 Johns Rd, Belfast: (03) 323 8640
Addington Accommodation Park (56 D9) – 47-51 Whiteleigh Ave, Addington, Christchurch: (03) 338 9770
Spencer Beach Holiday Park (54 G8) – Heyders Rd, Spencerville, Christchurch: (03) 329 8721
Amber Park (56 D9) – 308 Blenheim Rd, Riccarton, Christchurch: (03) 348 3327
Christchurch Top 10 Holiday Park (56 D9) – 39 Meadow St, Papanui, Christchurch: (03) 352 9176
Riccarton Park Holiday Park (56 D9) – 19 Main South Rd, Upper Riccarton, Christchurch: (03) 348 5690
South Brighton Motor Camp (56 D10) – 59 Halsey St, Christchurch: (03) 388 9844
All Seasons Holiday Park (56 D10) – 5 Kidbrooke St, Christchurch: (03) 384 9490
North South Holiday Park (56 D9) – Cnr Johns Rd & Sawyers Arms Rd, Harewood, Christchurch: (03) 359 5993
Alpine View Holiday Park (56 D8) – 650-678 Main South Rd, Templeton, Lincoln: (03) 349 7666
Akaroa Top 10 Holiday Park (56 G12) – 96 Morgans Rd, Banks Peninsula; off Old Coach Rd from SH75: (03) 304 7471
Duvauchelle Holiday Park (56 G12) – Seafield Rd, Duvauchelle, Banks Peninsula: (03) 304 5777
Okains Bay Motor Camp (56 F13) – Okains Bay, Banks Peninsula: (03) 304 8789
Kowai Pass Domain Camp (55 B4) – Domain Rd, Springfield; off SH73: (03) 318 4887
Glentunnel Holiday Park (55 D4) – SH77, Scenic Route 72, Homebush Rd, Glentunnel: (03) 318 2868

South Canterbury

Rakaia River Holiday Park (55 G5) – SH1, Rakaia; south end of Rakaia Bridge: (03) 302 7257
Coronation Holiday Park (55 J3) – 780 East St, Ashburton: (03) 308 6603
Abisko Lodge & Campground (55 F2) – 74 Main St, Methven: (03) 302 8875
Pudding Hill Lodge (52 J8) – SH72, Pudding Hill: (03) 302 9627
Ashburton Holiday Park (62 D8) – Tinwald Domain, Ashburton: (03) 308 6805
Grumpys Retreat N' Holiday Park (61 E5) – 7 Keen St, Orari Bridge: (03) 693 7453
Geraldine Holiday Park (61 F4) – Cnr SH79 & Hislop St, Geraldine: (03) 693 8147
Fairlie Gateway Top 10 Holiday Park (61 F1) – 10 Allandale Rd, Fairlie: (03) 685 8375
Lake Tekapo Holiday Park (60 E9) – Lakeside Dr, Lake Tekapo: (03) 680 6825
Lake Ruataniwha Holiday Park (59 H6) – Max Smith Drive, Twizel: (03) 435 0613
Omarama Holiday Park (67 A3) – 1 Omarama Ave, Omarama; junction of SH8 & SH83, closed in winter: (03) 438 9875
Ahuriri Motels (67 A3) – SH83, 5 Claycliff Dve, Omarama: (03) 438 9451
Temuka Holiday Park (61 G5) – 1 Fergusson Dr, Temuka: (03) 615 7241
Timaru Top 10 Holiday Park (61 J4) – 154a Selwyn St, Timaru: (03) 684 7690
Glenmark Motor Camp (61 J4) – 30 Beaconsfield Rd, Timaru: (03) 684 3682
Otematata Holiday Park (67 C5) – East Rd, Otematata: (03) 438 7826
Kurow Holiday Park (67 D7) – 76 Bledisloe St, Kurow; on SH83, west end of town: (03) 436 0725
Fisherman's Bend, Lake Aviemore (67 C7) – Nth side of Lake Aviemore (Oct to Apr only): (03) 689 8079
Knottingley Park (68 D12) – Waihoa Back Rd, Waimate; dump station at rear end of public toilets in camping area: (03) 689 8079
Victoria Park Camp and Cabins (68 D12) – Naylor St, Waimate: (03) 689 8079
Kelcey's Bush Farmyard Holiday Park (68 C11) – Upper Mills Rd, Waimate: (03) 689 8057
Waitaki Mouth Holiday Park (68 F13) – 305 Kaik Rd, Waitaki: (03) 431 3880
Oamaru Top 10 Holiday Park (68 H11) – Chelmer St, Oamaru; off SH1 near railway: (03) 434 7666
Hampden Beach Motor Camp (74 B13) – 2 Carlisle St, Hampden: (03) 439 4439
Moeraki Village Holiday Park (74 B14) – 114 Haven St, Moeraki: (03) 439 4759

Otago

Larchview Holiday Park (67 G5) – Swimming Dam Rd, Naseby: (03) 444 9904
Ranfurly Holiday Park (67 H5) – 8 Reade St, Ranfurly: (03) 444 9144
Blind Billy's Holiday Camp (74 D8) – Mold St, Middlemarch: (03) 464 3355
Waikouaiti Beach Motor Camp (74 E12) – 186 Beach St, Waikouaiti: (03) 465 7366
Leith Valley Touring Park (74 G11) – 103 Malvern St, Dunedin: (03) 467 9936
Dunedin Holiday Park (74 H11) – 41 Victoria Rd, St Kilda, Dunedin: (03) 455 4690
Lake Waihola Holiday Park (79 B6) – Waihola Domain: (03) 417 8908
Brighton Motor Camp (74 H10) – 1044 Brighton Rd, Brighton, Dunedin: (03) 481 1404
Aaron Lodge Holiday Park (74 H11) – 162 Kaikorai Valley Rd, Dunedin: (03) 476 4725
Portobello Village Tourist Park (74 G12) – 27 Hereweka St, Dunedin: (03) 478 0359

Clutha Valley

Lake Hawea Holiday Park (66 C9) – SH6; 500m north of Lake Hawea turn-off: (03) 443 1767
Aspiring Campervan Park (66 D8) – Studholme Rd, Wanaka: (03) 443 6603
Lake Outlet Holiday Park (66 D8) – 197 Outlet Rd, Wanaka: (03) 443 7478
Glendhu Bay Motor Camp (65 D7) – Mt Aspiring Rd, Wanaka: (03) 443 7243
Wanaka Lakeview Holiday Park (66 D8) – 212 Brownston St, Wanaka; on right just before camp: (03) 443 7883
Arrowtown Holiday Park (65 G6) – 11 Suffolk St, Arrowtown: (03) 442 1876
Glenorchy Holiday Park & Backpackers (65 F2) – 2 Oban St, Glenorchy; at the head of Lake Wakatipu: (03) 441 0303
Queenstown Top 10 Holiday Park 'Creeksyde' (65 H4) – 54 Robins Rd, Queenstown: (03) 442 9447
Shotover Top 10 Holiday Park (65 G4) – 70 Arthurs Point Rd, Queenstown: (03) 442 9306
Frankton Motor Camp (65 H5) – Yewlett Cres, Frankton; in front of Remarkables Hotel, Queenstown: (03) 442 2079
Queenstown Lake View Holiday Park (65 H4) – Breacon St, Queenstown; 150m from Gondola: (03) 442 7252
Kingston Motels & Holiday Park (72 B8) – 2 Kent St, Kingston: (03) 248 8501
Cairnmuir Camping Ground (66 H8) – 219 Cairnmuir Rd, Bannockburn: (03) 445 1956
Cromwell Top 10 Holiday Park (66 H9) – 1 Alpha St, Cromwell: (03) 445 0164
Chalets Holiday Park (66 H8) – 102 Barry Ave, Cromwell: (03) 445 1260
Alexandra Holiday Park (73 A2) – 44 Manuherikia Rd, Alexandra: (03) 448 8297
Alexandra Tourist Park (73 A2) – 31 Ngapara St, Alexandra: (03) 448 8861
Clyde Holiday & Sporting Complex (66 J10) – Whitby St, Clyde: (03) 449 2713
Balclutha Camping Ground (79 E3) – 56 Charlotte St, Balclutha: (03) 418 0088
Kaka Point Camping Ground (79 G4) – 39 Tarata St, Kaka Point; on coastal rd: (03) 412 8801
Owaka Motor Camp (79 G3) – Ryley St, Owaka: (03) 415 8728
Keswick Park Camping Ground (79 H3) – 2 Park Lane, Pounawea: (03) 419 1110
Pounawea Motor Camp (79 H3) – Park Lane, Pounawea: (03) 415 8483
Gold Park Motor Camp (79 A3) – Harrington St, Lawrence: (03) 485 9850
Curio Bay Camping Ground (78 H11) – 601 Waikawa-Curio Bay Rd, Curio Bay: (03) 246 8897
Catlins Woodstock Lodge & Camp (79 G2) – 348 Catlins Valley Rd, Owaka: (03) 415 8583
Papatowai Motor Camp (79 J1) – 2503 Papatowai Highway, Papatowai: (03) 415 8565
McLean Falls Eco Motels & Holiday Park (78 G12) – 29 Rewcastle Rd, Owaka: (03) 415 8668

Southland

Glenquoich Caravan Park (71 D7) – SH6; 1km north of Athol, beside Mataura River: (03) 248 8840
Mossburn Country Park (71 F5) – 333 Mossburn Five Rivers Rd, Mossburn: (03) 248 6313
Possum Lodge Motel & Holiday Park (70 E10) – 13 Murrell Ave, Manapouri: (03) 249 6623
Manapouri Motels & Holiday Park (70 E10) – 50 Manapouri-Te Anau Rd, Manapouri: (03) 249 6624
Te Anau Great Lakes Holiday Park (70 D11) – Cnr Luxmore Dr & Milford Rd, Te Anau: (03) 249 8538
Te Anau Top 10 Holiday Park (70 D11) – 128 Te Anau Tce & Mokonui St, Te Anau: (03) 249 7462
Te Anau Lakeview Holiday Park (70 D11) – 1 Te Anau-Manapouri Rd, Te Anau; opposite DOC Visitor Centre: (03) 249 7457
Fiordland Great Views Holiday Park (70 C11) – 129 Milford Rd, Te Anau: (03) 249 7059
Knobs Flat (64 H9) – SH94: (03) 249 9122
Tuatapere Motel (76 F12) – 73 Main St, Tuatapere: (03) 226 6250
Riverton Caravan Park (76 H14) – Hamlet St, Riverton: (03) 234 8526
Invercargill Caravan Park (77 E5) – A&P Showgrounds, 20 Victoria Ave, Invercargill: (03) 218 8787
Coachmans Inn Camp Ground (77 E5) – 705 Tay St, Invercargill; east end: (03) 217 6046
Beach Rd Holiday Park (77 F4) – Follow signs to Invercargill airport, 8km to the west: (03) 213 0400
Invercargill Top 10 Holiday Park (77 E5) – 77 McIvor Rd, Invercargill: (03) 215 9032
Amble On Inn (77 F5) – 145 Chesney St, Invercargill: (03) 216 5214
Lorneville Holiday Park (77 E5) – 352 Lorne Dancre Rd, Lorneville, Invercargill: (03) 235 8031
Bluff Camping Ground (77 G5) – Gregory St, Bluff; off SH1: (03) 212 8774
Gore Motor Camp (78 B9) – 35 Broughton St (SH1), Gore: (03) 208 4919
Dolamore Park (78 A8) – About 12km west of Gore: (03) 208 9080
Winton Golf Course & Camp (77 B4) – Sub Station Rd, Winton: (03) 236 8422

Motorhome Public dump station (wastewater disposal site)

NORTH ISLAND

Far North

Kerikeri Public D/S (4 A8) – Cobham Rd, by memorial hall, Kerikeri
Gibby's Place (4 A8) – 331 Kerikeri Rd, Kerikeri
Mangonui Public D/S (2 H8) – Beach Road, next to public toilets, 400m from SH10, Kaitaia
Omapere Public D/S (3 E3) – SH12 on harbourside next to Information Centre, opposite Opononi State School, Omapere
Kawakawa Public D/S (4 C9) – Waimio St, off SH1, on the right hand side past entrance to bowling club, Kawakawa
Kaitaia Public D/S (1 J6) – Behind Community Centre, corner of Mathews Ave and SH1, Kaitaia
Kaikohe Public D/S (3 C7) – Recreation Rd, Kaikohe; D/S on roadside at rear of Pioneer Village toilets

Northland

Dargaville Public D/S (3 J7) – Mobil Service Station on SH12 in town centre
Dargaville Public D/S (3 J7) – Caltex Service Station on SH12 in town centre
Dargaville Public D/S (3 J7) – Northern Wairoa Museum, Mt Wellesley; In public car park, Dargaville
Ngunguru Public D/S (4 F13) – Te Maika Rd, at North end of Ngunguru; Oppsite the school, near public toilets
Kamo Public D/S (4 F11) – On SH1, Lillian St, behind Fire Station, Kamo
Caltex Star Mart (4 F11) – Tarewa Rd, Whangarei
Whangarei Public D/S (4 G12) – Council Waste Water Treatment Plant; Kioreroa Rd, Whangarei
Recreational Concepts (4 F11) – 6 South End Ave, Whangarei
Waipu Public D/S (6 A8) – Langs Beach, next to public toilet, Waipu
Warkworth Public D/S (6 E10) – Kowahi Park, cnr of SH1 & Sandspit, Warkworth
Warkworth Hire Centre (6 E10) – D/S just inside main gate, Warkworth

Hibiscus Coast

Orewa Public D/S (6 G10) – South end of Orewa by KFC, Orewa
Whangaparaoa Public D/S (6 H10) – Gulf Harbour adjacent to public toilet by public boat ramp, Whangaparaoa

Auckland

Shelly Beach (7 A1) – Kaipara Harbour, Helensville; Beside public toilet
Waitakere Public D/S (7 D2) – McLeod Rd extension, Te Atatu South, fenced area in McLeod Pk opposite Riverglade Parkway road
Claris Landfill D/S (36 E5) – Gray Rd, Great Barrier Island
Manukau Mobil SS (7 F5) – Wiri Station Road, Manukau
Te Arai Point Public D/S (6 C9) – Beside public toilets, Te Arai
Wellsford Public D/S (6 D8) – Centenial Park, off SH1, Wellsford
Maraetai Public D/S (7 E7) – 188 Maraetai Dve, bowling club, Maraetai

Counties

Waharau Public D/S (8 G9) – Opposite Waharau Regional Park, Kaiaua Coast
Pukekohe Public D/S (7 H5) – Franklin Rd, Pukekohe; 400m past sports stadium
Tuakau Public D/S (7 J6) – In St Stephens Drive, Tuakau, opposite Police Station
Drury Public D/S (7 H5) – Tui St, behind shops, Pukekohe
Waiuku Public D/S (7 J4) – Jane Gifford Reserve, on bypass road to Manukau Heads, on right.

Hauraki/Coromandel

Ngatea Public D/S (8 J11) – On SH2 in village centre near public hall
Stuart Moore Motors BP Service Station (8 H11) – Thames, turn into Bank Street opposite the Toyota factory, East corner of parking area
Coromandel Public Dump Station (8 C11) – Wharf Road Scenic Reserve, Coromandel; Turn left towards Long Bay, 300m over bridge, near public toilets
Whitianga Public D/S (8 D13) – At rubbish station at Tin Town opposite airport
Pauanui Public D/S (8 F14) – Pleasant Point Boat Ramp (off Vista Paku) –
Whangamata Public D/S (8 J14) – Whangamata Domain, Whangamata; Turn off Port Rd into Aicken Rd, at public toilets
Waihi Public D/S (10 F10) – In Victoria Park, Waihi on SH2; Near public toilets in the park
Paeroa Public D/S (10 E9) – Marshall St, Paeroa; Near public toilet and information centre
Paeroa RV Centre (10 E9) – Coronation Rd, Paeroa
Tairua Public D/S (10 A11) – 175 Beach Road, Tairua
Cooks Beach Public D/S (8 D13) – Next to public toilets, Cooks Beach

Waikato

Te Kauwhata Public D/S (9 F5) – Turn off Mahi Rd into Domain in township
Te Aroha Public D/S (10 G9) – Next to public toilets on Lawrence St
Matamata Public D/S (12 C11) – On SH27, turn off Broadway into Hetana St; Near public toilets
Ngaruawahia Public D/S (9 J4) – In Waikato Esplanade Domain (The Point); On riverbank between Rowing Club & Railway bridge
Tirau Public D/S (12 E11) – Near public toilets down service lane from SH1, behind OK Tirau Motel
Te Awamutu Public D/S (11 E7) – On SH3, at Mobil Service Station at north end of town
Hamilton Public D/S (11 C6) – SH1, Lincoln St, entrance near model railway, Hamilton
Raglan Public D/S (11 C3) – Raglan Club, 22 Bow St, Raglan

Rotorua

Rotorua Public D/S (13 G4) – Entrance to Wastewater Treatment Plant, Te Ngae Rd
Tokoroa Public D/S (12 H12) – Whakauru St, Tokoroa; Next to sewerage treatment station
Wairakei BP Service Station & Truck Stop (19 C5) – On SH1 opposite hotel; D/S in parking area at the rear on left side
Kinloch Marina D/S (19 D4) – In Marina Car Park, Kinloch
Taupo Public D/S (19 D5) – 2 Mile Bay Boat Ramp, Taupo; 5 km south on SH1, next to public toilet
Tokaanu Public D/S (19 G3) – At boat ramp
Putaruru Public D/S (12 F11) – Market St. Heading south on SH1, first left turn after roundabout.

Bay of Plenty

Katikati Public D/S (10 G11) – North side of Katikati shopping centre turn off SH2 into roadway beside the A&P showgrounds
Mt Maunganui Shell Service Station (13 B4) – Hewletts Rd, Mt Maunganui on main route to Tauranga via Harbour Bridge
Tauranga BP Service Station (13 B3) – Chapel St end of Waihi-Mt Maunganui Expressway via Harbour Bridge, Tauranga
Te Puke Public D/S (13 C5) – Situated at public toilets
Tauranga Public D/S (10 J13, 94 D2) – Maleme Rd, can be reached from Oropi Rd or Cameron Rd, close to transfer station, Tauranga
Omokoroa Public D/S (10 H12) – Omokoroa Beach at west end of Peninsula in Omokoroa Domain Car and Trailer Park, Omokoroa
Omokoroa Public D/S (10 J12) – 1.9km from SH2 opposite Fire Station, turn left into road to main pump station 200m.
Mt Maunganui Public D/S (10 J14, 13 B4, 94 B3) – Tauranga Airport. Take first road on right past 'Classic Flyers NZ' Building.

Eastern Bay of Plenty

Kawerau Public D/S (14 G8) – Behind Bowling Club opposite information centre, town centre
Whakatane Public D/S (14 E10) – Caltex Service Station, Commerce St, next to fire station
Ohope Public D/S (14 E11) – Situated at public toilets, half-way along beach before bridge; In Maraetotara Reserve with play equipment;
Waiotahi Beach Public D/S (14 F13) – Waiotahi Beach Domain; On SH35 at public toilets
Opotiki BP Service Station (14 F13) – Cnr Bridges St & Church St; Past the last diesel pump
Murupara Public D/S (20 B11) – Behind BP Station, Pine Dr; off SH38, Murupara
Omaio Public D/S (15 D5) – Omaio Domain, off SH35
Te Kaha School House Bay (15 C6) – New toilet block, Te Kaha

Eastland

Gisborne Mobil Service Station (22 D10) – 49 Wainui Rd, Gisborne; East end of main road across bridge
Gisborne BP Service Station (22 D10) – Corner Ormond Rd & Sheridan St, Gisborne
Te Araroa Public D/S (16 B12) – Transfer Stn, 26 Te Arawapaia Rd, Te Araroa
Gisborne Public D/S (22 D10, 100 C3, 99 C2) – Hallrite Plumbing and Gasfitting Yard, 71 Awapuni Rd, Gisborne

Hawkes Bay

Napier Public D/S (28 D12) – Marine Parade by Ellison
Napier Public D/S (28 D12) – 104 Latham St, Napier; Beside Council Sewerage Pump Station
Clive BP S/S (28 E12) – Main Rd, Clive
Hastings BP S/S (28 F11) – Stortford Lodge; Corner Maraekakaho Rd & Heretaunga St
Waipawa Public D/S (28 J9) – 1 High St, Waipawa
Takapau Public D/S (16 F11) – 15 Nang St, Takapau

Taranaki

New Plymouth Public D/S, Mobil Service Station (23 B5) – Corner Leach & Eliot Streets
New Plymouth Public D/S, BP Service Station (23 B5) – 71 Powderham St, New Plymouth
Opunake Public D/S (23 F3) – Beach Rd, Opunake
Whangamomona Domain (24 C11) – 32 Whangamomona Rd
Normanby Public D/S (25 D1) – On Main Hwy, North of Hawera, Normanby
Aotea Park Public D/S (25 F4) – Cnr of Chester St & SH3, Waverley
Opunake Public D/S (23 F3) – Corner Napier and King Sts, Opunake

Wanganui

Taihape Public D/S (27 F2) – Linnet St, Taihape
Wanganui Public D/S (26 J8, 109 C3) – Springvale Park, London St, Wanganui
Ohakune Public D/S (26 C11) – Ohakune Club, 72 Goldfinch Ave, Ohakune
Taihape BP Connection (27 F2) – 80-88 Hautapu St, Taihape

Manawatu

Feilding BP Express Service Station (29 C7) – Corner Kimbolton Rd & Aorangi St next to KFC
Feilding Sewerage Treatment Plant (29 C7) – Kawa Kawa Rd Feilding; Past abattoir & Manfield Racetrack, on LHS down long drive, turn right at end of drive
Ashhurst Public D/S (30 D9) – Ashhurst Domain, SH3, Ashhurst
Palmerston North Caltex Service Station (29 E7) – Cnr Fitzherbert Ave & College St
Palmerston North Public D/S, Totara Rd Wastewater Plant (29 E4) – Behind Racecourse, Palmerston North
Foxton Public D/S (29 F5) – Inside the entrance to Victoria Park off Victoria St
Levin Public D/S (29 G5) – Sheffield St, Levin
Otaki Public D/S (29 J4) – Riverbank Rd, Otaki; Off SH1 just north of the Otaki River bridge

Wairarapa

Pongaroa Public D/S (30 G13) – Behind public toilets on SH52; not good van access
Woodville Public D/S (30 D10) – Swimming pool area, Normanby Rd, Woodville
Mawley Park (34 B9) – 15 Oxford St, Masterton; On bank of Waipoua River
Greytown Public D/S (34 C7) – At Arbor Reserve, Greytown; Rest/picnic area on SH2 opposite Kuranui college
Martinborough Public D/S (34 E7) – West end of Dublin St, Martinborough; Close to Motor Camp & swimming pool
Carterton Public D/S (34 C7) – Dalefield Rd, Carterton

Wellington

Upper Hutt Public D/S (33 D4, 111 B5) – On SH2 (River Rd), Upper Hutt; 500m north of Moonshine Bridge at Rest Area sign, beside toilets on gravel road by river
Tawa Public D/S (33 D2) – Tawa Swimming Pool, Davis St; D/S opposite pool entrance
Wellington Public D/S (33 F1) – 25 Urlic St, Plimmerton
Wellington Public D/S (33 F1, 110 D2) – Ngauranga Gorge, Hutt Rd, Wellington
Paraparaumu Public D/S (33 B4) – Mobil Service Station, corner SH1 and Kapiti Rd, Paraparaumu
Porirua Public D/S (33 D2) – Prosser St, Porirua
Lower Hutt Public D/S (33 E3, 110 D3) – Seaview Marina, Port Road, Lower Hutt

SOUTH ISLAND

Marlborough

Blenheim Public D/S (44 C10) – Mobil Service Station, Cnr of Grove Rd and Nelson St, Blenheim
Kaikoura BP Service Station (48 E12) – on SH1; north side of Kaikoura
Picton D/S (35 J3, 40 G10, 44 A11, 113 C3) – Challenge Service Station, Corner Wairau Rd and Kent St, Picton
Kaikoura Public D/S (48 E12) – South Bay Domain, Kaikoura

Nelson/Tasman

Collingwood Public D/S (37 C7) – At entry to Collingwood Motor Camp, at car park beside information centre
Takaka Mobil Service Station (38 E8) – Cnr Commercial St & Motupipi Rd, Takaka
Takaka Public D/S (38 E8) – Takaka Information Centre in the car park
Motueka Public D/S (38 G10) – Follow sign from High St into Tudor St to Hickmott Pl
Richmond Public D/S (43 A4) – Jubilee Park, Gladstone Rd, Richmond
Nelson Public D/S (38 J11) – Mobil Tahunanui, 28 Tahunanui Dr, Nelson
Nelson Public D/S (38 J12) – BP Truck Stop, Hay St, Port Nelson
Murchison Public D/S (42 G9) – On SH6 by entry to TNL Freight Yard, between Mobil Service Station and Matakitaki Bridge
Murchison Public D/S (42 G9) – Mobil Service Station, SH6, Murchison; on back fence past the truck diesel pump

West Coast

Greymouth Public D/S (45 F4) – Caltex S/S Tainui St, Greymouth
Hokitika Public D/S (45 H2) – SH6; north end of town, 1km from centre, adjacent to sewage ponds in large laybys on either side of road
Goldfields Tourist Centre (50 A11) – Ross; beside public toilet on roadside
Glacier Motors Mobil Service Station (49 G6) – Franz Josef, on SH6
Haast Public D/S (58 D9) – 3km from junction of SH6 & Jackson Bay Rd, Haast
DOC camp site, rest area (58 E12) – On SH6; 45km east of Haast beside the river, in front of toilet block, Pleasant Flat
Westport Public D/S (41 G3) – New World car park, Palmerston St, Westport
Nelson Creek Public D/S (45 E6) – Nelson Creek Domain, Nelson Creek
Blackball Public D/S (45 D5) – Adjacent to Sports Domain
Runanga Public D/S (45 E4) – Runanga Workingmen's Club, corner of Pitt and McGowan Sts, Runanga
Ross Goldfields Information and Heritage Centre (50 B11, 51 B2) – 4 Aylmer St, Ross
Greymouth Public D/S (45 F3) – New World car park, cnr High and Marlborough St
Greymouth Public D/S (45 F3) – Cobden Bridge rest area, north side of bridge

Canterbury

Cheviot Public D/S (48 J9) – Centre of village, accessed from service lane (key at Mobil service station)
Waikari Public D/S (54 B8) – in domain, Princess St; signposted off SH7 at Waikari (Key held by Mary Booker, 20 Princes St or Roger Mander, 18 Princes St)
Oxford Public D/S (53 F4) – High St, Oxford; approximately 800m from the cnr of Oxford Rd & Main St
Amberley Public D/S (54 D8) – Mobil S/S Carters Rd, Amberley
Kaiapoi Public D/S (54 G8, 56 C10) – Charles St, Kaiapoi
Rangiora Public D/S (53 F7, 56 B9) 22 Railway Rd, Rangiora

Christchurch

Christchurch Public D/S (53 F3, 56 D9, 119 C5, 120 E4) – Styx Mill Transfer Station, off SH1 between Belfast and Redwood, Christchurch)
Styx Mill Rd Transfer Station (53 H7) – Off SH1 between Belfast & Redwood, Christchurch; enter transfer station drive to kiosk and ask to use D/S
A & P Showgrounds (53 J6) – Curletts Rd, Christchurch; between motorway corridor and Lincoln/Halswell Rd intersection
Lincoln Club (53 J6) – 24 Edward St, Lincoln
Templeton Public D/S (56 D8) – at information kiosk; off SH1
Rolleston BP Service Station (56 E8) – Rolleston

South Canterbury

Washdyke Public D/S (61 J5) – Allied Truck Stop site, Sheffield St, Timaru
Fairlie Public D/S (60 F12, 61 F1) – Gladstone Grand Hotel, 43 Main St, Fairlie
Lake Tekapo Public D/S 2 (60 E9) – On road in Lake Drive, follow Motor Camp sign for 200m.
Rakaia Public D/S (55 G5) – Rolleston St, Rakaia; off SH1, beside public toilet
Rakaia Gorge Public D/S (55 D2) – SH72; at public toilet, north side of river
Methven Public D/S (55 F1) – Mobil Service Station (Methven Motor Services), Hall St, Methven
Lake Tekapo Public D/S 1 (60 E9) – Tekapo village; on roadside, 400m from village centre on SH8 towards Fairlie
Twizel Public D/S (59 H6) – Turn off SH8 to town centre, adjacent to Shell Service Station
Timaru Public D/S (61 J4) – Follow truck by-pass route off Marine Pde to Caroline Bay; adjacent to toilet and carpark by rollerskating rink
St Andrews Domain (68 B13) – Main South Rd, St Andrews; 250m south
Lake Aviemore (67 C6) – North side of Waitaki Lakes; closed May to Oct
Waitangi Bay (67 C7) – Waitaki Lakes; closed May to Oct
Gillies Caltex Service Station (68 H11) – Thames St, Oamaru

Otago

DK Auto Shell Service Station (74 E12) – Waikouaiti; at rear
Warrington Public D/S (74 F12) – Warrington Domain; off SH1 at Evansdale, follow signs to beach, at public toilet
Mosgiel Public D/S (74 H10) – BP Service Station, 77 Gordon Rd, Mosgiel
BP Dunedin North (74 H11) – one way system, south near gardens
Dunedin Shell Service Station (74 H11) – turn off SH1 for Andersons Bay Rd, adjacent to Old Gas Works between Hillside St & McBride St
Dunedin Shell Service Station (74 H11) – Kaikorai Valley Rd, Kaikorai Valley; off SH1, 3km
Fleetwood Motors (74 H10) – Shell Service Station, SH1, Fairfield Straight
Ranfurly Public D/S (67 H5) – Intersection of Northland and Charlemont St, off SH85, Ranfurly
Dunedin Public D/S (74 H11) – BP Truck Stop, 867 Cumberland St, Dunedin

Clutha Valley

Boundary Creek Reserve (DOC camp site) (58 J10) – Approximately 20km south of Makarora, 12km on Haast side of the Neck
Kidds Bush Reserve (DOC camp site) (66 A9) – Hunter Valley Rd, Lake Hawea
Arrowtown Public D/S (65 G6) – Behind the Lake Districts Museum at the public toilets
Queenstown BP Connect Public D/S (65 H4) – Cnr SH6 & Frankton Rd, Queenstown
Caltex Service Station (66 H8) – Village centre, Cromwell
Caltex Service Station (72 A13) – 50 Centennial Ave, Alexandra
Council Depot (72 D13) – Teviot St, Roxburgh; close to motorcamp
Lawrence Public D/S (79 A3) – SH8; on west side of town beside rest area
Clinton Public D/S (78 C13) – On the roadside adjacent to park, from SH1 turn at BP Service Station and War Memorial
Albion Cricket Club (66 D9) – SH6, Main Rd, Luggate
Omakau Public D/S (66 H12, 67 H1) – Omakau Recreation Reserve, 13 Alton St, Omakau
Cromwell Public D/S (66 H9) – BP Service Station, Sargood Drive
Queenstown Public D/S (65 H5, 125 B2, 126 B2) – Cemetery Rd
Clyde (66 J10) – Clyde Recreation Reserve, 7 Whitby St.
Tapanui Public D/S (73 J2) – Bushy Hill St.

Southland

Milford Sound Public D/S (64 D9) – In car park
Knobs Flat Public D/S (64 H9) – SH 94, Te Anau, Council operated
Te Anau Public D/S (70 C11) – Lake Front Dr, Te Anau; at boat harbour, adjacent to public toilets
Manapouri Public D/S (70 E11) – Hillside Rd, Manapouri
Otautau Public D/S (76 F14) – At public toilet, behind Plunket Rooms in Hulme St, just off Main St
Riverton BP Service Station (77 E2) – Bay Rd, towards Riverton Rocks
Invercargill Public D/S (77 E5) – Rockgas Invercargill, 20 Spey St, Invercargill
Riversdale Service Station (72 J9) – SH94, Riversdale
Gore Public D/S (78 B9) – Gore A&P Showgrounds; down first entry
Gore Public D/S (78 B9) – Richmond Rd, Gore; at kerbside, 750m upstream from SH1 Bridge and Trout Monument
Winton Public D/S (77 B4) – SH6; behind Mobil Service Station, Winton
Tokanui Shop (78 G9) – Southern Scenic Route through Catlins (old SH92), Tokanui

A

B

C

D

E

F

G

H

I

J

K

L

M

N

O

Q

R

S

T

Y